THE JOURNALS AND
LETTERS OF
FANNY BURNEY

DR. CHARLES BURNEY
By Sir Joshua Reynolds

THE JOURNALS AND LETTERS OF

FANNY BURNEY

(MADAME D'ARBLAY)

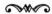

VOLUME VII
1812–1814
LETTERS 632–834

Edited by

EDWARD A. BLOOM

and

LILLIAN D. BLOOM

OXFORD
AT THE CLARENDON PRESS
1978

Oxford University Press, Walton Street, Oxford OX2 6DP

OXFORD LONDON GLASGOW
NEW YORK TORONTO MELBOURNE WELLINGTON
KUALA LUMPUR SINGAPORE JAKARTA HONG KONG TOKYO
DELHI BOMBAY CALCUTTA MADRAS KARACHI
IBADAN NAIROBI DAR ES SALAAM CAPE TOWN

© *Oxford University Press 1978*

British Library Cataloguing in Publication Data
Burney, Fanny
    The journals and letters of Fanny Burney
    (Madame D'Arblay)
    Vol. 7 : 1812–1814 : letters 632–834
    Index
    ISBN 0–19–812468–6
    1. Bloom, Edward Alan   2. Bloom,
    Lillian Doris
    823'.6   PR3316.A4Z/
    Burney, Fanny – Biography

*Printed in Great Britain
at the University Press, Oxford
by Vivian Ridler
Printer to the University*

ACKNOWLEDGEMENTS

WE are indebted to Professor Joyce Hemlow, to Althea Douglas, and the staff in the Burney Room, McGill University, for providing us with the headnotes and text of the journals and letters (numbers 632 to 834), the Diary Entries, and the transcription of M. d'Arblay's financial statement (Appendix II) that shape this volume. Twenty-five of the General's letters contained obliterations, some more than others. Yet many of these letters have been restored by the patience and skill of Miss Caroline Cronk, who worked over them many evenings in the Burney Room. We are grateful to Professor Hemlow, Mrs. Douglas, Professor Peter Hughes of the University of Toronto, and Mr. Warren Derry of Bath, all of whom read our annotations.

Many libraries have helped us to complete our research. Four have extended themselves beyond the call of institutional loyalty. For almost two years the letters of volume vii were literally closeted in the Upper Reading Room of the Bodleian Library, where staff members like Mrs. Sheila Gordon-Rae and Mr. William Hodges encouraged us and guarded our manuscripts and notes. At the John Rylands Library of the University of Manchester Dr. Frank Taylor and Miss Glenis Matheson allowed us free access to all the peripheral holograph materials—such as the letters of Marianne Francis and Mrs. Piozzi—that enlightened many of the obscurities of Mme d'Arblay's allusions. Dr. Lola Szladits of the New York Public Library's Berg Collection has permitted us to draw upon her expertise. The late James M. Osborn was, as always, generous in making available every pertinent item in his rich hoard now deposited in the Beinecke Library of Yale University: the sale agreement for *The Wanderer*, certain letters of Charles Burney, Charles Burney Jr., and his son Charles Parr. These have often provided the response to or provocation for a Mme d'Arblay letter. Finally, the detective process required by a volume such as this could never have been completed without our being able to use the resources of the National Library of Ireland and the Four Courts in Dublin, the National Library of Wales, the British Museum, the Probate Room of the Public Record Office (London), the Boston Public Library, the Harvard University Library, the Brown University Library in whose reference room we called constantly upon the bibliographical agility of Mrs. Elizabeth Schumann.

Countless archivists and librarians in England and France have contributed details dredged from records long lost from sight. What we know of the Pellapras came from the archivists at Caen and Lyon, each working separately to piece together a family history. For the exciting information found out about James Greene of Llansantfraed, we are obligated to Mr. William Baker of the County Record Office in Newport, to the Monmouth & District Field Club and Antiquarian Society, and to the Revd. David Williams of Llandygwydd, Cardiganshire. Miss Jane Langton, registrar of the Royal Archives at Windsor, has answered several questions, particularly those which concern Charlotte Beckedorff and Fanny Burney's pension. We have gone from the Revd. Canon D. Ingram Hill, Rural Dean of Canterbury, to Mrs. D. Gail Saunders, archivist of the Ministry of Education and Culture in Nassau, Bahamas, to inquire about the grandson of John Gregory. We have learned much about Alex d'Arblay's unhappy career at Caius through the effort of the college librarian, Mr. J. H. Prynne. Similarly Miss H. E. Peek, keeper of the archives of the University of Cambridge, has helped us to rediscover and identify various people in and around the University. Mme Jill Bourdais de Charbonnière of Paris Research Associates has been diligent in ferreting out biographical details about obscure French army officers and minor functionaries in Napoleon's government. Baron Franz von Lobstein of the Palazzo di Malta, Rome, has given us what bits he could find about the marquis de Thuisy. Miss Patricia Allderidge, archivist of the Bethlem Royal Hospital, has provided personalities for the last tenants of Camilla Cottage. Mme M. Vanneroy of the Bibliothèque municipale de Joigny gave us the documents that comprise Appendix III and describe the Cossack occupation of the area surrounding Joigny in early 1814.

One of the rewards of this volume involved our transcription of a section of Mme d'Arblay's Exercise Book III. Appendix I is a vivid, albeit slanted, account of Fanny Burney's association with Mrs. Thrale, an intimacy that ended with the emergence of Mrs. Piozzi in 1784. Evident just beneath the French words (with their ungrammatical structure and bizarre distribution of accents) is Mme d'Arblay's desire not merely to justify her behaviour but to regain a friendship that she once took for granted.

Ten hitherto unknown Mme d'Arblay letters came to light just as this volume had gone to press. Thanks to the scholarly good will of their owners—The Kestner Museum, Hannover, and Mr. Michael Burney-Cumming, Loughton, Milton Keynes, Bucks.—we are able to print them as Additional Letters: Numbers 633A, 639A, 640A, 685A, 689A, 695A, 722A, 735A, 775A, 789A. Others have helped us in last minute research and we hereby express our gratitude: Faith Cornwall, The Huntington Library, San Marino, California; Bruce Redford, King's College, Cambridge; the archivists at Aylesbury, Bucks.; at Auxerre, Yonne; Nantes, Loire-Atlantique; Saint-Brieuc, Côtes-du-Nord.

In the pursuit of information we have travelled frequently to Montreal, crossed the Atlantic many times, and the English Channel at least twice. We have followed indistinct trails that took us from Ireland to large industrial cities in south Wales and to beautiful but remote Welsh villages. At home we have had the help of our typist, Mrs. Virginia Bowers, who worked with us and selflessly catered to our demands. To defray some of the expenses that have made this volume possible, both Rhode Island College and Brown University have given us what subventions they could without depriving others of like support. To both these schools we are grateful.

CONTENTS

LIST OF PLATES

xi

ABBREVIATIONS

MEMBERS OF THE BURNEY FAMILY

AA   The Revd. Alexander Charles Louis Piochard d'Arblay, 1794–1837

CAB   Charlotte Ann Burney, 1761–1838
CBF   after 1786 Mrs. Francis
CBFB   after 1798 Mrs. Broome
CB   Charles Burney (Mus. Doc.), 1726–1814
CB Jr.   Charles Burney (D.D.), 1757–1817
CF   Clement Robert Francis, 1792–1829
CFBt   Charlotte (Francis) Barrett, 1786–1870
CPB   Charles Parr Burney (D.D.), 1785–1864
EBB   Esther (Burney) Burney, 1749–1832
FB   Frances Burney, 1752–1840
FBA   after 1793 Madame d'Arblay
JB   James Burney (Rear-Admiral), 1750–1821
M. d'A   Alexandre-Jean-Baptiste Piochard d'Arblay, 1754–1818
MF   Marianne Francis, 1790–1832
SEB   Susanna Elizabeth Burney, 1755–1800
SBP   after 1782 Mrs. Phillips
SHB   Sarah Harriet Burney, 1772–1844

SHORT TITLES

Add. MSS.   Additional Manuscripts, British Museum (Library).

AR   *The Annual Register, or a View of the History, Politics, and Literature . . .,* 1758–.

Barrett   The Barrett Collection of Burney Papers, British Museum (Library), 43 vols., Egerton 3690–3708.

Berg   The Henry W. and Albert A. Berg Collection, New York Public Library.

Berry	*Extracts from the Journals and Correspondence of Miss Berry from the year 1783 to 1852*, ed. Lady Theresa Lewis, 3 vols., 1866.
Bertaut	Jules Bertaut, *La Vie aventureuse de Louis XVIII*, 1949.
Bertier de Sauvigny	G. de Bertier de Sauvigny, *La Restauration*, 1963.
BM	The British Museum (Library).
Boigne	*Memoirs of the Comtesse de Boigne* [*1781–1814*, vol. i], ed. and trans. Charles Nicoullaud in 3 vols., 1907, 1908.
Clifford	James L. Clifford, *Hester Lynch Piozzi* (*Mrs. Thrale*), Oxford, 1941; 2nd ed., 1952.
Comyn	The John Comyn Collection of Burney Papers, The Cross House, Vowchurch, Turnastone, Herefordshire, England.
C.R.S.	Publications of the Catholic Record Society.
Dard	Émile Dard, *Un Confident de l'Empereur, le comte de Narbonne*, 1943.
Dean	Capt. G. G. T. Dean, *The Royal Hospital, Chelsea*, 1950.
DL (1842–6)	*Diary and Letters of Madame d'Arblay*, ed. Charlotte Barrett, 7 vols., 1842–6.
DL	*Diary and Letters of Madame d'Arblay* (*1778–1840*), ed. Austin Dobson, 6 vols., 1904–5.
ED	*The Early Diary of Frances Burney, 1768–1778*, ed. Annie Raine Ellis, 2 vols., 1907.
Forneron	H. Forneron, *Histoire générale des émigrés . . .*, 3 vols., 1884–90.
GEC	George Edward Cokayne, *The Complete Peerage . . .*, revised by Vicary Gibbs *et al.*, 13 vols., 1910–59; *The Complete Baronetage*, 6 vols., Exeter, 1900–9.
GM	*The Gentleman's Magazine*, 1731–1880.
Gontaut	*Memoirs of the Duchesse de Gontaut*, trans. Mrs. J. W. Davis, 2 vols., 1894.
Greatheed	Bertie Greatheed, *An Englishman in Paris*, ed. J. T. Bury and J. C. Barry, 1953.
HFB	Joyce Hemlow, *The History of Fanny Burney*, Oxford, 1958.
JRL	The John Rylands Library of the University of Manchester.
Judd	Gerrit P. Judd, IV, *Members of Parliament, 1734–1832*, New Haven, Conn., 1955.

Juniper Hall	Constance Hill, *Juniper Hall, a Rendezvous of Certain Illustrious Personages during the French Revolution Including Alexandre d'Arblay and Fanny Burney*, 1904.
Lefebvre	Georges Lefebvre, *Napoléon*, 6th ed., 1969.
Life	*Boswell's Life of Johnson* . . ., ed. George Birkbeck Hill, revised by L. F. Powell, 6 vols., Oxford, 1934–50, 1964.
Locks of Norbury	The Duchess of Sermoneta [Vittoria (Calonne) Caetani], *The Locks of Norbury*, 1940.
Lonsdale	Roger Lonsdale, *Dr. Charles Burney*, Oxford, 1965.
Madelin	Louis Madelin, *Histoire du Consulat et de l'Empire*, 16 vols., 1937–54.
Maurois	André Maurois, *Adrienne, ou la vie de Mme de Lafayette*, 1960; trans. Gerard Hopkins, 1961.
Memoirs	*Memoirs of Doctor Burney, Arranged from His Own Manuscripts, from Family Papers, and from Personal Recollections*, by his daughter Madame d'Arblay, 3 vols., 1832.
Nelson	R. R. Nelson, *The Home Office, 1782–1801*, Durham, N.C., 1969.
NYPL	The New York Public Library, Fifth Avenue and 42nd Street, New York.
Orieux	Jean Orieux, *Talleyrand ou le sphinx incompris*, 1970.
Osborn	The James Marshall and Marie-Louise Osborn Collection, The Beinecke Library, Yale University, New Haven, Conn.
PML	The Pierpont Morgan Library, 33 East 36th Street, New York.
PRO	Public Record Office, London.
Queeney Letters	*The Queeney Letters, being Letters addressed to Hester Maria Thrale by Dr. Johnson, Fanny Burney, and Mrs. Thrale-Piozzi*, ed. the Marquis of Lansdowne, 1934.
Rambuteau	*Mémoires de Comte de Rambuteau*, ed. M. G. Leguin, 1905.
Révérend, Ier *Emp.*	Vicomte Albert Révérend, *Armorial du premier empire; titres, majorats et armoiries concédés par Napoléon Ier* . . ., 4 vols. in 2, 1894–7.
Révérend, *Restauration*	Vicomte Albert Révérend, . . . *Titres, anoblissements et pairies de la restauration, 1814–1830*, 6 vols., 1901–6.

Révérend, *Monarchie*	Vicomte Albert Révérend, *Titres et confirmations de titres; monarchie de juillet, 2ᵉ république, 2ᵉ empire, 3ᵉ république, 1830–1908,* 1909.
R. H. I., Windsor	Royal Household Index, the Queen's Archives, Windsor Castle.
Robinet	Jean Baptiste Robinet, *Dictionnaire historique et biographique de la révolution et de l'empire. 1789–1815,* 2 vols., 1899.
Scholes	Percy A. Scholes, *The Great Dr. Burney,* 2 vols., 1948.
Six	Georges Six, *Dictionnaire biographique des généraux et amiraux français de la révolution et de l'empire (1792–1814),* 2 vols., 1934.
Solovieff	*Lettres de Madame Staël à Narbonne,* ed. Georges Solovieff, 1960.
Thiers	L. A. Thiers, *History of the Consulate and the Empire of France under Napoleon,* trans. D. Forbes Campbell, 20 vols., 1845–62.
Venn	*Alumni Cantabrigienses,* pt. 2: From 1752 to 1900, compiled by John Venn and J. A. Venn, 6 vols., Cambridge, 1940–54.
Vincennes	Archives du Service historique de l'armée, Château de Vincennes.
Vitrolles	*Mémoires de Vitrolles,* ed. Pierre Farel, 2 vols., 1950–1.
Walpole	*The Yale Edition of Horace Walpole's Correspondence,* ed. W. S. Lewis, 39 vols., New Haven, Conn., 1937–.
Welvert	Eugène Welvert, *Princesse d'Hénin, histoire d'une grande dame du temps passé,* Versailles, 1924.
Woelmont de Brumagne	Henri de Woelmont, Baron de Brumagne, *Notices généalogiques,* 8 vols., 1923–35.

Alexander d'Arblay
To Charles Burney

A.L.S. (Berg), 14 Aug. 1812
Double sheet 8vo   2 pp.   *pmks*   DEAL / 16 AU 1812   17 AU 1812
17 AU 1812   wafer
Addressed: To Doctor / Charles Burney / Greenwich
[*emended by* FBA:] ʌ / the Reverend /
Docketed in pencil, p. 1 : Son of FB.

from Deal, the 14ᵗʰ of August 1812.

Dear Uncle!¹

We are on the point of arriving at Deal from Dunkerque
where we have waited a whole month and more for the departure of the Mary Ann,² the American ship on which we are now
dining, after two days fasting. Mamma, whose bodily feelings
are sollicited by an excess of fatigue as much as her mental ones
by an excess of joy, incapable of holding herself the pen, has
put it into my hands to give you that happy intelligence. Her
intention is to go to bed for 24 hours immediately upon landing:
She hopes her debarcation can suffer no difficulty.:

Forgive me this bad English, dear Uncle, in favour of the
good tidings I announce: I am harrassed of fatigue and hunger,
and have been sick so long time that I now look like a ghost.
My pen trembles so that I am forced to relinquish ˡ it. God bless
you, dear Uncle, and may nothing trouble the joy with which
I shall see you after such a long, long separation!

Alex. d'Arblay.

Mamma will herself write to dear Grandpapa the moment she
is landed and less sick. — —³

Her love and mine to every body. — —

632. ¹ CB Jr. awaited the travellers at Dover rather than Deal. On 20 August,
however, he met them 'upon some common'. See L. 637 and Diary Entry, p. 507.
   ² FBA and her son had waited from early July to 13 August while the *Mary
Ann* acquired her full quota of passengers. See vi. Ll. 600–31.
   ³ By 24 August, as CFBt reported to MF (Barrett, Eg. 3702A, f. 162, 26 Aug.
1812), 'my dear Aunt [is] in good looks & spirits. Alec is silent & shy & brown &

To James Burney

A.L. (PML, Autog. Cor. bound), *n.d.*
Double sheet 8vo   1 p.   *pmks*   DEAL / 16 AU 1812   17 AU 1812
Addressed by AA: Captain Burney / 26 James Street / Westminster
Postdated, p. 1: Aug. 15. 1812
Annotated, p. 4: Dear Madame / D'Arblay on returning / to England—
1812

Who will be more sincerely rejoiced—except myself—than my dear kind James to meet again a so long lost sister?—no one, I firmly believe, no one! —& I can let no creature rob me of the pleasure of telling him that I am actually in good—dear old England!— I siezed a pebble to kiss when I touched the shore, & I shall guard it all my life—But alas—what is perfect?—the best & dearest of partners could not accompany me!—I have Alex, however, in raptures—Distribute my love—I shall spend to-morrow here to rest—for I have passed 3 Nights with my cloaths on,[1] & I must recruit in strength for supporting my approaching happiness.

thin. but his countenance very intelligent'. Five months later the initial portrait was altered only by the family's sensitivity to FBA's uncertain health. In a letter (JRL), MF reported to Mrs. Piozzi on 15 January that her aunt had 'grown very fat, & does not look more than 40 years old'. Despite her liveliness, she was in poor health, '& obliged to keep her room one day in two'.

633. [1] Along with other passengers, FBA boarded the *Mary Ann* the night of 12 August. The ship sailed early afternoon the next day and, soon becalmed, took two days and one night for the voyage from Dunkirk to Deal. Exhausted by sea-sickness, FBA spent an extra night aboard. The morning of 15 August she and AA were rowed ashore (L. 637).

To Mrs. Broome

A.L. (Diary MSS. vi, not numbered, Berg), 15 Aug. 1812
Double sheet 8vo   1 p.   *pmk*   17 AU 1812   red wafer
Addressed: Mrs Broome / N° 10. Cheynes Street / Alfred Place / Bedford
Square[1]
Endorsed by CBFB: Sister d'arblay / aug^t 1812
Edited by CFBt. *See* Textual Notes.
Also L., copy in hand of CFBt (Diary MSS. viii. 5852, Berg), 15 Aug.
1812.   Double sheet 4to   1 p.

Aug. 15—1812

In a flutter of joy such as my tender Charlotte will feel in reading this I write to her from England!—I can hardly believe it—I look around me in constant enquiry & doubt—I speak French to every soul—& I whisper, still, if I utter a word that breathes private opinion—[2]

Tell my other dearest Charlotte her charming Letter arrived just as I was preparing to depart, & has given firmness to my project, & satisfaction complete in its execution.[3] I shall announce this to my beloved Father in a Letter to-morrow.[4] And *after* to-morrow I shall set off to Chelsea. I can not lie down till my Pen has embraced you all—

my Charlotte—adieu for Two days!—[5]

634. [1] FBA had only an old address of CBFB, who in the spring of 1811 had moved from 10 to 23 Chenies Street, Bloomsbury. See the letter (JRL) of MF to Mrs. Piozzi, postmarked 15 May 1811.
  [2] Fearful of Napoleon, his police (whether headed by Fouché or his successor Savary), and the comte de Montalivet (L. 689 n. 4), FBA wished to safeguard the appointment of M. d'A in the ministère de l'Intérieur. CB encouraged FBA's prudence, urging her in a letter of 1810 (Osborn) to avoid 'any intercourse with your own country & relations [that] may injure your caro sposo' (vi, L. 568 n. 2). In the spirit of CB's advice, she wrote to her family with a mere '*guarded assurance* that she is alive'. See MF's letter (JRL) to Mrs. Piozzi, 3 Dec. 1810.
  [3] CFBt's letter, now missing, invited FBA to visit the Barrett household. On 24 August CFBt repeated the invitation in person and reported (Barrett, Eg. 3702A, f. 162b) to MF two days later that 'Aunt d'Arblay promises to spend a week with us at Richmond'.
  [4] On 16 August—Sunday—a letter 'could not go'. FBA wrote the next day, saying nothing about a projected visit to Richmond.
  [5] FBA would not in fact see her sister until the evening of 21 August, at CB's apartment (L. 637).

To Doctor Burney

A.L. (Berg), 17 Aug. 1812
Single sheet 8vo   1 p.   The cover is missing.
Edited by FBA, p. 1, *annotated and dated*:   ⊹·   ⊹·   1812   (2)   Return to England after 10 Years absence
Also L., copy in hand of CFBt (Diary MSS. viii. 5854, Berg), 17 Aug. 1812. Double sheet 4to   1 p.

DEAL!
in GREAT BRITAIN!
AUGst 17. 1812

Here I am, in dear—dear old England, my dear, dearer—dearest Father!—Here, with my Alex,—& to-morrow I hope to set off for London[1]— But I am somewhat fatigued, my Voyage having been very laborious, & it is possible I may yet wait a day to recruit— —not alone my body but my mind, for my joy is almost too much for me, & seems to want *rest* between the *LAND* & my dearest *Father*!—I can write no more— now,—I am hurried, adieu

My dearest Father for a very—*VERY* short time[2]

635. [1] FBA left Deal on 19 August and arrived at Chelsea College the following evening.
[2] FBA would not have delayed had she known that CB, believing rumour, expected her in Chelsea by the third week in July. In a letter (Osborn) SHB announced to CB Jr. on 21 July: 'My Father, ignorant of [FBA's] late dreadful sufferings, was in the highest spirits at the prospect of seeing her; and all Friday & Saturday neither he nor I could think to talk of any thing else.' His 'disappointment', continued SHB, became 'now proportioned to his preceding delight'. The reunion took place on 20 August (L. 637).

To Mrs. Waddington

A.L. (Berg), *n.d.*
Double sheet 8vo   2 pp.   *pmks*   CANTERBURY   19 AU 1812
Addressed: Mrs. Waddington, / Lanover, / near Monmouth, / Wales.
Annotated on address page: Miss sent to Monmouth.

No hand but my own shall tell my ever dear Mary—soft always to my recollection is that name—that I may yet hope to see & embrace her again—to thank her with the warmest gratitude for her dear & most interesting Letters—to press to my heart her lovely Girls[1]—to account for my forced silence[2]—& to rejoice once more in her constant Friendship, her unalterable tenderness.—

I write from—would you—Can you believe it—from Deal!—Deal in OLD ENGLAND! Dear—brave—incomparable old ENGLAND!— —I still doubt all my senses!—I have been here since the 15ᵗʰ—too much shaken by my Voyage to proceed: but I go on to CHELSEA to day or to-morrow.

Heaven bless my sweet Friend! — —

I have brought with me my younger—but alas not my elder Alexander!—

I have met with inexpressible kindness from Lady Lucy Foley, who I find more engaging than ever.[3]

---

636. [1] Only three of the six Waddington daughters were alive in 1812: Frances (b. 1791), Emelia (b. 1794), Augusta (b. 1802). Mrs. Waddington's first child, Harriet (b. 1790), died at the age of 5 months; her third daughter, Mary Anne (b. 1792), died in 1793; and her fifth, Matilda (b. 1797), lived only two weeks. See also v, L. 532 n. 4.
[2] The delivery of letters between England and France was so uncertain that MF in a note (JRL) to Mrs. Piozzi, dated 30 Jan. 1809, reported that her mother was 'anxious for letters from Paris. Nobody has heard of poor dear Aunt D'Arblay for an age.'
[3] See L. 637 and nn. 20, 23; vi, L. 631 and n. 53.

To M. d'Arblay

A.J.L.S. (Diary MSS. vi. 5856–[59], Berg), 22 Aug. (Journal for 12–22 Aug. 1812)

Double sheet large 4to   4 pp.   foliated in pencil 108, 109   *pmk*   3 Avril 1813   red wafer

Addressed: A Monsieur / Monsieur d'Arblay / Rue de Miroménil Nº 8 / Faub^g St Honoré / PARIS.

Edited by FBA, p. 1 (5856), *annotated and dated*:   ×   ⯂   Chelsea, *Aug^st* [*22^d*] *1812*   Nº ⌐33.⌐1   Detail of arrival in England after Ten year's absence

Edited also by CFBt *and the* Press. *See* Textual Notes.

22^d

Another opportunity already offers for writing to mon meilleur ami, ⌐but, most provokingly, I cannot send my prepared outline[d] first Journal Letter as the Paper is too thick & heavy.⌐¹ I will here therefore ⌐copy it, in part, to⌐¹ give, what I wish to receive, an idea from Day to Day of what passes, though necessarily leaving details for our meeting.—when will that be?—when?—¹

12th August. We were summoned on board the Mary Ann, & all called over, & all had our passports examined. I went down to the state cabin, with Me de Carbonnière,² & the Caillebots,³ & I made acquaintance with M^e & Mlle de Cocherell,⁴ & Me de Ronchorolle,⁵ & found them very amiable & pleasing. Alex

637. ¹ M. d'A returned to England only on 28 Apr. 1814. See Diary Entry, p. 510. But in L. 775 FBA says that M. d'A arrived on the 29th.

² Henriette-Marie-Anne-Louise-Alexandrine *née* de Bournon (b. *c.* 1781) was the wife of Louis-Eugène (1770–1826), *dit* comte de Carbonnière (vi, L. 603 n. 4). She was visiting her father Jacques-Louis (1751–1825), comte de Bournon, to show him her newest child, now 4 months old. A celebrated mineralogist and friend of M. d'A, the comte had, after the prince de Condé dissolved his army, emigrated to England and remained there until recalled by Louis XVIII.

³ Anne-Renée-Henriette *née* Desvergers de Sannois de Maupertuis (b. 1768) was married to Marie-*Louis* de Caillebot (1764–1831), 4th marquis de la Salle. She was accompanied by two of her children: Marie-Constance-Pauline (aged 3) and Armand-Louis-Constant (aged 21). See vi, L. 601 n. 1. For the purpose and subsequent difficulties of their voyage, see L. 647.

⁴ Françoise-Charlotte de Cocherel *née* Gallien de Préval (b. *c.* 1755) and her daughter Philippine-Louise-Geneviève (aged 22 and listed in the ship's register as 'Virginie'). See vi, L. 608 nn. 6, 7.

⁵ The eldest daughter of Mme de Cocherel, Louise-Élisabeth-Marguerite (b. *c.* 1772) had in 1790 married the Ultra Anne-*Charles*-Léonor (1765/6–*post* 1817), comte de Roncherolles, baron d'Heugueville (vi, L. 608 n. 7).

was very fortunate in being with his school-fellow, young Chancel;[6] Mrs. Gregory[7] & the Miss Potts[8] chose to stay upon the Deck. We expected to Sail every Moment, ⌐but alas¬, the night wore away while we were yet immoveable!—And when morning came, we were all dismissed to seek our fortunes till one o'clock at noon. I have told you that I dined with my interesting new friend at Dunkirk,[9] from whose hospitable board I wrote you my last Continental Letter. I sent Alex to regale himself at a Restaurateur's, for he was quite too voracious for such a Table as far MORE than sufficed for me. As my generous Hostess would not let me pay her, & I had no mark of remembrance I could part with left, I durst not present myself to her for a Breakfast, but I went to another very good person, where I had excellent Coffee & cream, & a hot roll & butter, just as if I had already crossed the Water. This Hostess, too, refused to be paid, after I had spent 2 Hours that were upon my hands in *gentle discourse* with her! The disinterested hospitality of the Dunkirkists is unexampled. She told me all her history, & seemed to take more delight in finding a social hearer than I could in her good fare. I was literally forced to leave my offering under a plate. How glad I shall be to return— if possible—by the same route, & to see again my worthy Flemish friends.[10] |

Alex chose to go to the Coffee house, where he wiled away his spare time in a Game at Billiards, very much to his satisfaction. At one he joined me, & we proceeded to the ship, where all was seriously ready, & we set sail—so much to my amazement, after such innumerable disappointments, that I really could not credit that we were in motion till—ah welladay! I was taken so ill that I was conveyed to a cabin!—I had just before given my *Second last* Letter to good Mr. Gregory[11] for my

[6] The 19-year-old Adolphe Delagrange Chancel (vi, L. 620 n. 13) was to join his mother in England (L. 638).

[7] Jeanne Gregory *née* Christian was born about 1772 in America (vi, L. 608 n. 11).

[8] The sisters Anna and Caroline Potts, aged 25 and 19 respectively (vi, L. 603 n. 3).

[9] Mme Thérèse-Élisabeth Goddefroy *née* Fockedey (b. 1758). See vi, L. 629 n. 2.

[10] When FBA returned to France in November 1814, she landed at Calais, not Dunkirk.

[11] For the various Gregory brothers of the Dunkirk mercantile house Gregorie et Fils, see vi, L. 608 n. 11. FBA probably had in mind David Gregory (1759–1822), whose wife Jeanne was also aboard the *Mary Ann.*

dearest—dearest Ami:—& just received one from that dearest which had followed me by a boat, in which had pursued us poor Mᵉ de Carbonière, who had arrived too late for the ship!—

Well, the *13th* was spent all in sickness;

14 August. All night, *même chose.* And all next Day. Imagine to what an excess of nauseous suffering I was reduced, when I could not hold up my head to ask, or hear, what was meant by *Ils viennent à bord.* Alex had been equally ill the first day; but the 2ᵈ he was tolerably alert: & when we were boarded by the English,[12] he tormented me with all his might to come upon Deck; but it was not possible. We were at Anchor, but my sickness was little diminished. All night I passed again in the same *triste état.*—

15 August. We now found we were in the Downs,[13] & near Deal. The officers who boarded the Vessel, & took us Prisoners,[14] had compassion upon the terrible state of the females, & ordered them boats to take them on shore. I was conveyed by Lieutenant Halford,[15] in his own boat, with Alex, & my luggage; with peculiar attention & politeness: but, the officers, very young men, having acted without consulting the Alien offices,[16] were afterwards reprimanded, & almost every soul was sent to

[12] Under '*SHIP NEWS*', *The Times* (17 Aug. 1812) reported: 'DEAL, Aug. 14. The ship *Castilian* has detained and sent into the Downs the American ship *Mary Ann*, from Dunkirk, with one hundred and one passengers on board.' For a full account, see Captain Risborough's deposition (vi, L. 631 n. 51) sworn before his Majesty's High Court of Admiralty of England at Dover (PRO, HCA 32/128Q).

[13] A roadstead in the English Channel off Deal between the North and South Foreland. Protected on the east by the Goodwin Sands and on the north and west by the coast, this anchorage has depths to 12 fathoms.

[14] On 31 July 1812 the Prince Regent 'order[ed], that a general embargo or stop be made of all [United States] ships and vessels . . . now within, or which shall hereafter come into any of the ports, harbours, or roads, within any part of His Majesty's dominions, together with all persons and effects on board all such ships and vessels' (*The Times*, 3 Aug.). See also vi, L. 619 n. 1.

[15] Probably Lieutenant Charles Halford (vi, L. 631 n. 52). Now 33, he was commissioned on 21 Mar. 1812, and the other 'young' officers also held new commissions. The ship's passengers were predominantly women because only they and their children were able to secure passports (at least to non-belligerent nations). By French law no adult males were allowed to leave France except with the army or on purportedly military business.

[16] The officers violated the Alien Act (given royal assent on 8 Jan. 1793), which had set up the Alien Office to screen foreigners passing through or residing in Great Britain (iii, L. 136 n. 11). This act directed that masters of ships 'provide lists of all foreigners to the custom office at the port of arrival'. The officers, who did not allow time for the ship's captain to prepare such a list, were guilty of another violation. By Order in Council of 23 Mar. 1796, persons without British citizenship could disembark only at Gravesend, Dover, Yarmouth, and (later) Falmouth. See Nelson, pp. 125–7. In taking the *Mary Ann*'s passengers ashore at Deal, the officers ignored the restriction upon locale.

Dover,[17] to be examined, & ordered, afterwards, to return to the Mary Ann! I must cut short all further detail here, or I shall never have done. Before the separation, I dined, at Deal, with Mᵉ de Caillebot & her son & Daughter, Mᵉ de Bue,[18] & Mᵉ de Carbonnière. We then all parted. Alex & I waited at Deal, for my Brother, to whom I wrote.[19]

16 August. It being Sunday, my Letters could not go; Alex & I visited Deal.

17 Augˢᵗ I heard that Lady Lucy cidivant FitzGerald was at Deal;[20] I wrote to beg news of my poor Mrs. Lock; she came to me directly, & spent all the rest of the Morning with me, & her first words, after the most affectionate embraces & welcomes, were 'And how is dear Mʳ d'Arblay?—' I thought I had never yet seen her so kind, so *polite*, so pleasing. She related to me all the sad history of our dearest Friends,[21] & invited me to be entirely *chez elle* while I stayed at Deal. In the afternoon, she sent her carriage, though I had made no engagement to beg & pray that I would come: so I could not refuse, though I had no *attire* fitting for her house. She had only with her one lady, who came purposely to meet me, ci divant Lady Louisa Hervey, sister to the husband of the eldest Miss Upton.[22] I had a charming afternoon. They made me promise to spend the whole of the next day there, if my Brother did not arrive. I now unpacked, to *adorn* a little matter better, & to fit Alex for sight. We dined & passed a delightful evening at Lady Lucy's, & I

---

[17] All non-British subjects were brought to Dover, where at an officially designated customs office they registered as aliens, surrendered any arms in their possession, and were detained at the port of arrival until a magistrate or the Secretary of State provided them with a passport to proceed inland.

[18] Mme St. Olimpe Dubue, aged 47, according to the passenger list of the *Mary Ann* (PRO HCA 32/128Q).

[19] Either this letter is missing or FBA refers to that written by Alex to CB Jr. on 14 August (L. 632).

[20] Lady Lucy Anne *née* Fitzgerald (*c.* 1771–1851) now resided in Deal (1811–14), where her husband Thomas Foley served as Commander-in-Chief in the Downs. See vi, L. 631 n. 53.

[21] Specifically the deaths of William Locke I in 1810 and of his two sons: Charles in 1804 and Frederick Augustus in 1805.

[22] Lady Theodosia Louisa *née* Hervey (1767–1821) was married to Robert Banks Jenkinson (1770–1828), 2nd Earl of Liverpool, who, as Lord Warden of the Cinque Ports, occupied the official residence of Walmer Castle in Deal. For the marriage of Lady Louisa to Jenkinson, see iv, L. 293 n. 5; for their current residence, vi, L. 631 n. 64.

Lady Louisa's brother Frederick William (1769–1859), *styled* Lord Hervey (1796), 5th Earl of Bristol (1803), cr. Earl Jermyn of Horningsheath and Marquess of Bristol (1826), had married in 1798 FBA's long-standing acquaintance Elizabeth Albana Upton (iv, L. 269 n. 11).

like her *Mari*, M. Foley, very well.[23] There was an assembly of all that is *comme il faut* at Deal in the evening,[24] & I was presented to every body,—though the only soul in a Hat.—But I was a traveller, & felt no shame from my joy at being thus safe landed.

18 August. Still no Charles: Lady Lucy warmly pressed me to stay on;[25] but I only passed the morning with her, & then, sure there was some mistake, set off the 19th for Canterbury, where we slept, & on the 20th proceeded towards Chelsea. While, upon some Common, we stopt to water the Horses, a Gentleman on Horse back passed us twice, & then, looking in, pronounced my name: & I saw it was Charles!—dear Charles! who had been watching for us several hours, & *3 nights* following, through a mistake.—Thence we proceeded to Chelsea, where we arrived at 9 o'clock at night. I [wa]s in a state almost breathless. John, the man servant, was in the court⟨yard⟩ looking for us; Becky came down,[26]—but I could not speak to any of them;[27] I could only demand to see my dear Father alone: fortunately, he had had the same feeling, & had charged all the family to stay away, & all the World to be denied. I found him, therefore, in his Library, by himself— —but oh my dearest Friend! very much altered indeed!—weak, weak & changed!—his head almost always hanging down, & his hearing most cruelly impaired.— — I was terribly affected,—but most grateful to God, for my arrival.

---

[23] Sir Thomas Foley (1757–1833) of Carmarthenshire was promoted to Vice Admiral in August 1812. He was a tall, attractive man. For a description of his 'fine presence and figure', see *DNB*.

[24] The assembly celebrated Wellington's victory at Salamanca, news of which reached Deal on 15 August 'and through the whole town . . . nothing during the whole evening was heard but congratulations and felicitations' (*The Times*, 19 Aug.).

[25] FBA refers to a letter (Berg [18 Aug. 1812]) from Lady Lucy: 'how have you slept? and how do you feel this morning my Dearest Mᵉ D'Arblay? The happiness it is to me to see you is so sincere that you *must* I think be aware of it; let me know *whenever you can* whether we may hope to see you and Dʳ Cˢ Burney at Dinner at 5 o'clock? The carriage will go *of course* for you.'

[26] Since 1798 CB lived in the Second Chaplain's apartment, adjacent to the Chapel, on the second floor of the Royal Hospital's main building. See iv *passim*; vi, L. 627 n. 6, and L. 790 n. 11 of this volume.

[27] FBA remembered John as CB's manservant when she left for France in 1802 (v, L. 505). See, however, Diary Entry (20 Aug.), where she names Becky (v, L. 505 n. 1) and George as the first two people she met in Chelsea. FBA was unfamiliar with George, who had been hired shortly before 1807, but she did know Beckey (Becky) or Rebecca More, who had worked for CB since 1794.

Our meeting, you may be sure, was very tender, though I roused myself as quickly as possible to be gay & cheering. He was extremely kind to Alex, & said, in a tone the most impressive, 'I should have been very glad to have seen M. d'Arblay!—' In discourse, however, he re-animated, & was, at times, all himself. But he now admits scarcely a Creature but of his Family, & will only see for a short time even his Children. He likes quietly reading, & lies almost constantly upon the sofa, & will NEVER eat but alone! —! —! — What a change![28] —— ⌐

21. August. My dearest Father seemed somewhat stouter today, & consented to step for a moment into the drawing room. Alex & I have 2 very pretty rooms in the College, at the other side of Burton's Court.[29] There was no possible accommodation for Alex, though I might have had Sarah's chamber, for Sarah is at Lymington, Bathing for her health, which I am most sorry to hear is far from good.[30] ⌐But I could not endure to send off

[28] Now 86 years old, CB had long suffered from rheumatism and bronchitis. Always given to bouts of depression, he was from 1806 plagued by 'the foul fiend Hypochondria'. Yet in 1808 MF found him 'as young and gay as ever, reading & writing without spectacles, (which he has never used *yet*,) and cheerful and entertaining, and sprightly, and kind, as if he had been 23 instead of *eighty three*' (Lonsdale, p. 462). In a letter of 1810 (JRL) to Mrs. Piozzi she had described CB as 'writing & reading the smallest hands without Spectacles—as industrious & occupied as ever, & though *confined* to his Library in Chelsea College, "The gold is not become dim, nor the fine gold changed." ' Within a year, however, he was in 'close seclusion' so that, according to SHB, 'He wastes, and enfeebles, I think, almost visibly; but he will not hear the slightest representation from anybody on the subject—and to fret him would be worse than to see how thin he grows' (*HFB*, p. 321). For a short while FBA's return had a therapeutic effect on CB. Clement Francis noted in a letter (JRL), postmarked 3 Sept. 1812, to Mrs. Piozzi: '[FBA's] arrival, has taken off near 20 yrs. from my Grand Father's looks.'

[29] FBA's rooms either looked north over Burton's Court or in the opposite direction over Figure Court. The former lies on the north side of what is now Royal Hospital Road (driven across Hospital property in 1846) and is bounded on the far side by St. Leonard's Terrace. This large piece of arable land (facing those Hospital buildings that constitute the North Front) was originally intended to be 'the chief ornament' of the Royal Hospital with its 'beautiful plantacons and walks'. While Burton's Court had been divided by avenues of lime and horse-chestnut trees, it was soon used for cattle pasturage. During FBA's long association with Chelsea College the Court was 'enclosed by a brick wall with an ornamental iron grille in the middle of each side' (Dean, pp. 85–6).

[30] She had planned her journey to Lymington before the arrival of FBA became imminent. In a letter (Osborn), dated 21 July 1812, she informed CB Jr. that 'Mosely has strenuously urged me to go for bathing to the sea-side, & previous to receiving this news, I had engaged to set out the 1st week in August with a friend who has secured me a lodging, & whose company on the road would be particularly desirable. Yet, were I going merely for amusement, I would at once give up the excursion rather than run the slightest hazard of losing my sister's society even for a single day. But every sensation of my relaxed little frame, tells me that bathing and change of air are almost indispensably requisite to enable me to get through the ensuing winter with tolerable comfort. I have been a cripple till

Alex alone.⁷¹ My dear Brother James came to greet me, which he did with Eyes filled with affectionate tears, early in the morning. Charles soon after followed, whose joy, equally strong, was far more gay. My charlotte came in the evening, & was *grave* & *gay* too, almost overpowered with tender feelings. And then, appeared sweet Fanny *Raper*,³¹ more lovely, I think than ever, her bloom more bright, her teeth more white, & her form more perfect, for all that menaced trop d'embonpoint has subsided into the most exact proportion that marks youthful health & beauty. I believe, indeed, she was glad at heart to see me, & for myself it was happy I had strength to bear so much reciprocated emotion, though All of joy, save at your absence; which constantly gave a checking sigh to keep off all perfection of happiness. My beloved Esther was in the Country. My Nº 3 will speak of Her & our sweet Friends, & my loved & lovely younger Charlotte.—I wrote directly to Windsor.³² When shall I hear from you? when see at least your handwriting?—I have This opportunity through that sweet second Charlotte,³³ & I have still in store one promised by my sister Burney, of whom by my next feuille³⁴—

adieu, & Heaven bless you!—Alex is quite well, *for him,*—& so is your own

F.D.A.

I cannot read a word of this—

within this last fortnight, ever since February, and even now am wearing what Mosely calls a *warm plaister*, and am often as rhumatic as an old hedger and ditcher.'

³¹ When last seen by FBA in 1802, Frances Phillips, aged 20, was much pampered by CB, with whom she lived. She had on 13 July 1807 married Charles Chamier Raper and in 1808 had borne Catherine Minette. For the marriage of Fanny Phillips and the birth of her child, see i, p. lxxi.

³² FBA's letter (see Diary Entry, 21 Aug.; and L. 639 n. 1) to the Queen affirmed loyalty and gratitude to the Royal Family. In addition to her affection for the Queen and the Princesses, FBA in 1812 was dependent upon them for her social acceptance elsewhere and the continuation of her pension, now more necessary than ever.

³³ CFBt.

³⁴ See L. 645 n. 1.

To M. d'Arblay

A.L. fragment (Berg), *n.d.*
Probably in the original a double sheet 4to, of which FBA later discarded the first leaf. After obliterating at least the last four lines of p. 3, she decided to preserve (or print) only the lower fold of p. 4, a segment (2·9 *to* 3·3 × 7·6″), which shows at the top part of an address panel and at the top right the ends of 6 lines of vertical writing characteristic of the right fold. 2 pp.
Edited by FBA, *who deleted the recto of the fragment, numbering and dating the verso*: 34 (34) AUGUST. 30th 1812. *See further*, Textual Notes.

. . . ⌈his grateful acceptance of the honour of being elected a Correspondent. Meanwhile, pray present his best compliments to M. La Breton,[1] to whom⌉ he had already written, & for whom he is preparing a long answer of comment to the publications with which he has been favoured from the *Secretaire perpetuel*.[2] ⌈But he has not yet had opportunity to send, nor time to read to me what he is getting ready.

<hr style="width:30%" />

638. [1] Joachim Le Breton (1760–1819) was admitted to the Institut in 1796 and in 1803 became secrétaire perpétuel de la classe des beaux-arts. Despite FBA's distrust of his politics, she was grateful to him for his efforts (begun in 1806 and successfully concluded in Apr. 1810) to have CB made a 'Correspondant' of the Institut and for other personal kindnesses (vi, L. 568 nn. 4, 5).
[2] Having received his diploma from the Institut on 23 Nov. 1810, CB was then sent in January 1811 some of its publications (among them Le Breton's *Notice historique sur la vie et les ouvrages de Joseph Haydn*, 1810). Impressed by Le Breton's kindness, CB in April 1811 wrote but did not send a nine-page letter (Osborn), which recalls the first performance of Haydn's *Creation* in England (1800).
'Je suis extrémement reconnoissant de la communication que vous m'avez fait l'honneur de me donner, de productions aussi importantes que celles de l'Institut National de France. . . .
'J'avois été long tems enthousiasmé de la musique de Haydn; mais je ne l'ai connu personnellement qu'à l'époque de son arrivée en Angleterre a la mort de son veritable Protecteur le Prince Esterhazi en 1791. . . . Je fus enchanté de trouver à ce grand génie un abord si simple, si uni, si complettement sans pretentions: ce premier apperçu me donna de lui une impression très favorable. . . .
'Lorsque Haydn nous a quitté pour la derniere fois, sa santé étoit très alterée: et il etoit si épuisé qu'il avoit pris la resolution de ne plus ecrire pour le Public. . . .
'Parlons actuellement du Chef-d'œuvre de Haydn—La Creation'; qu'il me semble n'avoir jamais été si bien appreciée que lorsqu'elle fut representee en Angleterre sous les auspices de Salomon: Mais alors même l'ouverture n'en fut pas parfaitement goutée du public. Quelques uns des mouvemens et des nouveaux effets devinrent cependant à la mode; ils etoient toujours choisies soit a raison de leur élégance, soit a cause de leur originalité, dans toutes les occasions ou les plus grands Musiciens s'assembloient tant en ville qu'à la Campagne.—'

You will be most glad to hear that good Mr. Burney is alive & well, & with what gratitude do I inform you that I have lost nobody of my family in this⊓ |

. . . every moment is filled up with interviews, family parties, & Letters! & never, never can I give you an adequate idea of the tender joy reciprocated from morning to night—scenes of continual emotion[3]—yet all, except for your absence, so sweet & so grateful, that they cannot hurt me, though I feel often hard-breathed & nearly stifled. But *you*, my dearest Friend, *You* keep off all *de trop* of Joy! I so miss, so sigh for you! so think of you from morning to Night!—And every one so wishes for you! —I am now at my dear good sister Charlotte's, to pass, with Alex, some days   Remember me to all my dear & truly loved Friends by whom you are *surrounded*—I have no room to name them, for Me de Chancel[4] can but enclose this petite Lettre

639 Chelsea College, 31 August [1812]

To Charles Burney

A.L.S. (Osborn), 31 Aug.
Single sheet 4to   1 p.   *pmks* T.P.P.U. / Chelsea EO   31 AU 1812 wafer
Addressed: Revd Dr Burney, / Rectory House / Deptford—
Dated, p. 1: 1812.

Chelsea College—Aug^st 31st
Monday—

This moment—calling to see my dearest Father, I receive the permission of Her Majesty to attend her at Windsor—in words the most gracious & condescending—but long travelling to me, from Miss Planta's distance.[1] I should have been very

---

[3] For an enumeration of the visitors received by FBA since her arrival in Chelsea, see Diary Entries, 21–7 August. FBA's popularity is indicated in a letter (JRL) by MF to Mrs. Piozzi (26 Sept. 1812): 'Clem writes me word every body is mad after her—Visitors Inquiries & Invitations to such excess that she leads the life of a besieged city. . . .'

[4] Mme Delagrange Chancel (L. 637 n. 6).

639. [1] Although she had ceased to be English teacher to the Royal Nursery on 5 Jan. 1812, Margaret Planta (i, L. 3 n. 2), now 58 and living at Cleveland Court,

glad to go *to-morrow*, but I fear your engagement is so arranged with our Etty that that will not be possible: therefore can it suit you, my kind Charles, to convoy me on *Wednesday*!²—I shall be glad to set off as early as you can make it convenient, on account of the length of the way, & the return. I shall go back to dear Charlotte's, & wait your answer: but if there be any impediment, *I* must still go, not to seem the reverse of all I feel.³ I shall therefore write your intention, as an explanation why I go not instantly. My kind Love to dear kind Rosette—

My Father joins to both *ditto*. ever & ever *à vous*

F B d'A.

640

To James Burney

[23 Chenies Street,
c. 9 September 1812]¹

A.N. (PML, Autog. Cor. bound), *n.d.*
Single Sheet 4to 2 pp. cut down to 4·5 × 7·2″
Addressed: Capᵗ Burney, / James Street.

My dear Brother—If you have not already made Sarah act, let me inform you That I am strongly urged, if forced to consult, *not* to consult one who is now by SEVERAL pronounced to have passed his best days, & to possess no longer his fine discernment

St. James Place, was again FBA's liaison with the Queen as she had been between 1798 and 1802. FBA refers to a letter from Miss Planta received on 27 August in which a royal audience had been arranged for the first week in September. On 1 September FBA wrote to Mme Beckedorff confirming the appointment (Diary Entry, 27 Aug.; 1 Sept.).

² Wednesday being a holiday, CB Jr. brought his sister to Richmond on Thursday, 3 September, and then to Windsor. FBA had last seen the Royal Family just prior to her departure for France on 15 Apr. 1802. Within nineteen days of her return to England she again paid her compliments to the Queen and Princess Sophia. 'Deeply affected' by the audience, FBA dined with Mme Beckedorff and returned to Richmond to spend the night with CFBt (Diary Entry, 3 Sept.).

³ Attendance upon the Royal Family was an obligation that FBA consistently honoured and CB Jr. abetted. In a letter (JRL) to Mrs. Piozzi on 26 Sept. [1812] MF wrote: 'Aunt D'Arblay went to Windsor, my Uncle Charles carried her thither, & they slept at Richmond, with Charlotte, in their way.' See also L. 657.

640. ¹ On 8 September FBA visited JB, who urged that she consult his physician. In order to forestall any action by JB, she here quickly but politely rejected his advice.

& sagacity. *Charles* is earnest I should rather advise with ⟨D⟩ʳ
⟨Astley⟩²—the Cambridges are wild I should see Dr. *Baillie*³—
my Father himself thinks our former Aesculapius no longer
himself⁴

And, thank Heaven, I still want no one at present. & while |
the directions of my own Doctor succeed, I should be mad to
change them for ANY one. Why, then, once again, apply for
counsel which I cannot answer to my understanding for following, unless my prescriptions fail? I am full of gratitude for your
earnest kindness & most affectionate solicitude: but — —
suppose you make me CHANGE my Larrey system,⁵ & then
that I should no longer amend? —? — ah, my dearest James,
who would be sorry like you? |

641   [23 Chenies Street], 10 September
                                              1812
To Doctor Burney

A.L.S. (Berg), 10 Sept. 1812
Double sheet 8vo   3 pp.   *pmks*   10 SE 1812   11 SP 1812   11 SP
1812   red seal
Addressed: Dr. Burney, / Chelsea College.
Endorsed by CB: Mʳˢ D Y   4
Edited by FBA, p. 1, annotated and dated: ⁎ 10 Septʳ 1812   (4)   Vic-
tory.

² Astley Paston Cooper (1768–1841), cr. Baronet (1821). In 1800 he became
surgeon to Guy's, giving much of his energy to the hospital and medical school.
Within a few years he built up what was said to be the largest private practice in
nineteenth-century England. He became a fellow of the Royal Society in 1802
and a founder of the Medico-Chirurgical Society in 1805.
³ Matthew Baillie (1761–1823), a specialist in thoracic and abdominal medicine,
had in 1795 published his innovatory *Morbid Anatomy of some of the most Important
Parts of the Human Body*. Four years later, his practice had grown so large that he
gave up teaching and resigned his post at St. George's Hospital. After helping
to attend Princess Amelia in her last illness, he was made Physician Extraordinary
to George III.
⁴ Sir Walter Farquhar (1738–1819) had once been an able if undistinguished
physician whose fashionable practice included the Prince of Wales. By 1813 he
was to limit his practice because of growing infirmity.
⁵ The 'general directions of preventive wisdom' given to FBA following her
operation by baron Dominique-Jean Larrey (1766–1842). See L. 668 n. 6, and
vi, L. 595 n. 9.

10 Septr 1812.

Huzza!

My dearest Father,

Huzza!

What a noble epoch for dear old England![1]

I long to embrace you with three times three.

Not bumpers,—but Cheers.[2]

Thanks for your kind Note, dearest Sir, & kind conference with Me Solvyns. I will go to her as soon as I can: but I am now in waiting for a rendezvous with the Duchess of Buccleugh,[3] upon a little business in which I have no personal concern, but for which her Grace has offered most condescendingly to come to me: however, our dear Charlotte Barret, | who negociates, through a third person, the MEETING, will insist for me that I shall save her Grace that trouble, as in duty bound.

Mrs. Solvyns is a most friendly creature; but I should wish no one else coming from her *dwelling place* to know of my Windsor honours. Innocent as they are, they would not there be popular.[4]

We had a most social & chearful & affectionate day on Tuesday at dear James's, whose hospitable board was surrounded by all of our tribe he could collect. I find his Wife *extremely improved*, instead of *fallen off*, in every way; assiduous to please, gentle in her manners, unobtrusive, yet rational [&] well read in her discourse, & full of marked & affectionate attentions [to] my Brother, who both meets & returns them with a pleased |

641. [1] FBA, to whom much of this information was new, implied the victories of Wellington in the Peninsula, the Anglo-Russian peace treaty, and the Tsar's return as an English military ally. All these events were reported in English newspapers in September 1812. See the following announcements in *The Times*: on the 7th, the Spanish government's presentation of the Order of the Toison (Golden Fleece) to Wellington; on the 8th, the English entry into Madrid; on the 10th, the Anglo-Russian peace treaty.

[2] FBA's strained jollity (a leitmotiv in her letters to CB) reveals her efforts to raise her father's spirits, to force him out of his solitude and self-absorption.

[3] Lady Elizabeth Montagu (1743–1827) married in 1767 Henry Scott (1746–1812), 3rd Duke of Buccleuch and 5th Duke of Queensbury. The bond between the Buccleuch and Fitz-James families was their descent from James II. For this relationship, see vi, L. 631 n. 29.

[4] FBA learned of Mary Anne Solvyns's gossip-mongering from various Burneys. In a letter to CB Jr. on 21 July (see L. 635 n. 2), SHB described her as 'That French-headed, fluttering bustler' who started the false rumour of FBA's arrival in England. Concerned about the position of M.d'A, FBA sought to suppress the news of her royal audience lest it be sent back to Paris by Mme Solvyns (L. 675 n. 5). For FBA's awareness of the latter's indiscretion, see L. 696.

distinction I was quite happy to observe.⁵ My Day gave me great pleasure.

> And we had dea[r] Etty with us besides.—
> And we drank your health;
> And M: d'Arblay's.
> So adieu, most dear Sir,
> I hope you heard the Guns?⁶
>   ever your dutiful
>   & most affectionate
>   FB d'Arblay.

10. Septʳ 1812.

⌐Remember me to good Beckey—I hope she is a little *purified*?⌐

---

⁵ Married on 6 Sept. 1785, JB and his wife Sarah *née* Payne were ill-matched. In May [1789], SBP wrote (Barrett, Eg. 3692, f. 13) to FB: 'I am sorry—very sorry to see, that however Duty and Prudence may operate in keeping them together, it is a Union truly ill assorted—She is by nature cold—unsociable— without affection—tho' good & well principled—her deficiencies are in points wᶜʰ I believe he can least of all forgive & wᶜʰ are the most opposite to his own character—wᶜʰ certainly with many excellent qualities, has some real imperfections, tho' he has a heart warmly affectionate towards those by whom he feels himself beloved—I believe with all this she does her *best*—& that what is wanting she cannot help—& I believe her fate is rather hard—& I am very sorry for her— I believe likewise that *his* is not very pleasant & for that I am more sorry.'

Having deserted his wife and children at least twice before 1798 (*HFB*, p. 282), JB ran off with his half-sister SHB on 2 Sept. 1798 and they lived together for five years (iv, Ll. 292, 295, 297). The 'Recluse Man & Maiden' were much in FBA's mind when she left England in 1802. Although JB returned to his wife in 1803 primarily because of his love for their daughter Sally, FBA herself saw for the first time a renewed cordiality between husband and wife.

⁶ The guns celebrated the cessation of hostilities between England and Russia, an event first announced on Thursday, 10 Sept. 1812. *The Times* reported: 'We subjoin an extract of an interesting letter from St. Petersburg, of the most recent date (6th (18th) Aug.):—"To-day peace is formally announced with England; and express orders are given at all the out-ports, that ships bearing the British flag shall be openly and amicably received. . . . The news from the armies is favourable. . . . It is expected that 700,000 men will be in arms in a few weeks." '

To Doctor Burney

A.L. (rejected Diary MSS. 5860–[5860c], Berg), *n.d.*
Double sheet 4to of which the conjugate leaves have been separated
4 pp. *pmks* T.P.P.U. / Tottenham CR 18 SP 1812 wafer
Addressed: ⌜à⌝ To / Dr. Burney / Chelsea College.
Endorsed by CB: Mrs D. B. from Mrs Broome's / 18. Septr
Edited by FBA, p. 1 (5860), *annotated and dated*: ⁜ 18. Septr 1812 (5)
Lady Mary Buccleuch Charlotte Greville.
Edited also by CFBt. *See* Textual Notes.

My most dear Father,
The World is pretty bad, already,—as we of the ancient
regime say——but it will be pretty much more topsy turvy
still, when I write a model of a Letter for my dear Father to
copy!——¹ Lady Charlotte Greville's Letter² is kind &
charming, but it is All TO you, & FOR You, Dear Sir; I had
never the honour of seeing her, though I had that of knowing
particularly, & of meeting with the most partial goodness from
her ladyship's Grand-Mother, the Dowager Dss of Portland.³
Nevertheless, when you have thanked her for this mark of
her affectionate regard for yourself, I shall be very glad if you
can add that I am much flattered in being the means of bringing
forth such kindness, & that I entreat her ladyship to do me the
honour to accept my grateful acknowledgments.
If you should think proper to add any thing else relative to
my return, I should wish it to be nearly confined to the principal

642. ¹ FBA's letter replies to one (Osborn) written by CB on 16 September: 'I
was hond wth the inclosed letter yesterday from Lady Charlotte Greville: will you
tell me how you wish I shd answer it? or rather will you send me a model—& wch
if it appears to me safe & prudent, shall be followed wth the utmost precision.'
Lady Charlotte's letter, now missing, had apparently invited both FBA and CB
to visit her at 31 George Street, Hanover Square.
² Lady Charlotte (1775–1862), eldest daughter of William Henry Cavendish
(afterwards Cavendish-Bentinck), 3rd Duke of Portland, had married in 1793
(with a dowry of £30,000) Charles Greville (d. 1832), youngest son of Richard
Fulke Greville, CB's early patron.
³ Lady Margaret (1715–85), only daughter and heir of Edward Harley (1689–
1741), 2nd Earl of Oxford, had married in 1734 William Bentinck (1709–62),
2nd Duke of Portland. The Dowager Duchess died two years after her meeting
with FB, who 'found [Lady Margaret] very charming, high-bred, courteous,
sensible, and spirited; not merely free from pride, but free from affability—its most
mortifying deputy' (*DL* ii. 198–9).

fact That, after waiting—in vain!—all these Years in the hope
of a PEACE by which I might have travelled *en famille*, a
dangerous & almost desperate illness from which I am still but
convalescente,[4] gave me so urgent a desire to embrace again my
dearest Father, that I could brook no further delay, & M.
d'Arblay generously yielded to my impatience, & procured me
a passport & means for coming over immediately. And further,
that my *head quarters* during my stay will always be at CHEL-
SEA,—but that I make thence excursions to visit all my dear
family, & particularly intimate Friends. |

Of Windsor, & Her Majesty's extreme & sweet graciousness
—touching as it has been to me, I believe it will be most
delicate, except in confidential *discourse*, to be silent.

And not only *delicate* with respect to the Queen, but, in my
situation, *prudent* for myself.

⌐I have been again at Deptford, & again to Richmond, &
spent a Day at lovely Charlotte Barret's, with our Etty, Mr.
Burney, Amelia, Rosette, & good Mrs. Baker.⌐[5]

I have made my visit to her Grace of Buccleugh, & she has
promised to do every thing in her power to favour & fulfil the
commission with which I was charged. She was very comfortable, & perfectly obliging.[6]

We are all going to day *en masse*, to see our Etty | ⌐at Turn-
ham Green,[7] where we are to meet dear Charles & Rosette, & I
suppose, il caro capitano,[8] / & his good compagne, Martin,[9] &
Saratina,[10] / to boot—I know not how to quit the kind house

---

[4] For FBA's illness and operation in late September 1811, see vi, L. 595.
Her reasons for considering herself a *convalescente* are explained in a letter (JRL)
by MF to Mrs. Piozzi on 14 Apr. 1813: 'A year ago—near two, now—she had a
lump in her left breast, which at first she neglected, but which afterwards encreased
so much, the french surgeons, who are very skilful, told her that if it was not speedily
extracted, it would become a *cancer* . . . she submitted.' Following a painful,
seventeen-minute operation, she continued to endure 'uneasy symptoms' in that
side. The doctors prescribed 'utmost quiet & peace of mind' as well as protection
against damp weather.
[5] FBA left Chelsea College on 2 September, and spent much of her time at
Deptford, with intermittent visits to Richmond and 23 Chenies Street. She returned
to CBFB on 17 September. See L. 654 for further reference to Sarah Baker.
[6] The 'commission' was the verbal petition of the princesse de Chimay (1744–
1814) on behalf of an English pension for her nephew Édouard (1776–1833),
duc de Fitz-James, pair de France (1814). This was the same pension granted to
his first wife (Élisabeth-Alexandrine *née* Le Vassor de la Touche), who had died of
tuberculosis in 1810 and left him 'a ruined widower' with two children. See vi,
L. 631 n. 28; *DL* vi. 67–8, 209.
[7] See Diary Entry, 18 September.   [8] JB (i, p. lxix).
[9] JB's son Martin, 24, a solicitor in London.   [10] Sally Burney, aged 16.

of little Hardy,[11] who, as you well told me, has become a pattern
of hospitality—Clement, too, clings to Alex with almost
brotherly fondness.[12] Nevertheless, I shall certainly come *next
week* to make my arrangements with good Beckey[13] for returning
again to my *Head Quarters*, previously to a long visit to the
Rectory.[14]

All join in Love & Duty—

I hope Sarah will seriously benefit by the fine weather,[15] &
that Fanny now, at last brought you her lovely little one.⌐[16]

adieu, Dearest Sir.—

⌐Charles the Younger tells me Lady Crewe is c[ome to] Town.
I hope I shall be able to see [her.]⌐[17]

643   [Paris, August–*pre* 23 September 1812][1]

M. d'Arblay
To Madame d'Arblay

A.L. (Berg), *n.d.*
Half of a single sheet 4to   2 pp.   The cover is missing
Edited by FBA, p. 1, *annotated and dated*: ⸬ 35 Sept[re] 1812 *See*
Textual Notes.

[11] CBFB (i, pp. lxxii–iii).
[12] Clement Robert Francis, now 20, and a student at Caius for the past year,
was early attracted to AA. According to CFBt (L. 632 n. 3): '[Alec] & Clem sat
making pot hooks & when we came away I asked Clem what he was writing.
Oh, said honest Clem, "doing an equation for me that I could not do myself."—
Clem says that Alec is very forward in mathematics & w[d] shine in any english
university . . . he & Alec are great friends & walk about together when Clem can
spare time from his private tutors of whom he has now 5. in the shape of two larks &
three canary birds.'
[13] On consultation with Rebecca More, FBA decided to establish 'Head
Quarters' elsewhere—at 23 Chenies Street, 'picnic' style with CBFB; at the Deptford rectory; at Norbury Park; and later at 63 Lower Sloane Street.
[14] FBA spent much of November and December at Deptford (Ll. 651, 662).
She and AA probably remained at the rectory for Christmas, AA having come
there from Greenwich School on 24 December.
[15] SHB suffered from a crippling rheumatism (L. 637 n. 30).
[16] Fanny Raper and her 4-year-old daughter Catherine Minette.
[17] When in town, Lady Crewe (1748–1818) had lived since the end of the
eighteenth century at an elegant address, 18 Lower Grosvenor Street.

643. [1] This is the third part of a long journal-letter (see Ll. 645, 646) that, according to CBFB, 'seems dated Aug[t]'. Parts one and two are missing, FBA never having
received 'N° 2'.

(3)

Ma santé, ma chere Bonne amie est excellente; et comme je te l'ai promis j'en ai le plus grand soin. Quant à la dissipation tous mes amis sans exception etant à la campagne j'ai pour toute distraction le soin de mon musée que tu trouverais un peu à la Dubster,[2] mais tu voudras bien être assez indulgente pour ne pas me le dire, parce que pour moi il est charmant; et je le prefererais au Musée National si avant de partir tu m'avais laissé ton portrait et celui de notre cher Alex. Dis tu quelquefois à nos parens et amis combien je regrette sincerement de ne pas avoir ma part des jouissances inapréciables dont votre reunion est la source. Dis leur bien qu'il m'en coute infiniment de les abreger en te priant de revenir avec M^de Solveyns que je te prie d'aller voir aussitôt que tu auras lu ceci.[3] Imagine toi ma chere amie que je n'ai reçu aucune lettre de toi ni d'Alex, et que sans l'aimable attention de la femme charmante que tu viens de nommer je serais encore à savoir si tu es ou non en Amérique, en Angleterre ou bien si tu es encore en mer.[4] Va la voir sur le champ je t'en supplie, et tache de t'arranger pour revenir avec elle dans notre hermitage, d'où nous sortirons à la paix pour aller ensemble revoir ⟨de tous⟩ nos excellens parens et amis. Dis leur bien que je les ai toujours portès que je les porte et que ⟨je les⟩ porterai toujours dans mon coeur; et qu'enfin je n'oublierai jamais toutes leurs bontés pour moi et que je sens comme je le dois le sacrifice que je leur demande de te laisser partir, et l'obligation de redoubler de soin pour les en dedomager, en epiant sans cesse tous les moyens de te rendre heureuse autant qu'il est possible que tu le sois eloignée d'eux. Comme je dois tout prevoir, et que quelqu'un m'a fait l'observation que le batiment sur le quel tu t'etais embarquée avec Alexandre pour New York ayant été pris par suite de la rupture avec les Américains, il serait possible qu'on ne voulut pas le laisser revenir avec toi. Que cela ¦ ne t'empêche point de profiter du retour de cette chère Mad^e Solveyns. Aye soin seulement de prendre les precautions necessaires pour qu'il ait l'argent que

---

[2] M. d'A refers to the clutter of his apartment at 8, rue de Miroménil by comparing it to the country house of Mr. Dubster (a comic character in *Camilla*), where clutter was equated with elegance. For Dubster's house, see the chapter 'Specimens of Taste', *Camilla*, eds. Edward A. and Lillian D. Bloom (1972), pp. 274–82.

[3] For an account of Mme Solvyns (1781–1844), see vi, L. 592 n. 2.

[4] Between 15 and 30 August, FBA had written five letters to M. d'A (Diary Entry, 24 Aug.; and Ll. 638, 645).

son oncle et Parrain Charle, que j'embrasse comme je l'aime jugera necessaire de lui assurer. La procuration illimitée⁵ que je t'ai remise à ton départ peut faciliter ces arrangemens. Le Cher et bien cher Frere au quel en ce cas tu le confierais, aurait seulement soin de lui donner un excellent maitre de mathematiques.⁶ [xxxxx 11 *lines*] Si tel etait le parti que tu te trouvasses dans la necessité de prendre malgré mon extreme chagrin de le savoir separé de nous avant d'être plus formé, laisse lui ta benediction et la mienne et dis lui bien de ne jamais perdre de vue le tableau que lui a toujours offert notre union et l'observation qu'il a si souvent été à portée de faire que lorsqu'on n'a rien à se reprocher, on peut, quand on n'a que des gouts moderés, vivre heureux avec bien peu de chose Amen! Une fois cette chere Mᵈᵉ Solveyns partie, je crois bien que je n'aurais de toi aucune nouvelle, or je ne puis passer ainsi l'hiver; ainsi *PARS* avec elle.⁷

[xxxxx 8 *lines marginal writing*]

644   [Hill Street, Richmond],
                                 23 September [1812]¹

Conjointly with Mrs. Broome
To Charles Burney

A.L. and A.L.S. (Berg), 23 Sept.
Double sheet 8vo   3 pp.
Addressed: Revᵈ Dʳ Burney / Deptford
Docketed in pencil, p. 1 :   (F. B.)
On spine: M. Benkovitz   5.3.62

                                          September 23ᵈ—
I have received this with a joy that almost shakes me—but I

---

⁵ On 3 July 1812 M. d'A obtained a procuration (signed by the duc de Masson *et al.*). Not 'illimitée', it allowed FBA to use discretion only in matters relative to the disposition of Camilla Cottage and the sale of *The Wanderer*.

⁶ For AA's mathematical prowess, see L. 645. M. d'A encouraged this skill as an aid to the military career that he anticipated for his son (especially Ll. 796, 821).

⁷ For FBA's reaction to this order and her reasons for rejecting it, see especially the conclusion of L. 646.

644. ¹ This letter may be dated 23 Sept. [1812]. It contains FBA's reaction to L. 643 and the missing 'Nᵒ 1', the only correspondence she had received from M. d'A since her arrival in England.

cannot keep the man while I read. I can only detain him to thank my dearest & dearest Charles[2] with all my soul—God bless & dear Rosette

[*By Charlotte Broome*]

My dearest Charles, our dear Sister is so flurried she cannot write more—& has not yet read the letter coolly—she is going to Chelsea to night—M. d'arblay seems well—the Lodging is taken at Chelsea[3] for to day—She sends you a Thousand Thanks—The | messenger is paid—

You had better to go to Chelsea the first day you can to learn the particulars of her letter.

I hope you are not the worse for your kind reception of so large a party yesterday—

kind love to dear Rosette from us all including

yours ever affectionately
my dear Brother
C. Broome |

There is no good news in the Letter—we fear it is to hasten the return of those dear Souls with Mrs Solven. The Letter seems dated Aug^t

645   Chelsea College,
                              31 August–*post* 23 September 1812

To M. d'Arblay

A.J.L. (Berg), 31 Aug. 1812–Sept^r

Single sheet 4to 2 pp. p. 1, the beginning of a Journal-Letter in French, p. 2, in English

Edited by FBA, p. 1, *annotated and dated*: 1812   (36)

[p. 2:] August. 31st 1812.   (36)

August 31st 1812.

It is through my dear sister Burney I am to send this *feuille*.[1]—

---

[2] The journal-letter of M. d'A (L. 643 n. 1) was delivered by Mme Solvyns to the Deptford rectory, whence CB Jr. had it sent express to Richmond.

[3] At Chelsea College.

645. [1] EBB's courier did not materialize and the letter was finally carried to Paris by the comtesse de Carbonnière. See L. 637 n. 2.

& though I have written to you so much of our first meeting, I cannot help recurring to her subject again.[2] She has had dreadful illness since I have been away, & cares that would have subdued any one else, from difficulties of life, through the changes of Fashion, & fickleness of the times with respect to her excellent husband;[3] but the inexhaustible gaiety of spirits with which Nature has endowed her, buoy her up against all evils that are not either immediate, or domestic: against what is *immediate* she necessarily sinks till she has devized some means to conquer them; &, against what is domestic her heart, with all its sportiveness, is too affectionate & too feeling to bear even the smallest shock. The good Mr. Burney is so conscious of her abilities, & so satisfied with their activity in his own & his family's service, that he casts every thing upon her judgement, which is happy for them all, for though he has a solidly good understanding, & can *think* as justly as any Man, he is so ABSENT & inexperienced, that he could never ACT till the season for all that should be done would be past by. Poor Esther therefore is often heavily laden, in defiance of the elastic spring that brings all round again—Oh my dearest—generous —noble ami!—what does not the prosperity & relief of her & her House owe to your exquisite disinterestness! it has elegantly provided for TWO of her dear Daughters, & is a standing Honour, Credit, & Happiness to all our Race. Maria, at Bath Easton, lives upon equal terms with all the highest & most opulent Personages that surround her.[4] In seeing this far-

---

[2] Probably in L. 638, of which only a fragment is now available.

[3] Charles Rousseau Burney had always been admired by FBA, who once referred to him as her sister's 'faithful Charles . . . one of the worthiest young men living' (*ED* i. 102). An able harpsichordist, he was for a time well patronized by CB's 'great Volk'. But by the last decades of the eighteenth century, his instrument was regarded as old-fashioned so that he, like many other music masters 'once in great business, [was] now wholly scholarless' (Lonsdale, p. 294).

EBB accepted her poverty, finding relief in what FBA called her 'gay exertions'. On 19 July 1819, EBB acknowledged to FBA (Barrett, Eg. 3690, ff. 126–7b) that 'my worthy & industrious partner has had *many* heavy [disappointments],—of which you may be certain I bore a share ——. On many Occasions where in—had merit received it's deserts, his Applications *must* have been successful,—which however was far from being the Case—19 times out of 20.—& this circumstance kept us long in straightened Circumstances.—'

[4] EBB's eldest child, Hannah Maria Bourdois, now 40, was a rich widow after a brief but financially successful marriage (1800–6) arranged by M. d'A (iv, Ll. 387, 392, 394). Within a year of her husband's death, Maria Bourdois on 14 June [1807] wrote to FBA (Barrett, Eg. 3697, f. 60): 'All my pecuniary affairs of which I likewise forgot to write about, are in good train, very shortly I shall have settled every thing and have my money in my own hands. my dear Sophy is as much

spreading good to my dear Hetty, my dear Mrs Locke now entirely gives up her early reproach in favour of Fanny[5]—That beloved Mrs. Locke, our *Non-pareil* Amine, & the ever good Natured & sprightly Augusta, must fill my next *feuille*. I know you will not like *a word & away* on their subject, & I have too much still to devellop upon our Alex for more room here. His extreme *sauvagerie* seems wearing away. Though open to endless commentary, he is universally a favourite here[6] |

I must remit all else of Journal—as I have only this half page permission for this occasion. What follows was written before I knew my narrow boundary.

[*post* 23] *Septr Chelsea College,*

Quand aurai-je encore de vos nouvelles, Oh mon ami! que deviennent toutes vos Lettres, et où vont elles?[7] car de les

overjoyed at the idea of coming to live with me as I am delighted with the prospect of having her.' The two sisters soon settled in Bath Easton.

EBB was always grateful to the d'Arblays for marrying off the dowerless Maria. As late as 19 July 1819 EBB wrote (Barrett, Eg. 3690, f. 127) to FBA: 'I do not forget your great kindness, thro' which our Dear first born,—gained a Prize, in the Matrimonial line—wch has shed a happy influence over all her family.'

5 Mr. and Mrs. Locke felt that M. d'A in 1800 should have arranged a marriage between Lambert-*Antoine* Bourdois (*c.* 1761–1806) and Fanny Phillips rather than Hannah Maria. With the death of SBP, the Lockes had worried about the future of the 18-year-old Fanny, on whom they had lavished affection when she was growing up in Mickleham between 1785 and 1795. At 25, Fanny Phillips also recognized her need to marry. About a month before her marriage in 1807 she signed a letter to MF 'still Fanny Phillips' and on 13 July 1807 reported 'that her name was that day scratched off the Old Maid's list'. See the letters (JRL) of MF to Mrs. Piozzi, dated 19 June and 21 July.

6 If a favourite, AA aroused more wonder than affection. CFBt—like other relatives—emphasized his intellectual accomplishments: 'Alec is promised admission into the Polytechnic school in Paris, in wch 300 young men are finished in Sciences &c. generally those who have distinguished themselves by previous attainments, & *those only*, in all France, are exempted from the conscription for life. that they may be literati & savans & so on' (L. 632 n. 3). Even MF acknowledged his scholarly interests. She described him on 15 Jan. [1813] in a letter (JRL) to Mrs. Piozzi: 'Alexander is 17; a very expressive dark-eyed, intelligent creature— a perfect Bookworm; his nose always in mathematics or Thucydides.'

7 Such lamentation runs throughout FBA's correspondence in this volume, even after the Restoration in April 1814. During the two preceding war years the difficulty of sending letters to and from France was reflected in CB's letter (Osborn) of April 1813 as he sympathized with FBA on 'uneasiness at the silence of her kind and worthy husband.' And on 5 Sept. 1813, CB Jr. wrote (Osborn) to his son: 'Poor d'Arblay has written 20 letters in the last two months, and has not received one line,—in reply.' On rare occasions letters could go through the post without cachet (L. 654); more often they were carried by hand or filtered through volunteers: Mme de Carbonnière and Mme Solvyns, John de Blaquiere, M. Saulnier, and the 'negociants'—M. Leconte, M. David, and M. Récamier. After the Restoration

posseder même ne me rendroit pas plus sûr que je ne suis de leurs existences. Cinq fois je vous ai écrit, sans savoir si jamais vous avez reçu une seule ligne de moi; cependant, il y a bien long tems depuis ma cinquieme Lettre jusqu'à celle-ci, faute de trouver aucune occasion de vous addresser encore mes jere-miades. De vous, neanmoins, j'ai reçu 1 et 3. Mais le N°. 2 m'a echappé. Si elle est perdue, ou si je l'aurai plus tard, c'est ce que j'ignore. Mais par Mad^e de Caïbot j'ai eu au moins la consolation d'entendre que son fils,[8] il y a à peu près un mois, lui a parlé de vous, et bien que ce n'étoit que pour dire "il y a quelques jours que nous n'avons pas vu M. d'Arblay;" c'étoit pour moi beaucoup, moi, depuis tant de semaines affamée de toute intelligence. Mon projet de Journal est, helàs, aneanti, par le cruel découragement de tant de difficultés C'est par Mad^e de Carbonière que ceci pass.—l'occasion offerte par ma soeur m'a manqué—Mon cher Charle me demande de vivre tout à fait chez lui, et d'être à moi toute la matinée, pour écrire à mon loisir et plaisir.[9] Il a une maison charmante à Deptford, où il est Recteur.[10] Il m'a engagé à mettre Alex chez son fils[11]—

C'est très couteuse—mais que faire?—

the exchange of mail between England and France continued uncertain (L. 794). In this period, FBA had other couriers: Sir James Mackintosh, the duc de Luxembourg, the staff of M. de La Châtre, Colonel Harcourt, M. Greffulhe, Barbara Planta, Mr. Entwisle.

[8] Probably Charles-Jean-Claude-Louis (baptized 14 May 1795 in Richmond).

[9] All of FBA's immediate family knew that she wished to give over each morning to the completion of *The Wanderer*.

[10] Ordained in 1808, CB Jr. was appointed Chaplain to George III in 1810. In the following year he was named vicar of St. Paul's, Deptford, in which rectory he lived (and at virtually the same time vicar of Herne Hill, Kent, and rector of Little Hinton, Wiltshire). See i, p. lxxi. In a letter (JRL), postmarked 28 May 1811, MF asked Mrs. Piozzi: 'Did I tell you of my Uncle Charles's strange goodfortune of having two livings given him in *one* day, with power to hold both & reside at neither? . . . & he will have had at 45, more than 2000 a year Preferment, after having been but 2 years in the Church.' See also her letter (Barrett, Eg. 3704A, f. 3–3b) to CFBt.

[11] The Greenwich School, of which CPB had been acting head-master since 1811 and which in his letters to Robert Finch (Bodleian) he often called 'the Gerund Mill'. His father did not officially resign until early in 1813 (Ll. 650, 676 n. 1).

Conjointly with Alexander d'Arblay
To M. d'Arblay

A.L. (Berg), *n.d.*
Double sheet 4to 4 pp. *pmk* 10 Décembre 1812
Addressed: À / M^r / M^r d'Arblay, / Rue de Miromenil, / N° 8. / f^g S^t
Honoré; à Paris.
Edited by FBA, p. 1, *annotated and dated* from *pmk*: Finished in Dec^{bre}
1812 (38) *See further*, Textual Notes.

Alex having undertaken to finish Clement,[1] I proceed to
speak of my poor Norbury. I cannot have the happiness to see
him, for I find that he is settled in Ireland, where he has
finished his education, as I believe, with great reputation, &
worth of every kind. He means to enter the Church, & is now
preparing for ordination.[2] He wishes ardently to live in England,
but, I am told, he would here find much more difficulty in
meeting with promotion than there, because he has not had the
advantage of an English University for completing his studies.
He has desired me, through his sister, to try my influence:[3] God
knows how joyfully I will do it, should I find any possibility.
But he must first settle his plan, & know what he can ask.[4]

William is at Sea,[5] *where*, is not certain, but it is believed he is
in the Mediterranean.

646. [1] At chess.
  [2] Charles Norbury (i, p. lxxi), the 'adored' child of SBP, had received his
B.A. from Trinity College, Dublin, in 1806. He was to be ordained deacon on
11 Oct. 1812 and a priest a fortnight later. For his death in 1814 and an explanation of FBA's epithet 'poor', see L. 749 nn. 1, 2.
  [3] Fanny Raper acted as intermediary between Norbury and FBA. His efforts
for preferment in England, however, came to nothing and he died in Ireland,
aged 29.
  [4] Ostensibly FBA was to petition the Archbishop of Canterbury to grant by
his special powers a mandate degree in lieu of the normal English university degree
on which Church advancement seemed to depend. She was to approach the
Archbishop through the Queen just as she had done—unsuccessfully—in 1791
for CB Jr.
  [5] John William James, the younger son of SBP, was now 21 and a midshipman
in the Royal Navy. He had already completed a three-year tour of duty in the
West Indies. See MF's letter (JRL) to Mrs. Piozzi, postmarked 28 Mar. 1810.

Ralph Broome is at school with Charles's son at Greenwich, & I have not yet seen him. But I am informed he is a shrewd & very original Boy.[6] And now for my eldest Nephew visible in these parts, Charles Parr; he is now Master of his Father's Academy, & with the happiest prospects. He is sensible & good, of pleasing & gentle manners, & an excellent scholar; he has married purely from inclination, a young lady who is pleasing & gentle, & rather pretty: but in no way striking.[7] She seems good, however, & adores her husband. They have a little Girl of 4 or 5 months of age.[8]

Richard, the Clergyman, who is the real *head nephew*, is well, & lives prudently & respectably at his living in Dorsetshire, with a new married Wife of whom I have yet had no account.[9]

Now for the neices. Maria, you know, is at Bath Easton, &, they say, grown handsomer rather than less handsome. She promises to come hither during my stay. Fanny has been 3 or 4 times to see me. She is not much altered in person, nor at all in manner; she is, therefore, still pretty, & full of spirit, information, knowledge, powers of discourse, & accomplishments.[10] She is, at present, at the attorney Generals', whose Lady, Lady Plomer, has conceived a warm attachment for her.[11]—D[r]

[6] The only son of CBFB and the late Ralph Broome (i, p. lxxiii), Dolph, as he was called, was a precocious 11-year old, given to respiratory ailments. As early as June 1810 he was taken 'to Richmond for a week to cure his war-whoop'— so MF reported (JRL) to Mrs. Piozzi. In March 1811 he studied at home, 'till Sir Walter Farquhar allows him to return to School'—another report (JRL) sent by his sister to Mrs. Piozzi. For his continuing decline, see Ll. 699 and n. 5, 713 n. 1, 718 n. 16, 724 n. 17, 735 n. 11.

[7] CPB received his B.A. (1808), M.A. (1811), B.D., and D.D. (1822) from Oxford. On 24 Dec. 1810 he had married Frances Bentley Young (c. 1792–1878). See i, p. lxxii.

[8] Frances Anne (1812–60), the first of CPB's six children, was born on [30] April.

[9] Richard Allen Burney (1773–1836), EBB's surviving son and FBA's eldest nephew, had no living in Dorsetshire. He was at this time Rector of Rimpton, Somerset (1802), and Master of St. Mary Magdalen Hospital, Winchester (1804). On 10 Oct. 1811 he had married Elizabeth Layton Williams (1786–1862).

[10] Frances or 'Fanny' Burney (1776–1828), daughter of EBB, was governess to the seven children of Sir Thomas and Lady Plumer at their estate Canons in the parish of Stanmore Parva, Middlesex.

[11] Marianne Turton (1775–1857) had married in 1794 Thomas Plumer (1753–1824), knighted (1807), attorney-general (1812). See i, L. 21 n. 10.

Sophy is with M[aria].[12] | And I shall see her at the same time. —Cecilia is always with Mrs. Hawkins,[13] but she has written the prettiest & most *naïve* Letter of delight upon our arrival, with her plan to induce Mrs. Hawkins to bring her, also, to London this winter, for a meeting; to which the good Mrs. Hawkins seems well inclined.

Amelia lives with her parents.[14] She is gay & pleasing, & perfectly good-natured; very fair, with pretty Eyes, fine teeth, & so many requisites of beauty that it is astonishing she should not be beautiful; yet she is not: au reste, I will not judge till I have seen her more particularly.

sweet Charlotte Barret is just what she was, i.e, charming. Marian[15] is on a visit at Mr. Arthur Young's,[16] & I have not

---

[12] See L. 645 n. 4.

[13] Cecilia Charlotte Esther Burney (1788–1821), daughter of EBB, was adopted by Ann Hawkins *née* Burney (iii, L. 132 n. 5). So attached had the two become that in April 1821, after Cecilia's death from tuberculosis, EBB wrote (Barrett, Eg. 3690, f. 142) that Cecy's 'dear remains are to be deposited with those of her beloved Aunt Hawkins. by her own desire (expressed long ago).'

[14] Amelia Maria Burney (1792–1868), the seventh and youngest surviving child of EBB. See i, p. lxix.

[15] Marianne Francis (1790–1832), younger daughter of CBFB, was given to evangelical piety and served as a secretary-guardian to Arthur Young (1741–1820), the agriculturist (i, L. 14 n. 1). See her letter (Barrett, Eg. 3704A, ff. 91–2) to CFBt, dated 31 Oct. 1812, or that (JRL) to Mrs. Piozzi, postmarked 22 Aug. 1811, in which Young is described as 'a man of high & exalted principle—firm & intelligent—Literature & Farming his delight—Think of such a man being seized in his latter days with *blindness*!—Not able to read his own books, nor see his own land—& yet as chearful & resigned as if he endured no privations at all—He is a beautiful specimen of what Religion will do for a man—For he *must feel* his loss deeply—but he says it is his duty to consider what he has left.' See also L. 719 n. 3.

[16] Since FBA last saw Arthur Young in October 1792 (i, Ll. 33, 34), he was permanently blinded following an operation in 1811 for the removal of cataracts. He remained devoted to FBA, according to MF in 1812 and as reported by CBFB (Barrett, Eg. 3693, ff. 88–9): ' "Mr Young desires me to say, that as his time approaches for returning to town [end of November], he passes all the friends he hopes to see in review before him—but very few afford him much pleasure in anticipation except *yourself*, his Richmond friends, Wilberforce, &, if he might hope for a little conversation with her, his old friend M^e d'Arblay, whom he much wishes to hear, & regrets he cannot *see*—in this respect he says she will have a great advantage—for should time have made any alterations in Her, they will be quite imperceptable to Him: but she will see only the wreck & ruin of a man—old, & blind, & helpless—but yet remembering, with no faint delight, the many happy hours he has passed with her—" '

yet seen her; but all agree she is a *prodige*,[17] though some with praise, some with censure; & all with wonder.

I come now to the youngest of the niece tribe, Sally, Daughter of James. This young creature, just 15, without the real beauty of fine features, has a face so very agreable that one cannot help calling it beyond its intrinsic right, *pretty*. She is fat, but not surpassing a full *embonpoint*, as much the result of health, lively spirits, & laughing ideas, as of flourishing Youth. She is by nature a perfect *espèigle*, but she has such good parts, so sincere a desire to be well thought of by those she esteems, & so good a heart joined to so gaily sweet a temper, that I doubt not but she will make, hereafter, a strikingly excellent wife & Mother, though she seems now to think only of sport & play & gambol.[18]

The truly worthy Mr. Burney, for whom we had suffered a false alarm, is even remarkably well; though his affairs, alas, are by no means prosperous as his merits ought to make them![19]

Mr. Barret & Mr. Raper I leave to some future Letter, when I shall have seen them better.

---

[17] According to CFBt (Barrett, Eg. 3702A, f. 163b), CB told FBA that MF was a 'prodigy'. At Bradfield Hall, she had 'a table and a great chair filled with books in all languages, as she reads in every language every day to keep them up— Greek, Latin, Italian, Hebrew, Arabic, German, Spanish, French, Dutch, etc.' See Amelia Defries, *Sheep and Turnips* (1938), p. 154. For an authoritative account of the friendship between MF and Arthur Young, see John G. Gazley, *The Life of Arthur Young 1741–1820* (Philadelphia, 1973), chs. xi, xii.

Between FBA and her niece there was a friendly suspicion. In a letter (Barrett, Eg. 3704A, f. 89) to CFBt, postmarked 10 Aug. 1812, MF feared her aunt 'would not tolerate *me*, just fresh from France, for I have lost all my relish . . . for gay company, & society in its usual state, music &c—& *rejoicing* in my loss, am not very likely to recover it. My pleasures now consist in going after the poor, & teaching children &c the society of religious people, reading & exercise.' Writing a letter (JRL) to Mrs. Piozzi in September 1812, MF admitted that she wished to see FBA out of '*Curiosity* . . . for to pretend affection for a person one never saw, is ridiculous; & I have not the most remote recollection of my celebrated Aunt'.

[18] Sarah or 'Sally' Burney, born in 1796, was JB's youngest child. For an example of her mischievous wit, see her letter (Barrett, Eg. 3700A, f. 140–140b) to CBFB, dated 4 Sept. 1813.

[19] For Charles Rousseau Burney's financial difficulties, see L. 645 n. 3.

All these, mon ami, make my Journal, for neither morning nor afternoon passes that some of them do not visit me. Kindness & affection such as they all shew would have warmed my heart had it been formed of marble. |

[*Alexander d'Arblay continued the letter*]

Dans ma dernière lettre que vous avez reçue ou recevrez plus tard, car j'ignore des deux laquelle partira la premiere, je vous détaillais fort longuement tout ce que je fais maintenant, et comme j'y parlais beaucoup d'Algebre et peu de Géométrie, Vous avez pu soupçonner que j'étais un peu enclin à négliger cette derniere, pour laquelle au contraire j'ai été saisi d'un beau feu et d'un dépit brûlant, en voyant que tout le monde ici la fasait six fois mieux que moi — Clément fait son Euclid sur le bout de ses doigts, *ad unquem*; et jusqu'à fatiguer Marianne, qui est a great scholar comme vous savez, qui fait parfaitement la Géometrie et même un peu d'Algebre. C'est un vrai prodige que cette Marianne; outre le Latin et le Grec, qu'elle entend à livre ouvert, elle parle Français, Anglais, Allemand, Italien, Et Espagnol, — chacun comme si c'était sa propre langue; et maintenant, — devinez ce qu'elle fait — elle apprend l'Hébreu et l'Arabe, tout cela, dit on, (car je ne l'ai pas encore vue) sans la moindre pédanterie; au contraire, ses lettres font on ne peut pas plus comique et plein d'une franche gaieté — Elle fait aussi, comme vous voyez, la Geom. et un peu d'Algebre — Elle est aussi très forte sur la Piano,[20] et compose — J'ai vu d'elle aussi de fort jolis dessins — Pour revenir à nos moutons, —

[*Madame d'Arblay concluded*]

I am obliged to take the pen, & seize this last sheet, to tell my dearest Friend, A *second* time, that I have, at length, heard from

[20] On 5 May 1812 MF wrote (JRL) to Mrs. Piozzi: 'I am working at Hebrew, with Dr. Kett to help me. . . . The Bishop of St. David's, Dr. Burgess, has instituted a Hebrew College, to promote the study of the sacred language, with premiums for the best translation, for calligraphy, &c &c. Kett says I must work hard . . . & he will send what I choose to the College, to try for the *Bishop's prize*.' By 10 August, she asked her correspondent: 'Did you ever think much of Arabic? that Hebrew cannot be perfectly known without it? And that roots, lost in Hebrew, are found in Arabic?'
For a time teaching distracted her from her music. In a letter (JRL) to Mrs. Piozzi, dated 28 Nov. 1812: 'I shall never play upon [the pianoforte], depend. Six months cessation from music has quite disabled my hands, & I am too lazy as well as too busy [teaching at "Mr Young's Schools for poor children"] to take the trouble of practising it all up again.'

him. *Septr 25th* I received, through Mrs. Solvyns, a long & delicious Journal Letter, & my joy at sight of your hand, after such long abstinence, was almost too powerful; yet it was soon *soberized*, when I saw that one Letter was missing; that I had N° I. & a small N° 3; but No 2. & that N° 3²¹ gives directions that have reference to N° 2, that I cannot clearly understand. All, however, about our Boy is exquisitely kind, & completely comprehended, & shall implicitly be attended to. But for MY return, if indeed your *santé is excellente*,²² as you assure me; every reason that *belongs* to reason opposes the change. for example; building upon the decided months, by yourself alone decided!— I have acted accordingly;²³ my dear Father *expects* them, so does All my Family; so do ALL my Friends; Maria & Sophy come at Xmas; Mrs. Hawkins brings Cecilia in November; Mrs. Waddington has taken a town house for December;²⁴ Sally comes from Lymington in a Month; Marian Franci[s] ˡ from Arthur Young's in 3 Weeks; all for meetings! I have not yet been to Norbury Park, where I am promised for a fortnight. ⌐I have settled nothing relative to my cottage,²⁵ I know nothing of *new* tenants²⁶ nor of the state of the property, all was to be arranged upon the spot, during my visit. Every thing is confused of my deposit in the

<hr/>

²¹ See Ll. 643 n. 1, 644 n. 2.
²² FBA repeated the opening statement of L. 643 to emphasize the logic of her remaining in England until spring.
²³ FBA had planned 'to stay in England *certainly* till the end of October, & all the winter if M. d'Arblay is well & can spare her'. See the letter, dated 26 Aug. 1812, of CFBt to her sister (Barrett, Eg. 3702A, f. 162b), and also the letter (JRL) of MF to Mrs. Piozzi, dated 26 Sept. 1812.
²⁴ See L. 658.
²⁵ Built in West Humble in 1796–7 with part of the earnings from her third novel, Camilla Cottage was rented during some of FBA's stay in France and so was a source of income. (See v, L. 536 n. 4, as an example of Mrs. Locke's successful effort to rent the cottage to the sisters of Baron Rolle 'for 6 months certain at 2 guineas & half p^r week' and later to Bolton Hudson.) Shortly after her return to England, FBA toyed with the idea of selling it, but in November 1812, CB wrote in a letter (Osborn) 'most urgently, to warn you against *selling* your Cottage at Norbury Park, you can settle, and receive, any money that has been rec^d, and is due to you, for *rent*; but by no means part wth the *Freehold* . . . think how creditable it will be for our student to have a little freehold in his Native Country.'
²⁶ The tenant of Camilla Cottage was Bolton Hudson (*c.* 1755–1820), the Receiver for Bridewell and Bethlehem Hospitals and Steward of Bridewell. According to the archives of both institutions, Hudson was named as Receiver (and hence Bridewell's steward) in July 1792 with an office at 14 New Bridge Street, the entrance to Bridewell. As Receiver he was responsible for keeping the financial records of both hospitals, collecting rents, etc. payable to both, and as steward for overseeing household management. For his son, see L. 831.

Strand,[27] that I wish to receive entirely, & must have to repay immediate expences; Charles is endeavouring to adjust it, but it is complicated, & I have no balance to shew or produce, not even in my memory!—And, added to all this, which demands so much time, I have had no leisure to unpack my small valise.[28] Imagine, therefore, how much confusion would result from so sudden a change of measures, & how much we should both have to regret at such important omissions—when my journey should so unsatisfactorily be ended. Think it over, my dearest Friend, & *if indeed* you are well, let prudence take the rein, for our future prosperity. Whatever may be the obstacles for a few months, they will not, in all human probability, extend to my half year, & then, at least, we shall not have been parted without fault.⊓ The avidity of my dear Family in our present union is as yet beyond any controlling. I am never an hour out of the arms of one or another of the affectionate tribe. I can only obtain leisure for my *Valise* by waiting till our common joy is less tumultuous, when I must try to shut myself up. If, therefore, You keep WELL, Think again ere you summon me to this change.[29] If *not*, every consideration upon earth is as NOTHING in the scale of eagerness for re-union.

The worthy & admirable Edward,[30] who is now in the room, begs to be remembered to you. He is always the same, i.e, as ignorant of his own worth as his cotemporaries are of their deficiencies. My dearest Father is rather better & rather stronger.[31]—Charles has preached 2^ce· to Day at the Chap^l roy^l.[32]

⊓James, Esther, & Charlotte talk of you incessantly, & also the young ones, & surtout Charles of Greek fame.⊓[33]

[27] Thomas Coutts and Company, the banking firm at 59 Strand. Here CB had an account into which several instalments of FBA's pension were paid—only to become entangled with her father's assets. See L. 653 n. 6.

[28] FBA's euphemism for *The Wanderer* manuscript carried in a small leather 'valise' twice across the Channel.

[29] See n. 23.

[30] Edward Francesco Burney (1760–1848), FBA's artist cousin (i, L. 10 n. 9).

[31] See Clement Francis's statement, L. 637 n. 28.

[32] On 27 September, CB Jr. preached in the chapel at Windsor before the Queen and the Princesses.

[33] When FBA judged her brother's scholarly renown, she considered his library, described by CFBt to MF (Barrett, Eg. 3702A, ff. 169b–170) as 'superb—nothing but english greek & latin tho—& Waltons Polyglot. ... The finest editions of all fine authors. So far it is delightful—but my uncles taste is to collect every edition. ... he has 25 different editions of Homer ... 30 editions of *Aristotle*.'
But more significantly, FBA acknowledged the recognition given to CB Jr.'s

Charles is inexpressibly kind upon the new idea—which I have just communicated to him, for Alex.[34]

⌐Mrs. Solvyns has behaved with a sweetness of good humour, & an openness of liberality in forgiving my seeming omissions of waiting upon her that fixes me her friend for life. I have really & truly had no power nor means to seek her.⌐[35]

647   [Chelsea College, 1 October 1812][1]

To Charles Burney

A.L. (Osborn), *n.d.*
Single sheet large 4to   2 pp.

Thanks for your ever kind zeal, my dearest Charles. I shall soon, I believe, have a summons to Windsor.[2] I had the honour of a long audience—& sweet as long—Yesterday, after the Eagle Feast.

I cannot help wishing earnestly something might be done for poor *Mᵉ la Marquise de Caillebot*. In being taken prisoner at Deal, She has already lost her passage on to La Guadaloupe, of which she is a native, & whither she goes, with two of her Children, to seek an asylum at her Mother's, Madᵉ de Maupertuis:[3] she has

three latest works: *Richardi Bentleii et doctorum virorum Epistolae, partim mutuae* (1807); *Tentamen de Metris, ab Aeschylo in choricis cantibus adhibitis* (1809); Philemon the Grammarian, *Φιλημονος λεξικον τεχνολογικον* (1812). FBA thought him pre-eminent as a Hellenist, next only to Richard Porson and Samuel Parr (*Memoirs*, iii. 410).
   [34] The 'new idea' concerned AA's enrolment at Greenwich School (L. 650).
   [35] FBA hestitated to visit Mme Solvyns (L. 641 n. 4) or even to establish formal relations with her family in Chelsea (L. 696 n. 11). It was not until 11 May 1813 that visits were exchanged by the ladies, and these were prompted by Mme Solvyns's planned departure for France (L. 692).

647. [1] The dating of this letter depends on the following: On 30 Sept. 1812 *The Times* reported that 'Her MAJESTY and the PRINCESSES will go this morning to Whitehall Chapel to see the French Eagles deposited.' The ceremony was a symbolic 'feast', a tribute to English military might. On that same day Charlotte Beckedorff sent a note (Berg) to FBA. Opening with the statement 'La Reine étant à Whitehall, pour voir la Ceremonie de la deposition des Aigles', she urged that FBA attend her Majesty and the Princesses that afternoon in the Beckedorff apartment at the Queen's House. FBA complied.
   [2] As anticipated, FBA was at Windsor for several days in November (L. 657).
   [3] Gertrude-Constance Desvergers de Maupertuis had married her cousin Nicolas-Pierre Desvergers de Sannois, seigneur de Maupertuis. For an identification of Mme de Caillebot and her problem, see Ll. 637 and n. 3, 654.

therefore a second passage to pay!—And her husband, the Marquis, who remains in France, with two other children,[4] both born in England, (at Richmond) is already a ruined man. Not only M. La Châtre,[5] but Lady Liverpool, upon my responsibility,[6] has interested herself in Me de Caillebots favour, for procuring her a passport first for London, & next for la Guadaloupe.[7] She has herself already sent a Copy of the inclosed petition to Deal, but received no answer. Could Mr. Reeves be prevailed upon to intercede for her?[8] He is so liberal, & seems to view I the innocent & hapless conquered people with so much humanity, & so strong a sense of impartial justice, that he is by no means a man immoveable.[9] I should be truly gratified in serving this poor lady, whose Mother, Mad^e de Maupertuis, is a lady of the first consideration at Guadaloupe,

[4] FBA was either inaccurate about the number of children remaining in France or one had died. The marquise de Caillebot bore three of her four sons in Richmond: Charles-Jean-Claude-Louis (L. 645 n. 8), Henri-Frédéric-Joseph-Laurent (1797), Georges-Louis (1799). See vi, L. 601 n. 1.

[5] Claude-Louis de La Châtre (1745–1824) was known to FBA by reputation from his brief stay at Juniper Hall (ii, p. xvi). He now attended Louis XVIII at Hartwell as 'l'agent confidentiel' (Vitrolles, ii. 499) and served primarily as liaison between the French King and the English government. So successful was he in this role that upon the Restoration he was appointed ministre plénipotentiaire en Angleterre.

[6] FBA informed Lady Louisa of the Caillebots' distress when they met on 17 August at Lady Lucy Foley's house (L. 637). Known for her charity, Lady Louisa had access to official circles through her husband, Lord Liverpool (appointed First Lord of the Treasury in June 1812).

[7] Apparently Mme de Caillebot was looked upon with suspicion by the officials of the customs office in Dover. While, according to a regulation of the Alien Act, she needed a passport to travel inland, she would be required to go to London for one purpose only, i.e. for further interrogation by the magistrates at Great Marlborough Street (see Nelson, p. 127). If she were cleared during that investigation, she would then be issued still another passport by either the Secretary of State or the Superintendent of Aliens that would permit her to leave the kingdom (*Statutes at Large*, 38 George III, *c*. 50).

[8] John Reeves (*c*. 1752–1829). Educated at Eton and Oxford, he was the author of *The History of the English Law* (5 vols., 1783–1829). In 1792, having recently returned to England after a term in Newfoundland as Chief Justice, he founded on 20 Nov. 1792 the Association for Preserving Liberty and Property against Republicans and Levellers. In that same year he served also as Commissioner for Bankruptcy, Chief of the Standing Committee of the Mint, and Receiver of the Police. On 30 Nov. 1792 the *Star* claimed that his annual salary was £1,000. In 1801 Pitt appointed him to a policy-making position in the office of the King's Printer. For his other appointments, see *DNB* and *GM* xcix² (1829), 468–71.

[9] At this time a Superintendent of Aliens (along with the two Under-Secretaries of State), Reeves had always been a vehement conservative and active in the association movement of 1792–3, which was responsible for detecting and suppressing activities deemed subversive and dangerous to property. FBA hoped he might out of sympathy for the aristocratic Mme de Caillebot and her children expedite the issuance of her passports, first from Deal (or Dover) to London, and then from London to Guadaloupe.

from whom she has been separated almost from Childhood, through circumstances of which I am ignorant, but who now eagerly expects a re-union,—& this poor Daughter, except her wardrobe, carries back to the maternal home—WORSE than NOTHING.

648   [Chelsea College], 13 October [1812]

Conjointly with Sarah Harriet Burney
To Charles Burney

A.L.S. & A.N. (Berg), 13 Oct.
Double sheet 8vo   2 pp.   a rectangle $(3.7 \times 3.4'')$ including the address is cut from upper right corner of second leaf   *pmks*   O[C] 1812   1812 wafer

My dear Charles,
    I am torn to pieces by the *embarras* not of riches! — — but of kindness—my Sister B. is just come from Turnham Green & claims me in John street[1]—Charlotte Broome is lonely, & demands me in Chenier street—& Charlotte Barrett pretends she LONGS for us at Richmond.
    —Norbury Park is yet unseen!—
    What shall I do?—
    Will you take me for *a Week at a time* till I have a little smoothed these kind difficulties?—
    Come to Chelsea on Thursday prepared in mind how to solve them for
                                          your ever affe^te
                                                FB d'A.
Best Love to Rosette.
        Octr 13. |

[By Sarah Harriet Burney]

    My dearest Brother, I must make use of this little corner, to

648. [1] No. 5 John Street, Oxford Street, to which EBB and her family had moved from Beaumont Street, *pre* 28 June 1805.

entreat that, if you ever invite me to Deptford, it may on no account be whilst that disagreeable person, Sister d'Arblay is with you!

Ever most affectionately yours

Kindest love   S. H. Burney.

     to Mʳˢ Burney.

649   [Chelsea College,
post 7 October–pre 30 October 1812]

To Mrs. Broome

> A.L. (Berg), *n.d.*
> Single sheet 8vo   2 pp.   wafer
> *Addressed*: Mrs. Broome. — / Chenier's Street —
> *Endorsed by* CBFB: Sister d'arblay / 1812
> *Annotated*, p. 2: to ⟨posted⟩ addresse⟨s⟩

My own kindest Charlotte—
To say Nay would be to have no heart — — —
I will write a delay to Mrs. Lock—[1]
Be not anxious, for I am better—& I have anticipated your idea, for I have applied for *opinion*—to Mr. Graham here,[2] of whom I think extremely well—he is delicate & gentle. Sarah has most kindly done this for me. And I shall have the receipt immediately for the doubtful dose—&c

---

649. [1] This letter can be dated shortly after 7 or 8 October and before 30 October. On one of these early October days CFBt sent a letter (Barrett, Eg. 3702A, ff. 169–70) to MF: 'Nothing yet fixed about Aunt d Arblays coming to us, & for what I see it is as far off as ever—She & Mama have managed between them. dear Mama all good ness to me, & meaning & wishing to secure her for me, & yet letting her promise to go to Deptford and offer to go to Norbury Park before we are to see her.' CBFB relayed this disappointment to FBA, whose visit to Norbury Park was therefore postponed in favour of '*half* a week' at Richmond (L. 650).
    [2] Richard Robert Graham (1734–1816) became at 13 the Apothecary at Chelsea Hospital, having succeeded his father Daniel (d. 1747). FBA's confidence is inexplicable, for Graham had no professional training and had to employ others to do his work. According to Dean (p. 221), Graham 'may be said to have been maintained by the Royal Hospital, from his cradle to his death-bed. . . .'

I shall be vastly glad of such another flannel as you have sent me, only *without any sleeves*. God bless ever & Aye

my dearest Charlotte |

I beg you to hurry Alex to Mr Achard[3]
& Home as yesterday—

650   Richmond, 2–3 November 1812

To Doctor Burney

A.L.S. (Berg), 2–3 Nov. 1812
Double sheet 4to 4 pp. *pmks* RICHMOND / 4 NO / 1812
4 NO 1812 4 NO 1812 wafer
Addressed: Dr. Burney, / Chelsea College, / Middlesex.
Edited by FBA, p. 1, *annotated*: ⋇ (7) Alex prevailed with to go to Greenwich School for a preparation for the University. *See further*, Textual Notes.
Also L.S. incomplete copy in hand of CFBt (Diary MSS. viii. 5862–[65], Berg)
Double sheet 4to 4 pp.

Richmond,
Novr 2^d 1812.

'Why, Fanny, you are Here, & There, & every where,—and no where!' says my dearest Father: well, and now I am at *another* where, for *me voici à Richmond*, chez our dear amiable Charlotte Barrett's.

This lovely love,—for such she is made such continual & plaintive representations of her desire that I would accellerate my motions, to pass a fortnight with her before her time & attention would be occupied by yet a third Baby,[1] that I could not resist them, & therefore made a compromize, which brought me hither on Friday for *half* a Week.[2] The rest of the fortnight is to be completed at some other period. To-morrow Charles fetches me back to Deptford.

---

[3] Jacques Achard-Bontems (1747–1828), born in Geneva, became a member of a small active group of 'Constitutionnaires' there. For some time he directed 'une maison de banque' in Paris and then in London, where he resided at 16 Bloomsbury Square.

650. [1] CFBt's third child, Richard Arthur Francis, was born on 12 Dec. 1812.

[2] From Friday 30 October to Tuesday 3 November.

Now for Alex.

To let him lose any more time before he resumed his studies was vexatious: this visit, nevertheless, had been promised ever since our arrival, & one to Norbury Park: but the good Boy, in consequence of a representation made by his Uncle, consented to forego *both*, & to begin his geometrical lessons without delay.[3]

This, however, was not all I wanted: I wished much ˡ that he should recover his general habits of early rising, & of regular study, as well as to ascertain the real state, by english judgment, of his classical attainments.[4] For all these purposes, I earnestly desired that he should undergo an examination at Charles's school.[5] But when I mentioned the plan to Alex, he recoiled from it almost indignantly. Had his Uncle himself, he said, still presided, he would not have hesitated; not only because he was his UNCLE, but because he was so renowned an Hellenist, that M. Hugot, (his own Greek Professor in Paris,) had declared him to be one of the most famous in the World: & to be known for a great Hellenist by *M. Hugot at Paris*, was a mark of such very extraordinary erudition & reputation, that to be placed under such a master would be an honour, not a discredit, however old, or otherwise advanced, might be the pupil: but that as to his Cousin, he was but his Cousin, however learned or clever he might be, & *he was unknown to M: Hugot.*[6]

Nevertheless, I eagerly wished & sought to overcome these obstacles. Two lessons, only, of an hour each, were very inadequate for employing his time, or finishing his education, & he

---

[3] Despite mathematical talent, AA was to have difficulty with geometry and calculus all through the sixth form at Greenwich School and during his years at Caius. He had been trained in French techniques that stressed Leibnizian analysis. Once in England, however, he had to acquire new procedures based upon Newtonian mathematics and its doctrine of fluxions. The mathematics of both countries were equally stylized but different enough from each other to cause hardship for a young person, trained in one, to shift to the other.

[4] After working with AA for almost a year, CPB was to be similarly concerned. In a letter (Berg) dated October 1813, he said that AA 'quits us certainly more HUMANIZED & ANGLICIZED & ACADEMICIZED by his residence amongst us:—but, oh!—that we could have made him more careful,—more regular,—more systematick,—more TIDY,—& oh!—above all,—that I could have persuaded him to give more mind & more time to remedy the defects of his early Classical education.—Too often does he trip even in the Elements of Grammar,—in which most essential branch of knowledge he seems never to have been well-grounded.'

[5] See L. 645 n. 11.

[6] Probably Pierre Hugot, 'Maître des langues étrangères' at the school of Jacques-Antoine Hix in Paris (see vi, L. 580 n. 8). M. Hugot (Hugo) was a resident in the rue de Quatre Vents. AA's regard for him as a classicist and master was not shared by CPB (see n. 4).

had got into idle ways of vague occupations, without any fixed pursuit, or methodised plan: young Charles, in ⌐ the mean time, was uncommonly good-natured & kind to him, &, on Thursday Morning, I saw my Boy beginning to soften, & to meditate upon the possible advantages of a little scholastic order: &, just at that time, by extreme good fortune, young *Mrs.* Charles proposed playing with him at Chess.[7] This was immediate conquest, &, voluntarily & gaily, he came to me himself with an offer of placing himself, till Christmas, at his Cousin's.

I could demand from him no longer period, till I see the result, & know better what project to form. But thus much has relieved my mind from much weight of care & perplexity. ⌐I have now time before me for arranging what will follow after the holydays.

Our Charlotte the elder has had an attack of cold & fever & pain in the side that has required some serious nursing, & several doses of James's powders, but this morning, *Novr 3^d* she is considerably better. We have all, here, such bad colds, that we think there must be an Influenza. For Heaven sake take heed that it does not reach you, my dearest Father.

1 o'clock. Charles is just arrived, & takes me back to ⌐ [Deptford] after an early dinner.⌐ He has left my Alex quite contented, & having acquitted himself amazingly well upon his examination: so as to enter at once upon the Sixth Form. This is a joy to me inexpressible.

In his usual absent manner, as soon as he was called to Breakfast, the first Morning, he took up his share, & walked off with it!—

You may imagine he was called to order.

Charlotte & Charlottina & Julia, & Mr. Barret & Dr.

---

[7] AA was fascinated by the mathematical precision of chess. The challenge of the game was always a lure and in this case a bribe. By early 1813 FBA was to lament the waste of 'hours and faculties' upon the game. See Ll. 678, 715, 790.

Charles, all, in their several ways, kiss your hands, my most dear Padre, with your ever & ever

dutifully affectionate
F B. d'Arblay.

Lady Anne Hamilton[8] has just sent me word she can convey a Letter for me to M.d'A. in a few days.—

My kindest Love to Sarah.

651   [Deptford,
c. 4–13 November 1812][1]

To Doctor Burney

A.L.S. (Berg), *n.d.*
Double sheet 8vo   4 pp.   wafer
Addressed: Dr. Burney, / Chelsea College, / Middlesex.
Edited by FBA, p. 1, *annotated and dated*: ⁂ 1812 (3) on Dr. B's kind Letter to M. d'Arblay. *See further*, Textual Notes.

My dearest—dearest Father—
Your kind Letter written with such exquisite tact of just ALL that will be most sweet & soothing to my dear *'temporarily widowed'* Mate, has drawn tears of pleasure into my Eyes, & forced my pen into my hand whether I would or no![2] You have precisely said every thing that will most gratify & comfort him. He will only be at a loss where to place the Letter so as always to have it at hand for frequent perusal, yet how to preserve it from accident or decay, as the choicest treasure of his varied collections of Things rare.

[8] Lady Anne (1766–1846), the eldest daughter of Archibald, 9th Duke of Hamilton and 6th of Brandon, was a devoted lady-in-waiting to Caroline. In residence with the Princess of Wales at Blackheath, Kent, Lady Anne would have called upon FBA to suggest that the Princess, planning to sail soon for the Continent, might be able to get a letter into France. See L. 651 nn. 3, 4.

651. [1] This letter can be dated shortly after 3 November, when FBA left Richmond for Deptford and before 14 November (see L. 655, wherein FBA says that she has seen Mrs. Hawkins).
[2] FBA's letter replied to an undated note (Comyn) by CB: 'I have scratched a bit of a letter to our worthy frᵈ at Paris,ˣ wᶜʰ I hope you will receive time enough for Lʸ A. Hamilton—you will do wᵗʰ it what you please—first distributing of my affectionate wishes to & for all around you.' (The superscript X, later inserted by FBA, identified M. d'A.)

I shall enclose it in a long *Epître* | of my own, which is now upon the stocks. Lady Anne Hamilton[3] has had the extreme kindness to let me know I shall have the latest intelligence when the person who is *going to Paris* sets out.[4] I am then to send my Letter to her ladyship. It is, I find, a *female* who is the traveller.[5]

Your approbation of my Boy's—*Heroism*, shall I say, or GOOD SENSE? in putting himself to school,—& to a Master unknown to professor Hugot![6]—charms me, &, I am sure, will pay the youth, as well as enchant his Father. |

I went yesterday to town to see [Mrs.] Hawkins,[7] but I could not get to Chelsea as Rosette waited for me at Mr Foss's.[8] Mrs. Hawkins is not in the least altered, & does not look a day older than when I saw her near 20 years ago! for I do not recollect to have met her before since my marriage. She offers as good a lesson as a Moralist need desire of the reward of good conduct & good temper, for every feature of her face speaks equanimity & benignity. I was very glad to see her at her dear & respectable Brother's[9]—not to mention MY own dear—spirited & amiable sister.— |

How excessively good you are to send me the Week's Register![10] I receive it most eagerly.

Good day, Good Day, my dearest Pappy!—

F B d'A.

[3] CB's letter to M. d'A was to be included in a packet that FBA planned to send to Paris through the agency of Lady Anne.

[4] Caroline of Brunswick (1768–1821), Princess of Wales and wife of the Prince Regent. She had married in 1795 but soon after the birth of the Princess Charlotte (7 Jan. 1796), the royal couple separated. Excluded from Court after her husband became regent (1811) and restricted in her number of visits to Charlotte, she decided to go abroad. In was not, however, until 9 Aug. 1814 that she embarked for Germany.

[5] For an explanation of FBA's reluctance to name the Princess of Wales, see L. 660 n. 5.

[6] AA's veneration of M. Hugo[t] was real despite FBA's amusement and CPB's distress. When matriculating at Caius College in 1813, AA acknowledged his preparatory work with only two men, 'Professor Hugo' and CB Jr. (Venn).

[7] Since the two cousins had last seen each other, Ann or 'Nancy' Hawkins (i, p. lxxiv), now 63, had been widowed in 1804.

[8] Brother-in-law of Rosette Burney, Edward Smith Foss (c. 1756–1830) had his law office and residence at 36 Essex Street, Strand. For his marriage to Rosette's sister Anne, see iv, L. 276 n. 2.

[9] The meeting of Ann Hawkins and FBA occurred at the John Street home of Esther and Charles Rousseau Burney, brother of Mrs. Hawkins.

[10] *The Weekly Register and Political Magazine, including a Digest of Politics, Literature and Fine Art* (9 Dec. 1809–6 Apr. 1811). FBA enjoyed reading back numbers of a periodical. In part, she wished to catch up on English events that she missed while in France. But also she had little sense of journalistic immediacy. See AA's letter (Barrett, Eg. 3701A, f. 8–8b, 14 Apr. 1816): 'You never write to me any

Pray thank Sally for her good—& very affectionate Letter,[11] with my best love into the bargain.

652   [Deptford, *post* 4 November 1812]

To Charles Burney

A.L. (Berg), *n.d.*
Double sheet 8vo   4 pp.
Addressed: Rev^d Dr. Burney.

My dearest Charles,

I must write to you—for when we are together your zeal & generous affection overpower even my judgment.

I must pay the masters of Alexander. All the obstacles you put in my way charm me with You, but do not the less dissatisfy my mind with itself.

Mr. d'Arblay, I know, will approve no other plan.

All obligation of a pecuniary sort, or *tendency*, must be to *YOURSELF*, & to yourself *ONLY*—since my Brother James, who, solely, would be else an exception, is not in a situation to shew, like you, the warm feelings that beat in his kind heart, as in yours, for the only child of a beloved sister.[1]

We have always paid all the Masters of Alexander, & they have been deeply expensive to us; but to his education, his honour, his good & his happiness, all our privations are chearfully directed, & for HIM we mutually practice the most daring oeconomy, since for him we set aside all similitude of appearance with the societies to which we belong.

public news—I wish you who read the Newspapers (if you are yet faithful to your laudable fashion of following up the train of "coming events" at the short distance of 2 or 3 months behind them) I wish you would now and then favor me . . . with a short abstract of the temporary state of things here and in France. Do you manage now to tread a little closer upon the heels of time, or does he still outstride the footsteps of your curiosity?' See L. 735 n. 3.

   11 SHB's letter is missing.

652. 1 CB Jr. wished to underwrite AA's education at Greenwich School and even to involve JB, a retired half-pay naval officer since 1785. CB Jr. was the richest of the Burney 'tribe' (Ll. 671, 716). In 1812 his library alone was worth almost £13,500 (6 years later it was bought by the British Museum for that sum). See L. 663 n. 11, for FBA's rejection of CB Jr.'s generosity.

In answer to what, with delicate adroitness, you have endeavoured quieting my scruples about in representing what you have done for your other Nephews upon this matter,[2] let me beg you to observe that that influence which, then, was exclusively yours, & which still, & always, must remain, solidly, yours, is, nevertheless, now ostensibly your son's, and ǀ neither you can look back, nor Charles look forward, with your hands fairly upon your Consciences, & wonder, or be displeased, at the nameless, yet unconquerable difference of sensation in owing obligation (of this sordid nature) to a Brother or a Nephew.

To Charles I shall still, but with pleasure, not pain, owe the kind admission of his Cousin to partake of the diffusion of those talents which form the Burney Club which I am so proud to see instituted:[3] And to you, my very dear Brother, to You— but too zealous for my *interests*, I must owe *aid*, not *opposition* to sustaining *propriety* with respect to my Boy according to *my own* conceptions. ǀ

Give me, then, your consent with one of those radiant smiles which Mrs. Lock celebrates, & let me go to Greenwich & arrange my business all by myself. Do-y-Willy?

I shall spend another day with you & dear Rosette, for the Arch[deacon][4] has fixed *Friday*

---

[2] Several other nephews of CB Jr. attended his school either at Hammersmith or Greenwich: Richard Allen Burney, Norbury and William Phillips, Martin Burney, Clement Francis, and Ralph Broome. In all likelihood CB Jr. paid the school costs for the sons of SBP and EBB.

[3] Informally organized in April (*c.* 1800–5), the membership of the Burney Club was limited to former pupils of CB Jr. Among these were CPB, John and Henry Bicknell, Francis Hargrave, Edward Foss, John Kaye, Martin Burney, George Arnold. For additional members, see the Records of the Shire Hall, Gloucester (D 18/672). Its meetings were occasional. CPB wrote to Robert Finch on 2 Apr. 1806 (Bodleian): 'Arnold dined with me at the *Burney-Club* on Monday,— we had a most pleasant meeting, & we had the pleasure of entertaining my Father as a Visitor. It was really delightful to see him enjoy himself so much amid his old Pupils.—Our Anniversary will be held on the 22nd my Father in the Chair, and we hope to muster about 50.'

[4] George Owen Cambridge (1756–1841), Archdeacon of Middlesex (i, L. 1 n. 6). Between 1783 and 1785 FB concealed her feelings for 'the young clergyman who seemed by his manner and actions to intimate thoughts of love, but who did not come forth with the offer of his hand, who did not . . . *speak*' (*HFB*, pp. 187–8).

To Doctor Burney

A.L. (Berg), 5 Nov. 1812
Double sheet 8vo   4 pp.   *pmks* T.P.P.U. / Deptford   6 NO 1812
6 NO 1812   wafer
Addressed: Dr. Burney, / Chelsea College, / near / London.
Edited by FBA, p. 1, *annotated*: ⁖ (8) *LADY CREWE*
p. 4, *scribbling in pencil*: Mad^e Gr< >. *See further*, Textual Notes.

Deptford
Rectory
Novr 5. 1812

My dearest Padre,

Yesterday I saw Lady Crewe, & I write to give you a short
hint of what passed. She made earnest enquiries about your
health, & way of passing your time; but when, in return, I
demanded whether you had had the honour of a visit from her,
she looked embarrassed, & answered, with a good deal of hesitation, That she always wished to seek her old friend, but was
not always sure she might not rather disturb than please him.

I ventured warmly to assure her that your real old friends,
like your Family, would always find the same kind welcome as
formerly, provided you were not *taken by surprise*, which you
had no longer the health or strength to ⎮ bear. She looked
quite delighted, & said if that were the case, though she was
now in town only for a limitted time, & that time was all
appropriated, she would lengthen it another day on purpose,
sooner than lose the pleasure of seeing you. And she spoke with
so much affection, & vivacity, that it was clear she only wanted,
& was happy to receive, an assurance of being welcome.

It was in Mr. Angerstein's Box at Drury Lane that we met.[1]

She has engaged me to her house on Tuesday, for a *Lunch*,
with the Miss Berrys.[2]

---

653. [1] On Wednesday 4 Nov. 1812, FBA and AA sat in John Angerstein's box at
the Theatre Royal, Drury Lane, for a performance of *Lionel and Clarissa* and the
farce *Who's the Dupe?*

[2] See L. 655, n. 10. The lunch took place on 10 November with Agnes (1764–
1852) and Mary Berry (1763–1852) present. For the Berry sisters, see iv, L. 389
n. 5.

I have no doubt but she will write to you, or send a message; pray, dearest Sir, do not disgrace my encouragement. She is a true, a faithful, & valuable ^l old Friend to You, and, hereditarily, for your sake, to all your family: and, besides & moreover, a charming & really worthy, as well as an excentric & peculiar woman.

I am more & more satisfied with the step I have taken for my dearest Boy, who is paid for his compliance by finding himself where he ought to be, upon the highest Form. To shew approbation, his Cousin very good naturedly allowed him to accompany us last Night to the play. And imagine if I am not as much rejoiced as surprised to hear that he is mightily liked by all his Comrades![3] I was afraid his shyness would have made him quite unpopular.

> Heaven bless my most dear Padre.
>
> My kind Love to dear Sarah. ^l

[⌐]I shall be extremely glad to have the other half of the 90£[4] at Mr. Turner's[5] when my dearest Father has a good day for writing the draft[6],—as Alex requires now a *penny or two pence* for his new goings on.[⌐] ^l

Imagine if I long to now have another set of News-papers!

---

³ CPB frequently assured FBA of AA's popularity. He wrote in October 1813 (Berg) about the boy's departure from Greenwich: 'He leaves behind him, dear Mʳˢ d'Arblay, many, many kind Friends, to whom his talents, his heart & his character have endeared him.'

⁴ FBA's royal pension.

⁵ Sharon Turner (1768–1847), F.S.A., associate of the Royal Society of Literature, author of the twelve-volume *History of England*, an attorney, who lived and practised at 32 Red Lion Square, London. For his tutorial relationship to Martin Burney as a law student, see vi, L. 576 n. 4. A copyright specialist, Turner became involved in FBA's legal affairs in 1812 and on 4 Nov. 1813 he and Martin Burney negotiated with Thomas Longman and his associates for the sale of *The Wanderer*.

⁶ When departing for France in 1802, FBA had arranged that her royal pension, paid quarterly, be banked by CB (L. 709), through whom she could draw money on need. But during her stay in France, her pension—until 1811—became entangled in CB's account. By July 1813, FBA was so concerned that she asked her sister Charlotte to write to her friend Thomas Mathias, treasurer to the Queen, for information about the pension payments. He answered (Barrett, Eg. 3700A, f. 169) on 14 July, enclosing 'the Papers you wished to have, relating to your Sister's Pension' and giving specific dates and amounts. See also L. 697 n. 6.

M. d'Arblay
To Madame d'Arblay

A.L. (Berg), *n.d.*
Originally a double sheet 4to, of which FBA later discarded the second leaf 2 pp.
Edited by FBA, p. 1, *annotated and dated*: 37. 10. Novembre. 1812.
See further, Textual Notes.

Quel bonheur inattendu ma chere chere Fanny! Une lettre de toi et d'Alex. Cette lettre n'est point datée[1] n'importe j'ai fort heureusement des nouvelles de toi beaucoup plus fraiches par cette excellente et toute aimable Mad^e Solvyns.[2] Je suis desolé ma chere amie d'avoir un moment troublé le bonheur dont tu jouis au sein de notre famille en te pressant de revenir.[3] Tu as bien et très bien fait d'user de ton droit, puisque je t'avais donné *carte blanche*. Je n'avais pas reflechi le moins du monde que tes affaires ne pouvaient etre terminées, et j'étais loin de soupçonner qu'elles n'etaient pas même commencées.[4] Tu ne me dis rien ma chere amie de ta santé, qui est le point essentiel. Je l'ai remarqué avec peine: mais j'espere que c'est parce qu'elle est bonne, et le besoin que j'ai de le croire fait que je fais tout ce que je puis pour me le persuader. Tu peus bien juger, ma chere Fanny que je n'ai pas été fort surpris de l'accueil que tu as reçu, et des projets de ta famille et de tes amis. Je te repons que ta lettre n'est pas moins bien reçue ici. Elle m'est arrivée aujourdhui 10 novembre par la poste et sans cachet. ⌐Je crois bien qu'il y a au moins six semaines qu'elle

654. [1] L. 646.
[2] M. Solvyns had close affiliations with important members of the Imperial government, such as Fouché and Montalivet, and in England with John Reeves. Because of these connections the passage of mail between M. Solvyns in Paris and his wife in London was surer than for others.
[3] L. 643.
[4] FBA was involved with the following: the disposition of Camilla Cottage, whether to sell or retain it; the transfer of rents from the Cottage and other capital held for the d'Arblays by Mrs. Locke and her son William (L. 721 n. 3); the ordering of the d'Arblay account with Thomas Coutts and Company; the untangling of her pension from CB's account; the completion and marketing of *The Wanderer*.

est ecrite.[5] j'en juge par ce que tu dis que M^de ⟨Hawkins⟩ doit
arriver, Cecilia ⟨viendra⟩ avec elle[6] et que Sally doit arriver
dans un mois.[7] Tu dois être à present avec Madame Wadington
et ses charmans enfans.[8] Je te prie de me rappeller au souvenir
de cette meilleure amie que je connais en verité comme si
j'avais passé une vie avec elle.⌐ Il faut, ma chere amie que je
t'avoue que j'ai un poids sur le coeur en pensant que je ne vois
point Amine[9] figurer dans la brillante et si aimable gallerie
que tu m'as fait parcourir. Je me crois en te lisant, au milieu
de nos amis; et je vois que pour des prisonniers vous n'êtes
pas très malheureux, Alex et toi. ⌐A propos de prisonniers: je
n'ai pas parvenu à savoir encore à quoi m'en tenir sur la capture
du batiment qui vous portait. J'ai oui dire que M^de de Caillebot
avait perdu tous ⏐ ses efforts, et j'ai dabord pensé que c'etait
parce que comptant rester longtems en Amerique elle voulait
faire provision de hardes neuves et même d'etoffes qui ont en
ce cas du être jugées de bonne prise. En fesant ce calcul, je me
disais que te trouvant dans une patrie tout à fait differente, tu
n'aurais pas du eprouver le même traitement. A present je
crains par un passage de ta lettre, celui où tu dis que tu as
besoin d'argent pour payer quelques depenses qu'il faut que tu
fasses immediatement, je crains, dis je que tu n'ayes été pillée
car je crois me rappeller qu'ayant emporté, et avec raison, tout
ce dont j'avais pu disposer tu me mandais qu'il te restait encore
pas mal d'argent.[10] De toute maniere, ma chere et toujours plus
chere amie, ce que je recommande par dessus tout, c'est de ne

[5] In L. 646 FBA mentions having just received on Friday 25 September a
letter from M. d'A. She held her own letter another two days to add further news,
one of the last items being that CB Jr. had preached twice on 27 September at the
Chapel Royal.
[6] In L. 646 FBA indicated that Mrs. Hawkins and Cecilia would arrive in
November.
[7] SHB had set out for Lymington during the first week in August and planned
to be away from Chelsea College for almost two months. See L. 637 n. 30.
[8] Writing on 10 November, M. d'A expected his letter to take about a month to
reach England. Because FBA informed him in L. 646 that the Waddingtons would
be in London during December, he expected his wife to visit her close friend
often.
[9] Amelia Angerstein *née* Locke, now 36. See v, L. 472 n. 2.
[10] For the assessment of their financial holdings, see the letter of M. d'A,
c. 4 July 1813, to FBA (Appendix II). FBA sometimes stressed her poverty when
writing to M. d'A, and for several reasons. His own yearly salary as one of the
chefs of the bureau des Bâtimens civils was only between 3,000 and 4,000 francs.
Moreover, he was—as his wife thought—over-generous to friends. As long ago as
11 July 1793, she later noted, CB had written to M. d'A (ii, L. 114a) 'the first
parental apprehensions of ⟨an⟩ insufficiency of Income'.

rien epargner absolument pour que vous soyez Alex et toi parfaitement confortables. A propos d'argent tu ne m'as encore rien dit de Mad[e] de Boinville et de celui qu'elle nous doit.[11] Rappelle moi je te prie à son souvenir et après lui avoir fait agreer mon hommage, tâche de l'engager à faire quelque chose pour sa malheureuse domestique qui se trouve en ce moment sans place et dans le plus grand besoin de 600[f] (25 pounds) que Boinville[12] lui doit. Sur ces 600[f] moitié seulement appartiennent à cette fille, qui ayant emprunté l'autre moitié est obligée d'en payer les interêts. Cette pauvre petite que nous avons vu si gaie est en ce moment bien triste. Ses pleurs sont excessivement rares. J'entens les bonnes, et elle en merite une par sa conduite. M[de] de Chastel[13] prend à elle le plus grand interest et la recommande à tout le monde mais jusqu'à present sans succès. Ce serait donc un veritable acte de charité comme de justice de la part de M[ad] de Boinville que de rembourser les 600[f] avancés par cette fille. Je n'ai pas trouvé non plus dans la charmante gallerie que je parcourerai plus d'une fois ni Melle ⟨Planta⟩ ni Miss Ba⟨ker⟩ ni son amie[14] que je n'ai pas besoin de nommer ni la belle soeur de cette amie,[15] ni Melle Crewe[16] ni Martyn qui j'espere continue *to be flourishing* in every way. Quant à Clement que j'admire presqu'autant que sa wonderful soeur,[17] je ne vois de lui dans ta lettre que ce qu'en dit Alex qui n'a pas été peu surpris de le trouver plus fort que lui sur la geometrie.[18] Ce pauvre Alex j'espere qu'en ⟨memoire⟩ de tant *d'accomplishments* reunis dans plusieurs individus de sa propre famille il s'efforcera de bien[π] |

[*The second leaf is missing*]

[11] Apparently Harriet Chastel de Boinville (d. 1847), while living in London, borrowed from the d'Arblays approximately £90 or £100, i.e. the sum of FBA's annual pension.

[12] Jean-Baptiste Chastel de Boinville died in Russia in 1813, aged 57. See v, L. 425 n. 8, and for a biographical account of his wife Harriet, v, L. 515 n. 21.

[13] Catherine-Françoise *née* Garaudé (b. *c.* 1763), the wife of Nicolas-Charles Chastel de Moyenpal (1749–1822), was Mme de Boinville's sister-in-law (vi, L. 595 n. 23).

[14] Known to the Burneys as early as 1784 and a life-long friend of Charlotte Cambridge, Sarah Baker now lived in Richmond in a house owned by Archdeacon Cambridge.

[15] Cornelia Cambridge *née* Kuyck Van Mierop (*c.* 1769–1858).

[16] Elizabeth Emma Crewe (*c.* 1781–1850), 'the sensible and amiable' daughter of Lord and Lady Crewe (i, L. 24).

[17] FBA admitted (L. 646) that MF was looked upon by all 'with wonder'.

[18] M. d'A refers to the statement in L. 646, written by AA.

To Mrs. Broome

A.L. (Berg), *n.d.*
Double sheet 8vo   4 pp.   *pmks*   T.P.P.U. / Deptford   14 NO < >
14 NO 1812   wafer
Addressed: Mrs. Broome / At Barrett's, Esqr, / Richmond — / Surry
Endorsed by CBFB: Sister d'arblay
Scribbling, p. 4

If I WROTE to you as often as I THINK of you, my most
dear Charlotte, how many letters of enquiry would you have
received! But I know not how to find a minute. Mornings I
have—*you know,*—none:[1] & the rest of the day seems so little
to my kind Hosts[2] that I cannot contrive to steal any part of it
without making them melancholy. Nevertheless, I have a constant lurking uneasiness to be more certain of your recovery.[3]
If you are *well*, you will write it without delay, I am very sure, &
tell me when ǀ your sweet namesake thinks of sending to the
Parsley Bed, for replacing the Noble Jew's little boy Bob[4]—&
what is become of Marian Marvel,[5] & all the plans & projects
for the close of the old Year.—

But—if you are *not* well—which Heaven forbid!—do not
fatigue yourself with writing, my beloved Charlotte. Your other
self, my other so dear Charlotte will take her pen, & give me
the news I anxiously await.

Our poor Brother Carlos has had an attack of cold & fever
that I have persuaded him to combat with James's powder. And
we have had success, though he is still quite confined & very
weak, & forced to a strict regimen[6]— ǀ but had he left himself

---

655. [1] Another of FBA's circumlocutions for work on *The Wanderer*.
    [2] CB Jr. and Rosette.
    [3] See L. 650. CBFB suffered 'an attack of cold & fever & pain in the side.'
    [4] See L. 650 n. 1.
    [5] MF was at Bradfield Hall in Suffolk with Arthur Young and would remain
there until shortly before the opening of parliament on 24 Nov. 1812. See MF
(Barrett, Eg. 3709A, ff. 91–2) to CFBt, 31 Oct. 1812.
    [6] CB Jr. had been overweight for years. As early as 1789, SBP had commented
in a letter (Barrett, Eg. 3692, f. 61b) to FB, 'how enormous he grows in Size—He
does not look like a Burney.' Over the years he underwent from time to time 'a
strict regimen' to combat obesity, severe attacks of gout, and headaches induced
by high blood pressure. In November 1812 he remained ill longer than FBA's

alon[e] I am convinced he would have had a high fever. Poor Rosette is low, but otherwise remarkably well.[7] My Boy is well at Greenwich. He had a congé for the play, to his great delight;[8] & another to go to see the observatory at Greenwich with his kind Uncle James; & another to accompany me to visit my dearest Father at Chelsea.

I, also,—but not my Boy—have been to our dear Esther's, to meet Mrs. Hawkins, whom I find quite unaltered in person, &, in manners, as usual, mild, amiable, & interesting.[9] I have also been at Lady Crewe's to a *Lunch party* made for my meeting the Miss Berrys.[10]

Adieu, Dearest, let me have news as soon as possible, for I don't write till I can bear with ignorance no longer. So pray be speedy. My kindest Compliments to Mr. Barrett, & my love when you see her to my dear Miss Baker: & Kiss my Babies.[11]

optimistic report indicated. On 26 November CBFB inquired (Barrett, Eg. 3693, f. 88) whether 'our dear Brother Carlos is recovered'. He continued to ail through December (L. 663).

[7] Rosette Burney endured periodically attacks of either nervous excitement or depression, during which CPB referred to her euphemistically as an *'invalide'*. See his letters to Finch (Bodleian), *passim*, and i, L. 10 n. 8. When Rosette became depressive, she hid from her family. But SBP describes a manic state to FB (Barrett, Eg. 3692, f. 61b) on 13 Aug. [1789]. '[Rosette] was in her best humour, wch is overpowering enough but when one considers how she *can* appear, her noise and incessant rattle is even welcome—I was a little secretly alarmed when almost as soon as they arrived, Charles asked for assafoetida for her; I had none, but produced Hartshorn wch he s^d w^d do as well—However she s^d she w^d have none—but being much pressed by him took the glass, tasted it, & flung the contents out of the window—Poor Charles exclaimed her childishness—but not discouraged, prepared a Second dose, wch at length she condescended to swallow.'

[8] See L. 653 n. 1.

[9] See L. 651 nn. 7, 9.

[10] On '*Tuesday, November 10th* [1812]', Mary Berry (ii. 508) 'went to Lady Crewe's, who gave a sort of *luncheon dinner*, to which we were invited, to meet Dr. [Charles] Burney and his sister Madame D'Arblay. They were neither of them there. When we entered a dozen ladies were sitting round the fire with Miladi. Lawrence, the painter, the only gentleman. Dr. Burney was ill and could not come, but at last Madame D'Arblay arrived. I was very glad to see her again. She is wonderfully improved in good looks in ten years, which have usually a very different effect at an age when people begin to fall off. Her face has acquired expression and a charm which it never had before. She has gained an *embonpoint* very advantageous to her face. We did not talk much about France; but with her intelligence there was a good deal she could tell, and much she could not, having a husband and a French establishment, to which she was to return after the winter.'

[11] CFBt's two daughters: Julia Charlotte, now 4, and Henrietta Hester, almost 2.

To Mrs. Waddington

A.L.S. (Berg), *n.d.*
Originally a double sheet 4to, of which the first leaf was later discarded
2 pp. *pmks* T.P.P.U. / Deptford   MONMOUTH   18 NO 1812   19
NO 1812   large red seal
Addressed: Mrs. Waddington, / Lanover, / Monmouth
Address page *annotated*: Miss sent to Monmouth

. . . advantage?

Alexandre will, *I HOPE,* answer the very pretty Letter of your
sweet Emily; but he is now at the shy age which makes him
as clownishly unfit for Mr. Greene as his whip made him
noisily so in his childish hardihood.[1] At this moment, & from
the beginning of this month, when my wintering here was
decided upon, he is, & has been, returned rigourously to his
preparatory studies for the Ecole polytecnique.[2]

Adieu—adieu—write me a less distressing Letter, & *aid* me to
turn my Eyes, while yet here, from the tragedy of my departure

ever ever Yours
F B d'A.

Deptford Rectory — —

I am again returned to my poor Brother Dr Charles, who is
wholly confined by a fit of the Gout. |

656.   [1] For James Greene's visits to the d'Arblays in Paris, see L. 697 n. 10. For his
history in Wales, see Ll. 684, 697 n. 9, 751, 788.
   [2] See L. 645 n. 6. The École Polytechnique, first called École des Travaux
Publics, had opened on 21 Dec. 1794. An institute of technology, its regimen was
paramilitary. Students were chosen by competitive examination. For four years
they 'went through a systematic scientific and mathematical curriculum, directed
toward practice . . . but under the foremost scientific minds, all formed in the
rigorous tradition which implants in the French intelligentsia something of the
Cartesian spirit, something of its mathematical imperative toward order, unity and
elegance in doctrine.' See C. C. Gillispie, 'Science and Technology', in C. W.
Crawley, *The New Cambridge Modern History* (1969), ix. 122. Under Napoleon the
school became increasingly militarized and often supplied officers for the artillery
and engineers.
   Apparently FBA had earlier written to her family that she was no longer fearful
of AA's being 'drawn into this dire conscription for [he] has distinguished
himself' by admission to the École Polytechnique. See MF's letter (JRL) to
Mrs. Piozzi, dated 21 Mar. 1811. Yet FBA acknowledged to herself (vi, L. 631)
that Napoleon's insatiable desire for conquest 'menaced a severity of Conscription to which Alexander . . . would soon become liable.'

With regard to the Miss Allen's,[3]—they will be *well off*, by all accounts, upon the banks of the Loire, & in many parts of the South, but *Paris* is now MORE, *much* more than doubled in all expences, as well as *London*, within these 10 Years.[4] The *same* income as before will suffice for **no** one.

657   Windsor,
                                           [24] November 1812

To Doctor Burney

A.L.S. (Berg), Nov. 1812
Single sheet 4to   1 p.
Edited by FBA, p. 1, *annotated*:   ⸫   (9)   Gracious Detention at Windsor
Castle by the Queen —

Windsor Castle,
Tuesday, Nov. [24] 1812.[1]

My dearest Padre will, I am sure, be happy to hear that Her Majesty has the extreme graciousness to desire to keep me here yet another day. I entreat, therefore, that my dear Sarah will be so good as to write FORTHWITH to Deptford, to beg that the Doctor Chaplain will let his Carriage come to fetch me some time in the afternoon, or evening of *THURSDAY*. The hour of my return none but the Great Gods can tell; but I shall at least embrace again my dearest Father before I re-visit the Rectory. The graciousness, goodness, sweetness I have met here are

---

[3] The large family of John Bartlett Allen (1733–1803) of Cresselly, Pembroke-shire, included two sons and nine daughters. By 1812 one daughter Mary was dead and three were unmarried—Jessie (*c.* 1778–1852), Emma (1780–1866), and Frances (1782–1875).

[4] The condition continued after the war. Mary Berry, who had last been in Paris in 1803, wrote on 14 Mar. 1816 from that city to Agnes Berry: 'I am sorry to say everything, even silks and millinery, which used to be cheap here, are almost double the price and every little thing costs money as it does in England, which formerly used not to be the case.' See *The Berry Papers*, ed. Lewis Melville (1914), p. 328. For an economic verification of the observations of FBA and Mary Berry, see A. Chabert, *Essai sur les mouvements des prix en France* (1945).

657. [1] This letter can be dated 24 November. FBA arrived at Windsor on this day and remained until Thursday, the 26th. Between Thursday 5 November (L. 651) and Thursday, the 19th (L. 656)—and possibly as late as Sunday, the 22nd—she had been at Deptford, presumably during an uninterrupted visit. On 26 November CB Jr. had his carriage call at Windsor and bring her to CBFB's house in Chenies Street. By 4 December FBA had returned to the rectory and from there went to Norbury Park.

indiscribable, & my beloved Padre has been enquired for with the most marked consideration, both by Her Majesty & their Royal Highnesses the Princesses Augusta & Elizabeth. The Princesses Mary & Sophia I am appointed to have the honour of seeing to-morrow, when again I am to be indulged with an interview with Her Majesty.[2] Adieu, most dear Sir; This will not reach you till to-morrow, *Wednesday*: & after to-morrow, Thursday, you will again bless your dutiful

& affecte.
FB. d'A.

658   Richmond,
                                    [30 November 1812][1]

To Mrs. Waddington

A.L. (Berg), *n.d.*
Double sheet 8vo   4 pp.   wafer
Addressed: Mrs. Waddington, / Hanover Street / Hanover Square.

I have felt nothing more of that little touch,[2] my dearest Mary—I am most happy to say: but it will put me upon my guard—I have thought of you—thought of your melting tenderness & too touching countenance almost incessantly since our meeting—We must have MUCH MUCH talk together—you must not leave permanently upon my mind the impression of sadness you have imprinted there at this moment.[3]

   [2] FBA's first extended stay at Windsor since her return to England had been anticipated as early as 1 October (L. 647 n. 2). She had had, however, an audience with the Queen and Princess Sophia on 3 September at Windsor and with the Queen alone on 30 September at the Queen's House.

658. [1] According to L. 646 Mrs. Waddington rented a town house for December. Probably arriving a few days in advance, she visited FBA and then by express arranged for another 'tête à tête' on 1 December. But AA was to return to Greenwich School early—on Wednesday 2 December—and to remain there until the 24th. See the letter (Bodleian) written on 21 December by CPB to Finch: 'My Troops are all on the retreat & my territories will cease to be infested after Christmas Eve.' Because of AA's impending departure, FBA could not see Mrs. Waddington until 2 December—hence the tea invitation for that Wednesday from CBFB to Mrs. Waddington and her three daughters.
   [2] FBA's 'bad cold' early in November (L. 650).
   [3] Mrs. Waddington never forgot that as the 17-year-old Mary Ann Port she had been rejected by Philip Goldsworthy, an officer in the First Royal Regiment of Dragoons (*HFB*, p. 258). In 1789 her family married her to the middle-aged

Your terrible man waited not for any answer.

I have my Boy only for today & tomorrow! He will not stay longer from his studies, & his Chief[4] adjures me not to tempt him, for reasons I shall explain in our tête à têtes.[5] For these two days I am wholly at his disposal; *you* are the last not to forgive that,—for my ǀ heart yearns after him. Absence there is so new! Never till this Greenwich plan had we been separated *3 days*, except at the moment of my dread calamity, when I sent him to Norbury Park, that he might not witness my despairing grief.[6]

I cannot get him to present himself to you: that sort of courage he cannot muster: & still less to your Nymphs: for he said 'if it were not for that P.S. on the outside—if Mrs. W. were sure to be *alone*—I think I could go to *her.*—'

They must not be affronted; he professed, *in Paris*, a mortal dislike to all GIRLS!—

O how he will pay for that blasphemy one of these days! The young ǀ persons to whom—to make them stare,—I there told it, always most gravely answered, while horrour sat on their brow —'Est il permis? ——'

I wish I could show you the savage—but know not how to arrange it. But he will be back in 3 weeks, when there will not be this hurry, as he comes to remain with me, here & elsewhere, for a month.

Benjamin Waddington, who, as Mrs. Locke reported in her journal (Barrett, Eg. 3697, f. 155), 'is a plain, worthy man his exterior has nothing *captivating* in it & he speaks in the Yorkshire accent—but he is kind hearted much attached to her & very tender & attentive at this time—. . . he has [not] a vulgar *mind* 'tho a vulgar manner.'

Mrs. Waddington never became reconciled to her marriage, wearing her sadness visibly. In a letter (Barrett, Eg. 3698, f. 316), dated 28 Aug. 1812, Emily described her mother: 'I am happy for her, that she will again be able to talk over . . . all the happiest days of her life—which, tho' it must awaken many painful recollections—yet, the feeling that there is still *one being* to whom she can say "Our heart-strings musically move / and thrill with like vibration!"'—must I think soften every pang!—& yet tho' I long for, I almost dread your meeting!—my poor Mother is so completely worn down by the 20 years of suffering mind & body—that have elapsed since you parted, that the sight of the only person except her children that she ever truly loved—after such a separation—& at a time when she had given up all hope of ever seeing her again—is a trial that her shattered nerves are ill able to support!'

4 CPB (i, p. lxxii).

5 AA's difficulties in the sixth form at Greenwich School arose from boredom, indolence, a disregard for classical grammar, and the disparities between English and French mathematics. See L. 650 nn. 3, 4.

6 On 8 Jan. 1800, two days after the event, FBA had learned of SBP's death. M. d'A, having been told of it by the Lockes, informed his wife. At the height of her grief, she allowed AA to be taken to Norbury Park, while she and M. d'A went to Chelsea. Within a few days the boy joined them there. See iv, L. 355 nn. 1, 2.

I dare *fix* nothing but for Wednesday—though I will *try* something for to-morrow.

My sister Broome, with her kindest comp^{ts} bids me say that on *Wednesday*, we hope you will come, with your Graces Three, if sweet Emily is well enough, to tea.—

If she is fatigued, let me know honestly, & I will come to you. pray be sincere, my dearest Mary—

Kiss them all round for your most fond [F d'A] |

Pray give my Comp^{ts} to Mr. Waddington. I am anxious to hear how your Emily bore the journey.[7]

This was designed for the post—but there comes your messenger— |

659   [23 Chenies Street,
                                       c. 1 December 1812][1]
To Charles Parr Burney

A.N. (John Comyn, unbound), *n.d.*
Single sheet 4to cut down to 2·9″   1 p.

. . .

N B. Would it be possible that Alexander could sleep in *another room*? I need not explain what I mean—though warmly & singularly I love his equally amiable & clever little Chamber Collegue.[2]

I earnestly beg of the Mathematical Master to make him once more go through Euclid, & not proceed in algebra, till he is a thoroughly good Geometrician.[3] This is the desire of Dr. Davy.[4]

---

[7] The frailest of the surviving three Waddington children, Emily or Emelia had become a confirmed invalid in early childhood and continued so throughout her life. On 12 Apr. 1819, she died, aged 25.

659. [1] This can be dated *c.* 1 December, just before AA returned to Greenwich School.

[2] Just as AA enjoyed games of skill and/or chance, such as chess and whist, so FBA sought to 'eradicate totally' (L. 678) these attractions. Apparently AA and his 'Chamber Collegue' spent study hours on games.

[3] FBA wished AA to become proficient in 'English' techniques of mathematical problem-solving. See L. 738 n. 5, and AA's statement in L. 646.

[4] Martin Davy (1763–1839), M.D. (1797), D.D. (1811), was master of Caius College, Cambridge, from 1803 to his death. His suggestion for AA's education at Greenwich was followed, for CPB wrote to FBA in October 1813 (Berg) that 'in

To Doctor Burney

A.L.S. (Berg), 4 Dec.
Double sheet 8vo   4 pp.   *pmks*   EPSOM   5 DE 1812   5 DE 1812
wafer
Addressed: Dr. Burney, / Chelsea College / near London.
Edited by FBA, p. 1, *annotated and dated*: ⁜ (10)   (1812)   Cruel
dearth of News from Paris—pss. of Wales.

Deptford, Friday Dec* 4

I am this moment setting off for NORBURY PARK, my dearest
Padre.[1] Charles takes me, & we shall stay a few days. I have
promised a longer visit in the Xmas holydays, when I can take
my Alexander.[2]

I had the happiness to hear some tydings of you last night
through our good & dear little Hardy; yet was grieved to find
that your—OUR old enemy, the Cough, is again harrassing
you.[3] Work at it well, Dearest Sir, by Lozenges & Toast &
Water alternately. I find nothing so serviceable. I am ǀ terribly
perplexed by the *extra*[X4] grandissima invitation I mentioned to
you: it is embarrassing in a thousand ways.[5] I *suppose Myself*

his mathematical studies, [AA] has implicitly followed yours & Dr Davy's directions,—& his time has really been turned to good account'.
   As early as November 1812, AA seemed destined for Caius College, not only
because it offered the Tancred scholarship but because its master and CB Jr. were
close friends, the former achieving the reinstatement of CB Jr. at Caius and putting
his name forward as a candidate for the degree of M.A. by Royal mandate in 1808
(vi, L. 592 n. 6). For the last four and a half years CB Jr. had been closely allied
to Caius, so that in November 1812 CB reported (Osborn) to FBA that 'D^r
Cha* has very kindly behaved for Alex at Cambridge'.
   660. ¹ The visit to Norbury Park had been postponed from early October. See
L. 649 n. 1.
      ² The visit was never made (see L. 663 and n. 3).
      ³ CB suffered from chronic bronchitis. In 1809 MF informed (JRL) Mrs.
Piozzi: 'His last attack he has quite recovered, but he coughs a great deal, and
what with coughing, & reading, & writing, spends his days in his solitary study....'
Even in the summer, when he usually secured relief, he wrote (Osborn) in 1813,
'Ah, my dear F. B. d'—y I am sorry to tell you I am not so well now, as when I
bragged of being freed from my cough.'
      ⁴ FBA supplied the superscript X and the explanatory note: 'X from the
Princess of Wales.'
      ⁵ An invitation from Princess Caroline of Wales was extended probably on the
recommendation of Lady Anne Hamilton. Because of the Princess's estrangement
from the Royal Family, FBA feared that her acceptance would affront the Queen.
Moreover, FBA probably worried about Her Highness's unpredictable behaviour,

absent, & have taken as yet no step upon it. But I should be very sorry, nevertheless, to return offence for condescendsion. I shall consult about it at Norbury.

But Oh—how I sigh for news of another nature! I long for a new batch of papers. I am told there are two new bulletins:[6] Judge if I am not impatient to read them! One great consolation I have received in the | mean time; Made de Caïllebot, my poor french lady, writes me word that her last Letter speaks of M. d'Arblay's being well.[7] Not a line—not a word have I!— And *your* sweet Letter, which would give his noble & affectionate heart such comfort, is still lying by me, for the reasons I have detailed to you.[8] *Three* Letters[9] begun for different opportunities lie by me also, unfinished, that I may add the latest intelligence when they go: but at this moment of utter darkness & uncertainty I can hazard nothing. yet how innocent of all public | matters whatsoever is our Correspondence![10] but there is no risking misconstruction, & I judge the forbearance I must use by that which He practices.

Heaven bless & preserve my most dear Father.

FB d'A.

My kindest Love to my dear Sarah.

---

detailed, e.g., by Mary Berry (ii. 388–9) on 7 Aug. 1809: 'She was in her very best manner, and her conversation is certainly uncommonly lively, odd, and clever. What a pity that she has not a grain of *common* sense! not an ounce of ballast to prevent high spirits, and a coarse mind without any degree of moral taste, from running away with her, and allowing her to act indecorously and ridiculously whenever an occasion offers!'

FBA overcame her scruples, and on 30 Jan. 1813 she and CB waited upon the Princess. According to Thomas Campbell, 'at the Princess of Wales's, I met Dr. Burney and his daughter, Madame d'Arblay. Her features must have been once excellent; her manners are highly polished, and delicately courteous—just like Evelina grown old—not bashful, but sensitively anxious to please those about her. I sat next to her, alternately pleased and tormented with the Princess's *naïveté*, and Madame D'Arblay's refinement. Her humility made me vow that I would abandon the paths of impudence for ever! Yet I know not that any body but herself could manage so much gentleness. I believe any other person would appear *designing* with it. But, really, you would love her for her communicativeness, and fine tact in conversation.' See *The Life and Letters of Thomas Campbell*, ed. William Beattie, 2nd edn. (3 vols., 1850), ii. 225.

  [6] See L. 661 n. 1.
  [7] See Ll. 637 n. 3, 645 n. 8.   [8] See L. 651 nn. 2, 4.
  [9] These letters are missing.

  [10] FBA's discretion was applied not merely to letters but also to conversation (L. 655 n. 10) and her fiction. Her reticence provoked censure of *The Wanderer* by those reviewers who had anticipated an exposé of Napoleonic France (Ll. 827 n. 5, 829 n. 6, Appendix IV). The known letters of M. d'A to offer insight into French life prior to the Restoration were those describing the reactions of the members of Mme de Laval's salon to Narbonne's death. See Ll. 736, 743.

To Doctor Burney

A.L.S. (rejected Diary MSS. 5866–[69], Berg), 10 Dec. 1812
Double sheet 4to   4 pp.   *pmks* T.P.P.U. / Deptford   9 DE 1812
wafer
Addressed: Dr. Burney / Chelsea College, / near / London —
Endorsed by CB: Mme d'A. B. from / Norbury Park
Edited by FBA, p. 1 (5866), *annotated*: ⋇· ⌐(11.)⌐ Perfect state of
long shut up Goods in closets at dear happy — lost West Hamble!
Edited also by CFBt *and the* Press. *See* Textual Notes.

Deptford Rectory,
Decr 10 1812

Two Letters from my dearest Padre!—what sweet kindness!
and O—what rare news is the news at this moment exciting it!
—I hardly yet breathe from the various and blessed hopes—
mixt nevertheless with nameless terrours which it has put into
agitation.[1] The first Letter greeted me on Sunday morning at
Norbury Park,[2] where, indeed, such cheering intelligence was
peculiarly seasonable, for most cruelly melancholy was the
change in all my feelings at that loved spot compared with
what formerly I had experienced. The virtuous & accomplished
Chief is missed every moment.[3]—Yet William is a truly worthy
successor,[4]—but William was there *besides*! And *Mrs.* Lock, my
constant, cherished & cherishing Friend, *she* also, was there
besides! Nothing, therefore, fills up the ¦ void[5]— —But I had
meant to keep to more chearful themes, and I have so great, so
unexpected a delight to give to Mr. d'Arblay, that I am sure
you will rejoice for him with all your heart,—i.e.—I have
visited the shut up Closet of Books at West Hamble, which

661. [1] CB's two letters provided FBA with news of France, specifically the 'two
new bulletins' that announced the defeat of Napoleon at Moscow and his army's
disorganized retreat.
    [2] 6 December, two days after her arrival.
    [3] William Locke I had died in 1810, aged 78.
    [4] William Locke II (1767–1847) was the heir of Norbury Park. FBA's attitude
toward him was to change when, in the process of selling Norbury Park, he forced
the sale of Camilla Cottage in 1814. See Ll. 776 nn. 3 and 4, 778, 782 n. 5, 805 n. 7,
831.
    [5] In FBA's mind, SBP continued to be associated with Mickleham and Norbury
Park.

contained our whole Library *in these parts*,[6] and which he had prepared himself to hear was a mass of moths, mildew, Cobwebs, & insects. — — I have visited it, my dearest Father, after an absence of Ten years & a half, during which period the door has never once been opened, and I have not found a single Book injured!—The few that were new, & handsomely bound, are as bright as if just bought; the many which he had himself sewed in various coloured paper, are dry, sound, | and clean: Not a pamphlet has a single leaf curled at the corner; not a label of the hundreds neatly written with his own hand, has dropt off, or is effaced. All the virtuous toils of his diligent leisure are now amply repaid. After the great & grand & incomparable good news which You have sped to me, there is none, perhaps, in the world—save what concerns his bosom affections — — that will give him such glee, such warmth such glowing satisfaction as this intelligence.[7] Ah, when can I send it him! — —

My Cloaths, too, that I expected to find half eaten by the Worms, & the other half in a wet, blue, mouldy, sticky, tatter-demallion state, are in perfect repair. I, therefore, am as much bodily, as He is intellectually richer than our joint hopes ventured to make us. |

I long to see you again, dearest Sir, but I went through so much in this visit that I want a little refitting. I hope to Heaven the Cough is better? — —

Adieu, most dear Padre, ever most dutifully

your affec^{te} Daught^{er}—

FB. d'A

all hence send love & duty.

My Alex is well—I saw him for a moment yesterday.[8]

My kind love to dear Sarah—

I had not time to tell you, in my multiplicity of tellings, that the Princess Elizabeth spoke to me[9] in high terms of Sally's last work, & with much praise, though not equal, of Clarentine.[10]

---

[6] At Camilla Cottage.

[7] FBA's statement became tragically ironic for M. d'A. See L. 831 for his tearful reaction to the architectural soundness of Camilla Cottage.

[8] FBA and CB Jr. apparently left Norbury Park on Wednesday 9 December, with a stopover at Greenwich School to visit their sons.

[9] See L. 657.

[10] SHB had by 1812 written three novels: *Clarentine* (1796), *Geraldine Fauconberg* (1808), *Traits of Nature* (1812). She was zealous not only in the composition of her novels but in their marketing. In a letter (Barrett, Eg. 3704A, f. 12b) MF, old

To Mrs. Broome
and Mrs. Barrett

A.L. (Berg), *n.d.*
Double sheet 8vo   3 pp.   *pmks*   T.P.P.U. / Deptford   16 DE 1812
wafer
Addressed in unknown hand: Mrs Broome / Barrats Esqr / Richmond
Endorsed by CBFB: Sister d'arblay. / 1812

My own dearest—
My two dearest Charlottes with what delight did I receive
last night the welcome intelligence of the new arrival. I began
to think the parsley bed had played us false, but I find, now,
that the procrastination, expectation, & indetermination were
merely a few airs & graces to give dignity to the introduction
of a Son & Heir.[1]
Nevertheless, the young Gentleman's initiatory caprices
embarrass me not a little with respect to my congratulatory
visit; but don't mention that to him, for I would not check his
roguish spirit at his first setting out ¦ in life; but what I could
have done in NOVEMBER[2]—the month appointed while we were
in ignorance of the little 'Squire's WHIMSYS—in *DECEMBER* is no
longer practicable: my Boy comes home to *me*[3]—for *HOME* has
he none at present but *ME* — — & 'tis quite out of the question
to take him so soon to parler françois with his young Cousin.

CFBt as early as 5 Mar. 1808 that 'Sally will annoy a Printer's Devil in her own
defence, I think: she is up to her chin in Booksellers.' SHB regarded her fiction
as a commercial asset that would free her from the need to be a governess. (For
her role as such to the Wilbraham family for approximately three years, see vi,
L. 584 n. 6.)

662. [1] CFBt's third child was born about a month later than expected. His
tardiness was forgiven for two reasons, as MF reported to Mrs. Piozzi in a letter
(JRL), dated 16 Dec. 1812: 'One, because she loves boys, and despises girls from
the bottom of her heart: the other because it disappoints the prediction of a super-
stitious old Frenchwoman, Madame de Thuisy.' For the identification of Mme de
Thuisy, see L. 764 n. 8.
[2] FBA was to serve as godmother to CFBt's child Richard Arthur Francis and
attend his christening if held in November or no later than the first two weeks of
December.
[3] AA's five-week Christmas holiday began on 24 December, and for that interval FBA would make no commitment requiring their separation.

Think of some new arrangement, my dearest Charlotte—⁴

And *you*—*I* should be quite unhappy not to be with you—but *HOW?*—your house will be full. & though only of *dearys*, you know my *snug* fashion loves the quietest modes & mansions. ⎮

I am called off by a gracious summons⁵ but cannot let the post miss my best felicitations to you all & Mʳ Barret with those of my Bro⟨ther⟩ & Rosette

663   Chelsea College,
                                      —31 December 1812
To Charles Burney

A.L. (Osborn), 31 Dec. 1812
Double sheet 8vo   4 pp.   *pmks* T.P.P.U. / Chelsea EO   To be Delivered / by 10 o'Clock / on Sund Mo[rn]   2 JA / [1]8[1]3   red seal
Addressed: Revᵈ Dr. C. Burney, / Deptford Rectory, / Kent.

How truly I am sorry for you, my dearest Charles! & how earnestly I shall long for news of your amendment,¹ & being able to undertake, *safely*, your so long planned & well-merited recreation.²

I entreat you to let me have a line, whether you go or not, to give me if possible better tidings.

My own plan is undergoing a change. I find that Mrs. Locke will not yet be alone³—& you know my passion for tête à têtes: —To this is added a desire of our excellent 'little hardy' that I should not go into the Country till quite freed from the remnant effects of the pang caused by my last excursion thither. I shall, therefore, visit Chenies Street before Norbury Park. I am not quite sure ⎮ when, but not before the 2ᵈ Week in January.⁴

---

⁴ FBA remained the boy's godmother but CBFB 'stood for' her (L. 667 n. 8).
⁵ She was probably called to Windsor on 20 December, when she could hear CB Jr. preach at the Chapel Royal (L. 663 n. 14).
663. ¹ CB Jr. had been ill intermittently since 14 Nov. 1812. At that time he suffered from 'cold and fever' complicated by the onset of gout (Ll. 655, 656).
² To visit Lord and Lady Spencer at Althorp.
³ FBA had last been at Norbury Park for a few days early in December, promising a longer visit with AA during the Christmas holidays (L. 660 and n. 2).
⁴ FBA did not journey to Norbury Park in January, when the cold weather confined her to the house and allowed her time to plan for AA's college career.

I am quite frightened by a Letter from Mrs. William Lock to hope I have received my first Cargo of Boxes safe!⁵—I have received nothing. I want to write her word so, but I know not her direction, & her Letter has no date.

I find, also, with much concern, that the Letter I wrote to prepare Mrs Locke of Norbury Park for a *retard*, has never arrived. Rosette was so kind as to undertake sending it. I cannot imagine how it has miscarried: but it is very provoking, for poor Mrs. Locke has been kept in the very uncertain expectation I wrote to spare her.⁶

I am strict to my regemen of Hours; ⏐ I never quit my small warm Fire side before one, & always return to it at 5.—And I take every other precaution also.

I shall apply to James about Coutts⁷ as soon as I see him again: he—Esther, & Charlotte have all been taking a *Chaste embrace*,⁸—& Mrs. James—fatty Sally, & Fanny Raper; & all are as well as they are affectionate.

Do you continue to take in the news paper?—what astonishing intelligence⁹—the reception & harangues!—¹⁰

I am truly glad dear Rosette is better. I beg her to accept my kind love.

If your own Charles is still within reach, pray tell him that I shall be extremely obliged if he will have the goodn[ess] to

---

⁵ FBA's possessions—clothes, letters, and books—had been stored for ten years at Camilla Cottage. Elizabeth Locke (iv, L. 385 n. 2) undertook to have them crated and sent to the Deptford rectory.

⁶ FBA doubted Rosette's capacity to fulfil an obligation, especially when she was 'low'—as she had recently been. See L. 655 n. 7.

⁷ See L. 646 n. 27.

⁸ In a youthful performance of Joseph Addison's *The Drummer* (1716), FB in the role of the prudish Lady Truman insisted that her husband Sir George (played by Maria Rishton) merely kiss her hand after an absence of about four years during which time he had been presumed dead. Maria protested against so unnatural a meeting and FB, faced with Maria's withdrawal, grudgingly allowed a '*Chaste embrace*' (*HFB*, pp. 239–40). The phrase became absorbed into the private language of the Burney 'tribe'.

⁹ The 'intelligence' recorded Napoleon's defeat at Moscow, the withdrawal of his soldiers from Russian territory, and on 24 December his desertion of the French army at Wilna. See *The Times* from 12 November to 31 December.

¹⁰ See under 'Parliamentary Intelligence' (*The Times*, 1 Dec.) the speeches of the Prince Regent, the Earl of Liverpool, and others in praise of Russia's military power. On 17 December (*The Times*, 18 Dec.) the Prince Regent asked both Houses for financial contributions to relieve the suffering of Russian civilians. The prince's request for £200,000 was debated and supported when written into a bill. But before the request was granted, there were parliamentary 'harangues', at least one *Times* editorial defending the Prince's proposal, and a sympathetic news report (23, 31 Dec.).

order me the Taylor's—the Bookes—& any other extra-accounts, that I may give him but one trouble at his Bankers.[11]

Alex is still—I think—rather alarmingly thin: | I am now trying Porter for him. our dear Padre is pretty well

A Merry New Year to-morrow to you & dear Rosette—& To Charles & Fanny—&—Fannittina[12] & your Mrs. Bicknell[13] |

How glad I am I liked your Sermon so much![14]

Chel. Col. Dec. 31, 1812.

664   [England, 1812]

To M. d'Arblay

> A.J. unfinished (Berg), *n.d.*
> Double sheet 4to   1 p.
> *Annotated by* FBA, p. 1: Commencement of Journal to Gen¹ d'A.

While no Folios procurable to Mortal hands could hold a millioneth part of all I want to communicate to my dearest of All dear Friends, if I include Thoughts, Feelings, & Comments with Facts & Events,—I am never allowed more than a poor mean Duodecimo for *all* my Adventures & Opinions. However, as no one can tell what Miracles may arrive I will amuse myself with *Supposing* this comely Quarto destined for the Eyes of Mon Ami, & fill it—& some of its *Semblables*, with Journal matter such as he loved to read, which I will sketch occasionally, when Recollection & Opportunity shake hands to call me forth —how well do I know the indulgent eagerness with which all I can transmit, however vague, or even vapid, will be received!

---

[11] Despite the urging of CB Jr. (L. 652 n. 1), FBA was adamant in her desire to pay AA's bills at school.

[12] CPB's daughter Frances Anne.

[13] For the early history of Sabrina Bicknell *called* Sidney (*c.* 1757–1843), see i, L. 7 n. 18. An impoverished widow in 1787 and the mother of two infant sons, she soon found work as housekeeper and overseer of CB Jr.'s schools in Chiswick, Hammersmith, and Greenwich. Her employer regarded her as an equal and a useful friend (v, L. 426 n. 2). In 1812 she managed the household at the Deptford rectory.

[14] The sermon preached by CB Jr. on 20 December at the Chapel Royal, Windsor.

But too much time has elapsed, in disappointed expectations of conveyances, since *mon retour desiré*, to let me even attempt chronological order in my relations. I can only throw them upon paper promiscuously, & let them jumble themselves into regularity by their connexions, allusions, & various contingencies.

665

[Paris, 31 December 1812
to 4 February 1813]

M. d'Arblay
To Madame d'Arblay

A.L. (Berg), *n.d.*
Originally a double sheet 4to, of which FBA later discarded the second leaf 2 pp.
Edited by FBA, p. 1, *annotated and dated*: ⊹ II ⌈1st Janvier *1814*⌉ 31 Dec^r, to Fev^r—1813 *See further*, Textual Notes.

Ah! mon amie—que j'eprouve en ce moment combien il est different d'exister ou de vivre! J'ai pu durant cinq mois et plus supporter l'existence eloigner de toi, mais ce n'est, je te jure, que par l'esperance de notre reunion. Combien ce doux moment me donne de courage! Adieu ma chere et adorable amie, toi que j'aime davantage à tous les instans, parceque toujours la reflexion ajoute encore aux raisons que j'ai de te trouver si superieure à tout ce que Je connais; et cependant qui peut se flatter d'avoir des amis plus aimables sous tous les rapports que ceux que j'ai. Personne, j'ose le dire. Aussi leur suis-je bien tendrement attaché: et cependant rien n'est plus vrai que ce que j'ajouterai ici; que je t'aime uniquement, parceque ce que j'eprouve pour eux n'est rien, absolument rien du moment où je veux le faire entrer en comparaison avec ce que je ressens pour toi! Bon soir, ma Fanny j'ai voulu finir l'année avec toi— à demain.

1er. Janvier, 1813 Je reprens la plume pour te dire que c'est avec un attendrissement dont je ne suis pas le maitre qu'en pensant à notre cher Alex, je veux commencer avec vous deux une année que je prie le Ciel de rendre aussi heureuse que celles dont il m'a fait jouir depuis notre Union; je t'avoue qu'il m'est impossible en ce moment de continuer; je vous quitte, mes amis, pour ne pas me mettre hors d'etat de remplir des devoirs aux quels je ne puis me soustraire. Je me porte physiquement à merveille; mais mon pauvre coeur est dans ce moment bien dechiré—

(4 Fevrier) J'ecrivais ce que tu viens de lire la veille du jour de l'an. Il y a consequement près de cinq semaines! Depuis ce tems je t'ai ecrit trois ou quatre petits billets—j'attendais pour t' envoyer cec⟨i⟩ une occasion qui se présente sans que j'aye la possibilité d'en profiter comme je le voudrais c'est à dire sans pouvoir causer avec toi un peu longtems — — *How do you all*— Comment vous portez vous? dans ces quatre mots, dans la reponse que tu y feras et que j'attens vainement est renfermé tout ce qui m'attache à la vie. Physiquement, je suis bien, très bien. Moralement, je devrais être beaucoup mieux: mais par une fatalité reellement inconcevable, j'éprouve le contraire. Occupé à compter non pas simplement les heures mais les minutes qui s'ecoulent par ce qu'elles tendent à nous rapprocher, je suis tourmenté à l'excès de la crainte que tu reviennes sans avoir achevé nos affaires. Ah ma chere Fanny, tu le sais si je soupire après l'instant où la paix, cette fille du Ciel nous permettra d'aller ensemble remplir des devoirs bien chers à mon coeur et passer quelques tems au milieu des parens et des amis dont tu es entourée, mais si cette paix se fait encore longtems attendre, je suis forcé de te l'avouer, je ne me sens | point la force de soutenir une seconde fois l'epreuve à la quelle le sort m'a condamné. Non les tourmens de l'Enfer ne peuvent surpasser l'horrible inquietude de n'avoir aucune nouvelle de l'unique objet de toutes ses affections—de tous les sentimens les plus tendres! Je te supplie donc, mon adorable amie, de rester plutot deux mois de plus, s'il le faut, afin de terminer ton ouvrage[1] de manière à ce qu'il ne soit plus question que de l'imprimer, ou du moins d'en achever l'impression. Ton frere, si bon pour nous,[2] voudra bien j'en suis sur, se charger d'en

---

665. [1] *The Wanderer.* For signs of M. d'A's growing impatience when the novel had not appeared by July 1813, see Appendix II.

[2] CB Jr. helped see FBA's first three novels through the press, and was particularly active during the marketing of *Camilla.* As her 'agent' he encouraged printing by subscription, pursued booksellers relentlessly, secured an advantageous contract with Payne and Cadell and Davies, distributed copies, and supported all efforts with 'warm zeal'. See *Camilla,* eds. E. and L. Bloom, pp. xviii, xxii.

67

corriger les epreuves.[3] ⌐En consequence, je te conjure de l'achever de manière à ce que tu n'ayes ensuite aucun regret de n'avoir pu en soigner toi meme l'impression, durant la quelle tu aurais pu y faire quelques changemens.⌐

Si tu prens le parti, je demande en grace à tes amis de prendre soin de ta santé, et de t'empêcher de travailler trop longtems de suite. Je me rappelle tout ce que j'ai souffert durant l'impression de Camilla;[4] et je tremble en songeant que si tu n'as pas cette fois cy la même raison de t'appliquer sans relâche pour ne pas *désappointer* le public et manquer aux engagemens que tu avais pris envers lui, tu en auras une bien forte, celle d'abreger mon exil. Songe, ma chere Fanny que la santé est le premier de tous les biens; car celui là seul nous peut faire jouir des autres; que tu as besoin de ménagements, et que si Mad[e] Solveyns ne m'apporte pas de ta part la promesse la plus solemnelle, de travailler avec moderation, et d'être arretée par la crainte d'eloigner l'instant si heureux de notre reunion en voulant trop la hâter, je ne pourrai supporter l'horrible inquietude à la quelle je serai livré. Ah je serai encore assez malheureux, et je partagerai tout ce que tu auras à souffrir en te separant—pour venir me rejoindre. Que ceux que tu laisseras doivent eux mêmes souffrir en te voyant t'eloigner. Ah mon amie, que mon coeur est dechiré, et de combien de manieres! ⌐Toi dont je partage tous les sentimens, dont je regrette de ne pouvoir en ce moment partager les tendres caresses, toi mon interprete ⌐

[*The second leaf is torn away*]

---

[3] M. d'A had no basis for assuming that CB Jr. would proofread *The Wanderer*. FBA consistently did her own proofreading.

[4] The difficulties of printing *Camilla* (published 12 July 1796) by subscription began with the announcement of the 'Proposals' in the *Morning Chronicle* (7 July 1795) and lasted until the postponement of publication advertised in *The Times* (6 July 1796). For the involvement of FBA and CB Jr. in this complex process, see iii, Ll. 168, 171, 172, 173, 174, 176, 178, 180, 182, 183, 186. The reasons for printing by subscription—namely, financial benefits for AA—are best explained in FBA's letter (iii, L. 173) to Mrs. Waddington. See *Camilla*, pp. xvii–xviii.

To Susan Adams

A.L. unfinished draft (Berg), *n.d.*
Double sheet 4to   1 p.

Had the smallest idea crossed my mind, upon quitting England, that my absence would have been so long, I should most undoubtedly have written a few lines of kindness to my good & excellent Susan,[1] with a desire to have some news, occasionally, of her health & welfare. But I had imagined that one year would have sufficed for my journey, my residence, & my return.

667   [23] Chenies Street,
                       13 January 1813
To Doctor Burney

A.L. (Berg), 13 Jan. 1813
Double sheet 8vo   4 pp.   *pmks*   Tottenham CR   14 JA 1813   red seal
Addressed: Dr. Burney, / Chelsea College
Edited by FBA, p. 1, *annotated and year 1813 retraced*: ⁛ (I) on a large projected Family assemblage.

Chenier's Street
Jany 13th 1813.

How is my dearest Father? I long to hear—through Sarah, (Mind that!) that he perseveres in the Graham System,[1] & with success.

We arrived safe & sound in Chenier's street,[2] where dear little Hardy had prepared her hospitable Bed & Board, & where Ralph was languishing for a Game at romps with Alex. to cure

666. ¹ Susan Adams was the maid who accompanied SBP to Ireland in 1796 and attended her there for four years until her death (iii, L. 216 n. 11).

667. ¹ Richard Robert Graham (L. 649 n. 2).
    ² FBA and AA had come from Chelsea College—a brief stopover between visits at Deptford and Chenies Street.

him of a little fever. Rather a new remedy; but our spirits have so much to do with our health, that the pleasure of the junction, if not of [the] exertion, has really been successful.

I am now upon the verge of a grand effort of strength & enterprize ᴵ for myself: good Mr. Burney's Birth day is to be kept to-morrow with a large family party, & a *Ball*, in John Street.[3] I know not exactly how many fandangos, or pas seul's, I may dance, but I cannot deny myself, upon such an occasion, being once more ABROAD & AMONGST them. I shall wrap myself up as warm as in the Furs of Russia, & I doubt not but that THE WEATHER will be REMARKABLY FINE.[4] How I long to know if any fresh intelligence is arrived![5]

I hope, at all events, the poetical spirit is still awake.[6]

I have had a Letter from Charles, in high flash, from Althorpe.[7] He says nothing of Gout & miseries, & therefore I flatter myself he has escaped this ᴵ time with the fright. He returns this week to Deptford.

I am invited to the Christening of the Son & Heir at Richmond;[8] but I dare not make a country excursion at this moment.

[3] The 65th birthday celebration of Charles Rousseau Burney, who in fact had been born in December (1747), had been postponed until FBA had returned to London (L. 671 and n. 3).

[4] On 13 January there was a penetrating drizzle with the temperature in the mid-thirties °F. The next day the rain had changed to cloudiness with the temperature unaltered (*GM* lxxxiii[1], 2, 8).

[5] FBA sought further news of the French rout in Russia, a presage of Napoleon's defeat and a subsequent peace between England and France.

[6] FBA was always aware of CB's depressive tendencies. As early as 21 July 1782, when he brooded over his wife's illness, FB wrote (Barrett, Eg. 3690, f. 11) to him from Ipswich: 'I was much afflicted to hear from [Hetty] the comfortless life you were leading,—Capt. Phillips, too, told me he found you *looking out of a window*,—dearest Sir!—can you not *force* yourself to collect papers, rummage memorandums, or do something or any thing to keep your mind from feeding solely upon its apprehensions?—I know too well what must be passing within it, & totally chearless it must feel, when I hear of *your* being unemployed.'

When in 1796 he mourned his wife, FBA suggested that he resume the writing of poetry. He responded by completing 'Astronomy, an Historical and Didactic Poem' (1796–9) and found his emotional equilibrium once more. See iii, L. 221 n. 6; *Memoirs*, iii. 249–51, 415–17. From that time on FBA urged intellectual and creative activity as a remedy for CB's flagging spirits.

[7] Althorp, Northamptonshire, seat of the Spencers (L. 663 n. 2).

[8] The christening of Richard, CFBt's third child, took place on 21 January. CPB in a letter (Berg) wrote to his mother on the previous day: 'My Father, I suppose, reaches home to-day, — as tomorrow he is to make his *baptismal* visit to Richmond.'

CB Jr. christened all of CFBt's children. On 21 Nov. 1808 MF had described (JRL) for Mrs. Piozzi the christening of CFBt's first child: 'The ceremony was performed very gracefully, and with a great deal of dignity by Uncle Charles; who came to Town on purpose, & professes himself ready to marry us, christen us, bury us;—in short, any thing he can [do] for us in that way, at any time.'

I shall pursue the directions of the kind & sagacious Mr. Graham unremittingly till I feel more my *own woman* again. I have been warned by my excellent M. le Dʳ Larrey that Winter will be very trying to me for some years to come.

And now—may I thank *YOU*, my dearest Padre, for all your paternal kindness & goodness?—no; for you will never hear me. Well! do you believe I thank you the less *within* because you cut short all words *withou*[*t*] ǀ No, no; I take my revenge there amply. Adieu, most dear, dear Sir:—

Charlotte joins in best Love & Duty.
Marianne is still at Mr. Wilbe[r]force's.⁹
M[y] Kind Love to Sarah. Alex is bearer, & will speak for himself. — — I hope! — —

668   [23 Chenies Street,
                                              21 January 1813]
To Charles Burney

A.L.S. (Osborn), *n.d.*
Double sheet 8vo   4 pp.   *pmks*   21 JA 1813   21 JA 1813   red seal
Addressed: Revᵈ Dr. Burney, / Deptford Rectory. / Kent.

My dear Kind Charles,
    This spirited effect of your promised deliberation has so astonished me I can scarcely believe mine Eyes!
    I had but begged you to think a little, & behold! every wheel is set to work in vigorous action!¹

---

⁹ William Wilberforce (1759–1833), philanthropist, had a house at Kensington Gore. The friendship between him and MF had been initiated by Arthur Young. See her letter (JRL) of 16 Dec. 1812 to Mrs. Piozzi: 'The Wilberforces are *his* friends, & he introduced me to them. Mr Wilberforce is one of the most charming characters I ever knew. So very cheerful & animated—& a kindness in his manner as superior to common urbanity, as gold to tinsel. . . . Wilberforce divesting himself of the Statesman & Orator, & playing like a child with his own young family, is very interesting & beautiful.'

MF was drawn to him as one of the affluent leaders of the evangelical Clapham sect who were dedicated in the Commons and the political arena to the liberalization of anti-Catholic laws, the abolition of the slave trade, and then of slavery itself.

668. ¹ The first intimation of activities to secure a Tancred scholarship for AA.

I shall write instantly to Lady *Keith*,[2] (not Gardner)[3] & I am hardly more sure of YOU than of HER, as far as previous engagements may not interfere.

But I am much at a loss with respect to our dear Padre; I have never dropt a hint upon this subject, & he is so timid, so apprehensive, that I fear a Letter can never be sufficiently | satisfactory to determine him upon action.

I think to tell him I entreat he will ask the Vote of the Governor for '*a Grandson now* under the care of his son the Rev^d Dr. Charles Burney.'[4]

And to Lady Keith,—or any other that may occur, I shall say—& beg you to do ditto—'That the hope of peace gives me courage to place my son at an English University, to finish his education, while I return to my husband.—'[5]

Beyond,—nothing must be written! —!! — — —

I have not yet opened to my Boy—but oh what a spur to regular study!—& what a softener to separation— | would such a prospect prove,—if separate we must! — — —

With regard to myself, I am again better. I wish you to comprehend, my dearest Carlos, that I have now no *actual evil*: but that I have cruel fears, from time to time, as I am a slave to care & precaution, or an instant sufferer: for the least cold—damp—extension of the right arm, bending down the chest,—quick exertion of any kind,—strong emotion, or any mental uneasiness, bring on either short acute pangs, or tolerable, yet wearing & heavy sensations.

[2] Hester Maria 'Queeney' Thrale (1764–1857) had married in 1808 George Keith Elphinstone, Lord Keith (vi, L. 594 n. 8). In 1813 he was Commander-in-Chief of the Channel Fleet. FBA successfully hoped that Lady Keith would urge her husband to write on AA's behalf to Admiral Samuel Hood, one of the Tancred voters (L. 670).

[3] Lady Susannah Gardner *née* Hyde (1749–1823), widow of Admiral Alan Gardner (1742–1809), Rear-Admiral of the Blue (1793), cr. Baronet (1806). Lady Gardner was not petitioned because as a widow she could not approach Lord Hood.

[4] See L. 670, in which FBA suggests that CB write to Sir David Dundas (1735–1820), Governor of Chelsea Hospital.

[5] So optimistic was the talk of peace following Napoleon's defeat at Moscow, the subsequent defection of the Prussian army (with nearly 30,000 men), and the plot against the Emperor's life, that on 1 Feb. 1813 Louis XVIII announced from Hartwell, 'The moment is at length arrived, when Divine Providence appears ready to break in pieces the instrument of its wrath. The Usurper of the Throne of St. Louis, the devastator of Europe, experiences reverses in his turn. . . . [my] re-establishment on the Throne of [my] ancestors will be for France only the happy transition from the calamities of a war which Tyranny perpetuates, to the blessings of a solid peace' (*GM* lxxxiii¹, 273–4).

None, however, last, nor are periodical, nor ever occur when
I cannot trace some thing that—I flatter myself!—is the cause.
It must be long ere a wound so dreadful (an operation of 17
Min. & a 1/2) can leave the spot as though it ne'er had been!
—yet how glad I should be of some hints how to guard against
evil consequences! My excellent ⏐ Dr. Larry was engaged to
give me some general directions of preventive wisdom, when he
was suddenly ordered to the Grand Army, with a new place of
Inspector General. He could only call to take leave, & generously to recommend to me change of Climate for my perfect re-
establishment.[6]

My kind love to Rosette— & Adieu, my
Dearest Charles — — F.B.d'A.

669   [23 Chenies Street,
                          25–26 January 1813]
To Charles Burney

A.L.S. (John Comyn, unbound), *n.d.*
Double sheet 8vo 4 pp. *pmks* 26 JA 26 JA 1813 27 JA 1[81]3
27 JA 1813 seal
  Addressed: Rev^d Dr. Burney / Deptford Rectory / Kent
  Annotated on address page: Missent to Newington Butts

⟨Chenies Street⟩ ⟨Monday⟩[1]

The hope you held out to me of coming hither, My dearest
Carlucci, has prevented my writing—(n:b: notwithstanding my
unwillingness ever to lose a post in answering a *Letter*) but the
continued bad weather[2] chills that hope, so here goes—
Your active proceedings charm me, come of them what may.

  [6] What FBA did not know was that baron Larrey (made inspecteur général
du service militaire de santé) was recalled to organize medical facilities for the
planned Russian campaign. He served as surgeon-in-chief not only during that
operation but also in the French occupation of Moscow, the retreat from that
city, the battle of Leipzig, and the long march back to France. If FBA and her
friends called him 'l'Ange', he was 'pour les blessés un père qui souffre des douleurs
de ses enfants' (Larousse).
  669. [1] Although postmarked 26 and 27 January, the letter was begun on Monday,
the 25th, and finished the following day.
  [2] From 15 to 25 Jan. 1813 the weather was cold, often with rain or sleet, a
sharp east wind, and temperatures for several days below freezing. On the 25th
the morning was clear but the afternoon became cloudy; the wind and cold
continued (*GM* lxxxiii[1], 2, 8).

And how they will make our dearest absentee exult!—Was I not SURE of him? he will cry.—[3]

Unfortunately, from a tour, my Letter for Lady Keith cannot reach her till to-day *at soonest*—perhaps & probably not so soon.

As to my dear Father—a visit from James intimidated me from writing: he has been so extremely ⎸ disturbed & harrassed by a request from James[4] for a Letter to Mr. Grant[5] soliciting for the Jem of India,[6] that it has almost made him ill!—&, at last, my Brother only could procure it, by writing word for word what he wished, & which, at length, he consented to copy.

Now in This affair, all is New to him: he has not an idea of my retaining your Godson—of *leaving* him, not a glimpse.

How write such a history? *You* only, can tell it.—for alas! I dare not venture thither!

I nurse myself night & day in case of a *call* for the 4th of next month, or to enable myself, as I *ought*, to present myself without ⎸ one:[7] & I am so prepared to catch cold on first going out, unless muffled as to Esther's, which was so very near, that I must not risk a previous attack,—for the 4th—to all its constant charms to my feelings, will now have an imperious demand upon my best hopes.[8] & *these*, also, I cannot write!—mine is a situation too complicate & too perilous for opening details that are not personal.

[3] M. d'A's gratitude was usually accompanied by tears (iii, L. 221).

[4] CB's reaction indicates morbid self-absorption and irritability but also unwillingness to forgive JB's involvement with SHB. For further evidence of CB's displeasure, see his minimal bequest to JB and Maria Rishton's interpretation of it (L. 769 n. 6).

[5] Introduced to CB by Arthur Young or William Wilberforce, Charles Grant (1746–1823) fused the evangelical piety of the Clapham sect with skilful activity as a member and often chairman of the East India Company's directors.

[6] Armed with CB's letter to Charles Grant, JB wished to secure either a cadet or midshipman rating for SHB's nephew James Christian (1797–*post* 1828), son of Richard Thomas Burney of India. In the Records of the East India Company (1823) James appears as a lieutenant in the 16th Native Infantry, retiring in 1828. SHB in a letter (Osborn) dated 26 Jan. 1814 remarked to CB Jr. that she could not in conscience apply to JB for help with still another of her nephews because he 'had such trouble with the other Cub who was here last year' (i.e. early 1813).

[7] FBA associated the Royal Family with 4 February, the day of the Queen's Drawing Room in honour of her birthday (her 69th in 1813). While FBA was not present at that event, she visited the Queen and the Princesses on three different occasions between 2 and 7 February (L. 672). During the lengthy audiences her cold was apparent. In a letter (Berg), dated 12 February, 'M^{rs} & Miss B[eckedorff] sincerely hope that Madame d'Arblay's cold has not increased since they had the pleasure of seeing Her at the Queens house.'

[8] The 'hopes' involved the Queen's intercession on behalf of AA and the Tancred scholarship. For the Queen's efforts, see Ll. 670 n. 7, 673, 677 and n. 3.

How unlucky this project had not occurred while you were at Althorp!⁹ It might have effected some change in our favour.

I am better, my dearest Charles, & working hard at Larrey, Farquar, & Graham, from their joint prescriptions

Do not be uneasy, kindest Charles, for I am seriously better from the measures I am adopting. They are not, I trust, adopted too late! |

Tuesday Morn^g I awoke with *de thot*: & I have ventured to write to our Father, & made a model,¹⁰ as well as I know how, to spare his cruel timidity, which afflicts me terribly. I will tell you the result when I know not. Not a word yet to poor Alex, whom I will not uselessly fidget. Love to Rosette & God bless you ever!—I receive no explanation whatever of my Box ⟨of letters⟩!¹¹

Pray entreat Chas to let me have transmitted hither my Taylor's & Book Bills &c that I may ⟨find⟩ & have but one ⟨job⟩¹²

670   [23 Chenies Street,
                                                26 January 1813]¹
To Doctor Burney

A.L. (Berg), *n.d.*
Double sheet 4to   3 pp.   red seal
Addressed: Dr. Burney / Chelsea College
Edited by FBA, p. 1, *annotated and incorrectly dated*: ⁙ 1812.   (6)
Desire of the Tancred Scholarship for Alexander—Dr. Davies

I am now going to write a very private Letter to my dearest Father, but which I premise he must not fatigue himself to answer to ME, except by *YES*, or NO;—That is the condition of this dispatch.

---

⁹ CB Jr. could have solicited the help of George John Spencer (iii, L. 136 n. 10), 2nd Earl Spencer, First Lord of the Admiralty (1794–1801) and hence able to approach Lord Hood. Alternatively, CB Jr. might have appealed to Lord Spencer's son, Robert Cavendish (1791–1830), who in 1813 was a commander in the Royal Navy with possible access to Lord Hood.
¹⁰ See L. 670.   ¹¹ See L. 663 n. 5.   ¹² See L. 663 n. 11.
670. ¹ For the dating of this letter, see L. 669 and n. 10.

And now

How I shall make my Padre stare till I explain myself hereafter, when I beg to know

Whether he is acquainted with the Governer of Chelsea
Hospital, & whether he can write to him a Letter to the following effect — —

Dr. Burney presents his respects to — — and hopes he will
have the goodness to pardon the solicitude of a Grandfather, if
he entreats the honour of his Vote, if it be not already engaged,
for a *Physical tancred Scholarship* which will be vacated shortly at
Cambridge, for Dr. Burney's Grandson, Alexander d'Arblay,
A youth who is just returned from France, to finish his education in the land of his birth, & who ardently desires that it
should ⎮ be at an English University, for which his studies
abroad have prepared him; but for which, unaided, his fortune
would be insufficient.

Now, my Padre, for some explanation.

An expectation of Peace is universal; & every body assures
me I had best try to place Alex at once where his acquirements
may lead to his advantage. *At all events* it cannot injure him,
ANY WHERE, for Education is every where necessary, and the
Mathematics[2] are no where so well taught as at Cambridge.

This *Physical tancred Scholarship*[3] will be vacated by its present

[2] At this time FBA, like M. d'A, approved AA's development as a mathematician.
On other occasions she either qualified her approval or withdrew it entirely.
See L. 686 n. 8.
[3] The scholarship was established by Christopher Tancred (1689–1754) of
Whixley, Yorkshire. After an argument with his five sisters, he disinherited them
and in 1721 placed his property in trust for the use of the masters of Christ's
and Gonville and Caius Colleges, Cambridge; the president of the College of
Physicians and Surgeons; the treasurer of Lincoln's Inn; the master of the Charterhouse; the governors of the Royal Hospital, Greenwich, and of Chelsea Hospital,
and their successors. The property settlement specifically provided for the creation
of the Tancred Hospital at Whixley for twelve indigent gentlemen and for the
establishment of twelve Tancred studentships. Despite efforts to contest the will,
the trustees on 8 Nov. 1757 established the trust and incorporated themselves by
Act of Parliament in 1762.
For several years the trustees honoured the provisions relative to Tancred
students who had to be natives of Great Britain, Anglicans, and in financial need,
as directed by the original Settlement of 1721. 'Four of which said Twelve Persons
should be Educated in the study of Divinity at *Christ*-College in *Cambridge*, and four
other of them in the study of Physic at *Gonville* and *Caius*-College in *Cambridge*,
and Four other of them in the Study of the Common Law at *Lincoln's-Inn*, *London*,
which said sums of Fifty Pounds yearly a Piece, should be paid to the said Twelve

possessor, Mr. Batty, in about a Month; Mr. Batty is going to the army.[4]

Charles is deeply anxious that you should write, if possible, to the Governor of Chelsea College.

He has written himself to 5 other Voters.
There are but 7 in all, viz.

1 The Governor of Chelsea Hospital,[5]
2 The Governor of Greenwich Hospital,—Lord Hood;[6] I
3 The President of the College of Physicians, Sr F. Milman.[7]
4 The Treasurer of Lincoln's Inn. Sir David Dundas,[8]
5 The Master of Christ Church, Dr. Brown,[9]

Persons, till they should have taken their respective Degrees of Batchelor of Arts, Batchelor of Physic, and Barrister of Common Law. . . . And that the said Twelve Persons shall be ever stiled **TANCRED'S STUDENTS.**' See the privately printed *Tancred's Charities*, ed. Simon J. Mosley, 28 Lincoln's Inn Fields, W.C. 2 (1964).

The £50 mentioned in the original bequest was not, however, fixed. The financial worth of the studentships depended on the income derived from 'the yearly rents and profits of Tancred Manor and Hereditaments'. The stipend fluctuated, but for most of the nineteenth century was approximately £100 per annum.

4 Robert Batty (1788–1848) entered Caius College as a pensioner in March 1808 and received his M.B. in 1813. Thereafter, he entered the army, served in the Grenadier Guards in the Pyrenees and at Waterloo, retiring in 1828 as a lieutenant-colonel. Interested in topography, he wrote several books combining his interest and career, such as *A Sketch of the late Campaign in the Netherlands* (1815). As an illustrator, he exhibited often at the Royal Academy.

5 FBA prevailed on CB (and on others as well) to write to Sir David Dundas, who in this case maintained his rigidity, living up to his nickname 'Old Pivot'. He never committed himself to AA despite these appeals. But Lady Dundas was more easily moved than her husband. Shortly before public announcement of the Tancred election result, CB in a letter (Osborn) revealed to FBA that 'This afternoon, while Sarah was reading to me the morn. Post, I was hon^d with the following note fr Lady Dundas, consort of Sir David K. B. our Governor (who s^d he w^d not be *teazed*, tho' he voted I suppose). "Lady Dundas has the pleasure to acquaint Dr Burney that M^r d'Arblay was this day elected to the Tancred Fellowship." '

6 Samuel Hood (1724–1816), 1st Viscount, entered the Navy in 1740. Made a lieutenant in 1746, he commanded the fleet in America (1763–7), served as Commissioner of the Navy at Portsmouth (1778–80), fought victoriously against the French off Dominica (1782), and was named Admiral of the Red in 1805. For his failure to act on AA's behalf, see n. 13.

7 Chairman of the Tancred electors, Sir Francis Milman (1746–1821) was liable to Burney pressure. As physician to Rosette Burney, he was a friend of CB Jr. Moreover, in 1813 he also attended Queen Charlotte, who informed him of royal interest in AA (L. 677 n. 3).

8 FBA incorrectly identified the Treasurer of Lincoln's Inn, who was Francis Hargrave (c. 1741–1821). He voted as a Tancred trustee for the last time in 1813; later in the same year he was declared mentally incompetent. See L. 683 n. 3.

9 FBA confused Christ Church, Oxford, with Christ's College, Cambridge. She was interested in the latter college, whose master from 1808 to 1814 was Thomas Browne (1766–1832). See also L. 674 and especially L. 678, which indicated that Lord Bute became the intermediary through whom Dr. Browne was approached.

6 The Master of Caius College, Dr. Davy.[10]
7 The Master of the Charter House, Dr. Fisher.[11]

Now

The Scholarship is at Caius College:

AND

The Master of Caius College, Dr. Davy,[12]
Has promised his interest,

AND

Engaged to give us his Vote.
This is what inspirits us.

Dr. Davy has even invited me to accompany Charles to Cambridge University upon the occasion. But I have not strength for travelling this cold season.

I dare not give a hint to Alex: lest it should make him wild with hope too soon.

I write now to Lady Keith, to interest her to plead to Lord Hood.[13]

Adieu, most beloved Padre.

simply Yes—or No. Mind!

[10] See L. 659 n. 4.
[11] Trained at Oxford, Philip Fisher (1751–1842) received his B.A. in 1770, his M.A. in 1772, and his B.D. in 1780. He became master of Charterhouse in 1803 and remained in that office until his death. Dr. Fisher was approached on AA's behalf by his brother John (1748–1825), Bishop of Salisbury, on the Queen's recommendation. The Bishop's wife Dorothea (*née* Scrivenor; d. 1831), an acquaintance of FBA, wrote on 19 February (Osborn): '[The Bishop] desires me to assure you, that he has not been unmindful of the command, with which the Queen has been so gracious as to honour him, relative to your Son. He applied immediately to his Brother the Master of the Charter House, & he desires me to enclose to you, the answer he has recieved from him.' The enclosure, now missing, revealed that Dr. Fisher, committed to another candidate at the March meeting, could support AA no sooner than the November election.
[12] See L. 659 n. 4, for Dr. Davy's interest as early as November–December 1812.
[13] Lady Keith had her husband write to Lord Hood (L. 673), who on 5 February replied (Berg) from Bath: 'I should be very happy to obey your Lordship's Commands in favor of your young Friend if it was in my power, particularly as my Vote is disengaged. I have not been out of my House (except in my carriage for exercise without which I can gett no sleep at night) since my return from Town in the Latter end of Nov.ʳ when I went to take my Seat in the new Parliament in order to give my Proxy.... From the infirm state of my health I have not attended a meeting of the Tancred Trustees for three years past, as they invariably take place in April and October, (when I am here) unless a vacancy for a student happens by Death or Resignation so as to occasion an extra meeting to be called in the Summer.'

London, 30 January [1813]

To Doctor Burney

A.L.S. (Barrett, Eg. 3690, ff. 110–11b), 30 Jan.
Double sheet 8vo   4 pp.   red seal
Addressed: Dr. Burney / Chelsea College—
Edited by FBA, p. 1, annotated, day and month retraced, year supplied: ⁂
1813   (2)   Entreaty Dr. B. would more *sans façon* admit his Family to his room.

30 Jan^y

My dearest Padre would allow of but one Letter a week; have I been observant & forbearing enough?

What nobillissima news!—

And how remarkable the explanation why the Duchess of Leeds did not follow up her kind & friendly intention![1] doubtless she is now engaged, & more than engaged, involved for every moment.

I long to know how this rigourous Season is supported by my dearest Father. For my part, I must own I do *not* find

The Weather remarkably fine.[2]

I am completely a prisoner to the house, & have been ever since the ǀ *once* when I went to our Etty, where the party had been deferred till my sojourn in town.[3] I was so immensely wrapt up, that, as I went & came in a Carriage, I did not find that I suffered; & I had true satisfaction in looking round again at our goodly tribe.

How I wish my beloved Father would permit himself to be more freely so surrounded by those whose first pride is to look up to him as their Chief! I often think he would be better, & feel his spirits lighter, if he could persuade himself to let them come in & go out, without taking the effort & ǀ forcing the

---

671. [1] Catherine Anguish (1764–1837) became on 11 Oct. 1788 the second wife of Francis Godolphin (Osborne), Duke of Leeds (1789), *styled* Marquess of Carmarthen (1761–89). He died in 1799, aged 48. CB knew his Lordship as a member of the Club and the Duchess for her musical skill. Her 'explanation' is revealed in *The Times* (15 Jan. 1813): the position of governess to the Princess Charlotte of Wales was soon to be filled 'by the Dowager Duchess of LEEDS'.

[2] 30 Jan. 1813 was a 'cold damp raw day' (*GM* lxxxiii¹, 98).

[3] On 14 January (L. 667 n. 3). Thereafter the month was mostly cloudy or foggy with the temperature going as low as the mid-twenties and never higher than the mid-thirties °F.

violence upon his feelings of receiving & entertaining them as
visitors. I would have them all permitted to offer what they can
find to say, & accept their relations or prattling, & be content,
in return, with sometimes a Nod, & Some times a wry face, just
as approbation or dissent might dictate;—& NOTHING MORE.

I am just informed of an odd circumstance. A Lady of our
acquaintance went lately to a Booksellers, who, hearing her
name was Burney, said 'Pray allow me, Ma'am, to ask if Mad^e
d'Arblay is really in England?—' She answered YES: 'Favour
me, then, Ma'am, with her direction: I want to write to her.'
This was 2 days ago. No Letter is | yet arrived in consequence.

Charles is returned from Lord Spencer's in high glee. I
could not possibly venture to Richmond, but I am Godmama,
& our Charlotte stood for me. Arthur Young & Clement were
the Males. Charles was the Priest.⁴

Adieu, my ever most dear of dear Padres—my kindest Love
to Sarah—affectionately & dutif[ully]

Yours F. B. [A.]

672   23 Chenies Street,
                                 [8 February 1813]

To Doctor Burney

A.L.S. (Diary MSS. vii. 5870–[73], Berg), *n.d.*

Double sheet 8vo 4 pp. foliated 1 2 *pmks* T.P.P.U. / Tottenham
CR 8 FE 1813 8 FE 1813 red seal
Addressed: Dr. Burney, / Chelsea College, / Chelsea.
Edited by FBA, p. 1 (5870), *annotated and dated*: ⁙ Chenies Street /
London Feb^y ⌐7⌐—8—1813 (3) ⌐Exquisite Graciousness & feeling of
The Queen & princesses.⌐
Edited also by CFBt *and the* Press. *See* Textual Notes.

Your dear & kind invitation, my dearest Padre, I should
instantly have answered, & not with my Pen, had all been as
favourable as my inclination & the Weather: but this last Week
has been wholly dedicated to the Queen & the Princesses: a
Letter came to me from Windsor to prepare me for their arrival,
&, consequently, to keep me always in readiness for the honour

⁴ L. 667 n. 8.

& the hope of a Summons. And, out of Their five days residence in town,[1] they have had the gracious indulgence to admit me Three days. And upon those occasions, I never quitted the Palace till they went to one of the Princes to dinner between 7 & 8 o'clock.[2]—Nor then, neither, in fact, I still stayed to dine myself, with my successor.[3]

But why, my dearest Father may say, not hasten to Chelsea NOW?—The fact is, I have been obliged to omit various precautionary measures during the whole of this week, & I now feel an absolute necessity to nurse again, & refit. To day I have entirely kept quiet & silent up stairs in my room, &, as these other days, I have kept wholly the reverse, my lungs, strength, & spirits all demand the recruit. I fear that for some days I must go on *DOCTORING* myself after these late excesses. But bad weather alone, after Wednesday, shall withhold me from embracing my dearest Father.[4] Don't let this intimation occasion any change in your *own Doctorings*, I entreat, for you know we settled, when I was with you last, that I *could take* a hint; & that There should be no *reserve amongst friends.*

I have quite been melted by the kindness, the condescendsion I have met with in these last long & precious visits. Never yet, after so many years of goodness, have I experienced quite so much sweetness & confidence. And in nothing was it so touching to me as in the earnest enquiries made by Her Majesty after my dearest Father, whom she spoke of with the most tender

672. [1] On Tuesday, 2 Feb. 1813, Queen Charlotte with Princesses Elizabeth and Mary 'arrived at the Queen's Palace, from Windsor' (*The Times*, 3 Feb.). On Sunday the 7th they dined early with the Prince Regent, 'and at five o'clock set off on their return to Windsor' (*The Times*, 8 Feb.).
[2] FBA did not see the Queen and the Princesses on 4 February, when Her Majesty held a Drawing Room at St. James's 'in commemoration of her birthday', but was in attendance on 2 February until the royal ladies went to dine with the Duke of Cumberland at his apartments in St. James's Palace. She waited on the Queen and Princesses on 3 February, for MF reported (JRL) to Mrs. Piozzi that on this day 'Aunt D'Arblay is with the Queen . . . & Alexander construing Thucydides with [me].' FBA also visited the Queen's Palace on 6 February, staying until her hostesses left to attend the Prince Regent's ball and supper.
[3] Charlotte Beckedorff earned £200 annually as Keeper of the Robes to Queen Charlotte from 3 Feb. 1802 until the Queen's death in 1818. (See BM, Add. MSS. 17879 [2]; Court & City Register 1804–19.) She served with Margaret Bremeyer until 1807 and thereafter with her daughter Sophia.
[4] Wednesday, 10 February, and the next day were fair, the noon temperature in the mid-forties °F. (*GM* lxxxiii[1], 98). Yet FBA did not visit CB on either of those two days, but tended AA, who had come down with 'influenza' (Ll. 674, 675), which she subsequently contracted. It is not likely that she saw CB until March (L. 683).

respect & consideration.—And from my Sire she went so gently
to my offspring, that I could hit upon no expedient in the World
for keeping my Eyes quite dry. Nor was even this all that she
did to moisten them; she enquired with interest & feeling after
my dear Partner, & permitted me to relate long details of his
situation & his noble conduct: & she listened like one who,
good herself, believed in goodness. |

I must reserve *reporting progress* as to the grand affair till my
next.⁵—How kind you were to tell me your Cough was better!
—*Better & better be it*, dearest dear Sir, prays

Your Most dutiful & affec^te

F B d'A.

My best Love to Sarah.
dear Charlotte's Love & duty—& Alexander's & Marian's.⁶
Alex was to take this, but is stopt by a cold.

673   [23 Chenies Street],
                              11 February 1813

To H.R.M. Queen Charlotte of England

A.L.S. and A.L. 2 drafts (Berg), 11 Feb. 1813
Double sheet 12mo   4 pp.   Draft I, p. 3; Draft II, pp. 1, 2, 4.

⌐Madam,¹
The delight, the gratitude—the astonishment with which

⁵ The combined efforts of FBA, CB Jr., and their friends (especially Mrs. Locke,
Mr. Angerstein, Lord and Lady Keith, Colonel Howard, Mr. and Mrs. Waddington through Professor Monk) to secure the Tancred for AA.

⁶ Although devoted to her mother, MF was at Chenies Street reluctantly.
Her letter (JRL), dated 15 Jan. 18[13], to Mrs. Piozzi admitted: 'indeed I only
left [Wilberforce's house] to-day—nor could have torn myself away then, had not
M^e D'Arblay been on a visit, for a short time to my mother.'

673. ¹ FBA's first draft acknowledging a letter, now missing, wherein Queen
Charlotte expressed her hope for AA as a Tancred scholar and her promise to
recommend his election to Dr. Philip Fisher and Sir David Dundas, who as the
'Governor of Chelsea Hospital generally votes as the Royal Family desires'.
See the letter (Berg) of Clement Francis to FBA, November 1828.

FBA's gratitude for the Queen's assistance in securing the Tancred for AA continued for many years. In a letter (Barrett, Eg. 3699B, f. 33b) to Princess Elizabeth,
FBA asserted, 'pleasure & pride upon the most gracious most benevolent interference, with which my venerated —& may I not say loved R^al Mistress forwarded, or rather decided my good fortune in obtaining a studentship without
which I had no means to place him at the University'.

I received the lines so graciously, so benignly penned by your Majesty's own hand, surpass all powers of description, & can difficultly even be imagined, though they found their way straight to my heart. The astonishment indeed, must ⌜indeed⌝ with time, wear away; but the delight will always be new, & the gratitude will be a part of my existence. Be the ultimate success of the enterprise what it may, I shall now always look back to its attempt as the cause of procuring me the highest honour of my life.

 with the deepest Respect & veneration,
I presume to sign myself
> Madam,
>> your Majesty's
>>> Most Obedient
>>> Most devoted
>>>> & most dutiful Ob^t Servant
>>>>> F B d'A.[2]

Ld Keith & Mr. Angerstein have written to Ld Hood, & Ld Keith & Mr. Greville Howard to S^r D[avid] D[undas]¹³ |

N° II

⌜March⌝ Feb. 1͢. 1813

Madam,
 The astonishment, the delight the gratitude with which I received the lines so graciously, so benignly penned by your Majesty's own hand, surpass all powers of description, & can difficultly even be imagined, though they found their way straight to my heart—there, I had almost said, to be housed for-ever; but the astonishment must, of course, with time, wear away; the delight, however, will always be new, & the gratitude a part of my existence.

 Be the ultimate success of the enterprise what it may, I shall

---

² FBA's letter (based on the two drafts presented herein) was received at Windsor by 12 Feb. 1813, for on that date the Keeper of the Queen's Robes replied (Berg): 'Mr^s Beckedorff presents her Compliments to Madame d'Arblay and begs leave to acknowledge the receipt of a letter for the Queen, which she has taken the first opportunity to present to Her Majesty.'

³ For the fuller relevance of this sentence, see the conclusion to draft No. 2 and nn. 4, 5, 6.

always look back to its attempt ǀ as the cause of procuring me
the highest honour of my life.

   with the deepest Respect & veneration,
   I presume to sign myself
                    Madame,
                    your Majesty's
                       Most obed^t most devoted
                       & most dutiful subject
                       & servant

   May I dare mention that L^y. Keith has just enclosed the L^d
Hood's answer to Ld K. in wh^{ch} he bewails his incapability of
travelling unless the election took place in Summer, in which
case his vote sh^d be at Ld K.'s service for the youth recommended:[4]
No proxys ǀ are permitted at Cambridge. Dr. Davy continues
always sanguine & encouraging. Sir D. D. has been 3 times
written to,[5] but has answered nobody.[6] His courtesy seems
universal. Mr. G. Howard[7] has promised Mrs. Locke to persecute Lady Dun, till he gets a reply.

674   [23 Chenies Street,
                        post 11 February 1813]

To Charles Burney

   A.L. (Osborn), *n.d.*
   Single sheet 4to   2 pp.

My dearest Charles—
   Lady K[eith] desires me to return Lord Hood's Letter
immediately, but I trespass upon her friendship for one day to
shew it to you, & to entreat you will communicate its contents
to our First Supporter, Dr. Davy. It will be needless to apply
further to L^d H[ood] as here is his promise for *us*, if for any
body.
   Yet, though there is one the less to canvass—& that one is an

   [4] L. 670 n. 13.
   [5] Sir David Dundas was written to by CB, Colonel Howard, Lady Keith, and
somewhat later by John Angerstein, William Wilberforce, and possibly the Duke
of York.   [6] Sir David never broke his silence (L. 670 n. 5).
   [7] Fulke *Greville* Upton Howard (1773–1846). See i, L. 16 n. 13; iv, L. 332 n. 9;
v, L. 464 n. 9.

engaged friend,[1] we want *4 votes* first the same. Lady K[eith] charges me to discover some relations, or friends, or even acquaintance & distant connexions of Dr. Brown, that either she or Lord K[eith] may attack them.[2] She is fervant in the Cause past description: entreat our sheet Anchor to give you, if possible, some documents.

As to Dr. Fisher—& Sir F. Milman—they have been so assaulted last Monday, that nothing less than impossibility can stand there in our way.[3] I *have* not heard the result.

Sir D[avid] D[undas] won't answer a Soul: a friend has undertaken to Dun his *Lady*, & try if that will produce some reply:[4] it has been said, by the wicked, that loquacity rather preponderates on the female side—I mean as a general remark; & one which I hold to be utterly slanderous: though, just now, I feel as if I could be in christian charity with her Ladyship should it, here, prove true. |

My poor Alexander is at this moment in bed with a cold & fever. I am giving him James's powders, which have so many times worked miracles in restoring him from similar attacks. If I succeed again, I am not quite sure, should other affairs go ill, but that, upon the next physical vacancy, I may enquire the proper Costume, & enter upon the lists as a Candidate myself.

675

[23 Chenies Street, 22 February 1813]

To Doctor Burney

A.L. (Berg), *n.d.*

Double sheet small 8vo   4 pp.   *pmks*   T.P.P.U. / Tottenham CR 22 FE 1813   23 FE 1813   wafer

Addressed: Dr. Burney, / Chelsea College, / Chelsea.

Edited by FBA, p. 1, *annotated and dated*: 23. Feb. 1813   ALEX   TANCRED

674. [1] Martin Davy (L. 659 n. 4).

[2] FBA wished to be certain of four votes since there were seven Tancred electors. At this time she felt confident of Davy, Sir Francis Milman, and Philip Fisher (see n. 3). Lord Hood, she knew, would not attend the election and Sir David Dundas would not reveal his commitment. The vote of Thomas Browne was therefore crucial.

[3] In fact Dr. Fisher was committed to another candidate (Ll. 670 n. 11, 677).

[4] Colonel Howard dunned so effectively that Lady Dundas, responsive to such pressure, broke the news of AA's election to CB before the official announcement (L. 670 n. 5).

What can my most beloved—my kindest Father think of this unnatural silence. Though thrice he has given me the blessing of his hand, & though he has sent me a packet of news for which I languished?

I must now to confession—my poor Boy has had an attack that I regard as an Influenza, & of a malignant nature. He kept his Bed wholly some days, & had high fever many more. The immortal James, however, has cured him, which, when persevered in attentively never has failed, in every illness he has suffered from his birth to this hour.

But alas—he was not yet recovered, when his nurse was seized with the sam[e] disorder. And mine is yet more obstinat[e.] I am but now getting about my room, & still unable to join the family down stairs, from the weakness left in my head & limbs through the violence of the assault. What a blessing of blessings my dearest Father escapes it! | James's Powders with me, also, is the only remedy, varied, latterly, by Nitre.[1] I thank God the seizure has not affected me where I most feel vulnerable. I have taken furious precautions, according to the severest discipline ordered by my D[r] Larrey. I shall now soon, I doubt not, be re-established.

But how cruel for my great business!—which has nearly lain upon the shelf for near a fortnight![2] — —

Yesterday Charles came & carried off my poor meagre Alex to Deptford, to try change of air. He is now so thin, that I seem to recollect him last week as a person tolerably fat!—

But now to pleasanter matters.—

Will not my kind Father rejoice when I tell him he sent me, in his delicious packet, 4 Letters from Paris!—from my own beloved Partner!—They are Scraps, some, but they are 4!— The oldest is | dated 20. November. After, 23[d] Then January 12. —And last of all, Feb[y] 4.[3]

This is a joy & consolation to me impossible to describe. I was secretly in anguish for some news since *the return*.[4]

675. [1] Nitre was used medicinally as a 'diuretic, sedative, and cooler' (*Enc. Brit.*, 3rd ed., iv. 472). FBA thought it would eliminate her persistent low fever.
[2] *The Wanderer.*
[3] Shortly before 12 Apr. 1813 FBA admitted having received seven letters from M. d'A. On that date he wrote another, which she later received (L. 689 n. 5).
[4] From *GM* lxxxiii[1], 78–9: 'It is a remarkable fact, that although Buonaparte reached Paris at half past 11 at night, on the 18th of December [following his

Yet, think how terrible that he is deprived of all participation of such satisfaction! Not a word from me has reached him! No, not a syllable! And, but that Mrs. Solvyns[5] has been so good natured & considerate as sometimes to mention me to her husband,[6] he would not know whether poor Alex & I were still in the land of the living!

5 long Letters of mine are lost. I am glad I never sent your precious billet.[7] Nor will I risk it till I hear that one line at least arrives safe. I am going to try an opportunity offered by Charlotte Barret.[8]

Mean while, friends are very active for me with respect to my Boy, & Charles is indefatigable. I am not without hope. It will be so superb a finish for our education. 120£ a year, during the term allotted, which I think is 3 years.[9] Dr. Davy is zealous beyond description, & Lady Keith is always at work. But your Dun—cannot be Dunned into answering any body.[10] Amiable

desertion of the French army at Wilna], no notice whatever was taken of his arrival either in the *Moniteur* or in any of the minor papers of the 19th. His arrival was kept a secret' until the 20th when he received his Senate and Council of State who congratulated him on a '*happy return*'. Apart from stating that nearly 300,000 men would in February 'be collected at Hamburgh, upon the Elbe, upon the Rhine, and upon the Oder, independent of 200,000 MEN WHO ARE WITH THE GRAND ARMY', and appealing for new Polish exertions in anticipation of a new campaign, Napoleon upon his return made no specific threats, either civil or military.

Because he had in fact miscalculated the number of troops left in Lithuania, Napoleon had immediately to recall 100,000 men of the 1809–12 classes, and the 1814 class (115,000 conscripts) would by March relieve the 1813 class in the depots (Madelin, xiii. 17 ff.).

[5] See L. 643. Through connections on both sides of the Channel—John Reeves in London (L. 696 n. 11) and various members of Imperial officialdom in Paris (L. 694 n. 2)—Mme Solvyns had access to couriers between France and England. Her gossip-mongering was less significant than her ability to supply the d'Arblays with information about each other. Thus, CB, as late as May 1813, wrote (Osborn) that his daughter had 'seen Mrs Solvyns—and that she seems perfectly cheerful and friendly . . . so safe a post-woman'.

[6] For François-Balthazar Solvyns (1760–1824), see vi, L. 592 n. 2.

[7] See L. 651 and nn. 2, 3.

[8] Some of CFBt's Richmond associates who could have served as couriers were Mrs. Aufrère (L. 720 n. 1) and a member of the large de Thuisy family (Ll. 764 n. 8, 803 n. 9).

[9] The Tancred Charity stipulated that its students could receive financial aid not only while they studied for a degree but for three years thereafter. Moreover, the payments varied every six months so that the annual amount could not be fixed, although AA in November 1814 reported in a letter (Berg) on 'my present scholarship of 110 pd^s per annum'. According to the 'Tutor's Account Book' AA received the following amounts as a Tancred student: £53. 14s. (11 Nov. 1813); £55. 14s. (6 May 1814); £52. 14s. (11 Nov. 1814); £48. 4s. (19 Apr. 1815); £57 (23 Nov. 1815); £52. 14s. (7 June 1816); £51. 14s. (14 Nov. 1816).

[10] A punning reference to Sir David Dundas, 'who s^d he w^d not be *teazed*' (L. 670 n. 5).

person! How can you endure such a Neighbour? You should teach him better manners. That i'n't good latin, I'm sure! I hope I sha'n't want him—for, *I'm very near* having a 2d. Vote! Now no Bunhill row!¹¹ Adieu dear[est] Sir.—

F[B d'A]

Good Charlotte's kind Love & duty—
& I thank both Becky & George for the exactness of the Par⟨cel⟩.

676   [23 Chenies Street,
                                    post 23 February 1813]
To Charles Parr Burney

A.L.S. (Osborn), *n.d.*
Double sheet 8vo   1 p.   wafer   tear mended
Addressed: To / the Rev^d Mr. Burney, / Greenwich.
Docketed, p. 4: M^rs D'Arblay.

If all the parents of all the bantlings who have the good Fortune to be under the care of the Revd. Mr. Burney,¹ are as

¹¹ In the Finsbury area of London, Bunhill Row was a large street with houses on only one side. FBA's allusion to Sir David Dundas in terms of 'Bunhill row' is cryptic. She might be implying the following: the temptation to fight him, for the row was adjacent to a military practice and parade ground; his negative behaviour, for the area and the Bunhill Fields Burial Ground had long been associated with dissenters; his inability to see or hear truth, for he was unlike Dick Whittington who in an early version of the story heard Bow Bells from Bunhill rather than Highgate and recognized his destiny. See Henry B. Wheatley, *London Past and Present* (3 vols., 1891), i. 301–2.

676. ¹ CPB was now officially master of Greenwich School, CB Jr. having resigned the title just before the start of the new term on 1 February. On 16 Feb. 1813 Samuel Parr wrote to his godson: 'I rejoice at your father's escape from the toils and vexations of a teacher; and whatever disappointment he may have suffered from the death of the Bishop of Ely, yet I am sure that his widely extended connections, and well-directed measures, will procure some valuable addition to his preferments. He has no theological heresies nor political crimes to expiate; and, whether Whigs or Tories have the ascendancy, he will neither be inactive nor unsuccessful in finding patrons.' See Parr, *Works*, ed. John Johnstone (8 vols., 1828), vii. 426. In turning his school over to his son, CB Jr. was preparing to concentrate on obtaining a bishopric.

Parr kept CPB ignorant of the burden carried by CB Jr. ever since he, as an undergraduate, stole books from the University Library in 1777 and was sent down (*HFB*, pp. 72–6). In a letter (JRL), dated August 1810, Clement Francis admitted to Mrs. Piozzi: 'However poor Man, though we can't grant him praise, he may be allowed Peace, for, that unfortunate Cambridge business has weighed hard down upon him through life. And indeed I almost think it might be buried in Silence. But it sticks to him like a leech.'

obedient to his ordinances as this present writer, he need not covet to keep better discipline within school than without;— For here—in defiance of all yearnings to mix a little domestic life, & a few lessons of The World, with your hocus pocus Mathematics, & Greek, & other outlandish lingos,—Here is my Alexander — — bowing himself to your opinion as chearfully & willingly, as it is subscribed to dolorously & reluctantly, by your

dutiful aunt

F B. d'A.—

So much in the dumps — —
And now, my dear Charles, let me thank you heartily for the *goût* you have given him for your habitation; & let me beg you, whenever it is possible, to send him forth for a *quick walk*: Mr. Thomas[2] recommends EXERCISE, & he does not take sufficient in the Grounds: as I learn from 'peaching Dolph.

My love to Mrs. Par & my name sake, & comp[ts], best, to Mrs. Bicknell

677 [23 Chenies Street, 26 February 1813]

To H.R.M. Queen Charlotte of England

A.L.S. draft (Berg), *n.d.*

Single sheet 4to, the cover of a letter bearing on the *verso* the *address*: Alexander d'Arblay Esq— / 23 Chenies Street / Bedford Square The single sheet was folded in a way to produce four 8vo surfaces, of which FBA used pp. 2, 3, and 4.

Edited by FBA, p. 1, *annotated and dated*: ⌐N° 2 March ⌐ / N° 2 Feb. 26. 1813

Madam,

With all my long experience of your Majesty's goodness it is not without trembling that I presume again to lay at the feet of your Majesty the actual position of my Son. But where

---

[2] Honoratus Leigh Thomas (1769–1846) received his diploma of the Corporation of Surgeons in October 1794 although two years earlier he had served as a naval surgeon. In 1799 he volunteered for medical service with the army in Holland. By 1800 he abandoned the military to take over the fashionable practice of William Cumberland Cruikshank (1745–1800), in Leicester Place. Between 1813 and 1822 Thomas frequently attended AA and JB. (For JB's sense of obligation to him, see L. 755 n. 3.)

the stake is so great, & success seems so near, may I not hope my very critical situation may plead some excuse?—

Dr. Davy

Dr. Brown   are promised to my Son.

Dr. Milman

    Lord Hood will be absent, or has given, also, his promise for him to Lord Keith.

⌈one of the opponents declines the contest⌉

His opponent has secured

Dr. Fisher &

Mr. Hargrave.¹

The casting vote therefore rests entirely with Sir David Dundas.

Several persons have addressed him, but he has never made any answer.

It seems therefore that he is not yet fixed—

Ah, Madam!——if I dared solicit your Majesty's permission to suplicate the intercession of their Royal Highnesses vote The Duke of York!²—Every one says a ⌐ hint from His R. H. would be decisive.—

Sʳ F[rancis] Milman has conducted himself with a cordiality & spirit truly engaging, & assured my Brother that my Boy shall have not alone his Vote & interest but his oratory, for that, as he is Chairman of the Committee, he shall make a harangue upon his eligibility, abilities, &c that must conquer Sir D[avid] Dun[das] ⌈who is said to be very tenacious in examining the rights & abilities & eligibility of the Candidates. And Sʳ F[rancis] gaily declares he is preparing an harangue to conquer him⌉—provided he does not come already engaged.³

677. ¹ See L. 670 nn. 8, 11.

  ² The Duke of York (1763–1827) became a friend of Sir David Dundas when both participated in the expedition to the Helder in 1799. In 1809 Sir David succeeded the Duke as Commander-in-Chief of the Army until the Commons acquitted the latter of charges that he had accepted bribes for the promotion of officers. Dundas understood the necessity of tendering his resignation upon the Duke's return to his command in 1811.

  ³ The Queen responded to FBA's plea. On 3 Mar. 1813, in a letter (Berg), Mme Beckedorff reported to FBA: 'My constant attendance upon Her Majesty, who, you will be sorry to hear, has been unwell ever since our return to Windsor, has prevented my writing to you before. I have taken the first opportunity to present your Letter to the Queen and am commanded to say that Her Majesty had done every thing you wished and hoped that it would succeed. Sir Francis Milman having been at Windsor on Account of the Queen's illness, Her Majesty has had an opportunity of receiving some directions about it from him which Her Majesty has sent with your Letter, and which will be attended to.'

The election is for the 16. of March.

The B^p of Salisbury & Mrs. Fisher—have sent me a letter of the extremest politeness, promising the Vote of Dr. Fisher for the next ⟨meeting⟩ in November — —4

but alas! — — — I shall no longer be here; I can make no arrangements for my Boy, must leave him hanging upon nothing in his uncertain destiny, & may not, myself by the cruel difficulty of receiving Letters; know his fate for months, if not years! I C^d extend my stay to the middle of May,5 for such an object as settling him satisfactorily; but further than that, I sh^d lose the benefit ǀ of my passport, & only arrive to be arretée— which I cannot look forward to without ⌐shuddering⌐ Horrour.

Sh^d my desire be indiscreet—impolitic—or improper—may I not still hope from the justness of Mind of Y^r Majesty in weighing the almost dreadful motives which urge me, forgiveness,—& even pity—rather than what wd. nearly break my heart, disapprobation & displeasure?—

With the most true & profound veneration,

I remain—for-ever,
Madam,
Your Majesty's
Most devoted
& dutiful
subject & servant
F. B. d'Arblay

678   [23 Chenies Street,
February 1813]

To Charles Burney

A.L. (Osborn), *n.d.*
Single sheet 8vo, being the first leaf of a letter (double sheet) to Alexander d'Arblay   2 pp.   p. 1, left margin and p. 2, right margin, have transparent mounting strips
Docketed, p. 2: February— / 1813—

I forgot to mention, my dearest Charles, that after rubbing

---

4 See L. 670 n. 11.   5 See L. 646 nn. 22, 23.

the Camphire into the part that is painful,[1] nothing will more relieve you than to have it immediately, & for a long time, slowly combed. There is no friction so good.

I am anxious about Alex: I hope to God he will not scamper about in the Wet. A relapse, thinner than the thin as he now is, would be frightful.

I languish to hear you are seeking another Horse,—& Horse Man!—I am inexpressibly vexed by that abomination.

If you do not return on Monday, let Alex write a word.

I am still in the same state: my fever is of the low sort, that is most difficult to cure, & my cough is cruelly obstinate.

I BESEECH you to make a point that our Alex be *orderly*, *tidy*, & *punctual*: do not spare him on those matters, dearest Charles. He will *more* mind you than any one, though alas! —! — his absence & carelessness grow upon him daily!—But don't seem to suspect them: be always *surprised*!—

I beg, also, that [2] he may not play *AT ANY GAME* whatever. I wish him to spend *all* his leisure in exercise, reading, or conversation. He has been drawn into habits here wholly new to him, & which I must positively now try to eradicate totally, for I find *moderation* out of the question.

His *Father* gave me this charge, if ever I perceived a love of any game gaining ground.

pray tear him off the other side—& pray give my kind Love to Rosette,

and for YOURSELF, my Charles, take your share that [is]closest to my heart.

Lord Bute had been written to for your *protegé*, to make him address Dr. B. —! —[3]

---

678. [1] According to current medical advice, 'camphire, and some other aromatic oils, have the power of allaying the pain, and of removing the inflammation from the part affected' (*Enc. Brit.*, 3rd ed., xi. 186–7).

[2] Specifically chess and, to a lesser extent, whist.

[3] John Stuart (1744–1814), 4th Earl of Bute, etc. could address Dr. Browne through his grandson John Crichton-Stuart (1793–1848), Earl of Dumfries, Viscount Air, Lord Crichton (1803), and 5th Earl of Bute (1814). Having studied at Christ's College, Cambridge, and receiving his M.A. there in 1812, Crichton-Stuart knew Dr. Browne.

[23 Chenies Street,
6 March 1813]

To H.R.M. Queen Charlotte of England

A.L.S. draft (Berg), *n.d.*
Single sheet 4to   2 pp.   written on both sides of address page of A.L.
addressed: Revd Dr Charles Burney, / Crooms Hill   wafer
Edited by FBA, p. 1, *annotated and dated*: March 5. 1813   No. 3—

Madam,[1]

The truly feeling heart of your Majesty will pardon—may I not venture to trust? that again I ⌈venture⌉ into the Royal presence, from a fullness of gratitude that casts me at your Majestys feet—I had nearly said more devotedly than ever; yet to what epoch can I look back, for many, many, years, in which my dutiful attachment to your Majesty has not been at once my happiness, my principle, & my pride? |

I fear nothing now! yet the opponents are far more active than fair: they have asserted, to Mr. Lyons,[2] the Lawyer of the Institution, that my English Boy was Born in *Calais*:[3] My Brother has taken the certificate of his baptism from the Vicar of G^t Bookham, Mr. Cooke.[4] But they say they must have a certificate of his Birth in G^t Bookham from someone present, & if such they dispute. Fortunately my kind Mrs. Locke was the first who received the ⟨promised⟩ Boy in her arms on the instant, which if they demand, she will depose before any, or every Justice of Great Britain.[5]

L^y Keith has written again—so has Col. Grev. Howard, so has Mr. Angerstein, & even Mr. Wilberforce,[6] who, by an

---

679.   [1] On 6 March (not the 5th as FBA later indicated), she wrote to the Queen in response to the information provided on 3 March by Mme Beckedorff (see L. 677 n. 3).

[2] William Lyon (*c.* 1763–1814), admitted to Gray's Inn in 1781, was the solicitor-clerk of the Tancred Charities at 7 Gray's Inn.

[3] See L. 670 n. 3.

[4] The Revd. Samuel Cooke (1741–1820) of Great Bookham (iii, L. 122 n. 8).

[5] Mrs. Locke was not required to make a deposition but she took the precaution of informing Mr. Ansell, the accoucheur, of 'the necessity of his affidavit that our Alex was born at Great Bookham'. She reported this to FBA in a letter (Comyn) dated 5 Mar. 1813. See also L. 680 n. 3.

[6] MF was the intermediary between the partisans of AA and William Wilberforce.

accident, has conceived a warm interest for my son, though he has never seen him; but to no creature has he[7] sent any answer. Oh, Madam! what do I not owe to your Majesty's gracious condesendsion! not alone in what I foresee will be the happy result, but in saving my aching head, nearly as much shattered as my heart, the terrible 10 days[8] further suspense how I c^d otherwise provide for the poor Boy from whom I must part!—
Blessed be your Majesty for ever & for ever! AMEN! |

I have been wholly spared the knowledge of your Majesty's illness till I hear, through the good Me Beckedorff, that 'tis almost past—Most assuredly else I should not even have thought of my late application.[9] I bless God that it is over, & with prayers the most fervant for your Majesty's perfect re-establishment, & long, & happier life!—a blessing to the Nation at large, a balm to the wounded, a support to the feeble,

I humbly presume to sign myself,
with the most heartfelt reverence,
your Majesty's ever gratefully dutiful
subject & servant,
F B d'Arblay.

680   [23 Chenies Street,
                          c. 6 March 1813][1]

To Charles Burney

A.L. (John Comyn, unbound), *n.d.*
Double sheet 8vo   3 pp.   *pmk*   T.P.P.U.   seal
Addressed: Rev^d Dr. Burney / Rectory / Deptford

Houra to your Worship![2] I shall have the Affidavit by to day's

[7] Sir David Dundas.
[8] The election was to be held on 16 March.
[9] FBA's ignorance of the Queen's illness derived from her preoccupation with AA's Tancred hopes. Newspapers wrote freely of the Queen's health, *The Times* on 27 February reporting that 'The QUEEN is indisposed, and is confined in the Castle. It is thought HER MAJESTY will not be able to hold a Drawing-room next week, as was expected.' And on 1 March *The Times* indicated that the Queen continued to ail.

680. [1] For the dating of this letter, see n. 4 below, and L. 679 n. 5.
[2] A whimsical reference to the fact that CB Jr. in 1799 had been named a justice of the peace for Kent County.

post.— Mr Ansell is alive & well,[3] & will give it.[4] The Earl of Rothes,[5] who remembers the transaction, & whose Mother was a constant friend to me,[6] is now Justice at Dorking,[7] & will sign the affidavit.

> Houra to your worship!
> This has put me into Paradise.

Mrs. Locke cannot be wanted—but—if some new trick made her necessary, she generously—sweetly says—she would come from her retreat, & in the Face of the whole University—or whole Universe, assert her taking on his birth ˡ into her kind arms, on the 18ᵗʰ of December, 1794, my male child, at 9 o'clock in the Morning. so

> Houra to your worship!
> What will they invent next?
> Shall I send the Affi— or keep it for you—? or what?
> Dearest Charles, how is your head?[8]
>   Adieu,—& Houra?

Love to Rosette

[3] William Ansell (1745–1830) was the surgeon-apothecary of Dorking (i, L. 6 n. 4).

[4] On 5 Mar. 1813 Mr. Ansell sent a note (Comyn) to Mrs. Locke:

'Mʳ Ansell presents his respectful Compliments to Mʳˢ Lock, informs her that he attended Mʳˢ Darblay Decʳ ⟨18⟩, 1794 and delivered Mʳˢ D. of a Male Child— Lord Rothes will come from London tomorrow Evenᵍ; will then wait on his Lordship, and make an affidavit to the above effect and send it by the Postman Sunday Mornᵍ.

'I will show your Note to Lord Rothes that the form of the affidavit may be drawn out properly.'

[5] George William Evelyn-Leslie (1768–1817), *styled* Lord Leslie, 11th Earl of Rothes (1810). See i, L. 13 n. 8; iv, L. 292 n. 45.

[6] Jane Elizabeth Leslie (1750–1810), *suo jure* Countess of Rothes, married in 1766 George Raymond Evelyn (d. 1770) and in 1772 Dr. Lucas Pepys (1742–1830), cr. Baronet (1784), physician to George III. See i, L. 12 n. 13; iv, L. 292.

[7] While presiding as justice of the peace, the Earl of Rothes lived at his estate Shrub-Hill, Dorking.

[8] Intermittently from February to August 1813, CB Jr. suffered violent headaches (see also Ll. 681, 698, 716, 717).

[23 Chenies Street,
10 March 1813]

To Charles Burney

A.L. (Osborn), *n.d.*
Double sheet 8vo 3 pp. *pmks* T.P.P.U. / Tottenham CR 10 MR
1813 wafer
Addressed in unknown hand: Revd Dr Burney / Rectory house / Deptford

I think, in sober reason, my dear Charles, *not a moment* should
be lost in announcing our Affida[vit]:—

Reflect but, had we been ourselves kept in suspense, how
uneasy we must have been. *Deduce*, that our antagonists are
all this time hoping *NO PROOF* exists, & thence redoubling their
bold assertions of Calais.

Besides, since Mr. *L.*[1] said it must have *legal proof*, it seems
distaining or defying his advice or opinion.

I do not ask you to *go* till convenient, but to *write* before you
sleep.

& briefly say—

I have the Affida[vit] of the Surgeon, a man of high respecta-
bility, & large fortune, (he gave his Daughter £20.000 in
marriage)[2] still living in Dorking—who has been sworn before
the E[arl] of R[othes] that my A[lex] was *Born* where he was
X^*tianed* at G[rea]^t Bo[okha]^m.

This will not cost you 2 minutes, & will be ready for the
ensuing visiting canvassers,—Dr F.[3]—or the W's[4]—who may
else, asserting *YOU KNOW*, yet have not *disproved* the report,

---

681. [1] William Lyon (L. 679 n. 2).
  [2] Ann Ansell (1774–*post* 1835), daughter of the surgeon, had married at Dorking on 13 Oct. 1796 Thomas Croft (d. 1835), a Londoner, living at the time of his
marriage in 'St. Ann Black Fryers Parish' (*GM* lxvi[2], 879) and at his death, in
Montagu Street. That his wife's dowry was £20,000 is probable since he was able
to bequeath the rents from sizeable estates in Dorking and elsewhere in Surrey and
about £170,000 in monies and annuities to his wife and two daughters. For the
exact distribution, see his will (Prob. 11/1855/f. 701), proved at London on 26
Dec. 1835.
  [3] Philip Fisher, Master of Charterhouse, was pledged to AA's rival. See Ll.
670 n. 11, 674 n. 3.
  [4] Burney family language for the 'Whoevers', in this case the supporters of
AA's opponent.

Caius College, from Ackermann's *A History of Cambridge* (1815)

gain over Sir D⁵—or even the D . Y⁶—as they would be very jealous of not having a Brit: born.—

& the evidence on the *Day* will be too late to decide votes already engaged.

Pray do this!—

I think you hurt your head by writing too soon after dinner— you must wander to your Library for an hour, to review it, &c—the moment the sleepy fit comes on—but not take your pen, believe me, just after eating

Pray Mind this!—

Adieu—adieu,

I must take care *I* don't go to Sleep, for I am ⎮ going to Sermonize myself.

682   [23 Chenies Street,
                                          16 March 1813]

To H.R.M. Queen Charlotte of England

A.L. draft (Berg), *n.d.*
Single sheet 4to   1 p.   on *recto* of the second leaf of an A.L. *Addressed*: Mᵐᵉ d'Arblay / ⌈at Dʳ Burney's⌉ / ⌈Chelsea⌉ [*Readdressed*:] 23 Cheines Street / Bedford Square /   with *pmks*   T.P.P. / Pall Mall   T.P.P.U. / Pimlico   4 MR 1813   red seal
Edited by FBA, p. 1, *annotated and dated*: March 16: 1813   No. 4.

Madam
Most humbly—yet with that chering confidence which your Majesty's ever gracious goodness has long mingled with my respect & awe, I now venture to write my happiness—Dr. Davy has just been brought to me by my Brother, to announce —what he goodnaturedly insisted upon aquainting me with himself, my Son's election.

The opponent, it seems, withdrew his petition.

All the Electors, therefore, voted for Alexander, even Dr. Fisher & Mr. Hargrave.

⁵ Sir David Dundas.   ⁶ The Duke of York (L. 677 n. 2).

The certificate of his Birth at G^t Bookham Surry, sworn by Mr. Ansell, my surgeon, before the Earl of Rothes, was formally read. My dear Mrs. Lock was not called upon or she would have come, she says, from her retreat, to take her oath of this fact to the whole University,—nay to the whole Universe, rather than My Boy should have lost the blessing of his Birth right.[1]

I feel sure of your Majesty's forgiveness that I write this joy of my heart—Alas! your Majesty would fain see such joy—all springing from your Majesty's own benificient graciousness,— more frequently. | Where, indeed, would be sorrow if success to the suppliant hung only upon the wishes of your Majesty? And such has always been to me—hereditary almost like their virtues—the condesendsion of Their R.H. the Princesses, that my heart now glows doubly in the trust that their R.H. will not disdain to take some share in my delight. Most humbly, & with soul-felt grateful attachment

I presume to sign myself Madam

683   23 Chenies Street,
                                                 16 March 1813
To Doctor Burney

A.L.S. (Diary MSS. vii. 5874–[77], Berg), 16 Mar. 1813
Double sheet 8vo   4 pp.   foliated 3, 4   red seals
Addressed: Dr. Burney, / Chelsea College.
Edited by FBA, p. 1 (5874), *annotated and date* 1813 *circled*:   ⁘   ⁘   (4)
Alex Elected a Tancred Student.
Edited also by CFBt *and the* Press. *See* Textual Notes.

March 16.

How will my Kindest Father rejoice for me! for my dear

682. [1] Throughout his Cambridge career AA was to be questioned about his birth-place. On 31 Dec. 1817 he sent a letter (Berg) to FBA: 'Here a pause ensued,—after which [Dr. Kaye, master of Christ's] said: Is your mother in England? —Yes, at Bath.—Pray what is her county?—Norfolk.—You are sure it is Norfolk? —Yes, indeed, perfectly sure, (and as I knew what he meant) I was born myself in Surrey, added I.—In Surrey? I had always imagined you had been born in France.—Oh! no. I was seven years in England before I ever went abroad, and then was 10 years in France.—This intelligence seemed to please him.'

Partner—for my Boy!—The Election is gained, & Alexander is chosen a student of the Tancred physical institution![1]—

He had ALL the votes—

The opponent retired.

Sir Dun[das], at last, behaved handsomely; came forward, & speechified for us. Sir Francis Milman, who was Chairman, led the way in the harangue.

Dr. Davy, our Supporter, leader, Inspirer, Director, Heart & Head patron & guide, spoke also.

Dr. Brown said a few words likewise.

Lord Hood was absent.[2]

Dr. Fisher gave his Vote. |

And ALL for Alex.—

Mr. Hargrave spoke, too,—but nothing, they tell me, to our purpose; nor yet against it. He gave a very long & elaborate history of a cause which he is to plead in the house of Lords, & which has not the smallest reference whatsoever to the case in point. Dr. Davy told me, in recounting it, that he is convinced the good & wary Lawyer thought this an opportunity not to be lost for rehearsing his Cause, which would prevent loss of time — — to himself;—or hindrance of business,—EXCEPT to his hearers.[3]

However, he gave us his Vote. |

'Tis a most glorious affair.—

Nevertheless, I still mean & wish to have it only known *where it now is*, till my fate is determined. Should it get into a news-paper, it might be in its effect as mischievous as it is now delightful. In about 2 or 3 months it may safely be published.

683. [1] From the 'Minute Books of the Proceedings of Tancred's Charities' for 16 Mar. 1813: 'Mr Robert Batty one of the Students in Physic on this Foundation at Caius College, Cambridge having entered into the Army since the last Meeting of the Governors & Trustees and thereby incurred a Forfeiture of his Studentship, and this day having been appointed by the Chairman for filling the vacancy occasioned by such Forfeiture / Proceeded to the Election of a Medical Student in the Room of Mr Robert Batty—and / Elected Mr Alexander Charles Louis Darblay to be such Student—.' It was not, however, until 12 Apr. 1813 that 'Alexander Carolus Ludovicus D'Arblay admissus est hujus Collegii Pensionarius Minor sub tutelâ Magr Chapman et Magr Gimingham' ('Gonville and Caius College Admissions Book', 1807–15).   [2] See L. 670 n. 13.

[3] Francis Hargrave, now senile, pleaded no case before the Lords. On 1 July 1813 his name was mentioned in the Commons when 'Upon the motion of Mr. *Whitbread*, 8000l. was unanimously voted for the purchase of the Law books, enriched by valuable notes, and 300 manuscripts, of Mr. Francis Hargrave, King's Counsel; to be deposited in the library of Lincoln's Inn, for the public use' (*GM* lxxxiii[2], 265).

I have HOPES but too delicious, from the present state & face of things!—but we must have patience & prudence.[4]

I can trust, however, to the discretion of Sarah, where she is warned of the importance of silence, & I feel already her kind joy in the intelligence. Relate it to her, therefore, my dearest Father, in your next tête à tête, with my love.

And pray give your benediction to my Alex. who comes to entreat it be[fore] ǀ he returns to pursue his studies à l'anglais, & prepare for the university, at Greenwich, whither he must go almost immediately.

This has so occupied me I have not been able to write sooner —I have so been tormented with doubts—addresses, replies, applications, cautions, &c &c

Now the first day & fine day I shall seek the *Cast*[5] I have hinted at, & the verbal blessing of my beloved Father to his

truly & lovingly dutiful

& affec^te FB. d'A.

684

To Mrs. Waddington

23 Chenies Street,
18 March 1813

A.L. (Berg), 18 Mar. 1813   18 Mar. 1813
Double sheet 4to   4 pp.   *pmks*   MONMOUTH   18 MR. .81⟨3⟩
Addressed: Mrs. Waddington, / Lanover, / Monmouth.
Annotated on address fold: Miss sent to Monmouth

My own hand alone must thank my kindest Mary for this last—& so satisfactory Letter, which has relieved me from sensations that saddened & perplext me. Yet have I no remembrance—nor comprehension of the *not for me only* so cruel to us both.—But I must let all research drop, for both our sakes, till

---

[4] FBA's hopes for peace were founded on some of the following: Louis XVIII's *Address to the People of France* (1 Feb. 1813), wherein he virtually proclaimed his Restoration; the occupation of Warsaw and other strategic points by the Russians; the penetration westward to the Elbe by a group of Cossacks; the rioting against the French occupation forces in Hamburg and in the states of Baden, Würtemberg, and Bavaria; the signing in late February of the Treaty of Kalisch between the Tsar and the King of Prussia.

[5] A favourite word of FBA signifying a chance ride, a lift in a carriage. The first 'very fine' day was 18 March with the temperature in the mid-fifties °F. (*GM* lxxxiii[1], 200).

we meet. An hundred Letters give not the explication that the EYE reveals in a moment in conversation. Yet I am utterly unable to FIX either my *time* or my *place* of embarking. My time will be later than my first purpose, my generous chieftain having written to me rather to prolong my sejour a MONTH, or even more, even two,[1] than fatigue myself in hurrying, or leaving undone by business here—& my sufferings from an Influenza,[2] which has assailed me ALMOST all winter, & will not quit me, though I am far better than I have been, have disabled me from business—& from all enjoyment of society, even in my family. I therefore gladly accept the furlough, though it doubles the grateful feelings which will soften the tragedy of my departure, let it happen when it may.—I go, indeed, from affection & worth, to worth & affection that can never be surpassed—& that consciousness must reconcile all round to the inevitable ǀ separation. If I must go by Morlaix, I shall embark at Plymouth, where my faithful old friend Lady Keith presses me to wait at the Governm^{t.} house, which she inhabits, for the vessel, winds, &c[3]—& this, to my feelings, would be very pleasant; but the Voyage to Morlaix[4] is so long, & I am *so dead*, rather than *ill*, at sea, that I cannot make it my choice, if I hear of means to go from the Downs, where Lady Lucy offers me every thing BUT a room, which she has not to spare, in the interval of waiting;[5] & she is so amiable, & this would be so feasible for the kind plan of my kindest Mary, that I shall certainly try for it: but still, I am not in my own hands, but in those of circumstances, & I must, definitively, go where I can be sure to find a vessel & means of departure.

When I know my fate, I will write it most surely.

What an *étourderie* of Sophia[6] that 30 Letters!—why did she not say 300 at once, her badinage would then have been clear

684. [1] See L. 665 wherein M. d'A advises FBA to remain in England for two or more months to finish her novel.

[2] FBA had a cold in late January and early February (L. 669 and n. 7). Through her exertions at the Queen's House and exposure to AA's infection (Ll. 672, 674), she became ill with influenza about mid-February (L. 675). She continued to ail with a low fever and a persistent cough, aggravated by anxiety over the Tancred election (Ll. 678, 686).

[3] As Commander-in-Chief of the Channel Fleet, Lord Keith lived with his lady at 'Governm^{t.} house' in Plymouth.

[4] Morlaix is a town in the *département* of Finistère. Its port lies five miles from the English Channel in a narrow valley. Morlaix is approximately 111½ miles from Plymouth (as contrasted with some 21 between Dover and Calais).

[5] See L. 637 n. 20.   [6] Sophia Elizabeth Burney (i, p. lxix).

to those who know not her turn to humour, which is *latent*, but extraordinary. She could mean only to say something agreeable, & she is so *good* humoured, as well as full of sly & satirical humour, than she never means otherwise. She wished to have it understood that where I was inexact to you no one should be surprized or hurt, not my nearest of kin, at my want of punctuality. Cecilia, who is a gentle & amiable & most affectionate character, I have seen but a moment: the oppression upon my breast makes all talking so fatiguing, so painful in its effect, that I have merely | ONCE embraced the good girl, & no more[7]— —you can difficultly conceive how I am forced to shut myself, from a cough that tears me to pieces when I talk.

How kind—how tender is your purpose to meet me where I am to embark!—yet should it be Plymouth—it will not be possible! For every reason I shall try for the Downs.—except for Lady Keith, whose friendship for me seems but warmed by my absence, & who herself will meet me at Deal, coming by sea, if I miss her at Plymouth; for she cannot this year visit London. She is *cold & wise*, & very reserved, but a friend upon proof of the brightest lustre & unshaken fidelity.[8]

Embrace your dear Girls for me, till I can take the pleasing office into my own arms—& adieu,

My ever dear Mary! Heaven bless & preserve you!

Pray don't let Mr. Greene[9] be angry with me—& never let it be forgotten I have at present no home, & am alternately at Chelsea—Deptford—Chenier's Street London—& Norbury Park—not to name Windsor—but never *chez moi*, & therefore in no state to give invitations. Besides which, I have real business, which—in part, you may divine, though if you do, you will feel how false & premature have been the reports that have been spread.[10]— |

Chenier's Street—23.
Alfred Place—   March 18. 1813.

But Chelsea is my surest direction.

[7] See L. 646 n. 13. FBA saw her niece in November 1812.
[8] Even when SB and FB first knew Queeney Thrale, she seemed reserved. The terms they had used were 'cold' and 'silent' (*HFB*, p. 119, and *ED* ii. 256). Despite her reserve, Queeney Thrale exhibited deep friendship, at least for FBA (see Appendix I).   [9] James Greene of Llansantfraed (Ll. 751, 788).
[10] Either that *The Wanderer* had been completed or that it had already been sold to a bookseller.

685   [23 Chenies Street,
                                          22 March 1813]
To Charles Burney

A.L. (Osborn), *n.d.*
Double sheet 8vo   4 pp.   *pmks*   T.P.P.U. / Tottenham CR   22 MR
1813
    Addressed: Rev^d Dr. Burney / Rectory House, / Deptford.

My dearest Carlucci,

We make use—than which nothing can be so right,—of the name of my dear absentee, why not do it according to his real idea?—which is, That he would have the offer be put fairly *to Auction?*

If not, in applying from one to another, the work will seem, to all who come second, bandied about, & rejected !!!

I would wish a short kind of circular Letter, to this effect—

That you shall have shortly *a work* to dispose of for your sister, which, as well as she can judge by the uncopied & yet not quite finished MS. will be about the length of her Cecilia;[1] & which, you frankly make known, you shall commit fairly to the highest bidder—or bidders.

Now this will admit no cavil, for 'tis the honest fact. And no one can be affronted, where all are treated alike.

I would wish it to go to Longman, Murray, Colborn, Robinson—PAYNE, White, Rees, Rivington, Williams, Hurst, Orme, Brown—Richardson, Hookham, Leigh, Mathews, Booker, Hatchard[2]— ╵ and as many more as you will; the more the merrier.

If you see this well, Charlotte will copy, & I will send the Billets, *all at the same moment.*

One or two a day, & one after another, will certainly incur an idea that the work is *under examination,* or *has* been, & is offered about *in Succession.*

685. [1] *Cecilia* appeared June 1782 in five volumes duodecimo; *The Wanderer* in March 1814 in the same format. FBA's last novel was about 60,000 words longer than *Cecilia.*
    [2] See Appendix V.

I would say nothing of *printing* for myself, though if dissatisfied I may *do* it:[3] but I hate all that looks like menace.

I know no other way than this that will really satisfy M.d'A.
that *the best has been done*:—

That we may not hear of some man who would have given
£100 more than the rest, when it shall be too late.

Colborn has been so civil & respectful, I would not affront
him by leaving him out: | & he is very obliging to my Father,
on lending him Books *Gratis*.[4]

This is a great stake to me! very great indeed, in its consequences!

I have taken these names from only one weeks news papers.
I hope you can add some others.

almost every work now, I see, even a play, has 5 or 6 publishers.[5]

The more, for Me, the better, because the pay comes quicker
and easier.

To Mr. *Payne*, perhaps, it may be more proper you should *tell*
than write this plan.[6]

As I am not ready, I should not be in haste, but for your
dont—& indeed, when I *am* ready, I have no time to lose, since
I wish ardently to superintend the Press.

PRAY call it a work: I am passed the time to endure being
supposed to write a Love-tale.[7] I will abide by the consequence. |

And also say nothing of *its* purposes, & all that. *It looks* like Puff.

[3] Motivating FBA's reluctance was her recollection that *Camilla* was printed
by subscription in 1796. See L. 665 n. 4.
[4] The books came from Colburn's English and Foreign Public Library.
[5] Co-operative publications had been advantageous to London booksellers
('the trade') and authors alike since mid-eighteenth century. By sharing costs,
the booksellers were able to reduce individual risks and monopolize copyright;
by utilizing the resources of all concerned firms, they were able to enlarge the
market for a jointly produced work. See Edward Dilly to Boswell (26 Sept. 1777),
regarding *The Lives of the English Poets*, in *Life*, iii. 110–11; Charles J. Longman,
The House of Longman 1724–1800, ed. John E. Chandler (1936), pp. 192–3; Frank
Arthur Mumby, *Publishing and Bookselling* (1954), pp. 190–3.
[6] FBA was sensitive to the fact that Thomas Payne II was Sarah Burney's brother.
More significantly, she remembered JB's ire when his brother-in-law, denied
exclusive printing rights to *Camilla*, had to share them with Cadell and Davies.
[7] FBA had similarly asked that *Camilla* be regarded as 'a work'. She objected
to the designation 'love-tale' or 'romance' because she believed she wrote realistic
fiction. She feared the moral stigma attached to the word 'novel', remembering
that the royal princesses were not allowed to read *Cecilia* (called a novel) until
it was first tested for purity. But see the advertisement of *The Wanderer* in the
Longman Catalogue (corrected to Mar. 1815) under the heading of 'Novels,
Romances &c.'

They will take it—or They Will let it alone, from public expectation—be its purpose &c what it may.

If you have not written already to Longman,[8] pray don't till *all the other* Billets are ready for the *same post.*

adio, dearest Carlucci.

Love to Rosette—

686   Norbury Park, 30 March 1813

To Doctor Burney

A.L.S. (rejected Diary MSS. 5878-[81], Berg), 30 Mar. 1813
Double sheet 4to   4 pp.   *pmk*   31 MR 1813   red seal
Addressed: Dr. Burney, / Chelsea College.
Edited by FBA, p. 1 (5878), *annotated*:   ⌗   (5)   Alex at Cambridge
Dr. Davy—Mrs. Lock
Edited also by CFBt *and the* Press. *See* Textual Notes.

March 30. 1813
Norbury Park,
near Dorking, Surry

I long for some news of my most dear Padre, & to hear that he keeps the same good looks that comforted me, after our long absence, when I was so happy as to see him last.[1] I had hoped, also, to send him an assurance that my tenacious Cough had instantly yielded to the salubrious air of Norbury park; but though I breathe its purity in the house, the Winds have most unkindly forbid my enjoying it abroad. The Cough is decidedly NERVOUS, for it is always least violent after eating. It is, therefore, as much less dangerous as it is more tedious than the other species. I have lost all expectation of its cure till the Zephyrs of the West waft us another atmosphere.

I am very sorry for the loss of the Duchess of Brunswick,[2]

[8] CB Jr. pressed for Longman, Hurst, Rees, Orme, and Brown as the publisher of *The Wanderer.*
686. [1] See Ll. 684, 691.
[2] The death of Augusta, Duchess of Brunswick, was reported in *The Times* (25 Mar. 1813): 'This venerable Princess . . . was in the 76th year of her age, and the last surviving sister of our Sovereign. . . . Her Royal Highness was confined to her bed only two days. . . . Dr. BAILLIE left the Duchess about six o'clock in the evening [23 Mar.], thinking her much better.' In three and a half hours she was dead.

who was reckoned extremely like the King.³ The Queen & the Princesses were much attached to her, & visited her whenever they came to town, & she was in Hanover Square.⁴ There are so few persons whom they can now see, & feel, & shew regard for, that to lessen the little number must be a real calamity to them.⁵ What must it not be to the Princess of Wales?⁶ |

I have had a Letter from a M. Lecointe,⁷ who, I am told, is a great *negociant*, to assure me that my dear Partner was *à merveille* in health on the 17ᵗʰ of February. This is a great comfort, though it is none to me to hear, at the same time, that he has never received but *une seule de mes Lettres*! Who, or What, has gotten them? It must be the Police, or the Flames.

I have just had a Letter from Alex, who assures me he is working hard at the Classics & at Mathematicks. The latter are what he most affections, but I prefer the study of the former for him, as leading more, when well attained, to sociality, & things of this world:⁸ the mathematicks lead to such abstruse pursuits, that they naturally incline their students to seclusion, *sauvagerie*, & absence of mind;—things not absolutely necessary

³ Charles Abbot (1757–1829), 1st Baron Colchester (1817), wrote in 1807: 'The Duchess, who is about a year older than the King, exceedingly resembles him in countenance, and still more in conversation and manner.' See J. H. Jesse, *The Life and Reign of King George the Third* (3 vols., 1867), iii. 518.

⁴ 23 Hanover Square was the London address of the Duchess since her arrival in England on 7 July 1807 (after she had been driven from her home in Brunswick by Napoleon).

⁵ Queen Charlotte inadvertently alienated people by her desire for privacy. As early as January 1782, Horace Walpole (ii. 325) could write to the Countess of Upper Ossory that 'Scarce any great ladies, except those immediately attached to the Court, were at the [Queen's] Birthday, in resentment for not having been asked to the Queen's balls last year.' From 1810 onwards the Queen required more solitude as she grieved over the death of Princess Amelia and the permanency of her husband's illness. In 1811 (as in 1788) she assumed responsibility for the King's person and the disposition of his household. Towards the end of 1812 and early in 1813, the Queen, even while performing her public duties, was further isolated by illness (L. 679), by the public discussion of the Princess Caroline's struggle with the Prince Regent over the education of their daughter, and by the reopening of the scandal that had culminated in an inquiry in 1806 into the morality of the Princess of Wales.

⁶ Caroline Amelia Elizabeth of Brunswick-Wolfenbüttel was the daughter closest to the Duchess of Brunswick.

⁷ The 'great *negociant*' was Louis Le Conte (1755–1842), who manufactured and marketed Chantilly lace. In 1810 he was conseiller de préfecture de la Seine.

⁸ For FBA's ambivalence towards AA's study of mathematics, see L. 670 n. 2. Her suspicion was supported by CB, who responded to this statement in April 1813 (Osborn): 'I think wᵗʰ you abᵗ Alexander's studies at Cambridge. Mathematics is the fashion there; but give me Classics and belles lettres, wᶜʰ are more the general taste of our united Empire.'

to check the gallant humour, or curb the foppish propensities of Alex, *for all* he is *justement arrivé de Paris!*

Imagine my delight, My dearest Father, knowing as I do, & trembling to know, his ignorance of the World, his extraordinary indifference to its knowledge, & the singular ˡ simplicity & *literality* of his character,—that Dr. Davy, the Master of Caius College, has promised me to take a general superintendance of his conduct when he is at the University! Dr. Davy, the excellent, perhaps best friend, of Charles, is one of the most pleasing & agreeable Men I have met with. And he has acknowleged himself to be quite struck with Alex, of whom he prognosticates all good.

So you don't wonder, perhaps, that I think Dr. Davy so agreable? You will have pleasure, also, my dear Father, to hear that Mrs. Lock has spoken to me in very high terms of Sarah's last work,[9] with which she has been so much pleased that, after having read it, she has bought it for her libr[ary.] Pray tell Sarah, who will be almost as glad as I am for Mrs. Lock's taste is as refined as her heart is feeling & bountiful.

We are quite alone together, at present, at which we are not much inclined to murmur, so much each has both to hear & to say. Yet my kind Friend allows me my Morning entirely to my own *Germans*,[10] which I 'mind' as well as my tormenting Cough will give me leave. I shall stay about a fortnight, & then Charles kindly promises to come & esquire me back. How I want, at this period, to double my existence! ˡ

I have just been told that Mr. Vansittart, Chancellor of the Exchequer,[11] has said to some of my friends, That it will be *no easy thing* for me to procure a passport for my son's return to France, now he is Eighteen years of age.[12]—

Adieu, My dearest—dearest Sir. If you should be able to indulge me with the sight of your hand, I quite beseech You to

[9] *Traits of Nature* (1812).

[10] *Germans*, 'those sprung from the same stock, near relatives', i.e. the fictional creations of *The Wanderer.*

[11] Nicholas Vansittart (1766–1851), 1st Baron Bexley, had been appointed Chancellor of the Exchequer as recently as 20 May 1812. See also v, L. 425 n. 1.

[12] At 18, AA was eligible for military service in France as a member of the class of 1812 or 1813. Evidently planning a return to that country during the summer of 1813 prior to his matriculation at Caius, he might well have been conscripted into Napoleon's army. The English were therefore reluctant to issue him a passport.

take the *littlest bit of paper in Nature,* that *my* good may not be *your* fatigue. Ever & ever most dutifully & affectionately

Your devoted daughter

F Burney d'Arblay.

My kind love to all of the family that ever get a peep at you.

Mrs. Lock, upon my chancing to mention that you take now & then a *tartine,* destines you a pot of the best strawberry jamm, made from her own Fruit by a particular receipt, that I ever tasted. I shall be its bearer. So, you see, *all* the sweetmeats of Mrs. Lock are not for Sarah![13]—I left Good Charlotte quite well. Poor Esther but so, so.—Love to James next Sunday Evening.

687   Norbury Park, 2 April 1813

To Charles Burney

A.L.S. (Osborn), 2 Apr. 1813
Single sheet 4to   2 pp.   six lines of cross-writing, p. 1.   *pmks*   3 AP 1813   3 ⟨AP⟩ ⟨18⟩13   3 AP 1813   black seal
Addressed: Rev^d Dr. Burney, / Rectory House, / Deptford,

Norbury Park,
April 2^d.
1813.

As to your Franking your Letters, my dear Carlos, *don't be in such a hurry!*—Let those murmur whose Frank prospects are dimmer![1]—

---

[13] CB commented on Mrs. Locke's gift and FBA's visit to Norbury Park in what FBA called 'a Fancifully pleasant Letter at 87' (Osborn), April 1813: 'Why, my Dear F Burney d'Arblay! what a happy effect has the kindness of your dear accomplished and elegant Friend Mrs Lock produced? She has poured balm into all your mental wounds, and healed every sore, wch having had no leonine tincture of March in it, now only breathes Zephyrs and the comforts of Favonius.'

687. [1] FBA's semi-serious pun refers to the concentrated efforts of CB Jr. to secure a bishopric, which would allow him the franking privileges of a member of the Lords. See L. 676 n. 1. As early as 21 Nov. 1808 MF jested (JRL) to Mrs. Piozzi that 'People have already settled that [CB Jr.] is to be a *Bishop*: and when I questioned him on his intentions, he pleaded the profoundest ignorance of his destiny; but that to please me he *would* try to be a Bishop as fast as he could.'

I am torn to pieces for *TIME*!—my life has not a third part of what my bounden occupations require. And now, a person[2] is arrived in town who has something to say to me from dear *absentee*—I would get thither to see him the soonest possible, though with the extreme regret of quitting this beloved spot & my most beloved Friend;—yet what I have to hear is perhaps, what it is essential I should know at once.

I beg you, therefore, to come the first day that is in your power. *Tuesday*, if then your toils extraordinary are over; if not, the first day after.[3] Mrs. Lock will receive you with great pleasure—or, rather, kindness, for she has small pleasure in what leads to my departure; yet she feels & acknowledges that there may be something important that is to be communicated, & that I ought to hasten to hear it. |

How truly sorry I am for poor good Mr. Walker![4] How dreadful a separation!—

Alex has mourning, in Becky's care, at Chelsea, which I shall desire he will write for, & deliver to the Greenwich attire-man. I recommend to my kind Rosette to give his attention *a jog*, should he neglect this matter. She will be again my kind Hostess, upon our journey back, though not for the *Week* till I have had this interview, & made up Mourning at dear Charlott's, for I set out without knowing the death of the poor Duchess; but here I am upon *articles* to see no company: therefore it is not material. Elsewhere, I cannot appear but in black. I am very sorry for this loss to the R[oyal] F[amily] for ye Duch^ss was loved by them all round.[5] Adieu, most dear Carlucci,—

Yours forever

F B d'A.

---

[2] M. Le Conte (L. 686 n. 7).

[3] Originally planning to remain at Norbury Park for a fortnight (L. 686), FBA was prepared to leave on 6 April after only a week's stay. Dissuaded, however, she did not return to Chenies Street until a week before 1 May (L. 690). But see the letter of MF, dated 14 April, that described her aunt's return from Norbury Park on the 13th.

[4] John Fortye Walker (*c.* 1782–1847), who received his B.A. (1803) and M.A. (1811) from Cambridge, was associated with St. Paul's, Deptford, in a secretarial capacity and was to be elected Lecturer there on 24 Oct. 1815. The 'separation' may refer to his sister Matilda, who died at sea on 10 Mar. 1813.

[5] Not only did FBA and AA wear the customary six-weeks mourning for the Duchess of Brunswick (*The Times*, 27 Mar.), but she sent condolences to the Queen, which were acknowledged on 4 April by Mme Beckedorff in a note (Berg) describing the Royal Family's shock at the unexpected death.

I did not fail to obey your order of thrice embracing your enclosed.

At all events, pray *WRITE* to say the Day you can—or even that you *think* you can come. You must endeavour to frank one day between your two Journies, if it be possible.

April 2ᵈ 1813. |

P.S. I had the extreme pleasure of shaking hands with our dear & good & sprightly & kind Dr. Davy just as I quitted London.

My dear Lettʳ that you have enclosᵈ:⁶ little allowing for my loss of time, because ignorant of my illness⁷—asks what my work will do for '*nos vieux jours*? which means for enabling us to *Live here*!! ultimately. — — for that, Sir, is the English of that Latin!—

yet he talks only of my return!—

688
To Charles Burney

[Norbury Park,
post 2 April 1813]

A.L.S. (Osborn), *n.d.*
Single sheet 8vo   1 p.   With traces of mounting tape, right margin
Docketed in pencil, p. 1: Mᵐᵉ D'Arblay / (Fanny Burney)   *in ink*, p. 2:
Autograph of Fanny Burne⟨y⟩ / (Mᵐᵉ D'Arblay) / Authoress of 'Evelina'. /
From the Autograph Book of her *great* great Niece
in pencil, p. 2: F. P. R.

Dearest Carlucci,
You can no where better enjoy a day or two of repose than in this now solitary, but always beautiful retreat, still presided by half the perfection of human excellence.— —And your late toils are of a species to be best appreciated here.¹ You are a great favourite with this sweet Hostess.

I write to beg you would be so kind as to bring with you the

---

⁶ A letter from M. d'A, now missing.
⁷ See L. 684 n. 2.

688. ¹ It is difficult to know whether FBA refers to CB Jr's 'toils' in readying a sermon for publication (L. 690 n. 1), exerting significant scholarly effort that might gain him a bishopric, or securing the Tancred studentship for AA.

last weeks news-papers, & up to your journey.—and also the
paper of 22 March, which has been [mi]ssed in my packet.[2]
So writing for no other intent
&c
I remain—what I was before—And intend to be after—
ever most affec[ly] yours
F.d'A.

Love to Rosy—
I have had a really delicious Letter from our dear Padre.[3]

689   [Paris, 12 April 1813]

M. d'Arblay
To Madame d'Arblay

A.L. (Berg), *n.d.*
A third of a single sheet folio   2 pp.
Edited by FBA, p. 1, *annotated and dated*: ⁂ 1   12 April. 1813.   1813.
p. 2: (3/1) (1813)   *See further,* Textual Notes.

Un mot seulement, ma chere Fanny, et c'est *encore* à mon cher
Mr Solvyns que je dois *encore* cet espece de tête à tête.[1] Ma
convalescence est bien établie.[2] C'est aujourdhui *Lundy. 12 avril*
[xxxxx 1½ *lines*] ⌐je suis sorti à pied hier et aujourdhui sans en
être fatigué. ⟨Deux⟩ fois je suis resté à diner chez Mad de
Grandmaison[3] avec la quelle je dine encore demain. [xxxxx ½
line] le grand bien de même que le plaisir.⌐ Avant hier j'ai vu
M. de Montalivet,[4] qui dès qu'il m'a apperçu est ⟨allé⟩ à moi

[2] FBA wished to see *The Times* containing the death notice of Matilda Walker
(L. 687 n. 4).
[3] See L. 686 n. 13.
689. [1] M. Solvyns, writing to his wife in London, enclosed the letter of M. d'A
within his own.
[2] M. d'A became ill in March with an ailment that occasionally recurred
during the late spring. On 4 July 1813 he wrote 'de ma longue maladie' that still
required convalescence (Appendix II).
[3] Marie-Pierre Sonnerat (1759–1848) had married first Pierre Descombes
(d. *pre* 1788) and second Alexandre-Paul Millin de Grandmaison (1739–1811).
For her third marriage, see v, L. 514 n. 21.
[4] Jean-Pierre Bachasson (1766–1823), comte de Montalivet, was in 1808
made comte d'Empire and directeur général des Ponts et Chaussées and in 1809
ministre de l'Intérieur. Despite his kindness to M. d'A, Montalivet would have

et m'a pris les mains comme eut pu le faire l'ami le plus tendre. Il voulait à toute force me renvoyer dans sa voiture en me disant qu'il allait sur le champ ordonner qu'on mit les chevaux. Sur la representation que je lui fis, que j'avais à la porte de son hotel une voiture de place bien plus economique que son equipage. Cela est vrai me dit il en riant, je n'y pensais pas; et il ajouta; Ne vous remettez pas trop vite au travail; et commencez par retablir tout à fait votre santé; je vous en prie, et s'il le faut je vous l'ordonne. Ces derniers mots furent prononcés avec le sourire le plus aimable, et il ne me quitta qu'après m'avoir reconduit sans s'en appercevoir jusqu'à sa second antichambre. Dans notre conversation qui avait été assez longue et sur le ton le plus amical il avait paru enchanté de ce que j'avais reçu si à propos une lettre de toi, ⌐et lorsqu'en se quittant je lui dis que j'allais prendre un bain, il m'en a dissuadé en me fesant l'observation que comme il etait près de quatre heures, il valait mieux, malgré qu'il fit très beau, attendre au lendemain p^r me baigner [xxxxx 1½ lines] ⌐J'ai suivi son conseil et le samedy et le ˡdimanche c a d hier et avant hier je suis sorti du bain à 1^h ½ et m'en suis parfaitement bien trouvé. J'ai cru ma chere Fanny que ce detail pourrait t'interesser. Il te prouvera que tu dois être sans le moindre inquietude ⟨sur⟩ ma santé. Puis je veux être egalement bientôt entierement rassurée sur ⟨la tienne et⟩ celle de ton chevalier. Au nom du ciel ne neglige aucune occasion de m'en donner des nouvelles et surtout ayez soin de m'ecrire toujours en français, comme tu l'as fait dans ta lettre du 8 qui m'est parvenue si promptement, tandis que je ⟨n'ai encore reçu qu'1⟩ ou 2 qui ⟨étaient en⟩ anglais [xxxxx ½ *line*]⌐ Tu n'as, m'as tu dit, reçu que 7 de mes lettres.[5] Eh bien ma bonne amie je suis bien sur de t'en avoir ecrit plus de SOIXANTE, quelquefois deux dans le même jour, quand deux occasions se sont presentées. Celle ci est la 3^{ieme} depuis l'arrivée de ton N° 8. c.à.d depuis 8 jours. Qu'elle te porte, ô ma fanni! l'assurance

tolerated no anti-Napoleonic sentiment in his ministry. Vitrolles wrote (i. 161–2), 'Le ministre de l'intérieur . . . tenait toujours présents à sa pensée et à sa mémoire tous les détails de sa vaste administration, au point d'en ouvrir à volonté la page à l'endroit que Napoléon voulait connaître. Il se refusait à regarder plus loin; en baissant la tête et levant les épaules—Que voulez-vous, disait-il, c'est la volonté de l'empereur.'

[5] Since FBA's arrival in England in August 1812, only eight letters between herself and M. d'A are now available to the editors: four from FBA to M. d'A (Ll. 637, 638, 645, 646); four from M. d'A to FBA (Ll. 643, 654, 665, 689).

du soin que je prens de moi, et qu'elle t'exprime à quel point je desire que tu veuilles bien m'imiter afin que rien ne trouble notre reunion, remise au tems où tu auras terminé toutes nos affaires, et où consequement nous ne serons plus exposés à une si triste et si douloureuse separation. Songes y bien ma chere et tendre amie, et songes y serieusement et ne vas pas croire que par là je veuille dire que tu sois condamnée à faire un adieu eternel à tant d'êtres qui te sont et me sont chers à tant de titres. Rien assurement n'est plus loin de ma pensée, mais la paix la bienfaisante paix reviendra sur la terre; et lorsque ce jour si desiré luira pour nous, ce sera ensemble que nous irons revoir ta chère patrie, et qu'après avoir joui des embrassemens de nos chers parens et amis, nous reviendrons dans notre hermitage jouir de tant d'heureux souvenirs aux quels se joindra l'esperance fondée de voir se renouveller un si grand bonheur. Amen, Amen! Tu dois sentir pourquoi je n'ecris point à ton chevalier dont je suis eternellement et bien tendrement occupé.[6] ⌐Dis lui que je le conjure de soigner bien sa ⟨santé⟩ et de ⟨m⟩'aimer comme je l'aime. Mille et mille tendres respects je te prie à notre bien et bien cher pere, [xxxxx 2½ *lignes, où sem-blent se poursuivre des salutations chaleureuses à la famille et aux amis anglais de M. et Mme d'Arblay*] Je t'ai ecrit sur ce chiffon p[r] ne pas trop abuser de ⟨l'admirable⟩ homme dans ⟨les mains de qui⟩ [xxxxx 1 *line marginal writing*]

690   [23 Chenies Street,
                                              1 May 1813]
To Charles Burney

A.L.S. uncompleted (McGill), *n.d.*
Double sheet 8vo (4·4 × 7·3[n])   2 pp.   *pmks*   T.P.P. / Unpaid / Totten-ham CR   1 MY 1813   1 MY 1813   red seal
Addressed: Rev[d] Dr. Burney, / Rectory House, / Deptford.

My dearest Carlucci,
A parcel is come for you, which I imagined the Proof sheet[1]

---

[6] At this time M. d'A wished to conceal AA's eligibility for conscription. See L. 752 n. 3 for the efforts of M. d'A to secure the postponement of his son's con-scription when the boy's age could no longer be hidden.

690. [1] CB Jr. talked of and expected the proof sheets of his latest work: *A Sermon*

you talked of: but I have peeped at a corner, & perceive 'tis some manuscript—therefore, as 'tis a sealed packet, I leave it to yourself for devellopment—only advertising you of the same as also,

in case you don't know it,
That I am always yours
F d A

Love to Rosette—
  & when you see him
    Alex—
& your Charles
  & his Fanny
  & our little Hopes of the Family,
  & Mrs. Bicknel.—
That cold north wind to Chelsea has not cured my tooth ache. very odd!—
But I am glad, *for all* that I went to my dear Father—& with YOU—
  Not odd at all. — — once more, &c |
    1000 thanks for what you have envellopped for my Dear Madam²—
  I am returned from Norbury Park last week, much

691   [23 Chenies Street,
             pre 18 March—3 May 1813]¹
To Mrs. Waddington

A.L. (Berg), *n.d.*
Double sheet 8vo 3 pp. *pmks* ABERGAVENNY BATH 3 MA 18⟨1⟩3 wafer
Addressed: Mrs Waddington / Lanover / Monmouth / Abergavenny
Readdressed: No. 2 / B⟨ ⟩ / Bath
Annotated on address fold: Miss sent to Monmouth

preached at the Anniversary Meeting of the Stewards of the Sons of the Clergy . . . May 14, 1812. To which are added lists of the nobility, clergy, and gentry, who have been Stewards . . . and the sums collected at the anniversary meetings, since the year 1721, pp. xxiv+39. Printed for F. C. & J. Rivington (1813).
  ² CB Jr. had sent FBA a draft of the circular he wanted distributed to the various booksellers interested in *The Wanderer*.
  691. ¹ According to FBA's near-concluding statement, this letter was written

Ah my dearest Mary!—kind, cruel—admirable—inexplicable Mary! Where are you?—What is become of You?—Have I lost you?—

Send me back, I earnestly entreat you, that terrible Letter which has thus inconceivably estranged you—send it back with frank & sincere marks upon the passage—or passages which have done me this mischief.

Every post I have been hoping—expecting to hear from you —& to receive some explanation. The severest reproaches, if you can THINK I merit them, would be balsamic in contrast to such an estrangement.

'Modify' — — good heavens! there is not a word I would not have altered, there is not a phrase I would have retained, could I have forseen an effect ˡ so disastrous. But let me enter into no recollections thus in the dark; be open & ingenuous, I demand it of your long friendship, which neither Time nor Absence have ever been able to affect—ah my dear Mary!—shall MIS-CONCEPTION—false judgment—undermine a confidence which I thought would have lasted while I last?

Can it be that You—so always & so closely within it, can have been hurt I decline to enlarge my circle of intimate intercourse?[2]

Would that be just?—or generous? or Mary?

Can you have taken ill I have not given you a written confidence upon subjects that require a detail for explanation which my existence here will be insufficient in this ˡ visit, to afford?—

But why conjecture? Give me the frank fact, I entreat, at once.

My poor Boy has been very ill—& I have been very ill—but we are now amending, though both confined to our rooms still.

May I have better news of my ever dear Mary & her dear ones

slightly more than six weeks earlier, at least prior to 18 March. On that date she had written to Mrs. Waddington (L. 684), in which many of the queries and doubts of L. 691 seem to be resolved.

[2] Apparently Mrs. Waddington took exception to what was for her FBA's inhospitality and breach of friendship. See particularly the last paragraph of L. 684, in which FBA refuses to invite James Greene of Llansantfraed to visit her. For the close friendship between Greene and Mrs. Waddington, see Ll. 751, 788.

ONE quarter of an Hours
conversation Tête à Tête
would solve whatever may seem to you a difficulty or strangeness: but how can I press your coming
for ME only?
when I am never at my own home—always surrounded by my
family—And in posession of so little time that my poor faculties
are often bewildered with the calls I cannot answer? I have
some reason to believe that indispensable business will uncontrol-
lably lengthen my stay. |
This was begun 6 weeks ago, & mislaid!—
How ashamed & sorry I am!—

692   [23 Chenies Street],
                                            11 May 1813
To Doctor Burney

A.L.S. (Diary MSS. vii. 5882–[85], Berg), 11 May 1813
Double sheet 4to 4 pp. foliated 5, 6 *pmks* T.P.P.U. / Tottenham
CR 11 MY ⟨ ⟩ 11 MY 1813 wafer
Addressed: Dr. Burney, / Chelsea College, / Chelsea.
Edited by FBA, p. 1 (5882), *annotated and redated*: ⁙· 11. May / 1813.
(6) Lady Crewe Lord Crewe crazy woman to the Queen— Mʳˢ
Piozzi. & Her Daughters. Mʳˢ Solvyns.
Edited also by CFBt *and the* Press. *See* Textual Notes.

Will my beloved Father be startled to receive a Letter from
me dated *May*, & Dated *Paris?*—one which I wrote to him
this time twelve month, & sent by a conveyance that was first
to reach Maria,[1] has *just now* been delivered to her, & she brings
it me to forward to its first destination.
Thank Heaven, my dear Mate's Letters now travel a little
less tardily; I have had two more since I saw you.[2]

692. [1] Maria Bourdois.
  [2] CB, in what FBA referred to as his 'Last Written Benediction' (Osborn,
July [1813]), responded to his daughter's letter: 'I expected a letter this mornᵍ
from our Capt. in James street, and the direction of both your epistles resembled
his autography so much, that my surprise was extreme on finding it dated "ce 29
Mai—Rue d'Anjou—Nᵒ 8, 1812! . . . I rejoice that Mʳ d'Arbʸ'ˢ letters travel now,
a little less tardi-ly than hereto fore.'

Mrs. Solvyns is now seriously preparing to depart. I saw her this Morning, & have invited her here to tea this evening. It is the very first day I have yet quitted Charlotte except for *you*, one single dinner to meet Mrs. Lock at her dear Amelia's excepted.[3] My own inclination & intention, therefore, kept in mind your charge, my dearest Sir, that as soon as I was able to go forth, I would wait upon Lady Crewe. Fortunately, I found her at home,[4] & in her best style, cordial as well as good humoured abounding in acute & odd remark, & well bred with perfect ease. I had also the good fortune to see my lord, who seems always pleasing, unaffected & sensible, & to possess a share of innate modesty that no intercourse with the World, nor addition of years can rob him of.[5] I was much satisfied with my visit. But what I shall do for time, now once I have been launched from my Council, or sick Chamber, I wot not!

What a terrible alarm is this which the poor tormented Queen has again received![6] I wrote my concern, as soon as I heard of it, though I have not yet seen the printed account, my packet of papers reaching only to the very day before that event. My answer has been a most gracious summons for the Queen's house for to-morrow. Her Majesty & two of the Princesses come to town for 4 days. This robs me of my Chelsea visit for this week, as I keep always within call during the town

[3] At 20 Great Cumberland Place, Hyde Park.
[4] See L. 642 n. 17. Lady Crewe, a brilliant Whig hostess, was a worldly woman. This quality intrigued FBA, less so MF, who commented (JRL) to Mrs. Piozzi in August 1815 that Lady Crewe 'looked dissatisfied with herself & the rest of mankind. I fear her heart is wholly set upon "this dim speck called earth," & that . . . Beauty & Literature & Fashion have all been tried in vain for Happiness.'
[5] Lord Crewe, now 71, had been an active Whig in Parliament for more than forty-eight years but remained unassuming. CB (n. 2) reported to FBA,'Your notions ab^t Ld Crewe, are perfectly correct—he is all steadiness, wth honour and propriety.' See *GM* xcix^1 (1829), 467.
[6] According to *The Times* (4 May 1813), an Assistant Mistress of the Wardrobe, who had lived always under 'the Royal protection', was emotionally affected by Princess Amelia's death. 'She slept in the tower over the QUEEN's bed-room. About five o'clock [2 May] HER MAJESTY was awoke by a violent noise at her bed-room door, accompanied with a voice calling loudly for the Queen of ENGLAND to redress her wrongs, and with the most distressing shrieks and screams imaginable. The QUEEN's bed-room has two doors: she used such violence as to break open the outer door, but found herself unable to break the inner one. . . . Mrs. BECKENDORF ventured to open the inner door and go out.' There she found the deranged woman clad in night clothing. During the commotion that followed, the Queen heard the noise and was greatly distressed. The shrieking woman was finally overcome by a porter and seen by a doctor, 'who ordered her a strait waistcoat; and she was sent off in a post-chaise, accompanied by two keepers, to a house at Hoxton for the reception of insane persons.'

residences, when I have royal notice of them.[7] And, indeed, there is nothing I desire more than to see Her Majesty, at this moment, & to be allowed to express what I have felt for her. My Letter from Made Beckerdorff says, that such an alarm would have been frightful for *any body*, but how much more peculiarly so for the Queen, who has experienced such poignant horrour from the effects of disordered intellects! who is *always* suffering from them, & so nearly a victim to the unremitting exercise of her duties upon that subject & those calls![8] |

I have had a visit this Morning, from Mrs. Piozzi — — who is in town only for a few days, upon business. She came while I was out: but I must undoubtedly make a second tour, after my royal 4 days are passed, in order to wait upon & thank her.[9]

Her two Daughters, the present Miss Thrale & Mrs. Merrick Hoare, have written to me that they will come to-morrow:[10] but I am forced to state my engagements, which vexes me, as I

[7] *The Times* reported on 10 May 1813: 'The QUEEN and PRINCESSES are expected in town to-morrow [11 May] from Windsor. It is said they will stay till Friday [14 May]. Cards of invitation are issued for a small party to a ball on Wednesday evening, at Carlton-house, to meet her Majesty the QUEEN.'

[8] The King suffered his first bout of mental 'derangement' (recently diagnosed as porphyria) in 1788 but recovered. From that time on, however, George III and the Queen dreaded the recurrent attacks. By October 1810, after the death of Amelia, he became incapable of transacting official business. In January 1811 the Regency Bill was passed and the care of the King's person was given to the Queen. He remained incompetent until his death in 1820.

[9] The estrangement between FBA and Mrs. Piozzi centered in the latter's marriage in 1784. Members of the Burney family, aware of FBA's pain over the rift, tried to effect a reconciliation, particularly MF, who first met Mrs. Piozzi in Bath in 1805. Between 1 Sept. 1812 and 17 May 1813, MF wrote at least 13 letters (JRL) to Mrs. Piozzi in which she announced the arrival of FBA, mentioned her name, or pleaded her case.

On 1 Sept. 1812, e.g., she wrote from Bradfield: 'Who do you think, my dearest Mrs Piozzi, is come to England?—to my amazement, as much as yours—Madame D'Arblay & her son Alexander! ! ! They are to be here till the end of October, perhaps all the winter. Mons. D'Arblay could obtain no passport. They waited 6 weeks for a vessel at Dunkirk & arrived last Thursday. She is with Grandpapa at Chelsea now & will be a week with my sister at Richmond, before she goes. I shall try to be there at the same time.'

Mrs. Piozzi remained seemingly indifferent. But MF, goaded by her mother, continued attempts in 1813 to arrange a meeting between Mrs. Piozzi and FBA. Admitting in a letter (JRL) dated 14 April, that she did not pass on Mrs. Piozzi's 'mention of Aunt D'Arblay to her, because I thought it would make her fret', MF then detailed the condition of FBA's health and concluded with the following plea: as she 'was so desirous of something kind & conciliatory, & is, perhaps, poor thing, in a most *dangerous* state, I think if you can bring yourself to send any-thing like a kind message, it would be a most christian act in you, & give great happiness to her.' Apparently this letter prompted Mrs. Piozzi to call on FBA on 11 May. (See Appendix I; L. 693.)

[10] Susanna Arabella Thrale (1770–1858) and her sister Sophia (1771–1824), who in 1807 had married Henry Merrick Hoare (1770–1856). But see L. 693.

love them both, & have proved their faithful attachment to me
from their childhood. Lady Keith is at Plymouth—& constancy
personified.[11]

I have gathered more lawrels again for Sarah — — Lawrels
by no means contemptible, but of the best growth & fragrance
— — for they spring from the approbation of Lady Templetown—a nice & dainty Judge. Tell Sarah, with my love, to bind
them well upon her brow.[12]

To Night, *by desire*, the daughter of our excellent old friend
Lady Strange is coming:[13] & two or three more of Charlotte's
Coterie, who will not be denied.

To Mrs. Solvyns I shall consign your precious lines for M.
d'Arblay.[14] My own Letters have been so erring in their
course, that I have never dared trust yours out of my sight,
since the intended opportunity offered by Lady ⟨Anne⟩
Hamilton failed.[15] With Mrs. Solvyns it will be safe—& oh how
welcome! — |

Adieu, most dear Sir—next week nothing *EARTHLY*—I answer
not further!—shall prevent my seeking a living embrace where
I now give one proxy for life—but with all my heart & soul—,
witness[16]

most dutifully
& affect[ly] your
F. d'A.

11 May—1813

11 The estrangement between Mrs. Piozzi and her daughters, particularly
the eldest, is suggested in a letter (Barrett, Eg. 3699B, ff. 22–24b) written by Lady
Keith to FBA on 6 Dec. 1816: 'I would advise your never referring in any way to
any of us. She could not bear to come so near to old Times which She knows *you*
must so well remember. To others she can say what she pleases, & no doubt as
she has invariably done, will ever continue to justify herself, in every Particular,
at our expence: but that, she well knows, would not do with you.' That FBA
regarded all of Mrs. Piozzi's daughters (with the exception of Cecilia) as close
friends was one reason why Mrs. Piozzi labelled her former protégée an 'aimable
traitresse'.
12 CB relayed to SHB Lady Templetown's praise of *Traits of Nature*. He wrote
(n. 2) to FBA: 'Your laurels for Sarah are now cleared up from the source—they
are very flourishing in L[y] Templetown's garden.'
13 Isabella Katherina Strange (*c*. 1759–1849), the daughter of Isabella *née*
Lumisden (i, L. 21 n. 13). In the sixth and seventh decades of the eighteenth
century, the Stranges lived in Castle Street, Leicester Fields, near the Burneys
in St. Martin's Street. The two families became close friends.
14 See L. 651 n. 2. 15 See Ll. 650 n. 8, 651 n. 4.
16 But see L. 696.

[23 Chenies Street,
                                            post 12 May 1813]

To Lady Keith

L., incomplete, an excerpt printed in *The | Queeney Letters | being | Letters
addressed to | Hester Maria Thrale | by | Doctor Johnson | Fanny Burney | and
Mrs. | Thrale-Piozzi |*, ed. the Marquis of Lansdowne (1934), pp. 115–17.

. . . Mrs. Piozzi, I suppose you know, is in town.[1]

Some time ago, when I believed I must depart in a few weeks,
my nieces[2] so much wished to say something to her in my name,
that, discarding my late resentment to the dark abyss whence
her 'Proserpine'[3] had brought it to me, I listened only to old
recollections of former kindnesses, and former friendship; and,
very willing myself to seek to turn an unjust enemy into a
recovered friend, I commissioned Marianne Francis, her
Correspondent, to assure her of my constant wishes for her
health, and constant interest in her happiness, and my unremitting remembrance of her former kindness: with an intimation
that had she been in town, I might have perhaps ventured to
call myself to her recollection in person.[4]

I had heard, at that time, that she had positively renounced
any London excursion this year: but, as chance is always
changing and reversing our plans, I thought it more civil to
let her see that it rested, thenceforth, with herself that we
should meet or not.

I was very uneasy, I confess, when I had taken this measure,
which, all things considered, had certainly not been merited

693. [1] This letter helps to clarify FBA's continuing pain at the breach with
Mrs. Piozzi.
   [2] CFBt and her sister, especially the latter.
   [3] The allusion indicates that FBA saw or rationalized Mrs. Piozzi as a queen of
the underworld who brought death to their friendship.
   [4] On 15 Mar. 1813 MF sent a letter (JRL) to Mrs. Piozzi: 'my Aunt D'Arblay
who is almost confined to her room, & has not for months known what it is to have
a day free from pain, besides the presence of mental uneasiness, & the constant
impression that she must traverse the ocean, to return to her husband, while at
the same time she is scarcely fit to walk across her bedchamber, has much congratulated me upon the honour of your correspondence, and charges me to say
from her, that your early kindness never has been obliterated from her memory,
& never can; that she always preserves amongst her favourite hoards, its eloquent
expression, & that if you were in town, she could with difficulty refrain from seeing
if no part of it still remained.'

from me: I had been to her the faithfullest and most attached of friends—all my connexions, and all my other friends had *bewailed* an intimacy that took me from them all; nor could I ever leave her 3 days without at least 3 letters to conjure me back . . . yet, when she took a step which called forth, by every tie of honour, my sincere disapprobation, she no sooner completed it, than she demanded my felicitations! I gave them;— warmly for her happiness, most coldly for its materials,—and she wrote me a letter of *reproach* for my want of cordiality!!!—In a Letter of ice, I own, I flung myself upon her memory for my vindication, but desired to close our correspondence by those letters of exquisite kindness which had preceded all but the last: or to resume it upon the same terms. To this, after a lapse of some time, I had a very friendly answer—beginning 'Quiet your kind heart, sweetest Burney &c.' and assuring me of her complete contentment. To that I sent an answer in kind . . . but I have never heard from her since!—never!—[5]

It is she, therefore, who dropt our intercourse: I was sorry— Oh how grievously sorry!—for what she had done, but I was not her guardian!—I had no right to control, nor to censure her; and I should never have dreamt of breaking off with her, which I should have thought even insolence, had she not first changed, and then fled herself.

But what led me to take this moment for addressing her by message, though so lately irritated by her unaccountable acrimony of injustice *wholly unprovoked*, was the little probability, as I was then preparing to return to Paris, that we should both live for being again in the same Kingdom, upon Earth. I felt, therefore, as one feels in going to take the sacrament. There is another than an Earthly Kingdom; 'Am I in charity for the translation with all mankind?'[6]—

No answer came for a considerable time; and if I felt more in charity than before my message, I frankly confess it was only with myself!—At length, however, imagine my surprise when Marianne told me that Mrs. Piozzi was in town, and had written

<hr/>

[5] See the preface to Appendix I.

[6] FBA's 'translation' converts into a question the priest's invitation to those of the congregation who wish to receive the Holy Communion. 'Ye that . . . are in love and charity with your neighbours, and intend to lead a new life. . . . Draw near with faith, and take this holy Sacrament to your comfort. . . .' Since the letter *confesses* the FB–Mrs. Thrale relationship to Lady Keith, the 'invitation', preceding the 'general confession' of the communion service, is appropriate.

to her from an Hotel in Jermyn Street,[7] but was just setting off for Streatham, to Mr. Davis's,[8] for the Easter holidays.[9] She *refers* to me, two or three times, in the letter, sending me her *good wishes*, which are *very sincere*, for my health and welfare, —and some other slight words, to that effect, alltogether embarrassed and cold indeed to what I had expected!—Well, you will not wonder that I charged my niece to name me no more. My feelings were disappointed, but my mind was easy, and I had done.

My sister Broome, affronted, would not call upon her; but Marianne went as usual, or perhaps *not* quite as usual, for I am told there is much more coolness in the air than there has been. They had 2, or 3, meetings,[10] and then . . . Marianne brought me suddenly word, that Mrs. Piozzi would *wait upon me, if I thought myself well enough to see her*!!

I then made my sister enquire what this meant, and heard that in conversing about me, Marianne had related a dreadful illness which had recently preceded my voyage, and from which it is truly wonderful that I should be recovered:[11] Mrs. P: uttered a loud shriek at the account, said I had never so suffered while she nursed and took care of me, and then sent the message.[12]

---

7 A letter (JRL) from MF is addressed to Mrs. Piozzi/Blake's Hotel/Jermyn Street/Piccadilly. The letter is dated 8 May.

8 Reynold Davies (1752–1820) was curate of St. Leonard's and schoolmaster at Streatham. In late November or early December 1798 he began educating five-year-old John Piozzi (later Salusbury), the nephew of Gabriel Piozzi and destined heir of Mrs. Piozzi. For eight years—until 1806—Mr. Davies saw to it that the boy had 'Companions & instructions just suitable to his capacity'. See the letter (JRL) of Mrs. Piozzi to Leonard Chappelow, written in [1798].

9 Easter Sunday in 1813 fell on 18 April.

10 See the letters (JRL) of MF to Mrs. Piozzi, dated 22 April and 8 May. The 'coolness' is certainly not apparent in the latter letter: '. . . I often think of the happy day I spent with you last Tuesday, & hope you will let me see you again soon—& that you get letters from Salusbury every day, & when you write tell him he is not forgotten by . . . Marianne Francis.'

11 MF not only talked to Mrs. Piozzi of FBA's illness, but wrote a vivid description of it and the subsequent operation endured by her aunt. See L. 642 n. 4.

12 One example of Mrs. Thrale's ministration occurred in 1781. In February of that year, after working to exhaustion on the first draft of *Cecilia*, FB fell ill at Chessington. According to Mrs. Thrale in a letter (JRL) to Mrs. Lambart: 'Here's sweet Fanny Burney very ill 20 Miles off, and desires to see me directly.' Mrs. Thrale accepted the summons, drove to Chessington over wintry roads, viewed the novelist with alarm, and arranged to have her brought home. When FB arrived at the house in St. Martin's Street, Mrs. Thrale was on the doorstep with a physician whom she had brought. For Mrs. Thrale's nursing of FB in Streatham as early as December 1779, see SB's account (Barrett, Eg. 3691, f. 54) that described Mrs. Thrale as 'all goodness and kind attention'.

There was no resisting being touched by a stroke such as this: and I should certainly have met her, upon it, with open arms once more . . . . but, most unfortunately, the first morning of my going out, after a confinement of nearly 3 months, was precisely the time she took for her visit.[13] I was really extremely vext, for she may think I was denied: which I could not have been for the world. The next day I meant to call; but I saw your dear sisters,[14] and heard she was to set off for Oxford.[15] I was appointed to go to the Queen's house: nevertheless, when Her Majesty went to the Prince's, to Dinner,[16] I hurried to Jermyn Street, in hopes of some change, or that she would not go till late: but she was already gone, and had left no permission nor address for cards or letters to follow her.

This is my history, up to this moment; Marianne has written my regrets, but directed them to Wales,[17] not knowing her actual dwelling.

[13] MF explained FBA's absence in a letter (JRL), dated 17 May. 'We were all sadly unfortunate in being out that morning you were so *very* kind as to call. I was at my school and Aunt d'Arblay had unhappily crawled out for some air, & was inexpressibly mortified & grieved, she desires me to say, at finding you had been, during the *only* absence she had made from home so long. She comforted herself, though, with the hope that she should see you the day after, & went the very next day to Jermyn Street: it was late before she got there, & you were gone!— The man said to Bath, but I could not believe that, nor could I believe my Aunt's report, & set off myself to enquire at the Hôtel, where I found the news but too true.'

[14] See L. 692 n. 10.

[15] Mrs. Piozzi did not go to Oxford but to Bath, remaining there 'just 25 Days'. See her letter (JRL) to John Salusbury, *c.* 15 May 1813.

[16] On 12 May the Queen and the Princesses dined with the Prince Regent at Carlton House and remained there that evening to attend a small ball.

[17] Although Mrs. Piozzi spent this late spring in Bath so that its waters might help 'Salusbury', she usually wintered there and spent the summer at Brynbella, the villa built by Gabriel Piozzi, in the valley of the Clwyd.

Apparently she responded to MF's letter, but her desire to ignore FBA was so blatant that her correspondent replied (JRL): 'I did not say I had heard from you to my aunt, because she was not mentioned & I thought she would be so much hurt. I know you wish her happiness—surely you will not refuse to promote it by sending her *some* kind message, if it be but *one* word, through [me].'

In reply, Mrs. Piozzi sent a conciliatory message (now missing) to FBA. Having left the letter at Richmond, MF wrote (Barrett, Eg. 3704A, f. 98) to CFBt on 2 July 1813: 'My Aunt d'Arblay is in the greatest distress to read the message to her. Pray my darling have the great kindness to look for it, & enclose it in a letter to Mama, without fail.'

Mrs. Piozzi made no further effort to see FBA at this time. In a letter (JRL) to her adopted son on 14 May 1813, Mrs. Piozzi admitted: 'When Connections are once broken, 'tis a foolish Thing to splice and mend; They never can (at least with *me*) unite again as before. Life is not long enough for *Darning* to me Friendships; and they are always a Proof however neatly done, that the Substance is *worn out.* A new Dress can better be depended on.'

694 [23 Chenies Street],
14 May 1813

To Doctor Burney

A.L. mutilated (Diary MSS. vii [5885b–87], Berg), *n.d.*
Originally a double sheet 8vo (7·2 × 4·4″), but with segments cut from
the top of the first leaf and bottom of the second leaf 3 pp. p. 3 (5886),
numbered (7) *pmks* 14 MY 1813 T.P.P.U. / Tottenham CR seal
Addressed: Dr. Burney, / Chelsea College, / Chelsea,
Docketed in pencil: 2—May 1813
Edited and mutilated by CFBt; *also edited by the* Press. *See* Textual Notes.

[*top of page 1 cut away*]
his most welcome & truly *aimable Lettre*, & more over newspapers, which are always treasures to me—and to say that,
with regard to the Institute, I most certainly wish your acceptance, as it is all prepared,[1] to go by Made Solvyns,[2] whose
conveyance is sure: & the opportunity is the only one.
She comes to me on Sunday after Church for my Letters to
Mr. d'Arblay, & yours.—
I hope you will send the acceptance. Sally[3] promises me a
little Drawing. I have got one from Charlotte Barret. These
remembrances will delight |

[*top of page 2 cut away*]
I have been received more sweetly & graciously than ever, if
that be possible, by my dear & honoured Queen & sweet
Princesses Eliza & Mary. The Queen has borne this alarm[4]
astonishingly, considering how great was the shock at the
moment. But she has so high a character, that she will not
suffer any thing that is personal to sink her spirits, which she
saves wholly for the calls upon them of others—& great &
terrible | have been those calls! The beloved King is in the *best
state possible* for his present melancholy situation;[5] that is,

694. 1 See L. 638 and n. 1.
  2 Mme Solvyns arrived in England early in July 1812 and departed for France
on 31 May 1813. See L. 697.
  3 JB's daughter studied drawing with Edward Francesco Burney. See her letter
(Barrett, Eg. 3700A, f. 140) to CBFB, dated 4 Sept. 1813.
  4 See L. 692 and n. 6.
  5 According to the bulletin issued at Windsor Castle, 1 May, His Majesty 'has
been in a tranquil and very comfortable state throughout the last month' (*The
Times*, 3 May 1813). On 5 June a similar bulletin was issued (*GM* lxxxiii¹, 584).

124

wholly free from real bodily suffering, or imaginary mental misery, for he is persuaded that he is always conversing with angels!—

Mad^e Solvyns expects a call to her vessel on Monday. She comes to procure Sunday for our last meeting. She desires a thousand respects to you.

[*Bottom of page 3 cut away*]

695   [23 Chenies Street],
                                                  15 May 1813
To Mrs. Waddington

A. L. (Berg), 15 May 1813
Double sheet 4to   3 pp.   *pmk*   1 ⟨   ⟩ MA 13   red seal
Addressed: Mrs. Waddington, / Lanover, / Monmouthshire.

                                               May 15—1813

How is this, my dearest Mary?—are you indeed changed?— shall I see you, at last, yet not find you?—Comment! the term of our separation is so speedily to end, so unexpectedly & suddenly, & you inform me of it by a few dry lines, as a matter of fact simply, or as a piece of business? You would not have me blame my Name sake, who knows so well how to write more feelingly; no, I go to the source, for I am well aware a Daughter who so adores her Mother, whether or not she uses her given words, catches her passing sentiments.[1]

After so many years of patient affection, & partial indulgence, must I see you suddenly become *exigeante* & punctilious? offended at a breach of punctuality in writing which I never possessed—& which I have too little time—too little LIFE, now to attain?[2]

Oh my dearest Mary, do not vex me—write me the kindest words immediately—such as belong to my assortment in your hand;—I will keep no other. Love me on SUCH as I am, for I am

695. [1] FBA had received a note from Frances Waddington with the news that she, her sisters, and parents planned a London holiday in June and July at 9 Holles Street, Cavendish Square.
[2] FBA's letter continues the apology (begun in L. 691) for dilatory correspondence.

no worse than while you have loved me so long. It is 13 years now that all Letter WRITING is oppression to me![3] My nearest family, and dearest Friends all make allowance for me; *YOU*, hitherto, have seemed to make it beyond all others: Retrograde, retrogade!—I would rather not meet than meet & not know you,—far, far! | The one would be a sorrow that a million of circumstances might end—the other, would be lasting disappointment.

REMEMBER ALWAYS—I am only a regular correspondent from the awe of ceremony—or the necessity of business — —

And

That I never *write* a Letter but when urged to it by my conscience! — — — — — c.a.d. when I feel I have no other method to claim—what still I prize as highly as ever—*receiving* one.

Be generous then, again, generous & kind.—Write to me in in your old style— let us have no draw backs at our meeting or explanations—apologies—susceptible queries—or—wearying pros & cons—sly inuendos, nor EVEN smiling reproaches—

BUT

Let us meet like two Friends long parted in person, but always faithful in mind equally eager to hear, & willing to relate the history of their separation.

Come to me, then, dearest Mary, with open Heart—open Arms—& open Countenance.

And then

In defiance of years & absence, we shall be to each other what we | have been.—

NB. To prevent all disappointment or misunderstanding, I must premise—That—for a constant rule—I see nobody but by appointment.—

My residence is uncertain—at Deptford, Chelsea, Mrs. Broome's & in Chenier's Street—or Norbury Park—But Chelsea is my constant direction.

a recent letter from Paris makes me believe I shall remain here till Autumn:[4] *certainly* till the end of August, to finish what you have been made believe Done so long ago—[5] but which illness has prevented my ever continuing. I was just going to

---

[3] All letter-writing reminded FBA of correspondence with SBP.
[4] See L. 689.   [5] *The Wanderer.* See L. 684 and n. 10.

write that intelligence to you, when the letter containing the good news of your intention—though I have quarrelled with the manner in which it was clad—arrived. I had had no hope of a meeting but by the sea side.[6]

696   23 Chenies Street,
                                           23 May 1813
To Doctor Burney

A.L.S. (Diary MSS. vii. 5888–[93], Berg), 23 May 1813
Double sheet 8vo and a single sheet 4to   6 pp.   *pmks*   T.P.P.U. / Tottenham CR   24 MY 1813   24 MY 18⟨13⟩   red wafer
Addressed: Dr. Burney, / Chelsea College, / Chelsea.
Edited by FBA, p. 1 (5888), *annotated*:   ·⁕·   1813 [*circled*]   (8)   Mrs. Solvyns Lʸ Harcourt Lʸ Crewe   p. 5 (5892), *annotated*: 8 Continued 8 (1813)
Edited also by CFBt *and the* Press. *See* Textual Notes.

                                            23ᵈ May,
                                        Chenies St.
                                        Alfred Place.

Oh how teized I am, my dearest Padre, by this eternal unwalkable weather! Every morning rises so fairly, that at every noon I am preparing to quit my conjuring, & repair, by your kind invitation, to prelude my promised Chatteration by a repast with Sarah—when, mizzling falls the Rain, or hard raps the hail,[1] & the Day, for me, is involved in damps & dangers that fix me, again, to my dry, but solitary conjurations. I am so tired, now, of disappointments, that I must talk a little with my Padre in their defiance, & in a manner, *NOW*, thank God! out of their reach. Ah!—how long will Letters be any safer than MEETINGS!—The little world I see all give me hope & comfort from the posture of affairs—but I am too deeply interested ǀ to dare be sanguine while in such a suspense.

---

[6] See L. 684, stating Mrs. Waddington's intention to see FBA at the Downs before she returned to France.
696. [1] During 19–20 May there were showers, succeeded by two days of heavy rain squalls (*GM* lxxxiii¹, 506; lxxxiii², 2).

I have made my long claimed visit to Harcourt House, & Lady Harcourt was so kind as to fetch & bring me home in her warm carriage.[2] She will not dispence with my passing a few days with her at St. Leonard's near Windsor, in the autumn, before my departure.[3] She introduced me to two officers lately returned from Spain, Lord Clinton[4] & Colonel Harcourt.[5] The latter, terribly wounded at Badajoz.[6] He is the destined heir

[2] Mary Harcourt (iv, L. 255 n. 10). Residing when in London at 15 Cavendish Square, she wrote twice before FBA consented to visit. On 4 April she sent a letter (Osborn):
'You was so very good & so kind as to say that I might hope for the pleasure of seeing you at Harcourt House before you left this Country.
'I know that now the time cannot be far distant—. . . May I beg that you will allow me to send the Carriage for you either on Wednesday next Thursday or Friday next—Sunday next or any day after that time, that will best suit your convenience—
'One thing I must entreat that you will have the goodness to stay all night— you shall have a well aired Bed, & I shall be quite delighted to see you—
'I will take care also C[ol] & M[rs] Harcourt shall have a peep of you, that you may tell our dear friends in France, that you have seen them.'
On 7 April Lady Harcourt repeated her invitation (Osborn). 'I am just come from Chelsea where I hoped to have seen you, & was much disappointed I did not find you at home—I want to know what day will suit you after I return, to give us the pleasure of seeing you at Harcourt House—I shall be in the Country, from Sunday the 19th 'till Wednesday y[e] 21st—but if you will let me send the Carriage for you either on good friday Evening, after y[e] Church is over, & will stay with me 'till Monday or let me see you on the 21st or 22nd—or any day after that you like, it will make me very happy.'
[3] 'In 1782 the Hon. William Harcourt was promoted to the rank of Major-General in the army. At the same period he purchased St. Leonard's Hill from the Duke of Gloucester, whereupon the King appointed him Deputy Ranger of Windsor Great Park, the Duke of Gloucester at the same time being made Lieutenant of Windsor Forest.' See *GM* c[2] (1830), 178.
[4] Robert Cotton St. John Trefusis (1787–1832), 18th Baron Clinton (1797). Entering the army in 1803, he became aide-de-camp to Wellington in the Peninsular War and sometime captain in the 16th Light Dragoons. Made a colonel in 1825, he served from 1827 to his death as Lord of the Bedchamber to George IV.
In 1812, he was fêted as the bearer of glad tidings—the victory of Salamanca. According to the report in *The Times* (28 Aug.), the Portuguese embassy celebrated with a religious service and 'a splendid dejeuné. No sooner had the ladies retired and the health of Lord WELLINGTON and the allied Army been drank, than Lord CLINTON entered, who was received by all the Portuguese present with the utmost enthusiasm.'
[5] Amédée-Louis-Charles-François d'Harcourt-Olonde (1771–1831), marquis d'Harcourt, pair de France (1830). Born in Paris, he emigrated to England in 1792 and in 1800 at St. Leonard's Hill married his cousin Élisabeth-Sophie d'Harcourt (d. 1846). They had three children: William-Bernard (d. 1846), Georges-Douglas-Trévor-Bernard (1808–83), Maria-Augusta (*c.* 1810–*post* 1833). Colonel Harcourt volunteered for service in the English army in 1793, rising through the ranks so that by 1813 he was a colonel and in 1819 a major-general.
[6] In March 1812 Wellington had attacked the French fortress at Badajoz in Portugal. 'In April he lost 5,000 men under a downpour of masonry, steel, lead and fire as he vainly tried to storm the great breach. The main attack failed completely. The fortress fell to a surprise move, intended only as a diversion. Picton and the 3rd Division climbed their 20-foot ladders up the walls of the castle. The attackers on the main front were sullenly acknowledging defeat when the

to Lord Harcourt's estate.[7] Lord Clinton, I believe, brought the news of Salamanca.[8] She presented me, also, to Miss Trefusis.[9] & Miss Rochford.[10]

But—M[e] Solvyns has deferred her setting out, she writes me word, to the 25 or 26th.—She invited me, for the Sunday last, when she had promised to come to me, to a dinner at her Brothers, Mr. Greenwoods,[11] to meet Mr. Reeves,[12] of the Alien office, & *sundry of my friends*, though personally unknown. These are arrangements, to me, intolerable: they embarrass & discountenance me; & I have really no longer health for

shrilling of the British bugles from within announced that the place was theirs.' See J. Steven Watson, *The Reign of George III, 1760–1815* (1960), p. 493.

[7] In a will signed 24 Mar. 1828, he ordered that, following the decease of his wife Mary, his principal heirs were 'Charles Amedet d'Harcourt' and his wife 'Sophia'. They and their children and their 'remote' issue were 'entitled' to the mansions, lands, and rents at St. Leonard's Hill and to the interests and proceeds of an additional £80,000. This bequest was contingent upon two conditions: that Charles and Sophia d'Harcourt and their children reside permanently in England (except for visits abroad to last no longer than six months or for travel in the service, civil or military, of the reigning British monarch); that within twelve months of their succeeding to the Harcourt estates, the family of the General (his rank so identified in the will) become members of the Anglican Church. Within two months the will was drastically altered. In a codicil dated 27 May 1828, Lord Harcourt by explicit direction barred Sophia from the inheritance and by omission her two sons William-Bernard and Georges-Douglas-Trévor-Bernard. The codicil, in effect, provided that, following the decease of Lady Harcourt, Charles d'Harcourt was to be the legitimate successor to the Harcourt estates, which he could retain only in his own lifetime. See Prob. 11/1773/f. 448 (proved 27 July 1830).
But Charles d'Harcourt died two years before Lady Harcourt. In 1833, therefore, the Harcourt estates devolved upon Edward Venables-Vernon (in 1831 Vernon-Harcourt), Archbishop of York and first cousin to William Harcourt.
[8] The battle of Salamanca was won by the British forces, who lost 5,000 men, while the French lost 14,000. After this battle, the road to Madrid was opened to the English so that on 12 Aug. 1812 Wellington entered the city as liberator. On 16 August the *London Gazette Extraordinary* announced that the aide 'to the Earl of Wellington, arrived his morning at the War Department with despatches, addressed by his Lordship to Earl Bathurst, dated the 21st, 24th, and 28th [July].' The most significant despatch, dated 24 July, began with the statement that Lord Clinton 'will present to your Lordship this account of a Victory which the allied troops under my command gained in a general action, fought near Salamanca, on the evening of the 22d inst. . . .'
[9] Probably Anne Matilda Trefusis (1790–1876), who in 1827 was to marry Edward George Moore (1798–1876), Canon of Windsor. Lord Clinton's other sister was Louisa Barbara Trefusis (1794–1885), who in 1822 became the second wife of John Rolle (1756–1842), cr. Baron Rolle of Stevenstone (1796). For Lord Rolle's first marriage, see L. 798 n. 13.
[10] Lucy Nassau de Zuylestein (1752–*pre* 1823), sister to William Henry (1754–1830), 5th and last Earl of Rochford, Viscount Tunbridge, and Baron Enfield [1695].
[11] Probably Charles Gregory (*pre* 1796–*post* 1819), the elder son of Charles Greenwood (1766–1818). At this time his address alternated between Swanbourne, Buckinghamshire, and Sloane Street, Chelsea. For his family background, see vi, L. 592 n. 2.
[12] See L. 647 n. 8.

whatever gives ⏐ me disturbance that is avoidable.—There is a full share of what is inevitable always at hand!—So I sent an excuse: she repeated the invite, with assurances *Mr. Reeves depended upon* me; but as I gave no leave for the engagement, I could not be responsible for its failure. I fear, however, she is affronted, for I have never seen nor heard of her since, though I have written to enquire whether your Letter for the Institute[13] should be sealed. To morrow, if I have no news, I must hie me, *Coûte qui coûte*, to try to find her, with our Letters. This is the 2ᵈ time she has made the same insistance! I think she will beware of the third! She is a good humoured, pleasing, friendly, lively woman, but without *tact*, or discretion.

I have the satisfaction to hear that my dear Alex goes on briskly with all his studies, & that he is more flourishing both in health & looks.

I have no more news from Paris, since my Letter of April 12ᵗʰ I begin to long!—[14]

Lady Crewe invited me to her party that ⏐ she calls Noah's ark: but I cannot *yet* risk an evening, & *dressed* too: she then said she would make me a small party, with the Miss Berrys;— of a morning! and now, she has written to Charles to make *interest with me* to admit Lord Lansdown, at his earnest request![15] —I am quite *non compos*, to know how I shall make my way, through these amazing honours, to my strength & re-establish-ment; for they clash with my private plan, & adopted system of quiet. However, she says the meeting shall be in the Country, at Brumpton,[16] & without fuss or ceremony. Her kindness is inexpressible, therefore I have not courage to refuse her; she has offered me her little residence at Brumpton for my dwelling, for a week or so, to restore me from all my influenzas.—She may truly be called a faithful family friend. I hope dear Sarah,

---

[13] See L. 694 and n. 1. CB's letter of acceptance written to the Institut, and carried by Mme Solvyns to Paris, is missing.

[14] See L. 689.

[15] Henry William Edmund Petty-Fitzmaurice (1780–1863), 3rd Marquess of Lansdowne. Active as a Whig in the Commons and after 1809 in the Lords, he was never thought a party man despite fifty years of political activity. He was a patron of the arts and literature, re-establishing the fine library and picture gallery collected by his father and scattered by his half-brother John Henry Petty (d. 1809). In 1808 Lansdowne married Lady Louisa Emma Fox-Strangways (1785–1851), fifth daughter of Henry Thomas (1747–1802), 2nd Earl of Ilchester, *styled* Lord Stavordale.

[16] See L. 697 n. 21.

& Fanny Raper will be of the party. If they are, charge them, Dear Sir, to let me hear their voices; for I shall never find out their faces.

I am advancing, though still far enough from ending, my conjurations. But as I have more time, I am more relaxed, which is wise, | perhaps, for my health, though not for my interest nor my book. But I relax neither wantonly nor wilfully.

What Weather! what weather! When shall I get to Chelsea, & embrace again my beloved Father!

This *freeborn Weather* of our sea-girt Isle of Liberty, is very incommodious to those who have neither carriages for wet feet, nor health for damp shoulders.

If the Farmers, however, are contented, I must be patient. We may quarrel with all our wishes better than with our Corn.

I have had another sweet visit from my kind Mrs. [Loc]k, who, knowing my situation, only calls by appointment, that she may be sure to be admitted.

To day I have had a visitor who left his card *Mr. John Gregorie*, & said he had been twice to seek me at Chelsea; & left me *Gregory's Legacy to his Daughters*!!¹⁷ I cannot imagine who he can be. I never knew any Gregory, in England, but the very agreeable Miss Gregory who lived with Mrs. Montagu, & who now is Mrs. Allanson.¹⁸

Adieu, My most dear Father, till the Sun shines drier!

ever & most dutifully

& affectionately your

FB. d'A.

Charlotte's kind Love & Duty. The *First*, from me to Sarah. |

⌐I should be much obliged to Beckey to send me my packet of

---

¹⁷ John Gregory (d. 1853) was a grandson of John Gregory (1724–73) and son of William Gregory (1759–1816), one of the six preachers in Canterbury Cathedral. FBA's visitor, who later became the Governor-in-Chief of the Bahamas (1849–53), probably brought with him the most recent edition (1809) of his grandfather's *A Father's Legacy to his Daughters* (first published posthumously in 1774), to which had been added 'Mr. Tyrold's advice to his Daughter', extracted from *Camilla*, 'A Sermon', pp. 355–62 (vol. iii, bk. 5, ch. 5) and 'A Picture of the Female Character', by George Horne, late Bishop of Norwich.

¹⁸ FBA, though unacquainted with John Gregory, had read his *Legacy* and knew his daughter Dorothea (c. 1755–1830), protégée of Elizabeth Montagu (*DL* i. 115). Identified in Mrs. Montagu's letter (*JRL*) to Mrs. Thrale, dated 15 Jan. [1781], as 'my spiritual Daughter', Dorothea had married in 1784 the Revd. Archibald Alison (1757–1839). For the marriage, see i, L. 3 n. 92.

old linnen by the carrier, when my dear Padre can send me the next batch of News.[19]

I keep them very carefully waiting an opportunity for return.⁋

697   [23 Chenies Street],
                                                    31 May 1813
To M. d'Arblay

A.L. (rejected Diary MSS. 5894–97, Berg), 31 May 1813
Double sheet 4to   4 pp.   red seal
Addressed: À Monsieur / Monsieur d'Arblay, / Rue du Miromenil, / Nº 8. faubᵍ St. Honoré, / À Paris
Directed in the hand of Mme Solvyn, *with a note*: sous couvert de J. Recamier le 8 juin / 1813 / —J R—
je prie Mʳ Recamier de faire remettre l'incluse en mains propres en disant c'est remis par le celebre Mᵐᵉ d'Arblay auteur d'Evelina, Cecilia &c
Edited by FBA, p. 1 (5894), *annotated*: ⁘ ⌈16⌉ (4/1)
Edited also by CFBt *and the* Press. *See* Textual Notes.

May 31ˢᵗ 1813

This very day, only, our kind Madᵉ Solvyns leaves London, & she has prepared me the means, through one of her friends, to send a Letter again to the dearest of mine to-morrow! how consolatory to the dearth of communication with which I feared I was threatened by her departure! And M. David,[1] the Gentleman whom she has engaged so obligingly in the interest of our happiness, appears to be of a nature so amiable & kind-hearted, as to take pleasure himself in snatching us from the abyss of doubt & anxiety, & fearful thoughts that hang upon silent absence. Alas, my dearest ami, now I know that you have been so ill,[2] I can no longer compose my mind in uncertitude

[19] CB loaned FBA the several newspapers that SHB read to him daily. Between 11 and 23 May, he sent her a 'large parcel of papers . . . by Errand cart' (Osborn [*post* 11 May 1813]).

697. [1] François-*Paul* David (*c.* 1778–1860) was the son of Marie Récamier (1748–1812), who in 1767 married Jean David (*fl.* 1740–1800), a merchant in Bordeaux. FBA's courier was also the nephew of Jacques Récamier (1751–1830), banker in Paris, who employed David (*c.* 1795–1806). After Récamier suffered financial reverses, David worked in the département des Finances until his retirement. Unmarried, he devoted himself to Mme Récamier until her death in 1849.
[2] See L. 689.

& suspence. It has always been difficult & irksome; but now it will grow painful & dejecting. Redouble, then, your admirable activity in finding means to write, or to give me intelligence of your health by message, for already it seems to me long—long—long since I have heard!—Your last is dated the 12. April: though I have *received* one since, dated the 4th—³ a Letter which I read almost daily, to assure myself again & again of the happy result of so much suffering in a perfect recovery. I am always charmed as well as consoled, to consider you under the care of the *feeling* & *sagacious* M. Esparron:⁴ for those are the two epithets that made me wish you in his hands. And if M. Le Noir⁵ has always been a peculiar favourite with me, from my high opinion of the integrity & the delicacy of his heart & his morals, what must he be now, when he has thus aided to nurse & cherish you? I am always seeing that Sallon that, you say, was never empty; on the frightful day that ⌐ preceded the blessed convalescence. How kind are our mutual friends! So, also, they came about for me! Ah mon ami!—who like you ought to have had your own true partner to have assisted you to bear your illness? who ever was comforted, soothed, aided, succoured, like that Partner when herself a sufferer! — — — —

Our Alexander is always at Greenwich. He has the advantage there, at present, of a Mathematical Master who has spent 8 years in France: & he is always so decidedly partial to French Mathematics, & mathematicians,—⌐à l'exception, pourtant, ne vous déplaise, of Newton, that that very circumstance cut short all obstacles & objections to his returning to that seminary. And particular instructors here are absolutely serious yet, you may well conceive he cannot remain much longer at Greenwich—Mon ami, when I object to sending the £200 abroad which is the *whole* of what now remains of Coutts' store,⁶

---

³ The letter dated 4 May is missing.

⁴ For Pierre-Jean-Baptiste Esparron (1776–1818), see vi, L. 617 n. 5. As a doctor he first met the d'Arblays in the early summer of 1812. He tended M. d'A during the latter's long illness in the spring of 1813. See Appendix II.

⁵ Marie-Alexandre Lenoir (1761–1839), who lived many years at 10, rue de Seine, was a long-standing friend of M. d'A. Lenoir was renowned as an archaeologist, a 'conservateur', and 'administrateur' of several museums, particularly the Musée des Monuments Français and the private museum of Josephine Bonaparte at Malmaison. He wrote widely from *c*. 1793 to 1833 on archaeology, hieroglyphics, and *objets d'art* in French museums.

⁶ Apparently FBA drew £200 not from her account at Coutts but from CB Jr., who after 1810 assumed responsibility for banking FBA's pension. On 13 Dec. 1810 Mathias wrote a letter (Osborn) to CB. 'I will pay M^{rs} D'Arblay's Pension to

believe me, were *you* the other, you would be the last to find
the sacrifice for Alex too much—I know you would go still
further yourself than I should. Can we not help M. de Tracy
some other way?⁷ I hope, ere long, to hear of his receiving the
twenty, & to see his writing to our Amine. For tis vile for *me*
to seem to demand! but it is all the effect of you believing us so
much richer than we are, from never having received the Letter
in which I stated, as soon as I knew it, what I found here. You
talked, in one Letter, & say you have in more, which, however,
have never reached me, of my sending you 25 by Coutts, *as a
means of hearing from me.* If *only* for that, it is surely not worth
while at such a discount especially as you would be grieved
past measure afterwards to impede any advantage to Alex.
The plain fact is, our little avoir in this country is not beyond
what I at present, & for the present, require, when *my* wants,
during my stay, & for my family, &c, are deducted.⌐ ⌐ How
unpleasant is all that belongs to Money! how constantly, to me,
wearing, wearying, & perplexing! I can never tell you how
embarrassed I am in seeming slack to do what you appear to
desire, yet how difficult to do otherwise! Oh that PEACE—
sweet Peace—amongst its other greater blessings, would allow
you to come over & settle yourself, as You could do in a week,
what should be done, & *how* to do it!

⌐I expected yesterday, Mrs. Waddington & her Children,
but had the grief to receive a Letter to tell me that she was
unwell, & her Emily, her second daughter, was taken dangerously ill, just as they were all packed & prepared for the
journey. I most earnestly hope the recovery will be speedy: but
they are always, alas, weak & sickly, the eldest daughter, my
name sake, excepted.⁸ Mr Greene lives always in their neighbourhood, & is turned a sour, severe, & disappointed character,

your Son Dr C. Burney with great readiness, instead of you, as has been usual.'
See L. 698.
⁷ Antoine-Louis-*Claude* Destutt (1754–1836), marquis de Tracy (v, L. 526
n. 21).
⁸ Frances Waddington, now 22, was to marry in 1817 Christian Karl Josias,
baron von Bunsen (1791–1860), a theologian and German ambassador to London.
She died in 1876.

as Mrs. Waddington writes me word.[9] He wrote to me at once, upon my arrival, with eager joy to fix a meeti[ng] as if he had been my most intimate friend.[10] I sent him my thanks through Mrs. W.[11] but said I was not at home, & could only hope to see my acquaintances by chance meetings. I hear he is much hurt, nay angry, but why? — —

The weather being now fine,[12] my cold & influenzas, & wintry heart &c—are removed, & I have *twice* been abroad to make visits. *twice* only!— Yesterday I saw, for the first time, L[y] Templeton, she & all the Uptons[13] remember you with unabated & flattering regard, especially Greville Upton, who has married a great heiress & bears the name of Howard.[14] He is determined to shew his esteem for you, he says, by kindness to Alex.[15] L[d] Templeton, also, is very friendly.[16] I think I have told you that I have not yet seen Mrs. Charles.[17] There is some

[9] James Greene had been hospitable and gregarious. William Coxe writes: 'Unacquainted with a single gentleman, when I first entered [Monmouth] county, I was introduced to Mr. Greene . . . his hospitable mansion was open to me at all times and on all occasions, without form or ceremony; I was left at full liberty to make excursions as my fancy or inclination suggested, and on my return, after the fatigues of the day, I enjoyed the comforts of an agreeable society. In this delightful residence, I first conceived the plan of writing a tour in Monmouthshire; Mr. Greene zealously encouraged and assisted me in the prosecution of the work; through his introduction, I became acquainted with the principal gentlemen and men of letters, and obtained access to various documents and interesting papers.' See *Historical Tour through Monmouthshire* ([first published 1801] 1904), p. 149. For the hidden causes of James Greene's change of personality, see Ll. 751, 788.

[10] For FBA's association with Greene in France, see the following letters in vols. v and vi: Ll. 517, 532, 533, 540, 542, 546, 551, 582.

[11] See L. 684 and n. 9.

[12] On 26 May 1813 there was hail and thunder. From 27 to 31 May, however, the days were 'fair' with mid-day temperatures ranging from 60 to 74 °F. (*GM* lxxxiii[1], 512).

[13] Elizabeth Upton *née* Boughton (1746–1823), Lady Templetown (iii, L. 216 n. 16) had three daughters: Elizabeth Albana (L. 637 n. 22), Caroline, and Sophia (L. 770 nn. 35, 37). For her two sons, see below nn. 14, 16.

[14] Fulke Greville Upton on 9 July 1807 had married Mary (d. 1877), only daughter and heiress of Richard Howard of Elford, Staffordshire, and Castle Rising, Norfolk. Upon his marriage Colonel Upton assumed the surname of Howard. His father-in-law possessed great wealth. According to the terms of his will, proved on 24 Nov. 1818, his capital mansion and park (known as Ashford Park) and all his lands and tenements in Surrey, his farms and other income properties in Stafford, his house in Grosvenor Square were all to go to the Honourable Fulke Greville Howard and after his death to 'the use of my blood daughter Mary Howard' and then to their children. The heirs received an additional £3,000 each, along with books, china, table linen, wine, and beer (Prob. 11/1610/f. 511).

[15] See L. 673 n. 3; L. 674 n. 4.

[16] John Henry Upton (1771–1846), 1st Viscount Templetown (1806).

[17] Cecilia Margaret Locke *née* Ogilvie (1775–1824). See L. 702 n. 3; v, L. 472 n. 2.

coolness, though no separation, in the family, but the Father[18] is what he is & therefore all intercourse is troubled.

People here, at present, talk much of what my heart is panting for—ever, PEACE!—Do they talk it chez-vous?[¶]

I saw L[y] Crewe the other day, & she pressed me to an assembly at her house; but I told her I had too lately quitted my room to venture out at night. She would have, then, she said, a morning party, naming the Miss Berrys, Lord Henry Petty (now Lord Lansdowne) & a great patron of PEACE,[19] & Mr. Rogers, author of the beautiful poem on Memory,[20] as persons who insisted upon being of the party; & that all objections on my part might be over ruled, she has just sent to tell me to fix my own day;—so it stands for next thursday, at one o'clock at noon. It is to be at a small *villa cottage*, she says, which she possesses at Brompton.[21] She is to fetch me herself, & bring me back to my sister Broome. How kind that good sister is! how she has nursed me through all the winter! And how my dear excellent elder sister has repined she had no room *chez elle* to take the same Charge! In some future Letter I must detail long accounts of both of them, & of Sally, who is extremely affectionate, & of both my very worthy & warmly attached Brothers. Oh how do

[18] William Ogilvie (*c*. 1740–1832), Cecilia Locke's father and second husband of the Duchess of Leinster, was reputed to be a dour Scot, an irritable person with an unprepossessing figure and a truculent personality. In the opinion of Cecilia's aunt Lady Sarah Bunbury, Ogilvie 'is very ugly and has a disagreeable manner' and yet loved his wife without equivocation (*Locks of Norbury*, p. 92).

[19] Henry Petty-Fitzmaurice was elevated to the peerage in 1809 on the death in November of his half-brother John Henry. While active in the Lords during this parliamentary session, he said little on behalf of peace. On 18 February, for example, he spoke briefly in support of England's war with America but urged its speedy termination. On 2 April he favoured an exchange of prisoners with the French. In private, however, he was ready to advocate peace. Mary Berry reports (iii. 7) that on 26 Mar. 1814 she visited Mme de Staël's. 'I found there', she said, 'Lord Lansdowne alone with her, and we had a very interesting conversation, and a very reasonable one, upon the affairs of France and the Allies.'

[20] Samuel Rogers (1763–1855), banker, poet, collector, host, and traveller. In his own day he was highly regarded as the author of *The Pleasures of Memory*, published anonymously in 1792. He was reputed to have exquisite taste, seeking out distinguished literary figures, and being sought out by them. See i, L. 24 n. 48.

[21] For a description of this party, see the note by George Eden (1784–1849) to his father William (1744–1814), cr. Baron Auckland (1793): 'The Lansdownes have been taking me to Lady Crewe's, at Brompton, to see Madame d'Arblay, who was exhibited to a select party. I found Lady Glenbervie there, who had dressed herself, she said, so as to be described as a heroine in the next novel. We had a great many other clever people, and passed a pleasant morning.' See *The Journal and Correspondence of William, Lord Auckland*, ed. Robert John Eden (4 vols., 1861–2), iv. 392.

they ALL—ALL long to embrace you! they brighten up at your very name—Adieu, most dear of all that are dear!— Move Heaven & Earth to give me news of your health, I most earnestly entreat. Mine is amended amazingly since the fine weather.

⌐I get on but slowly with our menage; you have charged me not to hurry, &c fatigue myself. How you are kind for that! You ask for poor Norbury & William—One is always in Ireland —the other is at sea. I wish earnestly & most vastly, to behold either of them—ind[eed I] do — —

Je pense à vous
—Sincerely & ever.⌐

⌐I shall long to hear that Me Solvyns found her little Boy[22] as flourishing & intelligent as she has been taught to expect.⌐ |

⌐Speak for me yourself to all our friends, mon ami, surtout à mon oncle.⌐[23]

698

To Charles Burney

[23 Chenies Street,
3 June 1813]

A.L. (Osborn), *n.d.*
Double sheet 8vo   3 pp.   *pmks* T.P.P.U. / Tottenham CR   3 JU
1813   3 JU 1813   wafer
Addressed: Rev^d Dr. Burney, / Rectory House, / Deptford.

My dear kind Charles,

I cannot answer for one moment of *Thursday*.[1] Lady Crewe will fetch me, & bring me home: all my day, therefore, is at her command & decision.

---

[22] Mme Solvyns had at this time one young son Charles-Balthazar, born in Paris on 6 July 1811. A precociously talented mathematician, he became a sous-lieutenant in an engineering corps of the Belgian army. He died in 1833 of typhus, contracted while he worked heroically during a hurricane to repair a damaged dike that threatened to burst and inundate the fort de la Croix.
[23] Gabriel Bazille, now 82.

698. [1] June 5. See L. 697 n. 21.

But *Friday* I will hold sacred & hoping to see you.

I am so grieved at your poor head's being still in pain! alas —I fear nothing but a real fit of the gout will do thoroughly![2]

Sir Joseph Banks is recovered, miraculously, they say, & wholly from resolving not to yield to his attack!—[3]

If you are prevented by business from coming on Friday, I will write my *idea*. But they[4] tell me we ought also to address our circular to Johnson, Miss Edgeworth's man who is a very good one—but I don't quite concur[5]

How I wish you were well enough for L^y Crewe—[6]

The sermon, helas came too late—the Q[ueen] & P[rincesses] go back to day.[7]

---

[2] FBA extends the premise, not widely accepted, of Dr. Thomas Sydenham (1624–89), who 'has given it as his opinion, that the more violent the inflammation and pain, the paroxysm will be the shorter, as well as the interval between the present and the next paroxysm longer' (*Enc. Brit.*, 3rd ed., xi. 186).

[3] Sir Joseph Banks (1743–1820), patron of scientific exploration and President of the Royal Society (1778–1820). Sir Joseph was so severely afflicted by the gout that his limbs were paralysed, but in this instance had regained mobility.

[4] FBA had consulted with Maria Edgeworth (1767–1849) and in all likelihood her father a few weeks earlier. On FBA's request, the Edgeworths arranged to see her and communicated their willingness in a note (PML), dated 17 May. 'Mr. & M^rs & Miss Edgeworth were flattered some time ago by a message from Madame d'Arblay intimating that she should wish to make their acquaintance—M^rs & Miss E will wait upon Madame d'Arblay any morning she appoints or if it suits Madame d'Arblay's convenience they would be particularly gratified by seeing Madame d'Arblay for breakfast at 10 o'clock any day except Monday or Wednesday when they are engaged—Miss E mentions breakfast because it is the only time when they are sure of being at home & would not on any account let Madame d'Arblay waste her precious time by coming merely to leave a ticket.'

[5] Since 1780 and until 1816, every book written by Maria Edgeworth alone or in collaboration with her father had been published by the firm of J. Johnson at 72 St. Paul's Churchyard. Although the founder Joseph Johnson had died in 1809, his name and reputation for fair dealing distinguished the firm. But FBA may have worried that the house of Johnson did not puff its wares and that, for broad circulation, it cheapened book production. Moreover, Johnson's lists tended toward political and religious nonconformity. The bookseller himself had been jailed in 1797 for publishing a political work offensive to the government. Had FBA affiliated with Johnson's firm, she would have joined the company of such dissenting or radical authors as William Cowper, John Newton, Joseph Priestley, Erasmus Darwin. For an extended obituary of Johnson, see *GM* lxxix[2] (1809), 1167–8.

[6] FBA expresses not only her concern for her brother's health but her willingness to abet his desire for ecclesiastical preferment through Lady Crewe, who had always wished to see him advance in the Church. MF indicated in a letter (JRL) to Mrs. Piozzi, dated 19 Feb. 1808, that CB 'corresponds still with his unaccountable Favourite . . . who writes him that her Garden is right reverend; & her trees all *bewigged*.' The passage of time only increased Lady Crewe's ambitions for CB Jr., as FBA was aware.

[7] For the sermon, see L. 690 n. 1. FBA could not deliver a copy of it to the Queen and the Princesses Augusta and Mary since they had left for Windsor on the morning of 3 June after having spent only three days at the Queen's House.

For Mercy's sake don't forget Mr. Mathias—[8]
I have sent off the £200[9]

Kind Love to Rotttete [*sic*]—

699   23 Chenies Street,
                                        13 June 1813
To Mrs. Waddington

A.L. (Berg), 13 June 1813
Single sheet 4to   2 pp.   *pmks*   T.P.P.U. / Tottenham CR   JU 1813
wafer
Addressed: Mrs. Waddington, / Holles Street, / Cavendish Square

June 13. 1813
Cheniers Street.

I need not—I am sure, tell my dearest Mary how I should
delight to meet her wishes—or, could I, to anticipate them—
but she MUST let me *name*, when we are tête à tête, how I am
situated with respect to any introductory efforts.—with a mind
liberal & delicate like hers, she will feel and conceive in a
moment the just claims of my family to my first exertions;—&
what are *mes devoirs*.

I enclose you my dear Mrs. Lock's note, to let you see how
inevitable is the delay of our excursion, as on *Tuesday* she will
return, from Lee,[1] to her still so dear, though no longer gay &
happy home. I have told my Sister Sarah, who was here to day,
of the delay. If your own engagements force you still to go that
road on Monday, to-morrow, I entreat that I may not entangle
your plans, for we will still go together another time. I, at all
events, must go thither in a day or two. I have postponed my

[8] FBA wanted CB Jr. to send his latest publication to Thomas James Mathias
(*c.* 1754–1835), librarian at the Queen's House.
[9] See L. 697 n. 6.

699. [1] Mrs. Locke visited her son, his wife Harriet, and their three children in
Lee, Kent, where George Locke had been appointed rector in August 1803 and
was to remain for over 40 years. For a listing of the Locke children and grand-
children (as of 1802), see v, L. 472 n. 2.

Richmond visit again. My dear Father has long lost sight of the professor Mehule[2]—He is shocked not to be able to aid you, & charges me with his affectionate compliments & excuses. He shuts himself | cruelly up from almost all the world.[3] Adieu, my dearest Mary—meet we must Tuesday or Wednesday, either in our excursion, or here, or *CHEZ VOUS*—only let me know what will be most commodious: & remember me most kindly to your three most amiable young Companions, with my comp[ts] to Mr. Waddington. I am anxious to hear how your Emily bears London—& that your head is better.

Certainly you must accompany your Fanny to Lady Crewe's— & Lady C. is *prepared* to like you, &, I feel sure, will meet any overture with pleasure. I question much, for myself, if I shall be able to indulge myself again with her society.—

Marianne is not returned[4]—poor Ralph continues to take James's powders every night.[5]

I dare make no offer for to-morrow Evening—as my dear Mrs. L[ock] will have my Morning. |

[2] Professor Étienne-Nicolas Méhul (1763–1817), a French organist and pianist, a music teacher and composer, a member of the Institut.

[3] CB was now aware of his withdrawal. On 29 Aug. 1813, he wrote to Samuel Wesley (BM, Add. MSS. 35027, f. 12): 'I cannot, at least immediately, bring myself, cordially to name any future time for such a meeting as you seem to wish. I have been long so much detached from the active world and weaned from musical delights, that I now no more wish to renew them than a child who has been several years deprived of the breast—unless coax'd by the civilities of such a performer as yourself.'

[4] As MF wrote (JRL) to Mrs. Piozzi in June 1813: 'I write from M[rs] Wilberforce's, with whom I am spending a fortnight, previous to our all leaving London for the summer. The Wilberforces for Sandgate. . . . Kensington Gore is always like a magic lanthorn; fresh spirits for ever flitting about us; "come like shadows & depart." I ventured to tell Mr W. the other day, that when he was canvassing so hard against the slave-trade, he forgot to exempt himself—working as hard . . . as if the whip was at his back.'

[5] FBA did not reveal the seriousness of Dolph's illness, but MF commented in a letter (JRL) to Mrs. Piozzi, 3 July 1813: 'I am here [Bradfield Hall] for two months, with Mr Young & his family, & I hope Mama is coming too, as soon as Dolph can bear the journey; for he has been very alarmingly ill.'

700   [23 Chenies Street,
                                               14 June 1813]
To Mrs. Waddington

A.N. (Berg), *n.d.*
Single sheet 4to   cut down to (4·5 × 7·1″)

O yes—I was sure you would *understand* what, in my place, you
would have *felt*—
Wednesday, my sweet Mary—because it is before Thursday.
To Mrs. Lock I will speak to-morrow—she was prevented
coming this morning—but will be here then:
And to Mrs. Angerstein when we meet.
Mrs. Br⟨oome⟩'s kindest thanks—adieu Adieu

701   [23 Chenies Street,
                                      post 14—*pre* 28 June 1813]

To Mrs. Waddington

A.N. (Berg), *n.d.*
A fragment (4·4 × 7·2″) torn from a single sheet 4to   1 p.
Addressed: Mrs / Waddington

Thursday is a very late day indeed, my dearest Mary—but
I shall hope still to make it either earlier—or very long—I am
in the midst of ⟨parting⟩ now with a ⟨branch⟩ of my ⟨family⟩
but[1]

                                              your ever & aye

701. [1] Rosette Burney and CPB's wife Frances and infant daughter were to
depart for Sandgate. CB Jr. was to go first to Cambridge for the Bishop of Ely's
visitation sermon on 17 June (L. 709), return briefly to Deptford, and as quickly
as possible join his family. In fact, he rushed to Sandgate on 13 or 14 July—
probably sooner than he intended—because of another of Rosette's depressive
attacks (Ll. 714, 715).

702   [23 Chenies Street,
                               post 14—*pre* 28 June 1813]

To Mrs. Waddington

A.L.S. (Berg), *n.d.*
Double sheet 12mo   3 pp.   corners torn   wafer
Addressed: Mrs. Waddington, / 9 Holles Street, / Cavendish Square.

And why, dearest Mary, settle 3 days beforehand whether
& when we shall pass together 3 hours in an evening?—
I so little like to break an appointment, that I love not to
make one unnecessarily. And, while my Brother is hovering
about, previously to so long an absence,[1] I do not hold myself
free. Yet I hope that | on Monday we may meet—if I shall not
be too much tired in the evening, for the Morning is destined
to some few of my visits that are of such old arrear—though to
such as I fear I shall else miss, only.—I have never yet been
able to return the call even of L^y Lucy [Foley], to whose kindness on my arrival I am so deeply in debt[2]—nor have I even
seen Mrs. Charles Lock[3]—⟨!⟩ &c &c But I have now got my
young Chev[alier] & I shall try to make some rounds—[&] |
if I cannot be with you in the evening I will embrace you in
the morning, if any way possible—but I entreat you to be sure
it has been beyond my forces & time if you do not see me. I am
the more anxious now to meet you, as my niece Barret claims
my long deferred promise for next week—as she is preparing
for a sea side excursion.[4] & I [hav]e given *you* for my delay, little
as I ha⟨ve⟩ [enjo]yed your society. Adieu Adieu | Love to
F[rances]. E[mily]. A[ugusta].

I shall give Alexander your beautiful note just as we are
setting forth to see you, whenever that happens.

702. [1] CB Jr. See L. 701 n. 1.
   [2] For Lady Lucy Foley's kindness, see L. 637 nn. 20, 23, 25.
   [3] FBA was consistently concerned over her failure to see Cecilia, the widow of
Charles Locke (d. 1804). See L. 697 n. 17.
   [4] CFBt and her family also went to Sandgate for their 'excursion' (L. 713 n. 2).

703   [23 Chenies Street,
                              post 14—*pre* 28 June 1813]
To Mrs. Waddington

A.N. (Berg), *n.d.*
A fragment (4·5 × 7·4″) cut from a single sheet 4to   1 p.

How my hopes are disappointed! you looked so well—so lovely. I thought only of old times.—

I am free from the smallest evil relative to my walk—We met an elegant Voiture that condescended to receive us almost immediately: & I am always best for exercise that is not exhausting. I shall long for good news of you to-morrow—if come to me you cannot, I shall be tempted to try to catch a glimpse of you again. Tell me, therefore, your hours—

Love to sweet Emily—& thanks to bright Augusta—

Her notes are touchingly affectionate.

704   [23 Chenies Street,
                              post 14—*pre* 28 June 1813]
To Mrs. Waddington

A.N. (Berg), *n.d.*
Single sheet 8vo
Addressed: Mrs. Waddington.

You are singularly right in your belief—we had no sooner got into the Coach than he exclaimed 'How I like Mrs. Waddington!' but you must not for the world intimate a *design* of a *parley* with him—He will shrink back into himself, IRRECOVERABLY, if he suspects any idea of observation. Your Fanny must *address* him in French, as if *sans y penser*, for even from that he will retreat, if he believes himself INTENTIONALLY listened to. The *thought* only would make him dumb for the Evening. He will again have to leave us for a commission; but he will not again lose his way. I shall be delighted if you can help me to *apprivoiser*

my *Sauvage*. But it can ONLY be by attracting him as if by hazard.
—We shall be happy to expect you. He is now with a private
Tutor.[1]

705   [23 Chenies Street,
                            post 14 June—*pre* 28 June 1813]

To Mrs. Waddington

A.N. (Berg), *n.d.*
A fragment (2·7 × 7·2″) cut from a single sheet 4to   1 p.

O that I had but Time of my own—sweet Mary! I am penetrated with sorrow by your note—
   We must write again to fix a meeting
   My Brother comes to me to-morrow but I know nothing yet
of Sunday, which however is a day I give to my Father when I
leave this 2d Home oh take Care of yours[elf] dearest Mary—
for y^r 3. & one more[1]

706   [23 Chenies Street,
                                            c. 29 June 1813]

To Mrs. Waddington

A.L. (Berg), *n.d.*
Double sheet 8vo   2 pp.   red seal
Addressed: Mrs. Waddington.

Your zeal—your kindness—can never surprise me, my dearest
Mary—but this does not appear to me a feasible project. My
Brother, charging me to present you his best Respects for the
honour of your note, defers answering it till he can come to
discourse with me upon it. But I must beg leave to give the

704. [1] For the purpose of AA's special tutoring, see L. 715 n. 3.
705. [1] FBA refers to herself and Mrs. Waddington's three daughters, thus excluding the 64-year-old Benjamin Waddington.

answer myself: I cannot think it right, if we negociate publicly in one Hemisphere,[1] to negociate privately in the other.[2]

Nothing, however, is yet done *here*: the work not being ready, I rather wish to defer than forward any | immediate arrangement, that I may not be hurried or tormented for the MS. should I, at last,—but we will talk over shoulds & woulds & ifs & ands—to-morrow—and as late as you please, for we, invalids, dine at the hour you lunch, & shall therefore be at liberty at any time before your own dinner. Ralph is abundantly better, though far from recovered.[3] I would I could hear similar words of your sweet Emily! To her & her excellent sister join the love that I here transmit to their very dear Mother.

707   [23 Chenies Street,
                                                29 June 1813]
To Mrs. Waddington

A.L.S. (Osborn), *n.d.*
Single sheet 4to, lower right corner torn away, but mended   1 p. with mounting tape on left margin, p. 1   *pmks*   T.P.P.U. / Tottenham CR 29 JU 1813   wafer
Addressed: Mrs Waddington / Holles Street, / Cavendish Square,
Docketed, p. 2: Written by Madame d'arblay / born Burney / to Mʳˢ Waddington born Port — 1813   Madame d'arblay rarely signed her name & often omitted even Initials —

What a melancholy Letter! I return it with real concern.

How kind is your zeal, my dearest Mary!—but my Brother & I are both of opinion that, till the English business is arranged, we have no right to treat upon any that is foreign. Should I, which is very possible, print for myself, the good offices of Mr.

---

706. ¹ See L. 707 for Mrs. Waddington's desire to effect an American publication of *The Wanderer*. For such publication, see L. 718 n. 15.
    ² While immediate negotiations for the English sale of *The Wanderer* were being conducted 'privately', the 'trade' had been aware of it as early as December 1811. For example, on the 8th Lord Byron wrote to William Harness (1790–1869) to say that his 'Bookseller (Cawthorn)' had just told him 'with a most important face, that he is in treaty for a novel of Madame D'Arblay's (the *Miss Burney*) for which 1000 Gs. are asked!' Byron was to read the manuscript if Cawthorne obtained it. There was also Byron's letter of the 12th to Francis Hodgson, in which the information was repeated. See *Byron's Letters and Journals*, ed. Leslie A. Marchand (1973–), ii. 1432, 146.
    ³ Ll. 699 n. 5, 713 n. 1.

Brevoort[1] may be highly benificial: but the work is [n]ot yet quite finished, & therefore we have come to no [so]rt of decision.

How grieved I am to hear so cruel an account [of] you! I could not have indulged [myself] with [ful]filling our project for to-morrow evening, as I [go] to the Q[ueen's] H[ouse].[2]— But I [wi]sh much to discourse with [yo]u, a few minutes previously to going thither. If, in [you]r morning rambles, y[ou]r amiable Fanny can call for [me] at two o'clock, I wil[l] have a few minutes tête à tête [wi]th my dear Friend, & go on, thence, to my destination.—

[T]uesday noon   ever her's is F.d'A.

708   [23 Chenies Street,
                                        1 July 1813][1]
To Mrs. Waddington

A.L. (Berg), *n.d.*
Single sheet 8vo   1 p.

'Tis well you gave me no commission, dearest Mary!—I arrived too late for the P[ss] El[izabeth]—& my other audiences

707. [1] Either Henry Brevoort (*c.* 1765–1841) or his son Henry (1791–1874), of the Bowery, descendants of Henrick Jansen Brevoort, who left Holland for New York about 1630. In the next century and a half the family, some of whom were farmers and others merchants, acquired great wealth in real estate. Neither Henry Brevoort nor his son was actively engaged in trade. Rather both were patrons of writers, e.g. Washington Irving. The younger Brevoort became in time a close associate of Walter Scott. See *Longworth's American Almanac, New York Register, and City Directory* (1813).

The reference to Brevoort is explained in a letter (PML) by Anna Letitia Barbauld to FBA, dated 6 July 1813: 'I hope you will not think me too officious if I address you on the subject I am going to mention. . . . I understand that M[r] Brevort an American merchant has asked whether you have made any arrangement for printing your intended work in America, & if not, offers to put you in a way to receive copy right for it there. If you have not thought of this before, I should imagine it may be worth attending to, for printed in America any thing of yours will certainly be the moment they can get it, & there is no reason you should not have the profit of it. . . . If you should give us any commands on this occasion I shall be happy to execute them.'

[2] According to *The Times* (29 June 1813), the Queen and the Princesses Elizabeth and Mary arrived at the Queen's House on 28 June 'at a quarter before one o'clock'. They remained in London until 3 July when, attended by the Duke of York, they returned to Windsor 'in consequence of its being the quarterly day, on which her Majesty's Council is held on the state of the KING' (*The Times*, 5 July).

708. [1] This letter may be dated 1 July 1813, the day after FBA attended the Royal Family (see L. 709 and n. 7).

were so circumstanced, that I had not the power even to name you.[2]—If I did not, you must be VERY sure I could not.—But I hope to be more fortunate to-morrow, when the Pss Eliza[beth] has appointed me for 12 o'clock precisely.[3] No *hour* had been named in my commands for yesterday; but I had believed, by former times, 3 o'clock the most favourable. I write this, that you may not be under any suspense—& to say how earnestly I wish to hear better news of you, & your Emily. Fanny was toute aimable & pleasing. My love to *both*.

709   [23 Chenies Street,
                      1 July 1813][1]
To Charles Burney

A.L. (Osborn), *n.d.*
Double sheet small 4to   4 pp.   *pmk*   2 JY .813   wafer
Addressed: Revᵈ Dr. Burney, / Caius College, / Cambridge.

My dearest Carlos,

I was immensely disappointed, upon opening your packet, to find no proposition but the rejected old one of £2000.—How can I *assent* or write, or study, in ignorance what they have to propose? By his Note, it is plain Mʳ Rees[2] means to submit some project to our consideration; but we must *hear* before we *speak*. It is evident, also, by his manner, that his *ultimatum* is not intended to *begin* in the treaty, unless he finds us very facile.[3]

I can make no proposition, nor even give any *assent*, thus in

[2] The audiences were 'circumstanced' because on 30 June the Queen and Princesses were engaged in preparation for the Prince Regent's ball and supper at 9 o'clock.
[3] There were no official duties on 2 July for the Queen and Princess Elizabeth, who were to return to Windsor the morning of the 3rd.
709. [1] Postmarked 2 July 1813, the letter was written on the 1st (see n. 13).
[2] Owen Rees represented Longman, Hurst, Rees, Orme, and Brown in his firm's negotiations for the purchase of *The Wanderer*.
[3] After four months of negotiation, FBA was able to secure a contract from Longman and his partners that she regarded as better than the fixed sum of £2,000, which they initially offered for *The Wanderer*. Had her hopes materialized for the work's long-continuing sale (i.e. through several editions) she would have realized £3,000.

the dark. I must know what your interview produces:[4] & he will certainly not be surprised that you should not close, without communing with me, as you have already told him that you should not.

I will write instantly your note, as you direct.

With regard to *hurry*, &c my dearest Charles, I would not keep you an hour from following Rosette, except for the ┊ conference, the result of which you can transmit to me at once, & I will ponder upon it as well as I can, & transmit result second to Sandgate. For I should be quite grieved to detain you. And I still adhere to saying That, while the work is not finished, the haste is not so great. For, After a satisfactory & explicit conference, the matter may be settled by two or three Letters.

Till I hear his propositions, I cannot send an answer to Colbourn.[5]

I have not information enough upon the subject, to *form* any offer. I can but listen, & beg a little time to weigh, before I decide. The matter is, to me, so many ways momentous!—

I am charmed you have that delightful *compagnon de voyage*, Dr. Young.[6] I flatter myself I shall be able to see him more comfortably; though even that peep enlivened, & did me good. I was yesterday at the Q[ueen's] H[ouse] till Eleven[7]—I go again to-morrow—& Saturday it is *inevitable* that I dine, at last, at Mr. Rogers, with Lady Crewe.[8] Think if I shall be harrassed afterwards for time! ┊

[4] CB Jr. was not only her 'agent' during the negotiations for the sale of *The Wanderer* but in the language of the subsequent 'Articles of Agreement' signed between FBA and her publishers, he became her 'executor administrator and assign', his role being to make a semi-annual inventory of the number of copies left in the bookshop to determine when and if new editions should be required.

[5] For Henry Colburn's terms, see L. 711.

[6] John Young, professor of Greek at Glasgow University, had long been a friend of CB Jr. and his family (iv, L. 292 n. 2). CPB in a letter (Bodleian) to Finch on 28 July 1805, described 'Professor Young & his Family; friends, whom we see only to regret, that we meet so seldom:—I love them and theirs within my heart of hearts. . . . I know not the Man, whom I have known so long, & loved so well, without diminution.' By 1819 as a last gesture of friendship, Professor Young had a bust of CB Jr. placed in the library at the University of Glasgow. See Parr, op. cit., vii. 428.

[7] See L. 708 nn. 1, 2. If FBA remained at the Queen's House until eleven on 30 June, it was not to attend various members of the Royal Family, who at nine left for Carlton House, but to visit Mme Beckedorff and her daughter.

[8] FBA wrote Rogers (Sharpe Papers, xiv. 226, University College, London), she 'cannot refuse herself the honour & pleasure of meeting Lady Crewe in the society of Mr. Rogers.'

The Coutts have been cleared by papers found of my dearest Mr. Lock, which, it seems, he had not found opportunity to send us[9]—But *MY* account is strangely entangled—from Mr. Mat[hias]—It appears that my dearest Father received the sums on the years unaccounted for—& I fear has mixed them with his own![10]—but I shall take no Measure till I can consult with you—as I dread inconceivably shattering him with any mark of failure of Memory.

God bless you, my dearest Charles. — —

Make the Conference as explanatory as you can—& then don't *grudge* crowning the whole with a few Epistles, blown hither by Sea breezes, rather than hurry off such an important concer[n to] *come to a finish.*

But, above all, be off as fast as possible, to refresh—& to change the scene.—

Adieu Adieu dearest Carlucci—

I had no opportunity to present the Sermon: but I have lodged it where it will be presented when the hurry of London is over.[11]

The whole talk of London is of Mad^e de Staël,—& her having lived Wholly [with] the opposition since her arrival[12]—yet being invited to the Prince Regent's Grand Ball last Night.[13]— |

---

[9] The elder William Locke and—after 1810—William Locke II, aided by his mother, assumed responsibility for certain of the d'Arblays' financial affairs while they were in France. According to M. d'A (Appendix II): the investment of £271 in 3 per cent consols and the interest accrued therefrom since 1803, the money received from the rental of Camilla Cottage, approximately £90 loaned to Mme de Boinville and returned to William Locke II or some other responsible party at Norbury Park. For the actual amount of money involved, see L. 721 n. 3.

[10] See L. 697 n. 6.   [11] See Ll. 690 n. 1, 698 n. 7.

[12] Harassed for her anti-Napoleonic attitudes and statements as early as 1803 (v, L. 541 n. 8), Mme de Staël (1766–1817) left France in May 1811 for Switzerland and Austria. Thereafter she journeyed slowly from Vienna through Russia (stopping over in St. Petersburg), and thence to Finland and Sweden (spending the winter of 1812 in Stockholm). She then went to England, where she received a brilliant reception during the season of 1813. At this time she was a sympathetic associate of the Princess of Wales.

[13] On 30 June 1813 the Prince Regent 'gave a ball and supper to a numerous and splendid party'. Invitations were sent to almost a thousand people; fresh flowers were brought from Kew, Kensington Palace, and Hampton Court to decorate Carlton House, and eighteen tents were erected upon the lawn where supper was to be served. (Because of the heavy downpour of rain, few individuals dared to use either the tents or the promenade that led to them.) Nevertheless the ball was a success, for the Queen and the Princesses, who arrived at half-past nine, did not leave until half-past five in the morning. Many of the guests stayed until after six (*The Times*, 1 and 2 July).

I am charmed that the visitation sermon did so well—but not surprised, for I liked it molto bene.[14]

Pray present my Compliments—with my regrets—& my hopes—to your amiable professor.[15]

And remember me in very best manner to Dr. Davy, if, fortunately, you find him at Cambridge.—

710   [23 Chenies Street,
                                              10 July 1813]
To Doctor Burney

A.L.S. (Diary MSS. vii [5904x–5905], Berg), *n.d.*
Originally a double sheet 8vo (7·2 × 4·4″), but cut and pasted as described in Textual Notes. 4 pp. *pmks* T.P.P.U. / Tottenham CR 10 J⟨ ⟩1813
Addressed: Dr. Burney — / Chelsea College, / Chelsea.
Endorsed by CB *in pencil*: M^rs d'A. / July 10th / 1813
Edited by FBA, p. 1 [5904x], *annotated and dated*: ⋇· 1813 (10) (2) The Wanderer. Lady Wellington Lady Crewe Mr Rogers Dinner
Edited also by CFBt, who by cutting and pasting, conflated the text with that of the A.L.S., FBA to CB, 24 Aug. [1813]. *See* Textual Notes.

My most dear Padre—

If the offering (2) I prepare for you should not meet with your kind approbation, what shall I have to recompense the absence it forces me to bear that will be soothing to my mind?—to my *affairs*, I trust, it will bring serious good; but

[14] The sermon to which FBA refers is described in the *Cambridge Chronicle and Journal, and Huntingdonshire Gazette* for Friday 18 June 1813: 'The Right Rev. the Lord Bishop of Ely [Edward Bowyer Sparke (1759–1836)] held his primary visitation and confirmation for Cambridge, Barton, and Shingay deaneries, at St. Michael's church, yesterday, on which occasion a sermon was preached by the Rev. J. Slade, rector of Teversham. His Lordship then delivered a very able charge to the Clergy, and afterwards confirmed the young persons belonging to those deaneries.' The 'charge'—i.e. the visitation sermon—was published later that year.

[15] FBA may have meant Professor Young, whose 'bonhommie' she admired (iv, L. 292), or she may have meant James Henry Monk (1784–1856), then Regius Professor of Greek at Cambridge. The latter and CB Jr. were friends, personal and professional. On 29 Mar. 1814, e.g., AA sent a letter (Barrett, Eg. 3701A, f. 5) to FBA: 'Pray tell my Uncle with Rose's respects & so forth that Prof^r Monk will be very much obliged to him for the Alcestis notes that he was so good as to promise him—& also some little notula for the Museum Criticism.'

I am almost sick of it, from the privations it demands to my heart.[1]

Next week, I trust, I shall spend a day with you—I really require that regale.

I won't send my love to Sally, for her being so wicked as not to send me the Newspapers by Alex. | But how could I help beginning with an *Houra*! to your patriotism! What glorious intelligence! how big with hope as well as honour![2] I was delighted by meeting Lady Wellington,[3] not long since, at Lady Templetown's.[4] Her very name electrified me with emotion. I dined at Mr. Rogers,[5] at his beautiful mansion in the Green park,[6] to meet Lady Crewe; & Mrs. Barbauld was also there,[7] whom I had not seen many, many years, & alas | should not have known! Mr. Rogers was so considerate, to my *sauvagerie*, as to have no party; though Mr. Sheridan, he said, had expressed his great desire to *meet again his old friend Mad^e d'Arblay*[8] — !— Lady Crewe told me she certainly would not

710. [1] FBA's offering was *The Wanderer* with its lengthy dedication to CB: 'With what grateful delight do I cast, now, at the same revered feet where I prostrated that first essay [*Evelina*], this, my latest attempt!' (p. vi).

[2] What CB and all England celebrated the week of 5 July 1813 was Wellington's triumph at Vitoria, which 'has insured the expulsion of the invaders from the Peninsula; perhaps it has laid open their own territories to a severe but just retribution' (*The Times*, 5 July). '[T]he public joy exhibited itself last night [the 5th], in a variety of illuminations, which were, probably, never exceeded for number, taste, and splendour' (*The Times*, 6 July). The Prince Regent gave a Gala and supper on 6 July (*The Times*, 8 July).

[3] Catherine Sarah Dorothea Pakenham (1773–1831) was married in April 1806 at St. George's, Dublin, to Arthur Wellesley (1769–1852), 1st Duke of Wellington.

[4] Lady Templetown's house was at 65 Portland Place.

[5] On Saturday 3 July.

[6] Samuel Rogers built his house in 1803 at 22 St. James's Street, overlooking Green Park. John Flaxman (1755–1826) and Thomas Stothard (1755–1834) helped with the decorations but all details were overseen by Rogers, who brought to his modest-sized house pictures, engravings, antiquities, and books, all collected with a connoisseur's judgement.

[7] Anna Letitia Barbauld (1743–1825) and FB first met in December 1783 through Mrs. Chapone. The two women rarely came together, the last time being in 1798 (iv, L. 280 n. 3). After the dinner party at Rogers's house Mrs. Barbauld wrote to FBA suggesting the American publication of *The Wanderer* (L. 707 n. 1).

[8] Richard Brinsley Sheridan (1751–1816), a Whig M.P. (1780–1812) and the author of *The Rivals* (1775) and *The School for Scandal* (1777). FB first met Sheridan in 1779 at Mrs. Cholmondeley's house (*DL* i. 190) and more often at the Thrales's. As FB commented in 1779 (Barrett, Eg. 3690, f. 2–2b) to CB, Sheridan—along with others—'vociferously urged me [to write a comedy] *immediately*, & promised to ensure the Sale of as many copies in Ireland as would pay.' She suppressed *The Witlings* on the advice of CB and Mr. Crisp, but this did not dampen her friendship with the dramatist. In 1795 he encouraged the production of *Edwy and Elgiva* at the Drury Lane Theatre (21 Mar.) and invited FBA to see the performance from his box. See iii, L. 148 n. 1 and iv, L. 364 n. 2; *HFB*, pp. 132–8, 247; *Thraliana*, ii. 916 and n. 1.

leave town without seeking another chattery with *her* old friend, Dr Burney, whom she always saw with fresh pleasure.

Adieu, my most dear Padre—

ever most dutifully
your affect^e
FB. d'A. |

I have spent two more days at the Queen's house,⁹ where all was gracious—kind—& sweet.

711   [23 Chenies Street,

12 July 1813]

To Charles Burney

A.L. (Berg), *n.d.*
Double sheet 8vo large   3 pp.   *pmks*   T.P.P.U. / Tottenham CR 12 JY 1813   wafer
Addressed: Rev^d Dr. Burney, / Rectory House, / Deptford.
Docketed in pencil, p. 1: 1813   From F.B.

My dearest Carlucci,
What is to be done?
We must settle to-morrow for one. That you may write on Wednesday.

I should like to look once more at Longman's Papers before I fix. I entreat you, therefore, to send me them immediately.

I lament my ignorance of events!!—O could I build upon PEACE & RE-UNION, I would defer, in either decision, printing till next spring.

But—if forced off—the work would considerably suffer by losing its author for the Proofsheets.

I am less sanguine about printing for ourselves upon deliberation, though still *harping* there on: but the fear of difficulties from ABSENCE—from death on their side or ours, for our successor, &c &c   vs. |

What, ultimately, is your most permanent idea?
I know you won't be offended if I don't follow it—

<hr>

⁹ See Ll. 708 nn. 2, 3; 709 n. 7.

Charlotte offers to consult her & James's good & confidential friend Mr. Turnour[1] before I decide—Could he help our uncertain judgment?

Colborn proposes payment by *installments*, not *editions*—which I much prefer.

I am quite against *Editions.*[2]

I am so terribly little skilled in money matters, that I am—often—almost ready to toss up!—.

God bless you, dearest Carlos—ever—we must not break your appointment for the reply ⟨Courteous⟩.

712   [23 Chenies Street,
                                              14 July 1813]
To Charles Burney

A.L. (Berg), including (on p. 3) a draft or model in hand of FBA of a L.S. (3rd person), CB, Jr. and FBA to [Henry] Colburn. *n.d.*
Double sheet 4to   4 pp.   *pmk*   14 J⟨ ⟩1813   wafer
Addressed: Dr. Burney / Sandgate, / Kent —

My dear—dear Charles!—I am more grieved at this cruel & unexpected stroke than I can express.—May you be able to parry it, dearest Charles, by your active & vigourous precautions!—Can you have advice there? or must you return? I am unspeakably anxious to know what you must determine.[1]

For my own affairs, I am in much perplexity: but, as you seem so bent against poor C[olburn] I have just resolved to write to *him* definitively—as you will see on the other side the paper: for, knowing his vehement desire to obtain the business, I think it utterly wrong to make any delay, where it must necessarily end in disappointment.—

711. [1] For Sharon Turner's knowledge of copyright law and of contractual relations between booksellers and authors, see L. 653 n. 5. Ultimately Sharon Turner and Martin Charles Burney signed the 'Articles of Agreement' for FBA with Longman, Hurst, Rees, Orme, and Brown.
[2] According to the 'Articles of Agreement' for the sale of *The Wanderer* FBA, against her better judgement, gambled £1,500 on the book's going through a number of editions. See L. 713 n. 5.
712. [1] CB Jr. had been called unexpectedly to Sandgate 'by the indisposition of poor Rosette' (Ll. 714, 716). For the nature of her illness, see Ll. 655 n. 7, 715 and n. 7.

This moment our kind Charlotte returns from Mr. Turner. We have named NO names, but given copies of the several propositions. He decided for Col.'s on account of the 1750£ *down*. For, he says, any one known to be liable to go abroad, had better run the least risk possible in times such as these. He is against *Editions*, for obvious reasons, & for *Instalments*. But the *Bookseller* is the most important, he says: a man of credit & probity: & there are but few such—those most to be trusted in great Concerns, are soon named — — he ran over a few, at the head of which he placed Longman & Cadell—[2]

I should much like waiting your return to fix with Longman but that—if I go in October—for which I must always be prepared, & which is in all human appearance at present my destiny—I should be truly grieved to spend the whole time previously to my departure in proofsheet correcting which I must do, in such a case.[3] It will be heavy work so to finish! Yet I am too anxious to omit correcting the press myself. I rather prefer your plan in your Letter from Greenwich—[4] & *something* must be written for *Friday*, as appointed.[5]

Mr. Turner says that if Copyright is not specified I have no claim upon it at the stated period![6]—

[2] The name of Longman belonged to one of the oldest and richest bookselling firms in London. Not only had it a profitable past (helping, for example, to publish Johnson's *Dictionary*), but under the leadership of Thomas Norton Longman, the company had acquired such valuable copyrights as Lindley Murray's *English Grammar* and the *Lyrical Ballads* of Wordsworth and Coleridge. See Appendix V.

The honourable reputation of Cadell and Davies descended from its founder Thomas Cadell (1742–1802) who, after retiring in 1793, passed management of the firm to his son. FBA knew Thomas Cadell I when he joined with Thomas Payne and Son to publish *Cecilia* (1782). She sold the copyright of *Camilla* on 6 July 1796 to Cadell and Davies (the newly reorganized partnership of Thomas Cadell II and William Davies) and to Thomas Payne II.

[3] FBA was not to return to France until November 1814. She always read her proofs and in 1813, preparing to publish *The Wanderer*, she wanted to avoid the grammatical errors, the Gallicisms, the repetitions, the unclear sentences for which the reviewers of *Camilla* (eds. E. and L. Bloom, pp. 915–27) had attacked her in 1796.

[4] CB Jr. sent FBA two separate letters that recommended stipulations for publication of *The Wanderer*; see L. 713.

[5] FBA did not wait for Friday 16 July, but sent Martin Burney to Owen Rees on the 15th with CB Jr.'s proposals. See L. 713.

[6] Sharon Turner, as a copyright specialist, insisted on the inclusion of the following in the 'Articles of Agreement' (Osborn) between FBA and her booksellers. 'Provided always and it is agreed that in case the said notes [of the booksellers] or any or either of them shall not be made or delivered as aforesaid or paid when due that it shall be lawful for the said Frances D'Arblay her executors administrators and assigns to give notice in writing of her or their intention to resume the copyright of the said work to the said Thomas Norton Longman

My state of health makes it IMPOSSIBLE for me to risk a later voyage than the heart of October it *ought* to be the beginning —for cold & destruction are *one* with me.—

Therefore—I am rather—all considered—for terminating— I can hear from you before I send off, if you can write by return of post—Shall I say

Dr. B. presents &c & is charged to — —

No—unless you have some reasons for delay or better hopes that I don't divine, I think I will write an acceptance at once! — — for affairs go on là bas so as to give no hope I can catch it rationally, & *therefore* it will be wise to *secure* what is offered. Could I *stay*, I should act just the reverse! but alas!—Let me hear at all events for at all events, I must, of course, write on Friday—& I don't like to trifle, when I do not see *2 paths* clearly. |

Dr. Charles Burney presents his Compliments to Mr. Colborn, & desires that the business in which they have mutually interested themselves, may no longer impede any arrangements which Mr. Colborn may have in contemplation, as his sister does not hold herself at liberty to part with the Copy right MS., upon the terms offered, without a fresh communication from Paris.

Dr. Burney & his Sister unite in offering their thanks to Mr. Colborn for his very obliging proceeding, & their concern for his useless trouble. |

Love to your dear Rosette & to Mrs. Parr & Fannetta—Is Carlino with you?

Thomas Hurst   Owen Rees   Cosmo Orme   and Thomas Brown or the survivors or survivor of them or the executors or administrators of such survivor who upon receipt of such notice shall lose and forfeit the copyright of the said work and shall not be at liberty to print or publish any future edition or to sell the copies of such editions as shall have been printed but that the said Frances D'Arblay her executors administrators and assigns shall and may after such notice be at full liberty to print and publish the said work or to enter into any fresh contract with any person whomsoever for the disposal of the copyright thereof.'

[23 Chenies Street],
15 July 1813

Conjointly with Martin Charles Burney
To Charles Burney

A.L. & A.L.S. (Osborn), 15 July 1813
Double sheet small 4to   3 pp.   *pmk*   15 JY 1813   wafer
Addressed: Dr. Burney / Sand Gate, / Kent,

July 15 1813—
My dearest Charles,
I am longing to hear how you go on—I need not, I am sure,
say, with what anxiety.
Mean while, after weighing both your Letters as well as I
was able, I preferred the counsel of the 1st i.e. making the
larger proposal, to the 2d i e. deferring the treaty for 6 weeks,
because of my terrible incertitude whether in that case I
should have time to revise, without being a slave to the Proofs,
at the very time that You—& Charlotte—& Esther & James
are all within reach. For now, Charlotte is gone off with Dolph
for change of air[1]—& Esther to Turnham Green, & James to
Richmond with Mrs. B[urney] & Sally; & Charlotte Barret, in
a fortnight, means also to take a 2 Months sea breathing.[2]
This weighed,—I gave the Commission, in your name, to
the good & active & amiable Martin[3]—to whom I transferred
the proposal you made, tearing off all above & below, as a
Credential to shew, in your own hand writing, with an excuse

713. [1] CBFB and Dolph were now with the Barretts in Richmond. Although mother
and son had planned to spend the holiday at Bradfield Hall, according to MF in a
letter (JRL) to Mrs. Piozzi on 23 Aug. 1813, 'Dolph fell ill, & had the sea-side
prescribed him by London Physicians; so they are gone to Brighton together.'
Dolph continued to ail. By 4 September they were in lodgings in Great Bookham.
Sally Burney sent her aunt a letter (Barrett, Eg. 3700A, ff. 140–1) expressing the
'hope [that] Dolph is getting better, and that Bookham air agrees with him'.
[2] See L. 702 n. 4. CFBt and her family spent about seven weeks at Sandgate,
for in a letter (Osborn) to FBA on 11 Sept. 1813 CB Jr. mentioned that 'Sarah
leaves me with the Barretts, on Monday Sennight', i.e. on 20 September.
[3] Martin Charles Burney, always in consultation with Turner and CB Jr.,
helped to negotiate with Longman and his associates until the 'Articles of Agreement' for the sale of *The Wanderer* were written. He affixed his signature on 4 Nov.
1813.

for your sudden absence, that you did not see or write yourself. It was most fortunate that bit was *shewable*, for it gave propriety to the Measure. N.B. I cut off '*Scrubs*.'[4]—Martin shall write what passed himself— |

[*By Martin Charles Burney*]

Dear Uncle

I called on Mr Rees in Paternoster Row this morning and made him the offer you prescribed in your Letter to my Aunt, viz £3000—£1500 to be paid immediately, £500 when the work is printed £500 in six months afterwards and the remaining £500 in six months after that. Mr Rees asked me if I had any authority from you to consent to any alteration.[5] I of course told him I had none, that I could hear his proposals and communicate to you or that he might write to you at Sandgate. Mr Rees said he would write by this night's post—I left him your direction written on the back of a piece of your Letter containing the offer which my Aunt cut off for the purpose of shewing him. This was all that passed. By Mr Rees' manner I do not think he intended proposing any material alteration, and I think the probability is that he will consent to the offer. I am Dear Uncle

Your very affectionate Nephew

15 July 1813 Martin Chas Burney |

[*By Madame d'Arblay*]

The post is going

[4] '*Scrubs*' is a colloquialism for 'One who pays not his whack at the tavern' or simply 'a shabby fellow'. See Eric Partridge, *A Dictionary of Slang and Unconventional English* (1961).
[5] These details were tentative. What was finally agreed to by both sides was the booksellers' payment of £1,500 for the first edition of *The Wanderer* (£500 on delivery of the manuscript, £500 six months after publication, £500 a year after publication), and of another £1,500 for five subsequent editions (£500 for the second and £250 each for the third to the sixth editions).

714

To Mrs. Broome *and* Mrs. Barrett

A.L.S. (Berg), *n.d.*
Double sheet 8vo   4 pp.
Addressed: Mrs. Barret

Dear Congress,
　　As a suppliant I now come before you—but not
　　　　as a Candidate for a Kingdom,
　　　　Not as a pilferer for spoil,
　　　　Not as a spinster for Royal alliance
　　　　Not as an Exile for violated property,
　　Those, & such minor claims, the modern demands of
hundreds, I leave to the Germanic body. Nevertheless, Dear
Congress! though excluding all these, I come for that in which
All ought to be included, Justice! — —
　　to deprecate your Wrath — — — — yet own, faintly,

I cannot come on monday!²—

　　I don't yet hear my own rights from the Clamour of hisses
that whizz in my Ears! Alas, alas, when may *I* speak?—When
will you listen? I ᶦ am so overpowered by wry faces, I know not
which way to turn my Eyes.
　　'And she said *I* should decide!' cries one,—'This is her
promise!'
　　''Tis abominable really!' cries another, whom I will not
name — —
　　Kind Host! fair Hostess,—
　　Dear Congress, all!
　　　Hear Me! — — —

---

714. ¹ This letter can be dated 16 July 1813. The 'appointment for yesterday'
to which FBA refers below took place on 15 July (L. 713). Moreover, she acknowledges the departure of CB Jr. 'the day before' the scheduled appointment. It is
possible that he left for Sandgate as early as 13 July, for FBA addressed her letter
of 12 July (L. 711) to the Deptford rectory but her letter of 14 July (L. 712) to
Sandgate.
　² 19 July.

Il est question, *in* this moment, of a little bit of property — —
elect,—

> To be transferred
>> from the present Possessor,
>> by a circuit, through an Agent far off,
>> to an Agent near at hand
> To an Actual Expectant.—[3]

This is the history.

Now, when Sancho Panca relates some wonders to an
Audience, who seem to marvel rather than believe,
>> he says
There stands My lord Don Quixote to say if I tell truth! [1]
Thus, DEAR CONGRESS! your humble suppliant says
Yonder stands Martin Charles Burney,
>> to certify whether this be a fact.—
>> And now, Dear Congress,
>> including the absent Member,
>>> Mr. ARCHDEACON CAMBRIDGE,
>> with whose Time, carriage, & kindness you make
>>> so free—
>>>> I remain, with a clear Conscience,
>>>> but a sorrowing spirit,
>>>>> Your affectionate suppliant
>>>>>> *F.B. d'A.*[4]

Really & most truly, Dearest Charlotte, I am much vexed:
but my Brother Cha[s] had made an appointment for *yesterday*
relative to a little affair of mine which shall be nameless, (&
which I dare say you cannot guess,) but the day before he was

---

[3] '[A] little bit of property [*The Wanderer*] . . . To be transferred from the
present Possessor [FBA] . . . through an Agent far off [CB Jr.], to an Agent near
at hand [Martin Charles Burney] To an Actual Expectant [Longman, Hurst,
Rees, Orme, and Brown].'
[4] The whole first part of this letter whimsically rejects CFBt's invitation to visit
Richmond; it rejects also the use of George Owen Cambridge's carriage at nearby
Twickenham Meadows as a conveyance from Chelsea to Richmond. FBA's
decision stemmed from the current negotiations with Rees for *The Wanderer*'s
sale.

called suddenly away to Sand-Gate by the indisposition of poor Rosette. Thus left to myself, neither chusing to appear, or to offend, I put the matter into the hands of my favourite Martin: whom I have seen twice, & who undertakes it with vivacity & intelligence. We cannot till next week have an answer to certain lines sent to Sand Gate,[5] thence to be else where transmitted, &c | 'tis a truly provoking, & unforseen circumstance, & I cannot, till after the post hour on Monday, even mention any day! But I must be upon the spot, in this first opening of debates & propositions, so unfortunately begun at a season so unpropitious. Martin is active, spirited, & sanguine.

I *fear Thursday*[6] will be the earliest day I can be free!—but I am not without *hope* to be sooner. *Your* time will be then so gone, that perhaps you would rather wait your return from the seaside? or will you accept 3 or 4 days?—Be sincere, Dearest Charlotte. Alex is almost non compos at this delay. Loves all round.

715   [23] Chenies Street,
                                          16–17 August 1813
To Charles Parr Burney

A.L.S. (Berg), 16–17 Aug. 1813
Double sheet 4to (9·2 × 7·7″), from the top of the second leaf of which a segment (3 × 7·7″) has been removed   3 pp.   wafer
Addressed: Revd Charles Burney, / Greenwich, / Kent

August 16th 1813.
Chenies Street,
to Day—
Chelsea, Je crois,
to-morrow.

Dear Nephew,
    Alexander has not been, I trust, more a truant than becomes the dignity of the first form: I will not, therefore, waste apologies upon that score, having matter abundant for them upon

⁵ Martin Burney's letter to CB Jr. (L. 713).
⁶ 22 July, just a week prior to CFBt's departure for Sandgate.

another: i.e, that I did not thank you for the most disinterested account[1] I ever received, nor give you notice when I had settled it at Mr. Child's.[2] I shall cut, however, short all confession of my misdemeanour, by letting it serve as a balance for your own, in promising a visit, & a chattery, that have never been performed.

So now we are quits.—

On MY Side, however, the scales again begin to weigh heaviest —again You will take my Boy under your tuition & protection, & again, therefore, have charge of a massy portion of my happiness.[3]—

My kind Brother has made me the welcome proposition of inserting your Name, conjointly with that of Martin, in the agreement in which his own stands as principal with Longman & Co.—& Martin assures me that your free consent seconds the motion. Thanks, dear Charles. I may travel far & near, & never find more honourable trustees.[4]

My last news of my dear Brother was very satisfactory—I will not now enter upon family subjects: yet I cannot refrain from telling you how much I honoured the exertion which spared your dear Father a melancholy & difficult journey, to which his health was really unequal.

I hear from Mrs. Barret—no small judge in those matters —nor, indeed, in any other—that my every way little niece— or great, which is it?[5]—is made up of engaging qualities. I long to hear that her amiable mother has recovered strength & bloom.

I entreat you, my dear Charles, if it be possible, to let Alexander walk forth to stretch his limbs. Mr. Thomas[6] declares

715. [1] FBA consistently refused CB Jr.'s offer to assume financial responsibility for AA's schooling (see, e.g., L. 652). In this letter she acknowledges receipt of bills accrued by AA at Greenwich School from November 1812 to June 1813.

[2] The banking firm for CB Jr. and the Greenwich School was Child & Co., Temple Bar, London.

[3] In preparation for his matriculation at Caius College (Michaelmas term, 1813), AA was about to return to Greenwich School for special tutoring in mathematics and the classics.

[4] If CPB's name appeared in preliminary documents for the sale of *The Wanderer*, it disappeared from the final 'Articles of Agreement'. The only Burneys named therein were FBA, CB Jr. as administrator, and Martin Charles Burney as a witness to the signatures.

[5] CPB's daughter Frances Anne (FBA's grand-niece) was now with her mother and grandfather at Sandgate.

[6] See L. 676 n. 2.

exercise to be essential to him: & his looks are visibly better or worse in proportion as he attends to that ordinance. It will make him, also pine less after that sedentary, seductive, & pondering thought-waster, Chess. I am by no means quite tranquil as to his health.—!

Adieu, Dear Nephew,

ever yours,

F B d'Arblay.

I beg my best compts. to Mrs. Bicknel.

I need not—I am sure, say how I shall rejoice in better news from the Rectory!⁷ |

[six or seven lines are cut away from the top of page 3]

Aug^st 17. 1813

I have this moment received your kind exhortation, my dear Charles, & I will only give Alex a hasty dinner, ere I obey its injunction. My heart aches at every separation, from a dread uncertainty relative to our future meetings. At present, my last Letter from Paris tells me to remain here till the end of October.⁸ —I hope, therefore, to see him safely installed at Cambridge before my departure — —

I have this moment a tolerably good account of dear Dolph. He does not find that sea bathing agrees with him: but he rides & drinks *Donkey*,⁹ & my sister Broome finds him better, both for that diet & that gentle exercise.

Thanks for your family intelligence—may it soon be more propitious—

I am here for some business, but proceeding as fast as I can to Chelsea.

---

⁷ Rosette Burney, still depressive, had left Sandgate and returned to the rectory at Deptford (see L. 716 and n. 5).

⁸ A letter from M. d'A, dated 4 May 1813 (see L. 697).

⁹ FBA refers to ass's milk, which was assumed to have curative value. See the work published in 1753: *A treatise on the extraordinary Virtues and Effects of Ass's Milk in the Cure of various Disorders, particularly the Gout and Scurvy; and of its nourishing quality in all Consumptive Diseases, and even the Decays of Old Age.*

716 [23] Chenies Street,
21 August 1813

To Charles Burney

A.L. (Berg), 21 Aug. 1813
Double sheet 4to   4 pp.   *pmk*   27 A⟨U⟩   ⟨18⟩13   seal
Addressed: Rev^d Dr. C. Burney, / Sand Gate, / Kent.

Aug^st 21st
1813
Chenies Street—Incog.

What a most unnatural silence would this have been, my
dearest Charles, had my heart & enquiries been as dumb as my
hand!—but I hear of you continually—*circuitously*, indeed,
which by no means rivals the strait forward *directly*, any more in
intelligence than in morals; but I am fain, when no uneasiness
urges me onward, to be content with any bye path that will
bring me but news of those I love. Am I flattered, dearest
Carlucci—or are you really stouter & better?[1] & able to cogitate
with omphos in a *brown study*, in the morning, & willing to be
frisky & agreeable, in your vulgar tongue, in an evening?[2] I
say *your* vulgar tongue, for I would not have you forget your
share in our common property.

What is your plan? I am very anxious to hear; & that
anxiety it is that brings me again into this high road—for tired
I am of my Pen! Oh tired! tired! oh! should it tire others in the
same proportion—alas for poor Messrs. Longman & Rees!—&
alas for poorer ME!—

The work, however, is done[3]—what fatigues me is copying
illegibilities; & that I am now labouring at almost incessantly,
& yet but little advanced.

---

716. [1] At Sandgate CB Jr. continued to experience headaches probably sympto-
matic of high blood pressure. Moreover, his gout (from which he suffered even
during the summer) had reached an advanced stage. For current medical prog-
nosis, see *Enc. Brit.*, 3rd ed., xi. 180.

[2] At this time CB Jr. was committed to contributions to *Euripidis Hercules Furens*
(Glasgow, 1820), *Euripidis Electra* (Glasgow, 1820), *Euripidis Opera Omnia* (Glasgow,
1821), and *Sophoclis quae extant omnia* (London, 1824).

[3] This is the first letter, available to the editors, that acknowledges the completion of an entire draft of *The Wanderer*.

163

What, however, is your plan? I long truly to see you—yet, before you return, my conscience worries my affection to represent that return you ought not at present! — — |

Certainly, my dearest Carlos, you have been too long harrassed with that pain in the head, to make it safe for you to risk losing your amendment, by feeding melancholy feelings. If your poor Rosette could benefit by the sacrifice of your nerves, that might pay any suffering; but your strength & spirits are her best support, as well as your own, &, for both your sakes, you must preserve them for the period when you may enjoy them together.[4]

She wants nothing—or, rather, alas, can partake of nothing but care & medical skill. She is in her own house, as she has desired, & she is super-intended & visited by her & your good & affectionate son, who will satisfy her, equally with yourself, that she is not abandonened;[5] &, when she is restored, she will be the first to feel & confess, that prudence & judgment, & therefore real kindness, call upon you, at this interval, to avoid all afflicting exertions.

Stay on, therefore, at Sandgate—or make some other excursion, till poor dear Rosette shall be able to appreciate your tenderness, & reciprocate every comfort. Your sight then will complete her recovery, without any longer endangering your own. May it be speedy! |

I am, my self, in a state of the extremest perplexity, with respect to my stay, or departure. I have received, lately, several Letters from Paris, but none are explicit: for example, the last 3 express themselves thus differently upon the subject. —The 1st says—We can so certainly never separate again, that I desire you to finish completely all our business, before your Voyage.—This seems unlimitted stay![6]—

---

[4] The ailments of CB Jr. were aggravated by his concern for Rosette's health. In a letter (Osborn), dated 11 Sept. 1813, he wrote from Sandgate to FBA: 'My gout has thrice renewed the attack;—but is *again* off—but I am horribly lame.'
[5] It was not unusual for Rosette, when severely depressed, to avoid CB Jr. In July 1812, she urged him to leave Deptford so that she could occupy the rectory alone. Such behaviour was implied by CPB in a letter (Bodleian), dated 15 July, to Finch: 'I cannot leave my Father, who is now mine & my Wife's guest.—My Mother, I am grieved to add, is quite an *Invalide* & my Father's Rectory is in no state to receive him.'
[6] L. 665, dated 31 Dec. 1812–Feb. 1813.

The last *but one says*:—When I desire you to finish all before you return, I don't mean that you should exceed September!— No, I would rather every thing went to ruin![7]—

⟶

The *last of all* says: You tell me you do not think you can be ready to come back before September:—I can easily believe it, as you have had so long a confinement with your influenza,— consequently, I give you to the end of October—when, well wrapt up, there can be no risk. *&c.*[8]

⟶

What can one make out of all this? Because I demand to stay till *September*, he voluntarily offers me to stay to the END of October!—6 weeks more than I claim—

I won't tell you my conjecture till I hear yours.[9]

But it is always terrible to have only conjecture for a Guide! Oh that he were here!—that he were here! — —

My dear son is with yours.—

My uncertainty of time perplexes & distresses my decision for printing. I would not take a *bad* moment, if I can be here for a *good* one. Mr. Rees says it is not well to come forth before Christmas— ׀ but before the meeting of Parliament would be quite *ill*:[10] nevertheless, that all is preferable to publishing in my absence.—

I know not what to do, but to wait to the last possible moment for fresh directions.

I hear an excellent account of my dearest Father—but Chelsea is not yet open.[11] My dear Esther is lively & well, & Amelia[12] is come to her fortune!—James is his own Man again,

---

[7] L. 689, dated 12 Apr. 1813.

[8] See the conclusion of the letter of M. d'A to FBA, dated 4 July 1813 (Appendix II).

[9] The conjecture is seemingly clarified in L. 718: 'There is a wish the present campaign should be over before my return, that I may go by Calais or Dunquerque.' But see L. 727, wherein M. d'A urged FBA not to depart before May 1814.

[10] The second session of the fifth Parliament of the United Kingdom of Great Britain and Ireland opened on 4 Nov. 1813.

[11] FBA last received in July 'a few "pleasing words" ' from CB in a letter (Osborn). For evidence of his desire to remain a recluse, see L. 699 n. 3.

[12] Having reached the age of 21, EBB's daughter Amelia Maria was eligible for £1000 bequeathed to her by her godmother the Hon. Mrs. William Bateman (v, L. 517 n. 5).

& his two Sarahs are bonny. Martin is excellent & most satisfactory in business. Mr. Rees sings his praise, though an antagonist.—

Messrs Longman are ready to sign whenever I am willing to print—but I had far rather lose a little interest of Money, than any I can avoid of something better: I am at this moment quite incog—because immensely busy, in Chenies Street. Poor Dolph and his mother are at Brighton, & they assure me the air strengthens him.[13] Remember me most kindly to the amiable Fanny at your side, & to her bright little one[14] My best love to my dear Charlotte—& kiss her lovely loves for me, & assure Mr. Barret of my sincere regard. If there be another personage of the Burney tribe within your reach, cast at her my Gauntlet![15] She did nothing but worry: skurry me to quit my dear Esther abruptly for Chelsea, while she was worry skurrying her self, all the time, to quit Chelsea at the same moment! an affront that demands solid satisfactio⟨n⟩ Pens & Pouts, till we Fire off Lampoons with whatever Weapon, Time & place she will name or, Parleyings & parryings till we rush forwards to an Embrace.

Adieu, my dearest Charles—

I miss my *sauvage*—Oh how I miss him! What shall I do at the end of October!—what terrible strings pull each way!—

What say the *Politicians*? I see none.

Do you meet Mr. Wilberforce?[16] |

Good Mrs. Cooke of Bookham, tells me that her daughter, who never could *get through a Novel* but of the first Water, could not part with Traits of Nature.[17]—I don't write upon business, for Martin says 'tis done.

---

[13] See L. 713 n. 1.

[14] FBA's oblique reference to Brightblossom, the nickname CB Jr. gave to his first grandchild. His devotion to the child is evident in at least two playful poems (JRL): 'To Brightblossom, my Grand-Daughter, on being left in the Gout, at Sandgate, when she returned home with her Mother, August 31st 1813' and 'To Brightblossom, July 15th 1814', addressed to 'Miss Burney, of Greenwich, at Ryde'. See L. 724A n. 3.

[15] SHB (see L. 713 n. 2).

[16] The Wilberforce family left for Sandgate in late June. See the letter of MF (L. 699 n. 4). For FBA's meeting with Mr. Wilberforce, see L. 723.

[17] Mary Cooke (1781–*post* 1820), the daughter of Samuel and Cassandra Cooke (iv, L. 263 n. 7).

717 [23 Chenies Street],
24 August [1813]
To Doctor Burney

A.L.S. (Diary MSS. vii. 5902–[02c], 24 Aug.
Double sheet 8vo (7·2 × 4·4″)   4 pp.
Addressed: Dr. Burney, / Chelsea College, / Chelsea—
Edited by FBA, p. 1 (5902), *annotated and dated*:   ⚬ 1813   (11)   a seal
Susan & Sophy Thrale   Marianne Francis—
Edited by CFBt, who by cutting and pasting, conflated the text with that
of the A.L.S., FBA to CB, [10 July 1813]   *See* Textual Notes.

Augs^t 24th

Your Seal, my dearest Padre, waits but for opportunity to
throw itself at your feet. I have brought it twice to you, in my
little Green bag, but I have found always so little time, & so
much to hear & say, that I have never recollected my poor
fellow-voyager till my return; & he never put me in mind of
my neglect. He was sulky, perhaps, & no wonder, for he
certainly is not used to be treated with such apathy. His
appearence, he well knows, is accustommed to excite gratitude,
& awaken hope & pleasure, as the sure Herald of Wit, Humour,
Information, or Kindness—who then can be surprised that he
should resent being | denied the light, which only shines upon
him for other people's profit?—

I am very, very busy indeed,—as I will explain when we meet.
I make one visit, to-morrow, nevertheless, from circumstances
that render it unavoidable: 'tis to my faithful old friends Sophy
& Susan Thrale, whom, from my illness, or theirs, or from my
absence from town, or their's, I have never yet visited in all this
time.[1] And they are amongst my most constant & affectionate
adherents. They are now in town only for a Week. They always
enquire most respectfully about my dearest Father: for they
have been to me *here*, & they write often. L^y Keith is always at
Plymouth to my great regret[2]— |

Poor Charles, the Rev^d, I hear with great concern is again
menaced with the Gout. I cannot but desire that a real fit,

717. [1] Susanna Arabella Thrale and Mrs. Henry Merrick Hoare visited FBA on
12 May 1813 (see L. 692 n. 10).
    [2] See L. 684 n. 3.

however painful, would liberate him from such continual threat & alarm, & make him completely his own Man again.[3]

I have lost my dear *sauvage*—& I miss him terribly.[4] I left our Esther & her excellent Mate, & good Amelia, quite well & blyth at Turnham Green,— they renew & revive every year by a rural breeze, that seems to *youngify* them from the noxious blights of their laborious winters. [7 *or* 8 *lines cut out*] | she [Marianne Francis] so loads herself with literary lumber, only to carry from her Bed room to her parlour, that she has fallen down stairs with her study upon her head, & hurt herself a good deal. May we not here say

'Tis folly to be wise?—at least, learned, to such an orkbornian excess.[5]

YOU pretended to be the Father, dear Sir, of that sect: at least you may now be styled the literal Grand father.

adieu, my ever dearest Padre! most dutifully &

affect[y] y[rs]

FB d'A

I hope you have good news from Sarah?[6] |—

718   [23 Chenies Street],
                                    26 August 1813
To Mrs. Waddington

A.L. (Diary MSS. vii. 5898–[5901], Berg), 26 Aug. 1813
Double sheet 4to   4 pp.   foliated 11, 12 *pmks* CHARLES STREET
24 AU .813   red seal
Addressed: Mrs. Waddington, / Lanover, / Abergavenny—
Edited by CFBt *and the* Press. *See* Textual Notes.

Aug[st] 26th 1813

I cannot yet reconcile myself to your flight, my dearest Mary, nor think of it without regret.[1] I had millions of hoarded

---

[3] See L. 698 n. 2.   [4] See L. 715 n. 3.
[5] Dr. Orkborne was the pedant ridiculed in *Camilla*. This is the most open FBA had been about her niece, whose intellectual interests made her a 'prodigy' (L. 646 n. 17).
[6] SHB sought remedy for rheumatic lameness in sea-bathing. In 1812 she went to Lymington (L. 637 n. 30). In 1813 she stayed at Sandgate with CB Jr.
718. [1] Mrs. Waddington and her family had left 9 Holles Street, Cavendish Square, and returned to Llanover. For their arrival in London two months earlier, see L. 699.

details, *in petto*, for demanding & recounting, & the fullness of my occupations, & the shortness of our meetings, & my reliance upon the approach of better opportunities, checked with me all but passing subjects.—yet I must not, I know, prolong this theme, nor give it its full weight, for the retrospection is now every way unavailing.—

I thank you for Mr. Sandford's entertaining letter;[2] I have not the most distant notion of the pathos of Miss Gubbins:[3] but I conclude she existed in some merry freak of imagination urged by your passionate taste—in those days—for sportive vagaries: Pray, however, thank Mr. S[andford] for remembering me. I shall never forget his worthy Mother, nor her reverence for our most loved.[4]

Your Charming Girls too—how I lament knowing so little of them! Fanny, by what I can gather, has seen, upon the whole, a great deal of this vast town & its splendours; a little more might perhaps have been better, in making her, with a mind such as hers, regret it a little less. Merit of her sort can here difficultly be known. Dissipation is so hurried, so always in a bustle, that even Amusement must be prominent to be enjoyed. There is no time for devellopment; nothing, therefore, is seen but what is conspicuous, & not much is heard, but what is obstreperous. They who, *in a short time*, can make themselves known & admired now in London, must have their Cupids—in Earle Dorsetes phrase, like blackguard Boys,

who thrust their links full in your face.[5] |

[2] Daniel Sandford (1766–1830) was born in Dublin, the second son of the Revd. Daniel (*c.* 1729–70) and Sarah Sandford (n. 4). Matriculating at Christ Church on 26 Nov. 1783, he received his B.A. 1787, M.A. 1791, and D.D. 1802. Made Bishop of Edinburgh in 1806, he remained in that position until his death. See i, L. 9 n. 3.

[3] Invented in the past by Mrs. Waddington for the pleasure of her friends, Miss Gubbins was probably a comic character noted for her crudity. Gubbins was a synonym for certain inhabitants near Dartmoor said to be unmitigated barbarians.

[4] FBA met Mrs. Delany's god-daughter Sarah Sandford *née* Chapone (*c.* 1732–93) on 7 July 1783. 'I spent the whole day with sweet Mrs. Delany, whom I love most tenderly. . . . We had no company but Mrs. Sandford, an old lady who was formerly her *élève*, and who seems well worthy that honour' (*DL* ii. 216).

[5] From 'Song' on 'Dorinda's sparkling wit and eyes' (1701), by Charles Sackville (1638–1706), 6th Earl of Dorset:

> Love is a calmer gentler joy,
> Smooth are his looks, and soft his pace;
> Her Cupid is a blackguard boy,
> That runs his link full in your face.

I had very much matter that I meant & wished to say to you upon this subject; but, brief—I do not, myself, think it a misfortune that your Fanny cannot move in a London round, away from your own wing. You have brought her up so well, & she seems so good, gentle, & contented, as well as accomplished, that I cannot wish her drawn into a vortex where she may be impregnated with other ideas, views, & wishes than those that now constitute happiness—& happiness! what ought to be held more sacred, where it is innocent? what ought so little to risk any unnecessary—or premature concussion? With all the deficiencies & imperfections of her present situation which You bewail, but which SHE does not find out, it is—alas, a MILLION to one whether, even in attaining the advantages & society you so sigh to see fall to her share, she will EVER again, after *ANY* change, be as happy as she is at this moment.[6] A Mother whom she looks up to, & doats upon—an Emily whom she so fondly loves,—how shall they be re-placed?—The chances are all against her, (though the World *has*, *I* know, such replacers,) from their rarity.

I am truly glad you had a gratification you so earnestly covetted, that of seeing Mad^e de Staël. Your account of her was extremely interesting to me. As to my speaking of you, my dearest Mary, I must much change my opinion of her penetration, if I can suppose that necessary, however little you might say when you have those looks called forth which express your feelings of admiration. And surely they were eminently called forth for Her!—As to myself—I have not seen her at all. Various causes have kept me in utter retirement. And, in truth, with respect to Me de Staël my situation is really embarrassing. It is too long, & difficult, to write upon,—nor do I recollect whether I ever communicated to [you] our original acquaintance, which, at first, was *INTIMATE*. I shall always, internally, be grateful, for the unbounded partiality with which she sought me out upon her arrival in this Country before my marriage: & still, & far MORE, if she can forgive my *dropping her*, which I could not help; for none of my friends, at that time, would

---

[6] FBA's opinion that Frances Waddington should be kept away from the London round or even be denied a London season inhibits the girl's attaining the wisdom and experience that came to the heroine of *Evelina* (1778) from such activity. In the case of Frances Waddington FBA was probably motivated by her own inability to chaperone the girl through a social whirl.

suffer me to keep up the intercourse![7] I had messages—
remonstrances—entreaties—representations Letters & Conferences, till I could resist no longer, though I had found her
so charming, that I fought the hardest battle I dared fight
against almost ALL my best connexions!—For Heaven's sake
let not a word of this transpire!—She is I now received by all
mankind—but that, indeed, she always was—all womankind,
I should say, with distinction & pleasure.—I wish much to see
her essay on suicide:[8] but it has not yet fallen in my way. When
will the work come out for which she was, she says, *chassée de la
France?*[9]—Where did your Fanny hear her a whole evening?[10]
She is, indeed, most uncommonly entertaining; & animating, as
well as animated, almost beyond any body. Les Memoires de
Mad^e de Staal I *have* read,[11] long ago, & with singular interest
& eagerness. They are so attaching, so evidently original, &
natural, that they stand very high indeed, in reading that has
given me most pleasure.—My Boy has just left me for Greenwich. He goes in October to Cambridge. I wish to install him
there myself. My last Letter from Paris gives me to the END of

[7] Enjoying the company of both Mme de Staël and M. de Narbonne in 1793,
FB yielded to the pressure of CB's friends that she end her 'Intimacy' with both.
See the letter (ii, L. 52) of James Hutton, who wrote of the 'Diabolical Democrate'
who 'came here to follow Mr de Narbonne'. Hutton's position was supported by
the Burkes, Mrs. Ord, *et al*. FB defended Mme de Staël before CB and James Hutton,
but soon capitulated (ii, L. 53; *HFB*, pp. 230–1). See v, L. 541 for her reluctance
to see Mme de Staël in Paris, but L. 735 for her continuing admiration of the
Frenchwoman's intelligence and generosity.

[8] *Réflexions sur le suicide* (1813) also appeared in an English translation that same
year.

[9] On 27 Sept. 1813 *The Times* announced that 'speedily will be published'
Mme de Staël's *De L'Allemagne* in three volumes. The work appeared in October
with its English translation *On Germany*. According to its Preface, the work,
completed in 1810, 'preserved a studied silence on the existing French Government. . . . and after 10,000 copies had, with [the censors's] permission, been printed,
Savary, the Minister of Police, seized and destroyed the whole impression, compelled Madame De Stael to give up the original manuscript, and ordered her to quit
France, her native country, within 24 hours.' See *GM* lxxxiii², 461. For a more
personal account of her book, see Mme de Staël's letter of 1810 to Juliette Récamier,
in *The Memoirs and Correspondence of Madame Récamier*, ed. Isaphene M. Luyster
(Boston, 1882), p. 72.

[10] Probably at the home of Sir James Mackintosh (n. 14), who was a friend of
the Waddingtons and an admirer of Mme de Staël.

[11] FBA had in mind Mme de Staël's *De l'influence des passions sur le bonheur des
individus et des nations* (Lausanne, 1796) or its English translation *A Treatise on the
Influence of the Passions upon the Happiness of Individuals and of Nations . . . to which is
prefixed a Sketch of her Life, by the Translator* (London, 1798). The English translation
was reissued on or about 16 Aug. 1813 in order to capitalize on Mme de Staël's
presence in England that year. For FBA's examination of her work in 1797, see
iii, L. 237.

October to stay in England. There is a wish the present campaign should be over before my return, that I may go by Calais
or Dunquerque. I dread inexpressibly the long passage by
Morlaix—Adieu, my ever dear Mary—Heaven grant you may
be enabled to send me better news of your own—& your poor
sweet Emily's health!—I had much to tell you of H[er]
M[ajesty] & P[rincess] E[lizabeth]—all *KIND* & desirable—I
spoke to L^y Crewe, as you will find, if ever you meet.[12] I made,
at last, my visit to Richmond, & was ill the whole time!—
keeping my room!—But I am quite well, now. I h[ave] a MS.
for you from our good Mrs. Astle[y][13] [*seal*]—adieu—My love
to yr dear Girls [*seal*] & Mr. Waddington. |

Was it YOU told me Sr J^s Mackintosh was very much *provoked*
that I would not speak with ⟨him⟩.[14] If so, make my peace,
I pray. |

NB My Brother has finally settled with Mr. Longman—
though all is still unsigned & in my hand, but pray can any-
thing be done—or proposed about Mr. Brevort?[15] in *concert* with
Mr Longman? or is it too late?

My dear Sister Charlotte is at Brighton with her lovely Boy—
I dare not think of your terrifying opinion! He is *better* at this
moment—but far from right!—[16]

Mr. Jeffreys Letter is very entertaining.[17] I am glad you forget
⟨poor⟩ Mr Alison.[18]

---

[12] See L. 699.

[13] Anne *née* Astley (*c.* 1748–1836) had been Mrs. Delany's gentlewoman-
companion. Mrs. Waddington, Mrs. Delany's great-niece, retained a friendly
interest in Mrs. Agnew, whose letter is missing.

[14] Sir James Mackintosh (1765–1832), first trained as a doctor and then as a
lawyer, was also a philosopher who enjoyed writing and reviewing for such
periodicals as the *Monthly Review* and the *Edinburgh Review* (L. 735 n. 9). He was
knighted in 1803 when he accepted Henry Addington's offer of the recordership
of Bombay; he remained in that post until 12 Oct. 1811.

[15] See Ll. 706, 707. Apparently Mr. Brevoort negotiated successfully with
Eastburn, Kirk & Company, who published *The Wanderer* in New York in 1814.

[16] Though Mrs. Waddington had diagnosed Dolph's condition as 'consumptive',
as late as 11 Mar. 1817 MF wrote (JRL) to Mrs. Piozzi that 'Dr Baillie says
he is *not* in a consumption, but that great care must be taken to avoid it, & he is
ordered into Devonshire at the end of this month.' Yet by the end of April he was
dead after his family's 'long agitations of hope & fear, & anxiety about this poor
boy', as MF reported (JRL) to her usual correspondent on 1 May 1817.

[17] Francis Jeffrey (1773–1850), born in Edinburgh, was a distinguished advocate
in his native city and editor (1803–29) of the *Edinburgh Review*. His 'entertaining'
letter must have been written shortly before he sailed from Liverpool on 29 Aug.

[*see opposite for note 17 cont. and note 18*

[John Street],
27 August 1813
To Marianne Francis

A.L.S. (Berg), 27 Aug. 1813

Double Sheet, 4to 1 p. *pmks* PIMLICO WITHAM MANNING TREE
28 AU ⟨ ⟩ wafer torn

Addressed: Miss Francis, / Arthur Young's Esqr, / Bradfield Hall / Suffolk /
Bury

Annotated on address page: Miss^t to [WITHAM, as above] / Returned from
[MANNING TREE, as above]

27. Augst
1813.

Have I received, by every opportunity, so much kindness
from my dear Marianne, & shall I pass by an occasion to shew
her a little?—though only by anticipation.—

Lord, de Blacquiere is safely returned to England! I have
this moment received a letter from him.[1]

I thought instantly of his amiable sister,[2] & of my dear
Marianne.

1813 for the United States in pursuit of Charlotte Wilkes, whom he married soon
after landing on 7 October. (When in 1834 he accepted a judgeship in the Court
of Session, he was named Lord Jeffrey.)

[18] The receipt of a letter from Jeffrey started up a series of recollections that Mrs.
Waddington had cast from her mind. Initially the letter reminded her that he had
reviewed *Essays on the Nature and Principles of Taste* by Archibald Alison (1757–
1839) in the *Edinburgh Review* for May 1811. In making this connection, she also
remembered the prebendary of Sarum's sense of loss when his daughter died in
1812. Always hypersensitive, Mrs. Waddington suffered with the curate until
she forced herself to forget his sorrow. FBA encouraged such forgetfulness.

719. [1] John de Blacquiere (1776–1844), 2nd Baron de Blacquiere of Ardkill,
county Londonderry. FBA justly spoke of his 'safe' return, for at the time of his
father's death—27 Aug. 1812—and for a period thereafter he was imprisoned in
France.

[2] Anna Maria de Blacquiere (1780–1843) had married in 1802 John Hamilton
FitzMaurice (1778–1820), *styled* Viscount Kirkwall. MF and Lady Kirkwall
became friends in 1811. As MF wrote (JRL) to Mrs. Piozzi on 27 May 1811:
'. . . there is *one* thing for which I believe I never thanked you, so now I must do
it most sincerely; & that is, for introducing me to Lady Kirkwall. I am hard to
like any body & a long time about it—& whether it was that I only saw her in
your presence & was then too much taken up in looking & listening to you to
observe her—I know not—but that dear Lady K has been so sweet & kind since
you left London that I am grown really to love her from my heart—'

At this time Lady Kirkwall was estranged from her husband, who in his departure took with him their two children. As MF continued her letter: 'I think there
is a nobility of *mind* about her—a generosity of Soul, & a *delicacy* of character,
which together with that sweet winning way of hers, are very uncommon, & to me,

He is so good as to bring me over some papers from M. d'Arblay.

I beg my kindest remembrances to my faithful old friend, who I hope is well, & whom I am sure you make happy.³— And my Compts. to Mrs. & Miss Young.⁴

My last News of dear Dolph was better. I know not yet when my dear sister will quit Brighton.⁵

Adieu, my dear Girl, ever yours affectionately

F B. d'Arblay

My sauvage is at Greenwich—polishing, I hope!—

How came you to play the part of Miss Orkborne with so little of your usual address, as to fall down with your study about your Ears? I thought you more perfect in the part.⁶

720

To Doctor Burney

[23] Chenies Street,
3 September—[1813]

A.L. (Diary MSS. vii [5912x–13x], Berg), 3 Sept.

Originally a single sheet 4to (8·7 × 7″), of which there are extant the three cuttings taken by CFBt for Pasteovers for the A.L.S. FBA to CB, 12 Oct. [1813]

Edited by FBA, *who had annotated and dated* p. 1 [5912x], *top margin*: ⁛ 1813 (12)

Mutilated by CFBt; *see* Textual Notes.

quite irresistible—& she has been so *wickedly* used—suffers so cruelly about her Babies—the tears stand in her fine eyes whenever she mentions their names— that it's hard to say whether most pity or indignation are excited at.'

³ At the very least MF made Arthur Young happy. According to Young's daughter, Mary: 'When at Bradfield she sleeps over the servants' hall, with a pack thread tied round her wrist, and placed through the keyhole, which he pulls four or five times, till he awakens her, when she gets up and accompanies him in a two hours' walk on the turnpike road to some cottage or other, and they take milk at some farmhouse . . . they return at half past six, as that is the hour Mr. St. Croix (his secretary) gets up. . . . My father puts children to school at Cuckfield, Stanninfield, and Bradfield. Every morning, summer and winter, she inspects and teaches at these schools' (Defries, op. cit., p. 154). See also MF's letter (JRL) to Mrs. Piozzi, dated 23 Aug. 1813.

⁴ In 1765 Arthur Young had married Martha Allen (d. 1815), the sister of CB's second wife. The daughter to whom FBA referred was Mary Young, now 47.

⁵ See L. 713 n. 1 for the date of CBFB's departure from Brighton.

⁶ See Ll. 646 n. 17; 717 n. 5.

September—Alas!—3ᵈ
Chenies St
Alfred place

NOTHING was ever more opportune, my dearest Padre, than
your NOTE & packet. I am *always* wanting news of YOU, & I
wanted most violently also news of the World, for I am now
pretty much shut out of it, copying Letters,

[*The text here is lost in mutilations. For segments of it, see Textual Notes.*]

A lady, Mrs. Aufrere,¹ whom I know not even by name, has
just sent me word that she desires to see me *de la parte de Mʳ
d'Arblay*, whom she saw in Paris, the 1ˢᵗ of August. I have
entreated her to hasten the interview, for which I am very
impatient, it will probably decide my fate with respect to the
time of my return to France. She had brought over a letter, also,
for Charles, which Charles Parr has sent to Sand Gate. She has
sought me at Greenwich. Charlotte is nursing poor Ralph at
Bookham! I am frightened to death for that fine Boy;² yet, *at
present*, he is better. May he recover entirely!—

[*The final text of the letter is lost in mutilations.*]

721   [23 Chenies Street,
                              5 or 12 September 1813]¹
To James Burney

A. L. (PML), FBA to JB, *n.d.*
Double sheet 8vo   3 pp.

My dear Brother;
I concur with you both in opinion & feeling, with respect
to preferring land to money, &c²— — But I can make no

720. ¹ Marianne Matilda Lockhart (d. 1850) had married Anthony Aufrère
(1757–1833) in 1791. A friend of both CBFB and CFBt, she was enlisted by them
to serve as a courier between FBA and M. d'A.
² See L. 718 n. 16.

721. ¹ This letter was written on a Sunday, either 5 or 12 Sept. 1813. By the
third Sunday of the month, FBA was already at Sandgate, having arrived there on
Friday the 17th.
² In September 1812 FBA thought of selling Camilla Cottage (L. 646 n. 25).
Now she recognized little choice about its sale. See L. 724 n. 16.

change, as I do not act from myself, but by positive commission from M. d'Arblay. The reasons Martin will unfold.

I am going to entreat a Transfer of my stock, now in the name of Mrs. Locke & Mr. William Locke,[3] as it is my intention to make a regulation of it that will facilitate our receiving it abroad, should it THERE be—at last—wanted—& I would have it placed at Mr. Hoare's,[4] as his house is eminently known for business with France — —

Will you, my dear Brother, be one of our Trustees, to this purpose, taking Martin, ⏐ who can best save you trouble, for the other?

Charles,—in case of my departure, will be Guardian to my Alexander, & with him I shall leave a power of Attorney for my Boy's service.

Whatever are my *hopes* of my future destination, I must ⏐ make my preparations for my *fears*, as I shall certainly go to Mr. d'A. next March, unless he writes to me to make another delay—with a view to join me here.

Such are his injunctions.

Martin will explain why I chose *Mr. Hoare* for my Banker

If you should be able, my dear Brother, to come to me on MONDAY, to-morrow, evening, in Chenies Street, for a dish— not of tea—but of chat, to talk over all these matters, & give me your opinions & counsels, & hear my circumstances, & views, & motives, you will much oblige me.

I shall arrive.

---

[3] That the transfer took place is indicated in a letter from Mrs. Locke to FBA, dated 4 Nov. 1813 (Barrett, Eg. 3697, f. 181): 'I copied all that related to business & dispatched it to my Willm I wanted likewise to mention the amount of your Stock which by the vigilance of *your Banker* who discovered a considerable error in the *Banks* acc^t amounts to £2,280.8.9.—I was struck with the smallness of the first sum of £1752.:15 4 & on my return to Lee had recourse to my accounts & discovered a total omission (to my horror) of £527.13 5. You know how immediately I flew to have this frightful error corrected & luckily stopped my W^m who was setting out for Norbury & we both again appeared at the *Bank* & with much difficulty I proved to the Clerks their omission & now my beloved Friend possesses the whole of her property—' For the discrepancy between this accounting and M. d'A's, see Appendix II and L. 709 n. 9.

[4] The allusion may be to the banker Charles Hoare (1767–1851) of 37 Fleet Street, or to his brother Merrick, who was married to the former Sophia Thrale (L. 692 n. 10). For the d'Arblays' complex use of their account at Hoare's between October 1814 and October 1815, see L. 822 n. 17.

722   23 Chenies Street,
                                     8 September [1813]

To Charles Burney
with notes to Mrs. Barrett
and to Sarah Harriet Burney

A.L. (Northwestern University, Evanston, Illinois), 8 Sept.
Double sheet (9·2 × 6·1″) 4 pp. A segment (2 × 6·1″) bearing notes to
CFBt and SHB has been cut from the bottom of the second leaf. The close
of the note to SHB appears on the right fold.   seal
Addressed: For the Reverend / Dr. Charles Burney, / SandGate, / Sussex.

                              23 Chenies ⟨St,⟩ Septr 8

How often—since your attack, my dearest Charles, have I
wished for telegraphic feet, or a *guideable* Balloon, that would
have cut short the eternal medlers with ones wishes, Time,
Money, & Convenience, & have let me down at once into the
chamber of my dear Brother, to help to nurse, or to cheer him!
And who could do it so well, so naturally, as one who, however
she sorrows for his sufferings, is all alive to the best hopes in its
present Cause? your Letter of yesterday so animated afresh my
desire to be with you, that I instantly set out upon an expedition
to Chelsea, to talk the matter over with our dear Father, to
whom I held myself engaged, & for whose summons I was
preparing. I found him delightfully well, in excellent humour,
& chearful spirits, & looking more healthy than I have yet seen
him since my return. He was all compliance with the proposition, acknowledging frankly that he had *rather* my purposed
visit of abode should take place when Sarah was returned[1] — —
which would appear to me quite SUPER natural as it seems so
much more probable, & genial, that he should require me
most when most alone, but that I think I perceive in him a
timid kind of apprehension that, if I should be under his roof
entirely, some rumour would spread that he had a Chamber
more than was *necessary* to his establishment! |

    Well—thus authorised, all my thoughts turned towards my
dearest Carlucci, & I felt already cordially shaking hands over

722. [1] SHB planned to leave Sandgate on 20 September. See L. 713 n. 2.

his respectable feet—& I drank tea in James Street, to take leave; & James & his Sallinette[2] accompanied me home to prolong the Adieu — —

When — — showers of rain that have been falling all night, & all this morning, have spread their humid influence so unkindly through the window cracks, & lock-holes, that I am seized with a great cold, & cough, & alarmed by a necessity of watchfully nursing *myself* ere I presume to aid that benign task to my dear Charles![3]

And now—all of difficulty that I had mocked, yesterday, in the midst of the sunshine, & with health & feelings blyth & bland, rises to affright & discourage me. There is no coach, they say, that sets out but at 5 o'clock in the Morning, or at 5 at night, & from the heart of the City:[4] so that I must either set off nearly in the middle of the night, or enter Sandgate at the same inauspicious hour. For the first, I no longer feel the strength—for the second, I have not the conscience.

Alltogether, in my state of precarious existence, 'twas but a wild idea, just at the opening of autumnal ǀ ⟨damps⟩. And I am very sorry, with all her youth & vigour, to hear that a certain sweet Nurse has a plan of a Coasting voyage home.[5] There are only 3 Months in the year in which such excursions should, for *pleasure*, or even with *safety*, be risked.

To the Rectory—at this period, my dear Charles, I cannot go—not even if *YOU* were there, for reasons I can detail when we meet. And that was a very principal motive with me for wishing to spend a quiet snug—social fortnight with you at SandGate.[6]

How wretched it is that my Letters all miss my best Friend!— & that *HIS* are so perplexing! this message by Mrs. Aufrère, whom I have seen, is not more explicit: he had heard, from Mrs.

---

[2] JB's vivacious, plump daughter Sarah or 'Sally'.

[3] The heavy showers began on 7 September and continued through the next day. The maximum temperature on 8 September was a chilling 54 °F. (*GM* lxxxiii[2], 302).

[4] According to the 13th edition of the *Post-Office Annual Directory* (1812), direct coaches for Sandgate left from the 'Golden-cross, charing cross' daily at 5 a.m. and from 'White-horse fetter-lane' at 5 and 6 a.m. Other coaches left either from the 'Angel, St. Clement's, strand' at 7 p.m. or Fetter Lane at 6 p.m.

[5] Probably Fanny, CPB's wife, who had spent the summer at Sandgate with her father-in-law, and left for home on 31 August. See L. 716 n. 14.

[6] Rosette Burney was at the Rectory. Her unpredictable behaviour had bewildered and frightened FBA and most of the Burneys for many years. See L. 712 n. 1.

Solvyns, I should be with him in September—well, he earnestly conjured her to see me, to *put aside* that project. He was so agitated, she says, that he extremely affected her, though she only saw him for a few minutes, just before she quitted Paris, Aug^st 11.th But when she asked if he had any particular reason against my coming in September, he said no, only he feared ǀ my catching cold!—she thought it *odd*, she said, as September is in general so mild a month—leaving out the equinoctial period. But to tell me—as he has done, in a Letter, I may come to the 10. of November[7]—! 'tis inconceivable, unless he wishes me to divine that I should stay to the end of this eventful impending Campaign.[8] Upon the whole, I have fixed to stay till Spring. God grant I may not have misunderstood him!—Heaven bless you, Dearest Charles—I long but know not how to contrive a meeting. ǀ

Charlotte & Dolph are at Bookham, riding & drinking Donkeys. ǀ

Millions of thanks my kindest Charles, for y^r most brotherly purposes upon my departure. ǀ

[*A note to Charlotte Barrett on page 3 has been cut away, leaving only the complimentary close on page 4:*]

My kindest Love ⟨to⟩ my d^r Charlotte

[*A note to Sarah Harriet Burney has been cut from the bottom of page 4, leaving only the heading (for—Sarah—). The close of the note appears on the right fold of the letter:*]

No parcel has come hither for you. *Surely* I will go through the *proving* work.[9] But there is no haste, now.

---

[7] This letter is missing, but possibly dated 17 Aug. 1813. See Ll. 724 n. 6, 728.
[8] See L. 724 n. 18.
[9] That is, the proofreading of *The Wanderer*.

[Sandgate, Kent,
post 23 September 1813]¹

To Doctor Burney

A.L.S. (Diary MSS. vii, 5906–[09], Berg), *n.d.*
Double sheet 8vo   4 pp.   paged 1–4   and foliated 15, 16
Addressed: Dr. Burney, / Chelsea College, / Chelsea.
Dated, p. 1 (5906) *in an unknown hand*: Septr. / or Oc^t
Edited by FBA, p. 1 (5906), *annotated and dated*:   ⁘   Sandgate   1813
(13 / 1)   residence at Sandgate with Dr. Charles Burney   Mr. Wilber-
force   Martellos
   Also edited by CFBt *and the* Press. *See* Textual Notes.
   *The change in the hand, the style, the ink, and the general appearance indicate
   that it was in her later editorial years (in the 1820s or 1830s) that* FBA *added the
   section pp. 2, 3, and 4 (Let me steal . . . adio, Padre mio.)*

I have time but for a word to my dearest Padre, by this
opportunity, which, nevertheless, I snatch at, to say how much
I hope he is well & bonny.—Charles recovers slowly, but
resumes the visiting system, which chears & does him good:
& not the least in the List to exhilarate his spirits stands his
Grace the Archbishop,² with whom he has twice dined this
last week.³ I have kept myself in the back ground, wanting
both Time & Disposition, & ONE THING besides too mean
to name—for visiting. I have therefore avoided going to the
Library, the general rendezvous of the Social, or upon The
Pier⁴—which I shall forbear ǀ parading till just before my
departure. I am to meet my Alex in town, to equip him for
Cambridge very shortly.⁵ I shall then settle with my dearest

723. ¹ The original letter (without FBA's account of her meeting with Wilberforce) was written from Ramsgate between 23 September and 6 October.
   ² For Charles Manners-Sutton (1755–1828), Archbishop of Canterbury (1805),
see iii, L. 199 n. 14.
   ³ The relationship between CB Jr. and his Archbishop, a royal favourite since
1794, was cordial. In 1810 CB Jr. 'abridged for the use of Young Persons' John
Pearson's *The Exposition of the Creed* and dedicated it to the Archbishop. Accessible
to his clergy, Manners-Sutton encouraged CB Jr.'s visits. See the latter's letters
(Osborn) to CPB (19, 21, 23 Sept. 1813).
   ⁴ 'But the principal object of remark at [Ramsgate] is its Harbour, which, as
a work entirely artificial, holds the first rank, for extent, grandeur, and, above all,
utility in the empire. . . . its form is nearly circular, and comprehends an area of
about 46 acres; that the length of the East pier is nearly 2000 feet, that of the West
about 1500, and the entrance-breadth 240 feet . . . and that the piers being 26 feet
in breadth, with a parapet on each side, they form the most charming promenades
for the company of the town.' See *Excursions in the County of Kent* (1822), p. 112.
   ⁵ From CB Jr. to CPB (Osborn, 23 Sept. 1813): 'You have gladdened Mad.

Padre my so long postponed happiness of being at Chelsea. Sarah will, literally, speak for herself[6]—but Charles is at St. Lawrence,[7] & cannot—therefore I add his Love & Duty to those of

> Dearest Padre,
> your ever most dutiful
> & affectionate
> FB d'Arblay.

Let me steal a Moment to relate a singular gratification, &, in truth, a real & great Honour I have had to rejoice in. You know, my Padre, probably that Marian Francis was commissioned by Mr. Wilberforce[8] to bring about an acquaintance with your F.D'A—& that, ǀ though highly susceptible to such a desire, my usual shyness—or rather consciousness of inability to merit the expectations that must have made him seek me, induced my declining an Interview—Eh bien—at Church at Sandgate, the Day after my arrival,[9] I saw this justly celebrated Man, & was introduced to him in the Church yard, after the service, by Charles. The Ramparts & Martellos around us became naturally our Theme,[10] & Mr. Wilberforce proposed shewing them to me. I readily accepted the offer, & Charles & Sarah, & Mrs. Wilberforce[11] & Mrs. Barrett, went away in their several carriages, while Mr. Barrett alone remained, & Mr. Wilberforce gave me his arm—and, in short, we walked the round from one to Five o'clock! 4 Hours of the best conversation I have, nearly, ever enjoyed. He was anxious for a full & true account of Paris, & particularly of Religion & Infidelity, & of Buonaparté & the Wars,

d'Arb's heart by your account of Alexander. As she cannot take him at Michaelmas, she wishes to add a *few* days to the time, which you allowed for his spending with her, for provision of necessaries, before he commences Cantab.'

[6] SHB was already in Chelsea, having left Sandgate on 20 September.

[7] CB Jr. was visiting or preaching at the chapel of St. Lawrence (the parish church for Ramsgate), a spacious building, partly of Norman origin.

[8] For MF's association with Wilberforce, see L. 667 n. 9. For her presence at Kensington Gore just before he and his family left for Sandgate, see L. 699 n. 4.

[9] But according to a letter (Osborn) of CB Jr., dated 19 September, 'M^rs d'Arblay arrived on Friday evening', which was 17 September. She must have met Wilberforce on Sunday, 19 September. In his letters to CPB at this time CB Jr. makes no mention of the introduction.

[10] 'The Ramparts and Martellos' refer to the Sandgate fortifications built in 1805 and 1806, when Pitt formed the scheme of erecting towers (armed with cannon and surrounded by parapets) to guard the Kentish and Sussex coasts against an anticipated Napoleonic invasion.

[11] On 30 May 1797 William Wilberforce had married Barbara Ann (*c.* 1772–1847), one of the nine children of Isaac Spooner (d. 1816) of Elmdon House, Warwickshire. The Wilberforces by 1813 had four sons and two daughters.

& of all & every Thing that had occurred during my Ten
years seclusion in France: & I had so much to communicate,
& his drawing out, & comments, & Episodes, were all so
judicious, so spirited, so full of information, yet so ⌜benignly⌝
unassuming, that my shyness all flew away, & I felt to be his
confidential Friend, opening to him upon every occurrence,
& every sentiment, with the frankness that is usually won by
years of intercourse. I was really & truly delighted & enlightened by him. I desire nothing more than to renew the
acquaintance, & cultivate it to intimacy—But, helas, he was
going away next Morning. | That his discourse should be
edifying could not, certainly, surprize me; I expected from
him all that was elevated in instruction; but there was a
mixture of simplicity & Vivacity in his manner that I had
not expected, & found really Captivating.[12] In contemplating
the Opposite—& alas hostile shore, which to our Fancy's
Eye, at least, was visible,—I could not forbear wafting over
to it a partial blessing—nor refuse myself beseeching one
from Mr Wilberforce, & the smiling benevolence with which
he complied has won my heart forever. Encore

adio, Padre mio.

724   [Ramsgate,
                              post 23 September 1813][1]
To Mrs. Waddington

A.L.S. (Berg), *n.d.*
Double sheet 4to   4 pp.   red seal
Addressed: Mrs Waddington / Lanover / Abergavenny.
Postdated in pencil, p. 1: Sept—1813
Annotated in pencil, p. 4: Mrs. Waddington—Lanover / Abergavenny
Docketed: W / circa 1812

Your Letter, Dearest Mary, has followed me hither within
these two days only—&, for once, I resolve not to let a 3d sun
set upon its request unobeyed.

---

[12] Apparently FBA's analysis of Wilberforce's personality is accurate. A remarkably charitable and pious man, he impressed his friends and acquaintances—
from MF to Mme de Staël—with his kindness and wit. See especially John S.
Harford, *Recollections of William Wilberforce* (1864) and James Stephen, *Essays in
Ecclesiastical Biography* (2 vols., 1849), ii. 203–86.

724. [1] This letter can be dated *post* 23 Sept. 1813; see nn. 2, 3.

I have now your two Letters, my kind Friend, to thank you
for, & the Portrait so singularly attractive of your Fanny, &
the very entertaining account of Mad^e de Staël. If I waited till
I could command two or three hours, I should write two or
three pages upon each: but I dare not give you the anxiety of
waiting any longer for the restoration of your treasure.

I have been summoned by my Reverend Brother to the sea
coast, where he has been, for some time, seeking to brace himself after a fit of the Gout, by sea breezes. We were some time
at Sand Gate,[2] & are now at Rams Gate.[3] I think we shall go
hence to Margate: but in the middle of October I must be in
town,[4] to meet my Alexander, & prepare him for Cambridge,
whither he goes on the 20th For me—alas, I fear I cannot
accompany him!—but my Brother will be so good, & see him
[es]tablished, & introduce him at the College, & present him
to various Masters of Colleges, & professors. If go myself I can
—which I much doubt—how happy would it have made me to
meet my dearest Mary!—But certainly Cheltenham must have
the preference, if preferable for the health of your invaluable
Fanny. The generous candour of the description which that
charming Girl has given of herself, & which ⌐ if written by any

---

[2] Written on 11 Sept. 1813, the letter (Osborn) that 'summoned' FBA to
Sandgate came from CB Jr.
   'But to business.—The Canterbury Coaches set off about 8—& get to Canter-
bury, in the afternoon—There my Carriage shall meet you.—So, negotiate quickly
. . . and get a place—& be set down at the Fountain Inn in Canterbury. . . . My
Man shall be there waiting for you; & shall bring you over to one who *always*
longs to see you.—
   'Now mark'—
Let your place be taken for Wednesday, Sept. 15th The Golden Cross, Char^g Cross,
is the Inn, I think— . . .
   'I am saddled with a whole house;—& so you may have an excellent Room,
with a Window to the Sea & work as you will.—'
   FBA made minimal changes in these instructions. She arrived at Sandgate
(via Canterbury) on 17 September. Almost immediately CB Jr. began to plan
their move to Ramsgate. In a letter (Osborn), dated 19 September, he had in-
formed CPB:
   'M^{rs} d'Arblay arrived on Friday Evening—I sent over my Chaise to Canterbury; & she performed her journey well.—She has too much cough about her—
& must nurse.—The weather is delicious.
   'Sarah marches tomorrow with the Barretts: and on Thursday, Gout willing,
Mrs dArb. & her Bro. begin their journey to Ramsgate—.'
   CB Jr. and FBA planned the 28-mile journey to Ramsgate for Thursday 23
September.
[3] A letter (Osborn) from CB Jr. to CPB, dated 23 September from Ramsgate,
indicates that CB Jr. successfully carried out his plan.
[4] Actually FBA wanted to be in Chelsea by the end of the first week in October.
According to CB Jr.'s letter (Osborn), 23 Sept. 1813, 'M. Alexander will be wanted
by my Sister, on the 7 or 8 of October.—'

one but herself, I should call a caricature, is strikingly extraordinary; but what I love most in it, is the blended fondness
& delicacy of the filial *eloge* implied by the word Education.
Oh do not hasten such a Daughter, such a friend, from You!
— — Wait till Time & Occasion present some one worthy of
her, by whom she may be sought, & won—& then the separation may, to both, be endurable.[5]

I hardly remember how I was situated when I wrote last;
but I have been, for about two months, in a state of inquietude
& incertitude with respect to my movements the most restless
& agitating. I can enter, here, into no details, but the result is,
that a Letter I have at length received decides me to spend here
yet a second Winter![6]—You will wonder—yet, could I see you,
one word would make wonder cease. The watch word given, or
known, how simple, often, do we find what, without it, appears
most complex! — — The little Book, therefore, will keep quiet,
till a better season. Yet the *Book man* tries to hurry me:[7] but I
think it would be injudicious to take a dead time, when I may
wait for one more alive. I shall remain here certainly till
March. You will turn, therefore, in your kind mind, what
chances may be forwarded by such a change to make me some
amends for the abrupt disappointment of your departure.

I dare not speak of your Emily—sweet angel! — — But I am
charmed at your augmenting hopes in your Augusta, who
appeared to me a lively blossom of fairest promise.

I must keep Miss Allen's Letter for the next opportunity, as I
am told a third sheet will be over-weight.[8]

Mad[e] de Staël has taken a house for 2 months at Richmond,
next door to my niece Charlotte Barret—who much regrets
losing all chance of seeing so celebrated a character, from
spending that time, herself, at the sea side, where she now is,
with her blooming young family. |

Do you remember any thing, formerly, of Julia Angerstein,[9]

[5] See L. 718 in which FBA comments on Mrs. Waddington's desire to have her daughter Fanny 'move in a London round'.

[6] The missing letter of M. d'A, dated 17 Aug. 1813. See L. 728.

[7] FBA wanted *The Wanderer* brought out in the spring of 1814. This may be inferred from CB Jr.'s comment (Osborn), 11 Sept. 1813: 'Your *Spring* decision is RIGHT.' For her confused and contradictory account of the booksellers' opinion of a good publication date, see L. 716.

[8] See L. 656 n. 3.

[9] Juliana Sablonkoff (1772–1846) was the daughter of John Julius Angerstein

once betrothed to poor Charles Lock?[10]—She married a Russian officer, a man of high merit; but without the consent, though without the positive refusal of her Father.[11] She has been living many years in Russia, where her husband, General Sublokoff, or some such name, has distinguished himself by his bravery & conduct:[12] but has had a fever, from fatigue, that has forced him to retire from the army, to refit: & he has taken the opportunity to bring back his wife to her native land, that he may try the Waters of Cheltenham. His gallantry, & good character, have now completely gained Mr. Angerstein, & they were all living in happy reconcilement, when Mr. A[ngerstein] was taken with a frightful illness, which is now threatening his life.[13] How happy, at last, for Julia, who was always tenderly, though not exclusively, attached to her Father, that she was thus fortunately & seasona[bly] returned! They are come from Cheltenham, by slow stages, to have advice from Town, & are now all together at Woodlands.[14] The whole family were just prepared to go for 3 Months to Mrs. Boucherett's, in Lincolnshire.[15]

Will you be sorry—I think you will, for I am at my very heart,—that I am going to part with my dear little Cottage on

and his first wife, the widowed Anna Crokatt *née* Muilman (d. 1783). See i, L. 9 n. 5.

[10] Of Juliana Angerstein's earlier relationship with Charles Locke, SBP wrote in her journal (Berg, on 20 Aug. 1791): 'Charles came down last night—& told me he *wished* much to marry Miss A—"I go to consult wth her Father on the subject—" [Mrs. Locke] trembling lest mortification & disappointment sh[d] await her dear son.' By November 1791 FB announced the engagement as a fact, although it was soon broken (i, L. 9 and n. 5).

[11] If John Julius Angerstein I had reservations about Juliana's marriage in 1804 to General Sablonkoff, he never revoked the handsome marriage settlement, dated 12 Nov. 1804, that he made for her.

[12] In his wife's will (Prob. 9/47), written 3 June 1841 and proved 11 Mar. 1847, Nicholas Sablonkoff (1776–1848) was described as a 'Major-General in the service of the Emperor of Russia and a Nobleman by birth of that country'. He married Juliana Angerstein on 20 Nov. 1804 (iii, L. 197 n. 7). They lived in Russia except for rare visits to England. In 1813 the General was much lionized at Woodlands, there talking of his experiences on the Russian front during the Napoleonic campaign ' "that made one's flesh creep!" ' (*Locks of Norbury*, p. 218).

[13] In 1813 John Julius Angerstein I was 78 and had been retired from business since 1811. Despite his illness at this time, he was to live another decade, dying on 22 Jan. 1823.

[14] After his retirement, Angerstein lived alternately at 102 Pall Mall and 'Woodlands', his villa at Blackheath. See also iv *passim*.

[15] Emilia Crokatt (*c*. 1761–1837) was Angerstein's adored step-daughter and the wife of Ayscoghe Boucherett (1755–1815), M.P. (1796–1803). See ii, L. 111 n. 2; iii, L. 150 n. 14. She and her husband lived at Willingham House near Market Rasen in Lincolnshire.

the borders of Norbury Park?—Imperious prudence forces my consent.[16] — —

My poor sister Broome continues wandering about, for change of air, to ease the cough of poor Dolph[17]—which has been aggravated by a pain in the side!—but is better, once more, for the moment — —! — My Alexander is gaining strength, at present, by ale beverage, which seems to agree with him. Wine has always agitated & *fevered* him. He is now at Greenwich. How I long to introduce him to you, & engage for him your kind interest!—

You may imagine I receive no Letters now—nor have received any | since the re-commencement of MISCHIEF: or— will it be GOOD in leading, at length, to the object of all our desires, sweet blessed Peace?[18]—I will take great care about good Mrs. Agnew. But she must wonder you should not mention her MSS. — — If I had any safe opportunity, I would send it you. It has, for Us, the deep interest of a subject always sacred to us.[19] And there is something always touching in her tender fidelity. I have a true regard for that excellent Creature.

— — I meant to have written 3 Letters to Night, & have now scribbled away, almost involuntarily, my evening in two short of my design.

[16] See Ll. 646 n. 25, 721 n. 2. Planning to live abroad, FBA had to invest her funds in readily negotiable stocks rather than in land whose value was determined primarily by the availability of a purchaser.

[17] CBFB and the coughing, feverish Dolph travelled first to Richmond in July, then to Brighton in August and to Great Bookham in September (L. 713 n. 1). After a short stay at Chenies Street, they returned to Richmond, where the boy found the air therapeutic. By early 1815 Dolph had 'been so ill with a cough' that CBFB had 'serious intentions of taking him to Cornwall for the winter'. Thus MF commented in her letter (JRL) of 26 January to Mrs. Piozzi, lamenting 'the Rolling-stone-Life' her mother led.

[18] From 4 June to 10 Aug. 1813, an armistice, arranged by Metternich, existed between the main forces of France and those of the allied coalition—England, Russia, and Prussia. Hostilities were, however, resumed in mid-August. The allies sought to drive 'the French from Silesia and back across the Elbe by a series of attacks on the front and flanks of their position. By 27 August the main armies faced one another at Dresden. After a head-on collision with Napoleon's 130,000 men the allies had to scramble back from Saxony into Bohemia' (Watson, op. cit., p. 558). The 'MISCHIEF' referred to by FBA consisted of many small but intense actions by the allies (over a period of six weeks) to recover the ground they had lost. She was accurate in her prognostication of a 'Peace', for by the middle of October the French were again pushed back to the Elbe and after the Battle of Leipzig (16–19 Oct.) Napoleon's army, having suffered thousands of casualties, retreated westwards towards the Rhine. See L. 733 n. 4.

[19] See L. 718 n. 13. FBA referred facetiously to Anne Agnew's letters as MSS. because they were long and garrulous, but they always spoke of Mrs. Delany, who was beloved by FBA and Mrs. Waddington.

Have any of the senators with whom you mix any idea when the Parliament will really open?[20] That will be the event to fill the town; & if I could know it, I would endeavour to prepare the little publication for it. But it will hang, I conclude, upon public affairs abroad. I am very glad you are likely to know Mrs. Hoare & Miss Thrale. They are dear & charming persons, & amongst the faithful & attached Friends whom I have known from their Childhood. I spent a day with them about 6 weeks ago most pleasantly.[21] Mrs. Hoare is now with Lady Keith— another of my faithfullest, &, strange to tell, warmest Friends! —for she bears a character of being not only as fair, but as cold as snow. Adieu, sweet Mary—remember me most affectionately to your lovely Girls—ever & ever yours

F B d'A.

724A

To Charles Parr Burney

23 Chenies Street,
9 October 1813

A.L.S. (John Wilson, dealer), 9 Oct. 1813
Double sheet 4to   4 pp.   *pmks*   11 OC 1813   T.P.P.U ⟨ ⟩,   seal
Addressed: Rev^d Mr. Burney, / Greenwich, / Kent.

[*first line*:] A thousand thanks to you, Dear Charles,[1] . . . [*a section about Alexander d'Arblay was printed in Christie's Catalogue of 1 Aug. 1973, p. 65*:]

I do not attribute wholly to perversity: his early scrapes, & the Glory flaming from them, in his years of adolescence, inflamed

[20] Parliament opened on 4 Nov. 1813, the day on which FBA signed the 'Articles of Agreement' with Longman, Hurst, Rees, Orme, and Brown. See L. 728.
[21] On 25 Aug. 1813. See L. 717.

724A. [1] FBA's letter, concerned with several family matters, also answers CPB's summary of AA's career at the Greenwich School. According to CPB's letter (L. 650 n. 4), the boy was capricious in his studies, neglecting especially the fundamentals of classical grammar. 'All his best exertions will be needed to overcome this disadvantage:—fancy & association are always at work,—but for sober nouns & verbs he has no relish,—& unfortunately Dr Davy has a strong affection for these old-fashioned Folks,—& Tutors & Proctors & Moderators somehow or other have imbibed a notion, that there is no other foundation for Learning & Scholarship.—Many, very many are the serious conversations, which I have had with Alex on the subject,—nor is there a remonstrance, which I have not urged.— He seems now fully conscious of the deficiency,—but I do entreat you to reason with him most stoutly on the business,—or he will disappoint his College,—discredit me,—& commit SUICIDE on his own ambitious views.—I should not write thus strongly, were I not seriously apprehensive that censure [may] devolve upon an ambition that pressed him, I am now of opinion, to an application too forcible & ardent for his physical fabric, &, by overstretching his powers, has now slackened their elasticity. Prosperity, also, in those days, & those studies, was gilt with such triumphant fame, that it has rendered all quiet & rational reward of toil insipid, & scarcely worth attainment. You will not . . . imagine I write this in defence of the System he has quitted; . . .²

I parted from my dear Brother at Sittingburn delightfully well in general . . . I am glad you *'piped'* as well as laughed at the prettiest verses he ever writ; for they surprised me I confess into tears.³ Sweet bright blossom! long—long may she enjoy Grandfather—Father—Mother—Uncles—Cousins—. . .

725   23 Chenies Street,
14 October 1813

To Charles Burney

A.L.S. (Boston Public Library, MSS. ACC. 16), 14 Oct. 1813
Single sheet 4to   2 pp.
Addressed: Revᵈ Dr Charles Burney.
Annotated, p. 1 by CFBt [*probably before giving it as an autograph*]: Revᵈ *Dr. Charles Burney.*
Annotated by dealer(?) *or* B.P.L.: Josiah H. Benton / Fd. / Apr. 11, 1939 / EE

me, when in fact I am but too keenly sensible of the mischief, & have tried every mode of cure, excepting positive punishment.'
  ² FBA alludes to AA's education in France and the ease with which he won prizes (L. 803 n. 4).
  ³ CB Jr.'s poem (L. 716 n. 14) to Brightblossom consists of twelve six-line stanzas of rhyming couplets:

> My sweet Brightblossom, fare thee well,
> May Puck to guard thee wave a spell;
> And watch thee, over dale and hill,
> By rugged road, through murmuring rill;
> And place thee, safe from mortal harms,
> Fraught with fresh smiles, in thy dear Father's arms.

>   ·   ·   ·

> Next Womanhood:— —but soft—no more
> The Vision deigns unfold her store;
> Nor may remoter scenes impart
> Their cheering raptures to my heart;—
> For, ere that day, thy tender tear
> Shall shed its tribute, on thy Grandsire's Bier.

(These are the first and last stanzas of the poem.)

Octr 14. 1813
Chenies Street—

As speedily as may be in your power, let me know, my dear Brother, your day of setting out for Cambridge, & your project of Rendezvous. Alexander is touched by your kind exertion for him with the warmest gratitude. His dear Father will participate in it:—his Mother alone feels it *not at all, at all!*—

I am wholly & undividedly my Boy's *NOW* & to the time of his departure:[1] — —

But I shall then be so harrassed for time—to treat of my house, which I have set wholly aside in the interval[2]—

& to adhere to my engagement for the 1st of November with Mr. Longman[3]—

For whom I have yet neither seen Martin,[4] nor over-looked innumerable new memorandums made *away* from Johnson's Dictionary,[5] & to which I must have recourse previously to parting with the MSS.—

That

unless you hold it *ESSENTIAL* that I should accompany you & Alex to Cambridge, I shall spare myself a weight of anxiety & apprehension by declining my visit there *now*, to let it take place at some future period. |

Dr Davy,[6] though he gave me a general invitation, does not now expect me.—I should scarcely see my Alex, with whom my whole mind would be fearfully wandering, for YOU will present him to the Professors, & Chiefs, & Clement to appendages: — — & you will so be taken up, that we shall have no time for our separate *gossiping*—

---

725. [1] AA arrived at Chenies Street on 9 October. See CB Jr.'s letter (Osborn) to CPB, dated October 1813. AA then left with CB Jr. for Cambridge about 20 October, took his Classical examination before the end of the month, and on Saturday (13 Nov.), he along with 248 other undergraduates 'admitted in the present term, were matriculated in the Senate-House, the greatest number ever known at one time' (*The Cambridge Chronicle and Journal, and Huntingdonshire Gazette*, 19 Nov. 1813).

[2] Camilla Cottage and its projected sale.

[3] A possible meeting prior to the signing of the 'Articles of Agreement' on 4 November.

[4] Martin Burney acted as FBA's solicitor in helping to draw up the 'Articles of Agreement' and as agent for CB Jr. in the negotiations with Longman and his colleagues.

[5] For each of her four novels, FBA tried to check word usage and spelling in Samuel Johnson's *Dictionary*.

[6] Martin Davy, Master of Caius College.

And for the HONOUR of my Boy, I can have nothing to wish, & nothing to gain, when YOU present him: & we are not even SURE that Dr Davy is there, who would be vexed as kindly as I should grievously should we miss Him — — for I know not, like you, 100 others—(not other *Dr. Davys!*—!) to see & meet there.

Alltogether, dispence with me this time, unless you see some reasons of adva[n]tage to Alex which I do not discern. Let all his Bills be made out for ME, but take him as your own personal Protegée.[7] Nevertheless, I will abide by your decision when you have considered my impediments.

To *Norfolk* I *certainly* cannot go:[8] I must prepare for nothing but Business, when Alex is deposited, or be ruined. I have an impending summons, also, for Windsor[9]—most graciously intimated, but not yet fixed.

Adieu, my dearest Charles,

ever & aye most affec^ty yours

FB d'A.

726   [23 Chenies Street, *c.* 14–20 October 1813]

To Charles Burney

A.L.S. (Osborn), *n.d.*
Double sheet 8vo   3 pp.   *pmk* T.P.P.U. ⟨ ⟩ wafer torn
Addressed: Rev^d Dr. Charles Burney, / Rectory House, / Deptford.

Thanks by the Million, my dearest Charles, for this most kind part you are acting with my dearest Boy.—Were my business less imperiously urgent,[1] with what delight should I have made a third in this most interesting—most momentous (to me) excursion! Speak for me, I beg, to Dr. Davy, if, happily, you

---

[7] That is, as AA's legal guardian. See L. 721.

[8] CB Jr. may have intended to visit his clerical step-brother Stephen Allen (i, p. lxxiv), who lived at 'the Rookery' in King's Lynn, or Maria Rishton (i, p. lxxiv), who resided at Hillington, near King's Lynn.

[9] See L. 730.

726. [1] Her business concerned the possible sale of Camilla Cottage and the final manuscript check of *The Wanderer* so that it could go to the printer immediately on her signing the 'Articles of Agreement' with Longman and his associates.

find him at his College. The anxiety of my mind at this enter-prize, from the singularities & incertitudes of Alexander, would nearly equal its satisfaction, but for the dread events around us,[2] which continually hurl into my Ears exhortations to gratitude for his extraordinary escape.[3] What a period is this!—how it works—with hope—alarm—& wonder, every part of my existence!

adieu, My dear kind Brother—
most excellent uncle, Adieu—
F B d'A.

I shall send Alexander's Trunk & Books by the Cambridge Coach, directed ǀ for him to the care of Clement, & to Clement's apartments, as I know not what will be Alexander's own address.[4] In his Sac de Nuit he will have a general change, in case of any delay in the delivery of his Cargo.

Pray *ask* him, if you sleep, as I conclude, upon the road, whether he has packed his night geer up the next Morning: he will else leave it in his room to welcome the next sleeping visitor.

My love to dear Charles & Mrs. Parr, & best Comp^ts to kind Mrs Bicknel. —. — —

When may I add the name of our dear Rosette? Alex thought her quite well. I long to hear that your arrival has not agitated her.[5] ǀ

I must now divert off m[y] solicitude with very serious occu-pation.

The Bills—While I am here! will be transmitted to ME—afterwards—till he is of age, to his kind Guardian—

---

[2] FBA refers to Napoleon's crumbling military machine: the defeat at Vitoria (June 1813), leaving France open to invasion from the south; the French retreat to the Elbe early in October; the declaration of war against France by Bavaria with her 30,000 troops; and Austria's new aggressions in Bohemia.

News of the Battle of Leipzig had not yet reached England. It arrived through a letter written by Lady Priscilla Burghersh (1793–1879), youngest daughter of William Wellesley-Pole (1763–1845). In Berlin with her husband (Commissioner to the Headquarters of the Austrian Army), she wrote to her mother on 27 October describing the havoc of the battle. Once the letter reached England, its news spread rapidly. See *Europe against Napoleon/The Leipzig Campaign, 1813 from Eyewitness Accounts*, ed. and tr. Antony Brett-James (1970), p. 254.

[3] FBA heard from M. d'A as recently as 5 September. See L. 728.

[4] See L. 728 n. 4.   [5] See L. 716 n. 5.

Paris, 28 October [1813]

M. d'Arblay
To Madame d'Arblay

A.L. (Berg), 28 Oct.
Originally a double sheet 4to, of which FBA later discarded the second
leaf   2 pp.
Edited by FBA, p. 1, *docketed, date retraced and year added*:   7   [28 octobre]
1813   *See further*, Textual Notes.

Ce 29 octobre

Sois sans inquietude sur ma santé, ma chere Fanny, j'en ai le
plus grand soin. Au nom du Ciel ma bonne amie menage bien
la tienne et ne neglige aucune occasion de m'en donner des
nouvelles. Helas! j'ignore absolument tout ce qui te concerne
depuis la petite lettre qui m'a été remise de toi en date du
[*blank*]. J'y ai dejà fait quatre reponses, ⌐dont une au moins
j'espere te sera parvenue. Je veus neanmoins te repeter en
substance dans celle cy que tu as toute raison d'être restée pour
t'assurer la derniere et peut être la seule ressource sur la quelle
nous puissions compter. Et qu'enfin sur tout ce qui est relatif
à cette affaire importante carte blanche ainsi que sur le reste.
Je te recommande seulement de prendre bien toutes tes precautions pour que l'arrangement que tu as fait soit solide, et que
la personne avec qui l'on a traité pour toi soit exact dans les
payemens qu'il devra faire à quelqu'un de soigneux qui nous
en rendra bon compte.[1] Tous les malheurs que nous avons
eprouvés rendent ces precautions[2] je ne dis pas seulement plus
necessaires que jamais, j'ajoute indispensables, ainsi que te le
prouve cette lettre ecrite à la hâte et dans un trouble extrême
qu'augmente encore l'inquietude du sort qu'elle eprouvera.
Quand et comment te parviendra t'elle? et de quel interest
n'est il pas pour moi de connoitre le plutôt possible d'une man-
iere certaine que tu | l'auras reçue et que tu sens la necessité de

727. [1] Aware that the 'Articles of Agreement' for *The Wanderer* would soon be
signed by Longman and his associates (as they were on 4 Nov.), M. d'A recommended to FBA that the negotiations be handled by a trustworthy agent who would
secure a profitable contract and subsequently render an honest account of sales
and payments.
[2] When Payne and Cadell and Davies brought out a second edition of *Camilla*
in 1802, M. d'A felt that he and his wife had been denied proper payment for the
laborious revision, that it had been virtually pirated.

me tranquilliser sur la crainte trop fondée que me donnera ta santé, jusqu'au moment où je serai tout à fait certain que je ne dois plus t'attendre qu'au retour de la belle saison.⌐

Ah! mon amie, je devrais d'après une de tes lettres dejà anciennes pouvoir compter que ton retour ne peut avoir lieu avant la fin de Novembre epoque à la quelle doit paraitre ton nouvel ouvrage; malgré cela, le moindre coup de vent me met dans une agitation inconcevable. Je me figure que tu es embarquée avec un tems epouvantable, que ce sein qui renferme une ame si belle si pure est de nouveau en danger par le froid que tu eprouves. ah ma chère Fanny au nom du Ciel—fais moi savoir que tu renonces à venir avant le mois de May, ⌐et sois à cet saison cy bien attentive afin d'eviter ces rhumes terribles et si dangereux aux quels tu es si sujette!³ J'*exige* absolument que tous les jours tu sortes mais en voiture. Je consacre à cet unique objet six francs par jour que j'espere pouvoir mettre de coté, car jusqu'à present je n'ai guere fait d'epargnes. Ma maladie et les necessaires que j'ai eu a payer tant pour toi que pour moi, joint à d'autres depenses en plus des prevues m'ont empeché de rien mettre de coté. Tandis que j'en suis sur ce vilain argent dont on est bien quelque fois forcé de s'occuper, je dois te dire une chose qui te fera sans doute un grand plaisir—c'est que tu n'as plus besoin de chercher et faire chercher les moyens d'en faire passer à notre cher ⟨Edmond⟩ de ⟨Beauvau⟩.⁴ Il a été envoyé sur sa parole dabord à ⟨Lobau puis⟩ à hambourg. Maintenant il est chez son oncle⁵ près de ⟨   ⟩⌐ |

[*the second leaf is missing*]
[*One line cut on spine*]

³ See Ll. 716, 722, in which FBA outlines the conflicting dates that M. d'A set for her return to Paris. His worried command that she should not return before May altered his earlier injunction: 'I give you to the end of October' (L. 716) or 'the 10. of November' (L. 722). By 8 September FBA had decided to stay until spring.

⁴ See vi, L. 619 n. 5 for the family of Edmond-Henri-Étienne-Victurnien de Beauvau (1795–1861). On 8 Mar. 1813, he entered military service as a sous-lieutenant in the first régiment des Hussards. By 27 August he was captured and taken to England as a prisoner of war but was released on 21 September.

⁵ Upon leaving England, Edmond de Beauvau arrived in Hamburg on 28 Sept. 1813 and was ordered to Wesel to await the decision of the Prince-Vice-connétable relative to his future. The young Beauvau, ignoring the order, went to stay in Dulmen (about ten leagues from Wesel) with his uncle Auguste-Philippe-Louis-Emmanuel de Croy (1765–1822), duc de Croy, prince du Saint-Empire, prince souverain de Dulmen (1803). On 23 October, an authorization signed by the duc de Feltre ordered Beauvau to return to Paris.

de lui et se montre reellement parfait. Ta pauvre soeur[6] qui vient d'envoyer chez moi à l'instant et qui comme tu la ⟨négliges bien⟩ sans doute est desolée t'embrasse. C'est de chez elle que j'ajoute ceci—

728   Richmond Hill,
                            12—[*c.* 29] October 1813
To Doctor Burney

A.L.S. (Diary MSS. vii. 5910–[13], Berg), 12 Oct. 1813
Double sheet 4to   4 pp.   foliated (17), and on P[1], (18)   *pmks*   30 OC 1813   To be Delivered / by 10 o'Clock / on Sund. Morn.   red seal
Addressed: Dr. Burney, / Chelsea College, / Chelsea.
Edited by FBA, p. 1 (5910), *annotated and dated*:   ✳·   1813.   (14)   M d'Arblay—MS. of the Wanderer
Edited by CFBt, who covered some of FBA's obliterations.
Edited also by the Press. *See* Textual Notes.

Richmond Hill,
Oct[r] 12 1813[1]

My most dear Padre will, I am sure, congratulate me that I have just had the heartfelt delight of a few lines from M. d'Arblay, dated Sept[r] 5th—I had not had any news since the 17th of August, & I had the melancholy apprehension upon my spirits that no more Letters would be allowed to pass till the Campaign was over. It has been therefore one of the most welcome surprises I ever experienced.

He tells me, also, that he is perfectly well, & quite *accablé* with business. This, for the instant, gives me nothing but joy; for, were he not essentially necessary in some department of civil labour & use, he would surely be included in some *levée en*

---

[6] Mme de Maisonneuve. See L. 731 n. 5.

728. [1] This letter, misdated by FBA, was written *c.* 29 Oct. 1813. On 3 October from Ramsgate, CB Jr. wrote (Osborn) to CPB: 'My present plans are these: To leave Ramsgate for Sittingbourn on Thursday, with Mrs D. A.—to take a place in the Canterbury Coach:—& on Friday morning, she will go off from the Rose, Sittingb[n] for London; & I shall decamp for Tunbridge.' CB Jr. and FBA left for Sittingbourne on 7 October; the next day she went to London, staying first at Chenies Street and then accompanying CBFB to Richmond (*post* 20 October). The postmark helps to date the letter as does FBA's reference to the peace rumours trickling back to London in late October after the Battle of Leipzig.

masse. Every way, therefore, this Letter gives me relief & pleasure.

I have had, also, this Morning, the great comfort to hear that my Alexander is *'stout & well'* at Cambridge, where his kind Uncle Charles still remains. ⌐My intelligence is from Charles Junr—I dispensed with any Letter from Alex till he lost his Uncle.¬

I am indiscribably occupied, & have been so ever since my return from RamsGate, in giving MORE & MORE last touches to my work, about which I begin to grow very anxious. —I | ⌐even feel my honour, now, engaged to finish it to the best of my power, to *'bring home'* as my dear Father expects. My Publishers forget they do not run all the risk themselves— in *half* the sum, we *share* the hazard—for it is only the first fifteen hundred that I am to receive by instalments; the rest is payable merely by succeeding editions, by 250 for every 2000 copies that shall successively be sold.

The real win, therefore, is dependent upon success.¬ I am to receive merely 500 upon delivery of the MS. The two following 500 by instalments from 9 months to 9 months, that is, in a year & a half from the day of *publication*:—not of delivery.[2]

If all goes well, the whole will be 3000—but only at the end of the sale of 8000 copies, ⌐three months after the last lot has disappeared.¬ Oh my dear Padre—if *YOU* approve the work— I shall have good hope.[3]

At my return from RamsGate, my purpose was to claim your permission for my so long delayed Fortnight: Alex. wished it also: but the sudden & unexpected arrival of Clement, ⌐to spend a week in Chenies Street, & of Charlotte to meet him¬ made Alex so earnest to gather documents & hints, for conducting himself at Cambridge, that he | thought it absolutely indispensable to his initiation in College *etiquettes* to stay & consult & confer with his Cousin.[4]— ⌐And just as I lost sight

---

[2] See L. 713 n. 5.

[3] See the 'Articles of Agreement' (Osborn): 'And it is agreed that the first edition of the said work is to consist of three thousand copies and no more and the five subsequent editions are each to consist of one thousand copies and no more and shall respectively be published within three months after two thousand nine hundred and fifty copies of the first edition and nine hundred and fifty copies of each of the immediately preceding five subsequent editions shall be sold.'

[4] Clement Francis, about to enter his third year at Caius College, was a reliable source of information about life at Cambridge. Moreover, he was a dedicated

of my dear Boy, & meant to chear myself by your Fire side, a new business broke out for me relative to a projected sale of my cottage at West Hamble,[5] which demanded Letters, & delibera-tions & a meeting at Mr Murray's,[6] solicitor, with Mrs. Locke & Mr. William Locke. And these interruptions joined to my vain endeavours to postpone printing the work till the spring[7] have cast me into as complete a *fidget* relative to some small changes & new touches, that still occur, whether I will or not, while the MS is in my hands & my power, that I deem it⌐ wisest to yet defer my promised visit, till I have fairly deposited my scribble with Messrs Longman—

I may then, with a mind disembarrassed, & spirits no longer so loaded, really enjoy the society of my beloved Father, & find in it—as I have ever done—all that is most endearing to existence, confidence & affection.

⌐I shall write to Beckey about my lodging,[8] for poor Sarah, I fear is sick of the subject.

But⌐ I have made no delay but for real business, & to come with greater comfort. I shall now probably pass a month, or two, at Chelsea, for I can only get to you upon fine days. I shall have ⌐plenty of prog for the interval.

As Charlotte has quitted Chenies street, I have followed her to Richmond, where I have a room in which I am wholly incog. & see only the two dear Charlottes, & Dolph, who is better. I have not visited the Cambridges & Miss Baker knows that I am here, I am so earnest to devote every moment to the Tribute I am preparing for my dearest Father,—and, I hope, two or three more.[9] — —

The day of delivery is fixed for the 4th—at the meeting of Parliament—can any thing be grander!

student. As he wrote (JRL) to Mrs. Piozzi in December 1811: 'I shall strive for a Wrangler's Degree, the greatest Honour in the Senate House. My success is of course uncertain—but on this depends Fellowships & Every other Academical Honour & Advantage, & therefore calls for much Exertion.'

[5] This is FBA's first awareness of complications attendant on her sale of Camilla Cottage. For the causes and far-reaching effects of these complications, see especially L. 776 and nn. 3, 4.

[6] Alexander Murray (d. 1830) of 3 Symonds Inn was in 1814 William Locke's solicitor, advising him on the sale of Norbury Park.

[7] See L. 724 n. 7.

[8] Rebecca More had been a consultant as long ago as 18 Sept. 1812. See L. 642 n. 13.

[9] In *The Wanderer*, the dedication 'To Doctor Burney, F.R.S. and Correspondent to the Institute of France'. See L. 710 n. 1.

Do give it your good wishes, dearest Sir!—I had best said your blessing—

Charlotte, now at my side, sends her love & duty—& joins with me in the *first* to Sarah, who I hope is recovered from her cold. & always most dearest Sir, ever most dutifully⌐

& most affectionately
Your F. d'Arblay.

⌐Many thanks for the news-papers. I will take the total storage of them & bring the whole 4 months gathering back to you.⌐

⌐They tell me Great News has again been afloat.⌐¹⁰

Mr. Stranghan is to print the MS.¹¹ Mr. Longman comes to me for it—in Chenies Street, on the 4ᵗʰ.¹²

729   [Richmond],
30 October 1813
To Doctor Burney

A.L.S. (rejected Diary MSS. 5914–[17], Berg), *n.d.*
Double sheet 8vo   4 pp.   *pmks* RICHMOND   30 OC 18 ⟨13⟩
30 OC 1813   wafer
Addressed: Dr. Burney, / Chelsea College, / Chelsea.
Edited by FBA, p. 1 (5914), *annotated and dated*: 30ᵗʰ Octʳ 1813   (15)
Alex obtains a Greek Prize at Cambridge.
Edited also at the Press. *See* Textual Notes.

I have a joy so great, my dearest Padre, that I cannot breath till I have communicated it to your kind paternal heart—

My Alex has obtained a Scholarship upon his opening career!¹—

---

¹⁰ L. 724 n. 18.
¹¹ FBA refers to Andrew Strahan (1749–1831), who carried on the business first established by his father William (1715–85) with printing offices initially in Bury Court, Love Lane, Wood Street, and then in New Street near Gough Square, Fleet Street. In 1813 the firm was listed as Strahan and Preston, Printers' Street, Gough Square. Andrew Strahan printed *Camilla* as well as *The Wanderer*. For FBA's meeting with Strahan, see iv, L. 292.
¹² L. 724 n. 20.

729. ¹ At Caius College there were several awards for excellence in written examinations. Since their inception in 1805, some of the prizes had doubled in monetary value (L. 740 n. 3). AA had won his prize of £10 in Classics.

> 'Tis the best that was vacant,
> & tried for, at Caius College
> by 10 or 12 Candidates,
> all entering the University
>   like himself,
> for the first time.
> His Exercize was pronounced
> the best—
> as was his Translation from
>   Demosthenes—
> His Name, therefore, stands first
>   in the List of This Year.—

⌒→

This Scholarship is of Ten pounds only, annually,—
But the Honour!— |

⌒→

Oh that to his Father as well as his Grandfather I could send such an exquisite piece of News!

This revives all my hopes of restoring him to the Literary pursuits which so often have crowned him with Laurels in France.

I think it may happily affect his Character & Temperament, to have this opening success in Greek: for all his present propensity is to the Mathematicks, which, with his thin person, & studious turn, & absence of mind, often made me fear for his health & strength & even existence. |

But if Literature takes its turn, the Sciences will no longer be so dangerous, because they will no longer EXCLUSIVELY absorb him.[2]

How kind has been Charles in staying with him so long!

He had himself the pleasure to tell Alex. his success:[3]—Oh how I envy that! Alex capered about the room with extatic joy

---

[2] See L. 686 and n. 8.

[3] CB Jr. told others of AA's success. Mrs. Locke—for one—wrote to FBA (Barrett, Eg. 3697, f. 181): 'I will now tell my beloved Friend how I joy in her joy & how proudly I feel Our dear Alex[rs] triumph—last Saturday my dearest George brought me the welcome news, for he had met D[r] C. Burney, who imparted it— . . . I must not omit my Georges sincere congratulations on your dear Sons preeminence—and how the victory that was announced yesterday will fill my beloved Friends heart with hope!'

& astonishment. How will his Greek Professor in Paris, M. Hugot,[4] who was warmly attached to him, & always pronounced that he MIGHT, if he would apply, be a second Dr. Charles Burney, as a *Helleniste*—how will he rejoice when this event may be told to him!—But his Father—Oh, his ' Father! —he will be in raptures!—

Adieu, Most dear Sir—

Your Genealogical Tree

   is not without some flourishing Branches—to wave around the honoured root of our Dynasty.

ever most dutiful & affecte

Your FB dA.

I am sure *Sarah* will be very glad.

730
To Charles Burney

Windsor Castle,
6 December [1813]

A.L. (Berg), 6 Dec.
Double sheet 8vo   4 pp.   *pmks*   WINDSOR   7 DE 1813
Addressed: Rev^d Dr. Burney / Rectory House, / Deptford, / Kent.

Windsor Castle, Decr 6^h

This is the very first moment I am able to write a word to my dearest Charles, whose Letter was put into the Chaise that I was mounting to obey the gracious commands that have brought me hither.

I am truly grieved at your new attack, my own dear Carlos— though I flatter myself, as you write in spirits,[1] it is passing off. What can I say about Lady Spencer?[2]—You know how little I like *gadding aside*—yet her Letter is so charming—her invitation at

---

   [4] For M. Hugo[t], see L. 651 n. 6.

730.   [1] On 26–30 Nov. 1813, CB Jr. told FBA (Osborn): 'The Gout . . . has gotten into my lower extremities.' Since in his letter he is wryly playful about its effects, FBA could minimize the nature of the attack. Both misjudged its duration. See L. 739.

   [2] Eldest daughter of Charles Bingham (1735–99), 1st Earl of Lucan (1795), Lady Lavinia (1762–1831) had married on 6 Mar. 1781 Lord George John Spencer (1758–1834) of Althorp Park, Northamptonshire. See iii, L. 136 n. 10.

once so ǀ cordial & so delicate, that I have not the strength, or, rather, the hardness to resist it.[3]—Two things, however, stand in the way of my propensity, though not one thing can in that of my gratitude — —

If my Alexander should be in vacation—my time with him is so precarious as well as precious, that I should not only be wretched, but think it wrong, to lose even one of the few moments I can pass with him: — —

And—there is a certain M.S. which is ceasing to bear that title—but which, without my superintendence, can adopt no other, that must positively detain [me] at Chelsea till it can walk alone. I have stopt ǀ the press to come hither—of course—but it is an immense inconvenience to Mr. Straghan, & disappointment to the Publisher, Longman, & I can do it no more. What time the printing may take is uncertain — —[4]

Now weigh all this in your most solemn sagacity, & for ME use your eloquence,—for Lady Spencer's has sufficed for herself —& make as clear as this haste—& vile pen—make obscure— That I am so sensible of her ladyship's goodness, & so attracted by the amiability of her invitation, That—should you be able to defer your own happiness till my two obstacles are surmounted, I shall be delighted—I *think*—& honoured, I am *sure*—(but don't use those phrases!) to wait upon her Ladyship under your auspices.—adieu—adieu—be well as ǀ as fast as possible—I left my dear Padre better than usual. Kind Love to Rosette

[3] The invitation, now missing, was conveyed to FBA in a letter (Osborn) by CB Jr. (26–30 Nov. 1813): 'I inclose a Letter from my dear clever Lady Spencer—Pray fail not to return it, & with it a reply to the part, which concerns you. . . . I kept it, in the hope of communing with you, on the subject.—She is my dear Ld Spencer's Wife—& must not be affronted.'

[4] FBA assumed the first two volumes of *The Wanderer* were to be printed before Christmas (L. 738), but by 2 February she was certain only of the first (L. 744 and n. 1). However, by 11 Feb. 1814 the other three volumes were off the press and the publication date set. Writing (JRL) to Mrs. Piozzi on that day, MF commented: 'The Wanderer will come out, I hear, in March: & my Aunt is still in England, correcting the proofs at Chelsea.' By 17 March the volumes needed 'only the sewing and stitching' (L. 753).

731   [63 Lower Sloane Street,
                              11–16 December 1813]
To Charles Burney

A.L.S. (Berg), *n.d.*
Single sheet 4to 2 pp. Once bound, and a binding strip (0·3 × 9″)
still attached at left margin *pmks* T.P.P.U. / Chelsea EO ⟨ ⟩ DE
⟨ ⟩ black seal
Addressed: Rev^d Dr. Burney, / Rectory House, / Deptford.
Annotated in pencil, p. 1: Burney / Mde d'Arblay / A.L.S. ⟨Journals⟩

Nothing can be more untimely for me, my dearest Charles,
than an invitation so every way impossible to refuse:[1] my head
is so harrassed by my House, my Proofs, & my internal affairs
of business, & my Heart is so saddened by the conscious misery
of its loved Partner — — Oh my dear Charles! the loss of M.
de Narbonne[2] will afflict him almost as I was afflicted at the
beginning of the year 1800![3]—as the tenderest of Brothers he
loved him—& as a chosen companion he adored him!—And
but the Week before, he lost the Friend EXCEPT Me. de

731. [1] CB Jr. would not allow FBA to reject Lady Spencer's invitation. In a
letter (Osborn) postmarked 11 Dec. 1813, he wrote: 'I am impowered by Lady
Spencer to invite you and Alexander to Althorp, from January 1st—She pledges
herself, that your time shall be *your own*.' He cites Lady Spencer, who promised
that FBA 'shall not be invaded by impertinent inroads or gossiping levity.— . . .
She shall have no *Wanderer* stroll into her apartment:—she shall have no female
difficulties thrown into her way.' CB Jr. continued: 'Read these extracts again—&
then remember that the post comes in every morning about *nine* and goes out
again between 3 and 4.—Strahan,—so *he* spells *his* name—can frank down, &
you can return *under cover* to him;—so that *no time will be lost*—and I shall have
seen my dearest of Sisters *happy* in the Society of the two first women I know, in
this country, Lady Crewe and Lady Spencer.— . . . Now, pray send me word
back to finish this arrangement with Lady Sp.—I will do the needful with Strahan
and Longman.'
   [2] Louis-Marie-Jacques-Almalric, comte de Narbonne-Lara, had died at Torgau
in Austria on 17 Nov. 1813, aged 58. The news that reached Paris is summarized
in Talleyrand's letter (2 Dec. 1813) to the duchesse de Courlande: 'Savez-vous,
chère amie, l'horrible nouvelle. Narbonne est mort. Quelle fatalité! Aller mourir
à Torgau d'une chute de cheval!' (Dard, p. 293). The fall was not the cause of
death. The General's troops were decimated by typhus but he moved among them
'gracieux et indéfatigable devant la mort, mais consterné par les désastres qui
s'accumulaient sur la France'. He contracted the disease but ignored his growing
weakness. 'En passant la revue d'un régiment provisoire qu'il venait de former, il
fit une chute de cheval.' A serious head wound aggravated his condition and he
died (ibid., pp. 288–9).
   [3] SBP died on 6 Jan. 1800.

Narbonne, the most valued, Genl La Tour Maubourg[4]—·
Brother to my own best Friend in France, Me de Maisonneuve[5]
—I have so been overset, that I have kept myself, except for
business & conferences with our dear Padre, nearly shut up.[6]

Yet I doubt not but the lively & kind, & yet feeling Lady
Spencer will revive & do me good—& to be again with YOU,
my own Carlos, who so kindly say that will, all together,
complete your cure—& to introduce my Boy to such a house—
Certainly the whole will do me as much real good as I am susceptible of receiving. Yet the exertion at this moment is tremendous to me of quitting my Cell. Arrange, however, all as you
will & can. I give you carte blanche from yours truly and
forever.

FB. d'A.

Longman &c hurry me to death. |

Our dearest Father was very ill while I was at Windsor!—
but, thank God, he is now tolerably recovered. Poor James is
confined with a slow fever! — —

The Arch[p] has again spoken very kindly of You at Windsor.[7]
My best Love to dear Rosette.

I remember with pleasure how much I used to admire the
sallies & vivacity of Lady Spencer, when Lady Althorp,[8] at
Mrs. Vesey's assemblies;[9] but I had no idea of her possessing

---

[4] Marie-*Victor*-Nicolas de Fay de Latour-Maubourg (1768–1850) suffered a
shattered thigh during the battle of Wachau (a village south of Leipzig) on 16 Oct.
1813. Although he required radical surgery, he lived another thirty-seven years,
filling several posts: ambassadeur to London (1819), ministre de la Guerre (1819–
21), gouverneur des Invalides (1821–30). His dedication to France is memorialized
on the south side of the Arc de Triomphe. For his earlier military career, see v,
L. 456 n. 9.

[5] Marie-Françoise-Élisabeth Bidault de Maisonneuve (v, L. 518 n. 10). Divorced
from her husband and living in near-poverty, she was regarded by FBA as an
intimate friend 'avec un jugement sain, et un coeur tendre, et donnée d'une
sensibilité' (v, L. 526, n. 15).

[6] For ease in visiting CB, FBA took 'a lodging in little Sloane Street, & in coming
backwards & forwards, has hitherto escaped cold. But the nights are terribly
damp, & I tremble for her'. See the letter (Berg) of SHB to CFBt (10 Nov. 1813).

[7] See L. 723 nn. 2, 3.

[8] Between 1781, the year of her marriage to Viscount Althorp, and 1783,
the year her father-in-law (John Spencer, b. 1734) had died.

[9] Elizabeth Vesey (*c.* 1715–91) was one of the 'blue-stocking' set of the 1780s
in London. Married previously, she became before 1746 the wife of Agmondesham
Vesey (d. 1785), M.P., whom CB knew as a member of the Club. FB met her in
1779 and from that time on went to several of Mrs. Vesey's parties, where she
was much amused by the old lady's hearing aids ('a collection of silver *Ears* to
serve instead of *Trumpets*'). See *HFB*, p. 188; *Memoirs*, ii. 262–8; *DL* i. 253.

this cordial & winning charm, nor of her retaining so kind a remembrance of me. She is really resistless.

I have had a charming & cheering account of my Alex from the Archdeacon Cambridge, through Miss Baker.

732   [63 Lower Sloane Street,
13 December 1813]

To Martin Charles Burney

A.L. (Houghton Library, Harvard), *n.d.*
Double sheet 8vo   1 p.   *pmks*   T.P.P.U. / Chelsea   EO   13 DE 18 ⟨13⟩ seal
Addressed: Martin Burney Esqr, / 16 / Mitre Court, / Temple,

All the Courtiers I have left at Windsor are men of business & punctuality, compared with a certain young Lawyer;—who made one appointment for a *wednesday* evening;—& another for a *Sunday*;—& observed neither!—leaving A FAIR YOUNG damsel vainly sighing for his presence! & who now will sigh on till he appear.

Monday Morn^g.

733   [63 Lower Sloane Street],
16 December 1813

To Mrs. Locke

L., incomplete copy in hand of CFB^t (Diary MSS. viii. 5918–[19], Berg), 16 Dec. 1813
Double sheet 4to   2 pp.   foliated (18)
Edited by CFBt *and the* Press. *See* Textual Notes.

To *Mrs Lock*   Decr 16. 1813

Ah, my dearest Friend—how is my poor Cottage—how are my proofs—how is every thing forced from my mind, except what necessity drives there, by this cruel—cruel stroke to my Heart's most suffering Partner! — — The World had power only in TWO¹ instances to have given him QUITE so deadly a blow, dear to his Heart of love as are some,—nay, many others: but *here*, [for *Monsr de Narbonne*,]—it was a passion of admiration, joined to a fondness of friendship, that were a part of himself.²—How he will bear it—& in our absence—perpetually occupies my thoughts. And I have no means to hear from, or to write to him! none, absolutely none!

Just before this, the deepest of wounds was inflicted, I was already overwhelmed with grief for my poor Madame de Maisonneuve—for M: d'A: himself, & for my own personal loss, in the death,—premature & dreadful, nay, inhuman, of the noble, perfect Brother of that Mad^e de Maisonneuve; General La Tour Maubourg. a Man who,—like my own best Friend,—was! is signalized among his Comrades by the term of a *vrai Chevalier | françois. He* was without a blot: and his life has been thrown away merely to prevent his being made a Prisoner! He had received a horrible wound on the first of the tremendous Battles of Leipzic & on the 2^d he suffered amputation—& immediately after was carried away to follow the retreating army! — — in such a condition,—who can wonder to hear that a very few miles from Leipzic he expired! — — —³

Oh my poor Mad^e de Maisonneuve!—She loved him with that exquisite sensation of perfect esteem & tenderness united, that I loved—LOVE—one in whom, as in him, I never saw a Blemish. Oh my sweet Friends—how much we think of Times to come! of blessed Futurity, to bear these strokes!—

Oh what a War is this!—when, when will it terminate!— I struggle hardly to bear up, for I am utterly powerless to offer any species of consolation to my dear unhappy absent sufferers.⁴ — —

733. ¹ FBA and AA.

² The friendship between M. de Narbonne and M. d'A increased when, as exiled Constitutionnels, they took refuge in 1792 at Juniper Hall (ii, pp. xiv–xv). After 1802 they met occasionally at Mme de Laval's salon, where their mutual friends included the comte Destutt de Tracy and his son, prince Victor de Broglie, marquis de Jaucourt, duc de Montmorency-Laval, comte de Choiseul-Gouffier, marquis de Riccé, etc. In 1805 Narbonne tried unsuccessfully to place M. d'A 'as Major-General in the Army of Poland' (vi, L. 572 n. 1).

³ See Ll. 731 n. 4, 735 n. 2.

⁴ Both sides suffered enormous casualties—dead and wounded—during the four-day battle for Leipzig: Russians—22,000; Prussians—16,000; Austrians—8,500; Swedes—300; the French in retreat about 100,000.

As for the 'retreating army', its troops 'soon gave themselves over to indiscipline. The impossibility of providing enough regular distributions of rations provoked and justified their actions. Each man's prime concern was finding food; and as all military spirit had been extinguished, and indescribable depression and disgust had

734   [63 Lower Sloane Street,
                            24 December 1813]
To James Burney

A.L.S. (PML, Autog. Cor. bound), *n.d.*
Double sheet 8vo   1 p.   *pmks*   T.P.P.U. / Chelsea EO   24 DE   seal
Addressed: Captain Burney / James Street, / Westminster.

Dear Brother,
    Alexander is not yet arrived, & I am in hourly expectation
of a visit from Clement that may tell me when to expect him.
    I cannot positively, therefore, say Yes, but I will not say,
No, to *our* keeping Christmas Day at your hospitable board.
    If we are not with you between 3 & 4, be sure my Boy is not
come,[1] & thus I still shall be awaiting him. If otherwise, you
will see him & your affe^te Sister

                                            FB d'A.

Kindest Love to Mrs. B[urney]
Sally & Martinus.
Friday morning.

735   63 Lower Sloane Street,
                            24 December 1813
To Mrs. Waddington

A.L.S. (Berg), 24 Dec. 1813
Double sheet 4to   4 pp.   black seal
Addressed: Mrs Waddington
Also L., incomplete copy by CFB^t (Diary MSS. viii, after 6676, and
numbered 292, Berg), 24 Dec. 1813
Single sheet 4to   2 pp.   numbered 292

taken its place, all those who had left the columns threw down their arms and
walked with a stick instead. Out of sixty thousand soldiers who still remained,
twenty thousand formed themselves into bands of eight or ten, scouring the
countryside and marching on the flanks of the columns, and camping on their
own account. . . . The Army gave these soldiers a nickname . . . *fricoteurs.*' So
General Marmont described the French retreat (as cited by Brett-James, op. cit.,
pp. 273–4). For the original statement, see *Les Memoires du duc de Raguse* (9 vols.,
1857), v. 702–3.

734. [1] AA, who had to complete his 'impositions' before leaving Cambridge, did
not arrive in Chelsea until 2 Jan. 1814. See L. 738 and nn. 2, 3, 5.

Decr 24th 1813.

You think, perhaps, my dearest Mary, that not to merit—by
exact returns—& not to EXPECT Letters is the same thing?—
But you did not think so *jadis*, & I have seen nothing in you I
have wished to change. Change not, then, kind Mary!—now
least of all, that I am so harrassed by multiplicity of calls, that
were I punctuality itself, I could not *earn* a Letter once a month.
But I,—you know, alas! am NOT punctuality itself!—&
though I claim not such interest as saucy Sophy¹ would have
me receive, I yet claim indulgence of long date which I should
be cruelly hurt to forfeit.

My heart has been almost torn asunder, of late, by the dreadful losses which the news papers have communicated to me of
the TWO DEAREST friends of my absent Partner,²—in these
late bloody conflicts!³ — — It has been with difficulty I have
forborne attempting to return to him; but a winter voyage
might risk giving him another loss, that, to his exquisite
partiality, might make the others, that are now sinking him
with misery, seem suddenly without interest or importance. But
that ¹ he should lose, forever, the two friends most dear to him
at the epoch when he generously indulges me with coming to
visit & enjoy all mine, is truly deplorable.

The loss of one of these so untimely departed favourites, how
will Mad^e de S[taël] ⟨support⟩!⁴—Pray tell me if you hear any

---

735. ¹ Sophia Elizabeth Burney. See L. 684 and n. 6.
² FBA refers to the comte de Narbonne and General Latour-Maubourg.
Of the latter *The Times* reported (22 Nov. 1813): '20 October: General Latour
Maubourg had one of his feet taken off [at Leipzig], and yet Napoleon forced
him to leave the place, in consequence whereof he died not far from hence.'
But see Ll. 731 n. 4, 736 n. 1.
³ FBA writes of these events almost three weeks after their report in English
newspapers. Her disregard of immediacy is described (Berg, 10 Nov. 1813) by
SHB to CFBt: '[FBA] reads Newspapers from morning till night: but Newspapers
of three or four weeks back, & will not let you say a word to her of present events.
"O, don't tell me—I shall come to it—I am reading up to it!" And by the time she
has read up to it, some newer intelligence will probably have arrived, which will
make what we are now rejoicing at appear stale, & put it all out of our heads.'
⁴ The liaison between Mme de Staël and Narbonne was probably ended by the
time of the Juniper Hall interlude, and certainly upon her leaving England (ii,
p. xviii). Within three days of her departure from Norbury Park, she sent a letter
(Berg, 25 May [1793]) to M. d'A: 'je n'ai pas reçu une seule ligne de lui, mon
Dieu serait il malade? . . . ce silence, c'est la mort.' Her love-letters to Narbonne
continued until May 1794, although she knew of his intimacy with Mme de Laval
in Lausanne (Dard, p. 135). On her visit to Switzerland in 1796, Mme de Staël
saw Narbonne a few times; but as she wrote to her husband, there was no intimacy
between them. Despite their separation they never forgot each other. In 1803,

thing of her, & *what*. I have no conception how she will endure such a blow![5]—Entre nous, this!—In beginning her Germany,[6] —in which I am only advanced to about a third of the first Volume, I perpetually LONGED to write to Her—but imperious obstacles are in the way[7]—&, next to you, to tell you, as the only person I know likely to sincerely sympathise with me, the pleasure—the transport, rather, with [which] I read nearly every phrase. Such acuteness of thought, such vivacity of ideas, & such brilliancy of expression, I know not where I have met before. I often lay the book down, to enjoy, for a considerable time, a single sentence. I have rarely, even in the course of my whole life, read any thing with so glowing a fulness of applause; but there I now stop; these two heavy misfortunes reached me, & I | have not had my mind enough at ease, nor my intellects enough at liberty, to take up the Book since. Whether it will carry me on, hereafter, with the same charm, I know not.[8] It is said, that Sir J[s] Macintosh has reviewed it in the Quarterly review. I thought your friend Mr. Jeffereys would have been its commentator.[9]

Narbonne protested to Napoleon against the exile of Mme de Staël from Paris (Solovieff, pp. 484, 487).

[5] On 7 Dec. 1813 Mary Berry (ii. 546) dined at Lord Stafford's with Mme de Staël, her son, and daughter. 'At dinner the conversation rather flagged. Madame de Staël was not excited enough; it appeared to me that she only wanted that to be brilliant as usual, though she had to day received the news of the death of Comte Louis de Narbonne. One must acknowledge that one could not lose an old lover more gaily, as it was said of Charles VIIth of his kingdom.' For her reserve at this time, see Dard, p. 135, Solovieff, pp. 489–90.

[6] See L. 718 n. 9.

[7] The 'imperious obstacles' originated primarily in France (L. 753 n. 8), although FBA knew that both CB and Queen Charlotte would frown upon a renewal of her association with Mme de Staël.

Nevertheless, she dominated English society during the season of 1813 and, despite her friendship with the Princess of Wales, was received by the Prince Regent at a ball attended by the Queen and the Princesses. As Mary Berry wrote (ii. 545): 'The Staël left Richmond . . . and wherever she is, there will society be also—if it is to be had within ten miles *à la ronde*. Except during her visit to Bowood . . . she has been constantly in town, giving very agreeable dinners and soirées, with two or three women and half-a-dozen men—*dont elle se charge toute seule*.'

[8] FBA's initial reaction to *De L'Allemagne* differed from that of MF, who on 11 Feb. 1814 admitted (JRL) to Mrs. Piozzi that while she found evidence of Mme de Staël's 'superior mind' in the work, yet 'she has shocked me, in several points, where principle is concerned, & disgusted me with an affectation of religion. . . . that though she may have some knowledge of it in her head, it stops at the brain, & never descends to her *heart*.'

[9] The review of *De L'Allemagne*, which did not appear in the *Quarterly Review* until January 1814, was by Reginald Heber (1783–1826). FBA had in mind the account of this work that appeared in the *Edinburgh Review* for October 1813. She correctly attributed it to Sir James Mackintosh. See W. A. Copinger, *On the Authorship of the First Hundred Numbers of 'The Edinburgh Review'* (Manchester,

I am just returned from passing a Week at Windsor, where those whom you know that I love & reverence have been all goodness to me, & all liberality for my peculiar feelings, & even sufferings, in the midst of their so just satisfaction.[10] You were named very graciously, with much regret that the fulness of their engagements prevented their seeing you, [espe]cially uttered by the Princess Elizabeth. I was quite sorry that, while at Windsor, I could not see our good Mrs. Astley. But I was lodged in the Castle, & had not a moment disengaged. Many thanks for the sprightly, spirited, nay, witty Letter of your Fanny. I join in her opinion through-out; though there is one stroke,—image, rather, I would efface, as not quite so scrupulously suited to my ideas of her refined mind and feelings, as to harmonize with my own portrait of her character & disposition. You will easily discover the *point*: but pray do not mention it to her *from me*: She seems full of sensibility *au fond*, & I would not hurt her gentle heart for 1000 universes. Of your too sweet, too lovely Emily I never dare speak: but give her, I pray, as to the accomplished Fanny, & lively Augusta, my kind love. I want to hear of all their healths—& of your's—how much! I expect my Boy home for the vacation in a day or two. You will wonder to hear—in the midst of so much occupation, that I am going to carry him, next month, for a week or two to Althorpe. But Lady Spencer is an Invincible. All opposition is thrown down by her fertile resources.—My Stuff is in the Press, & could not be set aside;—*n'importe*—the proofs shall come & return, Franked, daily: my son is coming to me, & my resolution & inclination, alike, forbid his not finding me;—*n'importe*, again, *he* must come too, & take the run of the Library:—I knew not how to travel:—*n'importe*, encore; I must accommodate my time to Dr. Charles's, & he his to mine, & we must come & go together. Thus the matter is arranged.—But always direct to Chelsea College, whence all finds, or follows. Poor Ralph is better—mais!—mais my poor sister has wholly left London for him.![11]—My Wanderer has been in the hands of the Publishers

1895), p. xx. She was surprised that so celebrated a work was not reviewed by the journal's editor, Francis Jeffrey.

[10] FBA refers to the military victories of the Grand Alliance. By the end of 1813 Napoleon's army had retreated to an area west of the Rhine for the first time since its movements eastward in 1805.

[11] CBFB's decision to leave London was made in November. In a letter (JRL), dated 9 Nov. 1813, MF informed Mrs. Piozzi: 'Poor little Dolph still keeps his

since the 4th of last Month. It will appear in February,[12]—I am inconceivably fidgetted about it. Expectation has taken a wrong scent,[13] & must necessarily be disappointed. I shall not fail to give my Cantab: your admonitions about Ale as well as Wine. Yet he is so even alarmingly thin, that I must wish him more fortifying beverage than water. I am always pleased—amused—or interested by your enclosures. Don't discontinue them, pray.

Adieu, ever dear Mary—ever most faithfully

Yours F B d'Arblay.

I have not yet seen Mrs. Montagu's Letters.[14]

My latest Letter is of *October*[15]—it talks, not, alas, of pleasure or comfort!—every friend a Mourner![16]

P.S. I open this Letter—which had been finished too late for the post, to say I have this very moment received your welcome & wished for one of Decr 22^d—Some part of it I have fortunately answered *d'avance*: but explain, I beg, how it is you seem to hold in equal admiration The Work[17]—and its ⟨suppressor?⟩—the Exiled, & the Exiler?[18]

alarming cough, which is always worse in London; so Mama comes to Richmond for good air; & here we shall remain, I believe, if any where, a twelvemonth.' Dolph seemed to improve temporarily, but by 18 Mar. 1814, MF wrote (JRL) to Mrs. Piozzi that 'neither Mama nor Dolph are well, both invalids nursing through this desperate winter.' By 27 July 1814, however, CFBt wrote (Berg), 'Dolph rows in the water & grows strong.'

[12] For the publication date of *The Wanderer*, see Ll. 738 n. 8, 753.

[13] FBA was aware that the reading public expected *The Wanderer* to present a realistic exposé of French life during the Napoleonic regime, and in the dedication to that work she repudiated any such intention.

'Such, therefore . . . who expect to find here materials for political controversy; or fresh food for national animosity; must turn elsewhere their disappointed eyes: for here, they will simply meet, what the Authour has thrice sought to present to them already, a composition upon general life, manners, and characters; . . . I have felt, indeed, no disposition,—I ought rather, perhaps, to say talent,—for venturing upon the stormy sea of politics; whose waves . . . with difficulty can be stemmed, and never can be trusted.'

[14] FBA is referring to *The Letters of Mrs. Elizabeth Montagu* . . . . Published by Matthew Montagu (4 vols., 1809–13).

[15] See L. 727, dated 28 Oct. 1813.

[16] For the number of French dead, see L. 733 n. 4. France was morally exhausted and disillusioned after almost twenty-one years of continuous wars. Resistance to Napoleon was growing. The Royalists, organized as Les Chevaliers de la Foi and Les Bannières du Roi, worked in the provinces to encourage a Bourbon Restoration. The Napoleonic ministers were paralysed by the growing lists of those killed in action or taken prisoner. The Assemblies and the bourgeoisie were disaffected. For many Frenchmen the defeat at Leipzig symbolized the defeat of Napoleon and their country.

[17] *De L'Allemagne* (nn. 8, 9).

[18] The 'exiled' was Mme de Staël; the 'exiler' Napoleon or, more specifically, Savary, the ministre de la Police. See L. 718 n. 9.

Madame de Maisonneuve
conjointly with M. d'Arblay
To Madame d'Arblay

A.L. & A.L. (Berg), *n.d.*
Double sheet 4to   4 pp.
Addressed: Madame / Madame D'Arblay, chez le Docteur / Burney. /
a Chelsey / près de London—
Edited by FBA, p. 1, *annotated and dated*:   ⁙   ⁙   (9)   (9)   (8)   (18)
Decembre   The terrible Death of M. de Narbonne—the Heart's dearest
Friend of my own Best Friend, & the God Father of Alexandre. The letter
is begun by Mme. de Maisonneuve
Annotated by CFBt, p. 4: Copied
Also L. copy by CFBt (Diary MSS. viii. 5918–5918x, Berg), Dec. 1813
2 double sheets 4to   5 pp.

Je n'avais pas pu jusqu'ici incomparable bien chere Amie!
obtenir la place de mettre une ligne dans la lettre de votre si
cher si excellent ami! aujourd'hui c'est lui qui ajoutera a ce
que j'aurai commencé et il veut faire l'essai si ceci vous parviendra mieux. il est bien affligé de la perte irréparable qu'il
vient de faire de son précieux et fidele ami le Cte de N[arbonne]
mais heureusement sa santé n'en souffre pas. il dit qu'il se sent
plus de courage et plus de force que vous ne lui en supposerez et
la crainte de vous inquiéter de vous causer une peine de plus le
porte a recevoir la consolation de ses amis et de sa voisine et a
soigner sa santé uniquement pour vous dont il ressent toute la
peine tout le tourment d'etre loin de lui dans cette triste circon-
stance. tâchez de lui donner de vos nouvelles. il en a bien
besoin; ainsi que de celles d'Alexandre: il vous Ecrit sans cesse
et il n'a pas la moindre certitude que ses lettres vous parvien-
nent. en vous parlant d'un si cher intérêt oserai-je vous parler
aussi de moi? j'espère que ce sera toujours avec amitié que vous
recevrez l'expression de mes plus tendres sentiments: je ne
pourrois vous dire tout ce que votre absence, la privation de
vos nouvelles me fait souffrir; combien je suis occupée continuellement de vous et du cher Alex — — je connois si bien votre
coeur que je ne doute pas que vous ayez été bien tristement

occupée de moi en apprenant la Cruelle Blessure de mon bien aimé frère; enfin il vit! il est encore a Mayence avec sa femme et incessament je vais aller l'attendre au Lys.[1] Si je ne suis pas a Mayence c'est parce que j'ai mon cher Maxime[2] ici avec moi, sain et sauf, ayant été exposé a tous les dangers de la Guerre, et d'un voyage comme il n'y en a jamais eu de si pénible, et de si dangereux. Florimond[3] est aussi ici; tous deux ont bien demandé de vos nouvelles, de celles d'Alex, tout ce que vous connoissez dans ce pays est affligé de la perte d'une des personnes les plus regrettables.[4] toutes vont bien quelques soient leur âge, leur delicatesse, ou leur chagrin.

Adieu chere bien aimée Madame, — n'oubliez pas des amies et une voisine dont le coeur est plein de vous et qui vous a voué une Eternelle amitié.[5]

[*M. d'Arblay continues the letter*]

Quelle perte, ma chere Fanni! et il faut encore y joindre le tourment que j'eprouve en songeant à l'inquietude que ma santé va te donner. Rassure toi ma tendre amie et compte sur le soin que je prendrai d'une vie dont tu as bien voulu embellir tous les instans. l'amertume de celui ci est adoucie par l'idée que

736. [1] Victor de Fay de Latour-Maubourg had survived the amputation of his leg and had managed during the rout of the French forces after Leipzig to cross the Rhine. He was now recuperating in a French hospital established in Mayence (later Mainz).

[2] Frédéric-Gérard-Benoni-César 'Maxime' Bidault de ◖Maisonneuve, though only 16 at this time, had already experienced almost a year of active military duty, beginning as a sous-lieutenant (Apr. 1813) in the 16th régiment de Chasseurs à cheval and then as a lieutenant (Sept. 1813) in the 19th régiment de Chasseurs à cheval.

[3] Just-Pons-*Florimond* (1781–1837) was Mme de Maisonneuve's nephew and a son of the comte Marie-Charles-*César*-Florimond de Fay de Latour-Maubourg (1756–1831). See v, L. 446 n. 12. A diplomat, Florimond began his career first as secrétaire d'ambassade in Copenhagen, then in Constantinople (1806). By 1813 he was ministre plénipotentiaire in Stuttgart, making a brief visit to Paris. In 1816 he held the same post in Hanover and in 1819 in Dresden. Named ambassadeur to Constantinople in 1823, but soon recalled, he was without employment until the Revolution of July. In 1830 he obtained the embassy in Naples and within a year the embassy in Rome.

[4] The death of the comte de Narbonne affected many people. 'Le 24 novembre 1813, Castellane écrivait dans son *Journal*, après avoir noté les nobles circonstances de la mort de son général: "Cette nouvelle me cause un profond chagrin. Je conserverai toujours le souvenir de ses bontés." Ce sentiment était partagé non seulement par la famille de Narbonne, mais par tous ceux qui l'avaient bien connu' (Dard, p. 293). See also Orieux, p. 113.

[5] Mme de Maisonneuve lived at 18, rue Basse in Passy (v, L. 518 n. 10). The d'Arblays bought and moved into an unfinished house at 54, rue Basse in October 1802 (*HFB*, p. 316).

lorsque nous serons reunis nous pleurerons ensemble cet ami incomparable, ce frere adoré, qu'un cruel accident vient de nous enlever si inopinement. Après avoir echappé aux ⏐ dangers si multipliés de la retraite de Russie,[6] qu'il a faite le plus souvent à pied, et couchant presque toujours au bivouac, au milieu des vieux militaires, tout à fait surpris de le trouver constament le même que nous l'avons vû, il est mort dés suites d'une chute de cheval,[7] et ce qui me désole le plus, il est mort isolé, n'ayant près de lui qu'un tres jeune aide de camp,[8] tous les autres ayant été placés, ou n'ayant pu parvenir à le joindre. Lui! la bonté par essence!—lui dont les soins si attentifs si recherchés en apparence, mais si naturels aimant tant à alleger les souffrances de ses amis, il est mort isolé, sans qu'un seul d'entr'eux put lui fermer les yeux, put recueillir sa dernière pensée, put recevoir son dernier soupir! Ah! cette cruelle pensée ne me quitte point; elle est déchirante. Je te l'avoue ma chere Fanny je regrette infiniment de n'avoir pas volé près de lui. Je ne puis être satisfait des soins qu'on aura pris de lui. Un bruit sourd se repand qu'Augustin[9] n'etait plus pour lui ce que nous l'avons toujours cru; que la prosperité l'avait gâté, et que son maitre, qu'il ne servait plus avec le même zele, et qui avait même d'autres reproches plus graves à lui faire, ne le conservait, que parce que son excessive bonté l'empêchait d'accueillir un seul

---

[6] While the Russian campaign was being planned, M. de Narbonne, then about 56, was asked to become Napoleon's aide-de-camp. To the surprise and suspicion of some (for he had been exiled from Paris for a short time), 'il ne s'y refusa pourtant pas, et la manière facile dont il en remplit les fonctions, la gaieté de son courage dans cette terrible campagne, ses bons mots, ses manières militaires et de si bon genre, tant avec les soldats qu'avec les officiers, lui gagnèrent complétement et les uns et les autres, et ceux-là mêmes à qui sa nomination avait inspiré le plus humeur et de jalousie' (Michaud).

[7] For the actual cause of his death at Torgau, see L. 731 n. 2.

[8] Anne-Louis-*Ferdinand* de Rohan-Chabot (1789–1869) became in 1809 sous-lieutenant des Hussards. Young Rohan (also entitled prince de Léon) served as aide-de-camp to the comte de Narbonne. As the Emperor's emissary, Rohan brought the Tsar *the ultimatum of France*. 'In 1812 he received the cross at Moscow, received ten lance wounds, lost all that he possessed, horses, effects, etc., was present at all the engagements, at the passage of the Beresina, at Torgau, where he had the grief of seeing . . . Comte de Narbonne die in his arms' (Gontaut, i. 161). At the Battle of Dresden he was captured. Released after a short imprisonment, he gained the rank of chef d'escadron. After the Restoration he was allied in a military capacity to the duc de Berry and the duc de Bordeaux. In 1824 he was made maréchal de camp.

[9] For Augustin, the valet of Narbonne, see ii, L. 68 n. 46; v, L. 511 n. 5; vi, L. 560 n. 9. An indication that the general felt abandoned and even ill appears in a letter (Berg, in the hand of M. d'A), dated 1813 from Torgau, and addressed to Mme de Fézensac: 'moi je me fletris comme une fleur detachée de sa tige.'

instant l'idée de se separer de ce vieux compagnon d'infortune. Je ne puis, ma fanni, t'exprimer à quel point ces revelations m'ont fait mal. Heureusement je suis loin d'être convaincu de la triste verité de ces bruits aux quels Mr de Choiseul[10] et moi refusons d'ajouter foi mais sans être moins tourmenté, de les voir si generalement accredités.

Lorsque j'ai appris cette à jamais lamentable nouvelle, j'etais chez M[de] de L[aval][11] avec Mathieu,[12] et trois ou quatre autres personnes. On vint prier M[de] de L[aval] de passer dans sa chambre, d'où le moment d'après nous vîmes sortir M[de] de Jaucourt[13] en larmes, pour nous prier de nous retirer parce que

[10] Marie-Gabriel-Florent-Auguste de Choiseul (1752–1817), comte de Beaupré, then de Choiseul-Gouffier (1771), had long been one of M. de Narbonne's closest friends. Before the Revolution they accepted Talleyrand into what Marie-Antoinette referred to as 'le triumvirat'. Usually together, 'les trois amis fréquentaient ensemble les mêmes maisons' (Dard, pp. 54–5). For the diplomatic and scholarly career of the comte de Choiseul-Gouffier, see iii, L. 130 n. 2.

[11] Appropriately M. d'A heard of the general's death at the salon of Mme de Laval (c. 1748–1833), who had been his mistress since their exile in Switzerland (iii, Ll. 184, 246). According to Rambuteau, pp. 25–6): 'J'y suis venu tous les jours, de 1808 à 1813: quelquefois j'apportais mon petit contingent de nouvelles, sinon je me glissais derrière les fauteuils et j'écoutais les histoires de l'ancienne Cour, les anecdotes de M. de Choiseul, les reparties de M. de Narbonne, les saillies de M. de Talleyrand dont Mme de Laval ne laissait pas de subir l'ascendant, ce qui me faisait dire à M. de Narbonne: "Pardieu, dans votre proverbe, il joue l'amant et vous le mari." '

[12] The son of Mme de Laval, Mathieu-Jean-Félicité de Montmorency-Laval (1767–1826), vicomte de Laval, had been associated with Narbonne when they were politically active in the last few years before the Revolution. While a member of the National Assembly, the vicomte voted with the majority and supported extreme egalitarian legislation. But when the republic was proclaimed, he emigrated first to England (ii, p. xv) and then to Lausanne. There he heard of the execution of his brother, the abbé de Laval.

When he returned to France about 1795, he seemingly abandoned a political life for one of pious charity. Yet by 1810 he had helped to organize the Ordre, which sought to bring 'au service de l'Eglise et du Roi l'organisation maçonnique qui avait été le principal instrument de succès des idées révolutionnaires'. Divided into three groups, the Ordre had at its pinnacle M. de Laval as grand master of the Chevaliers de la Foi 'qui seuls connaissaient toute l'étendue de l'Ordre et son double but politique et religieux' (Bertier de Sauvigny, pp. 18–19).

By 1815 he was openly political, named on 17 August to the Chambre des pairs, ministre des affaires étrangères (1821) and président du Conseil. In these offices and in the Chambre he repudiated his youthful liberalism. For FBA's personal portrait of the vicomte, see her French Exercise Book III (Berg), dated 1804.

[13] Divorcing the comte de La Châtre, Marie-Charlotte-Louise-Aglaé-Perrette *née* Bontemps (1762–1848) had married in Switzerland Arnail-François de Jaucourt (1757–1852), comte (1808), marquis (1817). For M. de Jaucourt's stay at Juniper Hall, see ii, pp. xv–xvii; v, L. 446 n. 14. He left England with an English passport in January 1793. According to FBA (iii, L. 131), he lived in northern France secretly, was discovered, and escaped to Switzerland some time before the end of 1793. Presumably he resided there for several years. At the latest he returned to France by 1799, entering the Tribunate, of which he was elected president on 25 Oct. 1802. The following year he became a member of the Senate. Although

—elle m'apperçut alors, et s'ecria: Ah! M^r D'Arblay—quelles nouvelles affreuses de notre ami—je te proteste que ce ne fut que plus d'un quart d'heure après, qu'en recueillant, ou plutot cherchant à recueillir mes esprits, je crus me rappeler avoir entendu prononcer le mot *mort*: j'etais de bout, le col tendu, ayant l'air d'ecouter, et n'entendant rien, en un mot comme une veritable statue. Neamoins je suis sorti machinalement avec les autres, et Me de Montalivet[14] a eu la bonté de m'accompagner. Ce n'est que lorsque j'ai été seul au coin de mon feu, que j'ai commencé à me rendre compte de ce qui venait de se passer. j'etouffais, mais sans verser une seule larme. Sur le champ j'ai pensé à toi, et effrayé de l'espece de suffocation que j'eprouvais, et de la crainte d'une horrible attaque de nerfs que je sentais venir; j'ai pris 7 à 8 gouttes d'offman, sur du sucre, et j'ai avalé deux analeptics puis je me suis mis au lit, où je suis resté sans aucune souffrance vive mais dans un malaise general.

Le matin je fis fermer ma porte et mettre le pot au feu pour avoir chez moi du bouillon. J'entre dans ces details pour te prouver le soin que j'ai pris de moi et le desir de me conserver dans l'idée que reunis un jour nous pourrons nous entretenir ensemble des chers amis que nous avons perdus. Je ne puis ma chere Fanny, te dire à quel point ceux qui nous restent sont bons pour moi. Cette adorable amie, dans la lettre de la quelle je t'ecris, est pour moi une veritable Soeur! Je reprends mon recit. Elle, Florimond | et Mr de Riccé[15] &c &c vinrent plusieurs fois, sans pouvoir entrer. Je n'etais veritablement pas en etat de recevoir même mes amis les plus intimes; Cependant j'etais levé, mais si foible, si souffrant, si etouffé par la frequence de ces soupirs brulans qu'un chagrin vif m'arracha que j'eus recours encore aux gouttes d'offman, mais sans succès. Ce ne fut que vers midi qu'ayant eu l'heureuse idée d'aller voir son portrait, certainement ressemblant, je me sentis soulagé par un deluge de larmes, alors j'envoyai demander des nouvelles de

maintaining ties with Mme de Staël's group in Paris after 1797 and until her exile from the city in 1803, he recognized the Bonapartes and actually served for a time as chambellan de Joseph Bonaparte.

[14] Marie-Louise-Françoise-Adélaïde Starot de Saint-Germain (*c.* 1780–1850) had married in 1797 Jean Bachasson de Montalivet, who in 1813 was ministre de l'Intérieur. See L. 689 n. 4.

[15] Gabriel-Marie de Riccé (1758–1832), comte de Riccé. For his enduring friendship with M. de Narbonne and his possible financial support of the general, see iv, L. 292 and n. 11; v, L. 453 n. 1.

M^de de L[aval]^16 et je sus: qu'à la suite de la nuit la plus terrible, elle etait encore très souffrante et desirait me voir. Après avoir pris une petite soupe et deux oeufs frais j'envoyai chercher une voiture et commençai par aller chez M^de de B[raancamp]^17 qui est aussi bien que son etat peut le permettre mais ne reçoit personne. De là je fus chez M^de de L[aval] qui heureusement n'avait avec elle que sa fidele Zoé.^18 Là encore je versai un torrent de larmes, et me sentis un grand poids de moins. l'instant d'après Mr de Choiseul Gouffier entra, les yeux et le coeur gonflés. Mad^e de Beaufremont,^19 soeur de celle que tu as vue à Cesy,^20 vint ensuite, la figure toute decomposée, et poussant des cris, puis Madame de Jaucourt &c. &c. Tout le monde pleurait. M^de de Jaucourt me demanda si j'avais reçu un billet de son mari, et sur ma reponse que non: elle me dit que c'etait pour m'inviter à diner chez elle aujourdhui Samedi avec Riccé et Mr de Montigny,^21 leur parent, attaché à la dernière ambassade de Vienne,^22 où il avait accompagné notre ami, et

---

^16 When Mme de Laval and the comte de Narbonne met in Switzerland shortly after the latter's deportation from England (iii, L. 145 n. 1), the result was a liaison that lasted for life. Neither, however, felt constrained by their relationship, Mme de Laval bestowing similar affection upon Talleyrand at the same time (Rambuteau, pp. 25–6).
FBA disapproved of the lady's morality and never mentioned her by name to CB (v, L. 513 n. 8). In her French Exercise Book III (Berg), dated 'Ce 6 mai [1804]', FBA compared Mathieu de Laval with his mother: 'actuellement il me reste un desir de savoir comment ce digne homme se conduit avec sa mere,— s'il sait tout ce qu'on dit sur son compte, s'il passe par tout cela en silence, ou s'il s'est melé de vouloir changer sa manière d'etre. Cette mere ne m'a jamais été nomée, mais le fils est toujours à la tête de tout-ce qui est pour le bien public relativement à la charité et la bienfaisance, pour le secours des malheureux, et le soulagement des malades. On ne peut pas passer la vie plus dignement, ni d'une manière plus faite en verité une meilleure.'
^17 Amable-Riom-*Louise*-Françoise de Narbonne-Lara (1786–1849) had married in 1806 the comte de Braancamp de Sobral (1775–1846). She served as official hostess in the French Embassy in Vienna while her father was ambassador there. 'Le tact et l'esprit [de Mme de Braancamp] auraient été pour lui de puissants auxiliares' (Dard, p. 261). ^18 Unidentified.
^19 The princesse Hélène de Bauffremont (1774–1836), at one time 'chanoinesse de Remirement', was in 1816 to marry the comte de Choiseul-Gouffier.
^20 The princesse Hortense-Geneviève-Marie-Anne de Bauffremont (1782–1848) had married in 1804 Joseph-Augustin de Narbonne-Lara (1767–1825). See v, L. 517 n. 11.
^21 Louis-Charles-François Levisse de Montigny (1786–1877) was legally adopted in 1821 by the marquis de Jaucourt and his wife. In 1860 Montigny assumed the title of marquis de Jaucourt.
^22 Narbonne was ambassador to Vienna from 5 Mar. to 11 Aug. 1813, occupying the largest house in the city and employing twelve body-servants and stewards. He was chosen for the post by Napoleon himself, who thought him shrewd enough to expose the machinations of Metternich. The ambassador soon recognized that Austria, while still an ally, was in fact an enemy. In April 1813 he sent this information to Napoleon at Mayence, who acted accordingly. See Madelin, xiii. 93 ff.

où consequement il avait appris à le connoitre et consequement à le regreter. Jaucourt, obligé de diner ailleurs, doit venir nous rejoindre le plutôt possible, car j'ai accepté. J'ai fait plus. J'ai diné hier chez Mad^e Helene de Beaufremont, avec Mr de Choiseul et M^r d'Ernaude.²³ Notre perte a fait tous les frais de la conversation, et nous avons donné de justes larmes à l'être incomparable qui nous reunissait. Tout cela, ma pauvre Fanny paraitra bien etrange dans le pays que tu habites; mais je le rep[ete.] j'entre dans ces details pour te prouver, que je cherche et que je trouve bien des consolations dans le malheur sans remede qui vient de m'accabler. Je reçois lettres sur lettres de tous nos amis. M^de de Cadignan,²⁴ que tu ne reconnoitrais pas depuis son abjuration vient de m'en ecrire une tout à fait aimable. Elle est dit elle un peu incommodée. Sans cela elle serait venue me voir. Ma chere M^de de Maisonneuve, est surtout d'une bonté que je renvoye à sa veritable source, à sa tendre amitié pour ma Fanny, et j'en jouis ainsi doublement. Nous esperons pouvoir bientot embrasser son frere si cher,²⁵ que notre excellent Larrey²⁶ a parfaitement soigné. Je regrette bien que ce dernier n'ait pas été de mon pauvre ami au lieu de Mr de Geneste premier medecin de l'Armée, un chirurgien,²⁷ et

²³ A misspelling of Jean-Baptiste Arnaud (1754–1823), baron de l'Empire (1809). He entered the army in 1772 and participated in the fighting of the armée des Pyrénées-Occidentales (1793–4), the armée d'Italie (1795), the armée de Hollande (1798–9), the armée du Rhin (1800–1). Made a colonel in 1804, he fought in the Prussian campaign (1806). By 1808 he was a member of the Légion d'honneur and général de brigade. Wounded many times over the years, he was at the siege of Badajoz in 1811. He was recognized as a chevalier de Saint-Louis in 1815 and retired in the same year.

²⁴ Catherine Dupleix de Cadignan *née* Hunter (1773–1860). See v, L. 513 n. 6. She had probably in the last year renounced her American citizenship in order to further her son's military career. See L. 747 n. 4.

²⁵ Suffering a head wound during the Russian campaign, fighting at Dresden, and seriously wounded again at Wachau, the marquis de Latour-Maubourg had been away from Paris since the spring of 1812. See L. 735 n. 2.

²⁶ For baron Larrey's medical efforts during the Leipzig campaign and the French army's retreat, see L. 668 n. 6.

²⁷ René-Nicolas Dufriche Desgenettes (1762–1837), chevalier de l'Empire (1809), baron de l'Empire (1810), inspecteur général du service de santé, médecin en chef aux armées (1803). He participated in the campaigns of the Grande Armée: Prussia, Poland, Spain, and Russia. Taken prisoner by the Russians on 10 Dec. 1812, he was freed by the Tsar in recognition of his medical services to the Russian troops. He became médecin en chef de la Grande Armée in 1813 and served in the Dresden campaign, during which he was cut off in the citadel of Torgau. He returned to France on 6 May 1814, two days after the departure of Napoleon. Despite his loyalty to the Emperor even during the Cent Jours, his medical skill was acknowledged by the Bourbons. His army career was only briefly interrupted, and his academic honours from 1819 to 1832 were many.

surtout un chirurgien comme notre cher Larrey, pouvant être d'une beaucoup plus grande utilité pour sauver des suites d'un accident comme celui qui a tué cette chère victime. Eux aussi le pleureront. Ah! que dis-je! jamais mortel n'aura plus universelement reçu l'hommage de larmes sinceres. C'est que son esprit, si justement admiré, etait la moindre de ses qualités; c'est que sa bonté si expansive animait ses moindres actions, c'est que d'une negligence excessive et même condamnable pour ses ǀ propres interets, il etait sans cesse occupé de ceux des autres. C'est enfin qu'avec quelques defauts et sans aucun vice, il reunissait aux vertus les plus rares toutes les qualités les plus brillantes et les plus attachantes; et que son ame etait un sanctuaire où l'on etait toujours sur de rencontrer tout ce qu'il y a de plus noble, de plus delicat, de plus chevaleresque, de plus grand et de plus aimable — adieu mes aimables et si chers amis! Quand nous reverrons nous? — Soignez vous bien. Je vous promets de vous en donner l'exemple. Je ne sais point, ma chere Fanny, si tu as reçu la lettre où je te mandais que notre ami Theodore de Meulan[28] a remplacé à Verdun le General qui commandait tous les prisonniers. Il me semble que leurs parens pourraient, quand ils leur ecrivent, donner de ta santé des nouvelles que je suis bien sur qu'il me ferait parvenir et qui me rendraient si heureux! Ton nouvel ouvrage doit être imprimé. Je te supplie d'en adresser sur le champ deux exemplaires à Mr Saulnier,[29] Secretaire genal de la police. Il en garderait un pour lui, et me donnerait l'autre, qui me ferait tant de bonheur, et me serait d'une si grande consolation en ce moment. Comme il me serait impossible de trouver le tems de le traduire, je desire infiniment en charger un Mr Dubuck,[30] qui ecrit à merveille et est très avantageusement connu dans la litterature par plusieurs ouvrages qu'il a dejà traduits de l'anglais entr'autres le Missionnaire.[31]

[28] Marie-Joseph-Théodore de Meulan (1778–1832), comte de Meulan (1818), who in assuming this post at Verdun was promoted to the rank of colonel (1814). For FBA's meeting with M. de Meulan at Joigny, see v, Ll. 532 n. 5, 537 n. 7.

[29] Pierre-Dieudonné-Louis Saulnier (1767–1838), secrétaire général du ministère de la Police (vi, L. 623 n. 2).

[30] M. d'A refers to Pierre-Louis Dubuc (*fl.* 1780–*post* 1820), a translator of Maria Edgeworth's *Scènes de la vie du grand monde* (1813–14): *L'Absent* (3 vols.), *Émilie de Coulanges*, and *Vivian* (3 vols.). He also translated Jane Porter's *Les Chefs Écossais* (5 vols., 1814); Mrs. Jane West's *Sidney, comte d'Avondel* (4 vols., 1813).

[31] For Dubuc's translation in 1812 of *The Missionary, An Indian Tale*, by Lady Sydney Morgan, see vi, L. 622 n. 5.

[Deptford Rectory],
30 December 1813—[1 January 1814]

To Mrs. James Burney

A.L.S. (PML, Autog. Cor. bound), 30 Dec. 1813
Double sheet 8vo   4 pp.   *pmks*   T.P.P. / U. Lombard St.   1 JA 1814
seal
Addressed: Mrs. Burney, / at Captain Burney's, / James Street. / Nº
26 Westminster.

Thursday Deʳ 30
1813

My dear Mrs. Burney,

I am quite anxious for news of my dear Brother.[1] I entreat you
to send me a line.

And I have no need of added anxiety—Alexander is not
come, & has not written!—

I am inexpressibly ill at ease. These fogs make me *desire* him
to defer his journey, could I but hear from him. I am going, a
second time, to write to him to that effect.

My dear Father, George says, is wonderfully collected &
well. What a mercy! for this Weather makes me a prisoner.
But poor Charles has ᒷ a new & severe attack of the Gout:[2] &
our Althorp visit is deferred for at least 3 weeks.

And probably, then, Lady Spencer will be come to town.

For *myself* this is a singular relief & convenience, as I am
harrassed with affairs, & as travelling in such weather would be
nearly Madness in me.

Rosette, thank God, keeps well, & is now a good Nurse.

I have heard that my sister of John Street, & Mr. Burney,
are well, also.

Try to send me a chearing account of my dear Brother
James; & give ᒷ him my kindest love: & tell him I write to *rou*
to save him the trouble of seeking his Spectacles—as well as to
assure you how much I am, My dear Mrs. Burney,

affectionately yours—
F B d'A.

737. [1] For JB's 'slow fever', see L. 731.
  [2] CB Jr. suffered an attack of gout at the end of November (L. 730 n. 1) but
was sufficiently recovered by 11 December to talk of FBA's accompanying him on
a journey to Althorp (L. 731 n. 1). The new attack, to which FBA refers, must have
occurred after 11 and before 30 December.

My love to dear Sally & Martin.

Clement is at Richmond—

And I know not even the *name* of any comrade at Caius College whom I could address.

He said he should come on *Monday*!—[3]

These dreadful fogs are what most disturb me. All travelling must, for some days past, have been dangerous. Would he were here!— ⎮

P.S. This moment it occurs to me, to beg of my dear Mrs. Burney to send, *for me*, some Messenger to the Inn at Charing Cross,[4] to Demand Whether any accident has happened to *ANY* Cambridge Fly, or Stage, since these Fogs,[5] as a young passenger is missing. This would relieve my greatest uneasiness. I will joyfully & thankfully pay the person. But I have no means to get one

I have just found a Boy to send ⟨2nd of⟩ ⌐Thursday⌐[6] night. I kept this till the Boy returned. He brings word no accident has happened to a Cambridge Coach. God be praised

Sat^y nig[ht]—no news!—

[3] 27 Dec. 1813.

[4] The Golden Cross Inn at Charing Cross was a terminal point in London for public vehicles from Cambridge.

[5] According to *GM* lxxxiv[1] (Jan. 1814), 87: 'The density of the atmosphere during the day, and the heavy fog at night, during the whole of last week, in London and many miles round, has been very remarkable, and has occasioned several accidents. On Monday night, the mails and other coaches were delayed unusually long, and proceeded on their way with great difficulty and danger. Many coaches were overturned. . . . There has been no instance of such a fog as last week pervaded the Metropolis, extending many miles round, since the Earthquake at Lisbon, 1755. . . . Yesterday [2 Jan. 1814], however, the fog disappeared, in consequence of a change of the wind.'

[6] 30 Dec. 1813.

738   [63 Lower Sloane Street,
                                      3–4 January 1814]
To Mrs. Broome
and Mrs. Barrett

A.L.S. (Berg), *n.d.*
Double sheet 4to   4 pp.   *pmks*   T.P.P.P. / Chelsea EO   4 JA 1814
wafer
   Addressed: Mrs. Broome / at Henry Barrett's / Esqr / Richmond / Surry—
   Endorsed by CBFB: Sister d'arblay / Jany 1814

Monday
My Boy is by my side—

My most dear Charlottes—kind, beloved, & every thing that
is amiable! — — Your 3 Letters are all arrived, & they gave
me the utmost of consolation I could receive while in a suspense
so painful—so alarming; for the news papers spoke of accidents
to the Northern Coaches,[1] without naming which they [w]ere.
My affright by Saturday was so great, that I could no longer
refrain from writing to Dr. Davy, to entreat him to make
enquiry for me what was become of my vainly expected son.
I have just received a kind, short answer—which followed, as
he knew it would, the naughty Boy's arrival.—naughty indeed!
For he always *INTENDED* writing, till Saturday,—when a
Letter of mine so shocked him, all at once, that he set himself
to finishing his *IMPOSITIONS*,[2] & worked for about 8 Hours
following, accomplished his difficulties in a time that, otherwise,
would have demanded a week or 10 days, obtained his leave
of absence, & set off, at 10 o'clock, by the *Night Coach*! which I
had especially charged him to avoid! He came through that
dreadful fog, stopt here about 12 o'clock[3]—& after a long

---

738. [1] According to *GM* lxxxiv¹ (Jan. 1814), 87: '. . . the York Mail twice [over-
turned], near Ware, notwithstanding the guard and passengers walked to keep
it in the road. The Maidenhead coach, on its return from town, on Tuesday
evening, missed the road, and was also overturned.'
   [2] The extra assignments imposed on AA by the College tutors—Chapman and
Gimingham—as a punishment. See n. 5.
   [3] Supposed to arrive on Monday 27 December, a stage route of 52 miles, AA
left Cambridge for Chelsea at 10 p.m. on 1 January. He reached Charing Cross
Sunday morning (the fog having lifted) and went from there to Lower Sloane
Street.

breakfast, went to the College to dinner & tea, & came to our dormitory in a rapidly advancing fever! with a cough that filled me with terrour!— He is *now Tuesday Noon*,[4] MUCH better, and James' powders has done as usual, wonders, & with analeptics, will complete his cure. But alas! he is come to me Thinner, paler, more meagre than [ever] be what may the consequence, I must tear him entirely from his Mathematics till I see him refitted in health. How many thanks I give you BOTH, from the bottom of my heart, for your most satisfactory communications![5] I had feared something yet worse—nay, much worse: Though this is very bad!—I shall never name this part of our commerce, to EITHER of the youths, for there is no need; Alex revealed the whole within 3 minutes of his arrival: &—as, alas, I may require your kind assistance again—& more than once—I would not put EITHER of them on their guard.

[4] 4 Jan. 1814.

[5] On 1 Jan. 1814 CFBt wrote (Barrett, Eg. 3702A, ff. 4–6) to FBA: 'I write at my dear Mother's elbow that I may have the happiness of joining to quiet your fears respecting our dear Alex's journey in this weather, as there can be no doubt that he is still at Cambridge. Clement left him there, & told us that Alex had so much to do, that he would hardly be able to leave College till *he* Clem returned thither. Clement left us yesterday morn^g Decr 31. . . . he solemnly promised to write on the first day & to send a long account of dearest Alexander. meanwhile I will tell you honestly my dearest Aunt all which we learnt from Clement & you will find in it more cause for triumph than regret.—Clement says that no one ever yet appeared there, who was so free from wicked thoughts, words, or deeds, as Alexander. & he says that his cousins mathematical talents & knowledge are matter of wonder & high expectation to the masters, as well as raising much admiration in his fellow students, all of whom he eminently excells. Mr Woodhouse, a mathematical *professor* at Caius College has conceived a real friendship for Alex, & has influence over him, which Clement wishes him to use in persuading dear Alex to study in the *Cambridge* way, that is to say, to lea[r]n to solve his problems & to give their proofs by *geometry* instead of *algebra* or the *analytical* method, wc^h is the french way & also the *best*. & Alex knows *that*. but unfortunately when his examination comes next year, he will be expected to bring geometrical proofs instead of analytical, & if he has not attended to them, he may lose the prize which he must else *infallibly* obtain.—Then, as a matter of *form* & *muster*, rather than devotion, the young men are all required to be in chapel at 8 in the morning 5 days out of 7.—& the heads of the Colleges make a great point of their conforming to this rule, & give *impositions* or long tasks to those who break it.—Clement formerly had an imposition for this sort of irregularity, & Alex has one now. This is no disgrace, & to *him* will be little trouble; but still if he has not learnt the imposition, he cannot yet leave College. . . . Alex's mind & talents are so superior to those of the other young men that he cannot be expected to listen to their *advice* . . . & even *Clem's* he receives from affection rather than conviction. The old Doctors are in the same predicament; & it is chiefly from Mr Woodhouse whom Alexander loves *and* respects, that Clement hopes to see him receive conviction of the expediency of conforming to College rules; & as this is really the only point on which he errs, we may trust that habit & example, now he has been longer there, will assist in making him adopt their regulations, even though his judgement discerns their futility. . . .' But see L. 740 n. 2.

I hope & trust Alex will reform—but it will not be COM-
PLETELY, I greatly fear, his mischievous habits are so dear
to him. How sweetly have you both tried to soften the business!
Oh yes, my dearest Charlottes twain! I will surely come & rest
& refresh myself some time at Richmond when I am at liberty.
I desire nothing more truly, for all there is perfect sympathy
with all my feelings.

Yet my Charlott*ina* has vexed me by her too generous zeal
of kindness in giving me her valuable time for my covering: will
it reach my heart? if so, I will unvex ¹ when I feel it on: & will
my *first* Charlotte arrange that I may not have double & REAL
vexation, by settling the *commission* part of the affair? BOTH my
Charlottes must know me well enough to be sure there is no
other way to save me from real disturbance. I shall now soon
be able to arrange my long arrears with my own dear sister.⁶
I have just heard our dear James is better, though he had been
worse, alas! & is fallen away most alarmingly.—I have no
fresh news of Carlos. I heard of our Esther last night, & she &
her's see[m] well.

The printing of V. II is finished. The rest wai[t] the termination of Xmas holydays even to begin.⁷ [I] *wish* to keep it back
till March—but the publishers are terribly of another opinion.⁸

O my friends—if you knew how unhappy I have been since
we met—& before I had the terrour of Alex—for my best of
Friends—who has lost his two dearest Heart favourites!—&
within 10 days of one another!⁹—I was already quite overpowered with grief. — —

Lady Keith is coming to town—purposely to grant me once
again a meeting. Faithful attachment can never go beyond
hers. It is fortunate I was not at Althorp.

I long for better news of my dear Dolph.¹⁰ our kindest love

⁶ For a considerable time after her return in 1812, FBA resided with CBFB
'pic-nic' style; i.e. the two sisters agreed to share living expenses. FBA, however,
had allowed her debts to accumulate, hoping to settle them from the advance
paid to her by Longman and his associates, or with the money gained from the
sale of Camilla Cottage.

⁷ *The Wanderer* appeared in five volumes 12°. It is probable that the printing of
the second volume was not yet completed. See L. 744 nn. 1, 6.

⁸ The booksellers wished a February publication, but FBA won her point.
The Wanderer appeared on 28 Mar. 1814. See L. 753.

⁹ Not having received L. 736, FBA still presumed the death of Victor de Fay
de Latour-Maubourg.

¹⁰ Between early November and the beginning of 1814, Dolph began to mend.
In February, MF wrote (JRL) to Mrs. Piozzi: 'Here I am at last [at Richmond],

THE

WANDERER;

OR,

FEMALE DIFFICULTIES.

BY

THE AUTHOR OF

EVELINA; CECILIA; AND CAMILLA.

———————

IN FIVE VOLUMES.

VOL. I.

———◆———

LONDON:

PRINTED FOR LONGMAN, HURST, REES, ORME, AND BROWN,
PATERNOSTER-ROW.

1814.

Title page of Mme D'Arblay's last novel

to him—& kisses to the 3 little charmers, & best remembrances to Mr. Barrett, & the two Cam[bridge]s & Miss Baker. ⟨For⟩ ever ever yrs

FB d'A. [1]

This moment comes George[11] with the very best made tippet I ever saw—the most perfect in size, shape & elegance throughout!—I am quite enchanted with its *propriety*. of taste & ⟨fitness⟩ with *all* its beauty for the quiet almost secluded Dame of other times for whom it is so kindly kindly wrought.—

739   [63 Lower Sloane Street,
                                   5 January 1814]
To Charles Burney

A.L. (Osborn), *n.d.*
Double sheet 8vo   4 pp.   *pmk*   5 JA 1814
Addressed: Rev[d] Dr. Burney, / Rectory House, / Deptford.

Let me begin with the only little word I have to say that is cheerful—My joy that my dearest Charles is better.—

But—that an excursion that at another time would be so agreeable, should now be so full of difficulty!—[1]

1st—I think it great imprudence in *you* to travel till the weather entirely changes—[2]

and for *ME*, it would be MADNESS. I cannot do it, my dear Charles: with my consciousness of my situation, I could not answer such an enterprise either to God or my Husband.—

If, therefore, you go till the elements are kinder, *I* am out of all question.

with my Mother & little Dolph, both of whom are pretty well, but would not long remain so, without the greatest care & quiet.' But see L. 735 n. 11.
[11] CB's houseboy.

739. [1] FBA refers to the journey to Althorp and the hospitality of Lord and Lady Spencer.
[2] On 26 Jan. 1814 Mary Berry wrote (iii. 3): 'The thaw commenced to-day, after four weeks and three days of continual frost, accompanied by a whole week of thick fog, and after a fall of snow such as I never remember to have seen before, even in the remarkable winters of 1788 and 1795. The streets have been in a state like a deep sandy road, and the few carriages that were out went in the same slow and silent manner.'

My poor wild Alex has travelled to me, at last, by the night coach, & thick fog of last Saturday!—& he is now under James's powders & analeptics! confined to his room, or mine, & I am ˈ now devoted to nursing him!— — nor, if all else were well, could I for the UNIVERSE quit him. That, you will not want to be told.

The other engagement I hinted to you, is with Lady Keith. She is coming to town, the end of next week, on purpose to see me!—

Nevertheless, as the other is a *prior* engagement, I would not —& will not make her arrival detain me, should all else be propitious—but can any thing be more cruelly ill-timed?— How she will be disappointed! & how am I shocked at once & grieved!

Perhaps, as the parliament meets so late,[3] Ly. Spencer may remain next month at Althorp, & you may change your time to *after* your *obligated* business, & go to her for a week, instead ˈ of a fortnight?

I am truly, truly vexed, to seem slack in accepting the honour of such kindness, when, in a natural state, I should be eager to show my sense of it, & my pleasure & gratitude: but my obstacles are not such as I can master!

Let us hope the Govt—the weather, & my Alexander, may yet dance the Hay to a better tune, if Lady Spencer can but admit us, *all three*, at a later period.

My dear Father continues wonderfully well, thank Heaven.

Some one day in next week I MUST go to great Charlotte Street Blackfriar's ⟨Mews⟩ to see a person who is going to Paris. Don't happen to come this way on that day! I can fix nothing, not even that, while Alex is ill. He is returned alas, thinner, paler, more bent than ever—His irregular, ˈ but violent application— has half destroyed him!—I take all study from him now whatsoever.

Adieu, my dearest Charles—my kind love to Rosette

---

[3] Parliament formally opened on 1 Mar. 1814 and then adjourned for three weeks until Monday the 21st. Lord Spencer was an active Whig in the House of Lords.

[63 Lower Sloane Street,
post 5 January 1814]

To Charles Burney

A.L. (Osborn), *n.d.*
Double sheet 8vo   4 pp.

Alas—My dearest Charles—alas!—

What step can I take to avert a blow so deplorably ruinous to all my hopes?—nay, almost to my powers of existence?—For where—& how can I finish his education for his future prosperity, if he is withdrawn from Cambridge? I am wholly without resource, for he is utterly unfit, nay, incapable for any mode of life that is not literary or scientific.

Mr. Chapman's Letter,[1] nevertheless, is narrow & cruel. He speaks of sins of Omission, as he would brand those of Commission, when he hurls a menace of so shocking a nature.

That Menace excepted, all the rest, all the detail, was already known to me, from *himself*, & from *Clement*,[2] since his arrival at Chelsea: but his health was so much my first object, that all my thoughts were given to that point—for he has returned to me like a Skeleton!— |

He disguises nothing: he has not an idea of art; he has not an idea, either, that he merits severity; for he has only, he says, pursued his studies his *own way*! He goes on with his Algebra, *Madly*: he seeks problems *night* & *day*: twice he has sat up *two whole Nights*! & *always*, as the time most undisturbed, he has sat up till 2 or 3 in the Morning!—Invited, also, by various youths, to their parties, which he concluded to be for learned chattery, they have ridiculed him into drinking wine—which his head cannot bear, nor his stomach; & the latter came home

---

740. [1] Benedict Chapman (1770–1852) had entered Caius College as a student in 1787, receiving his B.A. in 1792, his M.A. in 1795, his D.D. in 1840. He was a fellow of the College from 1792 to 1820, a dean in 1797, a steward in 1799, bursar from 1805 to 1807, master from 1839 until his death. He was ordained deacon (Ely) on 15 June 1794, priest on 22 May 1796, and served as rector of Ashdon, Essex, from 1818 to 1852.

[2] On 25 Dec. 1813 Clement Francis in a letter (Berg) to FBA recommended that AA be temporarily removed from Caius until he acquired a sense of purpose and discipline. This advice, continued Clement, was seconded by many of AA's friends at the College.

in a state so disordered, that he was perpetually sick!—To this
is added, that his pursuit of these problems have made him
nearly starve himself, for he has hardly ever gone to dinner: he
has only arrived as the students arose, seized a morsel of bread
& cheese, & — — at night felt ravenously hungry!—yet at *noon*,
when Mr. Cambridge called upon him, I *now* am told, his
Breakfast was untouched!—Can you wonder he came home,
—in a night coach through such a fog, more dead than alive,
I have been so frightened for his very life, that all else has sunk
as nothing before me, till his amendment. James's powders, &
analeptics, have cured his fever, & restored his stomach: & I
am now recovering him by Bark & Barley Broths. And he is
wonderfully recruited within these 3 last days. Till when, he
never even left my room.

He promises complete amendment upon his return—but
Alas!—

I wish him to try for the Classical prize in May:[3] if only to
scratch him from this absorbing algebra. He says he knows not
how to *set about* studying for it.

Will you, my dearest Carlos, invite him to pass 2 or 3 days
with you, & then put him in a way?

The youth who purposes being first, has dissuaded him from
the attempt. He is the dupe of every one! But if He were *3ᵈ* I
should be glad he *tried*: & clement says it would much appease
the Masters.

I have not told him of Chapman's Letter to I you.[4] I fear to
shake his just restored health by such a blow to his spirits. But
if you have him *with you*, while he is free from any *dread* of seeing
you angry, you could do it with more *effect yourself*, & with less
danger. for *apprehension* is what is most hurtful to an ardent, yet
unthinking Mind, like his.

He is capable, they all say, of every thing!—but this algebra
makes him forget EVERY body! himself, whom he demolishes,
most of all!—

I will not talk to you of my heart-aching terrour! — —

[3] See L. 729 n. 1 for competitive prizes and awards at Caius College. For the
result of AA's performance in this later Classics examination, see L. 790.

[4] The letter is missing but Chapman apparently presented a list of charges
(his own as well as those of William Gimingham and Martin Davy) that stressed
AA's indiscretions, his idleness, 'heedlessness', immaturity, his absences from
chapel, lectures, and hall, his 'braving all order' (L. 750).

I rejoice most profoundly—for I can do nothing gaily—you are better, my dear Carlos—& I long for further amendment:
I am quite vexed about L^y Spencer, Was it necessary to mention *my* impossibilities when *yours* sufficed, as my invitation was not separate?—I fear that has hurt her.

741
To M. d'Arblay

Chelsea College,
13 January 1814

A.L. (rejected Diary MSS. 5922–[23b], Berg), 13 Jan. 1814
Originally a small double sheet 4to (8·6×7·2″). The conjugate leaves were separated and a cutting (1·1 *to* 1·6×7·2″) was removed from the second leaf and pasted to the first. See Textual Notes. This cutting and a second segment (5·9×7·2″) of the second leaf are extant, though damaged by a seal tear. A segment (*c.* 1 *to* 1·5×7·2″) sliced from the top of the leaf is missing. 4 pp. *pmks* DUNKERQU[E] 7 Avril 1817 red seal
Addressed: À Monsieur / Monsieur d'Arblay / Rue de Miromenil / 8, f^g St Honoré / à Paris
Edited by FBA, p. 1 (5922), *annotated and year* 1814 *circled*: (1)
Edited also by CFBt.

Chelsea College—
Ce *13^m Jan^r* 1814.

M'est il permis encore de m'addresser à mon meilleur ami!—ou bien le plus cher!—non pas pour lui dire comme il me tarde de le revoir—cela ne peut pas se dire—il n'y a point de moyen—point de langage pour le dire—mais pour demander de ses nouvelles, et de lui donner des nôtres. Je me porte, à ce moment, très bien, mais, pendant ce mauvais tems, je ne suis que prisonière à la maison; et je ne manquerai pas d'observer autant qu'il m'est possible tout ce que me recommande mon tendre ami; en toute confiance que ces soins seront reciproques, et que malgré tous les maux—et les malheurs—qui peuvent nous arracher le bonheur, nous nous conserverons mutuellement, religieusement la santé, pour pouvoir, à l'époque de notre ré-union, jouir au moins de la consolation d'être encore l'un à l'autre. Ah, mon ami, si vous saviez comme—depuis quelque tems—vous occupez TOUTE mon Ame!—⌐Faites moi savoir, de manière ou d'autre, comment vous vous portez et surtout rassurez-moi sur cette tendresse qui m'est si précieuse et si *necéssaire*, et qui seule peut vous faire lutter contre l'affliction par tendresse, ici, je veux dire cet oubli de vous même qui vous mettra toujours devant les yeux un cher vous-même dont la conservation, pour tout ce qui est bonheur dans ce monde tient à la vôtre. Ah mon ami, quand serons nous reunis? A mon avis ⟨   ⟩ c à d : il y a ⟨   ⟩ la lettre où vous exigez de moi les soins les plus assidus de ma santé, en me promettant solonelle-ment une réciprocité d'attentions. Amen! voila l'engagement fait, qu'il soit accompli! Aux affaires ⟨1ˢᵗ⟩ pour le livre. Le ⟨press⟩ ⟨   ⟩ est imprimé[1] mais, ⟨pour seul moyen⟩, comme vous me dites les propos 'je n'ai point le moyen' le libraire ne veut pas qu'une seule page soit envoyé avant la publication. Il dit, je ⟨   ⟩, on peut le repandre, et lui faire tort. Le tout est à lui, maintenant, pas à moi. Même *le copyright*.[2] Tels sont les conditions. Je ferai autant qu'il me sera possible tout ce que vous m'avez indiqué quant aux copies mais je ne peut plus en reclamer au delà de la convention déjà faite d'ici encore ⟨   ⟩ possible et une autre Famille Respectée,[3] et mon compagnon m'a causé des dettes que je ne puis payer que par des copies. Cependant, je ferai de sorte de vous envoyer, coûte que coûte, 5 exemplaires :[4] le pʳ je me flatte que vous voulez bien garder à jamais : le 2ᵈ pour mon cher M. de Lally ;[5] le tʳ pour M Barbier[6] et les deux autres pour votre distribution. Nos chères dames, d'Henin, de Maison-neuve, de Tessé, attendront la traduction.[7] Mais je ne doute pas que Mᵉ Solvyns aura le 4ᵉ.[8] De plus [il a] été ⟨mentionné⟩

---

741. [1] *The Wanderer*. See L. 753.

[2] See L. 728 n. 2.

[3] The Royal Family were to receive six copies.

[4] According to L. 756, M. d'A received ten copies.

[5] For Trophime-Gérard, comte de Lally-Tolendal (1751–1830), see i, L. 17 n. 21. FBA, respectful of M. de Lally's literary judgement, wished to have his opinion of *The Wanderer*.

[6] For Jean-Pierre Barbier de Neuville (1754–1822), see vi, Ll. 567 n. 1, 595 n. 10. Now retired from the ministère de l'Intérieur, M. Barbier had been in 1805 chef de la Troisième Division where M. d'A went to work on 16 March as a rédacteur. That FBA wished him to have a copy is indicative of gratitude for past favours when the d'Arblays were most in need.

[7] Ever since the letter of M. d'A, dated 4 July 1813 (Appendix II), FBA was certain of a French translation of *The Wanderer*. It was translated in 1815 as *La Femme errante* by J. B. J. Breton de la Martinière and A. J. Lemierre d'Argy.

[8] FBA's token of gratitude to Mme Solvyns for passing letters to and from the d'Arblays between August 1812 and May 1813.

s'il faut en donner à M ⟨B ⟩[9] que je ne connais pas, il faut le *preter* à Mad^e ⟨Cad⟩;[10] | Mais il me faut absolument ⟨10⟩ pour la famille Burney: 5 à mon pere & mes freres et soeurs plus d'autres parens qui ont toujours eu des copies de ce que j'ai imprimé 5,[11] et 3 pour les amis qui ont travaillé,[12] et qui veulent bien travailler pour mon ⟨ ⟩ Je n'ai pas d'espace pour plus de détails mais tout est arrangé d'après ⟨ ⟩ qui me paroît ⟨ ⟩ une pareille distribution et certes personne ne nous remerciera d'acheter le livre pour en faire des cadeaux! Faites moi savoir, je vous en prie, comment je peux vous faire passer le p^r exemplaire et arrangez quelque chose avec quelque libraire quant à la traduction. Mr Longman était enchanté de l'idée que Mr de Lally en serait de la fête.[13] Mais pour l'envoyer avant la publication, voilà ce qu'il a refusé de faire pour l'amerique d'où l'on m'a fait l'offre de 500£ ^St pour avoir une copie tout de suite.[14] Il faut être juste, lorsqu'on paye £⟨3000⟩ ^St on a le droit à tous les avantages lorsque ces £3000 ne nous reviendront qu'après la 6th edition.[15] Cependant j'ai prévenu Mr Longman de votre intention, et il m'a assuré qu'il vous fera passer le p^r exemplaire où vous voulez, pourvu que vous lui indiquera le moyen. ⁋

Je tremble de voir l'attente publique sur ce pauvre petit ouvrage![16]

[9] Possibly M. Bachasson, comte de Montalivet. The presentation of *The Wanderer* to the ministre de l'Intérieur would be a prudent gesture.

[10] Mme de Cadignan.

[11] Only nine copies went to the Burney 'tribe' (L. 756 n. 1).

[12] Intending to give a copy each to Mrs. Locke, Mrs. Waddington, and Lady Crewe, FBA again had to alter her plans (L. 756 n. 1).

[13] FBA refers to the plan of M. d'A first described in his letter (Berg) to her dated 4 July 1813. At that time he proposed that *The Wanderer* be published initially in Paris as a translation by M. de Lally, Mme Allart, and 'quelques autres de tes amis', and after the peace be printed in London as an original English text. While FBA rejected this plan, she was now prepared—six months later—to regard a French translation as a financial asset.
For Marie-Françoise Allart *née* Gay, see vi, L. 597 n. 5.

[14] Through Henry Brevoort (L. 707 n. 1), with Mrs. Waddington as intermediary, FBA began to plan for an American edition in the summer of 1813. For the consummation of the plan, see L. 718 n. 15.

[15] See L. 713 n. 5.

[16] FBA feared public notice of her work. As early as 1779, she had told Samuel Crisp: 'I had always dreaded as a real evil my name's getting into print. . . .' Dazzled by the success of *Evelina*, she felt that nothing she could do thereafter would equal it. She once told SBP: 'you can't think how I tremble for what all this will end in! I verily think I had best stop where I am, and never again attempt writing: for after so much honour, so much success, how shall I bear a downfall?' (as cited by Edward A. Bloom, ed. *Evelina*, 1968, pp. xiii, xiv).

J'ai changé le titre, et j'espere que vous n'en serez pas mécontent: c'est actuelment The Wanderer. Le 2de titre, Female Difficulties, reste.[17]

À present, à notre ci-devant Hermitage. Le croyez vous, mon ami, — on en a fait une Valuation, et, le verger, les saplings, le Kitchen Garden, entier le tout inclus, on ne l'a fait monter qu'à 640 L^{res} S^t! — Et elle nous a couté £1000, moins 3 ou 4, livres. avant de rien planter, sans meubles, et sans les papiers! — [18] J'ai remis tout à fait tout projet de vente, avant que d'avoir vos idées la-dessus. ⌐La rente actuelle est à 73 L^{res} l'année, dont 26 sont toujours oté par les taxes, que nous payons nous même. Il nous en revient, ordinairement, 47 net. Mais à prèsent il en faut des reparations qui demandent, me dit-on, £200 L^{res}[19] Si l'on fait cela la valuation sera augmenté. La personne[20] qui ⟨   ⟩ et qui l'a ⟨vu⟩ il y a 7 ou 8 ans, m'a fait dire qu'il l'achetera au prix fixé 640 L^{res} [   ] il le quittera le Novembre prochain, car il ne peut plus le garder, il ne peut pas l'augmenter, et en acheter le terrain, &c pour que ce soit la peine, de faire lui même les réparations. William nous offre un bail de 21 ans. Il dit qu'il ne peut pas faire davantage, à cause de *l'entail*. Oh que vous ⟨passiez⟩ ici, pour voir et regler tout cela. William m'a chargé de vous dire qu'il n'y est rien qu'il ne fera pas pour vous montrer son vraie amitié, autant que de le faire est compatible avec sa position. Helas Norbury Park a besoin aussi des reparations, et bien besoin — et il ne peut pas en faire! ⟨Ait⟩ les 500st que notre meilleur ami avoit perdu, lorsque nous avions perdu notre 500'! Notre pauvre Hermitage ne peut pas rester comme elle est en ⟨   ⟩ et sans être habitée. ⟨Suffit à peine   ⟩ tombé. Il faut, ⟨l'hôte⟩ quiⁿ |

[17] As in all her other novels, FBA probably intended her heroine's name (Juliet) to be the title.

[18] By October 1813 William Locke decided to sell Norbury Park, informing FBA either directly or through his solicitor that Camilla Cottage was built on land for which she had no deed (L. 728 nn. 5, 6). He was, however, prepared to buy the cottage for its current appraised value, i.e. £640, despite the fact that the d'Arblays had spent almost twice that sum on its construction and grounds. In this letter FBA must have known that she had to comply with Locke's conditions. Nevertheless, she remained indecisive, leaving the matter to M. d'A. For the quarrel and misunderstanding provoked by this forced sale, see especially Ll. 776, 778, 781 n. 6, 820.

[19] For the later reaction of M. d'A to this version of the cost of repairs to Camilla Cottage, see L. 831.

[20] The present tenant Bolton Hudson (L. 646 n. 26).

[*The top of the second leaf is missing*]

┌actuellement, ⟨et⟩ non pas vous etonner.┐—Mon cher Pere se porte à merveille, le tout consideré: Mais—il est bien, bien faible! Il ne sort pas de sa chambre pendant tout l'hyver. Il ne reçoit presque personne. Il aime etonnament la solitude: et sa memoire, qui commence, quelque fois, a manquer d'exactitude, et toujours parfaite pour Vous. Je vous ai déjà dit qu'il vous destine son Encyclopedie: et, je crois même la plus part de ses livres françois.[21] Il a voulu m'en parler; mais cela m'a trop sensiblement touché; et, le voyant, il a coupé court le discours. — Cher—cher Pere!—

Notre excellent [Frère ainé, Jacques] [*tear*] ┌il n'en est pas encore remis et┐ garde sa chambre ┌mais son [homme l'avai]t fait quitter son lit. ⟨ ⟩┐ je ne suis pas sans inquiétude. [Il a une intrans]┌igeance ⟨affreuse⟩, et il┐ n'écoute pas les medecins. Quoique il a l'ad[miration de] Thomas, qui est son ami particulier,[22] et qui est l'homme qu[i a fait la] guerrisson dont je vous ai parlé, de la goûte, en donnant de l[a mouta]rde bien melée avec de l'eau. C'étoit à un gouteux, son propre Cocher, qui étoit enflé à l'estomach, et à la poitrine, et dans l'angoisse de la mort. Et il étoit guerri tout de suite! en 3 jours il a re-commencé son metier, ce qu'il suive encore. C'est une chose merveilleuse, et on ne peut pas plus vrai. M. Thomas le lui a donné après avoir vainement essayé et madeira, et de l'Eau de vie: et le pauvre cocher étoit à l'extremité.[23] Charles a la goûte—pas,

[21] According to CB's will, M. d'A did not receive as much as FBA described herein. He did receive *A New and General Biographical Dictionary; containing an historical and critical Account of the Lives and Writings of the most Eminent Persons in every Nation; particularly the British and the Irish.* The work appeared in several editions: twelve volumes in 1761–7, a similar number of volumes in 1784, fifteen volumes (edited by William Tooke) in 1798. But all of CB's French books, 'except the works of Voltaire many of which are unfit for the perusal of Females', were left to SHB and Fanny Raper.

[22] For JB's illness, see L. 731 and for his physician, L. 676 n. 2. FBA acknowledged the closeness of JB and his doctor when, at her brother's request, she presented Mr. and Mrs. Thomas with an inscribed copy of *The Wanderer* (L. 755 and n. 3).

[23] The coachman suffered from 'atonic gout', i.e. a stomach disorder whose pains and cramps afflicted 'the trunk and upper extremities of the body'. Mr. Thomas's treatment of this ailment was not as radical as FBA suggests, for one prescription advises that 'some wine also may be necessary; but it should be in moderate quantity, and of the least acescent kinds, and if every kind of wine should be found to increase the acidity of the stomach, ardent spirits and water must be employed' (*Enc. Brit.*, 3rd ed., xi. 187).

Dieu Merci, de cette manière, mais de sorte qu'il est prisonier à sa chambre, à Deptford:[24] sans quoi, nous aurions été, lui, Alex et moi, à Althorp, chez Lord Spencer: Lady Spencer ne voulant pas écouter d'obstacle: j'ai plaidé mon état de santé: elle m'a promis plus de soins que partout ailleurs: j'ai dit que le petit livre etant actuellement à l'imprimerie, je ne pouvais pas le quitter, sans desoler le Libraire: Elle m'a promis MES MATINS à moi, même le dejeuner, et point de *tap*, même, à la porte: j'ai dit que c'étoit le tems de vacation pour mon fils, que je ne pouvois pas manquer de nous faire passer ensemble: tout de suite, elle a fait invitation à Alex:[25] ce qui m'a decidé, car la Bibliotheque de milord Spencer est le premier, qui n'est pas Royale, de ce pays.[26] Mais la goûte du pauvre Charles a renverser tout cela. Esther est active, spirituelle, assez bien portante, et bienfaisante et gai, presque comme autrefois: et pour moi elle est bien chere. Charlotte est toute bonté, et d'une tendresse pour votre athanase qui n'a point de nomme. Sally est bien, et plus douce, et aussi spirituelle que jamais. ⌐

[The top of the second leaf is missing]

⌐l'espoir que vous m'avez ranimez car mon si cher ⟨père⟩ a bien besoin d'être encore ⟨rassure⟩, helas. Je pense à ma bien aimée Mᵉ de Maisonneuve nuit et jour mais quel noble enfant que Maxime. ⟨Tout le monde loue⟩ son fils à tous les égards, ⟨   ⟩ surtout ⟨   ⟩ et pas moi seule qui suis toujours en ⟨avance⟩ à ce sujet. Sa charmante mère est toujours presente

---

[24] Apparently CB Jr. suffered from what was then diagnosed as a rare combination of the regular gout (marked by an inflammation of the joints in the lower extremities) and the 'retrocedent' gout (marked by an attack upon some internal parts; in his case the head, occasioning apoplexy or palsy).

[25] L. 731 n. 1.

[26] The library at Althorp, founded by Charles Spencer (1674–1722), 3rd Earl of Sunderland, was rehabilitated and increased by George John Spencer, 2nd Earl Spencer (L. 669 n. 9). In 1814 the library occupied a suite of apartments on the ground floor: the Long Library made up of ancient classics, fifteenth-century books, and works on theology (especially large-paper copies of the Polyglot and other Bibles); the Raphael Library (named after a picture of the Holy Family by Raphael); the Billiard Library consisting of books on history and poetry; the Marlborough Library made up of travel literature, history, and the *Acta Sanctorum* in 55 vols. For a detailed description of this Library, see *Aedes Althorpiana* (vols. v–vi) of Thomas Frognall Dibdin, *Bibliotheca Spenceriana* (6 vols., 1814–22).

In 1892 a part of the collection, enlarged some time after 1814 by a fifth room called the Gothic Library, was bought by Enriqueta Augustina Rylands *née* Tennant (1843–1908) and moved to Manchester as a memorial to her husband John (1801–88).

a tous ceux qui ont eu l'honneur de la connaitre. L'aimable et
⟨   ⟩ est tranquille. Je me flatte ⟨   ⟩ trois
⟨   ⟩ De toute manière les 20 ⟨£⟩ que j'ai envoyés sont
rejetés comme de trop.[27] Cependant je ne veux pas les reprendre
de si tôt. Ah! si vous voulez *La Paix* chez vous comme on la
veut ici. Toutes nos affaires seront bientôt arrangées. On ne
pense pas d'autre chose. Dans ce pays Lord Castlereigh[28] a été
beni de la manière la plus attendrissante en partant de la ⟨   ⟩
une populace en ⟨   ⟩ moi! comme j'ai plus de joie et
d'espoir! Certes, mon cher ami, vous aviez ⟨   ⟩ comme à
votre ordinaire, bien noblement ⟨   ⟩ décision quant
à notre ⟨   ⟩ prisonier de toute manière possible
car, ⟨   ⟩ dans une eglise protestante en angleterre il est
regardé comme anglais et comme tel il ne peut pas repondre
aux pays avec lesquels l'angleterre est en guerre et si j'étois à
le réclamer comme votre fils, et ⟨   ⟩ il est ⟨   ⟩
tout à fait, avant et⌐

[8 *lines on the badly damaged right fold*]

⌐La paix! La paix! quand serons-nous réunis? tout le monde
la désire. Tous nos amis j'espere se [po]rtent bien et se sont
⟨   ⟩. Soignons bien toutes nos santés pour nous revoir.
Adieu! Adieu!⌐

[3 *lines on spine between pp.* 2 & 3, *sliced*]

⌐Dieu veuille que vous puissiez lire ⟨   ⟩.⌐

---

[27] The sum of money sent to M. Destutt de Tracy. See L. 697 and n. 7.

[28] Robert Stewart (1769–1822), *styled* Viscount Castlereagh (1796–1821), 2nd
Marquess of Londonderry (1821). The English government led by Pitt had since
1800 wished to secure a Bourbon restoration and to see, once Napoleon was
defeated, ' "a strong and prevailing disposition for the return of the Monarch."
Telle sera très exactement la ligne de conduite suivie par Castlereagh . . . qui a rejoint ses collègues sur le continent, au début de janvier, afin d'observer de plus
près le developpement des événements' (Bertier de Sauvigny, p. 23). FBA referred
to Castlereagh's departure and undoubtedly his intention.

742   Chelsea College,
                                   22 January [1814]
To William Lowndes

A.L.S. 3rd person (Osborn), 22 Jan. [*misdated*] 1813
   Single sheet 4to   1 p.   *pmks*   T.P.P.U. Chelsea   EO   27 JA ⟨1814⟩
red seal
   Addressed: Mr. Lowndes, / Bedford Street, / 38

Madame d'Arblay returns Mr. Lowndes[1] thanks for the
Copy which he has sent her of Evelina.[2] She cannot be so
ungrateful as to take ill a preliminary account that is meant so
well; but she would have been far more pleased that the
history of her Life should have awaited her death. There are
many errours in the relation; beginning with the very first line;
but none that are material.[3]

742. [1] William Lowndes (*fl.* 1784–1821) was a bookseller (iii, L. 179 n. 3) and
a son of Thomas (1719–84), publisher of *Evelina*.
   [2] FBA refers to the edition of *Evelina* issued in 1810 as volumes 38 and 39 of
The British Novelists. The series represented a co-operative venture led by F. C. &
J. Rivington and included such other booksellers as William Lowndes and Cadell
and Davies.
   [3] The 1810 edition of *Evelina* (vol. 38) included a biographical and critical
preface by Anna Letitia Barbauld. FBA probably objected to the following statements in the preface:
   a. 'Scarcely any name, if any, stands higher in the list of novel-writers than that
      of Miss BURNEY, now Mrs. D'ARBLAY, daughter of the ingenious Dr. Burney'
      (p. i).
   b. 'Miss Burney composed her *Evelina* when she was in the early bloom of youth,
      about seventeen' (pp. i–ii).
   c. 'The least natural character [in *Cecilia*] is Albany. . . . Dr. Johnson had
      supplied the part' (p. iv).
   d. 'The celebrity which Miss Burney had now attained awakened the idea of
      extending that patronage to her. . . . she was made *dresser* to Her Majesty.
      She held this post for several years, during which the duties of her situation
      seem to have engrossed her whole time. Her state of health at length obliged
      her to resign it, and she soon after married to M. D'Arblay, a French emi-
      grant' (p. vii).
   e. '. . . the propensity which the author had shown in all her novels, betrayed
      into it by her love of humour, to involve her heroines not only in difficult
      but in degrading adventures. . . . and the situations Camilla is continually
      placed in with the Dubsters and Mrs. Mittin are of a nature to degrade.
      Still more, the overwhelming circumstance of her father's being sent to
      prison for his debts seems to preclude the possibility of her ever raising her
      head again. . . . The mind has been harassed and worn with excess of painful
      feeling' (pp. ix–x).
   f. 'A writer who has published three novels of so much merit may be allowed
      to repose her pen; yet the English public cannot but regret an expatriation
      which so much lessens the chance of their being again entertained by her'
      (p. xi).

She will accept with pleasure the obliging offer of Mr. Lowndes for two more copies: one for M. d'Arblay, in France, another, for her Son, at Cambridge.[4]

Chelsea College,
Jany 22^d 1813[5]

743   [Paris, January 1814]

M. d'Arblay
To Madame d'Arblay

A.L. (Berg), *n.d.*
Originally a double sheet 8vo, of which FBA later discarded the second leaf   2 pp.   wafer or seal torn out of page
Edited by FBA, p. 1, *annotated and dated*: (2) (1814) *Jany^{re}* v—^{rr}*or Fev^r*⊓

Les papiers publiés, ma chère amie t'ont appris la mort de M de Narbonne, et je n'ai pas besoin de te dire l'état où m'a mis la nouvelle de la perte irreparable de cet ami pleuré generalement de tous ceux qui l'ont connu. Pour moi, je sais que rien ne peut m'en consoler, et pourtant je fais tout ce que je puis pour me persuader que peut etre il aurait pu etre plus malheureux. Nous n'avons absolument aucun detail sur sa mort si inattendue. Nous ne savons que ce qu'en ont dit les journaux— Madame de Brancamp est inconsolable. ⟨Daru en de⟩ [vient] presque mort de chagrin. Tout le monde ⟨autour⟩ le pleure, et personne actuellement ne manque une occasion de faire son eloge. Il semble qu'il entrait dans ma destinée de ne lui devoir que des choses agreables. Sa mort même m'a rendu plusieurs amis que je croyais avoir perdus, et qui se sont empresses à venir le pleurer avec moi. De ce nombre est Madame de Fezenzac[1] sa cousine dont tu m'as entendu [|] souvent parler. Je

---

[4] This coldly formal letter, silent about the forthcoming *Wanderer*, indicates FBA's continuing hostility to any Lowndes for Thomas Lowndes's high-handed treatment of *Evelina* and his inadequate payment to the author.
[5] See L. 745.

743. [1] Grief was shared by friend and relative.
Narbonne's friend was Pierre-Antoine-Noël-Bruno Daru (1767–1829), man of letters, soldier, and statesman. He entered military administration in 1784. By 1796

lui dois aussi de nouveaux amis que le besoin de parler de lui rassemble. De ce nombre est Mad Helene de Beaufremont et Mr de Choiseul[2] ses plus intimes amis qui ont voulu que je melasse mes larmes aux leurs. Dernièrement nous nous etions donné la tache impossible à remplir de citer une seule occasion où cet être adorable avait manqué une occasion de rendre service où bien celle où il lui serait echappé je ne dis pas une epigramme, mais ce [sarcas]me qui put, non pas nuire à quelqu'un, mais [le] ⟨gêner⟩.[3] Nous avons été forcé d'y renoncer; et d'un commun accord nous nous sommes ecriés que son esprit était le moindre de ses avantages, et que c'était sur tout par son ame par son obligeance qu'il etait reellement adorable. Son seul defaut, à la verité bien grand etait la plus complete negligence de ses propres affaires,[4] quand au contraire il etait toute activité pour l'interet des autres.[5]

[*The second leaf is missing*]

he was chef de division au ministère de la Guerre. Filling various official posts, he was named comte de l'Empire (1809) and ministre secrétaire d'État (1811). After the fall of the Empire he rallied to the Bourbon cause although he joined forces with Napoleon during the Cent Jours. In 1819 he became a pair de France.

Narbonne's cousin was Louise-Joséphine de Lalive du Châtelet (d. 1832), who had married in April 1783 Philippe-André-François de Montesquiou (1753–1833), *dit* comte de Fézensac. She was the daughter of Ange-Laurent (1726–1779) and Marie-Josèphe *née* de Nettine (d. 1827).

[2] See L. 736 nn. 10, 19.

[3] M. de Narbonne had a satiric wit. In 1805, as an instance, he ridiculed the Napoleonic regime and its ruler, his *lazzi* passing from one salon to another; indeed so widely were they circulated that in 1806 the satirist was made to retire to a distance of at least 35 miles from the capital. For Napoleon's ambivalence toward *les grands salons* and their members who derided him, see Madelin, xi. 67–8.

[4] Lacking financial responsibility all his adult life, and particularly between 1806 and 1809, 'Narbonne devait rester sans emploi. Il se débattait dans une gêne financière, dont sa générosité était la cause, tout autant que ses habitudes fastueuses' (Dard, p. 157).

[5] M. d'A remembered various kindnesses of Narbonne: his abortive attempt to see a Major-General d'Arblay in the 'Army of Poland' (L. 733 n. 2), his solicitude for FBA during her illness, his urging the d'Arblays to consult M. Larrey, his obtaining from the ministre de l'Intérieur necessary leave-time for M. d'A following FBA's operation (vi, L. 595 and n. 36).

The most telling evidence of M. de Narbonne's selflessness appears in several of his letters (Berg, in the hand of M. d'A) to his cousin Mme de Fézensac. Under a cover of cynical bravado he indicated the misery of his troops at Torgau and his effort to alleviate suffering. On 17 Sept. 1813 he wrote: 'Cela vous fait grand chose ma Cousine de savoir que je m'ennuye ici comme un chien, quoique je sois occupé de toutes les oeuvres de charité que vous aimez tant. Je suis un veritable soeur grise. Je couvra ceux qui sont nus, quand j'ai des habits; je donne à manger à ceux qui ont faim, quand j'ai du pain, je gueris les malades et les blessés quand ils ne meurent pas; et dès que tout cela est fait, je les envoye se faire tuer le plus heroiquement que je peus. . . .'

[63 Lower Sloane Street],
2 February 1814

To Longman, Hurst, Rees, Orme, and Brown, Publishers, Paternoster-Row

A.L.S. draft, 3rd person (Berg), 2 Feb. 1814
Single sheet 4to   2 pp.

N° I

2ᵈ Febʸ 1814

Madame d'Arblay acquaints Messrs. Longman & Co. that a rumour which has for some time alarmed her, has to day been confirmed to her for fact—that the first volume of her work is now in reading in various circles!—![1] How this has been brought to bear she knows not: she has regularly refused to shew even a page of it: even her Father, even her Brothers have not read one line:[2] but she is now in the deepest uneasiness at the offence that must necessarily be given amongst her best friends, by a refusal on her part which seems to exclude those only who ought least to have been excluded. The work must unavoidably risk unfair censures by being seen thus partially; & the sale will undoubtedly be injured by thus prematurely satisfying curiosity.

She begs leave, also, to observe that the Critics, & very able judges, into whose hands she is informed that the first volume is fallen, are the LAST who ought to see it in an unfinished state. Their approbation is the most difficult to obtain; & their censure stamps disgrace: She is peculiarly, therefore, vexed that the reading should have been begun under such disadvantages by Sir James Mackintosh, Madame de Staël, & Lord Holland.[3] |

744. [1] Apparently the first volume of *The Wanderer* without the dedication was printed in limited quantities either to favour chosen readers or to secure advance praise. As L. Baugh Allen explained in a letter (Barrett, Eg. 3700A, f. 208) to Mrs. Waddington, who in turn transmitted its contents to FBA: 'The *Wanderer*, too, I have gone thro nearly the 1ˢᵗ Vol of that. 'Tis all that is Printed & Mᶜintosh got it by favor. The beginning I thought [3 words obliterated] the better Part of the Vol. is exquisite, & interesting to a degree. if the Heroine gets thro', as well as she promises, she will eclipse all others hollow.'

[2] At least CB Jr. had seen portions of the novel, if not the whole. On 11 Sept. 1813, he wrote (Osborn): 'your WORK will do! No lack of incident.'

[3] Henry Richard Vassall Fox (1773–1840), 3rd Baron Holland (1774). See

Finally, Mad^e d'Arblay assures Messrs. Longman & Co. that the prefatory pages of which she has spoken, will lose all their purpose in being read AFTER the work which they are written to precede.[4]

Her other works she had the uncontested privilege of presenting to her own family & friends, before they were seen by those of her publishers, Messrs Payne & Cadell.[5]

She solemnly, therefore, entreats that they will call back the Volume, or Volumes,[6] which they have lent out; & not suffer another to go forth, till the Work, in its proper state, shall be delivered to the public at large.

Mad^e d'A. forbore making this remonstrance to Messrs. Longman till she had made enquiries of the Printer,[7] who has positively protested that from his house not a Copy has ever been sent, or lent, except to Messrs L:

If this application should be too late, & the Copy, or Copies, cannot be withdrawn, M^e d'A. must, at least, beg to have some of the 1st Vol^s designed for her own connexions & friends forwarded to her without delay; that she may soften the reproach of what is thought her undue reserve, which, in 5 Letters, from separate quarters, has reached her already.

It would be needless for Mad^e d'Arblay to add how much she has been flattered, nevertheless, by this eagerness. Her cautions are the mere effect of her solicitude to run less risk of ending it in disappointment & disapprobation: for, if this premature communication be not checked, all the interest of the narration will be broken; all illusion will be abolished; & the Work will be born old.

---

iii, L. 134 n. 8. His interest in *The Wanderer* arose from his own literary pursuits (primarily in classical and modern languages) and from a desire to find in the novel substantiation of his pro-Napoleonic attitude. See L. 754 n. 7 for still another reader of an advance copy of the first volume.

4 To FBA the dedication was significant not only because it contained her tribute to CB but because it provided a general history of the novel's evolution, a rationale for avoiding political controversy in literature, and, most significantly, a genre defence of fiction.

5 See L. 712 n. 2.

6 FBA in Ll. 730, 738 indicated that two volumes of *The Wanderer* had already been printed; now she was no longer sure (see n. 1. above).

7 Andrew Strahan.

745   *as of* Chelsea College,
                                             5 February 1814
To William Lowndes

A.L.S. 3rd person (John Comyn, unbound), 5 Feb. 1814
Double sheet 8vo   strengthened   1 p.   *pmk*   7 FE 1814   seal
Addressed: Mr. Lowndes, / Bedford Street. / 38.
Annotated in pencil, p. 1: Lowndes was Publisher of 'Evelina'.

Madame d'Arblay is much obliged to Mr. Lowndes for the
setts which he has sent her of Evelina: but she must entirely
decline correcting any mistakes in Memoirs which she so
little wishes authenticated, or printed, as those which would
bring her very obscure life before the public.[1]

Chelsea College
Feby 5th 1814.

746   [63 Lower Sloane Street],
                                        6 February 1814

To Longman, Hurst, Rees, Orme, and Brown,
Publishers, Paternoster-Row

A.L.S. draft, third person (Berg), 6 Feb. 1814
Single sheet 4to   2 pp.

N° 3   6—Feby. 1814—
  Madame d'Arblay is overwhelmed with confusion & gratitude by the perusal of the letter of Sir James Mackintosh.
Could she have foreseen such an honour, her nervousness would
have been changed into ⌜⟨pleasure⟩⌝ And if she may hope—as
Sir James politely intimates—for the favourable opinion of the
other two distinguished characters,[1] who have occasioned her—
so much alarm, she is perfectly conscious of the kindness of his

745. [1] See L. 742.
746. [1] Mme de Staël and Lord Holland, along with Sir James Mackintosh, secured
before publication volume one of *The Wanderer*. See L. 744.

observation upon so flattering an introduction of her new work to the public. Nor is she less satisfied with the justice of Sir James's remark that the truth will acquit her of any blame towards her own friends—who must find some other appellation if they will not rather rejoice at, than merely forgive, a loss of precedence redounding, by its event, so singularly to her advantage.

Neither Sir James Mackintosh, nevertheless, nor Madame de Staël can be surprised at her late affright, when they hear that the Ms. had never been shown to her Father's best Friend, Lady Crewe, nor to her own, Mrs. Lock: two ladies whose merits & claims they can peculiarly appreciate. ¹

Madᵉ d'Arblay, nevertheless, recommends to Messʳˢ Longman not to repeat so hazardous an experiment; for the lenity & candour with which this 'fragment' of her work has here been judged are nearly as rare as the talents & genius which give them weight.

She hopes Messʳˢ Longman will permit her to keep the Note of Sir James,² that it may be found, hereafter, by her son, in contact with similar marks of favour bestowed upon her earlier productions by Dr. Johnson³ & Mr. Burke.⁴

---

² The note is missing.
³ FBA refers to Mrs. Thrale's letter (Streatham, 22 July 1778) to CB: '. . . So far had I written of my letter, when Mr. Johnson returned home, full of the praises of the *Book* I had lent him, and protesting there were passages in it which might do *honour* to Richardson. We talk of it for ever, and he feels ardent after the *dénouement*; he could not get *rid* of the Rogue, he said! I lent him the second volume, and he is now busy with the other two' (*DL* i. 48; *ED* ii. 250, 252–3).
⁴ For Edmund Burke's letter to FB (29 July 1782), see *DL* ii. 92–3. He praised *Cecilia* for 'the natural vein of humour, the tender pathetic, the comprehensive and noble moral, and the sagacious observation, that appear quite throughout that extraordinary performance.' FB was excited about this letter, writing (Barrett, Eg. 3690, f. 15–15b) to CB on 4 Aug. 1782: '. . . I tell you I have had a Letter from Mr. Burke!—& *such* a Letter! . ! . . . Did I not say well when I said Mr. Burke was like *You*—for who, except You or He could, at a Time of Business, disappointment, care & occupation such as His a[re], have found leisure to read with such attention, & to command with such good nature, a Work so totally foreign to every thing that just now can come Home to his Business & bosom. . . . I could not, for some time, believe my own Eyes when I looked at his signature.'

M. d'Arblay
To Madame d'Arblay

A.L.S. (Berg), 10 Fevrier 1814
Single sheet 8vo 2 pp.
Edited by FBA, p. 1, *annotated and dated*: ⁑ N⁰ 16. 10 Fevrier. 1814.
Exquisite Testementary Leave taking to his Wife & Son on the Expected
Seige of Paris.

Paris ce 10 Fevrier 1814

Dans ce moment terrible d'une crise si menaçante[1] où ma
seule consolation est de penser que tout ce que j'ai de plus cher
est à l'abri non pas de tous les malheurs qu'elle fait présager
mais du moins de l'influence immediate que ne peut manquer
d'avoir la violence j'obeis au besoin imperieux de faire connoitre encore une fois à ma chere Fanny et à notre bien cher Alex
que quoiqu'il arrive, ils pourront toujours se dire que rien ne
les a remplacés et ne les remplacera jamais dans un coeur tout
à eux. Fier du bonheur dont ils m'ont fait jouir, et bien resolu
à m'en montrer digne jusqu'à mon dernier soupir, je ne rougis
point les larmes que me font verser en ce moment des souvenirs
à la fois doux et dechirans. Ô mes amis! quelle année—la
perte de Mʳ de Narbonne, de Madame de Tessé[2] et votre
eloignement, dont il faut que je me felicite!!! En verité bien
assez pour justifier ce petit instant de faiblesse qui ⎮ va faire

747. [1] Early in February, Napoleon—and hence Paris—appeared doomed. Murat,
his last ally, had abandoned the Napoleonic cause. From mid-January onward the
allies had advanced 250 miles and overrun a third of France; they had sent armies
down the Marne and Seine toward Paris and probed with Russian patrols as far
as Orléans. See E. V. Gulick, 'The Final Coalition and the Congress of Vienna,
1813–15', Crawley, op. cit., pp. 640–1, and L. 748 n. 10.
   [2] He expressed his regard for the comtesse in a eulogy 'Portrait de Madame de
Tessé' (Notebook, undated, Berg):

> L'homme le plus savant, qui prè, d'elle s'instruit,
> Et l'ignorant fieffé, qu'éblouit l'amalgame
> D'un corps aërien et d'un céleste esprit,
> D'accord, en la quittant disent:
> Elle est toute amen!
> Voilà ce que j'adore, et sans moins admirer
> Ce jugement si prompt, que rien ne fait errer:
> Et pourtant, de ce tout, chef d' [xxx 1 *word*] de nature,
> Une part est sans froide, et l'autre est sans mesure.
> > Par le Lⁿᵗ Genˡ d'Arblay

place à une fermeté dont mon incomparable Fanni m'a donné le si heroique exemple qui j'espere ne sera pas perdu pour notre fils, que j'embrasse ainsi qu'elle de toutes les puissances de mon ame et d'un coeur tout à eux. Adieu mes amis.

A.P. d'Arblay.

P.S. L'amie qui veut bien prendre ce mot en garde veut en bien aussi se charger de faire parvenir à ma Fanny, quand cela sera possible une petite tabatiere d'or p^r elle ainsi qu'une petite montre à repetition pour Alex. Cette montre est excellente. Cette même amie leur remettra par la suite—2,000^f—que je lui ai prêtés, J'en ai prêté autant à Madame de Beauvau.[3] J'ai aussi prêté—1,500^f—à Mad^e de Cadignan pour un an. Ce petit service l'a empeché de perdre p^r 4 à 5,000^f d'effets qu'elle avait été forcée d'engager pour faire face aux depenses de son fils à l'epoque de son depart pour l'armée où il a debuté de la maniere la plus satisfesante p^r ceux qui s'interessent à lui.[4] Il est dejà Lieutenant en premier dans la garde d'honneur.

J'ai encore prêté

à un Mr Vachier excellent sujet de mon bureau	200^f[5]
à Mr Maulnoir- - - - - - - - - - - - - - - - - - - -	⌜200⌝[6]
à M^r Le Noir -	⌜200⌝ 200[7]
à M^{de} Rigaud qui a perdu son mari - - - - - - -	130[8]

[3] Nathalie-Henriette-Victurnienne de Beauvau-Craon *née* de Rochechouart de Mortemart (1774–1854), at present 'une Dame du Palais' in the service of Empress Marie-Louise. See also v, L. 513 n. 2.

[4] Charles-Frédéric-Louis Dupleix de Cadignan, now 17, was at the start of a long army career. He was made an officer in the garde d'Honneur départementale in 1812, a lieutenant in the first or second regiment of the garde d'Honneur (1813), aide-de-camp of General Montesquiou (1815), sous-lieutenant in the lanciers de la garde Royale (1815), lieutenant in the same unit (1817), capitaine of the ligne Breveté (1818) and of the dragons de la Garonne (1820). He was retired in 1831 and received his pension in 1845.

[5] Pie-Casimir Vachier (1776–1851), born in Le Buis (Drôme), began his administrative career in the bureau de la Préfecture in the Drôme (1800–12). In 1813 he was employed as a rédacteur in the bureau des Bâtimens civils of the ministère de l'Intérieur, rising gradually in the ranks until his retirement in 1847.

[6] Louis-Joseph Maulnoir (1755–*post* 1815) worked from 1783 to 1791 in the bureau des Finances and the chambre des Domaines de Paris and from 1791 to 1794 in the bureau des Travaux publics. In 1801 he was employed by the bureau des Bâtimens civils et des prisons, from 1803 to 1811 he was a sous-chef, and from 1811 to 1816 (after which his name disappeared from the personnel lists) he was chef. See also vi, L. 611 n. 2.

[7] See L. 697 n. 5.

[8] Marie-Anne Villeneuve Rigaud (*fl.* 1780–1820), the widow of the Haitian André Rigaud (1761–1811). He volunteered for service in the French army in 1777 and became a commissioned officer in 1790. He rose steadily in rank,

à Desessars - 56[9]
à Mr Girardin - - - - - - - - - - - - - - - - - - - 100[10]
à un M[r] l'Eguille[11] neveu du M[quis] d'Argence[12]
et attaché à mon bureau - - - - - - - - - - - - 60

Total ‾‾‾‾‾‾946‾

Toutes les sommes cy dessus reunies forment à present tout
notre avoir, Mr Louis[13] et Mad[e] de Sim[iane],[14] nous ayant
remboursés ce qu'ils nous doivent. Pour le reste ainsi que nos

becoming commandant en chef l'armée du Sud de Saint-Dominigue (1795–1800). From 1801 until 1810 he spent most of his time in France. On 19 Apr. 1810 he returned to Port-au-Prince to resume the command of l'armée du Sud. Dying there on 18 Sept. 1811, he left behind in Paris his wife and six young children to educate.

[9] Probably Louis-Hyppolyte Ragon des Essards (*fl.* 1783–1819), the mayor of Béon, a village near Joigny. See vi, L. 561 n. 2.

[10] François Girardin (1776–*post* 1815), a relative of M. d'A. After two years as receveur des contributions in Chablis (Yonne), Girardin was employed in the ministère de l'Intérieur in October 1811, probably on the recommendation of M. d'A, who wrote to the comte de Montalivet to ask that his young relative be assigned to the bueau des Bâtimens civils so that his enthusiasm could be disciplined. Entering the bureau, he began as an expéditionnaire and was later promoted to a rédacteur. His employment was terminated in October 1815 for unknown reasons.

[11] Alexandre-Luc de Boyer d'Eguilles was born in Aix-en-Provence in 1774, became a Chevalier de Malte, and flourished until 1818 at least. He worked for a short time in the bureau des Bâtimens civils, his name appearing on the personnel lists for 1813. But he, like M. d'A, was forced to leave in March 1814 because of the changes planned by the monarchy.

[12] M. d'A refers to Jean-Baptiste de Boyer, marquis d'Argens (*c.* 1703–71). Despite a notorious and dissipated youth, he began to write prodigiously and seriously about 1734 and in time became chamberlain to Frederick the Great. A friend of d'Alembert and acquainted with Voltaire, he is best known for his sceptical *La Philosophie du bon sens, ou réflexions philosophiques sur l'incertitude des connaissances humaines* (1737), and for *Lettres morales et critiques* (Amsterdam, 1737), *Lettres juives* (6 vols., The Hague, 1738), *Lettres chinoises* (5 vols., 1739, 1740), and *Lettres cabalistiques* (6 vols., The Hague, 1741).

[13] Baron Joseph-Dominique Louis (1755–1837). According to M. de Vitrolles (i. 171): 'Parmi ceux qui se groupaient autour de M. de Talleyrand . . . était l'abbé Louis. Il n'avait jamais rien eu d'ecclésiastique, si ce n'est la fonction de conseiller-clerc au parlement de Paris et celle de diacre à la messe du 14 juillet 1789. Il avait quitté depuis longtemps le titre et le costume de son état. Ses principes et ses mœurs passaient pour relâchés . . . mais il était ferme et affirmatif; on ne doute jamais quand on n'a qu'une idée. Rude et grossier par caractère, il se croyait audacieux lorsqu'il n'était qu'insolent.' Emigrating to England, he returned to France after 18 brumaire. His financial talent made him at first invaluable to Napoleon, then to the gouvernement provisoire, and subsequently to Louis XVIII, who made him ministre des Finances.

[14] Diane-Adélaïde de Simiane *née* de Damas d'Antigny (1761–1835) was the sister of Joseph-François-Louis-*Charles*-César (v, L. 514 n. 17) and Joseph-Élisabeth-*Roger* (1765–1823). The widow of comte de Simiane (a suicide in 1787), she was the mistress of the marquis de Lafayette. Her financial difficulties, chronic during the Napoleonic era, were not alleviated until the Restoration: 'En 1814, elle fit nommer l'abbé de Montesquiou ministre de l'intérieur à la place de Beugnot' (Woelmont, i. 778).

meubles, si je venais à perir on ne peut qu'esperer de la recouvrer et il est prudent de se preparer à le perdre. Adieu mes chers bien chers amis. Mille tendresses à ceux que j'ai près de vous—adieu.

748   [63 Lower Sloane Street,
                                        15 February 1814]
To Charles Burney

> A.L. (Osborn), *n.d.*
> Double sheet 8vo   4 pp.   *pmks*   15 FE 1814   15 FE 1814   T.P.P.U. /
> [Chel]sea   EO   seal
>   *Addressed*: Rev^d Dr. Burney, / Rectory House, / Deptford.

The hope, according to his own intimation, of seeing my kind Charles could alone have prevented my answering—with all my hurries, his last Letter, & thanking him for having written to Dr. Davy. I long to know that correspondence at length.

Alex went on *Friday*. I would have kept him to the last moment, but he told me he wished to shew the respect to Mr. Chapman's desire of his arriving *previously to* the Lecture day, Monday, by arriving 2 days sooner.[1] I did not think it right to check so proper a notion, especially as he says he wishes to prepare for the Lecture, & to pay his visits to the professors previous to meeting them officially.

He is gone, poor Boy! with the best intentions!—but alas his terrible heedlessness & absence take from me all confidence in his steadiness.

For himself, he has not a fear! he thinks it enough to design right, to make right sure! & he said to me, in parting, 'How glad you'll be of the good accounts you'll receive of me, mama! — —'[2] & presently added—after seeing your kind wishes &

---

748. [1] AA left Chelsea on 10 February.
     [2] According to AA he performed well during the Lent term. On 29 March he wrote to FBA (Barrett, Eg. 3701A, ff. 4–5):
     'In triumph do I resume my pen! In triumph write to my Mam on the same day, & at the expense of a double post. . . .
     'As I was crossing the avenue to go to Chapel, Mr Gimingham passed by me & accosted me—"M^r d'Arblay, I shall be happy to speak to you a moment—If you

blessing in your Letter—'Don't you think Uncle Charles is disposed to grow quite fond of me,—when he shall hear, from the Professors, an account of my conduct being exemplary? ——'

You may be sure I did not say *no* to this sanguine artlessness! —He is gone off in the highest spirits & glee, with all this bright perfection before him.

He wrote 3 very proper Letters to Messrs. C[hapman] G[imingham][3] & D[avy] &, as they were solely on his own affairs I thought it right to pay the postage.

I also, in inclosing the 31.£ wrote a line or two to Mr. Chapman,[4] recommending, gently, some patience & lenity with a most unthinking, but well-intentioned young creature.

Sarah has written to a lady, a friend of her's & of James's, Mrs. Paris,[5] who lives at Cambridge, to entreat her to invite him, & to see after his health, & well doing; & to write if she perceives, or hears, any thing alarming, in any way.

will stop into my apartment, I shall follow you immediately"—What means this summons, thinks I to myself! What subject of complaint can the fellow have; I have been very regular with him—I dont know what he can be after—As I was ruminating, in he popt—"Mr d'Arblay," says he, (hear! hear!) as your Uncle thought proper at the beginning of this term to write a word in your behalf, & as I could not help expressing at the time what I thought upon the subject, I have now sent for you for a purpose very pleasant to me, to let you know that your present conduct & regularity has perfectly satisfied me in every respect,—& that I now look upon the irregularities of the former term as completely done away!—

' "It is the more pleasant to me, because now that the fine weather is coming you will have the opportunities to absent yourself from Lectures now & then in the course of the next term without irregularity.—& to save the trouble of a formal note, as I suppose you will see Dr Burney during this Vacation; I beg you will present my compliments to him & tell him that I am now perfectly satisfied in all points! . . ."

'There's for you now! There's for you! What say you? Chapman I hope too is very well contented—

'O Mammy! . . .'

[3] William Gimingham (1773–1838) was admitted as a pensioner at Caius in 1790, receiving his B.A. in 1795 and his M.A. in 1798. A fellow of the College from 1796 to 1820, he also served intermittently as Dean (1800), Proctor (1806), Bursar (1808–10). Ordained in 1800, he was Rector of St. Dionis Backchurch, London (1803–4), Prebendary of Wells (1817–38), Rector of Bratton-Fleming, Devon (1818–38).

[4] Recorded on 17 Feb. 1814 in the 'Tutor's Account Book' is FBA's cash payment of £31. 1s. 10d. This additional sum along with £1 'Excess of Caution' and £53. 14s. 'Tancred draft' was used to cover the following debts of AA: £3. 18s. 8d. (Admission fees), £3. 11s. 4d. (Midsummer term), £3. 17s. 4d. (Michaelmas term), £74. 8s. 6d. Apparently AA in this last term spent considerable sums of money on clothes and furniture.

[5] Elizabeth Paris *née* Ayrton (*fl.* 1770–*post* 1816) would be understanding of AA's difficulties since her own son John Ayrton Paris (1785–1856) was a Tancred student at Caius from 1804 to 1808 before he took his M.D. in 1813.

To Clement I have written a most solemn injunction to acquaint me immediately if the old course should be renewed; that I may TRY to stop its progress.

I have also applied to the *Gip*, to attend peculiarly to calling him, & to his affairs, & fire, & rooms, &c—with a promise of a handsome *douceur* per month for her extra good offices.[6]

And I have addressed Clement's private Tutor, Mr. Alty,[7] & begged that he will take the new pupil for This Term. Alex himself thinks that may remind him of his engagement to study mechanics, &c, & not abandon himself, as heretofore, to his eternal Algebra. If so, 'twill be £10 admirably employed.

The worthy Martin was so kind as to relieve my difficulties how to get him hence to ǀ the coach in time, by inviting him to sleep overnight at his chambers in the Temple,[8] whence he promised to conduct him himself to Fetter Lane, on Friday morning.[9] He left me, therefore, on Thursday Evening.

I am not at all anxious, you will believe!

He was extremely struck, he tells me, with your *manner* of haranguing him; it had 'a commanding kindness', he said, that made a powerful effect upon him.

May it last!—Amen!—Amen!

France, too! Good God! how will all end at Paris!—[10] I have had another Letter—& full of hope of Peace! written the end of Dec.[11]

Adieu, my dearest Charles.—God bless you.

Saturday. I dined at Chelsea. our Padre is delightfully cheerful [& w]ell. Love to Rosetta.

[6] See L. 824 n. 4.

[7] John Alty (1789–1815) entered as a pensioner at Jesus College, Cambridge, n 1807; he took his B.A. in 1811 and his M.A. in 1814, when he was elected a fellow of Jesus. In the same year he was admitted to Lincoln's Inn. Dying of fever in March 1815, he was buried in the College chapel.

[8] Martin Burney's chambers were at the Inner Temple, Chancery Lane.

[9] The coach for Cambridge left from the White Horse Inn, Fetter Lane, daily at 5 a.m., at 7.30 a.m., and at 8 a.m.

[10] From reading *The Times* (7 Feb. 1814), FBA would have learned that 'the Allied Armies have penetrated very deeply into France. . . .' One day later she read 'that bets are publicly laid at Paris on the event of an approaching change of the Dynasty'. On 11 February *The Times* reported that palisades, meant for artillery, were being built at the different barriers of Paris. The next day *The Times* quoted from a French paper: 'The works undertaken for the defence of Paris are at length completed. . . . The brave pupils of the Polytechnick school have offered to serve the pieces, and they are already sufficiently exercised.'

[11] See L. 736.

749   [63 Lower Sloane Street,
                                     16 February 1814]

To Mrs. Broome
and Mrs. Barrett

A.L.S. (Berg), *n.d.*
Double sheet 4to   4 pp.   *pmk*   16 FE   wafer
Addressed: Mrs. Broome, / Richmond, / Surry.
Endorsed by CBFB: sister / d'arblay / 1814

Alas my dearest Charlottes—what an unexpected blow is
this!—dear sweet—& *erst* nearly incomparable Norbury![1] how
short a race!—& of late, I believe, a melancholy one.—O may
his gentle soul but be permitted union with the Angel Mother
by whom he was nearly adored![2] With that hope, I stop almost
all regret, except for my poor dearest Fanny![3]—O what a stroke
for her!—the instant I am sure she knows it, I shall quit every
thing to go forth & seek her—

     He was not happy—he could not endure Ireland,[4] though,
with nobleness & piety joined, he determined to do his duty

749. [1] Charles Norbury Phillips, ordained as recently as 25 Oct. 1812, died on
3 Feb. 1814 (aged twenty-nine) in Ireland. His family thought him 'nearly
incomparable'. According to MF, writing (JRL) to Mrs. Piozzi on 13 Apr. 1814:
'. . . When that cruel Col. Phillips broke his poor wife's heart with unkindness,
she left behind her 3 children. Norbury, the eldest Son, went to Trinity Coll:
Dublin, & there, totally neglected by his Father, struggled with the greatest
integrity through the most distressing difficulties. At last he got a curacy. And his
first act was to take his half brother Molesworth [abandoned with the rest of
his family by their "unnatural father"] home, maintain, & give him, himself, a
classical education.' Ever since his ordination he struggled to obtain a church
living, preferably in England.
   [2] SBP's devotion to her precocious first-born son increased when they were
separated by Molesworth Phillips (iii, L. 202 n. 1). Before the age of seven, the
boy was sent to a boarding school at Portsmouth and rarely allowed home even
during holidays. In 1794 his father had him sent to Dublin and placed under
'Methodistical' tutors, the Maturins (*HFB*, p. 276).
   SBP's journals express her intense love for Norbury. When the child was ill in
October 1789, he said to her—as she records it in her letter (Barrett, Eg. 3692,
f. 89–89b) to FB—' "*I should have died*"—'And what would Poor Mama do without
her little Darling," said I—"*My dear Mother*," sᵈ he with a very composed countenance—"You would *find me in Heaven when you die*—because if *I am good*, I shall go
to Heaven." . . . While sick he was a little Angel.—I never saw a more sweet,
tractable, grateful, & affectionate little Patient.—The Joy of seeing him restored
to Health is such to me that I cannot bring myself to be *very* severe when he is
more overpowering wᵗʰ his noise & Spirits than I or others like, as yet.'
   [3] Fanny Raper, Norbury Phillips's sister.
   [4] For some hint of Norbury Phillips's unhappiness in Ireland, see L. 646 nn. 2,
3, 4.

there: but if the Preferment at which my elder Charlotte hints was in England—I must try to avoid hearing of it—for the very thought gives me a greater shake nearly than his loss.[5] Poor Fanny must have no such hint given her!—Alas—had I lost my Angel sister in Ireland, knowing *her* there to be wretched, how differently I should have borne the separation![6]

It is indeed consoling—greatly consoling that he departed in the house of such a person as Dr. Alcock is described to be.[7] It leaves no harrowing fears that he *might* have been saved—such as have always embittered MY heaviest calamity—[8] |

He was good, I believe, very good, & very pious, that sweet Norbury, & therefore fitted for death, however premature & sudden—yet how early a blossom to be lopped off!—Ah, if I thought not of his loved Mother—if I hoped not SHE may be where He may arrive!—[9]

Who is to tell this affliction to poor Fanny!—If it be not already done, it may be better to prepare her for it, by a Letter from her kind Cousin,[10] relating his illness, & hinting at his danger, yet mentioning his being well attended, &c & then—my excellent & most feeling friend, the Archdeacon,[11] may be prevailed with to break the truth to her. The sight of his hand,

---

[5] MF in a letter (JRL), dated and addressed as in n. 1: 'Mr. Archdeacon Cambridge had an old affection for Norbury's mother, which her melancholy death had tended to strengthen, & for some time he exerted himself to get church preferment for Norbury. After many trials, he at length succeeded, & was just finishing all' when he received word of Norbury's death. MF implies that the preferment was in England.

[6] SBP's tragedy was compounded for FBA when she remembered that her sister had endured the crossing of the Irish sea, was back on English soil, and on her way to the safety of the Burney family—only to die in lodgings in Parkgate (iv, Ll. 354–62).

[7] John Alcock (1731/2–1817) entered Trinity College, Dublin, in 1750 and received his B.A. (1754) and his M.A. (1759). When Norbury Phillips died in his house, John Alcock was rector of Drumhome, about four miles from Ballyshannon.

It was Dr. Alcock who wrote to the Archdeacon 'to say that his worthy young friend N° Phillips called on him lately, complaining of a pain in his chest & cold—that the next day a typhous fever declared itself, & in 5 more he was dead' (see the letter of MF, *supra*).

[8] FBA felt that Molesworth Phillips was responsible for SBP's death: his forcing her to live in desolate Belcotton among financial squabbles and difficulties, his separating her from Norbury, his own philandering. FBA regarded him as little short of a murderer. She was convinced that SBP, freed from the 'baleful visage' of the Major, would have lived (*HFB*, p. 291).

[9] That Norbury's piety fitted him for death is confirmed in MF's letter (JRL) to Mrs. Piozzi (*supra*): 'Another letter from a relation followed this to say that the state of mind in which he died was delightful. Entirely prepared, truly penitent & humble, & resting solely on the merits of our blessed Saviour for forgiveness.'

[10] CFBt.

[11] For George Owen Cambridge's feeling for Norbury Phillips, see n. 5.

after a previous alarm, would almost instantly lead her mind to a suspicion that would guard her from too insupportable a surprise. And the Archdeacon—always doing good, always tenderly loving poor Fanny, & the sweet Norbury, & tenderly revering their departed Mother, will not shrink from the melancholy office if he knows I am persuaded she will better bear it from him than in any other way.

My own Mind—left to itself—would be absorbed at this time by the situation of Paris—& the nameless fears—conjectures—hopes—horrours—& alarms that succeed each other, all day long, upon HOW the tremendous conflict will end.— though my turbulent ¦ Alexander takes care that ALL my anxiety should not be centred there!—He left me the 10th The good Martin made him sleep at his Chambers, in the Temple, whence he saw him set off on the 11th in the morning.[12] I followed your exceeding good idea, my dearest Charlotte, relative to the Gip: who is to persecute at His door in a morning, to watch him for meals, & to attend to his fires. I have applied, also, to Mr. Alty, the private Tutor of Clement,[13] to take him for this ensuing term, & to be kind enough to superintend his observance of the established rules of study. And I have written to Mr. Chapman, to beg his lenity for heedlessness & absence of mind that are unaccompanied by any vice, or any mischief save to himself. Charles has written to him also; & to Dr. Davy,[14] who has answered most kindly that he will try, himself, to lend a hand to snatching the wayward youth from threatening danger. And I have written to Clement, conjuring him to let me know immediately if again there is any failure. Alex has *agreed* that so he shall do; all points of very false notions of honour are, therefore, now settled. Alex went off in the highest spirits, sanguine that he shall now, as he cannot follow, unannoyed, his own excentricities, become EXEMPLARY for exactitude & regularity! poor simple youth!—he never sees

[12] See L. 748 nn. 8, 9.
[13] Clement Francis did not need a tutor as a goad. On the contrary, as MF reported (JRL) to Mrs. Piozzi on 14 Apr. 1813: 'the poor fellow studies so violently that he grows "pale as primrose" with those "blood-consuming mathematics"— & if he goes on so "his *inch* of *taper* will be burnt & done" so much sooner than he thinks for. So little exercise & so much reading gives him headaches & giddinesses that are very alarming.'
[14] CB Jr. wrote also to William Gimingham, the other college tutor responsible for AA's over-all performance.

fear, any way! had I time, or composure, to relate his own account of his motives for thus braving all order, you could not, even at ¦ this melancholy moment, forbear smiling at their singularity & simplicity. I dare not, alas, be sanguine! I am fear in every pore!—But not without hope!—

I have an earnest request to make to my dearest Charlotte, though I know it will worry her—but how can I help it? it is—to know, as nearly as possible, my *pecuniary* debt with her. I ask no account of any other! I want no memorial.—But I don't mean the £15.—but the *pick-nick*.[15] When was the date up to which we had settled? I am going to sell out.[16] & can take no fairer moment: my dear Charlotte can soon, by memorandums, see what time *she* spent in Chenies street after our account. I was there, except one fortnight at Norbury, & one at Sand Gate, or 3 weeks, from January.[17] But I have no species of memorandum when we were separate, & when together. I ENTREAT you, my love, to call to mind your time of absence—the rest, *I* can cast up. When once I am *clear*, if Alex is reasonable, I shall be able to go on upon my running income.[18] But I languish to be *clear*. You will therefore greatly oblige me by compliance at once: & then, I shall begin to turn my thoughts upon being again with you, as soon as I possibly can. But I shall NEVER come till this is arranged. The Book is fast advancing.[19] I have most interesting things to tell *ye* of it, had I time—but, in fact, imagine my panic to hear that Mᵉ de Staël has already contrived to get at the 1ˢᵗ vol.—!

Poor sweet Norbury—being *alone* in Ireland—& where none could lend it him, was upon my list!—embarrassed as it is with 50 claims more than I can pay.—adieu, my two dear Charlottes both! ⟨dear⟩, & most dear to me each.

F d'A. ¦

Very kind remembrances to Mr. Barrett & kisses to my three

---

[15] See L. 738 n. 6.

[16] FBA planned to sell a portion of stock bought by the d'Arblays prior to and during 1803: the 5 per cent 1797, the 5 per cent Navy, or the 3 per cent consols.

[17] Excepting sojourns at Norbury Park and Sandgate and a few shorter visits elsewhere, FBA lived with CBFB from 13 January until November 1813, when she moved to 63 Lower Sloane Street.

[18] FBA refers to the debts incurred by AA during the Michaelmas term (L. 748 n. 4).

[19] FBA at this time was reading proofs of *The Wanderer*. See MF's letter (JRL) to Mrs. Piozzi, dated 11 February (L. 730 n. 4).

little ones. I dined at Chelsea to-day, where my dear Father is remarkably well. I am sure Miss Baker[20] is very much grieved for poor Norbury.

750   [63 Lower Sloane Street,
                      23 February 1814]

To Charles Burney

A.L.S. (Osborn), *n.d.*
Double sheet 8vo 4 pp. *pmk* 23 FE 1814 seal
Addressed: Rev^d Dr. Burney, / Rectory House, / Deptford.
Docketed: p. 4: Feby 23rd

Dr. Davy certainly judged right, my dear Charles.—I would take his experience for a university student as reverentially as your's for a Youth in his preparatory studies. If Alexander were not encouraged as well as exhorted, he would be desperate.

Mr. Chapman tried dry menace—

& he defied it.—

Silly, alike, & wrong—yet not less, to me, terrifying & unhappy. — — He may be led—he won't be driven.

No — — if we have any chance it is Dr. Davy who will uphold it. |

Lady Keith is at length arrived. I have a Letter from her this moment, to tell me to fix my own *time & place* for a meeting —a goodness I cannot avail myself of before *Saturday*, on account of this OUTWARD part of my Mourning for my poor much-lamented Norbury.[1]

It was a KEY that you lent me, when this was mislaid, that opened the Closet.

I shall be much obliged by speed: as perhaps there will be all to order, for there may be nothing that will do.—My affairs are so dispersed I cannot tell where to search them.

[20] For Sarah Baker, see L. 654 n. 13. All the Cambridges—and therefore Miss Baker—were tied in affection to SBP and her children.

750. [1] FBA postponed her meeting with Lady Keith until Saturday 26 February. In that way she observed for slightly more than three weeks the 'OUTWARD part' of her mourning for Norbury Phillips.

Ah Charles!—in what a state is ' Paris [and] France!—²
I am happy to be as much alone, & as much employed *neces-
sarily* as possible, for my spirits are in an agitation of anxiety
unspeakable — —
  I hope, by your Note, you are better. I want to hear MORE
of the Arch^p & of Lambeth—
  Methinks it is time!—³
  How goes on the Greek work?⁴
  I am wofully worried about a work that is NOT Greek!—⁵
                        always love to Rosette
                          & always most affec^ly,
                                dearest Carlos, Yours F. d'A.

I have torn time to go twice to poor Fanny Raper—⁶
Keep your head very warm always after the leeches.⁷

751   *as of* Chelsea College,
                                  [2] March 1814
To Mrs. Waddington

A.L. (Berg), 3 Mar. 1814
Double sheet 8vo   one line (0·2 × 1·15 *to* 1·2″) and a rectangle
(0·15 × 2·15″) cut from 2nd leaf   3 pp.   *pmks*   2 MR 1814   2 MR. 814
black seal
  Addressed: Mrs. Waddington / Lanover, / Abergavenny —

Your Letter¹ fills me with horrour, my dearest Mary—though

  ² See L. 748 n. 10.
  ³ CB Jr. had become a close associate of Charles Manners-Sutton and a frequent
visitor to Lambeth Palace. FBA encouraged the association as a means by which
CB Jr. would gain a bishopric, an honour anticipated by all the Burneys (Ll. 645
n. 10, 676 n. 1). As early as 1808 MF reported (JRL) to Mrs. Piozzi: 'My Greek
Uncle Charles every body arranges into a Bishop. . . . Has been publishing an
Edition of his favorite Bentley to make presents of to his *learned* Friends. . . . his
chief Friend the Bishop of Rochester is promoted.—So soon, I suppose, we shall
see *him* bear his *sable* honours thick upon him.'
  ⁴ See L. 716 n. 2.   ⁵ *The Wanderer.*
  ⁶ Together they mourned Norbury Phillips.
  ⁷ CB Jr. continued to suffer from the gout. The attacks were more frequent
and severe, demanding the use of 'leeches' applied to the feet and/or the inflamed
part.
  751. ¹ This letter was precipitated by the unexpected death of James Greene,
aged 53, on 16 Feb. 1814, whose remains were buried in the churchyard of Llan-
santffraed, Monmouthshire. The letter was written after Mrs. Waddington had

it is all together dark & little intelligible but to combinations & conjectures—Poor unhappy Man!²—

You send me an envelope, & nothing to enclose in it.

No note of *Mrs. Chamber's*—³

None of Mr. *Prossero's*—⁴

What are become of them?

You seem evidently to allude also to some Letter I have never received from yourself.—

& you say not if you have received mine, written instantly upon your anxious & alarmed appeal.—

And you tell me not whether I may frank to you by *Mr. Hall*,⁵ or whether he is now in town? I dare not address a Member without authority.

I conceive your terrible situation, by the ⏐ dreadful catastrophe that the Letter signed W.P.⁶ makes too plainly to have

investigated the contents of his desk. According to his will (Prob. 11/1567/f. 186), dated 1 Jan. 1813 and proved 11 Apr. 1815: 'I desire that the key of my desk which I always carry in my pocket may be delivered to Mrs. Waddington of Lanover and I bequeath all my Manuscript Letters and papers to her and every thing contained in my desk & the great box in my Room.'

² See L. 697.

³ Elizabeth Chambers (*c.* 1770–*post* 1829) was the wife of Thomas Chambers (d. 1829), a 'farmer' who owned property in 'Ragland Town' and also rented farm land from the Usk Charity and Henry Charles Somerset (1766–1835), 6th Duke of Beaufort. See the 'Tax Schedule for the County of Monmouth in the Parish of Ragland' (1829), in the C.R.O., Newport. Greene recorded in his will that 'from Mr. & Mrs. Chambers of Ragland I have received kindness attention and assistance when I stood in the greatest need of it. I desire that my accounts with them may be instantly settled and if there be any balance in my favor I desire it may be paid to them as a testimony of my esteem and warm regard and also I request that all my wearing apparel may be given to them.' For further reference to Mrs. Chambers, see n. 8.

⁴ FBA's mistranscription of the family name of Edmund Bond Prosser (*c.* 1780–1855). According to Samuel Parr (op. cit., i. 773), Prosser was the 'skilful Surgeon of Monmouth' and an acquaintance of James Greene. Little is known of Prosser. In the 'Minutes of the Committee of the Dispensary—1810' (C.R.O. Newport), he was one of several surgeons given thanks 'for their liberal offer of gratuitous attendance' at the newly founded Dispensary, later the Monmouth Hospital. Admitted to the 'Burgess Lists of Monmouth' (1780–1818), he was also surgeon to the county gaol in that city from about 1824 onward.

⁵ Benjamin Hall (1778–1817), M.P. for Totnes (1806–12), Westbury (1812–14), and Glamorgan (1814–17), was probably in London at this time, Parliament having formally convened on 1 March.

⁶ The Revd. William Powell (1770–1838) of Abergavenny, Monmouthshire, was a friend of the Greene family, officiating 23 Sept. 1799 at the marriage of Greene's eldest daughter Arabella Penelope (1782–1865) to Peter Richard Hoare (1772–1849), then of the parish of St. Martin's-in-the-Fields, London. Powell had matriculated at Jesus College (Oxford) on 8 Apr. 1786, receiving his B.A. (1789), M.A. (1792), B.D. (1800). In 1814 he was rector at Llangattock-juxta-Usk, Monmouthshire. Kind and learned, he was described by Samuel Parr (op. cit., i. 773) as 'the best scholar I saw [in Monmouthshire]. . . . a very well-behaved, well-informed man'.

taken place—but, when your Mind is quieted, unravel the mystery that surrounds all this cruel business for it ⟨sobers⟩ my whole mind in perplexed doubts & shocking suggestions.

I shall keep safe the envelope for L^y M.[7] in case you may have found out the omission, & that what is meant for her may arrive.

The Letter WP. seems to be written by an angel.—How is it all?—& *who* is it?

Who is Mrs. Chambers?[8] who is Angelina?[9]

On re-reading your Letter, you mention having written to me on Thursday—what is become of that Letter? It was probably explanatory? Pray find out how it has missed me—& forward it. & tell me how to *Frank*—I am out of the way, here, of all Members. |

£2380!—good Heavens!—[10]

And Mr. W. '*already knows*' that *already* terrifies me—is there fear or possibility of even MORE?—I hope not!

Do not write till you are more composed—it will then rather calm than distress you to let me comprehend this dreadful affair—but let your good Fanny discover for me the Letter already written, & the papers intended for Ly. M.

I, also, with Mr. WP. think *apoplexy* certainly the end—unless some paper be found explanatory, addressed to *You*.—[11]

---

[7] In all likelihood Catherine Mackintosh (L. 718 n. 14), but possibly Frances Milman (d. 1836), daughter and heiress of William Hart (1741–1804) of Stapleton, Gloucestershire. In July 1799 she had married Francis Milman, physician to the Queen and other members of the Royal Family.

[8] Mrs. Chambers figures in another context in James Greene's will: in it he asks his daughters to pay £25 annually to Susan Hallon, 'Mrs. Chambers's Niece who served me from respect and regard and without hope of favor or Reward & if she be inclined to enter into Service my daughter Angelina will do well to take her   I know no person so honest or so capable of making an excellent housekeeper but it is not to be supposed that this request is made as remuneration for any criminal attachment   I have always respected Susan Hallon as I should have respected my own daughter.'

[9] Angelina Frances (d. 1846) was the third daughter of James and Anne Greene. In 1810 she had married George Matthew Hoare (1779–1852) of Morden, Surrey.

[10] Probably the sum of debts accumulated by Greene about 1802 and never repaid. The figure could have been derived by Mrs. Waddington from the subpoenas served upon him by the Court of the Exchequer (see L. 788 n. 2) and kept either in the locked drawer of his desk or his great box. The £2,380 could not apply to the debts acknowledged by Greene in his will. These added up to £2,200 and 'with interest [would] not amount to more than £3,500'. The will stipulated further that they be paid by Greene's daughters Angelina and Charlotte from an estate then worth about £250,000.

[11] Aware of his recent melancholy (L. 697) and now of his dark past, Mrs. Waddington perhaps suggested that Greene committed suicide. He was buried with full religious rites, 'apoplexy' being recorded as the cause of death.

Calm your dear—& too sensitive mind my dearest Mary—
[*a sentence cut out*] your Fanny!—What would become of you
without her!—[12]

I regard Her, now, to be as great a succour to you, as you
have been to Her.—Heaven bless you—!—

March 3ᵈ 1814
Chelsea College. — —

752   [63 Lower Sloane Street,
                                 post 8 March 1814]
To [Madame de Boinville][1]

A.L. (McGill), *n.d.*
A fragment (2·2 to 2·3 × 7·3″) obviously cut from the top of the second
leaf of a double sheet 4to [*Ends of cross-writing show on right fold*:] as / hope /
than / My / w / to ⟨   ⟩ 2 pp.
Recto docketed in ink: Madᵐᵉ d'Arblay
Verso docketed in ink: Madame D'Arblay

Recto of fragment:

so long-awaited & eventful termination. Alas—how many that
we both love have been, & still will be mowed down by the
slaughter of War, ere Peace, for which I live & pray, will leave
us to our still so short even when no longer untimely race! You
are most kind so to remember ǀ

Verso of fragment:

intercourse.—I am extremely glad that you have had a letter
from your very good & sincerely attached Alexander; I do not
dare venture to write at this perilous moment:[2] but if you still

---

[12] Mrs. Waddington's reliance on her daughter during a crisis was another
argument by FBA against Fanny's London season unaccompanied by her mother.
See L. 718.

752. [1] This letter replies to one (Berg) from Bracknell, Berkshire (postmarked
8 Mar. 1814), by Mme de Boinville; 'I had a few lines from my good Alexʳ dated
the 12ᵗʰ of Janʳʸ His silence respecting Mʳ d'Arblay proves to me that he was
well. I have two channels through which I make efforts to write . . . I shall have
the greatest pleasure in forwarding any letter for you my dear Madam.'
[2] The tension of FBA's letter stems from her recognition of an embattled
France, particularly Paris. For the French military crisis at this time, see Ll.
747 n. 1, 748 n. 10.

keep open any correspondence, I shall be very much indeed gratified that you would mention that *M^e d'A. & FAMILY* are well:

not AND SON!—!³

753   [63 Lower Sloane Street,
                                        17 March 1814]¹
To Mrs. Waddington

L. printed, 'A Burney Friendship II', *Monthly Review*, ix (Oct. 1902), 147–8.

The newspapers will tell you that the 28th is to be my day of trial.² All is entirely done, and waiting only the sewing and stitching. I have nothing more to do with it, and hardly a moment even for alarm, much as there is *de quoi*, but my whole soul is occupied with Paris! not with *what* will be the catastrophe, but with *which way* and *how* it will be brought about, with regard to the inhabitants.³ My own best friend has a martial presence of mind that makes me fear less for him than I should for any other human being, in case of difficulties that are

---

³ AA, now 19, was eligible—as FBA wrote (Berg, 1814)—for 'the conscription of Buonaparte'. Anticipating this by October 1813, M. d'A (through an intermediary) consulted with the Director of Conscription and gained a two-year postponement of military service for AA.

753. ¹ Because the letter was interrupted by the sound of 'the guns', it was written on 17 Mar. 1814. See n. 5.

² See, e.g., the advertisement in the *Morning Chronicle*, Thursday 17 Mar. 1814: 'On Monday the 28th instant will be published, dedicated to Dr. Burney. THE WANDERER: or, Female Difficulties. In 5 vols. duodecimo. By the Author of Evelina, Cecilia and Camilla. Printed for Longman, Hurst, Rees, Orme and Brown, Paternoster-Row; and at the British Gallery, 54, New Bond-street.'

³ On 4 Apr. 1814 *The Times* announced that a 'dispatch has been received by Earl Bathurst from Viscount Castlereagh, wherein his Lordship states, that the Negociations, which have been held at Chatillon between the Plenipotentiaries of the Allied Powers and the Plenipotentiary of the French Government [i.e. Caulaincourt] were broken off on the 18ᵗʰ ult'. For more than a month previous to this announcement it was obvious that the conferees could only disagree, and at the expense of the Bourbons. See Bertier de Sauvigny, p. 27.

Moreover, to FBA, who wished only an end to the war, Blücher's victory at Laon was ominous. Even *The Times* (17 Mar.) became bloodthirsty: 'if BLUCHER, if the Cossacks, get to Paris,—to Paris, the seat of BUONAPARTE's pride and insolence,—what mercy will they show to it; or why should they show it any mercy? . . . Perhaps the famous city of which we speak may even now be laid in ashes.'

personal; but he will be only one of an immense cluster, and must run all risks with those by whom he is surrounded. And the terrors of my female friends—some of the sweetest women in the world—affect me without measure. M. D'Arblay ceases not a moment regretting M. de Narbonne—all his late letters written since that event name no other subject. I am astonished beyond all words at the manner in which that event has been borne here by one who I thought devoted to his very shadow.[4] But let me enter into no other subj — —

I was stopt by the guns.[5]

I am in a state of frightful agitation relative to news. News of every turn and colour shakes me now in such dread uncertainty — —

Midnight. Imagine my gratification—I was stopt again to receive a letter announcing that M. D'Arblay was very well in Paris the 18th of February. This news seems quite recent, and has relieved me unexpectedly. An English lady has written it at his desire to Mr. Reeves of the Alien Office.[6] Nothing, therefore, can be more satisfactory. Yet what difficulties must there be of passing letters when, even so, a month is taken up for the delivery of a billet from Paris to London, though the Government receive their packets in three or four days! I am breathless now with expectation for the declaration to be made on the opening of Parliament relative to peace or war.[7]

That I do not write to Madame de S[taël] is not *prudery*, as

[4] Mme de Staël. See L. 735 n. 5.

[5] As reported in *The Times*, 18 Mar. 1814: 'Yesterday morning was ushered in with the welcome discharge of cannon, confirming the glorious intelligence which we had the happiness to announce the day before in our Extraordinary Edition.' What was in fact announced on 17 March was Marshal Blücher's victory at Laon, which *The Times* heralded as 'the prelude to the Tyrant's total downfall'.

[6] For evidence of Mme Solvyns's association with John Reeves, see L. 696 and n. 11. On 18 March FBA wrote her thanks to Mr. Reeves for 'his most welcome intelligence from the amiable Mrs. Solvyns' and added that she 'has had no direct news from M. d'Arblay since the end of Decr, nor even any that is circuitous since the 10th of January. If Mr. Reeves writes . . . to Mad. Solvyns, how kind an office he would perform by inserting "Madame d'Arblay & *family* not and *Son*! are well". . .' (A. L., third person, 8vo with integral blank leaf, an excerpt in *Maggs Catalogue* 971, dated 1976.)

[7] Parliament, formally opened on 1 Mar. 1814, adjourned until Monday, the 21st. On that day a motion was introduced by Lord Ossulston, ' "that an humble Address should be presented to his Royal Highness the Prince Regent, praying that he would direct an instruction to be given to the negociators at Chatillon, not to conclude any treaty with France, which should not contain a provision, that a general amnesty should be given to the subjects of that nation, on account of offences merely of a political nature" ' (*The Times*, 22 Mar. 1814).

you suspect, but *prudence*, and more than prudence, *far more.*[8] I should delight to let her know how truly and cordially I admire, nay, am enchanted with her work—and will try to do so through the Lockes—or by some means that won't involve me in personal renewals at this tremendous epoch.

You must lock up four vols. of the 'Wanderer';[9] that is Mrs. Locke's plan not to peep—and write a letter for every volume.

Adieu, dearest Mary.

754   [63 Lower Sloane Street],
                                      19 March 1814
To Mrs. Locke

L., incomplete copy in the hand of CFBt (Diary MSS. viii. ⌈5930–32⌉ [*renumbered*] 5923-1, 5923-2, Berg), 19 Mar. 1814
Double sheet 4to   3 pp.   Pages 1 and 3 numbered 21 22
Edited at the Press. *See* Textual Notes.

March 19. 1814
To Mrs Locke
I hasten to impart to my kind & most sympathizing friend that I received last night, tidings, good tidings, of my best Friend of Friends—they have been communicated to me, oddly enough, through the Alien Office!—Mr. Reeves wrote them to my Rev.d Brother, at the desire of an English Lady now resident in Paris, Made Solvyns, (wife of a frenchman)[1] at the request of M: d'Arblay: they assure me of his perfect health.—They

[8] FBA feared especially at this time that the news of her association with Mme de Staël (declared *persona non grata* by the French government) might jeopardize not only the employment of M. d'A but his actual safety in Napoleonic France.
[9] Mrs. Waddington did not read *The Wanderer* as soon as FBA thought she would, for, piqued at having received no presentation copy, she refused to buy it. In an undated letter (Barrett, Eg. 3700A, f. 241b), addressed to 11 Bolton Street, where FBA lived after 8 Oct. 1818, Mrs. Waddington admitted: '. . . The half of the first volume of The Wanderer . . . is all we have been able to read—I think as superior to every thing Mrs d'Arblay has yet published, as the Paradise lost is to the Paradise regained.' Once she received the set from Fanny Raper some time after October 1818, she was fulsome in her praise.
754. [1] François-Balthazar Solvyns was in fact born in Antwerp. He lived in Paris from 1808 to 1812 during the publication of *Les Hindoûs*. Continuing to reside there until April 1814 (L. 767), he returned to Antwerp, where he soon became port commandant.

are dated, Paris, 18th of February. It will not seem very recent news to me in a few days; but NOW it appears Yesterday; my last intelligence, & that circuitous, being of the 18th of January—& my last *direct* information, the end of December.[2]

At a time like this—when all public news, good or bad, of a Warlike nature, fills [|] me with almost equal alarm—though by no means equal joy or sorrow! — — an assurance such as this is more precious than words can say. I had had no hope of any information at all till the dire contest was over. When will that be?—

'Say the Bells—not '*at Stepney*' but the whole World over!—

> And the whole world over may answer
> I do not know!—
> as well as the Great Bell at Bow.[3]—

Nothing could be so well timed as this intelligence, for my inquietude was beginning to be doubly restless from the accession of time that has fallen to me by having got rid of all my proofs, &c: it is only real & indispensable business that can force away attention from suspensive uneasiness. Another comfort of the very first magnitude, my sweet Friend will truly, I know, participate in—my Alex begins to listen to Reason.[4] He assures me he is now going on with very tolerable regularity: & I have given him, for this term, to soberize & methodize him a little, a private tutor:[5] & this tutor has won his heart, by indulging [|] him in his problem passion. They work together, he says, with a rapidity & eagerness that make the hour of his lesson the far most delightful portion of his day. And this Tutor, he tells me, most generously gives him problems to work at in his absence: a favour for which every pupil, perchance, would not be equally grateful! but which Alex., who loves Problems

---

[2] At this time FBA had not yet received L. 743. Her last communication was L. 736.

[3] FBA's personal and topical alteration of two verses from the nursery rhyme beginning 'Oranges and lemons, / Say the bells of St. Clement's'.

> When will that be?
> Say the bells of Stepney.
>
> I do not know,
> Says the great bell of Bow.

[4] Even prior to his triumphant letter of 29 Mar. 1814 (L. 748 n. 2), AA assured FBA of his orderly conduct and his willingness to observe the rules.

[5] John Alty. See L. 748 n. 7.

algebraic, as another Boy loves a Play or an Opera, regards as the height of indulgence. He comes to me next week to stay till the 20ᵗʰ of April.⁶

No one is so unsettled in their prospects, so uncertain in their fate, as I am at this period. Upon public events my very private destiny is entirely hanging!—When—where will the Conflict end?—And how?—

I have had much worry by premature seizures of my poor book—which has been caught—I know not how—the moment the first vol: was printed, by Lord Holland—Sir James Mackintosh—Sir S. Romilly,⁷—& Madᵉ de Stael!!! I fear the latter is affronted at receiving no answer to her messages. When my kind Augusta sees her, I entreat she will make my peace. I should be truly sorry to return her long partiality by an appearance of real ingratitude or forgetfulness.

755   [63 Lower Sloane Street],
                                21 March 1814
To James Burney

A.L.S. (PML, Autog. Cor. bound), 21 Mar. 1814
Single sheet 8vo   1 p. trimmed   *pmks*   T.P.P.U. / Kings R. Slo. Sq
21 MR 18⟨ ⟩ seal
Addressed: Captain Burney, / James Street, / 26 Westminster.

March 21ˢᵗ
1814

Dear Brother,

It disagrees with me to refuse you anything; therefore, not having slept soundly upon it, I have come to a resolution to make a new arrangement, & do what you wish.

You shall have the set, with one of which I beg your own, &

⁶ For the change in AA's arrival and departure, see L. 761 n. 3.
⁷ Of Huguenot descent, Samuel Romilly (1757–1818), M.P. and law reformer, was knighted in 1806. Extremely active in the parliament that opened on 1 Mar. 1814, he found time to read an advance copy of *The Wanderer*, volume one. He was motivated by regard for FBA as a novelist who understood French life and by personal interest in French politics that altered from an early republicanism to a pro-Bourbon commitment.

Mrs. Burney's affectionate acceptance, on Saturday:[1] which is my first day of distribution, save one to Windsor on Friday.[2]

That it may look less like a FEE, & therefore give a more pleasant feeling, I purpose writing

For Mr. and Mrs. Thomas—[3]

unless you see any objection.

Adieu, dear James—

ever & aye your

FB d'A.

I have had—God be praised. News of M. d'A.—of the 18. of Feby when he was well, & still at Paris.

Alex goes on most delectably.

756   *as of* Chelsea College,
                                           22 March–2 April 1814
To Mrs. Broome

A.L.S. (Berg), 22 Mar.–2 Apr. 1814

Double sheet 4to   4 pp.   *pmks*   To be Delivered / by 10 o'Clock / on Sund. Morn   2 AP 1814   T.P.P.U. / Chelsea   EO   black seal

Addressed: Mrs. Broome, / Hill Street, / Richmond.

Endorsed by CBFB: sister / d'arblay / 1814

March 22^d 1814

Chelsea

What an Age since I have written—at least with my PEN, to my dearest Charlotte! with my heart, I have ten times answered all her dear Letters—& given good measure over, to

<hr/>

755. [1] Because the publication date for *The Wanderer* was Monday 28 March, FBA planned to distribute copies to the Royal Family on 25 March, to close friends and family on 26 March.

[2] The sets of *The Wanderer* destined for Windsor were misdirected by the printer and did not reach FBA for another week. By post on 2 April, the four sets for the Princesses arrived in Chelsea (L. 760). On the same day—but after the post— the Queen's copy arrived. The books were then sent to Windsor followed by a note written on 4 April (L. 761) explaining why they could not be personally presented —as *Camilla* had been. The books reached Windsor on 3 April and Mme Beckedorff distributed them the next day. In a letter (Berg), dated 6 April, she wrote to FBA: '. . . que je n'ai pu trouver le moment de Vous dire que le paquet de livre est arrivé Dimanche Soir et que Lundi matin, je les ai delivré et présenté a la Reine et aux Princesses. Sa Majesté et leurs Altesses Royales les ont réçu gracieusement.'

[3] For Honoratus Leigh Thomas, see L. 676 n. 2. His wife was Anne *née* Cruikshank (*c.* 1775–*post* 1846), the elder daughter of the anatomist.

boot. No one, I well know, will make more tender allowance for my epistolary failures; &, in truth, my very conscience acquits me, at this period, so little I have enjoyed any leisure, & so tired is my hand of holding a Pen—

March 27th

I sent off last night a mere note, to say my dearest Charlotte's sett awaited but opportunity to be cast at her feet: & to express, briefly but truly, my extreme concern that I could not send two other setts.—though I have 30:[1] but *10* are wholly for M. d'Arblay & his own distribution amongst our, now, mutual relations & friends in France: though the greater part, in fact, will go simply to persons who have aided our correspondence, & to whom we have no other mode of shewing our gratitude, & of exciting *a continuance of favours*—such as Me Solvyns—as, also, the secretary to the Police!—M. de Saulnier.[2]—M. Recamier, the Banker, who sends sometimes our Letters, M. David, his nephew,[3] whom Me Solvyns brought to your house —&c—Then 6. of my remaining 20. go to the R[oyal] F[amily] 2 to Cambridge, 2 to Camilla book holders, &c—[4]

April 1st—Again I lost the post, by an interruption, & now I have severely to regret that my kindest Charlotte should have sent to *Sloane Street*, instead of the *College*, where the packet has so long been waiting opportunity! I was in town with Mrs. Stuart, the Primate's lady,[5] who had the goodness to fetch me herself to see the excellent Susan Adams, now ill,[6] & admirably nursed, at her house in Hill Street.[7] How VERY unlucky the carrier should come at that moment! & not go on to the College! where, alone, I have any *acknowledged* direction, for I merely sleep in Sloane Street, now my Press business is over: except by

---

756. [1] The thirty sets given to FBA were probably distributed as follows: ten to M. d'A, five more than she originally intended (L. 741); six to the Royal Family; two to AA; one each to Lady Crewe, Mrs. Locke, Mr. and Mrs. Thomas; one each to CB, SHB, and the families of EBB, JB, CB Jr., CBFB, CFBt, CPB, Fanny Raper. FBA apparently kept no copy for herself (see L. 760).

[2] For Pierre-Dieudonné Saulnier, see L. 736 n. 29.

[3] For Paul David and Jacques Récamier, see L. 697 n. 1.

[4] Frances Boscawen, Frances Anne Crewe, and Frederica Augusta Locke had been active in securing subscriptions for *Camilla* and kept their lists of subscribers in bound books.

[5] For Sophia and Archbishop William Stuart, Primate of Ireland (1800–22), see iv, Ll. 421 n. 2, 422.

[6] Susan Adams was employed by the Stuarts in 1801 to care for their young children who by 1804 numbered four.

[7] The Archbishop and Mrs. Stuart lived at 18 Hill Street, Berkeley Square.

APPOINTMENT, you would not yourself find me there; & so it was I missed your two dear daughters, greatly to my concern.

I should have left all avocations apart, nevertheless, to answer you relative to the last sad offices of our dear regretted Norbury, but that I went to Fanny to speak of it, & she seemed certain he must have left more than sufficient for that melancholy purpose, & rather hurt than pleased even by a hint upon the subject. With regard to her half Brother,[8] on the contrary, she was very anxious: but there I could not interfere, except by counsel & discussion. Upon US, in my opinion, the children of our OWN half Brother have a far higher claim—higher?[9]— *This* has NONE, beyond the common humanity that would make it truly desireable to serve ANY child: for to US he is no way tied that is more binding than general good will to all mankind must make *him* in common with the whole human race. His own relations & friends are all in ¦ Ireland, as well as himself, & there, & to them he must belong, unless any prospect should open for placing him here, according to our Charlotte's plan, in the B.C. hospital:[10] or any other, that might educate him, & find him some provision, without undertaking a Guardianship & responsibility for which we have none of us any vacancy, nor any justly unengaged means.

Your account, my Charlotte, won't do at all!—I am tormented inexpressibly in having no substantial documents to rectify it but I will certainly suffer no diminution from James's equitable estimate. But where is Alexander's NAME? You omit it wholly. NOTHING is COMFORTABLE but the £1[5.] I can no where find the memorandum you speak of about our pick nick—nor made I ANY of any sort all that time: which I now much regret, though, even now, I cannot wonder at, my fatigued pen considered. I dare not trust to y^r *26th March*,

---

[8] Molesworth Phillips married Ann Maturin (*fl.* 1800–22) on 4 Oct. 1800 (i, p. lxxi). They had two sons and two daughters. Norbury Phillips gave a home to his half-brother Molesworth and educated him (L. 749 n. 1).

[9] The ten surviving children of Richard Thomas Burney, FBA's half-brother. But she sometimes bridled when confronted by this 'claim'. See L. 777 n. 3.

[10] FBA had in mind the Blue Coat School, Christ's Hospital, Newgate Street. The Hospital was so called because of the uniform worn by the boys (poor and/or orphaned). The uniform, originating as did the Hospital in the sixteenth century, consisted of a blue coat or gown, a red leather girdle round the waist, yellow stockings, and a clergyman's band around the neck. No boy was admitted younger than seven or older than nine, and most were made to leave by the time they were fifteen. For Charles Lamb's account of the school, see *GM* lxxxiii[1] (1813), 540 *passim*.

which seems said *au hazard*: —— our *real* account was *settled* the 1ˢᵗ November, 1813, as I see by your hand writing in the blue book, though it was not *paid*, nor is *paid* to this day. My other, i.e. my pick nick debt, cannot be less than £20, even supposing it to be but 11 weeks, when I include Alex.'s share. If we can find no clearer documents, *that* i e. £20, you must not refuse, if you would again make happy by a similar plan & reception,[11] my dearest Charlotte,—your most tenderly affectionate FBd'A— |

April 2d.—yet a new date ere I can conclude!

our dearest Father has been very unwell indeed—very alarmingly altered & shattered—& has much affrighted me: but yesterday—I finish this April 2ᵈ. he was sufficiently recovered to walk through his apartments! I was quite overjoyed! And —if I durst tell you my anxieties about Paris you would indeed rejoice for me!—yet I trust confidently in the peculiar character & presence of mind of M. d'A:, for else I should be wretched with terrour.

What a balmy relief have I also received—my Two dear Charlottes will participate in feeling—in an account of one of the Tutors, Mr. Gimingham,[12] of his perfect satisfaction with the corrected conduct & complete regularity of my Alexander!— Nor is even this ALL: Dr. Davy himself has just written to our Brother Charles, to say That even the learned Dons are now satisfied with him! God be praised! this is, indeed, a weight off my spirits & my fears that helps on endurance of that cruel burthen which still remains, & which PEACE alone can finally remove. I want to write a separate Letter to my Charlottina— but she will allow for my lengthened delay. Poor Mr. Burney mends slowly, but regularly.[13] I have very astonishing NEWS of my Book to tell[14] but no place this time—news almost incredible— My love to Marianne[15] & Mr. Barret:, & Julia—I expect

[11] For FBA's insistence on sharing household expenses at Chenies Street and CBFB's reluctance to accept any significant sum, see Ll. 738 n. 6, 749.
[12] See L. 748 n. 2.
[13] For Charles Rousseau Burney's ailments, see L. 773 n. 4.
[14] FBA would have reported that the whole of the first edition was sold out three days before the publication date.
[15] MF, having spent a long Christmas holiday with the Wilberforces, returned in early February to Richmond where, as she wrote (JRL) to Mrs. Piozzi, there are only 'empty heads and unploughed brains—cards and conversation . . . defecated of the grossness of meaning'.

Alex to-day for Easter. I shall then try to arrange my plans. We MUST go to Norbury Park—& were pressed to *Wimbledon*,[16] to L^y Spencer's; but the death of Dow^r Lady S.[17] has put the family now into retirement. Alex does not think Clem will come.[18] They seem firmly fast friends.—

757

To Charles Parr Burney

as of Chelsea College, 25 March [1814]

A.N.S. (Osborn), 25 Mar.
Single sheet 12mo   1 p.   with a mounting strip on the right margin of the *verso*

I feel sure that my dear Charles will grant an hospitable reception to a Wanderer who will seek it under his roof in the form of a travelling Companion in a post chaise with his dear Father, by the first opportunity.

My love to your amiable Fanny, whom I flatter myself, will lend an ear to the Wanderer's tale, when you can find time to be its recounter.

ever yours, dear Charles,

Chelsea College,   FB. d'Arblay.
March 25th

---

[16] George John Spencer, 2nd Earl Spencer, was born on the family estate at Wimbledon. According to *Boyle's Court Guide* (1814), Lord and Lady Spencer had four residences: 27 St. James's Place, Althorp, Wimbledon, Battersea in Surrey.
[17] According to *AR* lvi (1814), 'Chronicle', 132, Margaret Georgiana Spencer died on 18 March. 'This lady was daughter of the Right Hon. Stephen Poyntz. She married in 1755 J. Spencer, Esq. afterwards created Earl Spencer, by whom she had the present Earl Spencer, the Countess of Besborough, and the late Duchess of Devonshire. She became a widow in 1783, after which she chiefly lived in retirement.' For FBA's association with Lady Spencer at Bath, see i, Ll. 3, 4.
[18] In a letter (JRL) to Mrs. Piozzi, dated 18 March, MF described Clement as 'working hard at Cambridge; & they tell me . . . that it is expected he will be Senior Wrangler.' By giving up the Easter vacation, he hoped to spend 'the long vacation with a private Tutor, near Bradfield Hall' and help his sister conduct Arthur Young's schools for poor children. The death of CB, however, forced his return to London.

758   [63 Lower Sloane Street,
                                           31 March 1814]¹
To James and Charles Burney

A.N. (PML, Autog. Cor. bound), *n.d.*
Single sheet 8vo, being a cover addressed: Madame d'Arblay   1 p.
Addressed on the blank *verso*, apparently over a complex fold: Mr James /
Charles / Burney / ⟨26 James Street⟩ Westʳ

It is impossible for me to come to you, my dear Brother.
Brothers—Sister—Nephew & Niece—
I have Letters to write of necessity that wholly require my
day—
as to-morrow I go to see our faithful Susan Adams, the last
nurse & attendant of our lost sister—who lives at the Primate
of Ireland's—whose lady will herself fetch me & bring me home
—that will swallow my whole morning.
I am in a flutter of spirits inexpressible—PARIS—FRANCE
—my BOOK—!!!!
And,——but——
—Thank Heaven, *NOT MUCH*, my Alexander—! though he is
always an anxious subject.
What do you mean by getting the Gout again?
Lock up 4 Vols. & read fairly—& let no one peep.²
Why my parcel was not sent to Chelsea I cannot find out. It
is meant for Windsor—where it cannot go till *Friday*.³

758. ¹ This letter may be dated 31 Mar. 1814. See L. 756, under date of 1 April,
and nn. 5, 6, 7.
   ² The suspense of FBA's new work depended on the reader's gradually coming
to learn the identity of the Wanderer (not even named until volume 3) and the
causes of her difficulties, which were explicated only in the last volume.
   ³ See L. 755 n. 2.

759 [63 Lower Sloane Street,
2 April 1814][1]

To Longman, Hurst, Rees, Orme, and Brown, Publishers, Paternoster-Row

A. Memorandum incomplete (PML, Autog. Cor. bound), *n.d.*
Single sheet large 8vo (7·9 × 4·9″) 1 p.
Annotated in pencil, p. 1: early 1814

to be strongly printed for 3 times in ALL the Papers—for M^e
D. has perpetual inquiries whether the Book is put upon the
shelf[2]

Me D. begs to know when the Queen's Sett will be ready.

Various Booksellers say they are suspected of keeping back
the Book, Mr Colborurn in particular, who has only 30. setts out
of 100 that were bespoken, & who complains that his customers
reproach him—[3]

The advertisement should mention, to end 1000 false reports,
the truth—i.e. That the 1st Edition was all gone 3 Days before
publication.[4]

759. [1] This letter was written during the morning of 2 April after the delivery
of the post, which did not contain the Queen's copy of *The Wanderer*. (The copy
arrived in Chelsea in the early afternoon by Longman's messenger.) The bold
tone of the letter indicates that it was written shortly after FBA learned from
Martin Burney that the whole of the first edition of the novel had been sold out.
See Ll. 760, 761.

[2] Longman and his associates did not advertise as vigorously as FBA recommended. No newspaper now available to the editors puffed the book's publication
for three successive days.

[3] There would be particular demand for *The Wanderer* at Henry Colburn's
fashionable lending library at 50 Conduit Street, New Bond Street.

[4] The publishers of *The Wanderer* altered FBA's suggestion. See, e.g., the
announcement in the *Morning Chronicle* (15 Apr. 1814): 'Second Edition of THE
WANDERER in 5 vols. 12 mo. price 2 l. 2 l. [*sic*] bds. (dedicated to Dr. Burney),
the Second Edition of THE WANDERER; or Female Difficulties. By the Author
of Evelina, Cecilia, and Camilla. . . .' A similar advertisement appeared in *The
Times* on 21 and 28 April.

760   [63 Lower Sloane Street,
                                        2 April 1814]
To Charles Burney

A.L. (Osborn), *n.d.*
Double sheet large 8vo   4 pp.   *pmks*   T.P.P.U. / ⟨ ⟩   1814   black
seal
Addressed: Rev^d Dr. Burney, / Rectory House, / Deptford.

Your Letter, my dearest Charles, arrived just as I was
setting forth to the Queen's House; on Thursday,—where I
spent not only the day, but the night.[1] And the next day, I went
thence to Brother James's—from whom I did not return till
very late. Two posts were thus inevitably & unavoidably lost:
& this morning, Saturday, arrives your sett at Chelsea, ere I
had had a moment to order it to your Rectory. It must therefore
there wait, till you have the grace & the duty to present yourself
there in person.

I have been labelling for distribution my whole 30 setts—
though they must wait opportunities for delivery as I have
very small means of finding them.

I am charmed with your kind project relative to Windsor.[2]
The Queen's sett is the only one not yet arrived. The 4 princesses ǀ are already here. They came with yours, & my Father's:
which latter, as it is pill day, I defer presenting. Our dearest
Father is weak & suffering; but I hope & trust from a passing
complaint.

News from France is expected every hour of some decision
respecting Peace[3]—Oh how will my heart glow when that
PEACE, shall be announced! I hear you have made a noble &

760. [1] According to *The Times* (30 Mar.) the Queen and the Princesses Elizabeth
and Mary arrived at Buckingham House on Tuesday 29 March and they left
for Windsor on Saturday 2 April. FBA visited them on the 31st, leaving the next
morning.
   [2] CB Jr. offered to accompany FBA to Windsor so that she might make the
presentation of *The Wanderer* in person.
   [3] Having earlier announced the arrival of the duc d'Angoulême at Bordeaux,
The Times on 25 Mar. 1814 reported that the south of France was in revolt against
Napoleon and in favour of the Bourbons. On 29 March *The Times* wrote: 'We
are happy to add, that the prospect of a real, a solid, and a truly glorious peace,
replacing the French KING on his throne, and Europe on its ancient basis, also
becomes daily more distinct and well grounded.' On 2 April the same paper wrote
editorially: 'Everything announces the winding up of the great Drama.'

spirited attack upon the seizure of my property by certain purloiners: Is this true?

But—put on a Wig! That will warm the dear brains, & keep them clear & vigorous. And you cannot be a BISHOP without one: & it will look *de bon augure*—

Besides—

I have news for you that would lift it up! though, now, it must be content ǀ to make your own natural ringlets stand on end:— i.e. viz.—

The Longman's have sent to beg me to prepare my 2ᵈ Edition! —⁴ The orders are so vast, it must soon be wanted!—!

How stands the Hair?

Not quite in elevation?

Well, then,—a bit more

Martin hies to me from Longman's this morning, with the incredible tidings—That the whole edition—of 3000 Copies— is already all gone!—by the enormous orders sent from all the Booksellers, joined to their own customers, through out the Kingdom!—

! ! ! !

What say the Curls?—

Oh put on the Wig!

Here's yet another mounter:—

They entreat me to forbear seeing Revizes, or proofs; not to check the sail: For — — not only the whole is gone 2 days before publication—but ǀ more-over, They have already orders for 800 more!—⁵

Astonishing! incredible! impossible!

I was quite overpowered—Martin shed tears of delight & pride—crying: 'If my uncle & I had fore-seen this, you should not have had less than £4000—& ought not!'⁶—Am I really dear Carlos, Awake?

They must print, they say, the two next Editions together!—!⁷

---

⁴ The second edition consisted of 1,000 copies. (Since this was the last edition, only 4,000 copies of *The Wanderer* were ever printed.)

⁵ If an additional 150 copies of the second edition were sold, then according to the 'Articles of Agreement', Longman would have to pay FBA £500 and prepare immediately for the publication of the third edition.

⁶ Martin Burney now felt that he and CB Jr had sold *The Wanderer* too cheaply, for they had agreed to a maximum of £3,000 if the work went through six editions.

⁷ The 'Articles of Agreement' made no provision for printing two editions simultaneously. See L. 728 nn. 2, 3.

Kind love to Rosette. I shall like Wimbl[e]don well,[8] when Alex is returned to C[ambridge].[9] But I can never quit him.

761   [63 Lower Sloane Street],
                                         6 April 1814
To Charles Burney

A.L. (Osborn), 6 Apr. 1814
Double sheet 8vo   4 pp.   with mounting tape on right margin, p. 4

Wednesday, April 6. 1814.

O what NEWS, my dear Charles!—I scarcely breathe! scarcely know whether I wake or sleep!—

I received yours yesterday as I was dressing to go to spend the day with Lady Keith, to whom I have had the pleasure of presenting my Alexander. At her house the news reached us from its first source—& nearly overpowered me.—The entry into P[aris] without bloodshed—the *Capitulation* is a joy to my soul, that no words can paint[1]—yet shall I taste no repose till I have personal assurances of individual safety—none!—however buoyed up with delicious hope.—

You must be sure I know not how to refuse you any thing—though I heartily wish Rosette a | Collegue who could possibly —& indeed properly be more munificent, & like herself.[2] Nor am I fond of augmenting engagements in their nature so solemn, & which I have no sort of prospect of personally fulfilling. But if nothing better offers, I am always yours, & at your command.

8 To visit Lord and Lady Spencer.
9 See L. 761 n. 3.
761. 1 On 6 April, a letter signed by Charles Stewart, Lieutenant-General, appeared in *The Times*: 'After a brilliant victory, God has placed the capital of the French empire in the hands of the Allied Sovereigns, a just retribution for the miseries inflicted on Moscow, Vienna, Madrid, Berlin, and Lisbon, by the Desolator of Europe. . . . [H]is Imperial Majesty, the King of Prussia, and Prince Schwartzenberg . . . acceded to entertaining a proposition to prevent the capital from being sacked and destroyed. . . . and Count Nesselrode . . . went in at four o'clock this evening, when the battle ceased, to Paris' (Stewart's letter was dated 30 Mar. 1814).
2 FBA had evidently been invited to stand as godmother at the christening of CPB's second daughter Rosetta d'Arblay, born on 12 March. See viii, L. 844.

My Royal Copy arrived after the post on Saturday. I wrote on Monday to Windsor; but, in your precarious state, durst not—as I would otherwise have done, propose you for a convoy. On the contrary, I have hinted it will be FULL AS AGREEABLE, if I may make my own devoirs some time hence, & at present only SEND the Books. For I am terrified at the thoughts of being detained, when I arrive, from Alexander,[3] whose stay cannot be lengthened, to make me | any amends.

Mr. Chapman has not sent me the Bills yet. I am very anxious for their arrival, on many accounts. I believe, this time, as Alex has added no furniture, nor bought any Cloathes, & the term is short, they cannot surpass the Tancred. I have, here, to re-fit him, &c.[4]

I am rather surprised at not hearing of my next 500 from Long[man] as the edition is so clearly gone. But I suppose I must wait till the 2^d comes out. It will be 15 months ere I receive the instalments, of course.[5] And, after the *3^d* Edition, every body being supplied, I cannot expect the residu for a long, long time. Yet I think it *secure.*[6] Poor M. d'A—who thinks we have here so much more money than I have found, knowing neither our losses, *completely*, through the omnium,[7] nor our unexplained omissions of receipts, has sent to me to advance £25. to a french Prisoner in Shropshire! I am cruelly tormented by inability to let him know the real state of our affairs: but I conceive that | Letters now will soon pass freely—oh what

[3] AA arrived in Chelsea on Saturday 2 April, the day before Palm Sunday (see L. 756). He was free of college duties until the end of Easter week, i.e. until Monday 17 April. He did not, however, return to Caius until after CB's funeral on 20 April.

[4] AA's fees due on Lady Day were £27. 15s. 2d. and those for the Midsummer term £28. 19s. 9d. ('Tutor's Account Book').

[5] According to the 'Articles of Agreement', Longman and his co-directors guaranteed payment of £1,500 in three installments at specified times. See L. 728 n. 2. The booksellers never made advance payments on *The Wanderer*. The last £500 of the initial £1,500 was banked at Hoare's by Longman on 13 Apr. 1815 (see the d'Arblay account, 1814–16, at Messrs. Hoare).

[6] For the six editions of *The Wanderer* and Longman's conditions of payment for each, see L. 728 n. 3. Her present hopes proved to be unfounded. In a letter to Longman & Co. on 30 Aug. 1817 (Barrett, Eg. 3695, f. 97), she revealed that in three years only 3,500 copies of the book had been sold; i.e. the whole of the first edition and half of the second. She realized, therefore, £1,500 for her effort.

[7] M. d'A knew precisely how much he had lost 'through the omnium'. See Appendix II. He had shared in William Locke's and John Julius Angerstein's purchase of shares of the omnium. M. d'A lost £428. 4s. of his original investment of £700. Mr. Locke then reinvested £271 that belonged to M. d'A in 3 per cent consols.

Heaven will that be! I rejoice to tell you our dearest Father recovers—& renews his little walks through the apartments. Charles Parr has sent a great alarm to Mrs Lock, which, I thank Heaven, I am going to allay.[8] Alex. is gone to escort Sally to see good Mr. B[urney] who recovers very slowly indeed, alas! *but* recovers. An offer is *preparing* for me of L^y Holl^d's Box at the playhouse! — — I never saw her:—& I, also, am *preparing* only to return Thanks.[9]—

adieu, dearest Carlos

oh for a Letter from Paris!—Love to dear Rosette

del^ry of Ms.	for 3000		£
	copy—		500.
			p^d
6. M. after day of			
March 25. Publication.—			500 in 3^M
			p^d ⟨sight⟩
12 M^ths after publication			500 in 3^M
March 28—			p^d ⟨sight⟩
			£
on 2^d Ed. of	1000—		500
publi-	— —		£
cation 3 Ed.	1000.		250
	— —		£
4. Ed.	1000		250[10]
	— —		

---

[8] CPB wrote to Mrs. Locke of CB's critical illness. But FBA's optimism did not allow her to see her father as a dying man even six days before his death.

[9] Lady Elizabeth Holland *née* Vassall (1770–1845) was divorced by Sir Godfrey Webster (1719–1800), cr. Baronet (1780). On 6 July 1797 she married Henry Lord Holland (L. 744 n. 3) against whom Sir Godfrey had secured £6,000 damages in an action *crim. con.* The two defendants were found guilty of having lived in adultery and having produced a child, Charles Richard Fox (d. 1873).

[10] FBA's anticipation of *The Wanderer*'s sales and payments therefrom through four editions.

762   [Paris], 7 [April 1814]

M. d'Arblay
To Madame d'Arblay

A.L. (Berg), 7
Double sheet 4to   4 pp.   *pmks* 12 A 1814 13 AP 1814 14 AP 1814
wafer
Addressed: A Madame / Madame d'Arblay née / Miss Burney chez
le 2nd Dr Charles Burney Chaplain de / Roy a Londre / *Angleterre*
Readdressed: Madame d'Arblay / Rd Dr Burney / Chelsea College
Edited by FBA, p. 1, *annotated and dated*: ✳· 4/2 1814 April. *See
further*, Textual Notes.

7*eme*

Quel bonheur inattendu mon adorable amie! j'apprens
enfin par Made Victor de Maubourg¹ que ⌐Melle Wad[dington]²
sait d'une de ses amies que⌐ ton jeune compagnon de voyage³
et toi vous êtes en bonne santé. Puisse le Ciel me conduire
bientot près de toi — près de lui! Ma santé est bonne, mais mon
pauvre coeur est bien malade — à une joie folle ont succedé des
anxietés sans nombres. Je n'ai connu, au surplus que peu de
dangers personnels: mais j'ai eu tant de chagrins — J'ai éprouvé
des pertes si sensibles! Il ne me reste du meilleur et du plus
aimable ami⁴ qu'un portrait fort ressemblant et de ma chère
Madame de Tessé⁵ que le système du monde de La Place,⁶
qu'elle m'a legué. Pauvre Mr de Narbonne! quelle fin! — au
surplus, il n'est pas à plaindre; — tu le sais toi qui comme moi
as pu lire dans son coeur si peu connu! Ah mon amie — mon
adorable amie, combien je le regrette! combien helas il me

762. ¹ Petronella-Jacoba de Fay de Latour-Maubourg (1772–1844). See vi,
L. 557 n. 7 for a description of her marriage in 1804.
² Frances Waddington was planning a journey to Paris. See L. 791.
³ This appellation, like 'ton chevalier' (L. 689), was a euphemism for AA,
devised in part for gallant pleasantry but also as a continuing cover for the boy's
military exemption in France.
⁴ Comte de Narbonne-Lara (L. 736 n. 4).
⁵ The comtesse de Tessé, died on 1 Feb. 1814, aged 73. For the cause of her
death, according to FBA, see L. 791.
⁶ Pierre-Simon de Laplace's *Exposition du Système du Monde* (1796): 2nd ed.
(1798), 3rd ed. (1808), 4th ed. (1813). M. d'A inherited the 4th edition. It is
ironical that AA should publish in 1832 *The Apostolic Gift of Tongues . . . To which
is added, an Appendix, containing an Answer to Hume on Miracles, and to Laplace on
Atheistical Necessity*.

273

fait faute! et combien neanmoins je sens vivement qu'il etait tems qu'il cessât de vivre.[7] Ah ma chere Fanni — combien n'ai-je pas à m'applaudir | d'avoir été constant dans mes refus.[8] En ce moment ma pauvre amie je suis sans etat,[9] mais non sans ressources: Mais je suis assez embarassé du parti que je dois prendre Quoique bien portant, et vigoureux encore, chaque garde que je monte en ma qualité de grenadier de la garde national me prouve que le repos est desormais tout ce qui me convient. Tache donc de trouver quelque moyen de me le procurer sans trop de privations.[10] Si cela est impossible, je suis bien resolu de me les imposer toutes. il n'y en a qu'une à la quelle je ne me ferai jamais. C'est celle de notre separation, et pourtant le tems n'est pas venu où nous pouvons la faire cesser. Si tu etais ici je mourrerais bientôt d'inquietude! et tu sens bien que l'honneur me retient ici, et m'empêche de t'aller joindre: mais une fois la paix signée,[11] rien ne m'arretera, et j'irai vous embrasser et arranger avec vous le plan qui nous restera à suivre pour notre avenir. Amen!

J'espère, ma chere amie, que ton excellent pere n'est pas trop incommodé des infirmités inseparables de son grand âge. Mon oncle, qui t'aime bien tendrement, et veut que je te le dise dans toutes | mes lettres, va bien, et a supporté avec un courage heroique la rude epreuve à la quelle il a été mis par les cosaques,

[7] Even when excluded from Napoleon's army, Narbonne 'ne manquait jamais d'exprimer pour l'armée nouvelle son admiration passionnée' (Dard, p. 166). He died while a member of that army and before he could witness its total defeat. Moreover, 'Narbonne, resté royaliste de coeur et de raison, s'était rallié à l'Empereur par admiration pour sa personne et pour sa gloire.' As Talleyrand later commented: 'Narbonne était mort à temps, car, dévoué comme il était, il eût suivi, deux ans après, l'Empereur à Sainte-Hélène' (Dard, p. 291).

[8] M. d'A was loyal to the Bourbons. Yet his loyalty did not prevent him from swearing late in 1800 an oath of allegiance to the laws of the Republic before the Minister Plenipotentiary of the French Republic in Batavia (iv, L. 396 n. 2). Moreover, he had been prepared in 1802 to participate in the French military expedition against San Domingo, although he stated to Bonaparte that he would not bear arms against England. This proviso, though expressed in language of loyalty to the Napoleonic regime, excluded him from military service. See v, Appendix, items 14–21. The fact remains that M. d'A served neither in Napoleon's army nor in his court.

[9] After nine years of service in the ministère de l'Intérieur, M. d'A in the interim between Napoleon's defeat and the Restoration was relieved of his appointment, when the ministry was to be reorganized along Bourbon lines.

[10] Perhaps the first hint that M. d'A entertained 'the idea of the Consul français' for himself. See L. 769.

[11] Peace was signed on 30 May 1814 (L. 787 n. 10), but M. d'A, worried about FBA's health following the death of CB, did not wait for the signing of the peace before coming to England.

maitres à deux fois differentes du pays qu'il habite,[12] et qu'ils ont totalement ruiné, sans commettre neanmoins aucune des horreurs dont on les accuse.[13] Ne vivant que du pillage, ils sont assurément le fleau des contrées où ils se trouvent et mon pauvre pays qui n'est pas encore près d'en être debarassé souffrira bien longtems de leur sejour redoutable.

⌐Tous nos parens et amis se portent bien. J'aurais mille et mille choses à te dire mais, j'attendrai pour causer avec toi librement, que j'aye reçu ta reponse et que je sache si je puisse m'abandonner à cette douce confiance dont la privation m'a fait et me fait encore tant souffrir. Made de Maisonneuve est trés inquiete de Maxime.[14] Charles qui a de ⟨   ⟩ et est chef d'escadron a été fait prisonnier il y a environ un mois.[15] Florimond[16] est à ⟨   ⟩. ⟨Meulan⟩ est chargé des prisonniers ses compatriotes, et ce qui ne te surprendra point c'est qu'ils aiment et estiment leur honnête geolier.[17] Parlons donc un peu de ton nouvel ouvrage. Ce n'est que depuis 7 à 8 jours que j'en connois le titre que nous avons tous essayé de traduire en Français *The Wanderer or female difficulties* ce qui je crois veut dire | *Dangers aux quels s'exposent les femmes qui d'elles voyagent sans un but fixe.* Cette version est de moi et ne vaut rien: mais jusqu'à présent personne n'a pu trouver mieux. Donne nous ton avis et pour Dieu adresse moi l'ouvrage qui doit avoir paru.

[12] Russian troops were in the area of Joigny and neighbouring towns from 22 January to 12 February. Joigny was briefly occupied not twice but three times: 30 January, 2 and 7 February. See Appendix III for the nature of the occupation.
[13] Of all the allied troops who marched across western Europe in 1813 and France early in 1814, the Russians evoked the most apprehension. In October 1813 an English army officer noted in his journal: 'The country through which we are passing is in great distress. The Cossacks have devoured or destroyed the little that the stagnation of commerce had enabled, the inhabitants to provide.' The officer continued: 'In many parts of Germany . . . the Cossack terror is so great that prayers are put up: "De Cossaquibus, Domine, libera nos!" In other churches they have added the term Cossack to the original Devil as more expressive of his mischievous proceedings' (Brett-James, pp. 56–7).
[14] 'Maxime' de Maisonneuve (L. 736 n. 2) was in the Bayonne-Toulouse battle area defended by maréchal Soult against Wellington's army.
[15] Jules-*Charles*-César de Fay de Latour-Maubourg (1775–1846) had started his military career in 1789 as a cadet gentilhomme. By February 1814, he was chef d'escadron in the 8th régiment de Chasseurs à cheval. There is no military record at Vincennes to indicate that he was ever a prisoner of the allied forces but in March 1814 he participated in the 'campagne en France' where, at Laon, he was wounded three times. His treatment and recovery in an allied hospital may have been regarded by M. d'A as a form of imprisonment. For the comte de Latour-Maubourg's marriage to Lafayette's daughter Anastasie, see v, L. 485 n. 7.
[16] Just-Pons-*Florimond* de Fay de Latour-Maubourg. See L. 736 n. 3.
[17] For Marie-Joseph-Théodore de Meulan, see L. 736 n. 28.

Mad^e de Cadignan qui est dans la plus grande devotion a été bien malade et est assez bien à present. Elle a été bien sensible à la perte qu'elle a faite de si amere,[18] et les inquietudes que lui donnent son fils passé lieutenant en premier dans le garde d'honneur la tuent. Il y a quelques jours que je ne l'ai vue, mais tu peus faire dire à sa soeur qu'elle est *pretty well*.[19] Adieu ma bonne et adorable Fanny. Tache de m'obtenir un moyen sur et prompt de correspondance. Mille et mille tendres complimens à nos chers parens et à tous nos amis ⟨et connaissances toutes mes meilleures pensées et voeux⟩.[π]

763   Paris, 8 April 1814

M. d'Arblay
To Madame d'Arblay

A.L. (Berg), 8 Avril 1814
Double sheet 4to   4 pp.   wafer
Addressed: À Madame / Madame d'Arblay née / Miss Burney chez Monsieur son pere / Le Docteur Charles Burney / Chelsea College / *London* / *Angleterre*
Edited by FBA, p. 1, *annotated*:   5/1   *See further*, Textual Notes.

Paris ce 8 Avril 1814

Quel bonheur inattendu ma chere Fanny; une lettre de toi![1] à la verité sa date est ancienne puis qu'elle est du 1er. Janvier: mais n'importe c'est une jouissance bien vive bien chere que celle de la vue de caractères tracés par toi. Pourquoi donc Alex qui etait avec toi alors, n'y a t'il pas joint un seul mot. C'est à minuit 1/2 cette nuit que j'ai reçu cette lettre qu'on avait retourne à la Police generale. Ce qu'elle m'a fait eprouver ne peut se decrire. Je ne l'entreprendrai donc point et je passe

---

[18] Mme de Cadignan (L. 736 n. 24) still mourned her husband, who died in 1804, and her second son, who died the following year.
[19] Mme de Cadignan had two sisters (v, L. 513 n. 6), both of whom lived and died abroad: Elizabeth Hunter and Anne de Palézieux-Falconnet.

763.   [1] This letter is missing.

tout de suite à ce qu'elle renferme de plus important pour
moi. Mon dieu mon amie que le portrait que tu me fais de notre
cher Alex me fait peine. Quoi? il est encore plus défait plus
maigre qu'on ne l'a peint dans l'esquisse que tu m'as adressée,
et que je n'ai pu regarder depuis, parceque l'impression qu'elle
me fait eprouver est plus douloureuse que je ne pourrais la
supporter en ce moment. Quelle folie à lui de passer ainsi des
nuits entieres à des recherches satisfaisantes sans doute, mais
dont le succès incertain met sa santé dans un danger reel.
Cette santé d'ailleurs est elle bonne et n'y a t'il pas encore
d'autres raison de craindre qu'il ne la perde? Au nom du Ciel,
ma chere amie, reponds moi franchement sur ce point; et |
surtout dis moi comment toi même tu te trouves — N'as tu
aucun resentiment de ce qui nous a tant et si justement allar-
més? Je suis heureux de ce que tu me dis de la santé de notre
dearest Father. Sois je te prie, près de lui, l'interprete de mes
sentimens. Sois le de même de tout ce que je voudrais pouvoir
exprimer ici à tous nos parens et à nos amis que j'espere embrasser d'ici à trois semaines ou un mois.[2] Ecris moi en attendant
ton opinion sur ce que je t'ai mandé il y a quelques jours, car
je suis si fatigué de revolutions, que je voudrais bien m'assurer
d'un endroit où je serais sur de passer à l'abri des orages
qu'elles entrainent le peu de tems qui me reste à vivre. Tout ce
que tu me dis d'Alex tend à me prouver, de plus en plus, que ce
que nous pouvons faire de mieux pour lui, est de mettre s'il est
possible à execution le plan que nous avions toujours eu d'en
faire un bon et honnête *clergy-man*;[3] et dans ce cas, quelqu'avantage que puisse me procurer le changement heureux et ines-
peré qui vient de s'operer, l'impossibilité que j'eprouve à rester
separé de lui, me ferait preferer le sejour qu'il habite à tout
ce qu'on pourrait me donner ici. Il ne faut pas d'ailleurs se
dissimuler que les bonnes places vont être tellement courues
qu'il sera infiniment difficile d'en obtenir. | Tant d'intrigues
vont se mettre sur les rangs avec ceux qu'il est bien naturel que
le Roi veuille recompenser, que malgré que je puisse dire sans

[2] For the arrival of M. d'A in England, see L. 637 n. 1.

[3] When AA became a Tancred student in 1813, he had to proceed to the
degree of Bachelor of Physic. See the letter (Barrett, Eg. 3702A, ff. 18–19) of
CFBt to FBA in the summer of 1815. Yet from the beginning of his University
matriculation, AA and his parents presumed he had special dispensation as to
the curriculum he studied, the degree he took, and the career he was to prepare
himself for.

vanité que j'aurais bien quelques droits à quelque preference rien ne serait peut etre moins assuré que le succès de démarches aux quelles je ne suis point accoutumé et qui me repugnent infiniment. Quant à la place que j'occupe il est douteux que je puisse la conserver à cause de la quantité de réformes qu'on va faire et qui sont effectivement indispensables.[4] Pour la première fois, ma chere amie j'eprouve quelques regrets de n'avoir pas accepté quelques unes des places qu'on m'a offertes; parceque le retour de nos legitimes souverains me mettrait à même de les servir dans la carriere que je me suis fermée, et qu'il me parait impossible de me r'ouvrir en ce moment où l'on aura pour l'armée plus d'officiers et surtout de generaux que de soldats.[5]

┌Je [t'ai] ecrit dernierement relativement à la difficulté extrême [que] j'ai à traduire le titre de ton nouvel ouvrage. Quand donc le recevrai je — [ne] serait il pas possible que tu m'en fasses passer un exemplaire par Lord Castelreagh?[6] Tu peus juger de l'impatience que j'ai de le lire. Dis moi donc je te prie quel est l'arrangement que tu as fait. Il me semble que tu pourrais sans aucun scrupule accepter les 500 guinées que t'offrait ⟨   ⟩ si tu en eusses donné 100 à ton libraire à qui cela ne pouvait faire aucun ǀ tort et qui au contraire aurait gagné ces 100 guinées dont le sacrifice ⟨me⟩ sera reellement necessaire à ceux qui voudront imprimer l'ouvrage à Boston sur l'exemplaire qu'ils recevront de Londres.[7] Au demeurant, ma bonne amie, tu juges bien que ce que j'en dis n'est que par maniere de censure, car en verité j'approuve de toute manière tout ce que tu as fait sur ce sujet. J'en dis autant de tout ce que tu as pu faire sur les autres, et j'imagine d'ailleurs que pour ce qui concerne notre pauvre maison il serait trop tard de te faire connoitre et mon etonnement de l'estimation qu'on en a faite, et mon opinion sur l'alternative ou de nous en défaire ou de la repeindre convenablement. Nous n'avons pas de succes, ma chere amie, dans nos speculations d'argent. ⟨Car⟩ plus rien

[4] But in L. 762, dated 7 [April], M. d'A reported that 'je suis sans etat'.
[5] M. d'A obliquely states his regret that, having been named maréchal de camp on 22 July 1792, he never sought the confirmation of this brevet, that he had little hope of securing it in the spring of 1814 when there were more generals in the French army than privates. (The brevet was in fact confirmed on 14 July 1814.)
[6] Castlereagh (L. 741 n. 28), who had been on the continent since early January 1814, was familiar to the French for his work at Châtillon (4 Feb.–19 Mar.), his subsequent signing of the Treaty of Chaumont, and his current negotiations in Paris for a permanent peace.
[7] See L. 718 n. 15.

que dans le pays que tu habites. Ne t'allarme point cependant, j'ai assez heureusement tiré mon affaire du jeu mais ne compte pas sur plus de trois cent ⟨pounds au retour de⟩ ce que tu peus avoir autour de toi. Dans tous les cas ne bouge point d'où tu es, et attens moi. ⟨trouvons⟩ maintenant ensemble la meilleure maniere ⟨d'arranger, de finir⟩ [xxxxx 5½ *lignes, dont une partie consiste en* 'mille et mille tendres hommages' *à la famille et aux amis de M. et Mme d'Arblay, entre autres* 'notre cher Mr Locke, Augusta, Miss Cambridge, William, *et* Mr Charles et ses charmantes soeurs']⁷¹

Helas! tu sais *sans doute* que l'une des personnes qui aurait le plus joui du nouveau present que tu as fait à la republique des lettres, n'existe plus. Combien je la plains et combien je la regrette. Elle m'a legué sa nouvelle edition du système du Monde de La Place. Quant à mon cher et à jamais regreté Mr de Narbonne il n'a pu rien laisser à Personne:⁸ moi j'ai de lui toutes les lettres que pendant ses deux campagnes de Russie et d'Allemagne il a ecrites à mon amie⁹ qui m'a permis d'en prendre copie p^r toi et moi.

---

⁸ M. de Narbonne was so poor that 'on dut vendre ses chevaux de guerre pour acquitter les frais de ses funérailles' (Dard, p. 289).
⁹ M. d'A copied the letters sent by M. de Narbonne to 'sa cousine', the comtesse de Fézensac (L. 743 n. 1). The book (Berg) in which M. d'A transcribed them is bound in red morocco with gilt ornamentation, 27·7 cm tall, 11 cm wide, and is stamped in gold—'Subscriptions-Buch des Herrn Joh: Friedr: Reichel aus Berlin.'
In the book are copies of thirty-eight letters, dated from 31 Oct. 1812 (near Moscow) to 12 Oct. 1813 at Torgau. Except for a few from Torgau, where Narbonne indicates the sufferings of his troops, the letters are concerned primarily with family. They repeat his anxiety about his mother ('je vous recommande toujours un peu ma pauvre mere, qui ne doit souffrir des mes torts'); news about Mme de Fézensac's son Aimery ('. . . [il] était, tout simplement à présent, compté parmi les meilleurs officiers de l'armée'); his love for his cousin ('. . . mais au nom de Aimery, que je vous retrouva la même pour moi, c'est à dire, la plus delicate, la plus sensible des amies, et ne changez rien rien & celle que j'aime depuis si longtems avec tant de raisons et tant d'idolatrie'). For Raymond-*Aimery*-Philippe-Joseph de Montesquiou-Fézensac, see L. 770 n. 20.

Chelsea College,
11 April 1814

To Mrs. Broome

A.L. (Berg), 11 Apr. 1814
Double sheet 4to   4 pp.   *pmk*   11 AP 1814   wafer
Addressed: Mrs. Broome, / Hill Street, / Richmond.
Endorsed by CBFB: Sister d'arblay / 1814

Monday Morning, Ap. 11,
Chelsea College, 1814

I know that our Brother James has given my dearest Charlotte some idea of our actual alarm for our beloved Padre—
& therefore I will let her find to-morrow some further account.
I cannot—alas—make it chearful!—but suspense is still worse.
He has great muscular strength remaining in his arms & hands,
& many symptoms upon which *I* should build for his recovery,
& keep alive every hope, but that he will not take any nourish-
ment. He began a *regimen* of abstinence admirable in itself, but
which he has pushed to an extreme, & rendered more than
mischivous—dangerous in the hig[h]est degree. And now, the
disuse has caused a distaste, that amounts to absolute disgust.
This, indeed, terrifies me—for, though he has no disease, no
fever, no positive pain, without sustinance he must waste
away!—

Dr. Mosely[1] is far more comforting about him than Mr.
North[2]—& *I* side with Dr. Mosely.

All he has taken since yesterday noon, is a quarter of a drop
of old Malaga wine!—given, now, with a feather!—

Could you be of the least use, I would beg my other so dear
Charlotte to take charge of dear Dolph, & press you to come:
But you could be of none! otherwise, Sally, with her kind love,

---

764. [1] Benjamin Moseley (1742–1819), M.D. (1784), was in 1788 appointed
physician to the Royal Hospital at Chelsea, a post held until his death. Although
doctor to both SHB and CB, he was regarded as controversial in his medical
opinions and even eccentric.
    [2] Either William North, Sr. (1744–1816), an old friend of CB, or William North,
Jr. (d. *post* 1846). Both father and son were associated with the medical services
at Chelsea College, the elder serving as Surgeon's Deputy (1779–1802) and Surgeon's Mate (1802–9), the younger as Assistant Surgeon (1809–16) and Apothecary
(1816–46).

says you would be most welcome to half her apartment, & she should delight to have you in it. But alas—'tis uncertain whether he would speak to you! for today he has not, & some other days he has not opened his mouth but to Sarah, me, & Beckey; & it seems painful to him ǀ even to be spoken to. He was up half the day on Saturday: on *Thursday* he walked 3 times through the apartments—

Yesterday, for the 1ˢᵗ time, he kept his bed. — — — He dozes almost continually.

I have written to the same effect to poor Esther, who, wanted for poor Mr. Burney, as you to watch Ralph, I have solemnly assured would here be useless,—Sarah, the all-essential Beckey, Maria[3] & George being always about him, in turn; & myself all day in the house: & yesterday Fanny Raper[4] sat up with the maids, to send poor Sarah to Bed; who really wants more regular rest. I shall take her post to night.

I am not without thoughts of begging my two dear Charlottes to renew their kind invitations of Xmas to my Alexander for a few days this Easter—if Mrs. Locke does not take him to Norbury park, whither I was myself going to accompany him to-morrow—But now—stationed here, & known by my dear Father, to whom my services are therefore useful, I would not stir for the universe. I have written to inform Mrs. Locke of my situation; but if my letter does not arrive in time, & she comes —as she had planned to do, Alex must at least keep to the engagement. Otherwise, I feel sure you will unite to receive him during these days of watchful uneasiness—& fearful doubt —*Doubt?*—I, alas, alone use even that word![5]— ǀ

This next week—this *very* week, I mean, I shall hope to settle our tardy account—Martin my soliciter, agent, & steward, cannot act for me sooner.

What I feel about France—I am sure you fully conceive! *HOPE & JOY* that even this sad moment cannot extinguish—

---

[3] Probably Mary *née* More (*fl.* 1793–1819), CB's former servant. She had nursing experience and was the sister of Rebecca More, CB's trusted housekeeper. See ii, L. 68 n. 30; v, L. 505 n. 1.

[4] Fanny Raper, who lived with CB from 1800 until 1807, was the grandchild closest to him and singled out in his will for a monetary bequest of 'one thousand one hundred pounds' for, as he admitted, he had 'adopted' her 'as heiress to [his] affection and designs in her mother's favor'.

[5] FBA continued to hope for CB's recovery, although this time her hope was mixed with doubt. The others at his bedside accepted the idea of his imminent death.

but fear & uncertainty that *no* moment can curb from preponderating—

ALL then, is well—if M. d'A is still in Paris—if some baleful order has not previously removed him thence upon some indispensable—duty[6]

I wait in speechless anxiety for private news—which must now surely arrive in a few days. I entreat Mr. Barret to call with my congratulatory compliments upon M^e la comtesse d'Ennery,[7] & Me de Thuisy & family:[8]

Is Lady Acton at Richmond?[9]

I write in my dearest Father's Room—& by his Bed side— He is quiet, thank Heaven—his hearing is wonderfully good, but he has spoken only twice all day!

adieu, my own very dear sister—Heaven bless & preserve you—My tender love to my dear Charlotte—& best Compts to Mr. Barret—& to your neighbours my friends. — — Mr. Burney is much better.

[6] The newspaper reports confirmed that Paris had been spared by the allied armies and the city's inhabitants were safe. But fighting continued elsewhere in France: Bayonne was under siege and Toulouse attacked by Wellington's troops.

[7] Rose-Benedicte d'Alesso d'Éragny (*c.* 1750–*post* 1814) married in Paris in 1768 Victor-Thérèse d'Ennery (1732–76), son of Jacques-Thomas-François (1701–39). As marquis d'Ennery (1763), he became governor of Martinique (1765) and was assassinated in San Domingo eleven years later.

After her husband's death Mme d'Ennery returned to France, but with the Revolution fled first to Switzerland and then to London (Apr. 1795). She settled in Richmond where until the end of the Napoleonic regime 'elle réunissait chez elle le parti constitutionnel de l'Émigration' (Woelmont, ii. 198). Accompanying her to England was her niece Claire-Louise-Rose-Bonne de Coëtnempren de Kersaint (1778–1828), who was there to marry the duc de Duras.

FBA's congratulations were dictated by the honour bestowed on Mme d'Ennery's nephew-in-law, who had recently become premier gentilhomme de la chambre du roi (see Ll. 770 n. 24, 773 n. 25). For the relationship between the duchesse de Duras and Mme d'Ennery, see Louis-Joseph-Amour de Bouillé du Chariol, *Souvenirs et fragments pour servir aux mémoires de ma vie et mon temps . . . 1769–1812* (3 vols., 1906–11), i. 319–27.

[8] Catherine-Philiberte-Françoise de Berulle (or Berule, *c.* 1760–*post* 1824) married in 1780 Jean-Baptiste-Charles de Goujon de Thuisy (1751–1834), 4th marquis de Thuisy. See *Annuaire de la Noblesse* (1847), p. 211. They emigrated to Richmond about 1792 with their large family: Amable-Jean-Baptiste-Louis-Jérôme de Goujon, comte de Thuisy (1781–1829); Eugène-François-Sixte (1782–1809, d. at Cadiz); Charles-François-Emmanuel-Louis (1784–1857), 5th marquis de Thuisy; Albertine-Louise-Mélanie (1785–1847); Auguste-Charlemagne-Maccabée (1788–1836); Georges-Jean-Baptiste (1795, at Richmond–*post* 1814). FBA apparently wished to congratulate the de Thuisys for their unflagging devotion to the now successful Bourbon cause.

[9] Mary Anne (*c.* 1785–1873) was the elder daughter of General Joseph Edward Acton (1737–1808). In 1799 she married by papal dispensation her uncle Sir John Francis Edward Acton (1736–1811), 6th baronet.

[63 Lower Sloane Street],
14 April 1814

To M. d'Arblay

A.L. (rejected Diary MSS. 5928–[29], Berg), 14 Apr. 1814
Single sheet 8vo 2 pp. black seal
Addressed: A Monsieur / Monsieur d'Arblay, / Rue de Mirominel, /
8 / Faugbourg St Honoré / à Paris.
Edited by FBA, p. 1 (5928), *annotated and dated*: 1814 / 4 (4 / 1) p. 2
[5929], *dated by* FBA: April 14 = 1814. *See further*, Textual Notes.

April. 14 1814

Ah mon ami!—mon meilleur et tous les jours plus que jamais
cher ami!—si vous saviez mon inquiétude!—au milieu d'un
bonheur si éclatant¹—et d'une douleur si triste et si juste, c'est
vous, vous, toujours, plus que l'Espoir, plus que le Chagrin et le
Malheur, qui m'occupez sans relâche—Helas! en quel moment
ai-je perdu mon tendre pere!²—mon pere qui, à cet instan se
seroit trouvé en paradis avant la mort! [Il] m'a laissé Executrice
avec 3 autres de la famille.³ Me voilà donc forcé de rester ici
pour un an.⁴ ah venez—venez donc—dès que cela vous serez
possible—m'aidez à remplir les dernieres volontés de mon
excellent Pere!—⁵

ᴵᴵIl ne trouve pas son testament, qu'il n'a pas eu le tems où
la force de faire en votre faveur, l'arrangemen dont il a eu le
projet quant à ses livres françois.⁶ Mais il vous a toujours ᴵ aimé ᴵ
bien tendrement et il ne vous a pas oublié. J'ai bien besoin de
vos conseils—et *à tems*—il faut que je fasse en attendant de mon
mieux.

Alexandre va assez bien mais le bon & cher M. Burney

765. ¹ The 'bonheur si éclatant' refers literally to the events of 11 Apr. 1814,
when there was 'a general illumination . . . in the evening, to blazon the glorious
victory of England and her allies, in wresting the dominion of the whole of Europe
—save our own invulnerable island, from the grasp and power of the Emperor
Napoleon!' (*Memoirs*, iii. 428).
² CB died in his sleep 12 Apr. 1814, spared 'the apprehension of a long death-
bed agony' that had frequently 'disturbed [his] peace' (*Memoirs*, iii. 423).
³ CB's will named EBB and FBA 'residuary legatees' and JB and CB Jr. 'executors'. All quotations from CB's will are from Scholes, ii. 261–72, and checked
against the copy (Prob. 11/1554/202).
⁴ FBA did not remain in England for a year but returned to France in November
1814.
⁵ By 20 April (L. 768) FBA was in sufficient emotional control to 'unsay'
her desire for the 'instant' return of M. d'A. ⁶ See L. 741 n. 21.

est très dangereusement malade helas!⁷—comme Vous etes ⟨vraiment⟩ envers moi ⟨pour m'encourager⟩. Vous etes ⟨précieux⟩ dans ce moment ⟨difficile⟩. Ah mon ami! ⟨une cruelle⟩ mort. |

C'est à notre ange d'amie,⁸ Amine, que je dois cette occasion précieuse de vous écrire. M. Grefeuil, J'èspere, parlera pour moi à Madᵉ Grefeuil,⁹ et à Madᵉ sa fille, Madᵉ de Castellane.¹⁰ Ah mon ami écrivez tout de suite—et venez le plutôt possible. Charles est tout ce que vous l'avez toujours cru.

⟨N'adresse rien à Charles et continuons 26 James s'est chargé de tout⟩¹¹ Je suis charmée quant à l'aimable M. de Meulan⁋

Mille tendresses à mon cher oncle. des nouvelles—des nouvelles de ma Madᵉ d'Henin ma Madᵉ de Maisonneuve —Mᵉ de Tracy¹² doit etre bien heureuse. mais Mᵉ de⟨Broglie?⟩¹³ Je suis tranquille pour mon cher Genˡ Victor.¹⁴ Mais Charle-Maxime ⟨&c⟩.¹⁵

⁷ But see the last sentence of L. 764.

⁸ Here FBA supplied the superscript × and the editorial note: 'Mrs. J. Angerstein'.

⁹ Jean-Henri-Louis Greffulhe (1774–1820), comte Greffulhe, maire de Fontenailles, pair de France (1818). He was the brother of Mme de Castellane (n. 10); the son of Louis Greffulhe (1741–1810), banker, and the latter's second wife *née* Jeanne-Pauline-Louise Randon de Pully (v, L. 518 n. 9).

¹⁰ Esprit-Victor-Élisabeth-Boniface de Castellane (1788–1862), maréchal de France, married on 26 May 1813 Louise-Cordelia-Eucharis Greffulhe (d. 1847). Serving in the Grand Army, he rallied to the Bourbon cause during the Restoration, when he was named chevalier de St. Louis and officier de la Légion d'honneur. At this time Mme de Castellane bore her first child Henri-Charles-Louis-Boniface (1814–47) and subsequently three others: Louis-Charles-Pierre (1824–83); Ruth-Charlotte-Sophie (1818–*post* 1859); Rachel-Élisabeth-Pauline (1823–*post* 1861).

¹¹ M. d'A sent his letter to FBA in care of her brother at the Greenwich School. CB Jr., however, had not lived there since 1811, when he was presented to St. Paul's, Deptford, and his only address became the rectory. Not only would the letters of M. d'A have to be sent from Greenwich to Deptford (the loss of at least a day), but at the rectory they might fall into the hands of Rosette, who could not always be relied upon to forward them to FBA.

¹² Mme Destutt de Tracy (v, L. 526 n. 21) had two reasons for happiness: first, her husband Antoine-Louis-Claude (1754–1836) was a member of the French Senate that on 2 April voted the Emperor's *déchéance*; second, her son Alexandre-César-Victor (1781–1864), who had been a prisoner of the Russians since 1813, was now freed by special edict of Emperor Alexander (see L. 767 n. 4).

¹³ During this period of Royalist jubilation, FBA remembered the princesse Sophie de Broglie *née* de Rosen-Kleinroop (1764–1828), whose husband Charles-Louis-*Victor* (b. 1756) was condemned to death by the Revolutionary tribunal and executed on 27 June 1794. See ii, pp. xviii–xix.

¹⁴ FBA's reaction to the news that General Latour-Maubourg had recovered from the loss of his leg at Wachau and had returned to Paris.

¹⁵ See L. 762 n. 14.

766   [63 Lower Sloane Street],
                                       15–17 April 1814
Conjointly with Mrs. Locke
To M. d'Arblay

A.L. & A.L. (Berg), 15–17 Apr. 1814
Single sheet 4to   2 pp.   *pmk*   27 April 1814   black seal
Addressed [*in hand of Mrs. Locke*:] À Monsieur / Monsieur d'Arblay /
8 Rue de Mirominil / Faubourg St Honoré / à Paris
Edited by FBA, p. 1, *annotated*: (5 / 2)   *See further*, Textual Notes.

                                          April 15 1814.
Quelle consolation pour moi — oh mon ami! que les lettres
que je viens de reçevoir! Je ne puis jamais vous dire ce que j'ai
souffert de votre silence — ah revenez — s'il est possible — auprès
de moi — d'Alexandre — de tant d'amis qui soupirent — pas
comme Moi! — mais qui desirent ardemment de vous revoir —
aussi ai-je bien besoin de vos conseils — helas, mon ami! — mo[n]
pauv[re] p[èr]e vous a beni mille fois — mais il ne jouira pas —
ici — de mon bonheur à votre retour! — Alexandre va mieux —
tout le monde se porte bien — Je vous envoie votre croix de St.
Louis — ⌐Nos amies angeliques de Norbury vous aiment toujours
de meme — ¬ notre plus que jamais chere Mad^e Lock et Amine
vous feront passer cette lettre — adieu — Adieu — pour bien peu
de tems! Amen! — |

[By Mrs. Locke]
   Your old faithful Friend cannot ressist adding a line to say
that from the bottom of her heart she blesses God! for your
safety—your letters have been a powerful cordial to your
precious Wife who is better than I expected to find her—she
delivered your Croix de St Louis to me,[1] & I have sent it
entreating M^r le Comte de la Chastre[2] to convey it safely to
you — — I sent it this morn^g 17^h Ap^l it was yesterday evening
that my beloved Friend entrusted me with it—I am at present,
for two or three days, with my Amelia in G^t Cumberland Place
—[3] need I tell you her joy & my Augustas & my Wili^ms &

766. [1] M. d'A was made chevalier de St. Louis on 26 Oct. 1791.
   [2] See also L. 768.   [3] See L. 692 n. 3.

Georges—they are with their Mother most affec^t attached to you — —

I saw y^r d^r Alex for a moment yesterday—quite well & rejoicing in his Fathers safety—my Wili^ms wife⁴ also rejoices truely with us & All that know you

767   Paris, 17 April 1814

M. d'Arblay
To Madame d'Arblay

A.L. (rejected Diary MSS. 5930 renumbered 5934–[39], Berg), 17 Avril 1814
Double sheet and single sheet 4to   6 pp.   *pmks* DOVER   23 AP 1814   23 1814
Addressed: A Madame / Madame D'Arblay / chez le Doct^r Burney / Chelsea College / London. / *Angleterre*
Has a scribbled direction: inquire for Mr John / Murray Bookseller at Albermarle Street / just arrived. Dover / 22 April
Edited by FBA, p. 1 (5934), *annotated*: ⁖ (7) Written in Paris after the entrance of the Allied Armies, & the Emp^r of Russia, & King of Prussia p. 5 (5938), *annotated and dated*: 7. continued   of 17th Avril 1814
Edited also by CFBt *and the* Press. *See* Textual Notes.

Paris ce 17 Avril 1814

Je t'ecris, ma chere Fanny, chez Madame Solveyns n'ayant pas eu un seul instant pour causer avec toi depuis que je sais qu'elle doit partir. Imagine toi que j'ai passé près de cinq jours et cinq nuits sous les armes, et ce matin encore la revue de Monsr le Cte d'Artois m'a fait mouiller pendant près de 5 heures.¹ Il est vrai que point ne dedomage d'un service aussi

⁴ See L. 663 n. 5.

767. ¹ Charles-Philippe de Bourbon, comte d'Artois (1757–1836), had arrived in Paris only on 12 Apr. 1814. 'A la porte de la capitale, c'est Talleyrand, représentant du Gouvernement provisoire, qui va le saluer officiellement. . . . On forme alors le cortège définitif qui comprend les grands dignitaires, de nombreux membres de l'aristocratie, des généraux étrangers, et même des maréchaux de l'Empire en uniforme' (Bertaut, pp. 165–6). To enhance this triumphal welcome, the French Senate on 14 April 'convey[ed] the Provisional Government of France to his Royal Highness Monsieur Comte d'Artois, under the title of Lieutenant General of the kingdom, until Louis Stanislaus Xavier of France, called to the throne of

⟨forcé⟩, ce Prince a eu la bonté de me dire d'une maniere on ne peut pas plus gracieuse, que ma conduite etait d'un bon exemple et qu'il la voyait avec beaucoup de plaisir. Je te dirai malgré tout cela ma [|] chere amie, je t'avoue que je suis si fatigué que je donnerais ma demission si je n'etais sur qu'elle servirait de pretexte à quarante autres dans la Compagnie à laquelle je suis attaché. Rien assurément ne serait plus facheux dans la situation actuelle des affaires. Tout, je te le jure, va miraculeusement bien: mais cependant il s'en faut de beaucoup que l'esprit de l'armée soit aussi bon qu'on le desire et qu'il devrait être.[2] Beaucoup de jeunes oficiers, pour ne pas dire tous, s'imaginent tout perdre parcequ'ils, ne seront pas generaux d'ici à deux ou trois ans, et quant aux soldats, l'habitude du pillage qu'ils ont contractée[3] excite des regrets qu'ils expriment quelquefois d'une manière peu rassurante. [|] Cette mauvaise disposition des troupes rend moins empressé de voir partir celles des alliés.; de crainte de tomber de fievre en chaud mal Il est bien desirable neanmoins d'être promptement soulagé de l'énorme poids qui nous ecrase à la verité le plus doucement possible; car l'Empereur Alexandre le plus genereux comme le plus chevaleresque des héros passés presens et futurs.[4] En verité sa conduite a été et est encore sublime. Imagine toi que l'absurde tentative de deffendre Paris a couté aux alliés dix mille hommes et

the French, has accepted the constitutional charter' (*The Times*, 20 Apr. 1814). As King's representative he reviewed on 17 April the troops loyal to the Bourbon dynasty.

[2] Morale among professional French troops was so low that a pro-Napoleonic take-over would have been possible by the military in 1814. Yet M. d'A and others dismissed the possibility, relying now on the presence of allied troops and in time on the quieting effects of a permanent peace. From Paris on 11 May 1814, J. W. Ward (1781–1833) informed Mary Berry (iii. 15) that 'the army is still, in general, attached to the late Emperor. But the different bodies of which it is composed have no means of union, or indeed of communication; no individual in whom they confide, and round whom they could rally; and in peace . . . they will rapidly crumble away, so that I see no great danger from that side.'

[3] For a description of the 'fricoteurs', see L. 733 n. 4.

[4] On 31 March Alexander entered Paris. When he heard the rumour that the Élysée Palace had been mined, he took up residence in Talleyrand's house in the rue Saint-Florentin. The president of the *gouvernement provisoire* boasted that in that house, particularly in 'le salon de l'Aigle', he convinced the Tsar of the need for a Bourbon restoration.

Not only was Alexander visibly close to Talleyrand, but the Parisians were aware of the contrast between the Tsar's arrival in Paris and Napoleon's entry into Moscow. They followed Alexander's negotiations with Napoleon at Fontainebleu, realizing that the former eased his enemy's fate by allowing him the rule of Elba and an annual revenue from France of 2,000,000 francs. The Parisians interpreted as an act of generosity the Tsar's release of all French prisoners—about 200,000 men—still in Russia.

qu'ils auraient été les maîtres de s'epargner cette perte s'ils n'avaient pas été decidés à menager Paris qu'ils ont été les maitres de prendre de vive force.[5] Lorsque la capitulation a été signée Alexandre s'est jetté dans les bras du Roi de Prusse en s'ecriant ⎮ La ⟨cause⟩ de l'humanité est vue enfin gagnée et Paris est sauvé![6] Tout ce qu'on a vu depuis et tout ce qu'on voit de cet homme extraordinaire est parfaitement en mesure avec cet elan d'un noble coeur. Ce que je t'en dis te fera surement imiter l'envie d'arriver assez à tems pour voir ce heros et pour assister au plus grand spectacle qui puisse s'offrir dans l'espace de vingt siecles la regeneration d'un grand Empire si près de sa destruction totale.

Je te laisse donc la maitresse de decider toi même de ce que tu peus et dois faire. à présent que tu sais à peu près à quoi t'en tenir sur notre situation. Je n'ai pas besoin je crois de te dire que je serais l'homme du monde le plus ⎮ heureux de voir ainsi abreger le tems de notre separation: mais en même tems je te tromperais et je m'abuserais moi même si je n'ajoutais pas que dans le cas contraire c. a. d. si n'ecoutant que la prudence, tu retardais ton voyage, je trouverais dans l'absence des inquietudes que me donneraient ton arrivée une sorte de dedomage^t de ton absence Tu vois ma bonne Fanny que je te parle bien franchement. M^r le Duc de ⟨Duras⟩ ce bon

[5] On 29 Mar. 1814 the allied armies came before Paris and the next day engaged the French massed on the heights of Fontenoy, Romainville, and Belleville (to the allied right), and of Montmartre (to the allied left). Fighting uphill, the allied army made up of 107,000 men met strategic difficulties. Opposing them, Marmont had nearly 12,000 regular troops, Mortier about 11,000, and Moncey the garrison of Paris largely drawn from the National Guard. The French had about 42,000 troops of varying ability with 154 pieces of artillery.

By the evening of 30 March the capitulation of Paris was signed, Marmont, on Talleyrand's orders, undertaking to withdraw his troops outside the fortifications. On 31 March the allied armies entering Paris were welcomed as liberators. The number of allied losses varied with the narrator. The 10,000 allied troops killed during the Battle of Paris (according to M. d'A) was increased in the account of the comtesse de Boigne to 13,000 (i. 288). From the non-committal report of Charles Stewart: 'Our loss has been something considerable' (*The Times*, 6 April). There were 12,000 enemy dead, according to Thiers (xvii. 332).

[6] This incident, not reported in the English press, circulated widely as fact among Parisians. On 25 Apr. 1814, from Paris, the comte de Lally-Tolendal wrote to FBA: '. . . le moment où les souverains dont on avait incendié et détruit les capitales, furent baignés dans leurs larmes parcequ'ils crurent qu'on allait les forcer à détruire Paris—le mouvement qui, devant leurs armées pleurant comme eux, les précipita dans les bras l'un de l'autre à la première nouvelle que Paris capitulait—l'accent avec lequel ils s'écrièrent—"*La cause de l'humanité est gagnée!*"' (*DL* vi. 122).

et genéreux ami, a Sur moi des projets qu'il me ⟨parait⟩ bien difficile de faire ⟨à ce pᵗ⟩ Je puis au reste m'en rapporter à sa genereuse amitié. Il s'agit d'un plan pris de S. M.⁷—adieu ma chère et bonne amie je t'embrasse comme je t'aime ainsi que ton compagnon de voyage ǀ

768   63 Lower Sloane Street,
                                  20 April 1814
To M. d'Arblay

A.L.S. (rejected Diary MSS. [5939–40b], p. 3 being numbered 5940, Berg), 20 Apr. 1814
Single sheet 4to folded in a way to produce 4 surfaces 8vo, of which FBA wrote on pp. 2, 3 & 4   3 pp.   black seal
Addressed: À Monsieur / Monsieur d'Arblay, / Rue de Mirominil, / 8 fᵍ Sᵗ Honoré, / À Paris. / Favoured by the / Revᵈ Robert Finch. / [*with pencilled direction*:] Mʳ Finch, / 286. Rue Sᵗ Honoré, / 1ʳᵉ Chaussée.
Edited by FBA, p.1 [5939], *dated*: April 20—1814   pp. 2 [5939b] & 3 (5940) *each annotated and dated*: (6) 1814
Edited also by CFBt *and the* Press. *See* Textual Notes.

April 20. 1814

I hasten, my beloved Friend—to unsay all I have said of desiring your instant return—I have reason to think I have judged ill, & ought to resign my impatience to the higher call of your awaiting the return of your King.—

I am even advised to endeavour to make myself known to Her R. H. Madᵉ La Duchesse d'Angoulême.¹

I write at so heavy a moment I can add no more—oh mon ami! soignez bien—bien votre santé!—c'est tout-ce qui m'est

⁷ Amédée-Bretagne-Malo de Durfort (1771–1838), 6th duc de Duras, hoped that Louis would appoint M. d'A to the post of 'Consul français' in England (L. 782 n. 2). For a biographical account of the duc de Duras, see v, L. 440 n. 2.

768. ¹ The daughter of Louis XVI and Marie Antoinette, Marie-Thérèse-Charlotte de France (1778–1851) was imprisoned (1792–5) after the execution of her parents, eventually released, and in 1799 married to her cousin Louis-Antoine de Bourbon (1775–1844), duc d'Angoulême. She served as 'symbole vivant des horreurs de la Révolution, statue de la douleur figée dans une éternelle mélancolie' (Bertaut, p. 147).

le plus cher au monde!—Alex is still with me—I have kept him
for the awful last rites— |

⌐I have sent you a Letter by M. Grefeuil[2]
another by M. Mackenzie[3]
& your cross through M. de la Châtre
all this through our dearest

AMINE

& yesterday I sent you
a long Letter—
that and The Wanderer
by Louis de Harcourt—⌐[4]
adieu—Mon ami, adieu!—

hier MON PERE auroit completé sa 88me année—et
commencé sa 89me—Mais!—c'est ce jour meme That his
last Remains are deposited in the Earth![5]—The last Testament
of this Pere cheri leaves my sister Burney & your own FB d'A:
joint inheritors, after Debts & legac[ies] all that may still rest
—!— |

⌐My safest address at present
will be *Mad^e d'A—at Mrs. Burney's
John Street, Oxford Street.*[6]
never Greenwich,
in fact Charles has long since left—& Chelsea also—In May
when I know it will be let—that good Charlotte is my only
stall—⌐

[2] See L. 765 n. 9.
[3] Colin Mackenzie (1779–1851), a Londoner, had in 1810 served the British
government in Morlaix, arranging for a prisoner exchange with Napoleon. In
that same year he again served his government by receiving and entertaining prince
Lucien Bonaparte, who had been taken prisoner by the English. For several
years, until 1828, he presided over a commission appointed to investigate British
claims on the French government.
[4] Amédée-Louis-Charles-François d'Harcourt-Olonde (L. 696 n. 5).
[5] CB was buried on 20 Apr. 1814 in the Chelsea burying ground. JB and CB
Jr. walked as chief mourners; the leading pall-bearers were the Hon. Frederick
North (1766–1827) and Johann Peter Salomon (1745–1815); the others were
Sir George Howland Beaumont (1753–1827), Dr. Benjamin Moseley (L. 764 n. 1),
John Townshend (L. 787 n. 6), and Samuel Rogers (L. 697 n. 20). For a description
of CB's funeral, see *GM* lxxxiv², 94, and for his friendship with Frederick
North, see ii, L. 41 n. 4.
[6] In L. 765 (and n. 11) FBA had suggested that M. d'A send his correspondence
to her, addressed to JB in James Street. Because of JB's anger at CB's will and his
refusal to act as executor, FBA now wished M. d'A to send his letters to her in care
of EBB.

769   [63 Lower Sloane Street],
                                       22 April [1814]
To M. d'Arblay

A.L. (Berg), 22 Apr.
Double sheet 4to   4 pp.   black seal
Addressed: à Monsieur / Monsieur d'Arblay— / Rue de Mirominel /
8 / f^g St. Honoré / à Paris.
Edited by FBA, p. 1, *annotated and dated*: (8)   (1814)   *See further*, Textual
Notes.

⌐Pray always date⌐

                                                    April 22^d—

The joy & the sadness that mix in all the feelings of this
Great Moment makes one support—yet keep down the other—
Mon ami!—to see you again—& at liberty! to decide ourselves
upon our new way of life! — —

You will surely have now heard of the loss of my revered
Father!—& have received the *4* Letters I have sent—& the
Croix—& the Wanderer. — — ⌐1. by M. Grefeuil, 1 by Mr.
Mackenzie, 1 through M. de La Chatre, 1 by / Colonel /
Harcourt. In one of recent date, I add the *business*.⌐

My dearest Father never made the change he had projected
of leaving you his French Books,[1] & to Alex English—Italⁿ &
Latⁿ—&c

He has left the Will he made while at Bath in the year 1807—
& by this, legacies to all his Children & Grand Children &
Nephews & Nieces—amounting to above 7000£—1st of this, *we*
have 1000. & alex has 100.[2]

---

769. [1] But see L. 773, in which FBA regards M. d'A as a 'gainer, not a loser'
by CB's failure to alter his will.

[2] The will was drawn up in 'Bath. South Parade, 5' and dated 'Jany. 12th,
1807'. At that time, CB had £7,800 in funds. He distributed slightly less than that
in the following manner: to EBB and FBA each, 'the sum of one thousand Pounds,
five per cent. Navy'; to Frances Phillips [Raper], £1,100; to CBFB, £200; to
JB and CB Jr. each, £200; to Richard Allen Burney, £200; to SHB 'One thousand
Pounds and one hundred Pounds more for a wedding Garment if ever she marries';
to his twenty-one grand-children each, £100; to the four children of his brother
Richard each, £100; to his female servants Rebecca More and Lucy Band each,
£33; and to his 'Boy, GEORGE, but lately come to [him], Six Guineas and a
year's wages'.

You shall have minuter particulars when I am more composed & have time—⌜or space—⌝

It is *thought* the money left in the Bankers hands—about or near 1000, will pay the Debts & last rites!—[3]

But nothing is known—

For the Sale of the Books, & all else,

He has left my sister Burney & me residuary Legatees.[4] Dearest—dearest Father!

My Brothers are left Executers,[5] for us — — But James is occupied—perhaps disappointed[6]—& Charles alone ⌜has seen the Will, &⌝ acts.

Only on Wednesday the 20th the Funeral took place![7]

Nothing could have drawn me from obscurity at this sad

---

[3] CB had in cash £1,826. See L. 782.

[4] According to CB's will: 'It is my wish that MY TWO ELDEST DAUGHTERS . . . be my residuary Legatees and have an equal share in such of my property as, when my debts, Funeral Expences, and legacies are paid, shall remain.'

[5] Even in his will CB indicates a reluctance to appoint executors, certain of the affection of his heirs for each other, and the equitable distribution of his funds. 'However, as I am informed that such an appointment is necessary lest difficulties and litigation should arise, I hereby appoint as my Executors and Trustees my two eldest Sons, Captain James, of the Royal Navy, and Doctor Charles, of Greenwich, more to assist their Sisters with their advice how best to act and make the most of the Property I have bequeathed them than to be a check upon their inclinations.'

[6] In a letter (Barrett, Eg. 3697, f. 305) to FBA, dated June 1814, Maria Rishton explained JB's reaction to CB's will. 'I trust I shall not wound your feelings, or risk giving you offence, by saying I was very much *surprised*, as well as *disappointed* when I read the disposition he had made of his property—I would fain not have enter'd upon the subject, but your letter calls upon me for my sentiments—and I am sure your Candour would despise me, if I hestitated, or evaded the question— Dʳ Burney's Will certainly did not meet my Ideas of Parental impartiality; I think poor James hardly treated: what I understand my dear Friend by a Father giving a Son a good Education, and a profession, is when he is liberal in affording him every opportunity of compleating that Education either at the University. if intended for the Church or any of the learned professions, or at a Military or Commercial Academy—and then he either buys him a Living or thro' his interest procures him one, places him with a Solisceter or in a Merchant's counting-House,—if the Navy is his choice—makes him an Allowance till his promotion enables him to provide for himself—your Brother James I belive left the Lynn Grammar School at the early Age of Ten or Eleven, and fag'd thro All the gradations of the Service free of Expence to his Father, till he reachd his present Rank—and severely has he suffer'd poor Fellow! for the independence of his political Creed, tho' allowed by the best Judges to be one, if not the first Navigator now living of Capt Cooks School—his present laborious Work will hand him down as such, to posterity—. You will I dare say from the present filial regard, endeavour to excuse your Father by Urging, that at the time James enterd upon life, he had not the ability to assist his Son, which must plead his excuse; but why (as it appears to me) disinherit his eldest Son at his death? whose decline of life is embitterd by professional disappointment, broken health, and comparative Poverty!'

[7] See L. 768 n. 5.

moment but strong advice—advice irresistible to be presented to M^e la Duch^{sse} d'Angouleme[8]— |

I was yesterday with our indefatigably sweet Amine to make the arrangements—when your Letter of the 18th[9]

& a most polite note from the Duc de Luxembourg arrived.[10]

I am now going to dress to present myself—Lady Crewe is so VERY good as to take me, & will send her carriage for me at 11. o'clock[11] [Judge] if I have accepted?

[Yet] I can never miss an opportunity for the Duc tells me my Letter must be with him at 2 o'clock.

I am charmed with the idea of the Consul français, & will take EVERY step I can devise. I will begin with consulting the Angersteins & Lady Crewe—

as also for a Letter to Lords Castlereagh[12] or Ld Cathcart[13]— God bless for ever my dearest best of Friends! |

All the world joins to keep down my impatience for your arrival till the King is arrived, & your dear Country a little settled!—There is only one opinion upon this—& I yield to it! —We can write perpetually, for the intercourse is incessant

8 The advice was Queen Charlotte's but written in a letter by Mme Beckedorff.
9 L. 767.
10 Charles-Emmanuel-Sigismond de Montmorency-Luxembourg (1774–1861), *dit* duc de Piney-Luxembourg et de Châtillon (1803). He first established his position in the gardes du Corps as capitaine in 1789. Always a royalist, he was created a pair de France and made a maréchal de camp in 1814.
In April 1814, having recently arrived in England from France, he brought—according to FBA—'the offer To Louis 18 of the Throne from the French new Regency after the Abdication of Buonaparte'. (But see L. 793 n. 6.)
The letter (PML) from the duc de Luxembourg to FBA is dated April 1814 from the 'hotel de la Sablonière Golden Square'. 'J'ai l'honneur d'envoyer avec emprisement à madame D'arblay la lettre ci-jointe et je serai très-aise d'avoir l'honneur de me charger de toutes les commissions qu'elle voudra bien me donner d'ici à demain deux heures que je compte partir pour retourner à Paris. . . .'
11 Lady Crewe's letter (Osborn) is undated:
'The D^{ss} d'Angouleme receives company *tomorrow* at *Grillons Hotel*, & the Lady who accompanies me thinks that we had better *drive* first to *some shop* in the street & wait there until the *doors are open* so as to avoid *all Crowd*.
'I believe, 2 o'clock is the *time fixed* but *we* must *set off* much sooner *from Gros^v Street*, & I will send my Carriage for you between 11 & 12—as we must take up M^{de} de Gouvello, *my French Lady*,—The King will be in the *Pr^{ns} drawing room* & you may therefore get *easily presented* to him. . . .' Lady Crewe's letter is based on misinformation. On 22 April the duchesse d'Angoulême was not at Grillion's Hotel but was holding an audience at the house of the comte d'Artois in South Audley Street.
12 FBA hoped that Viscount Castlereagh as foreign secretary, who was also active among French diplomats, could use his office to further M. d'A's chances as 'Consul français'.
13 William Schaw Cathcart (1755–1843), Lord Cathcart (Scottish, 1776), cr. Viscount Cathcart (1807), Earl Cathcart (1814). As ambassador to the Russian court (1812–20) and confidential adviser to Castlereagh, he too might help M. d'A's consular ambitions.

I desire infinitely an opportunity to send a Wanderer to my dear M. de Lally[14]—as well as to M. Barbier Neuville[15]—

⌐P.S. This was written in extremest haste to go by the Duc de Luxembourg, but it did not arrive in time. Between Grief, Business, distance from town, & the want of any servant of my own, you have not any notion of my helplessness as to commissions. Have you authorized a M. de Billy to draw upon me for £50?[16] I have let him have £25 but till I hear you have received it, & know that you enjoin it, I can go no further. My present income is already insufficient for Alexander & me, & I am obliged to sell out for every extra expense, which keeps the current income from encreasing. You certainly never got my letter about my disappointment in money matters. You know, I hope, that the £3000 for the Wanderer will only be paid after the 6th Edition. Oh that you were here to arrange these affairs yourself! I have kept all proceedings about our House till I have your directions. With regard to our legacies, these [may not] be paid this year to come, as all others must be satisfied first— we rejoice that you have seen the inauguration of your most amiable King,[17] come dearest Friend—For my relief, my comfort, my happiness.⌐

[14] She did not have his address for reasons which he clarified in a letter (Berg), dated 25 Apr. 1814. 'Oui, chère Madame, je vous écris de ce Paris d'où j'étais exilé depuis un an, avec défense d'en approcher de plus de soixante lieues. Pour quel délit? allez vous dire. Pour avoir écrit dans la Biographie, et lû dans un cercle d'amis l'article de Charles I; pour avoir eu, en composant et en lisant cet article, *l'intention maligne* de reviver l'interêt public sur la mémoire, les malheurs, les vertus, les héritiers de Louis XVI.' [15] See L. 741 n. 6.

[16] Joachim-Nicolas Billy (1748–1837), born at Provins, Seine-et-Marne, was a legislator and a wholesale merchant of milled flour.

Elected (20 Mar. 1789) as a substitute member to the Estates-General for Provins, he was not seated until 17 May 1791, as a member voting with the left. In 1792 he was a municipal officer. In the following year he became an assesseur du juge de paix and a member of the conseil de la commune de Provins. His name appeared on the lists of the collège électoral de Provins for 1827.

[17] The postscript was written after 22 April and on or before 29 April (see L. 773). FBA in referring to the 'inauguration' may have been anticipating M. d'A's presence at that event to be held on 3 May, since he had invited her to Paris to attend it with him (see L. 773 and n. 32). On the other hand, she may have used the term loosely to indicate other possibilities: the French Senate's vote on 2 Apr. 1814 effecting Napoleon's *déchéance* and its decree on the same day to adopt a constitution indicating that Louis XVIII was *freely* recognized as King of France, but only after he had agreed to adhere to the principles of the new constitution; the arrival of a courier on 5 April at Hartwell, 'apportant la nouvelle de la déchéance de Napoléon et du rappel des Bourbons' (Bertaut, pp. 160–1); the triumphal arrival of the comte d'Artois in Paris on 12 April and his appointment as 'lieutenant-général du royaume' while France awaited the return of Louis (L. 767 n. 1).

770   Journal for 22 April 1814

For the Reverend Alexander d'Arblay

A.J. (Diary MSS. vii. 5950–6000, Berg). The date of the principal event described is 22 Apr. 1814, but the account, FBA says in her emendation, was written up in 1825.

Twenty-six single sheets 8vo (7·4 × 4·6″) foliated at the top 5950–6000; foliated at the bottom 25–50; paged at the top 1–51   51 pp.

Edited by CFBt *and the* Press. *See* Textual Notes.

When,—walking one morning in Hyde Park with my honoured Partner, I related what will here follow,[1] he earnestly called upon me to commit it to Paper, with my meeting with my own King in Kew Gardens;[2] that both interviews might be retained for, & by Alex.

Many, & sad![3] are the years that are passed since I had this, & many a similar injunction; but I have always meant compliance,—& now,—in the year 1825!—I call upon my memory for its observance:—for my Memory now grows reproachful—

While I was still under the almost first impression of grief for the loss of my dear & honoured Father, I received a Letter from Windsor Castle, written by Madame Bekerdorf, at the command of Her Majesty, to desire I would take the │ necessary measures for being presented to Son Altesse Royale Madame Duchesse d'Angoulême, who was to have a Drawing Room in

---

770. [1] Having left Hartwell in Buckinghamshire permanently and arriving in London early in the evening of 20 April, Louis XVIII held a series of receptions. The one attended and described by FBA occurred on 22 April. The last of Louis's English audiences, it was given in honour of the officials of London.

[2] For FB's meeting with George III in Kew Gardens on 2 Feb. 1789, see *DL* iv. 242–51.

[3] In the eleven years since FBA accepted her husband's 'injunction', she was to witness the deaths of many people close to her: Queen Charlotte, who died in November 1818; friends like Lady Crewe (1818), the princesse d'Hénin, Sophia Hoare, Claude-Louis de la Châtre (all three of whom died in 1824); members of her family like Dolph Broome (1817), CB Jr. (1817), M. d'A (1818), Ann Hawkins (1819), CRB (1819), Maria Rishton (1820), Cecilia Burney (1821), Rosette Burney (1821), JB (1821), William Sandford (1823).

London, both for French & English, on the Day preceding her departure for France.[4] The Letter added that I must waive all objections relative to my recent loss, as it would be improper, in the present state of things, that the Wife of a General Officer should not be presented: and, moreover, that I should be personally expected, & well received, as I had been named to Son Altesse Royale by the Queen herself. In conclusion, I was cherged not to mention this circumstance, from the applications, or jealousies, it might excite.

To hesitate was out of the question. To do honour to my noble absent Partner, & in his Name to receive Honour, were precisely the two distinctions my kind Father would most have enjoyed for me. I could not but grieve that the call ˡ had not happened a few Weeks sooner, that its pleasure, now so damped, might have been exalted.

I had but 2. or 3 Days for preparation. My first step was to beg my sweet Amelia Angerstein to write for me to M. Le Duc de La Châtre,[5] to whom I had formerly been known, to enquire whether I might appear in black Gloves: a thing in the *English* Court never permitted; & that he would address Mᵐᵉ La Duchesse de Serrent[6] on that point; for my private Letter ordered me to be presented through the means of that lady, the First in place about Mᵐᵉ d'Angoulême. The Duc sent full consent, in a very encouraging Letter; & my kind Amelia offered her assistance, & promised to take charge of my head Dress. My Sister Sarah procured ˡ me a Robe Maker, to whom I consigned all further arrangement.

At this moment, my Nephew Charles Parr Burney, now Dr.,[7] called, & instantly went to Lady Crewe with the account of my unexpected enterprize; & that most amiably active Friend of my dear Father came to me herself, &, missing me in person, alighted to write me word she would lend me her carriage, to convey me from Chelsea to her House in Lower Grosvenor

---

[4] *AR* lvi (1814), 'Chronicle', 35, records that on 23 April 'about eight o'clock [a.m.], his most Christian Majesty, the Duchess of Angoulême, the Prince de Condé, and the Duke de Bourbon, left London to embark at Dover for France.'

[5] Claude-Louis de la Châtre (L. 647 n. 5).

[6] Bonne-Félicité-Marie *née* de Montmorency-Luxembourg d'Ollone (1739–1823) had married in 1754 Armand-Louis de Serent (1736–1822), *dit* marquis de Kerfily (1741), duc de Serent, lieutenant-général, pair de France (1814). For many years she served as dame d'honneur to the duchesse d'Angoulême.

[7] The 'now' is 1825. CPB received his D.D. in 1822.

Street,[8] and thence accompany me herself to the audience. How sweet an attention!

Mean while, I received a most polite Note from M. Le Duc de Luxembourg, enclosing a long & delighting Letter from my best Friend, & offering to be himself *à mes ordres*, for carrying back to Paris my own *dispatches*.[9]

This was indeed a spur to counteract my dejection; & when the morning arrived, I set off, in Lady Crewe's carriage, with tolerable courage. I had already been informed that a Court Dress would be dispensed with, the Duchesse d'Angouleme having no apparel prepared for herself that could demand such an Etiquette.

I stopt at the house of my tender Amelia for my Cap, which was all I wore of white; save a Fleur de Lys, as a bouquet, which she had prepared for me. All I had assumed of ceremony, was a Bombazeen & crape Robe with an enormous long train.

Arrived, however, in Grosvenor Street, when I entered the room in which this very dear & even fondly attached Friend of my Father received me,—the heaviness of his loss, & my melancholy dress, sweeping mournfully after me, proved quite overpowering to my spirits, & in meeting the two hands of my Hostess, I burst into tears, & could not, for some time, listen to the remonstrances against unavailing grief with which she rather chid than soothed me. But I could not contest the justice of what she uttered, though my Grief was too fresh for its observance. Sorrow, as my dearest Father was wont to say, requires Time, as well as wisdom & Religion, to digest itself; and till that time is both accorded, & well employed, the sense of its uselessness serves but to augment, not mitigate its severity.

Miss Hayman,[10] a lady whom I knew little more than by sight, alone was present. She had been Treasurer to the Princess of Wales, & my Father was intimately acquainted with her. I think she could not be surprized at my emotion, for she might easily believe & conceive my deep cause of regret. Lady Crewe had yet, & *far* yet more reason to comprehend & partake of it, from an intercourse of confidential friendship which had begun with her very existence. My Father had acted as Parent at the

---

[8] See L. 642 n. 17. [9] See L. 769 n. 10.
[10] For Anne Hayman (1753–1847), Keeper of the Privy Purse to Caroline, Princess of Wales, see iv, L. 328 n. 11.

Altar—to her Father, or Mother; & he had represented the Duke of Beaufort,[11] as Sponsor to herself at her Christening: & a connexion of uninterrupted trust & affection had been kept alive from that period to the last of his honoured life. But, anxious to do me solid service, she desired to chase from me all indulgence of sadness, lest I should unfit myself from making essential use of an audience that she believed, might lead to some essential benefit.

She purposed, also, taking this opportunity of paying her own respects, with her congratulations, to Madame Duchesse d'Angouleme. She had sent me a NOTE from Mad[e] de Gouvello,[12] relative to the ⏐ time, &c, for presentation, which was to take place at Grillon's Hotel,[13] in Albemarle Street. I had met with M[me] de Gouvello at Lady Crewe's.

We went very early to avoid a crowd. But Albemarle Street was already quite full, though quiet. We entered the Hotel without difficulty, Lady Crewe having previously demanded a private room, by right of former knowledge of Grillon, who had once been Cook to her lord.[14]

This private room was at the back of the house, with a mere yard, or common Garden, for its prospect. Lady Crewe declared this was quite too stupid, & rang the Bell for Waiter after Waiter, till she made M. Grillon come himself. She then, in her singularly open & easy manner, told him to be so good as to order us a front room, where we might watch for the arrival

[11] Charles Noel Somerset (1709–56), 4th Duke of Beaufort (1745). Lady Crewe's christening took place on 28 Nov. 1748.

[12] Gasparde (Gasparine)-Louise-Julie de Bourbon-Busset (1779–1853) married in London in 1801 Louis-Paul de Gouvello (1754–1830), vicomte. Active in the army as early as 1775, he became a sous-lieutenant in the gardes du corps de comte d'Artois in 1788 and remained with Monsieur until 1794. He went to England in 1795 as capitaine in the hussards de Rohan, fought alongside the English in Saint-Domingue (1797–8). After the Restoration he was named sous-lieutenant in the gardes du corps de Monsieur (1814) and maréchal de camp (1815). Awarded several honours, he ended his active military career in 1816.

Mme de Gouvello was close to the French Royal Family by virtue of her husband's rank as commandant de la compagnie des vétérans émigrés (1798–1814) and his long association with the comte d'Artois.

In her letter (Berg) to Lady Crewe: 'M[ad] de Gouvello s'empressera de faire la commission de Lady Crewe, ce sera pour vendredie si le Roi reçoit alors Lady Crewe et M[de] d'Arblaye veroient M[de] la Duchesse d'Angouleme et S. M. Louis XVIII. M[de] de Gouvello sera presentée a Lady Crewe si la visite sera pour vendredi.'

[13] 7 Albemarle Street was the site of Grillion's Hotel from 1803 to 1860, when it was moved to 19 and 20 Albemarle Street. (FBA's was a common misspelling of the hotel owner's name.)

[14] The fashionable hotel was owned and managed by Alexander Grillion (*fl.* 1803–22).

of the Royals, & be amused, ourselves, at ˡ the same time by seeing the entrances of the Mayor & Aldermen, & common council men, & other odd characters, who would be coming to pay their Court to these French Princes & Princesses.

M. Grillon gave a nod of comprehension & acquiescence, & we were instantly shewn to a front apartment just over the street door, which was most seasonably supplied with a Balcony.

I should have been much entertained by all this, & particularly with the originality, spirit, good humour & intrepid yet intelligent odd fearlessness of all remark, or even consequence, which led Lady Crewe to both say & do exactly what she pleased, had my heart been lighter; but it was too heavy for pleasure; & the depth of my mourning & the little, but sad minute that was yet passed since it was become my gloomy garb, made me hold it a matter ˡ even of decency, as well as of feeling, to keep out of sight. I left Lady Crewe, therefore, to the full enjoyment of her odd figures, while I seated myself, solitarily, at the further end of the room.

In an instant, however, she saw from the Window some acquaintance, & beckoned them up. A Gentleman, middle aged, of a most strikingly pleasing appearance & polite address, immediately obeyed her summons, accompanied by a young man of a prepossessing & sensible look; & a young lady, pretty, gentle & engaging, with languishing soft, love-looking Eyes; though with a smile & an expression of countenance that shewed an innate disposition to archness & sport.

This uncommon trio I soon found to consist of the celebrated Irish Orator, Mr. Grattan, & his Son & Daughter.[15]

Lady Crewe welcomed them with all the alertness belonging to her thirst of amusement, & her delight in sharing ˡ it with those she thought intellectually capable of its participation. This she had sought, but wholly missed in me; & could neither be angry nor disappointed, though she was a little vexed. She suffered me not, however, to remain long in my seclusion, but called me to the Balcony, to witness the jolting out of their

---

[15] Henry Grattan (1746–1820), M.P. for Malton (1805), for Dublin (1805–20), and by 1814 a well-known legislator. Between 1810 and 1813 (and again in 1816 and 1817) he debated brilliantly against anti-Catholic laws. In 1814 he spent less time in parliament, using his freedom to translate some of Maria Edgeworth's tales into French. Married in 1782, he had four children: James (1783–1854), Henry (1789–1859), Mary Anne (d. 1853), Harriett (d. 1865).

carriages of the Alderman & common council men, exhibiting, as she said 'Their fair round bodies with fat capon lined;'[16] & wearing an air of proudly hospitable, yet supercilious satisfaction, in visiting a King of France who had found an Asylum in a street of the City of Westminster.[17]

The Crowd, however,—for they deserve a better Name than Mob,—interested my observation still more. John Bull has seldom appeared to me to greater advantage. I never saw him I *en masse*, behave with such impulsive propriety. Enchanted to behold a King of France in his Capital; conscious that *le Grand Monarque* was fully in his power; yet honestly enraptured to see that 'the King would enjoy his Crown again', & enjoy it through the generous efforts of his born & bred Rival, brave, noble old England; he yet seemed aware that it was fitting to subdue all exuberance of pleasure, which, else, might annoy, if not alarm his regal Guest. He took care, therefore, that his delight should not amount to exultation. It was quiet & placid, though pleased & curious: I had almost said it was Gentleman-like.

And nearly of the same colour, though from so inferiour an incitement, were the looks & attention of the Grattans, I particularly of the Father, to the black mourner whom Lady Crewe impressively called amongst them by Name. My Garb, or the newspapers, or both, explained the dejection I attempted not to repress, though I carefully forbade it any vent; & the finely speaking face of Mr. Grattan seemed investigating the physiognomy, while it commiserated the situation, of the person brought thus, rather singularly before him. His air had something foreign in it, from the vivacity that accompanied his politeness—I should have taken him for a well bred Man of Fashion of France. Good breeding, in England, amongst the Men, is ordinarily, stiff, reserved, or cold. Among the exceptions to this stricture—how high stood Mr. Windham![18] and how

[16] Misquoted from Shakespeare's *As You Like It* (ii. 7. 154): 'In fair round belly with good capon lined'. FBA draws on a popular tradition of the well-fed city official. See, e.g., Samuel Butler's *Characters and Passages from Note-Books* (1759, printed posthumously), ed. A. R. Waller (Cambridge, 1908), p. 109.

[17] According to *AR* lvi (1814), 'Chronicle', 34–5, on 22 April 'The Right Honourable the Lord Mayor, the Aldermen, Recorder, Sheriffs, City Officers, and Common Council of the city of London, waited upon his Majesty Louis XVIII. King of France, at Grillon's Hotel. . . .'

[18] William Windham (1750–1810), see i, L. 1 n. 11.

high in gaiety, with vivacity stood my own honoured Father!
Mr. Lock—who was Elegance personified in his manners, was
lively only in his own Domestic, or chosen Circle. |

All, however, now, followed the Example of Mr Grattan, who
had the tact to leave me to myself; & I should quietly have
awaited the arrival of *Son Altesse Royale*, but for a new scene
that both astonished & discomposed me.

A lady, accompanied, humbly, by a Gentleman, now burst
into the room with a noise, a violence, a self-sufficiency, & an
assuming confidence of superiority, that would have proved
highly offensive, had it not been egregiously ridiculous. Her
attire was as flaunting as her air & her manner; she was rouged,
& beribbonned as if decked out for my own poor Madame
Duval;[19] & seemed to have just as much of the French woman,
in her strangely mixt dialect, grafted upon very coarse English
materials, as that same Gentlewoman. But English she was not;
she was Irish, in its most flaming & untamed nature, & possessed
of | so boisterous a spirit, that she appeared to be just caught
from the Woods — — the Bogs, I might rather say.

When she had poured forth a volley of words, with a fluency
& loudness that stunned me by surprise as much as by their
noise, Lady Crewe, with a smile that seemed to denote she
intended to give her pleasure presented me by Name to
Madame la Baronne de Montesquiou.[20]

She made me a very haughty courtesie, & then, turning
rudely away, looked reproachfully at Lady Crewe, & screamed
out 'Oh fie!—fie, fie, fie!—' Lady Crewe, astonished and
shocked, seemed struck speechless,—& I, too much amazed at
a reception so new to me, as well as unaccountable, stood still,
with my Eyes wide open, & my Mouth, probably, so also, from
a sort of stupor rather than of affront or dismay, | for I could
annex no meaning, nor even any idea to such behaviour. She
made not, however, any scruple to devellope her motives, for
she vehemently inveighed against being introduced to such an
acquaintance, squalling out: 'She has writ against the *Emigrés*!
—She has writ against the Great Cause! O fie!, fie! fie!'

---

[19] The crude quasi-French woman in *Evelina*.

[20] Henriette-Mathilde Clarke d'Hunebourg de Feltre (1790–1831) had married
in 1808 Raymond-*Aimery*-Philippe-Joseph de Montesquiou (1784–1867), baron de
Montesquiou-Fézensac et de l'Empire (1809), *dit* vicomte de Montesquiou-
Fézensac (1817), 2nd duc de Montesquiou-Fézensac (1832).

Her violence & vociferation were such that Lady Crewe could not at first attempt to counteract them; but the indignant looks that accompanied her silence would have rendered it as forcible as eloquence to any one gifted with remark, or not run away with by their own humours, tempers, or wilfulness. For me, I stood aloof, with a scorn at such an assault that saved me from consternation, & enabled me to wait the explanation with something between resentment & contempt.

When she had made these exclamations, & uttered these accusations, till the indulged vent to her rage began to cool ǀ it, she stopt of her own accord, &, finding no one spoke, looked as if she felt rather silly; while M. le Baron de Montesquiou, her very humble sposo, shrugged his shoulders, but with what to me seemed a doubtful expression—whether it were of shame at the turbulent vulgarity of his fair Mate, or of participated horrour against poor ME. The pause was succeeded by an opening harangue from Lady Crewe, begun in a low & gentle voice, that seemed desirious to spare me what might appear an undue condescendsion, in taking any pains to clear me from so gross an attack: she gave therefore, nearly in a whisper, a short character of me & of my conduct, of which I heard no more than just enough to know that such was her theme; & then, more audibly, she proceeded to state, that, far from writing against the Emigrants, ǀ I had addressed an Exhortation to all the ladies of Great Britain in their favour.[21]

'O, then', cried Mme de Montesquiou, 'it was somebody else! It was somebody else!—'

And then she screamed out delightedly: 'I'm so glad I spoke out! because of this explanation:! I'm so glad! I never was so glad!'

She now jumped about the room, quite crazily, protesting she never rejoiced so much at any thing she had ever done in her life.

But when she found her joy, like her assault, was all her own, she stopt short, astonished, I suppose, at my insensibility, & said to me: 'How lucky I spoke out! the luckiest thing in the World! I'm so glad! A'n't You?—Because of this *eclaircissement*'.

'If I had required any *eclaircissement*—' I drily began—

[21] *Brief Reflections relative to the Emigrant French Clergy* (iii, L. 126 n. 4).

'O, if it was not you, then,' cried | she, "'twas Charlotte Smith?'[22]

I knew not what she might allude to, & with a sort of sullen superciliousness declined either enquiry or answer.

'Yes, Yes, 'twas Charlotte Smith!' she repeated; & again capered about the room, with a flightiness that might have amused me at a moment of less sorrow, but which now could not move me. Lady Crewe seemed quite ashamed that such a scene should pass where she presided; & Mr. Grattan, soon satisfied with his portion of this lady's extravagant squalls, quietly stole away.

Not quietly, nor yet by stealth, but with evident disappointment that her energies were not more admired, Madame la Baronne now called upon her attendant sposo, & strode off herself. I found she was a great Heiress, of Irish extraction & education, & | that she had bestowed all her wealth upon this emigrant Baron[23]—who might easily merit it, when, besides his title, he gave her his patience & obsequiousness.

Some other Friends of Lady Crewe now found her out, & she made eager enquiries amongst them relative to Madame Duchesse d'Angouleme; but could gather no tidings. She heard, however, that there were great expectations of some arrivals down stairs, where two or three rooms were filled with Company.

[22] For earlier references to Charlotte Smith (1749–1806), see i, L. 3 n. 48; iii, Ll. 123 n. 9, 126 n. 5. The two women as writers were often compared, Mrs. Smith's *Emmeline* (1788) considered an imitation of *Cecilia* (1782).

But what Mme de Montesquiou had in mind was Mrs. Smith's *The Emigrants, A Poem in Two Books* (1793). The first book sets its 'Scene on the Cliffs to the Eastward of the Town of Brighthelmstone in Sussex' on 'a Morning in November, 1792'; it describes through a narrator the straggling arrival of various French clergy responsible for 'Bigotry (the Tut'ress of the blind)' and concludes: 'yet unhappy Men,/Whate'er your errors, I lament your fate' (pp. 7–8).

Mrs. Smith feared that she might be attacked for her portrait of the French clergy. In the poem's dedication to William Cowper (p. vii), she vindicates her portrait and begs 'to be understood as feeling the utmost respect for the integrity of their principles'.

[23] FBA underestimated the importance of Mme de Montesquiou's family. Although Irish in origin, it had for several generations contributed to French military power. Her father, Henri-Jacques-Guillaume Clarke (1765–1818), comte d'Hunebourg, duc de Feltre, entered the military before the Revolution and by 1793 he was général de brigade. According to Vitrolles (ii. 486): 'Chargé, en 1796, par le Directoire, de surveiller Bonaparte, il sut gagner l'amitié de ce dernier, ce qui lui valut d'être destitué, mais d'en être récompensé après le 18 Brumaire. Il fut secrétaire intime de Napoléon. En 1807, il fut ministre de la Guerre. Il se déclara royaliste à l'arrivée des Bourbons. En 1814, il fut nommé pair de France. Il sera maréchal de France et, en 1817, gouvernera la 14ᵉ division militaire.' These royalist honours were bestowed upon him despite the fact that he served as Napoleon's ministre de la Guerre during the Cent Jours.

She desired Mr. Grattan Junior to descend into this Crowd, & to find out where the Duchess was to be seen, & when, & how.

He obeyed—but returned without any success; he had not met with any body who could give him any intelligence. There were many French Men of high rank, but he did not know them; & feared being troublesome or unopportune.

'Pho, pho, you must never fear that, Mr. Grattan—If the Duc de ‌‌‌‌‌‌‌‌ (I forget the ǀ name) is among them, he is my friend, & I beg you will send him to me.'

Mr. Grattan said he had not observed him; he had only heard the Name of the Duc de Duras.[24]

'The Duc de Duras?' I repeated; 'is he here?'

'Do you know him?' cried Lady Crewe.

'O Yes.—& M. d'Arblay is particularly acquainted with him.'[25]

'Run to him, then, Mr. Grattan, run to him directly, & ask him how & when Madame d'Arblay can be presented to the Duchesse d'Angouleme.'

'O, not for the World!' I cried, 'not for the World! I would not take such a step—such a liberty on any account.'

'Pho, pho;—go, Mr. Grattan; go directly. You must not mind all that. Poor Madame d'Arblay is very nervous just now'.

In vain I expostulated—though Mr. Grattan was palpably as unwilling as myself, for he appeared to me extremely modest & unobtrusive. But the vivacity ǀ of Lady Crewe could suffer no opposition, & he again obeyed.

I flew, however, after him, & stopping him at the head of the stairs, quite supplicated him not to name me. He smiled, good-humouredly, at these contesting requests, but with a look that shewed me I should not plead in vain.

But, when he returned, what was the provocation of Lady Crewe, what my own disappointment, to hear that the Duchess was not arrived, & was not expected! She was at the House of Monsieur, le comte d'Artois, her Father in Law!

[24] For the activity of the duc de Duras at this time, see L. 764 n. 7. 'Duras, fort entiché de protocole, souverain juge sur toutes les questions d'étiquette "plus duc que Saint-Simon lui-même", est chargé d'ordonner, de réglementer tout ce qui concerne ce chapitre, d'assigner à chacun la place qui lui revient. Lourde tâche avec un roi comme Louis XVIII que ces questions passionnent' (Bertaut, p. 176).

[25] See L. 767, wherein M. d'A describes M. de Duras as 'ce bon et genéreux ami'.

'Then what are we come hither for?' exclaimed her ladyship: 'expressly to be tired to death for no purpose! Do pray, at least, Mr. Grattan, be so good as to see for my carriage, that we may go to the right house.'[26]

Mr. Grattan was all compliance, & with a readiness so obliging, & so well bred, that I am sure he is his Father's true Son in manners—though there was no opportunity ¦ to discover whether the resemblance extended also to Genius.

He was not, however, cheered, when he brought word that neither Carriage nor Footman were to be found.

Lady Crewe then said he must positively go down, & make the Duke de Duras tell us what to do.

In a few minutes he was with us again, shrugging his shoulders at his ill success. The King, Louis 18, he said, was expected, & M. le Duc was preparing to receive him, & not able to speak or to listen to any one.

Lady Crewe declared herself delighted by this information, because there would be an opportunity for having me presented to his Majesty; 'Go to M. de Duras,' she cried, 'and tell him Madame d'Arblay wishes it.'

'For Heaven's sake,' exclaimed I, 'do no such thing! I have not the most distant thought of the kind!—It is Madame la Duchesse d'Angoulême alone that I — —'

'O, pho, pho,—it is still more essential to be done to the King! It is really important. So *go* & tell the Duke, Mr. Grattan, that Madame d'Arblay is here, & desires ¦ to be presented. Tell him 'tis a thing quite indispensable.'

I stopt him again & quite entreated that no such step might be taken, as I had no authority for presentation but to the Duchess. However, Lady Crewe was only provoked at my backwardness to be exhibited, & charged Mr. Grattan not to heed me. 'Tell the Duke,' she cried, 'that Madame d'Arblay is our Madame de Staël!—tell him we are as proud of our Madame d'Arblay as he can be of his Madame de Staël.'

Off she sent him,—& off I flew, again to follow him; & whether he was most amused, or most teazed by our opposing petitions, I know not; but he took the discreet side of not venturing again to return among us.

Poor Lady Crewe seemed to think I lost a place at court, or

[26] 72 South Audley Street, the residence of the comte d'Artois.

perhaps a Peerage, by my untameable shyness, & was quite vext. Others came to her now, who said several rooms below were filled with expectant courtiers. Miss Grattan then earnestly requested me to descend with her, as a chaperon, that she might see something of what was going forwards. | I could not refuse so natural a request, & down we went, seeking one of the commonly crowded rooms, that we might not intrude where there was preparation or Expectation relative to the King.

And here, sauntering, or grouping; or meditating in silence; or congratulating each other in coteries; or waiting with curiosity; or self-preparing for presentation with timidity; we found a multitude of folks in an almost unfurnished, & quite unadorned Apartment, The personages seemed fairly divided between the Nation at Home, & the Nation from Abroad, the English & the French; each equally, though variously, occupied in expecting the extraordinary sight of a Monarch thus wonderfully restored to his Rank & his Throne, after misfortunes that had seemed irremediable, & an Exile that had appeared hopeless.

Miss Grattan was saluted, *en passant*, by several acquaintance, & amongst them by the Son in Law of her dear Country's vice Roy, Lord Whitworth, the young Duke of Dorset;[27] to whom, as to all others, anxious not to have the air of wandering alone, she proclaimed she had descended from Lady Crew with Madame d'Arblay. And Lady Crew herself, too tired to | abide any longer in her appropriated apartment, now descended.

We *patroled* about, zig zag, as we could, the crowd, though of very good company, having no chief, or regulator, & therefore making no sort of avenue, or arrangement for avoiding inconvenience. There was neither going up, nor coming down; we were all hussled together, without direction, & without object; for nothing whatsoever was present to look at, or to create any interest; & our Expectations were merely kept awake by a belief that we should know, in time, what, & where, something or somebody was to be seen.

[27] George John Frederick Sackville (1793–1815), 4th Duke of Dorset, who was to die in less than a year, on 14 Feb. 1815, after a hunting accident near Dublin. He had been visiting his mother, who since 1801 was married to Charles Whitworth, Lord Lieutenant of Ireland (1813–17). For Whitworth's service as Ambassador to Paris, see v, L. 525 n. 13.

For myself, however, I was much tormented during this interval from being Named incessantly by Lady Crewe, while my deep Mourning, my recent heavy loss, & the absence & distance of my dear Husband made me peculiarly wish to be unobserved. Peculiarly, I say; for never yet had the moment arrived in which to be marked had not been | embarrassing & disconcerting, to me, even when most flattering.

A little hub bub, soon after, announced something new:—& presently a whisper was buzzed around the room of 'The Prince of Condé.'[28]

His Serene Highness looked very much pleased—as no wonder—at the arrival of such a Day; but he was so grouped around by all of his countrymen who were of rank to claim his attention, that I could merely see that he was little & old, but very unassuming & polite. Amongst his Courtiers, were sundry of the French Noblesse that were known to Lady Crewe & I heard her uniformly say to them, one after another, 'Here is Madame d'Arblay, who must be presented to the King.'

Quite frightened by an assertion so wide from my intentions, so unauthorised by any preparatory ceremonies, | unknown to my Husband, & not, like a presentation to the Duchesse d'Angouleme, encouraged by my Queen, I felt as if guilty of taking a liberty the most presumptuous, & with a forwardness & assurance the most foreign to my character. Yet to control the zeal of Lady Crewe, exerted by a belief that she was drawing me from an obscurity under which I ought not to be clouded, was painful from her earnestness, & appeared to be ungrateful to her kindness: I therefore shrunk back, & presently suffered the Crowd to press between us, so as to find myself wholly separated from my party. This would have been ridiculous had I been more happy; but in my then state of affliction, it was necessary to my peace.

[28] Louis-Joseph de Bourbon (1736–1818), 8th prince de Condé, only son of Louis-Henri de Bourbon (1692–1740) and princesse Caroline de Hesse-Rheinfels-Rothenbourg (1714–41). After the fall of the Bastille, he removed to Worms (1791), there instituting the *émigré* 'army of Condé', notable only for ineffectual anti-revolutionary campaigns (1792–6). In 1797 he went to Russia and subsequently (1799) served in its army. By 1800 he was in Austria but moved on to England in the following year, residing with his family at the Abbey of Amesbury. He accompanied Louis XVIII to Paris in May 1814, when his titles of 'colonel général et de grand maître de France' were returned to him, and then to Belgium during the Cent Jours. On his return to France in July 1815, he lived almost uninterruptedly at Chantilly until his death.

Quite to myself, now, I smiled inwardly at my adroit cowardice, & was ˈ quietly contemplating the surrounding masses of people, when a new & more mighty Hubbub startled me;—& presently I heard a buzzing whisper spread throughout the apartment, of 'The King!—Le Roi!—'29

Alarmed at my strange situation, I now sought to decamp, meaning to wait for Lady Crewe up stairs: but to even approach the door was impossible. I turned back, therefore, to take a place by the Window, that I might see his Majesty alight from his Carriage; but how great was my surprize when, just as I reached the top of the room, the King himself entered it at the bottom!—

I had not had the smallest idea that this was the Chamber of audience; it was so utterly unornamented. But I now saw that a large *Fauteuil* was conveying to the upper part, exactly where I stood, ready for his reception & repose.

Placed thus singularly, by mere accident; & freed of my fears of being brought forward by Lady Crew, I felt rejoiced in so fair an opportunity of beholding the King of my honoured ˈ Husband, & planted myself immediately behind, though not near to his prepared seat. And, as I was utterly unknown, & must be utterly unsuspected, I indulged myself with a full examination, my Eye Glass in my hand. An avenue had instantly been cleared from the door to the Chair, & the King moved along it slowly, slowly, slowly, rather dragging his large & weak limbs than walking:30 but his face was truly engaging; benignity was in every feature, & a smile beamed over them that shewed thankfulness to Providence in the happiness to which he was so suddenly arrived; with a courtesy, at the same time, to the Spectators, who came to see & congratulate it, the most pleasing & cheering.

It was a scene replete with motives to grand reflexions; & to me, the devoted subject of another Monarch, whose melancholy alienation of mind was a constant source to me of sorrow, it was a scene for conflicting feelings & profound meditation ˈ

His Majesty took his seat, with an air of mingled sweetness & dignity. I then, being immediately behind him, lost sight

---

29 According to *The Times* the King entered Grillion's Hotel at approximately 5.45 p.m.
30 Louis XVIII suffered from gout, obesity, and a hip deformity.

of his countenance, but saw that of every Individual who approached to be presented. The Duke de Duras stood at his left hand, & was le Grand Maitre des cérémonies; Madame de Gouvello stood at his Right side; though whether in any capacity, or simply as a French lady known to him, I cannot tell. In a whisper, from that lady, I learned more fully the mistake of the Hotel; the Duchesse d'Angouleme never having meant to quit that of her Beau-Pere, Monsieur, le Comte d'Artois, in S. Audley Square.

The presentations were short; & without much mark or likelihood. The Men Bowed low, & passed on; the ladies courtsied, & did the same. Those who were not known gave a card, I think, to the Duke de Duras, who Named them: those of former acquaintance with his Majesty simply made their obeysance. |

M. de Duras, who knew how much fatigue the King had to go through, hurried every one on, not only with speed, but almost with ill breeding, to my extreme astonishment. Yet the English, by express command of his Majesty, had always the preference, & always took place of the French; which was an attention of the King in return for the asylum he had here found, that he seemed delighted to display.

Early in this ceremony came forward Lady Crewe, who being known to the King from sundry previous meetings, was not named; & only, after courtsying, reciprocated smiles with his Majesty, & passed on. But instead of then moving off, though the Duke who did not know her, waved his hand to hasten her away, she glided up to his Ear, & whispered, but loud enough for me to hear, '*voilà*, Madame d'Arblay; *il faut qu'elle soit présentée.*'

I was thunderstruck. But Lady Crewe went gaily off, without heeding me. |

The Duke only bowed, but by a quick glance recognized me, & by another shewed a pleased acquiescence in the demand.

Retreat, now, was out of the question; but I so feared my position was wrong, that I was terribly disturbed, & felt hot & cold, & cold & hot, alternately, with excess of embarrassment.

Various presentations now followed of both French & English; but I heard no names, &, though close behind the Royal Seat, I gathered not a word that was said: my sight was dimmed, &

my Ears were stunned by astonishment at my own situation; & self-reflexions & doubts absorbed both my senses & my faculties.

I was roused, however, after hearing for so long a time nothing but French, by the sudden sound of English. An Address in that language, was read to His Majesty, which was presented by the Noblemen & Gentlemen of the County of Buckingham, congratulatory upon his happy Restoration, & filled with cordial thanks | for the graciousness of his manners, & the benignity of his conduct, during his long residence amongst them, warmly proclaiming their participation in his joy, & their admiration of his virtues. The Reader was Colonel Nugent,[31] a near Relation of the present Duke of Buckingham.[32]

But—if the unexpected sound of these exhilarating felicitations, delivered in English, roused & struck me, how much greater arose my astonishment & delight when the French Monarch, in an accent of the most condescending familiarity & pleasure, uttered his acknowledgements in English also— expressing his gratitude for all their attentions, his sense of their kind interest in his favour, & his eternal remembrance of the obligations he owed to the whole county of Buckinghamshire, for the asylum & consolations he had found in it during his trials & calamities. |

I wonder not that Colonel Nugent was so touched by this reply as to be led to bend the knee, as to his own Sovereign, when the King held out his hand: for I myself—though a mere outside auditress, was so moved, & so transported with surprise by the dear English language from his mouth, that I clasped my hands with rapture, & forgot at once all my fears, & dubitations, &, indeed, all *myself*, my poor little *Self*, in my pride & exultation at such a moment for my noble Country.

Fortunately, as it was singularly, for me, the Duke de Duras, probably urged by the sound of my clasped hands, & the view he could not but take of my enchantment, made this the moment

---

[31] Edward Nugent (1752–1819), was in 1814 either a Lieutenant-Colonel or Colonel of the Second, or Middle, Regiment of the Buckinghamshire Local Militia. He and the first Duke of Buckingham and Chandos were cousins. See *The Manuscripts of J. B. Fortescue, preserved at Dropmore* (H.M.C., 10 vols., 1892–1927), ii. 613 and index.

[32] Richard Temple-Nugent-Brydges-Chandos-Grenville (1776–1839), 2nd Marquess of Buckingham (1813), cr. Duke of Buckingham and Chandos, as also Earl Temple of Stowe (1822), M.P. for Buckingham (1797–1813).

for my presentation, &, seizing my hand,—no longer unwilling so to be seized,—& drawing me suddenly from behind the chair to the Royal presence, he said 'Sire, Madame d'Arblay.'

How singular a change, that what | but the instant before would have overwhelmed me with diffidence & embarrassment, now found me all courage & animation! & when his Majesty raised his Eyes with a look of pleased curiosity at my name, & took my hand—or, rather, took hold of my Fist—& said, in very pretty English 'I am very happy to see you.—' I felt such a glow of satisfaction, that, involuntarily, I burst forth with its expression, incoherently, but delightedly, & irresistibly, though I cannot remember how. He certainly was not displeased, for his smile was brightened, & his manner was most flattering, as he repeated that he was very glad to see me, & added that he had known me, though without sight, very long: 'for I have *read* you—& been charmed with your Books—charmed & entertained. I have read them often. I know them very well, indeed; & I have long wanted to know *You*!—'

I was extremely surprised,—& not only at these unexpected compliments, but equally that my presentation, far from seeming, | as I had apprehended, strange, was met by a reception of the utmost encouragement, nay, pleasure. When he stopt, & let go my hand, I courtsied respectfully, & was moving on; but he again caught my *fist* — — &, fixing me, with looks of strong, though smiling investigation, he appeared archly desirous to read the lines of my face, as if to deduce from them the qualities & faculties of my mind. His manner, however, was so polite & so gentle, & his air spoke him to be, at that moment, so happy, that he did not at all discountenance me; & though he resumed a warm praise of my little Works, assuring me had reaped from them not alone recreation & amusement, but instruction & information, he uttered | the panegyric[33] with a benignity so gay as well as flattering, that I felt enlivened, nay, elevated, with a Joy that overcame *mauvaise honte*.

The Duc de Duras, who had hurried on all others, seeing he had no chance to dismiss me with the same *sans cérémonie* speed, now joined his Voice to still exalt my satisfaction, by saying, at

[33] Louis XVIII summed up FBA's creative intention. As she argued in *The Wanderer* (i, p. xxiii), the novel was 'to make pleasant the path of propriety . . . snatching from evil its most alluring mode of ascendency'.

the next pause 'Et M. d'Arblay, Sire, bon et brave, est un des plus devoués et fideles des serviteurs de Votre Majesté.'

The King, with a gracious little motion of his head, & with Eyes of the most pleased benevolence, expressively said: '*Je le crois.*' And a Third time he stopt my retiring courtesie, to take my hand.

This last stroke gave me such exquisite delight—for my absent best *Ami*, that my vivacity gave place to melting tenderness, & I could ׀ not again attempt to speak. The King pressed my hand—Wrist, I should say, for it was that he grasped, & then saying, 'Bon jour, Madame la Comtesse', let me go.

My Eyes were suffused with tears, from mingled emotions; that mingled themselves with my astonished delight at this unlooked for favour:—the satisfaction it would give, ere long, to my honoured Husband was its first charm; but the rapture it would have caused to my beloved Father, only a Week or two earlier, I missed by so short an interval, that I could not repress the regret that stole away half my contentment. I glided nimbly through the crowd to a corner at the other end of the room, where I made a seat of a low Table, and strove to keep out of sight—for, almost, I wept. ׀ But oh! with tears how different to those I have since shed!

Lady Crewe joined me almost instantly, & with felicitations the most amiably cordial & lively. She had not heard what had passed, & was eager for information, having remarked, with friendly pride as well as pleasure, from the animated interest she had allowed to glide, ⟨hereditarily⟩, from Father to Daughter that the King had detained me longer at my Audience than any other person who had been presented that morning. She called upon me to give my account, & without delay, not conceiving my emotion, or concluding, & perhaps justly, that what was wisest would be to end it: she was obliged, however, to listen to my plea of postponement, though, not from its real motive; but she yielded when I whispered that all around us were awaiting to hear my answer with a curiosity as great, though not as kind, as her own. ׀

We then repaired to a side board, on which we contrived to seat ourselves, & Lady Crewe named to me the numerous personages of rank who passed on before us for presentation. But every time any one espied her, & approached, she named me also; an honour to which I was not insensible though very averse. This I intimated; but to no purpose; she went on her own way, not heeding me—The curious stares this produced, in my embarrassed state of spirits, my grief & melancholy from such recent grief; & a species of decorum I thought due to the depth of my Mourning, it was really painful, and I thought even improper to sustain; but when the seriousness of my representation forced her to see that I was truly in earnest in my desire to remain still unnoticed, she was so much vexed, & even provoked that she very gravely ⎸ begged that, if that were the case, I would move a little further from her, saying 'If one must be so ill-natured to people, as not to Name you, I had rather not seem to know who you are myself.'

It was impossible not to laugh at a turn so extraordinary & unexpected; yet I found she was so really in earnest, that I must either comply, or yield to her presentations: I therefore, though piteously shrugging my shoulders, glided gently lower down the room. ⎸

When, at length, her Ladyship's chariot was announced, we drove to Great Cumberland place, Lady Crewe being so kind as to convey me to Mrs. Angerstein. But now, I had, at last, so much grace as to communicate as well as I could, what had passed with his Majesty Louis 18—though still, the subject being awkward, because personal, I could not quite satisfy her cravings as categorically as she desired: but she gained enough to be truly cordial in her congratulations on the honour I had received.

As Lady Crewe was too much in haste to alight, the sweet Amelia Angerstein came to the Carriage to speak to her, & to make known that a Letter had arrived from M. de La Châtre, relative to my presentation, which, by a mistake of address, had not come in time for my reception.

I must here Copy the Note, which was written in answer to Mrs. Angerstein's enquiries relative to my Mode of proceeding. ⎸

À Madame Angerstein.

⟶

Je n'ai pu prendre que ce matin les ordres de Madame la Duchesse d'Angoulême, qui sera très aisé de recevoir M^de d'Arblay entre 3 heures 3. h^r et demie. Il faudra demander en arrivant au nº 72. South Audley St. M^{de} la Duchesse de Serrent.

Le Roi, qui désire voir M^{de} d'Arblay, et qui la recevra avec *grand* plaisir, sous le double rapport de son nom actuel, et de celui du charmante Auteur de Cecilia, &c, vera du monde depuis quatre heures jusqu'à cinq. Il faudra demander le Duc de Duras l^r Gentilh^{me} de la Chambre du Roi, bien connu de M^{de} d'Arblay.

M. de La Châtre a l'honneur de présenter ses hommages à Mad^e Angerstein, et de la prier de l'excuser de n'avoir pu lui faire plutôt réponse.

Ce 22e avril, 1814. |

This Note solved all of astonishment that had envellopped with something like incredulity my own feelings & perceptions in my unexpected presentation & reception. The King himself had personally deigned to desire bestowing upon me this mark of royal favour. What difficulty, what embarrassment, what confusion should I have escaped, had not that provoking mistake which kept back my Letter occurred! It was solely to Madame la Duchesse d'Angouleme that my gracious Royal Mistress had named me; but, fortunately as well as surprisingly, my own little Books had united themselves with the remembrance of the services of my honoured Husband, & led his Majesty, when he heard what was intended by *Son Altesse Royale*, to command my presentation to himself also.—What pleasure did this little narration give to my Partner in All!—the look of lively eagerness with | which he caught every word, & the anxious smile of his attention till I came to the Finale, are now before me!—he charged me to commit the whole to Paper for Thee; our Alex — —

All, however, was still to be done with respect to Son Altesse Royale the Duchesse. The truly unfortunate blunder which lost me the directions written by M. La Châtre, had lost me the hour appointed by *son Altesse*. My zealous Lady Crewe, extremely tired, though pleased, went home, & I accompanied my sweet Amelia Angerstein up stairs to deliberate upon what course to pursue.

I then heard that *Son Altesse* was to dine with the King & Princes, but would probably receive some of the presentations in the Evening that had failed in the Morning. This was the opinion of Mad^e de Gontaut,[34] who, upon its strength, was to accompany | Miss Upton[35] to make the attempt! Mr. & Mrs. Angerstein were engaged out to Dinner: but they offered me a small repast for myself, & the use of their carriage to convey me to Lady Templetown's, where I might join Miss Upton, & be under the Wing of Mad^e de Gontaut. This kindness I gladly accepted.

Miss Upton took her part in this little *manœuvre* most good naturedly & readily. She carried me to Mme de Gontaut, & we proceeded to—I think—South Audley Square, the House of M. le Comte d'Artois—(Now Charles X^th of France) (This June—1825).[36]

Arrived, however, we were peremtorily refused admittance. The Royal family was at dinner, & too much fatigued to permit even a Name to be carried in to them. Mme de Gontaut, however, by her high rank, high manners, commanding person, & dignified voice of insistance, obtained our *entrée* as far as the Hall: but could obtain nothing beyond. |

Not to appear myself a presumptuous intruder, I now made known that to my little party, which was encreased by the junction of Miss Upton's elder sister, Mrs. Singleton, & her sposo,[37] that it was by the sanction of Orders of Mad^e la Duchesse herself that I sought a presentation. Mme Gontaut,

[34] Marie-Louise-Joséphine *née* de Montault de Navailles (1773–1857) had married in England the *émigré* Charles-Michel de Gontaut (1751–1825), vicomte de Gontaut-Biron-Saint-Blancard, lieutenant-général (1814). God-daughter of Louis XVIII, Mme de Gontaut served as 'gouvernante des Enfants de France', cr. duchesse de Gontaut-Biron (1826). She was associated with the comte d'Artois and his family (even his grandchildren) all her life.

[35] For Sophia Upton (1780–1853), the youngest daughter of Lady Templetown, see L. 697 n. 13. Shortly after her arrival in England Mme de Gontaut met Sophia Upton, who was 'very warm-hearted, and . . . devoted to me. . . . She detested society; and eager as she was to please those whom she liked, she took no pains to conceal her absolute indifference to all the rest of mankind.' There developed between the two women a close friendship that would account for Miss Upton's presence—along with Mme de Gontaut's—at the house of the comte d'Artois (Gontaut, i. 98–9).

[36] The comte d'Artois became Charles X on the death of Louis XVIII (16 Sept. 1824) and was crowned at Rheims, 29 May 1825, with all the ceremony of the *ancien régime*. Even in 1814, the comte d'Artois, about to take permanent residence in France, was 'inféodé de toutes les vieilles idées d'avant la Révolution, qu'il ne paraît disposé à aucune concession, à aucun compromis avec les révolutionnaires nantis de leurs rapines ou avec les tenants du régime impérial exécré' (Bertaut, p. 167).

[37] Caroline *née* Upton (1778–1862) had married James Singleton (1772–1855).

with all her politeness, & early initiation into Court-Manners,[38] could not quite disguise an amazement that bordered upon incredulity at this information. I could not, however, abate it by relating that it was my own Queen who had excited this condescendsion in Son Altesse Royale, because I was enjoined not to name that honour: I was forced, therefore, to leave the workings of Doubt to their own operations.

Mme de Gontaut could not prevail with any of the attendants to mention her to M. Le Duc de Grammont,[39] who was of the Royal Repast: but when it should be over, a promise was made to take in a little whisper. |

Tired of the Hall, & its multitude, we now mounted some steps of a Stair Case, upon which the anti-room to the Dining Parlour opened. Here, leaning upon the Banisters, we remained, one above another, yet grouped for discourse, a very considerable time, amusing ourselves with our own remarks.

At length, when the Dinner was taken away, & the Desert was served, we forced our way a little forwarder, getting into the anti-room, whence we had a peep at the Royal Table & its Guests, as the Door was wide open, on account of the heat. All there was nearly dead silence; excess of exertion, & of fatigue, after the lives of quiet & seclusion which had so long been led by the Royal Chiefs,[40] having so completely over-powered their strength & spirits, that sleep, heavy sleep, seemed fastening upon their Eye-lids, unbiden, yet unopposed. And, of course, since They could not hear, no one of their Court ventured to speak. |

The Duc de Grammont, more awake & alive, because,

[38] Mme de Gontaut was virtually born into court life. Her father, comte de Montault-Navailles (d. 1790), superintended the education of the Children of France (Louis XVI, Louis XVIII, and Charles X). At the age of seven she was presented for baptism by His Royal Highness (Louis XVIII) and Her Royal Highness (the comtesse de Provence) in the chapel at Versailles.

[39] Antoine-Louis-Marie de Gramont (1755–1836), *dit* comte de Louvigny, duc de Guiche (1780), duc de Gramont (1799). Emigrating with Louis XVIII, he had been premier gentilhomme de la chambre du roi, becoming in 1814 lieutenant-général and pair de France. In 1820 he was made ambassadeur extraordinaire de France.

[40] The house and grounds at Hartwell looked more like a small town than a gentleman's estate, several of the servants having opened shops in the lesser houses on the grounds. While the strictest etiquette was observed in the royal household, life was simple and even dull. Even when guests were present, the Royal Family ate plain food and Louis himself did the carving. The same table napkins were used for several meals. After dinner the King often played whist at three pence a point while the courtiers played at billiards or ombre. At eleven in the evening the King went to bed and therefore the rest of his company as well. See Margery Weiner, *The French Exiles, 1789–1815* (1960), pp. 178–9.

probably he had less been weaned from the World's hours & customs, when he learnt that Mme de Gontaut was in waiting, contrived to steal out: & they had a sprightly & very agreeable chattery together; but he declined being the bearer of any message to the Duchesse even from Mme de Gontaut, as he said S. A. Royale was absolutely dying with weariness.

My authority being so high for Notice, though known only to myself, I could not consent to forfeit my claim so tamely; & therefore, when the Duke was returning to the Royal Room, I assumed courage to call him back; &, making a brief apology, I named myself, & said I had received the commands of *Son Altesse* to attend.

He stared with the utmost amazement, but bowed a civil compliance, & went on.

He soon returned, & assured me he had tried vainly to execute my commission, for the moment he attempted to speak, the Duchesse had stopt him, & [|] begged him, in pity, to forbear naming a human soul, as she was half dead: & indeed, he added, her head dropt with sleep before she finished her injunction.

All now being hopeless, & very vexatious, we gave up the point, & severally parted to our several abodes.

Not here, nevertheless, closes this subject, for an audience afterwards took place in France, which, like this, I have been charged to commit to Paper.[41]

771   [63 Lower Sloane Street],
22–27 April 1814

Alexander d'Arblay *with a postscript by*
Madame d'Arblay
To M. d'Arblay

A.L. & P.S. (Berg), 22–27 Apr. 1814
Double sheet 4to   4 pp.
Addressed: A Monsieur / Monsieur d'Arblay / Rue de Miroménil N° 8 / Paris.

[41] FBA's audience with the duchesse d'Angoulême was to take place in Paris in February 1815.

Chelsea, Londres, Vendredi 22
Avril, 1814.

Cher Papa,

Maman vient de recevoir hier une lettre datée du 18, par M. le Duc de Luxembourg, précurseur de la paix—c'est elle seule, j'espere, que vous attendez—et cela ne sera pas long; car le Roi part demain pour Douvre où l'Amiral Foley doit le recevoir[1]— Avant hier il fit sa grande entrée à Londres, dans un superbe carrosse à huit chevaux qui lui avait été donné par le prince Régent qui l'accompagnait assis sur le derriere—Il est impossible de se faire une idée de la foule immense qui s'y portait et resta 4 heures à attendre la procession tout le long de la large rue de Piccadilly aussi longue que la rue St Honoré, tandis que toutes les maisons et toutes les rues adjacentes faisaient flotter des drapeaux blancs déployés avec diverses inscriptions en l'honneur de la famille des Bourbons, et que les toits et les greniers étaient tous aussi remplis que les plus superbes appartements et les balcons les plus magnifiques. Toute la noblesse Anglaise s'y étalait dans une longue file non interrompue de carrosses—resplendissants stationnés dans la foule qui irrésistiblement en remplissait tous les sieges, et les faisait presque crouler sous eux. Concevez quels cris une telle foule doit avoir fait retentir à la vuê de cette auguste famille si longtemps souffrante et calomniée, et si heureusement, quoique tard, rendue à ses premiers honneurs et à ses premiers droits![2]—Au sortir du carrosse, Louis, au milieu des— | acclamations *inappaisables* de la populace qui traînait son carrosse après en avoir ôté les chevaux, arracha de son habit le Grand ordre du

---

771. [1] *The Times* (21 Apr. 1814) reported from 'DEAL, April 19.—Orders have just now been received by the Port Admiral, FOLEY, to prepare for the reception of LOUIS XVIII, his suite, and the Duke of CLARENCE.' On 25 April it announced that Louis and his party had arrived at Dover about 6 p.m. on Saturday 23 April. 'His Most Christian Majesty was to sleep in the state apartments of the Castle, where Lord Liverpool, the Lord Warden, would be in readiness to receive him.'

[2] The procession, according to *The Times* (21 Apr.), formed at 3.20 p.m., at Stanmore on 20 April. The King of France and the Prince Regent rode in a state carriage 'drawn by eight cream-coloured horses, and surmounted by the Royal Standard of England.' They were escorted by a large body of ceremonial troops.

'Though . . . it became generally known in the morning, that the train could not reach town till between five and six o'clock, such was the impatience of the multitude, that the principal avenues were crowded from noon. But this multitude was not the mere populace; persons of the first distinction lined the road with their equipages. . . .'

Sᵗ Esprit avec son étoile, et en décora le Prince Régent;³ dont la conduite, depuis qu'il a tenu ici les rênes du gouvernement, a été admirable. La Gazette vous donnera des détails de tout cela sans doute; mais je n'ai pû me refuser le plaisir de vous détailler moi-même une si belle scene, si inattendue, si méritée par de longues souffrances, par une si noble résignation, par le rang et par la vertu. Louis XVIII y versa des larmes de joiy, et déclara que depuis cette entrée qui lui avait manifesté si pleinement les sentiments de la nation où dans des temps moins heureux il avait trouvé un refuge, toute son agitation, toutes ses peines, ses infirmités semblaient s'évanouir devant une joie presque céleste pʳ le présent et un calme parfait sur l'avenir.— Maman vient de recevoir une autre lettre, du 17, écrite chez M⟨ʳ⟩ Solvyns,⁴ qui est justement arrivée à Douvres presque 5 jours et 5 nuits sous les armes! C'est trop, beaucoup trop, malgré les compliments les plus flatteurs—Mais ⟨le⟩ Consulat! Ah espérons que vous y réussirez—Cela comblerait tous nos voeux, et serait bien préférable à un poste militaire auquel les troubles, les fatigues, & l'envie, inséparables de la régénération d'un grand Etat, arracheraient tous ses agréments—Quel spectacle sublime et imposant la semaine prochaine doit offrir! Et ce héros, cet Alexandre, quelle joie pure doit le pénétrer! Que l'autre Alexandre parait petit dans la balance!—ce n'est pas seulement que 'Magnus Alexander *corpore* parvus erat', mais *anime* en le comparant à celui-ci. Mais quand cette touchante cérémonie sera achevée, et tout, pour un long temps, j'espere, établi sur des bases fermes et tranquilles, alors

> Anglia ⟨seu⟩ placidos renovet, te Consule, menses,
> Gaudeat et rabidum claudere Martis iter;
> Seu juret Saturos restinguere passus honores,
> Tranquillos agitans, non sine laude, dies;
> Ah! Quâ te cumque animus, quâ Gloria cumque vocabit,
> Ah! memori repetas arva Britanna pede!

As reported by the *Morning Chronicle* (21 Apr. 1814), this act occurred on 20 April in the principal ballroom of Grillion's Hotel: 'His Majesty again expressed his gratitude [to the Prince Regent], and taking off the Cordon and Star of the Order of the Holy Ghost, which he wore, he personally placed the Star upon the breast of the Prince Regent, and with the assistance of the Prince de Conde, and the Duke de Bourbon, invested his Royal Highness with the Cordon, this being the first investiture since the revival of the Order.'

⁴ See L. 767.

Non haec te falsos inter numerabit amicos
Quis ⟨Lethea⟩ fuit pacifici unda maris;
Neve illam felix tu dedignabis arenam
Quâ portus misero, perfugium que fuit.
Diemque sonaret adhuc horrenda tonitrua belli
Fulmineosque Furor praecipitaret equos,
⟨Jactaretque⟩ ferox flagrantibus Horror in armis,
Undique sanguineum fervere Mortis opus;
Quâ Tamais tumidos gelido trahit agmine fluctus,
Quâ ⟨Ievioris⟩ Habri mollior unda fluit;
Dulcibus haud parcens, lambit quas Sequana, ripis,
Nec quâ funereum Rhenus aravit iter:
Haec ⟨   otum⟩, varias plorans longo ordine gentes
Hectore servili tristia colla jugo,
Haec tantum, sparsis Europa Orbisque ruinis
Imposita, ⟨exeruit⟩ nobile sola caput;
Nuncque orat, ut reduces agitat Victoria pennas,
Semper honore novo, semper amore frui.
Armorum fremitus, Mavors, bellique furores,
Et quicquid stolido fertur in orbe decus,
Suspende, immeritasque Neci parce addere, pennas:
Tam satis erubuit fusa cruore Ceres!
Tu que, optata ⟨diu! fessis⟩ te tradere terris,
Dum decorat teneram ⟨nobis⟩ oliva manum,
Ne dubita, Pietas, ⟨caeloque⟩ illabere aperto;
Sic, modo quâ sanie, flore rubebit humus!

Eh bien? Qu'en dites-vous.—There's for you, now—voilà pour
nous remettre, vous et moi, à notre Latin—ce qui est très
nécessaire pour moi dans ce moment, comme vous saurez
bientôt, si vous obéissez à mon Apollon. En attendant, vous
avez envie de voir des journaux Anglais; ça viendra. Je n'ai pas
encore pû voir ce fameux *Morning Chronicle* du 13 qui Vous a
tant réjoui.[5] Mais adieu: maman voudra absolument y mettre
un petit mot: je n'ai plus que deux lignes à ajouter, qui renfer-
ment tout le reste:

[5] This edition of the *Morning Chronicle*, available now in Paris, reported the
arrival and friendly reception of the English naval brig *Cadmus* and her men by
the inhabitants of Calais. It described Elba, 'the place of Napoleon's retreat', the
illuminations in London in honour of Wellington's victory at Toulouse, and the
Easter Fête at the Mansion House, where Mme de Staël was a guest.

⟨Huc ades⟩, ô precibus votisque calentibus acte!
⟨Huc ades⟩, ô animi ⟨fons⟩ et ⟨origo⟩ mei!
Carior et juveni fervet quo Sanguine pectus,
[xxx 1 word] quo ⟨non⟩ lux melior, non mihi nocte quies!
—te nec ⟨incerti⟩ popularis aurai
Turgeant flatus, sed inermis aetas
Fauno, et agresti nemorum susurro
Tradat, et umbris:
Hîc, levi turbâ procul et profanis,
Conjugum, et natum, placidos ⟨que⟩ amicos,
Altior Regum, foveas, recepto
Rure beatus;
Centies donec revoc⟨ârit⟩ annos,
Centies brumas Charon, et recentem
Spiritum, et famam, memorique nomen
Raptet Olympo!![6]

J'avais une longue histoire, à vous raconter des forêts de Cambridge; mais je crains qu'il me faille d'abord l'arranger en style pompeux; car, comme vous savez, Si canimus Sylvas, Sylvae sint Consule dignae.—Adieu!

[By Madame d'Arblay]

27th Avril. I make up this Letter. adieu—adieu—

P.S.
Si vous venez ici, je serai un bon clergyman, et j'aurai toutes les chances du monde d'un bon living qui nous suffira à tous les trois, pr nous maintenir heureux et contents à l'abri de tous les orages de la cour, de la guerre, et du sort. (J'espere avoir bientôt une occasion de vous expliquer comment—)et c'est de la maniere [p]our moi la plus agréable de toutes, par ⟨mes⟩ études ⟨   ⟩

[6] AA's Latin poem is an occasionally ungrammatical paean to peace and an earnest prayer that M. d'A will soon rejoin his family in England.

772 [63 Lower Sloane Street,
pre 28 April, 1814]
To Mrs. Waddington

A.L. (Diary MSS. vii. 5924–[27], Berg), *n.d.*
Double sheet 8vo   4 pp.   foliated (23) (24)   *pmks*   T.P.P.U. / [Kin]g's
R. Slo. Sq   30 AP .814   30 AP 1814   black seal
Addressed: Madame [*emended to*] Mrs. Waddington / Lanover / Abergavenny.
Edited by CFBt *and the* Press *and dated incorrectly*, p. 1 (5924), *top margin*:
Ap¹ 3. 1814 *See* Textual Notes.

Alas—my dear—fervant—but too precipitate Friend—if you
have written such a Letter, you have undone us all! — — M.
d'Arblay belongs to the National guard, & he has written me
word that Honour keeps him to his post till a proper moment
for giving in his resignation! Judge, then, what sort of consolation I should receive from his presence, when I should know
that he would EVER after—if he found me tolerably well, repent
having taken such a Treason![1]

Be not uneasy for me, my tender friend—My affliction is
heavy, but not acute: my beloved Father had been spared to us
something BEYOND the verge of the prayer for his preservation
which you must have read—for already his sufferings had far
surpassed his enjoyments! I could not have wished him so
to linger!—though I indulged almost to the last hour a hope
he might yet RECOVER, & live to comfort. — — I ⎮ last of all
gave him up!—but never wished his duration such as I saw him
on the last few days. Dear blessed Parent! how blest am I that
I came over to him while he was yet susceptible of pleasure—of
happiness!—Many thought I had given 10 years more to his
life![2] — — alas! — — my best comfort in my grief—in his
loss—is that I watched by his revered side the last night—&
hovered over him 2 hours after he breathed no more—for though
much suffering had *preceded* the last hours, they were so quiet,
& the final exit was so soft, that I had not perceived it, though

---

772. ¹ Mrs. Waddington, concerned about FBA's health after CB's death, urged
M. d'A to journey immediately to England, regardless of his military obligations.
² See Clement Francis's statement (L. 637 n. 28) that FBA's return from France
'has taken off near 20 yrs.' from CB's appearance.

I was sitting by his Bedside —! — and I would not believe it—
when all around announced it — —

I forced them to let me stay by him, & his reverend form
became stiff before | I could persuade myself to believe he was
gone hence for-ever — — —

Yet neither then, nor now, has there been any violence, any
thing to fear from my grief—his loss was too indubitably to be
expected—he had been granted too long to our indulgence, to
allow any species of repining to mingle with my sorrow—& it is
repining that makes sorrow too hard to bear with resignation—
Oh! I have known it! — — —

You will easily believe with what pain I must have torn
myself from my retirement in little more than a week—in 11
days—after this separation, to enter into the very midst of the
World, to be presented to Mad^e la Duchesse d'Angouleme. —
— but those who ought best to know remonstrated against my
repugnance, & assured me it might be lastingly injurious to M^r
d'Arblay, since every body who had any pretence to that
Honour came eagerly forward. I found the effo[rt] | however,
less trouble than I had expected, for though the Crowd was
immense, & I was kept in it all day, it was of NEW faces—I met
NO ONE, save Lady Crewe, who took me, that I had ever
beheld in the same apartment with my dearest Father. Nothing,
therefore, called forth his image save my own constant recollection.

Adieu—dearest Mary!—you have frightened [me] into
writing—but I am better, not worse for it. [I h]ave now had 6
Letters from M.d'A.—

My kind love to your dear Children—

To M. d'Arblay

A.L. (rejected Diary MSS. 5942–[49], Berg), 29 Apr. 1814
Two double sheets 4to   8 pp.   black wafer
Addressed: À Monsieur, / Monsieur d'Arblay, / Rue de Mirominel, /
8 / fᵍ St. Honoré / à Paris.
Edited by FBA, p. 1 (5942), numbered I, *annotated*: 9   *and the date
retraced*
p. 5 (5945), *numbered* 2, *and annotated*: 9. continued April 29ᵗʰ 1814
p. 9 [5949], *numbered* II
Edited also by CFBt *and the* Press. *See* Textual Notes.

April 29ᵗʰ 1814
Chelsea still!

The sweet Amine has just sent me word that an intimate
acquaintance, a Russian officer, will set off for Paris to-morrow:
—perhaps Mr. John Angerstein himself—

I shall, therefore, at length, write quite openly & entirely
upon matters of business—many of which I have long been
almost pining to discuss with my ever most dear Friend.

The loss of my beloved & revered Father must, surely, now,
have reached your Ears?—I have written 4 Letters with what
details I could relate. I will confine this sheet to essential
concerns.

This dear Parent has left, as nearly as he could calculate it
his whole *revenu* in Legacies to various branches of his family.
The sum amounts to between 7 & 8 thousand pounds. ⌐And
hundreds which were in the Banker's hands, will be apportioned
to the last sacred rites, & to debts. Whether there is sufficient
for the purpose, we do not yet know.[1]

The change in his Will, which was, (the last,) signed at Bath,
in the year 1807,[2] which he had *intended* of leaving you all his

773. [1] After making individual bequests, CB added in his will: 'Though at present
I have only £7,800 in the Funds, yet if I live to return to Chelsea I shall leave in
my Banker's hands, in arears of Salaries, Pension, and Jany. dividend at the
Bank, more than sufficient to complete the Sum in the Funds mentioned above.'
   [2] CB wrote and sealed his own will in Bath, where he had journeyed on 20
December 1806 to recover from a mild paralysis of his left hand and depression.

french Books, never was executed. But you are a gainer, not a loser, by the original design, for⌐ he has left the sale of the whole library, after particular bequests, to his *residuary legatees,* my sister Burney & myself: to whom fall every thing not named for any other person: prints, &c.[3]

Dear, kindest Father! to *me* never was bequest so unexpected! ⌐To Esther, it is now become *essential*—for poor worthy Mr. Burney is dangerously lingeringly & hopelessly ill![4] we are all in grief & alarm for him & his ⟨fond & dearest⟩ wife, who never quits him. Smaller details of the Will & legacies I will write by some less ⌐ important opportunity. I am eager to give this to solid concerns.⌐

My 2 Brothers are named Executers, ⌐but only as advisors, my dearest Father leaving them as an added complement, & saying both, & I, should agree too well to want arbitrators, though we may counsellors.⌐[5]

James, who is only mentioned for £200, is hurt & disappointed, & declines acting. Charles has only the same sum, in money, but sundry legacies, is therefore, sole acting Executer.[6]

You must not be angry with poor James—should our sale be productive, I shall earnestly desire to find some means of shewing him my affection:[7] but, till the sale is over, I have no power: &, indeed, he would, NOW, be very difficult to treat with. He always requires, when discontented, to be left

---

[3] See L. 769 n. 2. In addition to the £1,000 that FBA and EBB each inherited, they were also the beneficiaries of other items in CB's will, the most important of which were the two libraries: 'The miscellaneous books in various languages (particular books hereafter excepted) . . . it is my wish that they should be disposed of, entire or by auction, for the profit of MY TWO ELDEST DAUGHTERS, as they shall themselves amicably settle, the produce of which all to be divided equally between them. . . . It is my wish that all the books, tracts, and treatises on the particular Faculty of Music . . . should be separated from those on all other subjects and disposed of together to some liberal collector or public library for the advantage of my two eldest daughters, ESTHER AND FRANCES.' For the other items bequeathed to them, see L. 822 n. 7.

[4] See Ll. 764, 765. CRB continued to ail for another five years.

[5] See L. 769 nn. 5, 6.

[6] CB Jr. was also left the following: 'Walther's Lexicon Diplomaticum Folº . . . together with all such Classics and splendid editions of learned and scientific books of which he is not already in possession as are in the glazed book-case standing in the parlour' of the Chelsea apartment; 'The remaining copies in sheets of the 4 Vols. in 4to. of [CB's] general Histʸ of Music', together with 'the frontispieces and ornamental plates' in the hope that a new edition would be brought out, the profits accruing to the 'Proprietor of the work'; CB's 'Silver Standish, a present from the late Earl of Macartney'. (Johann Ludolph Walther's *Lexicon* was published in Göttingen in 1745.)

[7] See L. 777 n. 1.

WHOLLY to himself, & his own excellent heart then sets his frequently wayward head to rights.

Charles is all activity & zeal.

Poor Charlotte, also, has but £200, & not one bequest! This astonishes me, for she was high in the opinion of the revered Testator: but he thought her far richer than she really is.[8]

His own design—Heaven bless him ever!—has been to do what he himself thought *strictly just* by All: but peculiarly kind & serviceable by Hetty & me.

Blessed be his immortal Spirit, Almighty God!—

How thankful am I that I came over! that I had the joy of enlivening the last year & $\frac{1}{2}$ of his precious life! that I sat up with him the last night that he yet breathed! & watched over him two hours when be breathed no more! — —

To business—to business! — —

My personal legacy is £1000 in the 5 p^r c^{ts}.[9] Alexander has £100.

What the sale may produce, no one can yet calculate.[10]

All the finest books, with the noble Glass case, are left to

---

[8] The £200 bequest was justified in CB's will: 'This was my intention at the decease of the worthy Mr. Clement Francis, as it was always my wish to proportion my female family bequests to the wants of my Children, and Charlotte, being left in possession of a certain and ample dowry for herself and considerable improving fortune to her Children during their minority, she was in no want of parental assistance and her second marriage has not altered my Opinion.'

Clement Francis in his will, proved 22 Dec. 1792, left the bulk of his large estate to his wife. She could, however, draw only £100 annually from the interest on the property bequeathed to her. Similarly each child—Charlotte, Marianne, and Clement—until reaching majority (L. 787 n. 4) had only £100 yearly. For the details of Clement Francis's will, see Prob. 11/126/f. 607.

For a time Clement thought it prudent to defer a university career. As MF wrote (JRL) to Mrs. Piozzi on 11 Oct. 1809, Clement 'will, I believe, soon be engaged with some Merchant. . . . For what could Clem do at College with 100£ a year?—a Sum that would not keep him in "Greek Books"—and as he is *not* Erasmus, he must have "*cloathes*" too.'

That his 'fate' was altered was due to the urging of three persons close to his mother. In a note (JRL) to Mrs. Piozzi, Clement in November 1811 indicated that 'Tomorrow will enclose me within the walls of Caius Coll. Cambridge. . . . I did intend to defer residence till Next October, but Mr Cambridge, Mathias, & my Uncle deem it best for me to begin immediately, & in deference to their opinion I consented to it.'

[9] On 30 Apr. 1814, the day on which CB's will was proved, the 5 per cent Navy was listed at 94¾ a share. FBA therefore acquired ten shares and the half-yearly dividends therefrom—approximately £45 annually.

[10] The money realized on the sale of CB's entire library was £2,353. 19s. See Scholes, ii. 273–4. The individual sales brought in the following: the non-musical books sold by Leigh and Sotheby, £1,414. 18s. 6d.; the music manuscripts sold by John White, £686. 0s. 6d.; the books on music also sold by White to the British Museum, £253. See Ll. 796, 822 and n. 2 for the sum gained by FBA from the sale of CB's miscellaneous library.

Charles: the Glass Bookcase, of French Books, between Sarah & Fanny Raper:[11] & another Glass case & Books to Sarah.[12]

I have never yet, myself, read the Will, & cannot, therefore, be more accurate. It is now in Doctors' Commons, copying, &c—the stamp will cost £110.!—

Now to the Wanderer. The 3ᵈ Edition is already printed & in sale.[13] I have sent it you by Col. Harcourt. ⌐but you must try to indicate how I can send it to M. de Lally, M. Barbier Neuville & others for your own presentations. I have much more to say on this matter when I have time & opportunity.

But what most presses is to entreat that you will not authorize my being drawn upon, at present, for money unless it is indispensable to *yourself*: I have nobody to act for me, but by solicitations I am ashamed to make: & I cannot act for myself with any propriety, in this moment of deep mourning. I have *no money, none*, but for *unavoidable* personal expenses. I have left nothing at Coutts, or any other Bankers, & to sell out can only be done by Trustees, whom I have named, for Alex when I thought I must leave him; & whom I cannot now change till our own dwelling & decision is made. My Trustees are both men of business,[14] & I had only requested of them to go to the Bank for me *once a year* to receive my dividends & *then* to transact any further business. I cannot, therefore, call upon them to quit their affairs oftener, merely for mine, but on reasons of resistless moment. The City is so distant, it is a day lost to them.

---

[11] To Fanny Raper and SHB went all the French books in 'the Glass Book Case of [CB's] Parlour marked E, except the works of Voltaire many of which are unfit for the perusal of Females, and Bolingbrokes Philosophical works.' The works of Voltaire denied to them were, as listed in Leigh and Sotheby's *Sale Catalogue*: Micromegas (1752); Lettres Inédites a Frédéric le Grand (1802); Candide (1749); Abregé de l'Histoire Universelle (1753); Histoire de la Guerre de mil septant quarante et un (1756, 1767); Pucelle d'Orleans (1762); Oeuvres (an incomplete set: 1757, 1788); Vie (1789); Essay upon Civil Wars & Letters on the French Nation, in one volume (1727, 1741); Philosophy of History (1766); Henreade (1732); Ingenu, or the Sincere Huron (1768). CB owned *The Works of the Right Hon. Henry St. John, Lord Viscount Bolingbroke* (5 vols., London, 1754).

[12] This further bequest to SHB is designated in CB's will as 'one of the glazed book cases in [his] bed room'.

[13] Yet on 30 Aug. 1817 (Barrett, Eg. 3695, f. 97) FBA was to ask 'Messrs. Longman & Co. whether a third edition was printed or halted, and whether Dr. Burney misunderstood Mr. Strahan to say that another edition—the fifth—has been ordered to Press'.

[14] FBA deliberately avoids telling M. d'A that JB and Martin Burney are their trustees, that CB Jr. is guardian for AA. But see L. 807, wherein FBA indicates the substitution of Edward Francesco Burney for JB.

I did it, nevertheless, for *M. de Billy*,[15] only upon seeing your hand to writing my name. I sent him, with the aid of Mar[ianne] Fr[ancis], £25 s^t!—but he now demands another £25—which I shall at least decline sending till I hear from you, as you have never named the commission, nor acknowledged that the 1st 25 have been repaid. Unless *You* require—which God forbid that £50 entire, M. de Billy may easily now have money passed to him from his friends by the Bankers.⁋ |

£.300, you tell me, is ALL you have been able to save! Alas, my dear Friend, had I listened to your tender urgings, & kept a femme de chambre, & lived up to 50 or 60 £ a month, & spent 5^s daily in a Carriage[16]—Where should we now be? — —

Yet, with all the œconomy I have been able to practice, our running small revenue is utterly insufficient for Alexander & me!—But I had indeed hoped that *without us*, & without his Education, you would have been able to save for our reunion that which I could by no means consent to use in separate luxuries. In those I have no pleasure! my sole desire, delight, design, is to accumulate a sufficiency for our meeting to PART NO MORE!—

Every day of my life, I more earnestly sigh for that BLESSED MOMENT.

At present, with all our long forbearance upon my pension, with all the accumulated interest of the £202.[17] placed by dear Mrs. Lock,[18] & of the house rent of Westhumble, with the 70 or 80 £ of ⟨   ⟩ & with £.500 for the Wanderer, which is all I have received,[19] & which I instantly united to the rest, we have only £83. pr. ann.!—added to which, my pension of £90[20]—& the house rent of 47.—for the rest is all given to Taxes & small necessaries. This is £.220.—But the £90 is only upon 2 lives the Q[uee]n's & mine.[21]

---

[15] See L. 769 n. 16.   [16] See L. 727.

[17] FBA cites £202 for the £271 (as recorded by M. d'A) invested for the d'Arblays by Mr. Locke in 1803 in 3 per cent consols. See Appendix II, L. 709 n. 9.   [18] See L. 721 n. 3.

[19] FBA received £500 for the delivery of *The Wanderer* manuscript to Longman and his associates. See L. 761 (and n. 5) in which she expresses her disappointment at not receiving an additional £500 when the first edition was sold out.

[20] On 7 July 1791, after five years of service to Queen Charlotte, FB was granted an annual pension of £100. Her reference to £90 is explained by M. d'A: 'ta pension de 100£ sauf la diminution qu'elle a subie à dater de l'epoque de l'impôt sur les pensions' (see Appendix II).

[21] The reason that FBA's pension did not terminate with the death of Queen Charlotte on 17 Nov. 1818 may be found in *Parl. Deb.*, xxxix. 295 ff., 608. On

The 2500 in arrears of the Wanderer will not be paid till the 6ᵗʰ Edition is sold.

⌐The Legacy & sale &c will be a year, perhaps, before being settled⌐

But, ultimately, we must needs have a decent competence.

our Alexander, if steady! —! —! may do perfectly well! if not, let us leave him an independence. He could only be contented by going to Cambridge—I was told that that would cost £200 a year—but, with the zealous help of Charles, & with exertions of my own such as I never made before, we have procured him a 3 year's scholarship of more than £100. per ann. In 3 years, if industrious, he may take his degree, & then we may seek him some Church benefice.[22]

⌐I shall take no steps about selling or repairing the house till you direct me. ¦

I write all this detail before I come to the consul general.— If ALL sorts of places are so precarious, & so transient, then I would fain, we work at assuring ourselves a *real* Independance, of all but our own œconomy, before all things.

This, if you can let me place, as fast as I receive the sums, all that arises *here*, till we meet, may be done.

And at all events, you will surely procure permissions to come over to settle our most deranged affairs, in a short time.

With regard to the Consul General, the very idea is enchantment to me. I shall *sortir de mon apathie*, as You call it, more willingly for that than for any other inducement. Alexander is enraptured at the plan. He has just left me for Cambridge, & better, but far, far from robust—

I have already taken every step in my power by Letter— but as yet there has been no time for answers.⌐[23]

4 Feb. 1819 the Prince Regent sent a message to the Commons saying that he had placed the annual sum of £58,000 at Parliament's disposal and asking that, out of this sum, provision should be made for those who had been members of the Queen's household. A select committee, set up to examine this matter, recommended on 23 March that £18,244 annually should be set aside for 'payment of pensions and allowances to the ladies of the bedchamber, maids of honour, and other attendants on' the late Queen. The recommendation was accepted by the Commons. The Treasury then disbursed this sum from the Civil List to the various recipients.

[22] M. d'A was already dead when on 11 Apr. 1819 AA was ordained a priest. Five years passed before he secured his first living in a new chapel in Camden Town. He obtained his preferment in part through the efforts of the Bishop of Salisbury, Archdeacon Cambridge, and the Revd. George Locke (*HFB*, pp. 419–20).

[23] See L. 769 and nn. 12, 13.

I have no spirits for detailing, or I could both charm & touch you—& amuse you also—but my heart keeps very heavy—my dearest Father is still always before me!—I must briefly, however, say that M. de Luxembourg sent me a Messenger express with a Letter from you, dated the 18ᵗʰ & a note of very flattering politeness to myself. ⌐I wrote—but he was gone ere my answer arrived—for the day I received his & your Billets, I was gone⌐ to town, perforce, to enquire about presentations to Madame La Duchesse d'Angoulême: for I had been advised, by Excellent authority, to force myself from my sadness & retirement, in order to have the honour of being named to Her Royal Highness. It was a furious effort—& made, at last, in vain!—I missed the opportunity, by accidental circumstances the most provoking:—yet the whole of the effort was attended with pleasing & soothing particulars.—& the *result* surpassed all my expectations, in a presentation to his Majesty Louis XVIII, that filled me with much delight, yet emotion, that those who saw me when I retired from him thought I was taken ill—when I was only taken happy!—a feeling almost ungenial, at this sad period, to my heart.

M. le Duc de Duras was amiable past all description—after the King had spoken to me in terms of boundless condescension—holding my hand while he spoke—M. de Duras said—in full court—'Et M. d'Arblay, Sire, est un des plus devoués des serviteurs de Votre Majesty.—'[24]

I knew not, till 2 days afterwards, that le Roi himself had even deigned to *desire* I should be presented to him. So had Mᵈᵉ la duchesse d'Angoulême,—whom I wholly missed!—

How do I now trebly rejoice that, when I first came over, I found means to make known ⌐—in case it was not known already to le Roi,⌐ that, though printed in All the Gazettes, it was positively false that M. de Duras was one of the Chamberlains.[25]—I begged not to be named, on account of *your* situation in Paris, but it was M. le Commandeur de Thuisy to whom I

[24] See L. 770.

[25] The duc was a distinguished member of an old and illustrious family that numbered among its members five marshals of France, many army officers, bishops and archbishops, several 'chevaliers du Saint-Esprit'. The Napoleonic image would have been enhanced had the allies and the *émigrés* still abroad believed that the duc de Duras served as chambellan to the Emperor. In order to still this gossip quickly, Louis XVIII had the duc serve prominently in the audiences held in London between 20 and 22 April.

gave the commission. ⌐He had already *conjectured* the fact, from a Letter of his Brother's,[26] but I was happy to ascertain it. M. de Mun[27] himself having assured me, in Paris, that not only the Duc de Duras *was not* chamberlain, but had never received the order, nor even a request! Yet could not have the paragraph contradicted!—

I shall send you if possible, by this opportunity a Letter of our Alexander, & one I had written for le Duc de Luxembourg.[28]

I will take *every* means in my power to forward the consulship oh with what eagerness!—Write by *every* opportunity, but n[umber] your Letters. I have written 6 by M. de Grefeuil, M. MacKenzie, M. de la Châtre, M^r ⟨Lauriston⟩[29] & Harcourt & *intended* for M. de Luxembourg. *This* is the 7th.⌐ |

M. de La Châtre has conducted himself with a friendly politeness, nay, kindness, that cannot be surpassed.

⌐Tell me what Letters you receive from me—Let us try ardently for this consulship — — but let no prospects diminish our moderation & forbearance till we have secured à l'abri *des plans* et of circumstance, an independence personal, & a security of provision for our Alexander.⌐

My friends have behaved nobly for our boy with respect to the scholarship at Cambridge: but in 2 years that ceases. I will live with *parsimony* rather than œconomy, till our revenu suffices without selling out.[30] My ease, comfort, spirits, & health

---

[26] Amable-Jean-Baptiste-Louis-Jérôme de Thuisy (1749–*post* 1815), chevalier de Malte (1787), chargé des affaires de la réligion de Malte en Angleterre. See *Liste de messieurs les chevaliers, chapelains conventuels et servants d'armes des trois vénérables langues de Provence, Auvergne, et France* (Malta, 1787), p. 160. For his brother, see L. 764 n. 8.

[27] Jean-Antoine-Claude-*Adrien* de Mun (1773–1843). See v, L. 514 n. 18. As a chambellan he would know that the duc de Duras did not serve Napoleon in an official capacity.

[28] For FBA's letter 'written for le Duc de Luxembourg', see L. 769 and for AA's letter to his father, see L. 771.

[29] Jacques-Alexandre-Bernard Law (1768–1828), comte de Lauriston, was captured during the Battle of Leipzig on 19 October and imprisoned in Berlin. After his release, he was made aide-de-camp to the comte d'Artois in April 1814 and so was in England when the Bourbons prepared to return to France. For his early career, see v, L. 425 n. 5.

[30] For the stocks now probably owned by the d'Arblays, see L. 749 n. 16 and Appendix II. FBA had not yet received her share of the 5 per cent Navy bequeathed her by CB. From the letters available it is difficult to assess precisely how many shares of stock bought between June 1796 and July 1803 were retained, sold, or diverted into other funds. See iii, Ll. 193, 222, 249, 250 n. 1; iv, Ll. 264, 267, 288, 409.

all hang on living without debts, & without positive depen-
dence upon circumstance.

Oh mon ami! mon ami!—vos 5 jours & 5 nuits sous les armes
m'ont fait bien Mal!—ah! that you could c[ome] to honourable
repose![31]

I will not think of such a sort of gay regale as a tour to Paris
to see the inauguration[32]—though I am now almost bewitched
by le Roi, & enthusiastic for the Emp^r of Russia: but it would
swallow all our œconomies, ⌜& reduce us to accept almost any
proposition, for sustaining ourselves. Besides, I do not dare hope
I am well enough for the voyages that are indispensable! Yet
I take care of my health since I think, always persuaded you
sympathise with me in that first & best mark of warm attachment.⌝

(Oh for our re-union!)

Alex ⌜grows up to the Ceiling of the Room. He⌝ is, *AT TIMES
ALL* we can wish: & much liked by the world. ∣

⌜The questions I would like to have answered:—Mad
d'Henin—& Me de Maisonneuve, Genl Victor de Maubourg
Me de Tracy—de Beauvau[33]—de Chastel[34]—de Grandmaison,[35]
de Meulan[36] et notre cher oncle & cher M. de Lally! M.
Gallais où et s-il?[37] M. de Lajard—[38] Enfin—enfin—Mais M^d
de Tessé!!—oh adieu—Je la regrette—adieu—adieu— —⌝ ∣

Direct ∣ Made. d'Arblay ∣ 26 at capt. Burney's James Street,
Westminster.

---

[31] See L. 767.

[32] In declining the invitation of M. d'A (L. 767) to witness the coronation,
FBA missed the pomp, as described in *The Times* (5 May): according to plan,
Louis was to enter Paris on 3 May. 'After the keys of [Paris] have been presented
to the King, and his Majesty has been complimented by the Prefect of the Department, the procession. . . . will repair to Notre Dame by la Rue de Faubourg, St.
Denis, &c. . . . After the *Te Deum* the procession will move to the Thuilleries in the
same order as before. He will there be conducted to the throne, upon which he will
seat himself, surrounded by the Princes of the Blood, Marshals, Ministers and
Chief officers.'

[33] For the gossip concerning Mme de Beauvau, see L. 808 n. 4. For a description of the members of her immediate family, see v, L. 513 n. 2.

[34] Catherine-Françoise Chastel de Moyenpal (L. 654 n. 13).

[35] See L. 689 n. 3.

[36] For Alexandrine de Meulan *née* de Turpin-Crissé (d. 1846), see v, L. 532
n. 5.

[37] Jean-Pierre Gallais (1756–1820), historian and publicist, occupied in Napoleon's government 'la chair d'éloquence et de philosophie à l'Académie de légis-
lation'.

[38] For Pierre-Auguste Lajard (1757–1837), see iv, L. 291 n. 5; v *passim*.

774   [63 Lower Sloane Street,
                                             29 April 1814]

To Mrs. Broome

A.L. (Berg), *n.d.*
Double sheet large 8vo   4 pp.   *pmks*   To be Delivered / by 10 o Clock /
on Sund. Morn.   T.P.P.U. / Chelsea EO   black seal
Addressed: Mrs. Broome, / Hill Street, / Richmond.
Endorsed by CBFB: Sister / d'arblay / 1814

My ever kindest Charlotte will be amongst the foremost &
the truest to congratulate me that my Heart's dearest Partner
is returned.—He came yesterday—wholly unexpected at the
MOMENT, but yet not much sooner than I had secretly hoped
for his arrival. He looks well in health, but terribly thin, worn,
& fatigued.

He is anxious to see you, my Charlotte—& my other Charlotte—& Marianne—Clement—Ralph—& Julia—Hetty—
Dick—& Mr. Barret—

And we hope to go together to Richmond ere long for all
these tender embrassades — — —

My own dear tender Charlotte what grief I have to still
defer even my pic-nic ship! In a manner utterly unaccountable,
Martin has ceased to come or write about my affairs—& they
are all in his hands — — He had promised me a second payment from Longman, from which I was ¦ to deduct my *wants*;
—or, to sell out for me.—He knows my situation, & has not
even answered my appeal to him. If his new avocations absorb
him, he should say so. He has obliged me both to *owe* & to
borrow, when I have no occasion to do either, & detest both.—!

Yet I will not judge him unheard—

But I am forced to speak the truth to you, lest you should
believe it even *possible* I could cease a moment to think of your
rights. M. d'A. shall, if possible, remain ignorant of this
strangeness—his kind heart instantly lamented both for you &
James your small legacies—& joined with ALACRITY in my
wish, after the sale, to double them. But till then, there is no
possibility, all the *money* being bequeathed [by] my dearest
Father. Most unfortunately, Rapin is amongst the Books in the

333

Glass Case | left to Charles.[1] Endeavour to think of some other, that may be *every way* valuable to my dearest Charlottina. I will immediately mark it to be bought in. Tell Her to make no scruple in her choice, as my dear Father himself, Sarah has told me, said he would leave her a Book.

I have taken from the sale with my own hand the folio Gray[2] for my dear Ralph.

Hetty & I have agreed to look out for something for Clement & Marianne—as a memorial of their dear Grandfather. I must not ask THEM, as Hetty gives me that carte blanche only for Charlottina, but I shall be very glad of *your* private opinion to guide me.

I would there were any thing we could offer to my dearest Charlotte—but M. d'A. & I, in our confabs. think some little matter that is *solid* will be best.

our plans—&c are all yet unsettled, or even discussed. A delightful one presents itself to my hopes—that of a place under the French Government, but in England: i.e. Consul General français en Angleterre.[3] For this we are now making some attempt. My love around—& my kindest compts. to dear Miss Baker, the arch[deacon] & Mrs. G. C[ambridge]

adieu, my ever dear |

Poor—poor Mr. Burney I think very ill of indeed!—he has hardly any ⟨face⟩ left! Hetty is forced to nurse him incessantly. She has only one day been here.

M. d'A. is going to Cambridge 1st of all.—

774. [1] Of the works by René Rapin (1621–87), CFBt may have desired one of the following, all of which were in CB's library: *The Whole Critical Works of Monsieur Rapin . . . Newly Translated into English by Several Hands* (2 vols., 1706), or the 2nd ed. by Basil Kennet in 1716; *Oeuvres diverses . . . concernant les belles lettres* (2 vols. Amsterdam, 1686), or the corrected edition of 1693; *Les Comparaisons des grands hommes de l'antiquité, qui ont le plus excellé dans les belles-lettres* (2 vols., 1684); *Réflexions sur la poétique d'Aristote et sur les ouvrages des poètes anciens & modernes* (1674); *Les Oeuvres du P. Rapin* (3 vols., 1709–10); or *Réflexions sur la philosophie ancienne et moderne* (1676).

[2] Either *The Poetical Works of Thomas Gray* (Glasgow, 1787), fol., or *Designs by Richard Bentley for Six Poems by Thomas Gray. With the poems, and explanations of the prints* (1753).

[3] See L. 793, which explains the failure of M. d'A to receive this office.

775

To Mrs. Locke

L., an excerpt in the hand of CFBt (Diary MSS. viii. 6002, Berg),
30 Apr. 1814

Single sheet 4to   1 p.   numbered 54

Edited by the Press. *See* Textual Notes.

April 30. 1814

My own dearest Friend must be the first — — as she will
be among the warmest to participate in my happiness—M.
d'Arblay is arrived.—

He came yesterday[1]—quite unexpectedly as to the day, but
not very much quicker than my secret hopes.—He is extremely
fatigued with all that has passed—yet well;—& all himself—i.e.
All that is calculated to fill my heart with gratitude for my lot
in life.

How would my beloved Father have rejoiced in his sight—&
in these glorious new events!

776

To Mrs. Locke

A.L. draft (Barrett, Eg. 3695, f. 93), 16 May 1814

Written on a leaf (6·3 × 3·7 to 4″) removed from a Memorandum and
Account Book, 1814, being an accounts page ruled for the dates 3–9
January 1814, the *verso* of which is ruled for the Diary entries 10–16 January,
1814. Other leaves from FBA's mutilated Memorandum Book for 1814,
extant in the Berg Collection, are printed in Appendix I

p. 1, *Docketed in unknown hand in pencil*: From the / *Lock Correspondence* /
Temporary misunderstanding / about lease of cottage

—Mrs. Lock—

May 16, 1814—

Your last arrived just as M. d'A was setting off for Cambridge,
where I hope he is now solacing himself with his darling

775. [1] But see Diary Entry, 28 Apr. 1814.

Alexander, after a very, very severe blow[1]—received the moment before he left me, through Martin Burney, from Mr. Murray,[2] who thinks there must be *some mistake* in the promise of the 99 Years lease asserted by M. d'Arblay!!! What inadequacy of powers there may now be in Mr. W[illiam Locke] I am no judge, but *mistake in the origin* of the little building there could be none. Not only M. d'A. could never, he says, have been so mad as to build, at so large a sum, from a pittance such as ours, upon any other terms than its lasting possession, but Mr. L[ocke]—the wisest of Men as well as the best.of.friends, could never have permitted, much less invited, such a transaction.[3] of This we shall always feel gratefully convinced, whatever be the result. M. d'A. was so greatly hurt, as well as astonished, that he could not finish the Letter. He took it with him.

He longs to see you—&c

777   [63 Lower Sloane Street,
20 or 21 May 1814]
To Esther Burney Burney

A.L. (PML, Autog. Cor. bound), *n.d.*
Single sheet 4to   2 pp.   trimmed   black seal
Addressed: Mrs. Burney, / John Street, / Oxford Street
Docketed in pencil, p. 1: Mrs. Esther B. Frances Sister

My dear Esther,

We are extremely sorry that James declines receiving for himself this mark of our affectionate concern at the late distribution:[1] but M. d'Arblay is of opinion that we cannot, upon deliberation, be justified in making an offer, in the second line

776. [1] See Diary Entry, 14 May 1814.
[2] See L. 728 n. 6.
[3] Between 5 and 19 May 1814 M. d'A wrote three letters (Berg) to William Locke, in which he protested—as FBA later commented—against 'the award of Mr. Murray Lawyer, which robbed him of his Rights to a House [Camilla Cottage] Built by himself on Ground accorded him [for 99 years], by Mr. Locke Sen[r] with a Ground Lease of £5. p[r] ann.'

777. [1] FBA wished JB to share in the proceeds and value of CB's 'Irish mortgage'. See L. 781.

ourselves.[2] It will lay us open to general murmurs, & our very anxiety for Harmony will produce discord: Charlotte, already chagrined that her 4 children, alone of the second race are not mentioned, will be still less satisfied; Sarah, already sorrowful for the 2 omitted Grand Children in India,[3] will think their case still harder; the Motherless, & worse than Fatherless William Phillips[4] would hold himself authorized also to some added consideration; & even Charles, though acquiescent to the proposal made to James, talks pointedly of his own—what he calls diminished £750, the moment the second line is mentioned.

But if James will accept for himself, his Eldership, which admits no rivalry, & his hospitable character, which endears him to his family, would make every one contented. And *He*, the next minute, may do blamelessly, what *We* can only do to incur fresh demands & new difficulties. We will make no insistence upon his ⎮ superintendence. We will all agree to commit the affair to M. de Corcey[5] in Ireland, & here, to Martin, whom M. d'Arblay will be both able & willing to assist. OR—if that will be more agreeable to James, I will with pleasure, if you approve, propose to Mrs. Burney the 3d we have offered vainly to himself. That, perhaps, would obviate all objections, as from Her it could descend, at once or hereafter, as was judged best, to her children. And it would give me pleasure to shew her my esteem & friendship though I had far rather it should reach her through its primitive channel.

Adieu, my dear Esther—M. d'A. is gone to West Hamble, to visit, & take notes upon his premises.[6] He will probably sleep at Norbury Park, where Mrs. Lock is now alone. There was a mere mistake, I thank God, yesterday, & no accident.

I have shown this to M. d'Arblay, who approves it.

---

[2] Upon receiving JB's rejection of a third share of the 'Irish mortgage', FBA and EBB thought his share should be given to his children, 'the second line'. Despite the objections of M. d'A, this is precisely what FBA and EBB did. See L. 781.

[3] Although CB made provision for eight of Richard Thomas's surviving children, he neglected two others, who had been born before the will was drawn up. SHB's concern was that of an aunt for her late brother's children.

[4] William Phillips, now at sea, might have felt entitled to all or a share of the £100 bequest to his brother Norbury, who had died in February 1814.

[5] John de Courcey (*c.* 1787–1822) was a solicitor in Chancery, who in 1814 worked and lived at 34 Dame Street, Dublin. He was a reputable lawyer and an active member of the Law Club, which had been 'instituted in 1791, for the better regulation of the practising solicitors' (see PRO, Dublin, 'Index to Prerogative Wills, 1811–58'). [6] See Diary Entry, 20 May 1814.

778   [63 Lower Sloane Street],
                                              24 May 1814
To Mrs. Locke

A.L. copy in the hand of FBA (Barrett, Eg. 3695, f. 94–b), 24 May 1814
Single sheet large 8vo   2 pp.
Edited by FBA, p. 1, *annotated*:   ×   *To Mrs. Locke.* p. 2: N.B. / This was
copied to shew, in Future, to the wounded writer's BEST & NOBLEST Friend,
in case of a breach irreparable—
It is an answer to a most unlooked for Letter of Reproach from my dearest
Intimate Friend in her misconceived resentm^t of M. d'Arblays high &
forcible reclamation to Wm. Locke Junr

To Mrs. Lock.

24th of May 1814[1]

Ah Heaven—to Me is this Letter?[2] & from Norbury Park?

What can there have been—to me as unknown as unintended
in 'the first page'—What in the Last—What in my whole life
to have merited it?

No—there was no CHANGE—I merely sustained & sustain
my husband: & the fond Mother who sustains her Son—& the
affectionate Sister who sustains her Brother—should surely
pardon The Wife who firmly believes that no human being that
breathes has a higher sense of honour than her husband.

& that even the 3 Ang[e]l friends whom she forever deplores.
Mr—Locke—Mrs. Delany—& her Sister[3]—

No, nor all the angels that now surround them— | had not,
& have not intentions more pure.

I earnestly conjure that Amelia[4] may not write to me at this

778. [1] The whole of this letter concerns the reluctant contretemps between the
d'Arblays and the Lockes over the forced sale of Camilla Cottage.

[2] Mrs. Locke's letter, now missing, is described by FBA as one 'I deplore about
our Cottage' (Diary Entry, 23 May 1814). It defends William against d'Arblay's
indignation, which culminated in the protest of 19 May 1814. See L. 776 n. 3.
Mrs. Locke must have confirmed the spirit of Amelia Angerstein's letter (Barrett,
Eg. 3697, f. 72), dated 4 May 1814, of which a fragment remains: '. . . let it not I
conjure my dear M^r d'Arblay be the means of sullying a friendship so valued by us
all so long & so sacredly established—. For Heavens sake . . . let him not again
write in so cruel a manner to William, who is still willing to attribute his last
letter to any cause but unkindness & if he feels it will be satisfactory to himself to
submit the case to a higher law authority let it be done *for* the sake of *elucidation*
in a cause which is ours as well as yours. . . .'

[3] William Locke (d. 1810), Mary Delany (d. 1788), SBP (d. 1800).

[4] Amelia Angerstein wrote twice more to FBA on this subject. In one letter
(Barrett, Eg. 3697, ff. 74–5b), dated 28 May 1814, she expressed her concern

338

period If the vindication of Mr. William must be my condemnation for *Mine* of M. d'Arblay's, I implore her Silence.

To see her hand also trace characters of reproach in which no word of kindness is blended—would do me more harm than can possibly be meant.

For *abler*—or for ANY NEW friends I am little—at this moment—disposed to Wish: I sigh, I sicken to be restored to those I have thus deploraably—thus unexpectedly lost!⁵—

779 [Calais], 26 May [1814]

M. d'Arblay
To Madame d'Arblay

A.L.S. (Berg), 26 May, including a copy by M. d'A of a letter from Claude-Louis, duc de la Châtre, to M. d'A, 25 [May 1814]

Single sheet 4to 2 pp. [possibly sent with L. 780 in a cover now lost]

Edited by FBA, p. 1, annotated and dated: ⋕ 10/1 II 1814 MAY on quitting F. d'A. upon a summons from the Duc. de Luxembourg to enter the Body Guard of Louis 18. *See further,* Textual Notes.

over the misunderstanding but also the Lockes's 'respect & confidence' in Mr. Murray, 'however dry & technical [he] may have appeared to you as he always did to me, in his intercourse.' When both sides were represented by solicitors, she wrote again on 31 May (Barrett, Eg. 3697, ff. 76–7b). 'Spare Mr d'A. the irritation of those feelings which you allow to be *distempered* in the subject of Lawyers, & let Mr Martin B . . . transmit to you the result of his conference [with Mr. Murray]. . . . Let us call Mr M. B. not a lawyer but *your Nephew,* the little arch blue eyed boy I remember at dear Mickelham, & Mr Murray, something very near a friend of My Angel Fathers, that will divert him at once of *some* of his odiousness in your Eyes; & let the whole painful business be concluded. . . .'

⁵ Mrs. Locke replied (Barrett, Eg. 3697, f. 183) on 26 May 1814: 'I will not lose a moment in assuring my ever beloved Friend that she has *certainly not "lost"* those whom she wishes to retain—

'I had anticipated her—*apology*, if I may use the word, for an unusual manner, which I cou'd not but feel most painfully; conscious that neither myself, nor *any* of mine, had, or cou'd ever deserve it from her or hers—my dearest Willm is so desirous for my sake, as well as for his own, that this misconceived business shou'd be satisfactorily settled, that I trust in Heaven! you will *both* revert to the Old & invaluable kindness, that I had looked towards, as one of my first consolations, and one that I considered as *immortal*—May I not revert to that persuasion, my ever most dear Friend? How promptly does my heart obey the call of yours, and confess itself, tho' wounded, yours with faithful affection.'

Mrs. Locke wrote three more letters (Barrett, Eg. 3697, ff. 185–7, 191–2) on 30 May, 9 June, and 19 July. These were always conciliatory even while defending William.

Ce matin à 4^h ½ ce 26 May

Copie du billet de Mr de la Châtre

Je vous prie mon cher d'A. de bien soigner les deux paquets dont vous voulez bien vous charger. Ils sont tellement pressés à remettre que je vous prie de ne pas perdre de tems en route et si cela vous coutait plus cher que ne le ferait un voyage ordinaire, sans compliment je le rembourserais; point de fausse delicatesse entendez vous.

Ce 25 au soir

Tu juges bien que je ne perdrai pas un instant,[1] d'autant qu'en effet il y a un de ces paquets très très pressé comme me l'a expliqué Mr de L. C. qui allait se mettre au lit, et m'a dit de prendre une voiture et la poste à Calais. Il a même ecrit sur mon passe port que je devais être servi sur la route, de preference à tout autre courrier.

[*On peut distinguer, à travers cinque lignes, plus tard oblitérées par Madame d'Arblay, des réferénces à* 'une requête à Deptford p^r demander à Charles . . . TEN POUNDS' | *et à des autres arrangements financiers.*]

Je suis raffraichi par les trois heures de sommeil que je viens de gouter fort heureusement, et vais vite m'habiller — Adieu — toi que j'aime au delà de tout ce qu'on peut exprimer, mais toujours en dessous de ce que tu mérites. Embrasse pour moi Alexandre, et écris moi, par notre ambassade. adieu adieu au revoir, toi que j'aime mille et mille fois plus que la vie!—Au revoir.

A. P. D'Ay

779. [1] M. d'A received his passport for France with unusual speed through the efforts of the French embassy in London and the office of John Reeves. On 23 May 1814 he wrote (Berg) to an unidentified correspondent: 'Il [notre ambassadeur] a eu la bonté de me donner en même tems un billet de sa main pour Mr Reeves qu'il a prié de vouloir bien m'expedier un passport. Aussitôt je suis allé à l'allien office, afin qu'à la première nouvelle je pusse partir.'

M. d'Arblay
To Madame d'Arblay

A.L.S. (Berg), 27 May 1814
Single sheet 4to   1 p.
Edited by FBA, p. 1, *annotated and year date* 1814 *circled*:   10/2   3

Calais ce 27 *May* 1814
à 9ʰ du soir.

Je suis arrivé en six heures, sans être malade un instant. Je
n'ai fait que manger, et cependant tous les marins français
excepté un ont été malades. dans deux heures je serai en voiture
avec un Mʳ Catoire[1] cet eleve de l'Ecole polytechnique dont
je t'ai parle dans le mot que tu as reçu de moi. Je te prie de
l'aimer, il est impossible d'être plus aimable et meilleur pour
moi. Je te quitte pour souper. Tu vois que je prens des précau-
tions pour te faire à croire. Je t'embrasse comme je t'aime et ton
fils egalement.[2]

A. P. d'Arblay

780. [1] The roster of students at the École Polytechnique for the year 1814 (and
for several years before and after) contains none named Catoire. Fatigued by his
journey, M. d'A may have been uncertain about the educational background of
the *two* Catoire brothers whom he met at Calais. He returned to Paris in a carriage
with one (L. 793), who was probably Henri Catoire (1792–*post* 1820), born at
Verdun (Meuse). Trained at the École Militaire de St. Cyr in 1809, he became a
sous-lieutenant in 1811 and joined the 61st infantry regiment. For unstated reasons
he left the military in 1813 and applied for the Légion d'honneur, which he received
with the duc de Feltre's approval.
    [2] The unexpected return of M. d'A to Paris on 24 May is noted by MF to Mrs.
Piozzi in a letter (JRL) written on 2 June 1814. 'Mʳ d'Arblay has been in England
& is returned to France to enter the army again. At least this is what I hear.'
For a fuller explanation, see L. 781 n. 3.

[63 Lower Sloane Street,
28 May 1814]

To Martin Charles Burney

A.L.S. (PML, Autog. Cor. bound), *n.d.*
Double sheet 8vo   3 pp.   trimmed   *pmk*   28 MY 1814   wafer mended
Addressed: Martin C Burney Esq / James Street / Westminster / 26

Dear Martin,

As no means we can devise or propose will induce my Brother
James to accept for himself or my dear sister in-Law our earnest
offer that he would share with us the produce of the Irish
Mortgage; we now, as what best shews our affectionate meaning,
offer the same portion, *a third*, to yourself & your sister.[1]

That we should not have begun with you; your own filial
feelings will easily explain, but, as my Brother's refusal is
positive, & has been re-iterated, accept now, without scruple,
at first hand what, finally, was always meant for you from your
affectionate Aunt

F. B. d'Arblay.

My sister Burney is not here to subscribe, but she has given
me her full consent in a note I have just received from her: &
the kindest & Best of Men left me, should his *own* second proposi-
tion fail,[2] like the first, permission to take this step, and to join |
to it his love & kind wishes to you & your sister.

My papers arrived safely, but we were both, unluckily out:
I am very sorry you missed seeing M. d'Arblay that last—& to

781.   [1] In March 1795 CB loaned Molesworth Phillips £2,000 on a mortgage of
£3,000 on the latter's estate at Belcotton in county Louth. For this investment
CB was to earn £80 as an annual dividend. So infrequently did he receive this
interest that by the first week in January 1800 Phillips already owed him £160
and CB thought his initial investment lost. See the Berg letter of CB to CB Jr.
on 20 Dec. 1799; also iii, iv *passim*, especially L. 329 and n. 4.
   By 19 Nov. 1814, when the foreclosure proceedings were begun, CB Jr. agreed
to accept as full payment £1,700 'with interest on the said sum of £2,000 at four
per cent from 25 June 1814 making together the sums £1,754'. Phillips was also
to have paid the legal costs that amounted to £184. 4s. 7d. The legal action was
completed on 25 Mar. 1815 ('Registry of Deeds', Ireland, bk. 694, p. 439, no.
476713). For distribution of the proceeds, see n. 7.
   [2] M. d'A suggested that EBB and FBA 'propose to Mrs. Burney the 3d' share
in the 'Irish mortgage' that JB rejected for himself.

me most unhappy day[3]—He would have talked the matter over with you.[4] He has made a proposal to Mr. Hudson in person,[5] for which we wait the answer, previously to any further procedure, though he has made another[6] for Mr. William Lock in case of a negative from Mr. Hudson.

You will draw up a little agreement that your Aunt Burney & I will sign, in case any accident should happen to either of us before our intentions are fulfilled. |

The prop[erties ar]e to revert to you [*tear*]

That M. d'Arblay will advance £100 for the immediate prosecution of the affair, *if*, or *as* wanted.

This £100, with 5 p^r c^t to be what is first paid from its produce.

Any & all other costs to be paid next, to Mr. de Coucy & yourself, that may further be incurred.

£100, then, to be deducted from each share making in all £300, for my sister Mrs. Broome.

After which

The residue to be equally divided in 3 shares, for my sister Burney, myself, and *you*, with your sister included.[7]

[3] M. d'A left for Paris 'Nearly at Midnight' on 24 May 1814, having been with FBA only since 28 April. As CPB described the departure (Bodleian) on 4 June to Robert Finch: 'D'Arblay is in Paris again:—he was summoned unexpectedly,— quitted home in haste,—& I knew not even of his departure till some days after the time, at which he must have reached his old domicile.'
M. d'A in a letter (Berg), dated 23 May 1814, explains the reason for his haste. While visiting FBA, 'à moitié chemin j'ai rencontré M^r et M^{de} de Brancamp, qui m'ont dit qu'arrivés depuis hier soir, ils m'avoient ecrit sans trop savoir où m'adresser leur lettre, dans la quelle ils me mandaient que Mess. [*tear*] et de Luynes me donnaient l'avis de ne pas perdre une minute p^r me rendre à Paris, parce que M^r de L[uxembourg] qui m'a reservé la place [*tear*].'
[4] Although Martin Burney represented the d'Arblays in the legal negotiations for the sale of Camilla Cottage, he consulted frequently with the more experienced Sharon Turner, who sanctioned acceptance of Murray's final 'proposition'. See the letter (Osborn, undated) of JB to Turner; also L. 653 n. 5.
[5] See L. 646 n. 26.
[6] In his proposal M. d'A set the forced sale price at £1,000, apparently pointing out that Camilla Cottage, exclusive of his own fees as 'Architect, Designer, Surveyor', cost £1,300 in labour and materials when built in 1796-7. See *HFB*, p. 351.
[7] Each of the three beneficiaries of the 'Irish mortgage' received approximately £569. Each would contribute from that share, allowing CBFB to realize £300 from the foreclosure. Thus EBB and FBA each gained about £469, JB's two children each about £235. However, before the 'Irish money' was shared with CBFB and JB's two children, it was divided between FBA and EBB. Thus on 21 Oct. 1816, FBA received from CB Jr. a sum of £500 and on 27 October an additional £354. 17s. 6d. from CPB. (There is no evidence that CBFB agreed to the sisterly offer or accepted any money when the 'Irish mortgage' was foreclosed.)

782 | 63 Lower Sloane Street, 30 May 1814

To M. d'Arblay

A.L. (Berg), 30 May 1814
Double sheet 4to 4 pp. *pmks* 9 Juin 1814 E. 4 ⟨ ⟩ black seal
Addressed: À / Monsieur / Monsieur d'Arblay, / Rue de Miromenil, / 8 / fg St Honoré, / à Paris.
Edited by FBA, p. 1, *annotated*: II *See further*, Textual Notes.

63 *Lower* Sloane Street, Chelsea
Sunday afternoon
May 30. 1814.

What a kindness—what a delicious kindness my dearest dearest Ami! to have written to me so speedily! From a state of lowness indiscribable, my spirits immediately re-animated at the unexpected sight of the most loved of all hand writings. ⌈Yet I can never tell you half my vexation when first I recollected not having given the bank notes! I had refrained from opening the dossier in which I keep them, at the moment of your demand, because some one was in the room, &, afterwards, neither of us thought of them again. But when, too late, the thought came across me, my concern was inexpressible. I was comforted, however, when I saw your ingenious resources for borrowing, leaving your *montre*,[1] &c. I shall languish to hear how you go on, & where you make your first entrance, and above all, what will pass with M. le duc.⌉[2]

782. [1] See the obliterated passage in L. 779 in which M. d'A had apparently requested a loan of £10 from CB Jr. The reference to the 'montre' is lost in the obliterations.

[2] It is difficult to know to whom FBA refers: the duc de Duras, who could have supported M. d'A's desire to become 'Consul français', or the duc de Luxembourg, who wanted M. d'A as a commissioned officer in his company. That the latter's career was dependent on both men is indicated in his letter (Vincennes) to Louis XVIII, dated 9 June 1814 from Paris. But as early as 23 April, the duc de Duras—through his wife—expressed a desire that M. d'A should resume h. military career. In his letter to Louis XVIII, M. d'A noted:

'D'après l'assurance que je devais être porté sur la liste des candidats pour la place de Consul general en Angleterre, j'ai prié Monsieur le Duc de Duras de mettre sous les yeux de Votre Majesté ma demande de cette place, qu'il me serait peut être plus facile qu'à tout autre de bien faire, à cause des liaisons que mon mariage avec Miss Burney m'a mis à portée de former. Mais plusieurs des serviteurs les plus zelés de Votre Majesté pensent que je puis la servir plus utilement dans l'artillerie de la garde, et Monsieur le duc de Luxembourg veut bien me proposer pour commander celle qui doit être attachée à sa compagnie de gardes du Corps.'

Till the thrice happy period when we meet—for which already I am impatient as if already 21 months[3] had again separated us, I shall regularly begin my Letters upon the 3 subjects I think you will most anxiously wish to have discussed: i.e. Alexandre; Camilla cottage; & our Residuary Legateeship.

Of *Alexander* I have, as yet, no news whatsoever. ⌐I fear, therefore, the examination has been unauspicious. I will not send off this till after the arrival of the post to-morrow. Yet why rouse up false hopes? silence, in such a case, is speech. He has certainly either not tried, or failed.⌐[4]

For *Camilla Cottage*, Mr. William, ⌐it seems,⌐ has made a proposal—but he has desired it may be communicated through Mr. Murray, by Martin. ⌐We cannot much wonder *now*, though *at first* such a measure was so wrong. Nevertheless,⌐ to Amelia, who has written me word of this, I have still pleaded my own wish to receive the proposal *through HER*.[5] And she will do what she can to that purpose, I am sure, for she anxiously—& kindly desires me to call it, *to YOU, a final arrangement*, not,—since that term so disturbs you, a *LAWYER'S* proposal. She is full of sweetness & feeling, & writes me daily long letters upon the subject, with great candour & gentleness. But Mrs. Lock took very ill, indeed, your Letter to Mr. William.[6] Since my answer, however, to what she has said of it, she has written again with her old kindness, & her desire of restored Harmony all around.[7] | ⌐I have stopt, in the interval, Martin from going to Mr. Murray.⌐ I have frankly said that I still & invariably felt sure that Mr. Lock never meant to call in a Lawyer at the end, or he would have made *US* call in one at the beginning. Amelia says that, in the midst of her concern, she is

[3] From July 1812 to 28 Apr. 1814.

[4] AA took his examination in Classics at FBA's prompting but failed badly. For his contrition, see his letter (Berg) to FBA: 'i can Write but to or three Words my dear mamma . . . i am resolute to take a quite new change of conduct to you, and to do ⟨directly⟩ what you will please to bid me, whatever may be your orders, but let not these orders, though sacred as they are, seem orders, but admonition, that i, once more called by you your brother, may fulfill them, not only with respect, but with pleasure. ah! be! be, my dear mamma, from this day . . . a consoler in his unhappiness. . . . Restore then, restore once more your once so dearly bestowed favour to your happy / Alex. d'Arblay. / Alas—!—!—!!— —'

[5] In this proposal William Locke asked that assessors should evaluate Camilla Cottage and its site so that an equitable price might be established by their estimate. There was in fact nothing new about this proposal. See L. 741 n. 18. For Amelia Angerstein's letter, see L. 778 n. 4, specifically her letter dated 31 May, where she reiterated her interpretation of 'a *LAWYER*'s proposal'.

[6] See L. 778 n. 2.   [7] See L. 778 n. 5.

much gratified at the *kind justice* which you do to the feelings & friendship of her husband, which are invariable.[8]

⌐I long to see what is William's new proposal. But my letter to demand it sans M. Murray is not yet finished. This must take place.

Our newspapers speak of a French Gentleman who dropt his despatches into the sea by orders.[9] I hope you do not know him?—⌐

Now to our *Residuary Legateeship*.

⌐I have taken courage, this very morning, *May 31*st to address Charles very warmly, first by Letter, & next, as he called ere he received it, by speech, upon the subject of separating the Music from the Musical Books, & sending one to an auction, while the other went to the Museum, according to the Letter of the Will. He resisted very peremptorily, but I got the Will, & read him the article[10] so precisely that he was staggered, & after many representations of the ill effects of any such irregularity, & the evil upon himself to which it might lead, I at length induced him to consent to accompany me to the College, where Mr. White[11] was making out the Musical Catalogue, & luckily, while we were there, 4 *connoisseurs* came to entreat to view the Collection of Mr. White, who, also, begged our leave to consult them upon the arrangement of the articles—and this curiosity

---

[8] Apparently M. d'A expressed his eagerness to entertain John Angerstein while the latter was to be in Paris (L. 773) in late summer. According to Foreign Office records (PRO) Angerstein's passport, no. 1163, was issued on 19 August.

[9] From Dover, 24 May 1814, as reported in *The Times* (27 May):

'The following trait of boldness in an English sailor deserves to be made public:— A French Gentleman who was charged with despatches for the King of FRANCE, in getting down the ladder to go on board a passage vessel, let them drop into the water, and the tide running very strong, drove them under the arch of one of the sluices which communicates with the outer and inner harbour of Dover pier in the farther end of which they lodged, and, as the tide was rapidly flowing, it was impossible to get a boat under the arch to save them; at this moment one of the seamen on board stripped off his jacket and shirt; and . . . plunged into the basin, and entering the sluice at the hazard of his life, brought out the despatches in his mouth; had they remained a few minutes longer, they would have sunk and been totally lost.'

[10] For CB's desire that 'all [his] books, tracts, and treatises on the particular faculty of Music be sold to a . . . public library', see L. 773 n. 3. FBA won her point so that on 22 July 1814 CB Jr. wrote Mr. White (BM, Add. MS. 18191, f. 20): 'If a Person should come to you commissioned by Mr. Baber of the British Museum, to value the Books on the subject of Musick, on the part of the Trustees of that Institution, pray let him see them—as often as may be needful.' This collection was purchased *en bloc* by the Museum in 1815 for £253. See L. 773 n. 10.

[11] John White, 3 Prince's Street, Storey's Gate, Westminster (v, L. 498 n. 7).

& interest made so clear the advantage of an Auction, that my sturdy Brother, at length, though very reluctantly, gave way, & my friend Mr. White is to be himself the auctioneer.[12] The Prints alone of the 12 famous Musicians, which had already been sent to the Bookseller, are countermanded, & to be sold, as they ought to be, with the Music.[13] This conquest has given me much satisfaction. It is the Letter of the Will, & it is ˩ also evidently the method that will be most advantageous. The 4 connoisseurs speak of the restoration in the highest style.

The Picture of ⌐ Handel, also, is to go to the Musical sale—[14]

⌐But⌐—imagine my consternation, 2 days ago, when Sarah shewed me a Letter from Charles, to tell her that he could not pay her her Legacy till the middle of July!—because, he should not receive the money of the *Sale of the Books* sooner!!!!!

This drew me from my sad seclusion & ruminating retirement, which, since your departure, had till then possessed me: &, in ⌐yet⌐ warmer terms ⌐then for the vexation,⌐ I this

[12] The sale of items 'on the particular Faculty of Music' (L. 773 n. 3) was first advertised in *The Times* (13 July 1814): 'The late Dr. BURNEY'S MUSICAL LIBRARY.—To be SOLD by AUCTION, by Mr. WHITE, in the last week of this month (July), pursuant to his will, the valuable and very fine COLLECTION OF MUSIC, printed and MS. . . . in which are many scarce, curious, and excellent [unedited] compositions for voices . . . and for instruments . . . with many rare articles not to be found in any other collection. Catalogues are now preparing, and due notice will be given of the day of sale, viewing, &c.'

The sale did not take place as scheduled, and new advertisements, repeating the same information substantially, appeared in the *Morning Chronicle*, beginning on Saturday 6 August, and resuming on 8 August for daily publication until the 13th.

The sale began 8 August and was to last nine days. The manuscripts sold quickly and apparently during the sale the British Museum committed itself on the printed music. By 15 August, White's advertisement was drastically altered in the *Morning Chronicle*. What was now offered for sale were those items left over from the first week's auction and personal items left to various members of CB's family. 'Miscellaneous Books and Articles, including 136 vols. 12 mo. of the Words of Italian Operas from 1637 to 1783, and others from the Pinelli Library; curious Italian Sacred Dramas, with rare wood cuts, 1550 to 1583, &c., Musical Tracts, Books on Dancing 1581, &c. an ancient MS Catalogue of Musicians, 180 engraved Music Plates, a Capital grand piano-forte with additional keys, having six octaves by Broadwood; a tenor by Banks; two violins by Merlin; a small silver prize harp, a fine original Portrait of Handel, by Wolfgang; a ditto of H. Purcell, by Closterman; a rare . . . Indian picture from the Collection of Governor Holwell; fine scarce Prints of Musicians and Performers, an excellent music table and chair, with machinery by Merlin. . . .'

[13] The prints were originally to be sold as part of CB's miscellaneous library in June 1814. They were, however, recalled and sold by John White during the week of 15 August.

[14] FBA refers to a half-length portrait of Handel, painted by Wolfgang at Hanover in 1710. The portrait did not sell quickly. According to an advertisement in the *London Gazetteer* (24 Aug. 1814), White intended to sell that day the portrait of Handel along with certain other remaining articles and books of CB.

morning addressed him. Charles, I said, I must now speak to the purpose, & with a firmness called upon by absolute Duty. Sarah, in losing her home,[15] ought to be the *FIRST* considered: & Hetty, you, & I, ought to consider her, with respect to this business, as under ou[r] protection: And, if you do not pay her in time for her to rece[ive] her Dividends, I shall hold them as a Debt to her from Esther [&] myself.' ⌐Much more, to the same purpose past, but I could procure no promise, though he seemed struck, & I cannot doubt that I have succeeded *au fond*.

'Next, I said, 'what is it you mean by paying the legacies from the sale? The sale is *ours, Esther's & mine*, & not amenable to any legacy.

'But if there is not money enough without?'

'I can make no such but! at the Bank there was £800—& at the Bankers, 900, & odd, & 126 in the house.—'

'But the debts?—'They do not call for £200—'

'But the funeral?'—'Not quite £100—'

'But the stamps, & the Taxes?—'

'All together, cannot amount to the whole of the money left.'

This he disputed, but could not prove. And, finally, I said 'I consider the money from the sale as the immediate right of Esther & myself, & shall expect it neither to go to the Debts nor the Legacies, nor to the Executors!—but to come straight to us.'⌐16 |

You will easily believe this was neither heard without surprise or reply; but I was steady, & courageous, & added: Resume again, my dear Charles, the candour & the kindness with which you have always behaved towards me till this distinction from my dear Father, which seems to have an alienating effect upon all the family.' He disavowed this strongly; but I continued: 'Expect from me,' I said, 'more exertion, now, in this business. Its result is of deep moment to my comfort & welfare: while I was passive, you called me asleep; when I gave my opinion, you called me troublesome:'—again he disavowed: he could not possibly, he cried, have called or

[15] SHB vacated the apartment in Chelsea College that she had shared with CB since 1807 and rented a smaller, less costly one. The original apartment was designed for the Second Chaplain's use although in late 1814 it was renovated as wards for the pensioners (L. 794).

[16] At issue here is the provision of the will that CB's property be shared by FBA and EBB after the 'debts, Funeral Expences, and legacies' had been paid.

thought me troublesome, very kindly adding 'I should listen to *you* if you were NOT my sister, after a friendship such as our's; or I must stand alone!' We then affectionately embraced; ⌐yet nothing was fixed. I obtained no positive satisfaction. Nevertheless,⌐ I flatter myself the remonstrance, ⌐with my declaration I should follow it up,⌐ will prevent any mischief at the sale. Oh that you were here! ⌐It will certainly have to take place, in *June*,¹⁷ yet has never been advertised, much as I have urged it! I think, sometimes, it is very well, but I gather no positive intelligence. This is all, up to the moment, I have to tell you. I am most impatient for news of you—

adieu mon ami, mon bien cher ami, adieu.⌐

⌐No news from poor Alex.—Pray remember me in the tenderest manner to la Psse. d'Henin & to Mᵉ de Maisonneuve —et à toutes ces dames who have the goodness to think of me, Alas! not to name Mᵉ de Tessé! I rejoice in the appointment of M. Vic. as Govr. des invalides. Mr. Burney goes on amending —& wishes M. & Mᵉ joy—

adieu—adieu⌐

783
To James Burney

63 Lower Sloane Street,
[31 May 1814]

A.L.S. (PML, Autog. Cor. bound), *n.d.*
Double sheet 8vo 1 p. trimmed *pmks* [T.P.] P./U. / Chelsea EO 31 MY 1814 black seal
Addressed: Captain Burney, / James Street, / Westminster. / 26
Postdated in pencil, p. 1: May 31 · 1814

With '*PERFECT CORDIALITY*'¹

My always dear James — —
Your doubts have caused me unspeakable disturbance & surprise: but I have been patient, for I was sure that your

¹⁷ CB's non-musical books were sold by auction between 9 and 16 June 1814.
783. ¹ FBA's response to JB's letter (now missing) in which he avowed his feeling of 'perfect cordiality' toward her. The exchange of letters indicates at least a truce in the hostility between brother and sister precipitated by CB's will (see L. 785). However, JB refused to honour his promise to act as a trustee for the d'Arblays when they were abroad. See Ll. 773, 807.

reflexions with a fair retrospection of the whole of my sisterly life, would do me justice in your honest heart—which no one breathing values more kindly than

Your affectionate sister
F.B. d'Arblay.

I hope we shall meet very soon. I will drink tea at your house as soon as my young Beau arrives to give me *le bras* home.

My love round your breakfast table.

63. Lower Sloane Street,
Chelsea.

784 [63 Lower Sloane Street, May 1814]

To Martin Charles Burney

A.L.S. (PML, Autog. Cor. bound), *n.d.*
Single sheet large 8vo 1 p.
Addressed: Martin Burney Esqr

My dear Martin will, I feel sure, pardon my sincerity that I grieve not to put this in the hands of my dear Brother, for his own use, or at least, destination*ing*, & decision—but I have not the opportunity to discuss it in public—Do, therefore, what you can yourself with my very dear Brother for me—

Should that, unfortunately, be nothing, you must beg his *digne fils* to relieve, me at least, from a burthen to my CONSCIENCE which could not weigh upon it without doing me a serious injury.

At all events, *I* will see the enclosed no more![1] I solemnly Vow I have done with it for-ever! And neither remonstrance nor persuasion shall EVER induce me to take back what I would far rather wish threefold further to send forth. So help me God! signs

Your affec^te Aunt, FB d'Arblay—

---

784. [1] The agreement in which FBA and EBB made over a third share of the 'Irish mortgage' to Martin Charles Burney and his sister Sarah. See L. 781.

785   [63 Lower Sloane Street,
                                              1 June 1814]
To Mrs. Broome

A.L.S. (Barrett, Eg. 3693, ff. 90–91b), *n.d.*
Double sheet 8vo   4 pp.   *pmks*   P.P.P.   1 JU 1814   black seal
Addressed: Mrs. Broome, / Hill Street, / Richmond. —
Endorsed by CBFB: Sister d'arblay / 1814
Docketed, p. 1: 1814

So busy—so occupied, as well as so sad have I been since I
lost my best of all best of Friends, that I have not been able to
settle any time for seeing my dearest Charlotte with any peace
or comfort. And even now I must postpone it till next week, as
I never make any positive engagement when the R. F. are in
town.[1]

Let me therefore, name Tuesday the 7th—or Monday the 6th
and expect you on one of those two days, unless you write to the
contrary.

My uncertainty of the arrival of Alexander—who never writes
any thing to the purpose in the shape of business, makes me
still ignorant when he will come: but if he should not be here,
it will be so true a delight to Me to keep my dearest Charlotte,
that I entreat her to leave word at Richmond that she must not
be expected after 9 o'clock. ǀ

Imagine how I have been mortified, after my pressing offer
to my other Charlotte, to find 1st that Rapin is Charles's,[2] &
next that Metastasio is Sarah's,[3] & last that Molière is incomplete!—The Booksellers, however, are trying to make it perfect.[4]
If they fail, she shall chuse something from the Catalogue.

785. [1] According to *The Times* (30 May 1814): 'The QUEEN and PRINCESSES after
being present at the Eton Montem to-morrow, will come to town in the evening.'
Because of the sudden illness of Princess Elizabeth, the Queen and her daughters
delayed their journey to London by a day, arriving in the city on 1 June at noon.
They returned to Windsor on Friday, 3 June (*The Times*, 1, 4 June), for the
monthly report on the King's health.
    [2] See 774 n. 1.
    [3] Since SHB and Frances Raper were to divide 'the French books in the Glass
Book Case . . . marked E', SHB probably chose *Didon abandonnée*; traduite de
l'Italien . . . par . . . M. Grignon. Together with an extract from *Memoirs of the
Life and Writings of . . . Metastasio*: by C. Burney . . . 2nd ed. (1810?).
    [4] The set of Molière was probably completed and given to CFBt since an
incomplete set was never sold with CB's other books.

our excursion proved utterly impossible, by the immensity of avocations that filled up the time of M. d'A. But he took the 3 Letters that arrived very kindly—

James, at length, thank God! is come to his senses. He has written me a very kind & cordial Note, & I am expecting a visit from him every hour. Poor James! where might he hope for faith in friendship if he doubted mine? But he *could not* doubt it: the bitterness of his feelings wanted some vent, & I, unfortunately, ˡ came most easily in his way, from my own restless anxiety to soothe or soften his chagrin. Hetty & Charles, who left him to himself, were soonest received into his returning favour. He could not misinterpret their efforts, for they made none. It will be a lesson to me in future, with him; though one that so opposes my real & warm affection, & fixed esteem for his person & character & disinterested integrity, that I hope I shall be spared putting it into practice. The distinction, however, shewn me by my dearest Father has, as yet, brought me as much pain, as his loss has affliction. It seems to have cast a kind of general though undefinable cloud over the Family Harmony. Yet who had ever a right to make a Will by his Choice, if HE who himself inherited NOTHING; whose whole possessions were the result of his labours & his talents, might not do it?⁵ None of his family were in distress; & he *believed* 3 of them to be in affluence.⁶

I defer speaking of our scheme till we meet [.If] ˡ it could be better worth offering, how much happier I should be in the proposal!—& yet, were it more considerable, your own too

---

⁵ FBA concentrated on the image of CB as the self-made man. At the conclusion of the 'Preface' to the *Memoirs of Doctor Burney* she promises to trace 'the progress of a nearly abandoned Child, from a small village of Shropshire, to a Man allowed throughout Europe to have risen to the head of his profession; and thence, setting his profession aside, to have been elevated to an intellectual rank in society, as a Man of Letters—

"Though not First, in the very first line"

with most of the eminent men of his day,—Dr. Johnson and Mr. Burke, soaring above any cotemporary mark, always, like Senior Wranglers, excepted.'

⁶ FBA tried to justify CB's bequests of £200 each to CB Jr., CBFB, and JB. That she was, nevertheless, aware of their inequity is indicated by her desire to have JB and CBFB share in the proceeds of the 'Irish mortgage'. Of CB's three children who received only a token inheritance, CB Jr. was the most affluent. Needing no financial aid, he was remembered in other ways in the will. CB also explained his behaviour toward CBFB (see L. 773 n. 8). For JB, on half-salary from the Navy, there was no explanation. Consequently, JB felt he was being punished for his former intimacy with SHB and for political sympathies that CB felt had ruined his son's career. See also L. 769 n. 6.

nice scruples might stand in its way. It hangs upon the Irish Mortgage, & therefore, alas, will not be forth coming for 15 Months,[7] according to Charles, or even 2 years, according to James: but neither of them doubt its security.[8] The Book Sales we immediately appropriate to ourselves, for these are not our Residuary lot, but a *Legacy* [re]ally mentioned as such.[9]

[Adi]eu, my dearest Charlotte—for-ever yours is

F B d'A [1]

[Marginal writing]

How I am grieved to hear you talk of a Cough! Get rid of it, dearest Charlotte, with all care & speed.

You would not catch Cold here—the change w[d] do you good, for this is airy & wholesome

I am glad M. d'A. saw Mr. Barrett, whom he calls '*un jeune homme d'un très jolie tournure*'. He was very sincerely sorry he could not get to Richmond.

Where is my dear Miss Baker? Still at Brighton?

I hope dear Ralph is well?

786   63 Lower Sloane Street,
                                        1 June 1814
To Charlotte Beckedorff

A.L.S. (?), 1 June 1814
Double sheet 8vo   1 p.

From the Francis Edwards Catalogue, number 915 (1968)

D'ARBLAY (Frances, Mme. *Fanny Burney*) AUTOGRAPH LETTER SIGNED, 1 *page*, 8vo 63 *Lower Sloane Street, Chelsea* 1 *June*, 1814, to Madame Benckendorf [*sic*], requesting a position 'in some corner whence I may have a view of the Emperor of Russia' (Alexander I) on the following day, saying that only thus will she get a view of 'the illustrious Pacificator' since she goes 'no where at present in public' etc.,[1] *silked on verso*   £45

---

[7] See L. 781 n. 1.   [8] See L. 781 n. 7.
[9] This is a restatement of the position held by FBA during her argument with CB Jr. (L. 782 n. 16).
786. [1] Miss Beckedorff replied (Berg) to FBA's request. 'The Emperor is coming

787   [63 Lower Sloane Street,
                                        post 2 June 1814][1]
To Charles Burney

A.L.S. (Osborn), *n.d.*
Double sheet 8vo   4 pp.
Addressed: Rev^d Dr Burney, / Rectory House, / Deptford.

Dearest Carlos,
Your going to the Drawing room fills me [with] satisfaction
& surprise. I had no idea you felt up to such an undertaking.
1000 thanks for the note to ⟨Leigh⟩.[2]
Also for my £19:10—which, (unluckily) is but too—apropos.
But how I am grieved at that cruel shake you must have
had!—Poor—poor Rosette! When will she be well enough to
calm & sooth instead of shattering you?—
The adv^t has never appeared in THE TIMES, which was my
dear Father's own paper, & is that of almost all his Friends.[3]
This I have added to your note.
I can add nothing else till I enquire what Books will do for
Charlotte Barret—Marianne—Clement[4]—Mr Graham[5] & Mr.

to the Queens house at half past five o'*Clock*. If you will have the goodness to come
to our room before that time, you will have an opportunity to see His Majesty.'
For FBA's reaction to the Queen's reception, see L. 790 and Diary Entry, 8 June.

787. [1] The dating of this letter depends on the occasion of the Queen's Drawing
Room, 2 June 1814.
    [2] CB Jr. requested George Leigh, bookseller and auctioneer (Appendix V)
to settle final details for the sale 'of the Miscellaneous Library of the late Charles
Burney' conducted by Leigh and Sotheby between 9 and 16 June 1814.
    [3] In L. 782 FBA first expressed her concern over the failure of Leigh and
Sotheby to advertise the impending sale of CB's 'Miscellaneous Library'. But the
Morning Chronicle on Thursday, 2 June carried the following: 'By Leigh and Sotheby,
Booksellers, at their House, No. 145, Strand, opposite Catherine-street, on Thursday next, and eight following days (Sunday excepted), at 12. The Miscellaneous
Library of the late Chas. Burney. . . .' This advertisement was repeated on Saturday, 4 June, and Tuesday, 7 June 1814.
    [4] The Francis children were not mentioned in CB's will on the assumption that
they had been well endowed by their late father. During their minority, they were
allowed £100 annually (L. 773 n. 8), and they received large sums of money upon
their coming of age—the two daughters each receiving £5,000 and the son £10,000.
See the letter (JRL) of MF to Mrs. Piozzi, dated 23 Aug. 1813.
    Because the will stipulated that CB's miscellaneous books were the property of
FBA and EBB, the two sisters decided that certain of these should be presented
to the Francis children as a token of their grandfather's regard.
    [5] See L. 649 n. 2.

354

Townshend.[6] But as you have prepared him for that little list from us, I will send it in time. ┃

I am not certain of the authors name of the history of France that I miss—but it began with a V. & was in 20 or 30 volumes, or more, always in an under Cupboard.[7] *Mezeray's* I have found, according to your hint.[8] The missing the Catalogue is quite pernicious, it would so help memory.

The mistake about the Residu for Legacy, was *my own*. But Hetty had already set me right.[9]

I thank you for your instructions how to get the Books set aside that are meant for Charlotte, &c. ┃

I am extremely glad indeed you went to Court, & was seen by my poor tormented Royal Mistress—What a dreadful business is brewing & fermenting, to *keep off* peace just as it arrives![10]

I have not yet heard from Paris.

Adieu, dearest Charles—This last note is such as I *patronize*, & always expected—it is open, kind, candid, & such as *encourages*, not *intimidates*, our addresses to our bequeathed adviser & aid.

So God bless you, dearest Carlucci,

Yours ever
FBd'A

I should like, now, to have the Prints all sent us back, for a [*tear*] ┃ & then sell them by Mr. White.[11]

---

[6] The second son of George (1723/4–1807), 1st Marquess Townshend (1787), John Townshend (1757–1833), was, like his father, a friend of CB and served as a pall-bearer at the funeral on 20 Apr. 1814. He was an M.P., successively, for Cambridge University, Westminster, and Knaresborough.

[7] In the *Sale Catalogue* Item No. 967 was 'Laureau, Velly, Villaret, et Garnier Histoire de France, 32 tom.'—1761, 89. The work was sold on 14 June, the fifth day of the sale, for one guinea.

[8] Item No. 1179 of the *Sale Catalogue* is 'Mezeray abregé de l'Histoire de France, 8 tom (1674)'; i.e. Eudes de Mézeray (François), *Abregé chronologique ou extraict de l'histoire de France* (6 tom., Amsterdam, 1673, 1674). To which had been added two additional volumes (Amsterdam, 1720) on the Reign of Louis XIII and of Louis XIV (by H. P. de Limiers). [9] See L. 782 n. 16.

[10] The allied armies entered Paris on 31 Mar. 1814; fighting elsewhere in France generally ended by mid-April. On 20 April Napoleon left for his 16-day journey to Elba and the Bourbon restoration was under way. But among the allied powers a mutual suspicion of aims so hampered peace negotiations with France that the First Treaty of Paris was not signed until 30 May. Despite this accomplishment, bickering among the Allies only increased so that the Treaty of London (signed on 29 June 1814) prohibited the convening of the Congress until they had reached agreement among themselves. It was not until November 1814 that the Congress officially opened, although its various committees began to meet in September.

[11] For White's advertisement and sale of the prints, see L. 782 n. 12.

or, if that does not please you, sent back again to M^{ssrs} Leigh—but I should gladly take a list, & make an examination by my own papers which I shall search to-morrow.

Can you not order this, as they are not advertised in the Catalogue?[12]

It will surely be better, if possible, to reserve them for Mr. White, as they will still be in time for *HIS* Catalogue. But *YOU* only can give this order now.

I hope you are not really ill?[13]

shattered is full enough.

788   63 Lower Sloane Street,
                                          3 June [1814]
To Mrs. Waddington

A.L.S. (Berg), 3 June
Double sheet 4to   4 pp.   *pmks*   T.P.P.U.   7 JU 1814   7 JU .814
black seal
   Addressed: Mrs. Waddington, / Calwich, / Ashbourne / Derbyshire.
   Also L., incomplete copy by CFBt (Diary MSS. viii not numbered, Berg),
3 June 1814   Single sheet 4to   2 pp.

My kind Mary will not have been angry, I am sure, at my silence, many as are, & continually accumulating the interesting motives to break it. But the arrival of my best Friend, though it gave a peace to my mind from the most laborious suffering, gave me not TIME! on the contrary, it swallowed up every moment in essential occupation, that was not devoted to the solace of a meeting that ended such dread anxiety.—But alas—he is already gone! he came with such a precipitance, from an unfortunate mistake, which led him to believe some evil had befallen either myself or Alexander, that he left his affairs in an undetermined situation, that made him liable to a recall—which has now happened, & abruptly separated us. My own affairs are so circumstanced, by my being left residuary

---

[12] 'A Catalogue of the Miscellaneous Library of the late Charles Burney, Doctor of Music, and Fellow of the Royal Society; Removed from his Apartments in Chelsea College.'
[13] See L. 792 n. 2.

Legatee, with my sister Burney, that I am necessarily stationary. What our ultimate destiny will be is all in the dark. I have told you, I believe, our application for a new place, of *Consul Général français en Angleterre*? This is yet unanswered: or, at least, HERE unknown: but my first or 2^d Letter from Paris may bring me the negative I expect. As yet, I have only heard from Calais:[1] That, however, is the date to ME the most important.

The communications concerning Mr. G[reene]—are tremendous. They open my Eyes to the clue to his *fate*, Forgery[2]— which I had not conceived; but not to his *character*. I mean not as to its moral failures; of those I have heard a terrible history that renders the ultimate act venial; but as to its intellectual faculties. Was he weak enough to think Forgery ever lastingly prosperous? or did he love Life so well as │ to cling to it even day by day, though sure it might be forfeited even hour by hour? That he did not run away;—that all was not always ready for his departure, remains yet more astonishing than all the rest. There must have been a mixture not only of good & bad qualities in the heart, but of feeble with shewy *compartments* in the head.

How happy am I he had sufficient self-command not to distress you by any last appeal, or address!—

His plea of friendship with You; his kindness in conveying English Letters; his confidential openness; his inexhaustible good humour & gaiety; & his unremitting restlessness to oblige, worked him an entry into our little dwelling, where he became

---

788. ¹ See L. 780.

² FBA may have used 'Forgery' to connote 'deception' as well as to mean (2 Geo. II. c. 25) a felony affecting 'any forged deed, will, bond, writing obligatory, bill of exchange, promissory note, indorsement or assignment thereof, or any acquittance or receipt for money or goods with intention to defraud any person'. In 1802 James Greene, despite his wealth, contracted various debts. Rather than fulfil his financial obligations and to avoid his creditors, he fled to Paris. Toward the end of 1802 he was subpoenaed to testify personally in a Chancery lawsuit (*Frere* v. *Greene*) against two illegitimate children of Anne Brigstocke Greene and an unnamed man; in short, to give evidence against his wife as an adulteress. Having so testified, he was arrested 'upon process issuing out of the Court of Exchequer at the suit of Thos Hill Esqr & others'. Within the first two months of 1803, then, James Greene was involved in at least two separate law cases (*Thomas Hill & others* v. *Greene*; *Charles Geering* v. *Greene*) in which he was charged with 'contriving and fraudulently intending craftily and subtilly to deceive and defraud' his creditors. His arrest, however, was illegal since he had been granted immunity to testify in Chancery. Once released, he returned to Paris, his debts unpaid. In 1814 Mrs. Waddington unlocked the drawers of his desk to find briefs and documents whose contents she communicated to FBA. See Monmouth Misc. MSS. 308 (C.R.O., Newport, Monmouthshire).

an intimate acquaintance, and—had he been less forward to make the claim before time or circumstance had earned it— would have become, a welcome Friend. But in treating himself as such too soon, he made us draw back doubtfully, & confine both our reception & opinion of him to that of a merely enter-taining anecdote-monger.[3]

The name of *Bridgestock* in one of the Letters,[4] leads me to mention a very odd circumstance. A French lady begged me to bring over a paper for her maid servant, an English woman,[5] who was married in France. As I brought no sealed Letters, this paper is open; but it has so strange a direction, I have never been able to forward it. in it, however, the Writer says, to her Mother, a Mrs. Mary Lawrence,[6] 'Pray tell Mr. Bridgestock[7] that Mr. Owen[8] is the ∣ *finest* boy that ever was seen; but poor Mrs. Green is dead.[9] *Mr. Green* & the children are well. &c— Is not this odd? Where does *Mr. Bridgestock* live?[10] something is said, in the same paper, of *Wooten Fair*—or Feast.

[3] For a biographical account of James Greene and his first meeting with FBA, see v, Ll. 517 n. 1; 532 n. 2.

[4] One of the documents in Greene's desk, headed 'Brigstock—ag^t—Greene', detailed his relationship with his wife: 'Soon after the date of the Articles of Separation the Deft advanced to Mrs Greene thro the hands of her Trustees the Amount of £1500 which he intended as Gifts but they were paid to her Trustees *generally* for her Use—Since that Time the deft has remitted to Mrs G. the quarterly Payments of that [Annuity] as they became due till on Consequence of his having become insolvent they were stopped—Mrs Greene has been living in a State of Adultery with another Man almost ever since her separation from her husband the deft who is now suing for a Divorce in the eccles^l Court' (dated 11 June 1803).

[5] The English woman was born Margaret Lawrence (1781–*post* 1812).

[6] The wife of John Lawrence (*fl.* 1812), who was overseer of the poor in Llandyg-wydd parish and farmed approximately 85 acres of land (Pentregewine) belonging to the Brigstocke family. See 'Baptisms and Burials, 1803–12, in Llandygwydd Parish' (St. Tygwydd Church).

[7] William Owen Brigstocke (*c.* 1761–1831), high sheriff of Cardigan (appointed for 1794), was Anne Greene's oldest brother and her trustee after she and James Greene were separated.

[8] According to 'Frere ag^t Greene' in the Court of Chancery (Dec. 1802) Owen Brigstocke Greene was an illegitimate child of Anne Greene. He was named in the brief by his half-sister Mary Anne Frere and her husband Edward so that the child would be excluded from legal inheritance. In his will drafted years later James Greene stated: 'I think it right solemnly to declare that no child which my late wife Mrs. Greene has borne since her separation from me can be mine as will be seen in my Examination before Commissioners of the Court of Chancery every word in that Examination is strictly true as I hope for Eternal Salvation' (for the identification of his will, see L. 751 n. 1).

[9] Anne Greene died probably in France in 1810, aged 48. She had deserted her husband about 1800 to live in Paris with Thomas Gunter Browne (1756–1834), described as 'a sensible shrewd man to all appearance'. Browne established per-manent residence in France after having retired from the British army on half-pay in 1783. See Greatheed, p. 111.

[10] William Owen Brigstocke lived on an estate called Blaenpant in the parish

How I long for better news of sweet Emily!—And how shall I interest your feelings, so tender, so alive upon even the smallest occasions in which those you love are concerned, when I tell you that, at this instant, I am wholly ignorant even of where I shall fix my residence! Whether in Paris, or London,— at Montpellier, or at Bath,—or upon the banks of the Loire, or at the foot of a welsh mountain! — — —

Were M. d'Arblay younger, or less worn with revolutionary events, & the dreadful fatigues, mental & bodily, of the last 12 months, there could be no doubt of our destiny, for his character, services, fidelity, & friends would all combine to restore him to his military rank; which his constant refusal to serve the last Dynasty had made him preferably sink into becoming a *Chef de Bureau*: but, after 20 years lying by, I cannot wish to see him re-enter a military career, at 60 years of age, though still young in all his faculties & his feelings, & his capacity, in private life, of being as useful to others as to himself. There is a time, however, when the poor machine, though still perfect in a calm, is unequal to a storm. Private life, then, should be sought, while it yet may be enjoyed. M. d'Arblay has resources for retirement the most delightful both for himself & his friends. I cannot, therefore, wish for the short blaze of a transient re-instatement, that must risk his strength & health, or become soon necessarily null. ˡ

I earnestly, therefore, hope that a domestic, literary, & rural lot will be his choice. He obeys, however, for the moment, a call the most honourable, made to him by the Duc de Luxembourg, who is just nominated Capitaine du Corps de Garde.ˡˡ

of Llandygwydd, Cardiganshire (grid reference SN 22 254444). The house, made of gray Pembrokeshire stone and said to contain fifty-two rooms, still stands on grounds of approximately 400 acres overlooking the Tivey Valley. In addition to Blaenpant, William Owen Brigstocke owned twenty-nine farms, covering 2,500 acres in the same parish (i.e. half of all the privately owned land in Llandygwydd).

ˡˡ The military post given to the duc de Luxembourg in May 1814 was part of a larger plan described by Vitrolles (ii. 24): 'Le général Beurnonville, que Sa Majesté avait chargé de dresser le projet concernant la formation de sa maison militaire, le présenta au Roi dans les séances suivantes du conseil privé. Ce plan fut discuté et particulièrement éclairé par monseigneur le duc de Berry. Il en résulta le rétablissement des anciennes compagnies de la maison du Roi. Celles des gardes du corps furent portées à six compagnies au lieu de quatre. Les premières étaient commandées par les titulaires anciens et portaient leur nom: le duc d'Havré-Croï, le duc de Grammont, le prince de Poix (Noailles) et le duc de Luxembourg (Montmorency). Le Roi avait donné les deux autres au maréchal Berthier, prince de Wagram, et au maréchal Marmont, duc de Raguse.' (For the other units that completed the 'maison militaire', see Vitrolles, ii. 24–5.)

He set out for Paris the 25th What resolution will there be formed, Heaven knows.

I have now so many of your dispatches, & all, in their several ways, so interesting, or amusing, or explanatory, that I know not with which to begin for returning. I have no way to send to Mrs. Hall[12] at this moment, but by post. I live recluse RE-CLUSE—though I have promised myself to a *private VERY* snug breakfast at Lady Crew's Brompton Cottage next week, to meet L[d] & L[y] Lansdowne[13] on their return from Paris, whence they bring the newest intelligence of the state of parties & affairs, to me, at this moment, so critically interesting. How deeply should I have been some time ago, & shall I be, possibly, some time hence, pleased by what you have written of The Wanderer;[14]—but it seems to me now a something foreign, so entirely has the loss of my dearest Father, & the subsequent danger—return—& departure of my FIRST Friend, engrossed all my faculties. I have lost sight of all my solicitude upon the subject, & know nothing of how it fares, either for censure or partiality. I am saved—but not by happiness!—much fidget & anxiety, for I think of it so little as never to make any enquiry. I shall soon have my *Sauvage* for his long vacation. That I forget not!

How could any one send *YOU* that odious Letter? And was *SHE* the principal favourite?—It is not to *HENRY* but *Merrik*, that my friend Sophia is married.[15] How can you let any one

[12] Charlotte Crawshay (*c.* 1772–*post* 1817), of Cyfartha, Glamorganshire, married Benjamin Hall (L. 751 n. 5) in 1801.

[13] See L. 791 n. 6. The Lansdownes received their passport on 28 Apr. 1814 and left shortly after for Paris to attend the coronation of Louis XVIII.

[14] Mrs. Waddington enjoyed sending on to FBA favourable comments about *The Wanderer* (L. 744 n. 1). These comments were made by others, for Mrs. Waddington herself did not read the novel until sometime late in 1818 or thereafter (L. 753 n. 9).

[15] Whether the Thrale daughters married for 'establishments' is difficult to determine. In a letter (JRL) of MF to Mrs. Piozzi, dated 10 June 1810, reference was made to Archdeacon Cambridge, who 'Says he never can recover his astonishment at *Lady Keith*, because she might have been a Peeress, if she had chosen it; when she was young. Swarms of swains used to follow [the Thrale girls, particularly Susan, "who was the handsomest *then*"] . . . till being always *finally* rejected, they ceased to persecute & found it was only *lost time.*'

Almost three years earlier Mrs. Piozzi took a more cynical attitude toward the marital ambition and success of Sophia and Queeney. Writing to the Revd. Leonard Chappelow (1744–1820) on 1 Dec. 1807 (JRL), Mrs. Piozzi commented: 'I am glad the eldest marries my Lord Keith—if *any* body is safe, they are Safe that anchor under Protection of a brave British Admiral. Sophia seems to like her Husband too . . . but there are so many Brothers I never know which is which.'

persuade you *the Miss Thrales* would marry for establishments?
They were as much above it in their fortunes & consideration
as in their minds & sentiments. Lady Keith is just going—or
gone to Bordeaux.

Adieu, dearest Mary! embrace your loves for me—& bid
them return the embrassade for yʳ faithful

F B d'A

June 3ᵈ—Ah, my [Mary] at this moment of making up my
⟨paper⟩ I receive the catalogue of my beloved Father's *Books*
for sale!— |

All *June* I *believe* myself certainly here—of *July* I know nothing
whatsoever—but how happy, how very happy shall I be if you
can accomplish that hint of London while I am yet so near it!—
I am lodged as near to the lost college as I can, for business in it!
63, Lower Sloane Street.

789   [63 Lower Sloane Street,
                                            7 June 1814]

To James Burney

A.L.S. (PML, Autog. Cor. bound), *n.d.*
Double sheet 8vo   trimmed   1 p.   *pmk* 7 JU 1814   wafer
Addressed: Captain Burney, / James Street, / Westminster. / 26
Postdated in pencil, p. 1 : June 7 1814

I would gladly have adopted, provisionally, the *Beau* & the
Bras offered me for yesterday, had not there been too much
damp in the air to make my using them prudent. I must wholly
shun all Evening walks till the sun resumes its right station, &
knows better what is expected from it in the month of June.

I am much obliged to dear Sally & her kind Mama for
their intentions. I have *pending* engagements, hanging not only
upon the weather but circumstances, for every morning till
Friday;[1] but Rain, or Illness, shall alone, then, prevent my

789. [1] FBA made no appointment while the Royal Family was in London. Intending to arrive at Buckingham House on Tuesday 7 June, the Queen and the
Princesses Augusta and Mary did not come until the next day to participate in
several of the celebrations for the Russian Emperor and the Prussian King. The
Queen and the Princesses returned to Windsor on Friday 10 June. For FBA's
attendance at one of these celebrations, see L. 790 and Diary Entry, 8 June.

hob nobing in a dish of tea with my dear Brother and all his—²

FB d'A.

I cannot dine out at Present.

If this were better worth 2ᵈ I should have let *Sally* pay for it.

790   63 Lower Sloane Street,
                                         9–10 June 1814
To M. d'Arblay

A.L.S. (Berg and Diary MSS. vii. 6004–[07]), 9–10 June 1814
Double sheet 4to 4 pp. *pmks* T. 5ᴱ 18 Juin 1814 black seal
The right and lower folds were cut by CFBt from the second leaf and pasted as P³, P⁴, and P⁵ to L. 798. *See* Textual Notes.
Addressed: À Monsieur / Monsieur d'Arblay, / Rue de Miromenil, / fᵍ St. Honoré, / Nᵒ 8 / a Paris.
Edited by FBA, p. 1, *annotated*: 12   On the Princess Charlotte—& Emperor of Russia
Docketed in unknown hand, p. 4: June 18.

63 LOWER Sloan Street, Chelsea.
Thursday, June 9ᵗʰ 1814.

Not a line yet from Paris!—how does the eternal post, always coming, yet never bringing what I wish, disappoint me!—Had the news from Calais been as slow of passage, I know not how I could have borne such painful inquietude. ⌜Sometimes I fear some mistake in the address to Lady K[eith]. Cannot you have said *Upper*, instead of *Lower* Sloane street, which occasioned her to drive from one end to the other of the street, in vain. Mᵈᵉ Braamcamp¹ sends me word she has done the same thing, & I am going to appoint her to my little Parlour in *LOWER* Sloane Street, Chelsea, 63,⌝ And, besides all my first, closest, bosom motives, of impatient tenderness for news how you have borne your journey, & how you now are, I am languishing for intelli-

---

² On 10 June, FBA went to JB's house to drink tea and then, accompanied by him, to see the illuminations in honour of the peace and the visits of the foreign monarchs and dignitaries. For a lengthy and detailed description of these illuminations, see the *Morning Chronicle* (10 June 1814). See Diary Entry, p. 515.

790. ¹ She and her husband had arrived in London on 22 May. See L. 781 n. 3.

gence relative to the consulship. ⌐But you, also must require News. Let me tell you, therefore, what most presses. *Alex. cottage.* College.⌐

Our poor *Alexandre* failed wholly in the Examination²—& is quite disconsolate; but I try to spirit him up by hopes of *next term.* He has *Carte blanche* from me, to arrive when he will;³ but I have begged him to gather *des* ⌐*renseignmens*⌐ *how* to work, & *what* to study, for repairing this disgrace next term.⁴ I am far less eager for his arrival than I should otherwise be, from hearing he has returned to his remissness about the Chapel, & that he wastes his hours & faculties upon *chess.* This last rage, will open the door to the same temptation that has ruined his time & his progress during all his other vacations: & now, less than ever, when *here,* can I impede the meetings that lead to *that,* & to consequences so much more serious. I leave him, therefore, master to come, but without daring to urge his arrival, till he makes the Reform.

⌐With regard to the *College,* I have only vexatious subjects to mention. The sale of the Books *begins to Day.*⁵ And I had no intimation of its approach but a week ago!! There are but 2092 Books in the Catalogue, forming 4000 volumes! out of 20,000 volumes! Many volumes are missing, imperfect, & out of order. There will be 8 days sale. Alas! that you were here!—

Esther & I have both, of late, exerted ourselves with great spirit, upon every occasion &, at length, have obtained the payment of the legacies of James & those of Charlotte & Sarah take place to-day & perhaps, of *Blue,*⁶ & others. |

But, now to my most immediate embarassments: My Hostess,⁷ Fanny Raper, Mrs. Haggit,⁸ & Sarah have all inquired for a spare room for our store of Furniture: but on account of the Freight & size of the Drawers & the Wardrobe, no small garret in a small House will suffice, for the very stairs, in such, are so narrow that the Goods could not be mounted, without being

---

² See L. 740 n. 3.
³ AA arrived in Chelsea on 13 or 14 June. See L. 791 and Diary Entry, p. 515.
⁴ For AA's study habits during his summer holiday, see L. 800 and n. 1; for his contrition and promise of reform, see L. 782 n. 4.
⁵ See L. 787 n. 12.
⁶ Elizabeth Warren Burney, called 'Blue', received £100 as a bequest from CB.
⁷ See n. 10, below.
⁸ Sarah Haggitt, now about 52, was the wife of the Chaplain of Chelsea Hospital. See i, L. 21 n. 18.

taken to pieces or apart.[9] Yet a room down stairs is unobtainable, because 3 times the price. Unless, therefore, we fix in *London*, every one says we had best part with the whole, not, like poor eager Hetty, to a shabby cheating village appraiser, but at a fair Auction in town.

For — — if we do not fix in London, we shall not only have some months to pay, for the hire of any empty apartment, but the packing & journeying of the goods to Bath or elsewhere & that with the risk of finding half of them, at least, broken & battered by the Carriage, so as to be worth little or nothing on arriving. Hand Cartage is so enormously dear that nobody here uses it but for *new* or *fine* & valuable Furniture.

Your plans of my taking apartments here is not cheaper, & is full of other expenses that, unless we finish here, will be useless. I have not one article that will do for a drawing room, neither Chairs, Tables, looking Glasses, Carpets, Grates, pokers & Tongs, Fenders, &c, &c — — all I possess are Bedroom Goods, & even there, I must purchase Beds, Chairs, & Tables. ALL these, if in London we fix, may be bought at once, though by *me*, not, I fear, to your pleasure as you will want things finer than I shall, & not be aware, till too late, of the difference which indulgence of taste makes in the expense. But if we remove from London, *all* will be to be sold, or cost as much by Carriage, & accidental destruction, to buy new wherever we settle ourselves. And indeed, mon cher ami, unless you return very ǀ quickly, which God grant!—what I have intimated when Alex ought to make *you*, as well as myself, wish him where he may be urged to study, not allured to idleness & dangerous amusements.

With regard to the melancholy article which cost us both so much pain on the night of our separation—I have vainly sought to dispose of it through Mrs. Hirst,[10] or otherwise, at such a price as meets your expectations; but I forced myself to consult with Mr. White, the musical auctioneer, who is making a Catalogue of all the music at the College. He told me it seems

---

[9] FBA is concerned with the storage and/or disposition of her share of CB's furniture to be acquired when the apartment at Chelsea College would become vacant during the week of 20 June.
[10] Hannah Hirst (d. 1845), the landlady of 63 Lower Sloane Street. See the 'Poor Rate Book', Midsummer 1813, in the archives of the Old Town Hall, Chelsea. The 'melancholy article' was a violin made by Merlin. Since EBB also inherited one, White's advertisement in the *Morning Chronicle* (15 Aug.) implied that two such violins were for sale.

a valuable commodity, & that he would undertake to sell it for me, after the music auction. This, as he will convey it to town for me in the cart that carries the Music, appears to me an admirable method. He will take with it one that Esther means to sell also, for it will be much the most advantageous method of disposing of the re[maining] goods of all sorts, he himself says.

Now could I but get news of our consulship! If that is attainable, & if we settle in London. There is no sort of doubt but that it will be highly desirable to keep all our possessions & then, coûte qui coûte, I would engage some apartment. But in *every* other case, c.a.d. in ANY removal, no matter whither, we would best take this fair opportunity to turn our little store into [good] prices, for Mr. White will see, in that case, to the packing up of all.

I shall take no resolution upon all this till the last moment but when Mr. White has done it is thought the Chelsea rooms will be claimed & ought to be *offered*, as they are to be new papered & painted. Therefore, answer to this as quickly as possible, I shall mostly be distressed if forced to act, by circumstances, before I hear from my best Guide. Donnez-moi donc votre avis le plus vite possible. Dieu ǀ permette que je ne sois pas forcée de prendre ma partie avant que vos instructions n'arrive! Have you yet received my *Seven* Letters?

Quant à notre Hermitage, rien ne s'est encore passé, sinon qu'on ne à veut absolument me fair savoir ce que c'est que le proposal de William que par M. Murray, & je n'ai pas encore vu Martin. Mais le bon M. Haggit,[11] Chaplain of Chelsea College offers me his counsel & assistance in your absence. I mean, therefore, to have a conference with him before I see my lawyer, Martin, again, though I am longing to see the proposal.

Je remettrai jusqu'à ma troisieme Lettre de vous parler de larmes—Alors, je vous copierai notre derniere correspondance avec Alex. First, tout va bien dans ce moment, et nous nous rencontrerons dans [*tear*] car j'ai promis de l'aller voir *to drink to*!ꟲ

[11] The Revd. William Haggitt (1756–1834), whom FBA had known as early as 1788 when he became Second Chaplain at the Royal Hospital. Their friendship survived despite a contretemps. In 1798 CB and the priest (now made Chaplain) quarrelled over possession of the apartment designated as the Chaplain's, which CB, having occupied for eleven years, was required to vacate for Haggitt. See iv *passim*.

Hier, j'ai quitté ma retraite, très volontiers, pour indulge myself with the sight of the Emperor of Russia.[12] How was I charmed with his pleasing, gentle, & so perfectly unassuming air, manner, & demeanour! I was extremely gratified, also, by seeing the King of Prussia, who interests us all here, by a look that still indicates his tender regret for the Partner of his hopes & his toils & his sufferings[13]—but not of his victories & enjoyments.—It was at the Queen's Palace I saw them, by especial & most gracious permission.[14] The Prussian Princes, 6 in number,[15] & the young prince of Mecklenburg,[16] & the Duchesse of Oldenbourg were of the party.[17] All our Royal Dukes assisted, & the princesses Augusta & Mary.[18] The princess Charlotte[19] looked quite beautiful. She is wonderfully improved.

[12] FBA saw Alexander I (1777–1825) on 8 June 1814. The Tsar and the Prussian King 'landed from the Impregnable and Jason, on the British shores at Dover, this afternoon [6 June] at half-past six.' See *GM* lxxxiv[1], 612.

[13] Friedrich Wilhelm III (1770–1840). His wife Luise of Mecklenburg-Strelitz had died in 1810. In the dark years that followed the Treaty of Tilsit (1807), when he lost half his territory to the French, his wife helped save him from despair, encouraging the reorganization of the Prussian army so that it could withstand French pressures. After her death, however, the King could no longer resist and was forced to join Napoleon in the war against Russia. Finally breaking with the French in late February 1813, he responded to English urging and joined a coalition with Alexander, to whom he was always subservient.

[14] On 8 June 1814, 'Between five and six', the visiting monarchs, 'with their respective suites, attended the Court of her Majesty, held, expressly for their introduction, at the Queen's Palace. Her Majesty, the Princesses, the Allied Sovereigns, their Families, &c. dined afterwards with the Prince Regent, at Carlton House' (*GM* lxxxiv[1], 613). See also Diary Entry, pp. 514–15.

[15] The Prince Royal Friedrich Wilhelm (1795–1861), who became Friedrich Wilhelm IV; Prince Wilhelm (1797–1888), who became Wilhelm I, the King's second son; Prince Wilhelm (1783–1851), the King's brother; Prince Friedrich (1794–1863), nephew to the King; Prince Augustus (1779–1843), the King's cousin; and Prince Heinrich (1781–1846), the King's brother.

[16] Georg Friedrich Karl Joseph (1779–1860), Grand Duke of Mecklenburg-Strelitz (1816), nephew to Queen Charlotte.

[17] Catherine Paulowna (1788–1819), the fourth daughter of Emperor Paul I, had married in 1809 Georg, the Grand Duke of Oldenburg. Widowed in 1812, she married in 1819 King Wilhelm I of Würtemberg (1781–1864) and died suddenly in the same year. She was the favourite sister of Alexander and one of his few confidantes. Arriving in England on 29 Mar. 1814, she was the first of the foreign dignitaries to appear in London, where she became a controversial figure among the visiting royalty. According to MF in a letter (JRL) to Mrs. Piozzi on 2 June: 'The Duchess of Russia, as she is called, rises at 6 in the morning, goes all over London to see whatever is curious & instructive, asks questions that puzzle the learned, & make the unskilful stare, avoids assemblies, & leaves every place at 11 oclock.'

[18] The Prince Regent (1762–1830); Frederick, Duke of York (1763–1827); William, Duke of Clarence and St. Andrew (1765–1837); Ernest, Duke of Cumberland (1771–1851); Adolphus, Duke of Cambridge (1774–1850); Edward, Duke of Kent (1767–1820); Augustus Frederick, Duke of Sussex (1773–1843); William Frederick, Duke of Gloucester (1776–1834); Princess Augusta (1768–1840); Princess Mary (1776–1857).

[19] The Princess Charlotte Augusta of Wales (1796–1817). Her attendance

It was impossible not to be struck with her personal attractions, her youth, & splendour. The assemblage was highly magnificent. The invitation was confined to sovereigns, Princes, Princesses, & the immediate officers of the crown & the court. The Duchess of York looked amongst the happiest.[20] The King of Prussia is her Brother. I was admirably placed for the view, where every one passed close me, yet without my being *en evidence*

[Adi]eu, my dearest dear Friend! When shall we [mee]t— when part no more? Be your Health your first [care] by all your love of your own

F. d'A.

Ah, mon *ami*—La *Paix*—et le *Repos*—ne devons nous pas les reunir?

What would have become of me if the Letter from Calais had travelled as slowly as this I so impatiently wait for from Paris? Mon ami, mon ami, ecrivez moi!

⌐It is Vendredi, June 10—et pas un mot de Paris! Helas! Ecrivez donc¬

Votre F.d'A.

791

To Mrs. Waddington

63 Lower Sloane Street,
15 June 1814

A.L. (Berg), 15 June 1814
Double sheet 8vo   4 pp.
Addressed: Mrs. Waddington,

June 15. 1814
63 Lower Sloane Street
Chelsea

I am very glad my dearest Mary spared herself & me her own pen upon the gloomy subject of the Deputy Letter I have

was virtually commanded by the Prince Regent. She was reluctant to appear because her mother, to whom she was sympathetic, had been excluded from the celebrations in honour of the visiting monarchs.

[20] Frederica-Charlotte-Ulrique-Catherina (1767–1820), eldest daughter of Friedrich Wilhelm II, King of Prussia, had married the Duke of York in 1791. Long separated from her husband and living in retirement in Surrey, she was invited to the festivities because of the King of Prussia. See L. 677 n. 2.

just received from her dear amanuensis,[1] who has so candidly & sensibly described the fatal scene,[2] as to shew me, very explicitly, it is a shock; but not sorrow, my dear Mary has just suffered.[3]

But poor sweet Emily! that *her* sufferings should have been augmented by this journey afflicts me sincerely.

But what is this note of which my dear Fanny talks relative to Mr. W. Locke?[4] None is enclosed. I have had no interrogatories, I have not even seen Mr. W. L.[5]—I secluded myself almost entirely from all the world during the latter period of my dear Father's existence, & I have not yet had either spirit or opportunity for returning to it. I am absorbed in business of Executorship, or in circumstances relative to my own affairs: & I have neither carriage to go abroad on visits, nor a *home* for receiving | visitors *chez moi*. I took a mere sleeping apartment, last November, in Sloane Street, because my revered Father

791. [1] Fanny Waddington.

[2] The obituary of Mrs. Waddington's mother (d. 9 June 1814) appeared in *GM* lxxxiv[1], 699–700: 'Aged 68, Mrs. Mary Port, relict of the late J. P. esq. of Ham-Hall, co. Stafford, daughter of [John] Dewes, esq. of Welsburn, and niece of the celebrated Mrs. Delany, by whom she was educated, among the wits and cognoscenti of that age. She was, in consequence, a woman of very superior intellectual attainments; but a marriage contrary to her taste, followed by domestic discord, produced an alienation of mind, which for many years deprived her friends and family of that social converse which she was qualified to adorn, by her rare intelligence, and by the rich stores of anecdote with which her memory was fraught.'

[3] Mary d'Ewes (1746–1814) married John Port of Ilam (formerly Sparrow), who died in 1807. The union was unhappy. As Mrs. Waddington wrote (Osborn) to FBA on 25 Sept. 1795: 'My Mother is here [Calwich] her health good tho' her Spirits are low & I am sorry to say no place is yet fixed upon for her Residence as my Father absolutely refuses to receive her in his House & as she is at present thank God too well to need Doc[r] Willis's advice.'
Probably the Revd. Dr. Francis Willis (1718–1807), who cared for the insane in his private asylum in Lincolnshire.

[4] On 9 June 1814 Mrs. Locke sent a letter (Barrett, Eg. 3697, f. 187) to FBA: 'My dearly loved Friend, I was preparing to obtain the proposal from M[r] Murray that I might transmit it to you, when, on hearing of the good Clergyman whom you mention to my Amelia, my William begged that he might be requested to hear it from M[r] Murray, before you receive it. . . . I need not, I trust, assure you of my desire, my zeal, to do any thing that may tend to forward, & terminate this business in the manner most acceptable to you, & your dear Partner; but, as there is a trusty Friend upon the Spot perhaps he will at once communicate with you.' It was probably to the contents of this letter that Mrs. Waddington referred, although FBA appears to be ignorant of the letter's existence.

[5] Mrs. Waddington had known William Locke ever since 23 Oct. 1786 when, as Mary Ann Port, she had been brought to Norbury Park by Mrs. Delany. Both families hoped that a match could be arranged between the two young people. Their hopes were frustrated, but Mary Ann—whether as Miss Port or Mrs. Waddington—never remained aloof from the Lockes. See *HFB*, p. 257; *Locks of Norbury*, pp. 33–41.

had not one to offer me under his roof: but I spent with him ALL the time that was not wasted in illness, or seized by affairs. Since his loss,—recur to + for my subsequent & present history.

I have not heard from M. d'A[rblay] since he left Calais, the 27ᵗʰ May—& I am far, far from easy at a silence so unaccountable. With regard to Paris in July or Augˢᵗ I am ignorant, at this moment, whether I shall go thither at all. should he obtain the Consulship for which we have been seeking, *certainly not*. But all, with regard to me, is in the clouds!

Should Fanny go thither, my dear Friend, without *you*, you should secure her some domestic as well as brilliant protection. I have already explained my own insufficiency from such an undertaking, which I look upon as of so religious a nature, that to satisfy my notions of it's demands, I must sacrifice my whole ǀ form & system of life—and, as I have already intimated, JUSTLY offend & disappoint those who have the nearest claims upon me, not alone Those *left*, here, but *RESIDENT*, there: all covetting a chapronship that requires Time, HEALTH, spirits, & FORTUNE that I possess not. This subject is very painful to me —it seems so ungracious—so unlike the promptitude I should wish to show to a request *of* yours, & *for* yours: but—to raise false expectations, or tacitly permit them, I have ever thought a cowardice of friendship unworthy the sacred Truth & Courage of its high character.

I have been strongly invited to meet Lord & Lady Lansdown,⁶ at Lady Crewe's, on a quite private party, to talk over the present state of affairs & par[ties,] &c in Paris: & nothing could be more interesting to me: but the dispersion, at this period, of all my dearest Father so valued, his Library—cast a damp upon my mind that made me send a declining answer, for the moment. Indeed, *except* to Lady Crewe, whose Brompton Cottage is close by, & to which she fetches me, I have been no where, yet, out of my family.

I have no doubt of the delight of Mᵉ de Staël in your commentaries & approbation, nor of her active pleasure in receiving your Fanny at Paris, in her society. And her parties, are, probably, amongst the most varied & popular of France. Since

---

⁶ In *The Times* (28 May 1814), the '*SHIP NEWS*' from Dover (26 May) reported, 'The Marquis and Marchioness of Lansdowne, Lord Hill, and an immense number of passengers have landed from France.'

I have quitted it, the head & Flower & first pride of my own parties, alike from her Intellects & her partiality, M^e ^l de Tessé, is no more.[7] She sunk in the first horrours of the approaching Siege of Paris. And Moscow & Leipsic[8] have so deranged the happiness of my other close connexions, that I shall never recover what I left!—

Adieu, dearest Mary, I am very glad you all so love my dear Fanny Raper. She is amongst my most affectionate comforts at this period.

My Alexander came for the vacation yesterday. How shall I rejoice to embrace you, if you arrive before I go into the country! I keep on this forlorn spot only while my [aff]airs command my attendance. Alex will, however, revive me.

792   63 Lower Sloane Street,
                                                16 June 1814

To Charles Burney

A.L.S. (Osborn), 16 June 1814
Double sheet large 8vo   3 pp.   *pmks*   T.P.P.U. / Chelsea EO   17 JU 1814   17 JU 1814   seal
Addressed: Rev^d Dr Burney / Rectory House, / Deptford. / To be / forwarded / if absent

My dear Carlos—

Sally has just communicated the unwelcome tidings that the College apartments will be demanded next week! I know not the day—& am *non compos* with perplexity how to dispose of my affairs there, while in utter ignorance *where* I shall rest my weary limbs — —

weary indeed! of being so long without a fixed home! — —

And not a line do I receive from Paris!—to-morrow it will be *3 weeks* since my Letter of Calais was dated!—

---

7 See L. 762 n. 5.
8 The French were aware of the suffering of their troops in the Peninsular War but the campaigns of Moscow and Leipzig epitomized their humiliation. In the autumn of 1812 Napoleon had lost 400,000 men dead or wounded and 100,000 as prisoners. For the number of French casualties at Leipzig, see L. 733 n. 4.

The Books intended for the Museum must now be offered as fast as possible, that we may know where to *stow* them; &, should they be rejected, that they may be added to the Catalogue of those for the Auction.[1] I beseech you to | appoint time & place for arranging this with Mr. White as fast as possible. If your jaunt must take place immediately,[2] pray try to settle it by Letter, & give him Orders, & me directions how to help expediting them.[3] He is nearly ready, & can be *quite* so if hurried, he says, very soon indeed: Especially for the museum part: which cannot too soon be arranged, lest the Governors should quit London: besides our desire to escape unnecessary expense from Warehouse room.

His Catalogue for the Auction cannot be made out till the disposal of the Books for the Museum is settled.

I hope you are well, my dearest Charles—& that you preached well—& was heard well, | and will well hear of having so done.

Your ever FBdA.

Alexander is by my side, at his Mathematical pothooks—He would certainly send you his respects if he ever sent any thing to any body.

I hope dear Rosette continues amending?

63. Lower Sloane Street Chelsea,
Thursday, 16. June, 1814

---

792. [1] 'The books, tracts, and treatises on the particular Faculty of Music' (as cited in John White's *Sale Catalogue* of CB's musical library) were intended for auction when no institutional buyer seemed available. By August, however, the British Museum decided to purchase the books, and pending completion of negotiations they were stored in White's warehouse until 1815. See L. 782 n. 12.

[2] FBA seemed unaware of the precariousness of CB Jr.'s health, and the concern it gave his son at this time. On 4 June CPB wrote (Bodleian) to Robert Finch: '[My father] is in tolerable case,—but not so well as I wish him to be.—At times, indeed, I feel most painful uneasiness respecting him,—but then again his spirits mount,—his looks brighten,—his heaviness vanishes,—& I think him not only one of the most delightful Men, whom I ever saw,—but the youngest Man for his age, who is known to me.—I hope, however, to get him to the Seaside during the summer with me.—& then I shall interdict Collations—excepting *cold ones*, & shall make him wander & idle it with me on the shore.' The 'jaunt' was to the Isle of Wight.

[3] CB Jr. wrote to John White on 22 July 1814. See L. 782 n. 10.

[Paris, 18 June 1814]

M. d'Arblay
To Madame d'Arblay

A.L. (Berg), *n.d.*
Double sheet folio 4 pp. wafer
Addressed: À Madame / Madame d'Arblay *to the care of* / *Miss Burney,*
Chelsea College / *London* [*but address covered by cross-written continuation of the text*]
Edited by FBA, p. 1, *annotated and dated*: 15 4 4 June. 1814 Detailed
narrative of General d'Arblay's entrance into La Garde du corps de son
Roi, Louis 1814 *See further*, Textual Notes.

Je dois commencer, mon adorable amie, par te rendre mille
et mille graces des details dans les quels tu es entrée sur nos
affaires; et je dois convenir que j'ai été aussi surpris qu'enchanté
du courage que tu sais si bien déployer quand une fois tu t'es
determinée à agir. Un si beau debut et les succès dont il a été
couronné doivent ce me semble t'engager à continuer. Amen!
Je reviendrai sur cet article que je quitte pour te conter à mon
tour tout ce qui m'est arrivé depuis ma derniere lettre où je
t'annonçais *my safe debarkation at Calais*. Je crois t'avoir dit aussi
que ne pouvant avoir une voiture pour prendre la poste j'ai eu
le bonheur de rencontrer un Mr *Catoire* qui m'a donné dans la
sienne la place qu'occupait son frere assez bon pour nous
laisser partir, au risque de ne pouvoir nous suivre de plusieurs
jours, parceque les places de plusieurs diligences étaient toutes
retenues. De cette manière, et en fesant courir devant nous
pendant la nuit un postillon, je n'ai pas été *trois jours entiers* en
route; et j'ai pu remettre le dimanche matin de bonne heure les
depêches dont j'etais chargé. *C'est bon*, m'a dit en traversant son
antichambre M^r le Comte de — et entrant dans son cabinet
après avoir pris ce que je lui presentais. Voilà me suis-je dit
aussitôt à moi même un charmant debut, et 5 à 6 louis bien
placés, car c'est là ce qui m'en a couté et certe je ne suis pas
tenté d'en reclamer le remboursement malgré tout ce que m'a
dit à ce sujet M^r le Cte de la Châtre. Passons à quelque chose
de plus serieux. En quittant M^r de — qui probablement etait

trop affairé pour s'appercevoir de l'effet qu'avait produit sur moi son accueil, je descendis à la chapelle ou bientôt je fus occupé de toute autre chose en y voyant reunis toute la famille Royale à l'exception du Duc de Bourbon¹ inconsolable de la perte de son fils et ne se laissant presque jamais voir. Mad⁰ la Duchesse de Duras² à la quelle j'eus l'obligation de jouir pleinement d'un spectacle si touchant et dont j'ai été attendri aux larmes fut la seule qui, à deux fois differentes, s'attira l'attention marquée de S.A.R. M^{de} la D^{esse} d'Angouleme Ô mon amie, que tu aurais été frappée et touchée de la melancolie qui m'a paru l'expression dominante de sa noble figure, sur la quelle, sans cela on ne verrait regner que la douceur et la bonté. Je n'ai point reconnu d'abord M^r le Duc d'Orleans³ dans qui j'avais trouvé de la grace jointe à l'elegance. C'est encore un fort bel homme; mais il me semble qu'il n'est point heureux, et qu'il doit avoir dans le commerce intime quelque chose de trop severe. Tout le monde au reste en dit tout le bien que j'en ai toujours pensé, depuis tout ce qu'on m'a dit qu'il avait fait tant en Suisse qu'en Amerique.⁴ Que dirait ici M^{de} de L[aval] si elle pouvait lire ce que j'ecris. Ne m'accuserait t'elle pas d'être le plus ingrat des hommes en voyant que je ne t'ai pas encore parlé d'elle et que j'en suis encore à te raconter que c'est elle que j'ai vue la premiere, pour l'entendre de se récrier:

793. ¹ Louis-Henri-Joseph de Bourbon (1756–1830), the 9th and last prince de Condé, continued to mourn the death of his only son Louis-Antoine-Henri (1772–1804), duc d'Enghien, tried without counsel by a military tribunal on 20 March for treason and executed by Napoleon's order.

The Prince's sorrow was augmented by the shock of first learning about his son's death from a newspaper account which he read in his London apartment. Thereafter his grief continued with 'fits of rage and cries for vengeance' (Boigne, i. 175).

² The duchesse de Duras (vi, L. 631 n. 4). See L. 764 n. 7.

³ Louis-Philippe (1773–1850), duc d'Orléans, King of the French (1830–48), was the oldest son of Louis-Philippe-Joseph (identified during the Revolution as Philippe Égalité).

⁴ Accompanied by his sister Mme Adélaïde in 1793, the young Louis-Philippe went first to Switzerland. With the execution of his father in November 1793, he became the 6th duc d'Orléans and the centre of intrigues by the Orleanist party. By 1795, he was in Hamburg, where he rejected the notion of his followers that he be named king. Between 1796 and 1800 he resided in Philadelphia but travelled widely in the United States. Upon his return to Europe, he declared his loyalty to Louis XVIII.

In 1809 he married Marie-Amélie of the Two Sicilies (1782–1866). Remaining self-conscious about his father's disloyalty, he returned to France only after the 'inauguration' of Louis XVIII and was received at the Tuileries. In 1814 his military rank was confirmed as colonel-général des Hussards, and many of his vast estates were returned, all as evidence of Louis's regard.

'Ma foi vous êtes l'homme le plus extraordinaire, et rien effectivement ne vous arrive comme à un autre. Quand on veut vous retenir près de soi, et vous eviter une inquiétude sans fondement, on vous trouve delogé sans tambour ni trompette, et dejà au delà des mers, et quand au contraire on reconnait qu'il peut vous être prejudiciable de n'y pas rester, et de faire ici une course tout à fait inutile, vous ne manquez pas d'y tomber comme une bombe, et cela à l'instant même où l'on vient de vous mander de ne point bouger parcequ'il ne peut plus être question de la place qui vous y fait venir. C'est ce que je vous ai ecrit cette nuit même dans le plus grand detail. Au surplus tâchez de joindre le plutôt possible le duc de Luxembourg qui est desolé de ce contretems'—Preparé comme tu te rappelles sans doute que je l'etais à quelque chose de ǀ semblable, je l'etonnai par mon calme, qui pourtant, je dois en convenir n'etait qu'apparent: car dans le fond je n'y etais rien moins qu'insensible. Je me rabattis alors sur la place de Consul et lorsque je l'eus assurée que tout paroissait concourir au succès de ma demande de l'autre coté de l'eau, elle me promit d'employer tout son credit pour y contribuer de celui cy. Revenons au Chateau c.à.d. à la fin de la Messe, d'où j'allai au Ministère Mad^e de Fezensac[5] qui etait sortie J'y retournai deux fois encore. La derniere elle etait à table; Je lui ecrivis sur un chiffon de papier qu'il fallait absolument que je la visse; et que j'avais aussi le plus grand besoin d'obtenir une audience de son frere.[6] Sa reponse rapportée verbalement, fut qu'on n'en etait qu'à l'entremets, et qu'en consequence elle me priait de repasser au bout de trois quart d'heures. A peine etaient ils ecoulés, que revenu pour la demander, j'appris qu'elle etait

---

[5] The wife of Philippe-André-François de Montesquiou, *dit* comte de Fézensac (1783), she was a sister-in-law to the politically powerful abbé de Montesquiou. For a biographical account of Mme de Fézensac, see Ll. 743 n. 1, 763 and n. 9.

[6] François-Xavier-Marie-Antoine de Montesquiou-Fézensac (1756–1832), the abbé de Montesquiou. An old friend of Talleyrand, the abbé held convictions bound to throne and altar. 'Il n'avait ni sou, ni maille et vivait de l'hospitalité de la princesse de Poix. Son aimable et indéfectible espérance dans le prochain retour des lys le tenait en joie. . . . [qui] lui n'était qu'un rêveur' (Orieux, p. 561). He served first in the provisional government established on 1 Apr. 1814 by the French Senate that had been convened by Talleyrand as Vice-Elector General, and he was chosen by that body to make the announcement at Hartwell that 'the Senate had called to the throne of France Louis Stanislas Xavier, brother of the late King, and after him the other members of the Bourbon family, in the former order of succession' (Gontaut, i. 138). With Louis's return to France and the formation of a permanent government headed by Talleyrand, the abbé became ministre de l'Intérieur.

sortie pour aller voir son fils[7] qui arrivait de Berlin où il etait resté prisonnier, mais qu'elle avait laissé l'ordre de me laisser entrer chez son frere. J'y rencontrai le Vte d'Agoult[8] qui dabord ne me reconnut point mais qui dès qu'il m'eut entendu nommer se montra tout ce qu'il a toujours été pour moi, et même parait chaque jour rencherir sur sa *fondness* pour ton athanase. Mais continuons: Le lendemain je fus de bonne heure chez le duc de Luxembourg qui me dit à peu près tout ce que tu dois avoir lu dans la lettre que m'ecrivait mad^e de Laval, et que sans doute tu as reçu. Tu dois y avoir vu que cet homme pour moi si bienveillant se trouvait arreté par diverses considerations politiques, dont il me parut regretter beaucoup l'influence; et nous nous quittâmes les meilleurs amis du monde après qu'il m'eut assuré avec l'air le plus penetré, que ce serait l'obliger reellement que de lui fournir une occasion quelconque et cela promptement, d'acquiter d'une maniere utile pour nous la dette qu'il aimait à reconnoitre avoir contractée envers moi. Il n'etait donc plus question que de la place de Consul general, et je me mis aussitôt à y penser serieusement. Je fus le même jour voir Mr de Talleyrand,[9] chez qui je fis antichambre pendant deux heures ½ inutilement. A la verité il avait assez d'affaires sans la mienne, et sans compter une foule d'etrangers de la plus haute distinction qui ne fesaient que traverser l'appartement je crois bien avoir vu entrer et sortir plus de cent personnes de marque dans son cabinet, ou dans une autre grande piece

---

[7] Raymond-*Aimery*-Philippe-Joseph de Montesquiou-Fézensac (L. 770 n. 20). Joining Napoleon's army as a volunteer (1804), he was commissioned as a sous-lieutenant in 1805, becoming général de brigade in 1813. He fought wherever the need was greatest and was taken prisoner on 11 Nov. 1813 in Saxony. Although he had been released earlier, he returned to France only on 30 May 1814. FBA saw him at Louis XVIII's reception for the officials of London on 22 April.

He was promoted to lieutenant-général (1823), made ambassadeur de France (1838-9), pair de France (1832).

[8] Antoine-Jean [Gabriel] d'Agoult (1750-1828), vicomte, was a member of one of the most illustrious families of Provence. He entered the army in 1766, rising in rank so that by 1783 he was a mestre de camp de cavalerie in the gardes du Corps. Emigrating in 1790, he served in the armée des Princes and was promoted to maréchal de camp in 1795.

Retired from the army in May 1814, he was given the honorary rank of lieutenant-général and made commandeur de l'ordre de Saint-Louis three months later. His familiarity with the royal household stemmed from his role as premier écuyer de la duchesse d'Angoulême.

Created pair de France (1823), baron-pair (1824), he ended his career as gouverneur de Saint-Cloud (1825).

[9] Charles-Maurice de Talleyrand-Périgord (1754-1838), who, for his efforts on behalf of the Bourbon restoration, became ministre des Affaires étrangères, most important officer in Louis XVIII's cabinet.

où etaient reunis les membres du Gouvernement provisoire lui excepté.[10] Le lendemain j'y retournai, et m'en allai tout aussi peu avancé que la veille. Le jour suivant, je n'eus pas la force de suivre le conseil de M^{de} de L— qui voulait que je prisse patience et que je continuasse cette maniere d'exister à laquelle j'avoue qu'il m'est impossible de m'accoutumer. Je mis donc quelques jours d'intervalle au bout des quels je fesais de tems à autre de courtes aparitions, et m'en allais lorsque j'avais vu que la nombre des *attendans* etait toujours à peu près aussi considerable. Ce qu'il y avait d'assez remarquable c'est que les gens me fesaient beaucoup valoir la faveur dont je jouissais, je ne sais trop pourquoi, de pouvoir penetrer jusqu'à l'appartement que je ne pouvais passer. Cet appartement etait effectivement precedé par plusieurs autres où d'autres personnes qui probablement enviaient mon sort etaient comme moi à attendre, jusqu'à ce qu'on vint leur annoncer que son Altesse serenissime[11] etait passée chez l'Empereur de Russie, ou bien qu'elle allait sortir sans pouvoir s'arrêter, c.à.d. sans vouloir se soumettre à l'ennui de les ecouter. Le moins plaisant de l'aventure, pour moi s'entend, est que presque tous les jours je rencontrais chez Mad^e de L— l'inabordable grand personnage qui n'a guere encore avait été si aimable. mais une politesse froide et même repoussante, etait tout ce que je pouvois trouver sur sa figure,[12] de sorte que loin de chercher à l'aborder ce qu'il avait tout l'air de vouloir eviter, j'etais plutot tenté d'être presqu'impertinent que prevenant et surtout courtisan. Je ne puis t'exprimer tout ce qui m'en a couté pour ne pas eclater, et pour me contenter de l'air glacial avec le quel je contemplais

---

[10] On 1 Apr. 1814 the members of the French Senate were called into extraordinary session by its president, Talleyrand. 'They passed a decree, "that there shall be established a provisional government, charged to provide for the wants of the administration, and to present to the senate the plan of a constitution which may suit the French people." ' See *AR* lvi (1814), 'General History', 22. The five members of the provisional government were Talleyrand; the abbé de Montesquiou; Émerich-Joseph Wolfgang-Héribert (1773–1833), duc de Dalberg; Pierre Riel de Beurnonville (1752–1821); and Arnail-François de Jaucourt (L. 736 n. 8). For a description of the members of the provisional government, see Thiers, xvii. 350.   [11] The duchesse d'Angoulême.

[12] Talleyrand was usually characterized by a stern rationality that could be described as 'l'air glacial'. Napoleon wrote of him that he had the gift of inscrutability and silence. See *The Memoirs of Napoleon I*, ed. F. M. Kircheisen, tr. Frederick Collins (1929), pp. 190–1. Talleyrand was so well known for his inscrutability that Mrs. Piozzi in her 1817 notebook (JRL) wrote: 'Jamais Visage ne fut moins Barometre is cleverly said by Lady Morgan of Talleyrand, who . . . is scrupulously careful to avoid *all* Expression lest some should escape which might trop reveler.'

le manege j'ose dire ridicule de cette *mock*-grandeur. ⟨J'avais, au
reste, entierement cessé de me presenter chez son Altesse qui
je ne sais pourquoi redoute surement mon caractere et mes
manieres selon lui un peu trop libres. Du moins j'en juge par ce
que m'a dit il y a six à 7 ans le Dᵣ Bourdois,[13] ainsi que je te l'ai
raconté dans le tems. Son Altesse, au surplus n'a pas tout à fait
tort; et quoique j'aye assez de confiance en ma maniere d'etre,
pour oser croire que jamais cette confiance ne me porterait à
la familiarité, j'avoue que je ne sais point vivre avec ceux vis-
à-vis des quels, il faut toujours paraitre guindé et sur ses gardes.

Cependant Madᵉ de L— qui presque tous les soirs, suivait
Son Altesse pour causer un moment avec elle en particulier, me
disait toujours de ne pas me décourager, et qu'elle etait sure que
avec de la perseverance on venait à bout de tout. Comme
neanmoins il n'etait question de rien, je ne pouvais raison-
nablement penser qu'il resulterait de tout cela quelque chose
de très avantageux pour moi. Quelques jours encore se pas-
sèrent, au bout des quels, cette amie reellement toute bonté pour
moi m'assura que Mᵣ de Tal. lui avait positivement dit: *qu'il
me porterait sur sa liste*; et elle ajouta: le tems est venu de faire
tout ce que vous pourrez auprès de *Madame La Duchesse
d'Angoulême et du Roi*. C'etait à peu près tout ce que je pouvais
attendre de Mᵣ de T. mais il m'etait impossible de ne pas
sentir que cette espece de condescendance de sa part ne me
menerait pas loin. Quelques personnes à qui j'en parlai augurè-
rent mal de son affectation à ne me point dire lui même ce qu'il
consentait à faire. Je n'en avais pas meilleure opinion. Je ne
m'occupai pas moins le soir même d'un memoire que je priai
Madᵉ la duchesse de Duras de faire remettre au Roi par son
mari[14] qu'il m'avait été impossible d'aborder encore, et que je
n'avais vu qu'entouré de personnes qui ne lui laissaient pas une
minute dont il put disposer. Une seule fois il m'avait fait signe
de la main qu'il etait desolé de cette contrarieté et qu'il n'en
etait pas moins continuellement occupé de moi et de mes affaires
ce qu'il m'a au surplus bien prouvé et de la maniere la plus
positive. Quel metier bon dieu que celui d'un homme vraiment
souple dans de pareilles places, surtout dans l'instant d'une
restauration. Imagine toi que Madᵉ de Duras est quelquefois

---

[13] The physician Edmé-Joachim Bourdois de la Motte (1754–1837). See iv,
L. 381 n. 1; v, L. 450 n. 6.　　　　　　[14] See L. 770 n. 24.

deux jours entiers sans avoir pu causer avec lui un quart d'heure. Du reste elle m'assurait que dans ces momens de liberté, il y avait toujours de sa part quelque chose qui m'etait relatif, et que continuellement il etait occupé de mes interêts. Peu de jours après je fus presenté, et comme nous etions plus de 400 ainsi montrés processionellement c.à.d. bien que je ne devais pas m'attendre à un seul mot de la part du Roi qui ne ferait qu'incliner la tête avec [cet air] de bonté que tu lui connois. Neanmoins lorsque Mr de Duras m'eut nommé je l'entendis repeter mon nom, avec quelques mots que je ne pus distinguer, mais qui très certainement n'avaient [rien] que d'obligeant à en juger par l'air gracieux avec le quel ils furent prononcés par S. M. et plus encore p[eut-]etre par la maniere dont ceux qui me suivaient me traitaient ensuite. De ce nombre etait un Mr le Cte d'Ambruzac¹⁵ qui depuis ce tems parait me faire une sorte de cour et a vis-à-vis de moi un ton qui contraste singulièrement avec sa conversation ordinaire pleine de morgue et peu en mesure avec le genre de son esprit assez cultivé. J'ai retrouvé ce jour là les deux Vergennes,¹⁶ avec qui j'ai été comme si nous nous fussions jamais quittés. Quant à Made la Desse d'Angoulême, j'ai été un peu desapointé, en trouvant qu'elle ne se rappellait ou du moins qu'elle avait l'air de ne se rappeller ni mon nom ni ma figure. D'Agoult, au surplus, ne m'avait point du tout reconnu non plus lorsque je l'avais

¹⁵ Louis-Alexandre-Marie de Valon du Boucheron d'Ambrugeac (1771–1844), comte d'Ambrugeac, a sous-lieutenant in the régiment du Maine in 1786, emigrated in 1791 and was at Coblenz as capitaine in the régiment Allemand de Wittgenstein, then in the uhlans Britannique from 1793 to 1796. Reinstated by Napoleon in 1810, he fought in the Spanish campaign. By 1813 he was a colonel, receiving the cross of the Légion d'honneur in March 1814. Immediately after the Restoration he rallied to the Bourbon cause and was named colonel-général in June 1814. During the Cent Jours he repudiated Napoleon and worked with the duc d'Angoulême, who saw him as a model of bravery and monarchical devotion. In 1815 d'Ambrugeac received the brevet de maréchal de camp, in 1818 became commandeur de Saint-Louis, and five years later was promoted to lieutenant-général. Created pair de France in 1823, he served in the Upper Chamber until his death.
¹⁶ Jean-Charles Gravier (1756–1822), marquis de Vergennes, was born in Dijon. He began his military career as mestre de camp in the régiment Royal Vaissaux, becoming a colonel in 1788 and a maréchal de camp in 1814. Constantin Gravier (1761–1832), comte de Vergennes, was born in Constantinople and died in Sablonville. In 1783 he was made capitaine-colonel des gardes de la Porte, the following year admitted to the honours of the court. He functioned as ministre plénipotentiaire first in Coblenz (1787) and then in Trèves (1788–91). An *émigré* for a decade, he returned to France in 1802 to become inspecteur des Eaux et Forêts. In 1814 he commanded the gardes de la Porte, another corps of the maison militaire, becoming in 1818 maréchal de camp. The two men were cousins.

rencontré chez l'abbé de Montesquiou; et Certes j'aurais été bien injuste si j'en avais conclu qu'il n'avait plus pour moi la même amitié. Le lendemain de ma presentation, nous eûmes une assez longue conversation sur mes affaires, qui me prouve bien tout l'interêst qu'il a toujours pris à ce qui me concerne. Sans me dire precisement qu'il pensait que j'echouerais dans mon projet relatif au Consulat; il m'en fit envisager les difficultés et selon lui le peu d'avantage, sans trop apuyer neanmoins sur ses regrets de ne nous voir reunis que pour nous separer de nouveau. Le lendemain nous reprîmes la même conversation; et il commença ⎮ par me faire entrevoir qu'il pensait que je ne pouvais guère rester au Ministère de l'Interieur. J'eus d'autant moins de peine à en tomber d'accord que le jour même j'avais reçu une lettre de M^{de} de Montagu[17] qui me priait de m'informer dans quel Bureau etait entré le fils de son cuisinier à qui l'abbé de Montesquiou avait accordé une place de surnumeraire, sur la recommandation de Mad^e de Simiane. Nous etions dans la cour, et interrompus à tout moment par les plus grands seigneurs qui venaient saluer mon compagnon à qui j'en fis compliment. Je suis me dit il à ce sujet obsedé d'une bien autre maniere chez moi par des gens qui me croyent bien plus influent que je ne le suis reellement: car je ne suis plus rien. J'ai donné à S.M. ma demission, et me contente de la retraite qu'elle a bien voulu m'accorder. Au surplus je ne trompe personne et dis à chacun qu'il aurait tort de compter sur moi, parceque je suis très resolu de ne faire usage du peu de credit qui pourrait me rester qu'en faveur de quelques parens et de quelques amis comme toi. Alors il m'a dit: il faut absolument que tu songes à quelqu'autre chose que ton Consulat qu'il est possible qu'un autre obtienne, d'autant que la place de Consul general exige un genre de connoissances dejà acquises sur les lois maritimes et autres, dont sans te faire tort on peut croire que tu ne t'es pas beaucoup occupé. Aussitôt ce qu'il me disait m'a rappellé que La Jacqueminiere[18] m'avait representé quelques jours auparavant, que non seulement je serais en bute à la jalousie des Consuls particuliers et mème generaux ainsi que

---

[17] Anne-Paule-Dominique 'Pauline' de Montagu-Beaune (1766–1839), marquise de Pouzols. See v, L. 515 n. 13.

[18] Louis-Charles Gillet de la Jacqueminière (1752–1836). See v, L. 448 n. 10. A cousin of M. d'A and a chief adviser in the Court of Accounts, he was alert to bureaucratic intrigue.

de toute la burocratie ministeriele mais qu'il y avait tout à craindre qu'ils ne me tendissent quelque piège, dans lequel il me serait d'autant plus difficile de ne pas tomber, que la place que je sollicitais etait celle de juge en dernier ressort de beaucoup d'affaires souvent litigieuses et très delicates. Je m'etais dit aussi à moi même sur ce sujet: que l'air froid de M. de T— provenait probablement de son interêst personnel, et de sa connoissance de mon caractère peu pliant et point du tout ⟨aux⟩ souplesses d'un agent d'affaires. d'Agoult alors me temoigna d'une maniere plus prononcée le regret de ce que je n'etais pas entré dans la Comp^e de Luxembourg. Ma reponse fut que la seule proposition m'en avait dabord enchanté; et que toi-même tu n'avais pas paru insensible à l'honneur que je ne pouvais manquer de tirer d'une distinction aussi flatteuse après une revolution dans la quelle aux yeux de ceux qui ne me connoissaient pas particulierement je pouvais être regardé comme ayant été l'ennemi d'une cause pour la quelle j'avais toujours fait les voeux les plus ardens, et comme le defenseur de brigands que j'ai constament combattus. d'Agoult m'interrompit pour me dire que c'etait encore plus pour le Roi lui même que pour moi qu'il aurait voulu me voir avec Mr de Luxembourg, si ta santé t'eut permis de revenir parmi nous. Je ne lui cachai point alors que j'avais l'esperance et la presque certitude que cet obstacle ne serait pas eternel. Dès lors il me pressa beaucoup, et me dit qu'il fallait absolument que j'allasse chez Mr de Luxembourg, qui s'en etait rapporté au M^al Marmont[19] pr la place du sous Lieutenant qui devait être chargé de l'artillerie mais que l'off^er presenté par le M^al n'avait pas été agrée par le Roi. Alors la tête montée, je courus à l'hotel de Luynes[20] et

[19] Auguste-Frédéric-Louis Viesse de Marmont (1774–1852), duc de Raguse (1808). Long associated with Napoleon's military campaigns, Marmont was made a général in 1798 and maréchal de l'Empire in 1809. By 1813 he was Napoleon's chief strategist. Commanding the final battle at Paris, he accepted the orders of Talleyrand, deserted Napoleon within four days, and surrendered to the Allies. On reporting this disaster to the house on the rue Saint-Florentin, he was congratulated by Talleyrand, who arranged that the duc de Raguse be given one of Louis XVIII's newly formed gardes du Corps.

[20] The Hôtel de Luynes was presided over by Guyonne-Élisabeth-Joséphine d'Albert *née* de Montmorency-Laval (1755–1830), the widow of the duc de Luynes et de Chevreuse (d. 1807). The Hôtel 'se trouvait rue Saint-Dominique, dans la partie qui a disparu, à l'endroit où le boulevard Raspail rejoint le boulevard Saint-Germain' (Orieux, p. 410). For the role of the Hôtel during the Empire, see v, L. 469 n. 8. After the Restoration it became the official address of the Compagnie de Luxembourg.

j'appris qu'en effet L'off^{er} proposé par le M^{al} Marmont n'avait pas été accepté, mais que malheureusement il avait fait la politesse de s'entremettre encore pour le choix d'un off^{er} d'artillerie au même Marechal qui lui avait nommé deux autres sujets. Il ajouta qu'il souhaitait de tout son coeur que je pusse etre presenté en troisième; et il m'engagea à voir à ce sujet M^r le M^{al}. Je le quittai dans cette intention, mais je ne tardai pas en changer; et après avoir rendu compte de tout ce que tu viens de lire au Vte d'Agoult je resolus de reposer tranquille et de n'y plus penser mon D'Agoult, ne songe plus à autre chose et deux jours après il arriva chez moi pour me dire: que je passasse chez Mr de Luxembourg et que mon affaire etait faite. J'y courus et Mr de Luxembourg en effet me dit que des lors que cela me convenait et qu'il etait laissé maitre de decider la chose c'etait à moi à preciser. je dis un *oui*, que j'espere que mon aimable amie ne dementira point. Dès le lendemain Mr de Luxembourg que j'etais nommé par le Roi, et aujourdhui 18 Juin nous avons été presentés à sa Majesté, et nous avons preté serment.—²¹

Tu peux juger si j'ai le desir et le besoin d'avoir des nouvelles de mon cher Alex, à qui une visite qui m'a tant fait de plaisir a surement nui. J'en suis desolé. Embrasse le pour moi ainsi que le cher Clement. Mille choses tendres à nos parens et amis. Je t'ai surement dit combien G[reville How]ard a été aimable pour moi.²² Dis à Alex d'aller le voir et de lui dire mille chos[es aimab]les pour moi.

(ce 18 à Minuit) Ame de ma vie! cette lettre attendue avec tant de bonté et d'impatience par toi c'est à dire par tout ce qu'il y a de plus aimable et de plus aimé dans le monde allait partir, quand la tienne est arrivée. Que n'ai-je pas eprouvé en la lisant! Quelles emotions contraires elle a excitées! Ô ma chere Fanny, je le repete, ame de ma vie! je ne veux te repondre que lors que la nuit m'aura rendu un peu plus calme. Je vais en

²¹ In joining a company of Louis XVIII's bodyguards or household troops, M. d'A became part of an aristocratic but unpopular organization despised by professional militarists and laughed at by all but the most committed royalists. By the King's desire General Dupont executed the programme of General Beurnonville, abetted by the duc de Berry, and recruited many men without difficulty for a maison militaire modelled after the one established by Louis XVI. Most of these recruits were middle-aged *émigrés*, politically anachronistic and quite unable to cope with current military conditions.
²² M. d'A had in mind Greville Howard's unceasing efforts to secure a Tancred studentship for AA. See especially L. 673 and n. 7.

consequence tâcher de me reposer ⌐et demain matin de très bonne heure je causerai froidement avec toi de tout ce qui nous concerne. à demain donc. Seulement, il faut que je te dise encore avant de me mettre au lit que je suis *indigné* mais non *surpris* de ce qui nous arrive. Rappelle toi ce que je t'ai dit après avoir fait l'observation qu'on emportait les livres non seulement sans en avoir fait un catalogue mais même sans les compter. J'ai des lors prevu ce qui devait en resulter. J'avoue neanmoins que ma sagacité n'a pas été jusqu'à craindre que plus de 20,000 volumes puissent être reduits à moins de *5,000*.[23] Il y a certes plus que de l'imprudence à presenter un semblable tableau à des gens qui tous ont du comme moi entendre ton pere dire qu'il en etait au 21eme mille, parlant ⟨alors⟩ de ses livres. Et il y a douze ans au moins que je le lui ai oui dire. à moi ⟨même 4⟩,600 volumes dont encore plusieurs sont depareillés !!! Ils ne le seront pas longtems, je le parie bien, car ce que je pourrais te dire à ce sujet arrivera surement trop tard. Dans le cas contraire, voici ce que je te conjure de faire c'est d'acheter des ⟨recueils⟩ avec ta soeur et si elle refuse, d'acheter seule tous les volumes depareillés et qui seront vendus à très bon marché et peut être *pour rien*; et de faire mettre tout de suitte dans les journaux que ceux qui pourront te fournir le moyen de completer les ouvrages ainsi ⟨retablis⟩ recevront en retour le double de la valeur des tomes qu'ils auront ainsi vendus. Ah combien ⟨est il⟩ reflechit aux suites facheuses et si bien prevues par moi d'une negligence. Par exemple, Charles sera bien faché un jour! Et que je plains ta soeur ainée qui souffrira encore plus que nous du tort que cela lui fait comme à nous. Je dis qu'elle en souffrira plus que nous parceque quoi qu'il arrive et ⟨en etant⟩ sage comme je suis bien scrupuleux de l'être ⟨ceci⟩ suffira toujours à Alex de quoi vivre honnorablement et confortablement. à propos, ⌐ je ne t'ai pas encore dit que la place que le Roi a bien voulu me donner est infiniment honnorable mais on ne peut pas moins lucrative, puisqu'elle ne me rapportera que—6000^f et qu'elle m'oblige à avoir un valet et deux chevaux, dont à la verité on me payera la nourriture. je crois qu'on nous payera aussi le logement.

Mon oncle est venu ici exprès pour me voir. Il se porte bien et me demande tous les jours si j'ai de tes nouvelles. Donne m'en promptement je te prie; et ne m'en veux pas d'avoir été si

[23] See L. 790.

longtems sans t'ecrire c.à.d. sans faire ce que j'aime le plus loin de toi. Sous peu de jours j'entrerai dans plus de details.

794   63 Lower Sloane Street, 24 June 1814

To M. d'Arblay

A.L. (Berg), 24 June 1814
Double sheet 4to 2 pp. The signature, a strip (0·8 × 2·1″), is cut out of the first leaf *pmk* 2 Juillet 181⟨4⟩ 3 black seals
Addressed: À / Monsieur / Monsieur d'Arblay, / Rue de Mirominil, / fauxbourg St. Honoré, / 8 / à Paris.
Edited by FBA, p. 1, *annotated*: ⁂ ⌐5.⌐ (13) *See further*, Textual Notes.

Friday—June 24ᵗʰ 1814

This Day concludes the 4ᵗʰ Week since my beloved Friend arrived at Calais, & wrote to me thence!—& not a line—not a word has he written that has reached me since!

I grow so sick with alarm & uneasiness, that I know not how to send off any more Letters—yet I am not *bodilily* ill, my dearest DEAREST ami!—if ever this meets your Eye, assure yourself I follow strictly your injunctions, to take the utmost care in my power of my health—that WHEN we meet we may not still have misery! for this silence—this suspensive state is now nothing short of misery!—

⌐All my Letters, I conclude, fail to arrive. You would else try some other route for yours, this might make them at length greet me. This is a new mode I have found for one of mine, & I shall try it with this note. But I wrote yesterday a very long letter through M. de la Châtre, which he has promised to forward instantly by his courrier.⌐

[*cut*] which God Almighty forbid!—entreat Mᵉ. [*cut*] [w]rite —& to indicate how I had best travel to you. [*cut*] you are only absent from Paris—sent upon some commission, & that your Letters have been neglected by some accident. That you have *written* I am very sure!—Alex is at his Algebra by my side, and quite well. He waited yesterday, in my name, upon Monsieur ǀ de La Châtre,¹ who promised to write to a Friend of your's

794. ¹ As ministre plénipotentiare to England, M. de la Châtre provided courier

for news of you that very day. Oh ere his answer comes may one arrive to relieve my cruel inquietude! ⌐sometimes I think you at Joigny²—& some mistake of the post is then more easy to conceive. But⌐ I have not an instant of the day any occupation for my thoughts that dissipates them from that *UNIQUE OBJET* of my *attente*. I employ my *time*, nevertheless, as well as I am able—& to watch & guide & take care of Alex is a constant source of interesting business. I think without that I should scarcely know how to exist in this torturing disturbance.

⌐Next week, if I hear not, I must necessarily act, both for Camilla Cottage & for the College. The first will else lose the season for repairs—the 2ᵈ must be emptied for the new purpose to which the apartment is determined. Mr. Yates,³ the 2ᵈ Chaplain, declines inhabiting them, & they are to be prepared, I am told, for wards for the pensioners.⌐

M. de La Châtre assures me he has heard of your safe arrival at Paris—That is my sole support.

O how well I now conceive the sufferings from want of news that brought you so precipitately over!

But what can become of our Letters?—

Heaven bless you my dear dear Friend!—far too dear when not at the side of your own

[*Signature cut out*]

O never be we again separated when once again united!

Lower Sloane Street, Chelsea.

63:

---

service for FBA. The appointment was still new to him, for it was only on 8 July that 'The Count DE LA CHATRE was introduced to the PRINCE REGENT, at Carlton-house . . . as Ambassador from his Most Christian Majesty LOUIS XVIII' (*The Times*, 9 July).

² FBA would expect M. d'A to return to Joigny, his native village, to visit family members who remained there—particularly his maternal uncle Gabriel Bazille, then about 83, who had, however, come to Paris in June to see M. d'A (L. 793). See genealogical table, vi, *facing* p. 476.

³ Richard Yates (1769–1834). A Cantabrigean (B.D. 1805, D.D. 1818), he was ordained deacon (1796), priest (1797), made rector of Ashen in Essex (1804–34). In March 1798 he was appointed Second Chaplain of the Royal Hospital in Chelsea and remained in that post until his death, when the position was abolished. Marrying well in 1810, Yates lived in easy circumstances and 'chiefly in London, where he was in great request as a preacher at the fashionable chapels' (Venn). There was little need for him to reside at the Hospital, daily services having been abolished since 1802, and most of the pastoral duties being performed by the Revd. Mr. Haggitt.

795
To M. d'Arblay

63 Lower Sloane Street,
29 June 1814

A.L. (Berg), 29 June 1814
Single sheet 4to   2 pp.   *pmk*   9 Juillet 1814   black seal
Addressed: A Monsieur / Monsieur d'Arblay, / Rue de Mirominil, /
8 f⁸ St. Honoré / À Paris.
Edited by FBA, p. 1, *annotated*:   ⁝·   ⌐6⌐   (14)   *See further*, Textual Notes.

63 Lower Sloane Street, Chelsea
June 29ᵗʰ 1814.

One word only can I now write—in the dreadful belief that
my Letters never arrive—Oh mon ami! objet unique de tout ce
qui pour moi est bonheur sur la terre—where—whither do my
Letters wander? You could not receive them without discover-
ing that *your's* never reach me—& the knowledge of my misery
—my anguish—my aching restlessness of soul, would urge you
to devellop the strange—inconceivable cause that deprives me
[of a]ll intelligence. This is the 5ᵗʰ Week that we have been
separated! This is the 5ᵗʰ Letter I have written, according to
our agreement, by weekly conveyance through M. de La
Châtre! ⌐And one Letter I sent by a private hand, M. — — —
who set for France last Sunday, the 20ᵗʰ⌐ Mon cher Cher ami!
if *this*, at last, meets your Eye—entreat instantly some one—
Mᵉ de Maisonneuve—M. d'Esparron[1] to write, if you are ill!—
which is my continual dread—& tell me at once *HOW* to come
to you! What is all I shall leave of our mere worldly interest in
such a scale?—or, are you absent from Paris upon some commission? and are *your* Letters, now, as *mine* were before the
happy restoration, mis-sent? *This* hope alone keeps me from
Despair—& alone prevents every | risk, both of Fortune & of
precarious Health & safety, to leave All & fly to you! ⌐But, till
the answer arrive for M. le Comte de La Châtre, which cannot

795. [1] Perhaps the doctor Pierre-Jean-Baptiste Esparron (see L. 697 n. 4) or
the related Jean-Charles d'Esparron (1746–1835), a lawyer, who handled many
financial affairs for M. d'A and FBA. On 1 Nov. 1814 AA wrote (Berg) to FBA
from Cambridge: 'I have opened a *check* book upon w- I have entered every thing
belonging to y- *grocer*, the *Cook*, all these expenses of the journey &c & will go on
with it every day. . . . So I hope good M. Esparron will not trouble himself for
nothing, w- I fear to be very likely.'

be later than this Week, I must force myself to be patient. This recluse is well. He is going to carry the note to M. L'ambassadour. I speak no more of our affairs in either college or Cottage, I direct now, alas, not for myself! the Book sale is over at £⟨1414⟩² & the Music sale is advertized for the last week in July.³ We are waiting, before it takes place, the refusal or acceptance of the Governors of the British Museum for the Books upon the ⟨nature⟩ of Music. ⌐

796   Paris, 3 July 1814

M. d'Arblay
To Madame d'Arblay

A.L. (Berg), 3 Juillet 1814
Double sheet 4to 4 pp. seal
Addressed: A Madame / Madame D'Arblay née Burney / *Lower Sloan Street*, Nᵒ 63 / Chelsea: / London—
Edited by FBA, p. 1, *annotated*: 16   *See further*, Textual Notes.

Paris ce dimanche matin 3 Juillet 1814.

Quoi mon adorable amie, ma chere et bien aimée toujours plus aimée Fanny, tu n'as recu aucune des trois lettres que je t'ai ecrites. En verité cela n'est pas concevable et m'allarme de toute maniere. ⌐Je regrette surtout ma bien longue lettre.¹ Ou plutôt un ⟨mauvais⟩ paquet dans le quel j'entrais dans le plus grand détail, ⟨absolu⟩ment toute mon affaire. Aujourdhui j'ai une excellente occasion; ⟨bien bien clair⟩, mais je n'ai que bien peu de tems à ma disposition, et j'en viens d'employer une partie à te copier l'article des precautions à prendre contre *le mal de mer* cité dans la lettre du cher docteur Larrey, dont je te donne ma parole de n'avoir pas du tout influencé l'avis. J'ajouterai que c'est de son propre mouvement qu'il t'a ecrit et qu'en verité j'ignorais absolument ce que recommande sa

---

² The sale of CB's miscellaneous library was completed on 16 June. The total sum realized was £1,414. 18s. 6d. For FBA's share, see L. 796.
³ See L. 782 n. 12.

796. ¹ See L. 793, the information of which is summarized in the four items listed in this letter.

lettre que j'ai cru pouvoir ouvrir pour te la faire passer plus facilement.

Dans l'impossibilité de pouvoir causer bien longtems avec toi je ne puis que te dire en gros

1° que j'ai été reçu avec bonté par S. M. mais sans que rien n'ait pu faire croire qu'il se rapellait de moi.[2]

2° que Mad^e la D^esse d'Angoulême n'a point paru non plus se souvenir de moi.[3]

3° que⌐ Mr de Talleyrand a été inabordable pour moi, tant que j'ai cherché à le joindre pour lui parler concernant la place de Consul gen^al, que neanmoins je le rencontrais presque tous les soirs chez M^de de Laval, à qui neanmoins il avait promis de me mettre sur la liste qu'il devait presenter au Roi pour cette place

4° que le Vte d'Agoult dont l'amitié pour moi est plutot augmentée que diminuée a fait lui même et à mon insu pendant quelques jours les demarches | necessaires pour que je fusse officier des Gardes du Corps; que M^r le Duc de Luxembourg a été et est encore pour moi excellent; que S. M. m'a accordé la place de sous Lieut^nt attaché à l'artillerie de la compagnie qu'il commande; ⌐que cette place très honorable ne me rapporte que 6000^f mais que comme je suis l'un des plus anciens Sous Lieutenants il est presumable que je serai bientôt Lieutenant avec⌐ 12,000^f par an.[4]

Je te temoignais en consequence, et je te temoigne encore le plus ardent desir de te voir arriver ainsi que notre cher Alex au quel j'ecrivais aussi à ce sujet, en le laissant le maître comme je le laisse encore de retourner à Cambridge à la fin de ses vacances. ⌐Je prevoyais de loin ce qui est resulté de la vente de la bibliotheque!!! Je n'ai pas meilleure opinion à present de l'affaire d'Irlande, et quant à notre pauvre Cottage, je te suppliais de persister, coute que coute, à ne la traiter que directement et non par l'intermediaire d'un homme de loi que Mr Lock n'a pas plus que moi jugé necessaire quand nous l'avons commencée!!!

---

[2] Named on 17 June 1814 sous-lieutenant in Luxembourg's 'compagnie de gardes du Corps', M. d'A was presented to Louis XVIII the following day.

[3] The duchesse d'Angoulême recognized few and gave the impression of haughtiness. 'In reality she was full of virtues and kindness, a French princess at heart, but she managed to make people think that she was disagreeable, cruel, and hostile . . .' (Boigne, i. 349).

[4] See L. 806 n. 2.

Je pense comme toi qu'il n'y a pas ⟨entierement⟩ à perdre pour les reparations à faire à cette malheureuse maison, et je crois que le mieux, c'est de s'en rapporter à la personne honnête qui l'occupe. Si tu te decides, ô mon amie, à venir me retrouver avec Alex, je pense comme je te l'ecrivais que ce qu'il y a de mieux à faire *de nos meubles* dont nous ¹ ne tirerions que bien peu de choses, seroit de les envoyer à Camilla Cottage. Fais au surplus sur cela comme sur tout le reste tout ce qui pourra te paraitre le plus convenable. J'avoue que malgré tout ce que j'ai fait pour m'y preparer, il m'est impossible de m'accoutumer à l'immuable idée que plus de vingt mille volumes dont mille au plus avaient été legués separement se sont trouvés reduits à 4,600 et n'ont produit que £1441 dont il nous reviendra à peine 500 que j'echangerais bien volontiers contre ⟨*Un grand mille*⟩ qu'on a jugé à propos de nous retirer.

Dieu le sait! si c'est la mendicité de cette somme qui excite mes regrets? La verité est neanmoins que le traitement que nous eprouvons dans cette ⟨tant⟩ aimée Angleterre m'a fait et me fait encore bien du mal, et qu'il a bien et trop influé sur mes idées de bonheur à venir.⁋ Quant au moment actuel, j'ai fait mon amie ce que ma conscience, l'honneur et ce que j'ai cru mon devoir me dictaient. Je desire par dessus tout au monde l'approbation de l'unique amie, de la dearest partner of my life! Je sens tout ce que doit te couter une separation aussi douloureuse: mais songe que lorsque ta santé sera retab[lie] tu pourras aller chaque année passer quelque tems avec les amis veritables qui nous sont restés; et que notre fils t'y tiendra compagnie; Car s'il trouve son avantage à continuer la carriere qu'il a embrassée, je ne m'y opposerai point. Ma seule condition c'est qu'il viendra passer avec nous la plus grande partie de ses vacances, et l'autre avec toi seule qu'il ¹ menerait en Angleterre jusqu'à ce que j'allasse te rechercher à Douvres.

J'avoue que j'aimerais encore davantage qu'il revint ici, et je dois ajouter que dans cette esperance je l'ai fait inscrire dans la compᵉ de Mʳ de Luxembourg. Qu'il fasse ses reflexions avant de refuser cette place qui lui donnerait tout de suite le grade de Lieutenant, et me procurerait l'inexprimable bonheur de ne plus me separer de deux êtres dont l'honneur seul me tient eloigné. Songez tous deux que je n'exprime ici qu'un

388

desir mais bien tendre bien profondement senti. Quant à toi
mon ange Rens moi le plutôt qu'il te sera possible la tranquillité et toutes les jouissances celestes d'une union tous les jours
plus chere. Amen!

J'ai lu ton ouvrage, et je t'avoue que plus d'une fois j'ai été
tenté de le trouver moins attachant que ses ainés: mais je dois
à la verité d'ajouter que le plus souvent j'ai reconnu mon tort,
et qu'après l'avoir achevé, mon idée predominante a été que
tu y as deployé autant de talent que dans tout ce qui l'a precedé;
que ton plan bien conçu est superieurement executé, et que
cette nouvelle production peut etre de la plus grande utilité.
Personne ce me semble, ne suit mieux que toi le precepte
d'Horace de mêler *l'agreable à l'utile*;[5] et je suis bien certain que
tôt ou tard le Public sortira de l'espace d'apathie où il reste
concernant *the Wand*[*erer*][6]
    4 lettres me sont parvenues.
    La derniere porte le N° 5. et consequement il en manque 1.[7]

Tous les Maubourgs avaient ecrit sur une des feuilles de
l'enorme paquet que tu aurais du recevoir de moi par M.r le C.te
de La Châtre à qui j'ecrivais.[8]

[xxxxx 3 *lines*]

ᵣ⟨mon oncle qui t'embrasse est venu ici hier pour me voir.⟩ᵔ

[xxxxx 1 *line*]

---

    5 M. d'A refers specifically to Horace's *De Arte Poetica*:

        omne tulit punctum qui miscuit utile dulci,
        lectorem delectando pariterque monendo.
                        (ll. 343–4)

Implicitly M. d'A refers to the financial rewards and fame attendant upon the
proper mixture of the sweet with the useful.

        hic meret aera liber Sosiis, hic et mare transit
        et longum noto scriptori prorogat aevum.
                        (ll. 345–6)

    6 In a letter now missing, FBA must have mentioned the tepid—even hostile—
notices of *The Wanderer* in *The Quarterly Review* (Apr. 1814) and *The British Critic*
(Apr. 1814). See Appendix IV.
    7 M. d'A received L. 782 (30 May), L. 790 (9 June), L. 794 (24 June), L. 795
(29 June) designated by FBA as No. 5.
    8 The notes of 'Tous les Maubourgs' are missing.

63 Lower Sloane Street,
6 July 1814

To Charles Burney

A.L.S. (Osborn), 6 July 1814
Double sheet 8vo   4 pp.   *pmks*   [T.P.P.] U. / Chelsea   EO   6 JY ⟨ ⟩
Addressed: Rev⁴ Dr. Burney, / Rectory House, / Deptford.

63 Lower Sloane Street Chelsea.
6ᵗʰ July 1814

Certainly, my dear Charles, I shall be very glad to have an
£100—and, for reasons good, as soon as may be; for I should be
glad to be enabled to *write* & to *hear* again from Paris before I
make my new arrangements in the funds. I had only declined
this offer when you made it me some time ago, from scruples
not to precede Hetty in any receival:¹ but as that scruple is
done away, I shall gladly avail myself of the convenience. But
I shall be much obliged if you can give it me in £20 Drafts, &
not in the gross sum at once.

How I rejoice at the hearty word you are now able to use for
our dear Rosette! *bravely*! My kind love to her, I beg; I ¹ hope
& trust the sea air will wholly establish *her* & strengthen *you*.
Were Ryde nearer, & were I not in search of a Tutor,² I should
be tempted to join you. But my extra means must all be con-
secrated to my Boy. Where-ever I can do best for Him I shall
fix my remnant summer.

I called yesterday upon Lady Crewe, but had not the good
fortune to find her at home. I was more fortunate with my old
friend, ci-devant Miss Anguish now Dˢ of Leeds,³ who received
me, after an absence from each other of *26 years*, with a cordiality
the most gratifying! I am engaged to her again next week.

The princess Augusta has condescendingly invited me to

---

797. ¹ Because several of CB's legacies were already settled (L. 790), CB Jr.,
as executor of his father's estate, paid EBB and FBA the first instalment of the
money earned from the sale of their father's miscellaneous library.

² FBA felt an indolent AA needed tutoring during the long vacation. Her
sense of urgency is indicated in Ll. 798, 803, 804, 805.

³ See L. 671 n. 1. The Duchess of Leeds in 1814 lived at 69 Lower Grosvenor
Street. FBA had last seen her on 13 Aug. 1787 when she was still 'the eldest
Miss Anguish'. At that time she was considered 'a good-natured girl, and so warm
in her affections, that she seems made up of nothing else' (*DL* iii. 303).

take a quiet view of the Fête & Fireworks from Her R. H.⟨ness⟩ apartment.[4] So I am beginning to peep again from my Cell. The relief of my Letter from Paris no words can express, though its ǀ contents would by no means have been of unmixt pleasure[5] but for my dreadful fears. However, I have still hopes of an arrangement after my own desire ULTIMATELY—The present season of exertion from *the FAITHFUL & LOYAL* over, resignation, at 60 odd years of age, will never be ill viewed, should our affairs here authorise the prudence of such a measure. At all events, M. d'A. will have a furlough to come over, not alone for *Me*, but to finally settle our poor Cottage.

Pray don't forget to thank dear *Parr* for his kindness in trusting me with his friend's Letter.[6] It was really precious to me at that time. My poor shy Algebraist owns you gave him *unspeakable* relief in opening for him his business of the Exchange of the Dictionary![7]—

Adio, Dear Charles; I wish you a STALL That may serve you for Rose, Parr, Fan, Bright, Tit, & All!

F B d'A.

How is it there are so few learned wights that I can't get a Tutor? or, that learned wights are so rich, they will not sell a little leisure?

[4] FBA anticipates the Fête on 21 July 1814, which the Prince Regent gave at Carlton House in honour of the Duke of Wellington. The Fête is described in *AR* lvi (1814), 'Chronicle', 63–5.

[5] L. 793, dated [18 June]. What FBA implies is her disappointment that M. d'A was not made 'Consul français' and her concern that he must fulfil an arduous and expensive military role (i.e. buying uniforms, keeping a groom and two horses on an annual salary of 6,000 francs).

[6] Armed with a letter of introduction (Bodleian) from CPB to M. d'A, Robert Finch (1783–1830) reported to his friend, he had visited M. d'A in Paris. Finch, an Oxonian (B.A. 1805, M.A. 1809), was an antiquary, who in 1814 travelled through France, Switzerland, Italy, Greece, and the Holy Land to study fine arts and antiquities. See Diary Entry, 24 June.

[7] Inheriting from CB *A New and General Biographical Dictionary*, M. d'A turned it over to AA, who wanted to trade it for a book on mathematics. See L. 741 n. 21.

63 Lower Sloane Street,
8–11 July 1814

To M. d'Arblay

A.L. (Diary MSS. vii. 6004–[07], Berg), 8–11 July 1814
Originally two double sheets 4to (9·5 × 7·8″) paged 1–8   6 pp. The first
leaf of the second double sheet (pp. 5 & 6) is cut away and missing; other
leaves (pp. 3–4 and 7–8) were mutilated. See the Textual Notes.
Edited by FBA, p. 1 (6004), *docketed and redated incorrectly*: ⟨17⟩ June 18.
Edited also by CFBt *and the* Press. *See* Textual Notes.

8ᵗʰ July 1814

Ah mon ami! You are really then well? really in Paris?
really without hurt or injury? What I have suffered from a
suspence that has no name from its misery shall now be buried
in restored peace & hope & happiness. With the most fervant
thanks to Providence that my terrours are removed, & that
I have been tortured by only false apprehensions, I will try ⌐to
recover from this shake, &⌐ to banish from my mind all but
the joy, & gratitude to Heaven, that your safety & health
inspire. Yet still, it is difficult to me to feel assured that all is
well! I have so long been the victim to fear & anguish, that my
spirits cannot at once get back their equilibrium.

⌐Every one takes for granted some Letters I send miscarried
& I cannot humble myself by proclaiming my disappointment
in it, therefore press not, rude people are only Agents of ridicule
when they publish their ridiculous reports abroad.⌐

I am charmed your dear excellent uncle is come to you. What
an active zeal of warm friendship! presentez lui mes hommages
les plus tendres ainsi que les plus sincères.

Quel bonheur pour moi qu'Alex a été à mon côté at this
trying interval!—He is well, but, as usual, incurably irregular
in his pursuits & unequal in his application. He dreadfully
wants a private Tutor to steady his studies, & direct them: &,
non obstant the expence, I am now endeavouring, through the
good Mr. Hagget, to procure him some lessons.

Far, far, indeed, am I from insensible to the Honour &

distinction[1]—so justly merited, so long earned, of the place you now occupy; yet, for me, what a calamity! for how am I to join you? I set aside all objections relative to my health, which, you well know, will always suffer yet more from the anxieties & *ennui* of separation | than from any risk that may be feared with regard to my health. But hear, & direct, if possible, the difficulties of my situation.

1st For our son. Can you really think him adapted to a military life?[2] the *brusqueris* of his character, ⌈yet timidity of his Nature,⌉ joined to an unconquerable ignorance of the ways of the world, & an absence & thoughtlessness that make him never ready for any appointment; nor steady to any engagement —surely seem bars insuperable, without counting my own repugnance to a Son of the Two Nations entering that career. He has never, also, mounted a Horse, & daily he grows more near sighted. Yet I venture not to make the positive proposition, till I hear from you more deliberately. It would be cruel to unhinge his present happiness in his actual pursuits & prospects, by telling him he might *follow mathematics at his pleasure*, & *play at Chess* as much as he desired. Catching at those 2 ideas, he would not be able to ruminate upon any other.

Yet 2dly How quit him? Oh my dear friend! every day, every hour shews me the danger, the evil, the even cruelty of leaving without a Guide, an Adviser, a Confident, a young creature so imminently in want of all, so unformed, nay, unformable, yet so valuable, so full of ULTIMATE promise, & so precious! — — even now, when he is by my side, & my whole time & thoughts are given to him, it requires a vigilance the most UNREMIT-TING to save him, alternately, from consuming himself by an application that disclaims SLEEP food, exercise, or rest — — OR from a dissipated idleness, that, without constraint or *bût quelconque*, wastes Hour after Hour, Day after Day, in idleness, positive nothingness, or dangerous visits to a place where his vanity is attracted, though his approbation is withheld—What, what can be done! the whole of | my happiness hangs upon

---

798. [1] See L. 788 n. 11 for the reasons that FBA acknowledges the 'Honour & distinction' of her husband's 'place'.

[2] FBA's negative response to the hint expressed by M. d'A in L. 793 that AA might have an honourable military career in France. The hint became a statement in L. 796 (not yet received by FBA): 'je l'ai fait inscrire dans la compe de Mr de Luxembourg.'

YOU and your society—yet all my peace of mind will be broken, & even my conscience will [be] deranged, if I quit this dear impracticable Boy till the moment I am always awaiting arrives, of his awakening to Reason & Common sense & Order. ⌐You built much upon Clement, but after you were gone from Cambridge,[3] the old fit of poor example, Alas returned, & Clement, after vainly remonstrating, left him wholly to himself, & even quitted Cambridge for the long vacation without taking leave of him.⌐

At this moment, however, he is repentant of his folly;[4] ⌐For if I was present here, & some help, I think he is disposed to seriously work this vacation, which lasts to the 20th October, to his sure & unrestricted good!⌐ But it is only with *watching* & *urging*, & *soothing*. There is no voluntary *Suite* in any pursuit.—

Yet, once again, if we can keep him from peril till he is a more fixed character, There is nothing we may not hope, ultimately, to repay us for patience & perseverance in rearing him.

But Exhortation & Counsel are vain; his own promises, nay, his good intentions, are vain! vain, because never remembered. Watching & reminding are all that serve him.

[*About 9 lines cut away and missing*]

⌐. . . mutual *appreciation* gave, & our long absence joined to our previous seclusion from the World, has prevented us forming any other. In what manner, that without destruction to all interests, can I quit the country [with] the *accession* & the *Cottage* unsettled?

The melancholy, oh mon ami!—how melancholy a prospect of penury,—& of loss of independence for our Boy, ever is ours! —! —

11 July The *Cottage*: To This you must give your most immediate attention as the Repairs must take place at all events during the *belle saison*.

I have never had *any* answer from Mr. Hudson. But I will relate you Martin's account of Mr. Murray's last conference:

---

[3] For the visit of M. d'A to Cambridge in May, see L. 776 and Diary Entry, 14 May. M. d'A hoped also that the industrious Clement would set AA an example of scholarly behaviour. Indeed, Clement's zeal stunned MF, who wrote (JRL) Mrs. Piozzi that 'poor Clem . . . has studied & fagged himself for this Senior-wranglership, more than his strength would bear, reading, sometimes . . . till he fainted away' (21 Dec. 1814).

[4] See L. 782 n. 4.

to work as quickly as possible, that the ruin of Nature may not mar the little Building, & double the expence of repairs! oh that you could be here to superintend!——⁵

Remember to *Play the field* at the price offered to Mr. Hudson, if Mr. Hudson, or William would not give £1000 for the⌐⁶

[*About 9 lines cut away and missing*]

[*Pp. 5 and 6 are missing*]

Your Letter, mon ami, had not it's tardiness so terribly distressed me, is all I could wish—interesting, full of intelligence, satisfactory, instructive, & amusing, while full of kindness & feeling. You make me *aimer* not *un peu*, as she is so good, in her Letter, as to desire, but *beaucoup*, et *de bon coeur*, Madame de Laval—her amitié for you has an activity of zeal, & a delicacy of *tacte*, with a spirit of constancy, that are truly charming.⁷

[*The remainder of the page is missing*]

⌐Have you been paid the 25 £ˢᵗ de M. de Billy?⁸

I hope Madᵉ de Simiane has had the consolation & happiness of seeing her Brother⁹ [*wafer stain*] Madᵉ de Damas¹⁰ & extremely *soulagée* by the re[turn] of M. le comte Alexis¹¹ & a return so honourable. Madᵉ de Cadignan I hope is well & happy. My comp to her. I beg'd Miss Planta¹² to call & Lady R⟨olle⟩¹³ with her. I am always uneasy at the fate of my Letters, written, in 6 I have extreme confidence. 7 that preceded your journey Letter—[*cut*] of these 2. This again is my 9ᵗʰ since⌐

[*The remainder of the page is missing*]

⁵ See L. 831 for the reaction of M. d'A to the condition of Camilla Cottage and William Locke's assessment of its state of disrepair.

⁶ See Ll. 646 n. 26; 781 n. 6; 808.

⁷ See vi, Diary Entry, 24 June 1805.   ⁸ See L. 769 n. 16.

⁹ Charles de Damas d'Antigny (L. 747 n. 14). With the return of the monarch, she enjoyed seeing him created pair de France, one of only six so honoured (Boigne, i. 366). Additionally he was given in 1814 a new military assignment as lieutenant-général in the maison militaire of Louis XVIII. 'Les deux compagnies de chevau-légers et de gendarmes de la garde, dites *Compagnies Rouges* à cause de leurs uniformes, avaient été accordées au comte Charles de Damas et au comte Étienne de Durfort' (Vitrolles, ii. 24).

¹⁰ Marie-Joséphine-Catherine Collet married Alexandre, comte de Damas, in 1783.

¹¹ Alexandre, comte de Damas (1755–*post* 1816), began his army career in 1771. In 1792 he emigrated with the prince de Condé, accompanied the latter to England, and did not return until the Restoration, when the rank of lieutenant-général was conferred.   ¹² Barbara Planta (d. 1834). See L. 803 n. 3.

¹³ Judith Maria Walrond (1751–1820) married in 1778 John Rolle, 1st Baron Rolle of Stevenstone. See L. 696 n. 9.

799   63 Lower Sloane Street,
                                  [*c.* 7] July 1814[1]

To Mrs. Locke

L., imperfect copy by CFBt (Diary MSS. viii. 6008–10, Berg), July 1814
Double sheet 4to   3 pp.   pp. 1 and 3 foliated: 57, 58
Edited by the Press. *See* Textual Notes.

                                     London
To Mrs Locke   July. 1814
Norbury Park.

After a most painful suspense I have been at length relieved by a letter from Paris. It is dated the 18th of June, & has been a fortnight on the road. It is, he says, his 4th letter—& he had not then received one of the uneasy tribe of my own—

The Consul Generalship is—alas—entirely relinquished—& that by M: d'Arblay himself, who has been invited into the *Corps de Garde* by the Duc de Luxembourg, for his own *Compagnie*; an invitation he deemed it wrong to resist at such a moment—& he has since been named one of the Officers of the Corps de Garde by the King, Louis XVIII, to whom he had taken the customary oath that very day, the 18th—[2]

The Season, however, of danger over, & the Throne & Order steadily re-established,[3] he will still, I trust & believe, retire to civil domestic life. May it be speedily! he is dreadfully worn & fatigued by the last year; & he began his active services at thirteen years of age, He is now past sixty. Every propriety therefore will abet my wishes, when the King no longer requires around him his tried & faithful adherents. And, indeed, I am

799. [1] This letter was written *c.* 7 July, when the Thanksgiving for peace was celebrated at St. Paul's.   [2] See L. 793.
  [3] Almost from the day of Louis XVIII's return to France, there was unrest. In the salons of the Bonapartists the disappointed generals and other supporters of the Empire ridiculed the pretensions of the *émigrés*. Mme de Staël gave dinner parties usually three times a week at her house in Clichy for the leaders of the Liberal Party. At these gatherings François-*Charles*-Louis Comte (1782–1837), the editor of *Censeur*, Benjamin Constant (1767–1830), Lafayette, and their hostess accused the new regime of reactionary tendencies. But the real danger to the Bourbon dynasty came ironically from royalist newspapers. *La Quotidienne* and *Le Journal Royal*, e.g., denounced the men and institutions of the Revolution, undermined the significance of the Charter, and hinted at retaliatory measures against anyone associated with liberal causes. Such journalism provoked open discontent among most of the general public. Shopkeepers and workers had other grievances. They felt their ability to manufacture and sell was hampered by Church decrees that banned work on Sundays and certain Holy days.

by no means myself insensible to what is so highly gratifying to his feelings, as this mark of distinction: *bien plus honorable, cependant,* as he adds, than *lucrative,* for the appointment is only of 6000 francs—and he must have 2 Horses & a Groom. Their *nourriture,* however, is by the Government, but the Uniforms, &c, are scarcely paid by such a stipend.

I must remain here till my own many affairs are settled, & till he sees the turn likely to accelerate or retard his final projects abroad. But he will obtain a short leave of absence in the Autumn, should matters wear a procrastinating aspect.

I shall quite grieve if you have never been tempted from your retirement to view the Good and THEREFORE really Great Emperor. I delight in the unpretending simplicity of his manner & conduct. The King of Prussia made friends of all who most nearly approached him.[4] Blucher is still the general Idol.[5] And he seems to ˡ enjoy as well as merit so being. Platoff is the only one of the noble set I have not had the pleasure to see.[6] Nothing else has yet taken me forth. But my own kind Princess Augusta graciously asks me to see the fireworks from her R.H's apartment.[7] And to that I gladly consent. Rejoicings for PEACE!

800   [63 Lower Sloane Street,
                      c. 11–17 July 1814]
To Mrs. Waddington

A.N. (Berg), *n.d.*
Double sheet 12mo   2 pp.   black seal
Addressed: Mrs. Waddington, / 65—Welbeck Street

To-Morrow, my sweet Friend—&, after 1 O'clock—(I have business at 12) at what hour you please, & for as long as you

4 It was not difficult to see the visiting monarchs, who made London their base, 8–23 June. For the various opportunities to observe the visitors, see L. 804 n. 3.
5 Field Marshal Gebhard Leberecht von Blücher (1742–1819) arrived in London 7 June 1814 and did not leave for home until 11 July. FBA saw him not at the Queen's Court 8 June but perhaps on his arrival in London and later at the Covent Garden Theatre (Diary Entry, pp. 514–15, 516). Of all the visiting dignitaries he attracted the greatest public affection (*The Times*, 8 June).
6 Count Matvei Ivanovich Platoff (or Platov, 1751–1818), the hero of the Moscow campaign, arrived in Dover early on the morning of 6 June and remained in England until 16 July.
7 In honour of the Duke of Wellington (L. 797 n. 4).

can. I shall let you into my little Nut shell parlour whence I exclude NEARLY all others—for I came to this place—in better times! merely to *sleep*, while I *lived* at the College!—Alexander has *no* mornings at his disposal[1] but for occasions that are indispensable | but I hope you will engage him to you in an Evening—I dare not tell him how kind you are—it would frighten the poor *sauvage*—not *savage*—100 miles away—[2]

My kind Love to your 3 dear children, & comp[ts] to Mr. W. —It will truly charm me to embrace you my dearest Mary!——& I trust we shall always fix a re-meeting at every interview.—à demain!—

801   [63 Lower Sloane Street,
                                          11 July—28 August 1814]
To Mrs. Waddington

A.N. (Berg), *n.d.*
Single sheet 4to   cut down to (4·2 × 7·3″)   1 p.
Addressed: Mrs. Waddington / Welbeck Street / 65

Be still better, my sweet Mary, on *Friday*—for I have already disposed of Thursday, knowing my dear Fanny Raper means then to be with you: she had commissioned me to enquire, yesterday, for her when she might be sure to find you on that day. She breakfasts in town,[1] & therefore could suit herself to any time. Pray give her a line. And me one, also, relative to *Friday*, & yet more to your continued amendment. How wounded I feel that your MUCH amended looks were not more true Heralds of emended health & strength!—

If unfortunately your Friday should be gone, & you let me know in time, I will make a new arran[ge]ment & close in with Thursday.

800. [1] Watched over by FBA, AA spent many of his mornings in study. At this time he was preparing for a new examination in Classics to be taken next autumn. In a letter (Berg) to M. d'A, dated 7 July 1814, AA reported: 'I am here with Mamma reading for the next term, & the following—nos sujets pour l'Examen Classique sont Hérodote et St Luc; l'auteur latin n'a pas encore été nommé.'

[2] FBA emphasizes the French meaning of 'sauvage'—a shy, unsociable person, although in L. 658 she called AA a 'savage'.

801. [1] Fanny Raper lived in Chelsea at Cook's Grounds, King's Road.

802

To Mrs. Waddington

A.L. (Berg), *n.d.*
Single sheet 4to   1 p.   wafer
Addressed: Mrs. Waddington.

I have time but to thank my dear Friend & both her amiable daughters—a person being just entered who comes to me with a message from Paris.—

Let me know, if possible, that you are better.—

N B—

Unless your friend has resigned all his LEGATION plans, his coming hither upon this project will not forward them!—*here*, nor *there*![1] — —

Weigh—but only *yourself*, this N.B.

803

[63 Lower Sloane Street,]
13 July 1814

To M. d'Arblay

A.L. (rejected Diary MSS. 6012–[17], Berg), 13 July 1814
Originally a double sheet large 4to   4 pp.   and, conjecturally, a single sheet 4to, a large cutting from which was used as a paste-on for p. 3 (6014) in all 5 pp.   wafer
Addressed: À Monsieur / Monsieur le Chev[r] d['Arblay]
Edited by FBA, p. 1 (6012), *numbered*: 18
p. 5 (6016), *annotated*:   ⁂·
Edited also by CFBt *and the* Press. *See* Textual Notes.

July 13th 1814—Yesterday I received my *2d Letter* from Paris![1] *2* in near 7 Weeks!—Alas! I must re-make myself, or be worn out by absence, distance, & silence thus united! And how act?

802. [1] In the back of FBA's mind was the failure of M. d'A to secure the post of 'Consul français'. Despite her acquaintance with Castlereagh and Cathcart, and her husband's with Duras and Talleyrand, the d'Arblays had no influence in diplomatic circles and could, therefore, be of no help to anyone with 'LEGATION plans'.

803. [1] See L. 796, dated 3 July 1814. The previous letter (793) was dated [18 June 1814].

—my perplexity & embarrassment only encrease, for I see no way that is clear; *Danger* menaces on one side—that of quitting our Boy; *Sorrow* abides always in the other, that of staying away from my best Friend.—I have written copiously upon all by Mr. Entwisle[2]—Miss B. Planta will take this, & sets off to-morrow, July 14th.[3]

I must keep exclusively to business, as it is late when I receive the Notice for writing, & my Letter must be off this afternoon. And upon business of such varied interests, such opposing calls, I cannot write quick. I try to weigh all I say, that I may be explicit, & make my difficulties clearly understood.

After what I have already represented about our chief Care, will not your own recollections join to shew the impossibility of a military career? His slowness in every sort of preparation; his insuperable disregard of *appearance* or *opinion*, which daily, hourly, fill me with vexation, in the midst of all my ultimate hopes from Time & Reason, would absolutely rob *YOU* of rest or peace, if you witnessed them where their ascendance would be so destructive. Exhortation is UTTERLY vain; constant watching, spurring, goading, alone have any chance: for argument & persuasion, or even Menace, are useless, because, though acquiesced in from their truth, & acceded to from his own candour, they are positively & literally forgotten the next moment! He promises with facility, for he Means to perform: but neither performance nor promise occur to him the next half hour! Yet is he full of a thousand qualities that—if he escape the Quick sands of his slack & tardy formation,—may

---

[2] John Entwisle (1744–1817) of Foxholes in the parish of Rochdale, Lancashire; Hamer Hall of the same county; and Cadoxton near Neath in Glamorganshire. A man of great wealth derived from investments in textile manufacture and landed property, he was also interested in the arts. He collected a fine library and maintained a gallery of 'paintings, engravings, prints, philosophical instruments, arms, etc.' (See his will, proved at Chester 10 Jan. 1818, a copy of which is now in the National Library of Wales.)

M. d'A may have become acquainted with him through mutual friends (e.g. James Greene, Mrs. Waddington, Benjamin Hall) or through Entwisle's nephew James Heywood Markland (1788–1864), who resided at the Inner Temple as did Martin Burney.

Entwisle received his last passport for France on 3 Aug. 1815, and because of his textile interests, it was endorsed by W. Tate, a muslin merchant and ware-houseman, of 8 Old Jewry.

[3] On 13 July 1814 AA also wrote to M. d'A regarding Miss Planta's departure as courier. 'Miss Planta part demain (Jeudi) au lieu de Lundi comme elle avait projeté.' Her departure was delayed because the Foreign Office did not issue her and Lady Rolle a passport (No. 921) until 12 July.

end in all that we can wish, & make him ONCE AGAIN the pride & comfort of our lives. Such he was, till those fatal 6 prizes turned his understanding into presumption, & his application into caprice.[4] He thought—& still thinks—he could, & can, do *what* he pleases *when* he pleases. This perverse secret vanity casts him upon indolence & whim, & he never begins any thing, little or Great, in time, or with sufficient diligence to make it even possible to obtain Success.[5] How, else, could your poor 3 days at Cambridge have 'made his happiness his ruin?'[6]

At this time, we are living wholly together, & I believe he is going on so as to retrieve his credit next term, October: but he requires my entire attention, with all I possess of address, affection, reason, & still to keep him to any sort of steadiness & regularity. His pursuits, naturally, are so desultory, as to leave them all superficial. He loves ONLY problems, & quits all else for their operations, without learning what should lead to them, or weighing what may result from them.

I am seeking him, now, at whatever expence, a *private Tutor*; not to live with, but to give him lessons 3 times a week. The good Mr. Haggitt will find me one.[7] We have no chance, otherwise, that his studies, however ardent, will so be regulated as to turn to account at his next examination.

[4] FBA traced AA's 'presumption' to France in 1806 when, as a schoolboy, he won honours for general excellence: specifically, first prizes in Memory, Geography, History, Version, and Thème (vi, L. 580). Between 1806 and 1814, FBA's attitude toward these prizes underwent drastic change. In 1806 her pleasure was so evident that CBFB wrote (JRL) to Mrs. Piozzi on 9 June [1806]: 'My Father has received a Letter from my Sister d'Arblay lately in wch she says her Son Alexander, now *rising thirteen*, has been a Competitor for Prizes at the School at Passy, & in the presence of 700 Spectators my Sister & M. d'Arblay had the Happiness of hearing every Prize adjudged to their Son for Learning, Good Conduct, &c.—'

[5] This evaluation of AA's behaviour is verified by the way in which he prepared his Tancred speech for delivery on 28 Oct. 1814. Despite eight months of forewarning, he made no attempt to prepare his oration until two days before its delivery. In a letter (Berg), dated 1 Nov. 1814, he told FBA how he searched frantically for suitable materials to be interlarded with 'this & that commonplace remark of my own'. The task finished, he calmly 'went to bed'.

[6] M. d'A went to Cambridge on 14 May and returned to Chelsea on 17 May. See Diary Entries, p. 511.

[7] According to AA writing (Berg) to M. d'A on 13 July 1814: 'Mais heureusement nous avons eu, Maman et moi, le *good luck* la bonne fortune, grâce à l'obligeance du respectable Mr Haggitt, de faire connaissance avec un jeune Gradué de l'Université que je verrai 3 fois par semaine, et avec qui j'étudierai les parties seches et Geometriques qui je n'aurais guères le pouvoir, ou la Courage, d'étudier tout seul. Nous commençons Lundi [i.e. 18 July] et je me prépare en attendant.'

M. Ch. de Thuisy,[8] who has sent me your Letter, says he has a Box of Books for Alexander at Richmond. I shall get them as quickly as possible. He is in extacy of delight at their prospect.[9]

But let me leave you to cogitate upon this First subject of our hearts, & go to one upon which no time must be lost for decision.

Your desire to keep the Cottage *as it is*, & send to it our few goods, makes me still think you certainly mean to come over? My perplexity, however, reaching the good Mr. Haggitt, I was invited to discuss the matter at his house, 2 days ago, *legally*; as he is as well versed in Law, nearly, as in Theology, from having had the arduous task of being Guardian to 4 Minors, who had landed property in difficult positions to arrange by Law.

I told him our whole history, from the beginning: I can only have room to give you the *result* of his opinion, after a conversation *pro* & *con* of 2 or 3 Hours. Our case, he says, is extremely hard, but our injury, though great, is irremediable! Our *fault* must pay its *forfeiture*; i.e. of building before we had secured our right of possession!! The History of our Trust may make us *pitied* but cannot make us *righted*: setting Friendship & equity, as moral circumstances, aside, Mr. William Lock, he says, as a *Gentleman*, & according to *Law*, acts fairly & honourably, in letting us sell the house by This valuation; for *WE* can *never* sell it ourselves! *NOBODY* would buy of *US* without a Title!—And if 21 years are suffered to elapse, from the time of building, without any deed being drawn, he *believes* the property becomes *LEGALLY* Mr. William's!—for an entailed Estate can only be leased for 21 years de suite!—[10]

---

[8] See L. 773 n. 26.

[9] In gratitude AA wrote (Berg) to M. d'A on 13 July: 'M^r le Ct. de Thuisy est venu en Angleterre, il est allé droit à Richmond, d'où il écrit pour savoir l'adresse de Maman et lui pouvoir envoyer les livres que Vous avez eu la bonté de lui confier pour moi—ainsi je n'ai que le tems de vous en remercier sans les avoir vus.'

[10] Without a title deed, the d'Arblays never owned Camilla Cottage, but were lessees. '[I]n order to secure the full benefit of the lease the tenant had to perfect his title by entry and until then he had no estate in the land, but only a right, which was known as *interesse termini*.' See Halsbury's *Laws of England*, 3rd ed. (1958), xxiii. 466. Since the d'Arblays were 'tenants in tail', they 'had all the rights of enjoyment of a fee simple owner. . . . A statute of 1540 empowered [them] to grant leases binding on [their] issue for terms of not more than twenty-one years or a period of three lives'—theirs and AA's. See R. E. Megarry and H. W. R. Wade, *The Law of Real Property*, 3rd ed. (1966), p. 95. Even if the d'Arblays considered their land to be agricultural, 'farming leases were generally granted for terms up to twenty-one years' (ibid., p. 620).

Considering, therefore, the shortness of life, & the minority of the young William: with YOUR absence, my impossibility to act against that Family, & Alexander's unconquerable inexperience & helplessness in affairs: Mr. Haggitt says 'You have only, Madam, to *try* to have £700—or to *accept* the £640.— for where there is no *TITLE*, you can have no *claim*: & a single Death may annihilate in an instant all chance, or even possibility of redress.'[11]

ᴦI mentioned the Auction, & buying ourselves the 5 Acres, to which Mr. W[illiam Locke] now agrees—To That he answered, that unless you could come over & superintend the sale yourself, then strangers I must trust; the general propensity of all mankind to pay [their] court to the more gainfull, their house expenses of commissions, surveyors, documents &c would make the *result* in the *receipt*, not more lucrative, in the end than the sum now offered—The reparations, alone, he says, unless superintended by yourself, may be charged so arbitrarily, from my ignorance, & from the loss of ⟨the⟩ help *essential*, that we had far more wisely take & make best some sum offered *at once*, than risk the many chances & accidents of any delay. Take it then, he said, at once, or you may leave your son a Law Suit— that he can never gain!'

To this melancholy counsel, which sent me home in desperation, & yet full of indignation at our unjust position, I must now add, [that] though, at first, I revolted from it, I am now brought over to ⟨believe⟩ it best, for what else is to become of the poor Cottage this Winter? It is Mr. Hudson's only to the 1ˢᵗ of November.[12] He will *hire* it, he has openly declared, *no longer*: he will *purchase* or *quit* — — and how shall we let it when this Autumn is over? Who will take it for the Winter? And what can it be worth after a winter—unheated, & unaired?

Even if we *had* a Tenant [again] we should certainly not let till next | Summer,—Where is now our Steward? Could we apply any longer to Mrs. Locke? Impossible! she has been so hurt & offended by your Letter to William that, though all is reconciled again, she wrote, at the moment, a Letter of reproach that forbids us ever applying to her again if we would

[11] After protracted negotiations, William Locke agreed to £700 as the selling price for Camilla Cottage. See his deposit to the d'Arblay account at Hoare's for that sum on 26 Oct. 1815.
[12] See L. 646 n. 26.

not give up all character & dignity of conduct.[13] Who then, would receive the rent? pay the Taxes? oversee the Repairs? secure the premises from pillage, devastation, or abuses?

'Tis impossible for us to rent an ⟨untended⟩ house so situated.⊓

Alas, my dearest Friend, we must surely accept this miserable £640—Mr. Haggitt says 'twill be *throwing it away* to hesitate! An appeal he says will be vain, though half the World would pity us as victims, none could help us, & the other half would but smile at us as romantic dupes.

⊓Were *YOU here*, nevertheless, this summer, I should still persist to press for buying the 5 acres & selling them & the house by Auction—but another winter uninhabited, may make the poor Cottage really one half its value — — And, in fact, said Mr. Haggitt, a light building MUST have lost something of its prime value by the *wear & tear* of 17 or 18 years.[14]

Mr. Haggitt finished by saying that, however really hard & cruel was our case, he never heard one in which he saw less hesitation, for we had NOTHING better to gain, & ALL to risk by delay.

Weigh this with Mr. Entwisle — — Think how Time flies & how reparations made by *US* will diminish our poor gain, for they will never be allowed for; & then force yourself to decide.

Our own Auction[15] has sickened me of my first earnest desire to sell thus by that mode; the pr Ctage, stamps, duties, taxes, &c &c so endless, & so confused & we are so entirely without *business heads* to advise & aid us, that my courage on that side is worn out.

And if it rests in our hands, the loss of support of the *Mère*,[16] she who kept the rents well paid, & the place well kept, may be destruction.

Weigh, weigh, & decide—& *then* write unequivocally, yet deliberately⊓ ⏐

[The top of the next leaf is missing]

[13] See Ll. 776 n. 4; 778 nn. 2, 5.
[14] Construction of Camilla Cottage was finished in November 1797 after about a year of effort.
[15] The recent sale of CB's miscellaneous library by Leigh and Sotheby in June 1814.
[16] Frederica Locke, William's mother. For an example of her concern for the d'Arblay cottage in 1803, see v, L. 536 n. 4. Mrs. Locke had also rented the cottage to Bolton Hudson seven or eight years before (L. 741 and n. 20).

Oh what will, at last, be our fate? When shall I again have a Home?—a Family? my own bosom Friend—Consoler—& all that is most beloved on Earth in one? — — when—when? & where? and How? — — — My whole soul wearies & sickens of this indefinable absence—

> yet—till the Cottage is finished—
> & the sales are over, & paid—
> as we have no Agent—
> James declining to act,

& Charles overwhelmed with other matter, & unfit—it would be absolutely throwing away all our little independance, both for ourselves & our Boy, to be BOTH away from all our most important worldly concerns.

I will hasten my part of finishing all that I can.

And, mean time, let us unremittingly reflect & watch for our dearest Alexander—adieu, mon trop TROP cher Ami!—

I am *well*, however, *pour ainsi dire*—save that, by a too long walk I have given myself a strain that I often feel very sensibly, though its swelling & pain are both always dispersed by the use of camphorated spirits. Is your Wrist quite cured—

[*The top fold of the page is missing*]

. . . found a regime for Alex [on whic]h he flourishes *à vu d'oeil*—

804   63 Lower Sloane Street,
                                            14 July 1814

To Charles Burney

A.L.S. (Osborn), 14 July 1814
Double sheet large 8vo   4 pp.   *pmks* T.P.P. ⟨ ⟩ 14 JY 1814
14 JY 1814   seal
Addressed: Rev^d Dr. Burney, / Ryde, / Isle of Wight.

                                    63 Lower Sloane St. Chelsea,
                                            July 14. 1814

I need not say with what trepidation I read your Letter, my

dearest Charles—Alex was out—& as he drank tea in James Street, I knew I should not see him till very late.¹ To wait was insupportable; I opened His Letter—& such had been my alarm, that I was *relieved* by the contents, as I found in them nothing new, & nothing that he had not himself avowed to me, save the *Eleventh* place, which I hope is still an exaggeration, as he told me the *Eighth*.²

At this time, & ever since his return to me, he is, and has been, going on perfectly well. He has given every morning completely to study, except when I have myself sent him out, either to see The Emperor,³ or to Mᵈᵉ La Châtre.⁴

As you had given me no hope of a Tutor, I had already applied to Mr. Haggitt, who has found me one, with whom he is to begin next Monday. I thank you, therefore, & dear Parr, but I have no occasion now for Mr. ⟨Iremonger⟩.⁵ The present person lives at Tower Hill! But that is nearer than Islington. He will meet Alex. in York Street Covent Garden at 10 o'clock in the morning, three times a week. The Terms I have left to Mr. Haggitt, & do not yet know. But all expence with me shall take that Channel, while things are in this alarming state. I shall hesitate therefore at nothing. What could to me be dear that would bring him into a better train?

I have not yet given him your Letter, I expect it to work upon him powerfully, as I know his high value for your good opinion & affection. I would not, therefore, waste it upon *mere* repentance; I reserve it for the first failure with his new Instructor: *now* he is really doing the best he can: but I foresee too painfully how soon he will be tempted to run riot again, when under controll: & this phillipic, which I have carefully re-

804. ¹ JB and AA met whenever possible to play whist or chess.
² AA's ranking among those who took the Classics examination in May 1814.
³ Arriving in Chelsea on 13 June, AA would have had many opportunities to see the Emperor: on 16 June, Alexander rode in state to St. Paul's to attend a special service for charity children; on 18 June he visited the Military Asylum and Chelsea Hospital, thereafter the Greenwich Hospital and the Observatory; on 19 June he drove in an open carriage to the Russian private chapel in Welbeck Street and to the Quaker meeting house in Peter's Court, St. Martin's Lane; on 20 June, his last public appearance, he reviewed the 'regular troops, with most of the Volunteer Corps in the metropolis' in Hyde Park. See L. 799 n. 4.
⁴ FBA's hasty writing of M. de la Châtre.
⁵ Either the Revd. Richard Iremonger (1779–1819), Oxford M.A. 1801, or his brother Frederick (1783–1820), Oxford M.A. 1810. Both were the grandsons of CB's friend Joshua Iremonger (1716–1804), of Wherwell, Hampshire, and London.

sealed, shall happen to arrive—by a private hand, just as his wavering genius is beginning to meander from the strait path prescribed by his preceptor.

Could I hope this Letter would make a lasting & indelible impression, I would end my cares & fears, by delivering it at once: but alas!—with the best intentions he has the frailest resolutions, & must forever be spurred, watched, Coaxed, or goaded, | to be kept from new mischief. He has not the smallest foresight of evil, or thought of consequences: & unhappy, nay, full of remorse as he felt at the abortive examination—3 Days over, it occured to him no more! Something MORBID certainly hangs about him; his health, therefore, is my first considera- tion: for he is either eager to petulance & rashness, or he has an apathy that leads to no cure but from Desperation. If he is now tractable, studious, & pursuing the strait line, it is, partly, at least, because the regimen, hours, &c that I super- intend for him, better his health, as his looks evidently shew, & in having his Nerves & system in a less irritable & disordered state, his mind & faculties are *serened* & more open to reason. My hopes, therefore, are always alive for better Days.

Mr. Bellamy, his Tutor-elect, is himself a Cantab. & has only left the university 2 years.[6] He is perfectly, therefore, *au fait* as to the reigning modes, & expectations, &c.

I have heard again, thank Heaven, from Paris.

I am extremely glad you are so well housed in the beautiful little Island.[7] I hope my dear Rosette feels her strength [returning] Daily; & Parr, & the | two Fannys & rising rival bloomer.[8]

But what am I to do for my dividend in the 5.ᵖʳ? & to change, as I desire, into the 4.?[9] They have refused Hetty hers, without a procuration from Mr. Burney? How can I get one from Paris? Is it inevitable? or will your presence & hand writing suffice, upon your return? What should I do? I received safely the

[6] James William Bellamy (1788–1874), a Cantabrigean, B.A. 1812, M.A. 1815, B.D. (Oxford, 1821). Ordained a deacon in 1813, he was in 1814 a priest at St. Mary Abchurch, London.

[7] Some time after 6 July (L. 797) and prior to 14 July (L. 804), CB Jr. and his family set up their summer quarters at Ryde.

[8] FBA's play on the name Brightblossom that CB Jr. gave to his older grand-daughter.

[9] By transferring her inherited 5 per cent Navy to the 4 per cent consols, FBA would receive a quarterly rather than a half-yearly dividend. But see L. 805 and n. 1.

drafts for the 100,[10] & thank you much for the mode devized. No news from the Archy?[11]—adieu

> yours ever
>
> F B. d'A.

805

63 Lower Sloane Street,
[15 July 1814]

To Mrs. Broome

A.L.S. (Berg), *n.d.*
Double sheet large 8vo   4 pp.   *pmk*   15 JY 1814   black seal
Addressed: Mrs. Broome, / Hill Street / Richmond.
Endorsed by CBFB: Sister d'arblay / 1814

63. Lower Sloane Street, Chelsea

How cruelly is this vexing, my dearest Charlotte! I cannot receive either principal or Dividend without a procuration from Paris![1] Esther has been denied payment for going without one from Mr. Burney.— —Your most kind service, therefore, must be at least put off, till I can procure advice how to proceed. In my uncertain situation & expences this is peculiarly uncomfortable. Perhaps Martin, who has promised to see me on Sunday, will be able to point out some remedy.

I have again, twice, I thank Heaven, heard from Paris. One Letter has been sent me by the Chev[r] de Thuisy, who has a Box of Books for Alexander—May I entreat you to send him, to the house of his Brother, the Marquis,[2] the enclosed | NOTE, requiring the Box, & then—will you have the goodness to let it be directed to me, here, & Booked, & be sent in such way as you deem safest? I know not why this Chevalier has taken it

---

10 See L. 797 n. 1.

11 The Archbishop of Canterbury (L. 723 n. 2), frequently so designated in vol. viii.

805. 1 FBA needed a 'procuration' or proxy from M. d'A to reinvest her inherited capital because 'by *marriage* the chattels real and personal of the wife are vested in the husband, in the same degree of property, and with the same powers, as the wife when sole had over them; provided he reduces them to possession' ('The Law of England Epitomised', in *Enc. Brit.*, 3rd ed., ix. 632). Apparently the procuration secured in Paris on 3 July 1812 (L. 643 n. 5) was either no longer valid or insufficiently comprehensive.

2 See Ll. 764 n. 8, 773 n. 26. The enclosed note is missing.

to Richmond, knowing my address here, & being first in town, whence he wrote to me.[3] But as I have no redress to hope from his awkwardness, I may as well *not call him to account*. Especially as a long interview might be the consequence: & then the explanation might be more troublesome than the obscurity.

All the World, in town, I am told, is occupied in discussing the history of the Royal Fugitive.[4] How melancholy is all that unhappy business! |

None of our affairs are settled—poor Charles is gone for sea air, by advice of Dr Baillie,[5] to the Isle of Wight. His head is so often disordered, that I am far from easy about his present state of health.

Of my own destination I am still very doubtful: but I am procuring Alex a private Tutor, whom he is to meet in London 3 times a week; & all my eagerness to quit this little habitation —& shake myself from its melancholy recollections by change of scene, give way to the hope of fixing his attention upon those dull bases of science which he wishes to skip over, to arrive by a short cut at its embillishments & flowers.

M. d'Arblay is not yet sure what his duties, his confinement, or his liberty may be; we put off all final arrangement till those previou[s] circumstances are ascertained. |

Whatever be the result, YOU, my dearest Charlotte, remain constantly amongst my first & warmest inducements for still wishing—though, of late, cruelly weaned[6]—to fix in England my remnant life.—

so witness your forever most affectionate

F B. d'A.

[3] See L. 803 n. 9.

[4] The Royal Fugitive is the Princess Charlotte of Wales. According to *AR* lvi (1814), 'General History', 218: 'the Prince Regent, accompanied by the Bishop of Salisbury, repaired to Warwick House, his daughter's residence, on July 12th, and announced the dismission of all her attendants, and his intention of taking her to Carlton House. This declaration . . . had such an effect on the young lady's feelings, that requesting leave to retire, she took the opportunity of escaping by the back stair-case, and rushing into the street, where she got into a hackney coach, and drove to Connaught House, her mother's residence. The Princess of Wales, much embarrassed by this unexpected visit, immediately drove to the parliament house to consult her friends what was proper to be done on the occasion. The result was, that the Princess Charlotte was persuaded to accompany her uncle, the Duke of York, to Carlton House.' For the notoriety that accompanied this event, see the 121 quatrains by Peter Pindar, *The Royal Runaway; or C—tte and Coachee!!* (1814).

[5] See L. 640 n. 3.

[6] FBA's disappointment over the failure of M. d'A to become Consul français in England.

15 July 1814

I have not seen James this fortnight. All goes unprosperously about our poor Cottage.[7] Alex joins in Love and compt[s] to all around you, [Twickenham] Meadows & Richmond Hill included.[8] Sally calls once a week—Esther is well, lively, spirited & ⟨alive⟩ as if still 25.— ¹

806   Paris, 17 July 1814

M. d'Arblay
To Madame d'Arblay

A.L. (Berg), 17 Juillet 1814
Double sheet 4to, greenish 4 pp. *pmks* FOREIGN 25 JY 25 JY 1814 wafer
Addressed: *Angleterre* / a Madame / Madame d'Arblay née Miss Burney / Lower Sloan Street N° 63 / *Chelsea*. / à Londre—
Edited by FBA, p. 1, *annotated*: ✴ 8 7 19

Paris ce 17 Juillet 1814.

Chere et admirable amie, je m'empresse de te faire passer une copie de la lettre que vient de m'adresser mon incomparable Capitaine le Duc de Luxembourg.

    "*Gardes du Corps du Roi,*
       Comp[e] de Luxembourg

"M[r] le Chevalier, j'ai l'honneur de vous prevenir que sur ma proposition le Roi, par ordonnance d'hier (14 Juillet) vous a accordé le brevet de Marechal de Camp pour prendre rang du mois de juillet mil sept cent quatre vingt douze, epoque

---

[7] The disposition of Camilla Cottage had not yet been determined. On 19 July 1814 Mrs. Locke (Barrett, Eg. 3697, ff. 191–2) wrote to FBA: '[William] very soon conversed about your business, which he is very anxious shou'd be settled: but, for *his satisfaction*, he begs that a person who is intirely approved by M[r] d'Arblay may be prevailed on to meet M[r] Murray, that the whole may be laid before him, as he must have his conduct perfectly understood by one whose opinion M[r] d'Arblay will defer to—after that, he trusts that y[e] business will be terminated to his, & your, satisfaction—it wou'd be considerably accelerated if the meeting cou'd take place at M[r] Murrays Chambers in Symonds Inn, as all the Deeds are there.' Through the efforts of JB, Sharon Turner became the supplementary 'opinion'. See JB's letter (Osborn, f.c. *post* 19 July 1814) to him.
[8] Archdeacon and Mrs. Cambridge lived in Twickenham Meadows; CBFB lived on Hill Street, Richmond.

410

où vous avez obtenu ce grade des bontés de Sa Majesté. Je vais en adresser la demande au Minstre de la Guerre.

J'ai l'honneur d'etre M^r le Chev^er avec attachement votre tres humble et tres obeissant Serviteur

Signé
Le duc de Luxembourg

Lorsque j'ai été lui en faire mes remerciemens, il m'a pris la main, et m'a dit avec la grace qu'il sait mettre à tout, ce serait à moi à vous en faire car aussitot que j'ai eu fait ma demande et que j'ai eu prononcé votre nom. S.M. s'est mise à sourire, et me l'a accordée avec l'air de satisfaction le plus marqué.

Tu sens bien ma chere Fanny que je ne manque point de reconnoitre la très bonne et très grande part de ce qui te revient ˡ pour la cause qui a produit et m'a valu cet air de satisfaction d'un si bon augure. J'espere qu'Alex y sera sensible, et je ne suis pas tout à fait sans me flatter quelquefois que cela pourra lui faire naitre l'idée de mettre le comble à mon bonheur en venant s'etablir tout à fait près de moi. Mais je ne puis trop le lui repeter ainsi qu'à toi ma bonne et toujours plus chere Fanny, son sort est absolument entre ses mains, et je me resignerai d'autant mieux à ce que vous aviez decidé tous deux à ce sujet, que pouvant disposer d'au moins six mois chaque année, nous serons toujours toi et moi les maitres de visiter l'angleterre quand une fois ta santé sera totalement rétablie.

La justice que le Roi a bien voulu me rendre est une veritable faveur; et cette faveur est pour nous très importante, puisqu'elle me donne la certitude d'avoir en peu de tems la facilité de mettre à execution notre projet de faire chaque année une course dans ton pays. En effet je me trouve avoir en ce moment 22 années de ˡ commission de M^al de Camp,¹ et comme aucun

806. ¹ The title of maréchal de camp had been conferred on 22 July 1792. But having deserted with Lafayette on 19 August and having resigned from the army on 1 September, M. d'A did not enjoy its rewards (v, L. 450 n. 9). In seeking to regain it—retroactive to 1792—he was supported by General Lafayette. In a letter (Vincennes), dated 28 May 1814 (with a postscript by Lafayette), M. d'A wrote to Gouvion-Saint-Cyr: 'Nommé Maréchal du Camp dans l'intervale du 21 Juin au 10 Aout 1802, mon brevet n'a point été expedié par la seule raison qu'à cette epoque tout a été bouleversé dans les bureaux de la Guerre. Je vous supplie, Monseigneur, de vouloir bien me faire confirmer ce grâce que l'Empereur a si bien reconnu lorsque j'ai sollicité ma retraite par ma memoire où j'esposais le droit que j'y avais, il a demandé un rapport pour *le Genal* d'Arblay. En vous faisant, Monseigneur, une demande si juste, mon intention n'est nullement de chercher à rentrer au activité, dans un tems où le nombre des places d'officiers generaux conservés se trouve si peu en proportion avec la quantité si considerable

des sous Lieutenans des gardes du Corps n'a ce grade, il est indubitable, que si Dieu me prete vie, je ne tarderai pas à être Lieutenant avec un traitement double de celui que j'ai actuellement.[2] Je ne dois pas non plus être bien longtems sans être general de division c.à.d. Lieutenant general.[3] A propos de tout cela je t'ai dejà mandé que pour peu que j'eusse cru que cela t'eut fait plaisir j'aurais pu te donner le titre [de] Comtesse, en laissant insérer dans mon brevet la qualité de [comte] que le Vicomte d'Agoult s'obstine à me donner.[4] Je me suis conten[té] du titre de chev^ier que j'ai porté et qu'on ne peut me disputer. Au surplus si cela pouvait tenter Alex, je ne doute pas qu'il ne me soit facile de te faire Baronne et consequem^t de le mettre lui même dans le cas de prendre par la suite le titre de Baron, non pas simplement par courtoisie, mais en fesant attacher ce titre à un cy devant fief de mon nom, après avoir achete ce fief qui ne couterait pas cher. Je te demande le secret sur ce dernier article mon oncle etant le seul à qui j'en veuille parler. |

Adieu ma bonne et adorable Fanny. N'est tu pas bien etonnée de tout ce que renferme cette lettre et ne seras tu pas tentée de croire que je suis bien changé, et que je suis tout à coup devenu ambitieux. Rassure toi ma chere chère amie; je suis et serai toujours le même; et te donne ma parole, que je ne ferai pas plus ma cour à présent que par le passé; et toujours quand tu me verras attaché à un Ministre, tu pourras etre assurée que je suis traité par lui comme un homme franc et loyal doit vouloir l'être: mais j'avoue que je ne suis pas insensible à l'agrément que me donne la perspective assurée d'entrer pour quelque chose dans l'amelioration de notre sort futur, et que c'est avec bonheur que je pense que le *canonicat* que j'occupe

d'excellens sujets dont les droits sont infiniment superieurs à ceux que je pourrais faire valoir: mais j'ai besoin de justifier d'un titre que je me suis cru autorisé à prendre, et que l'on m'a toujours donné lorsque des bureaux de l'artillerie il m'a été fait quelque proposition relative aux commandemens que le General Gassandy m'a offerts à diverses epoques. J'attache donc Monseigneur le plus grand prix à une justice que je considerais comme la plus grande faveur, et je le sollicite comme la recompense de services que j'ai cherchée à rendre et qui m'ont pas toujours été sans quelqu'utilité.'

[2] The salary of M. d'A as sous-lieutenant d'artillerie was 6,000 francs (see L. 793). He hoped to receive an additional 4,000 to 6,000 francs by promotion to the rank of lieutenant.

[3] It was not until his retirement on 31 Oct. 1815 that M. d'A was named lieutenant-général honoraire and pensioned as a maréchal de camp.

[4] For FBA's reaction to the title of 'Comtesse', see Ll. 807, 811.

me mettra à même de te placer p^r la fortune [apte à te] maintenir au rang pr le quel tu es si bien [faite et tout] le monde ici
le desire te [dire toutes ses amitiés].

Desire tu que j'aille vous chercher. Ecris le moi, et je pars
malgré que j'aye ici mille choses à faire. Si telle est ta volonté
manifeste le promptement parce que le 15 aout je serai de
service au Chateau⁵ jusqu'au 1er d'octobre ainsi que je te l'ai
ecrit.

807   Chelsea, 20–25 July 1814

To M. d'Arblay

A.L. mutilated (rejected Diary MSS., the final page foliated 6016,
with one segment mounted in a Scrapbook, Berg), 20–25 July 1814
Originally probably two double sheets 4to. Of the first double sheet two
segments are extant, one (2·9 × 2·9″) cut from the first leaf, the other
(6 to 5·75 × 7·9″) torn from the second leaf. From the second double sheet
the second leaf or address cover has been cut away and is missing.
Edited by FBA, p. 1, annotated and dated: +++ 1 [July] 20
Edited also by CFBt. See Textual Notes.

63. Lower Sloane Street
⌜July 20th 1814⌝

'Approve' what you have done?[1] Oh yes, mon ami! it is
impossible to do otherwise: your motives to every deliberate
action are always so pure, so noble, they cannot but engage
approbation, even when mingled with regret—and REGRET!
how shall I escape regret, when your Honour—which is mine,
& is my ⌐ your ¬ son's, has led you to a position that separates us
by an absence I know not how either to endure or to break? ⌜I
have written you a sheet upon this subject by Mr. Entwisle &⌝

[*Line sliced, remainder of leaf missing*]

⌜scholarship, of 10, or 20 £ S^t a year. I was obliged while you
were here, to sell out & had I not made the exchange with you

---

⁵ All during the Restoration the Tuileries was called the Château.

807. ¹ FBA's response to the statement made by M. d'A in L. 796: 'Je desire
par dessus tout au monde l'approbation de l'unique amie, de la dearest partner of
my life.'

for £25, I must now sell out again[2]—to the eternal exclusion of fixing a steady revenue for our old age. I ponder.

WHY being thus advanced, you will wonder I am not richer but Martin & Edward[3] have not yet been able to find conjointly, a day for going to the Bank for my dividend.[4]

And my legacy, I can neither receive principal nor interest till [the estate is settled].[5] |

[*The bottom of this leaf and the top of the next leaf are missing*]

July 22. I receive this moment a Letter from Mad. [*tear*] [most aim]able & like herself. Tell her I am extremely obliged: but that I missed M. Cacherd,[6] & have no chance to see him, as I am already so distant from town, & am preparing to go to Wales. Tell her, too, that here, as at Paris, I mix only with a chosen & very small set, of Relations & old friends, & have lived in such retirement since I lost my dear Father, that I fear I have very little chance to serve M. Cacherd; especially as our own artists are all at work upon the same heroic Emperor. Nevertheless, I will surely not fail to name him wherever I have a voice. I will endeavour to get her a Letter from Maria Bourdois; which she must kindly accept as from myself, for I now write only to *you* & my old correspondents, writing still being hurtful to me. Maria is always at Bath but well & happy.

Explain to every one who would apply to me in person, That I have *no home*, at present, & receive no visits. I am wholly devoted to Alexander, my residuary business, & my old friends. |

[*The top of the page is cut away*]

our journey take place.

How much all the world here is disposed to favour & like our Alexander is truly extraordinary. He pleases almost every

---

² As early as 16 Feb. 1814, FBA talked of 'sell[ing] out' stock that she and M. d'A owned (L. 749 n. 16). On 29 Apr. 1814 (L. 773), she repeated her intention. Apparently in May, while M. d'A was in England, some shares were sold, probably of the 5 per cent 1797.

³ JB continued his refusal to act as executor of CB's will and now to function as FBA's trustee. JB's duties as trustee were assumed by Edward Francesco Burney.

⁴ The semi-annual dividends for the 5 per cent stocks and the 3 per cent consols were paid in January and June.

⁵ See L. 805 n. 1. FBA needed a procuration signed by M. d'A to receive both.

⁶ Probably FBA's mistranscription of Pierre Cochard (*fl.* 1763–1814), a painter who entered the Académie de Saint-Luc in 1763 and trained there. In the early summer of 1814, portraits of the Tsar were in great demand and many were available in Parisian and London print shops. M. Cochard hoped to avoid the competition by securing a commission through people like FBA, who had influential connections.

where. With the *family*, without the exception of a single Individual, he is a particular favourite: & all my friends are full of kindness & indulgence towards him. *Amine* invites him to her Box at the play; to see the shews & fine sights at her house & in Pall Mall; & even *courts* his esteem & affection: Lady Keith has *written* him (like our revered & dear Madame de Tessé!) an invitation to be always my chevalier whenever I visit her: Mrs. Waddington presses him to be of the party to Wales: Lady Spencer had asked him to Althorp, & her husband's noble Library, in company with my Brother Charles & myself: Mrs. Hoare & Miss Thrale invite him: Mrs. Haggitt would make him l'ami de la maison; Lady Harcourt desires to know him: & Lady Crewe calls him *my charming son.*— |

July 25th This is now going, by Alex, to Mr. Waddington.[7]

What can be the reason I never hear from you of what is to be done? Can M. Entwisle have lost your direction? Is it changed? Ought I to say au *Chevalier* d'Arblay?—I shall do it with pleasure, for dearly I love the title by which you were first named to me—though *titles* are now so sunk into ridicule, that I have a sort of mèpris for all that are not RESTORED,— the *created* seem all farcical, & calling for some new Moliere. For Heaven's sake hasten me a Letter upon THE COTTAGE: remember, whatever may be your ultimate plan of residence, *I* am a positive captive till the Cottage & the Sales are over, & till I have finished with the legal forms relative to the Executership.

In the interval of all that, we may discuss our Alexander— But we must never, to his versatile mind, & capricious humour, give a choice by *coaxing him with his own indulgencies*:—we must see clearly ourselves what is BEST, & then make such representations as suit the experience & prudence of the parental character. If then his feelings oppose our opinions, I join with you completely in finally leaving him his own Master. But against the ARMY—I AM—& YOU will be, believe me! Search, therefore, something else for *him* — — or give us here the *8 months* you have mentioned in a former Letter the first of the 3 only Letters from Paris![8]—and we must resign you for the 4

---

[7] See L. 819 n. 1.

[8] '[O]f the 3 only Letters from Paris' now available—Ll. 793 ([18 June]), 796 (3 July), 806 (17 July)—not one specifically mentions 'the *8 months*'. The statement is, however, repeated in another context in L. 808, wherein M. d'A speaks of '6 mois entiers et peut être 8' for FBA to choose her place of residence.

months remaining—till he is fitted to be left to himself. And
Then—only for another World will I again be torn from the
object of all my happiness in This!—

adieu. adieu. adieu—

write—write—write. |

ᴵᵀPS—I have said Adieu 2ᶜᵉ or 3ᶜᵉ, yet know not how to forbear
writing on & the less, as you no longer encourage me to write
by M. de la C.[9] though your only Letters through him he had
the goodness to send me *Express*, with a very civil Note, & an
assurance no other had ever arrived, for he opens all his despatches himself.

Pray remember me as you know my feelings to all our kind
Friends, & chiefly to my very dear & respected uncle. Me. de
Braancamp, told ⟨Alex⟩ M. de La Tour du Pin was going,
Ambassadour to Holland[10]—will our dear valued Princess
accompany him[11] — — I learn nothing of Me. de Boinville
though I have written again.[12]

Mr. Burney is considerably better. He hopes to try country
air next week.[13] If that succeeds, He & his family will quit
London entirely—Charlotte also has now quitted it.[14] James
only remains as a fixture.

Judge then, in the Easter & Christmas vacations, ⟨how Alex⟩
is to be housed—be fitted up, if I were to abandon him? His
uncle Charles kindly offered him his house for *all* the vacations,
when we came over—but even then, he must come occasionally
to town, or see nothing of the World, & arrived there, he must

---

⁹ M. de la Châtre, through whose embassy FBA sent several of her letters to
M. d'A.

¹⁰ Frédéric-Séraphin, comte de la Tour du Pin-Gouvernet (1759–1837). For
his other titles, see iv, L. 334, n. 6. Mme de Braancamp anticipated by almost a
year the comte's new diplomatic assignment. Named as conseiller d'ambassade to
the Congress of Vienna in November 1814, he worked closely with Talleyrand
in writing 'the Treaties of 1815' to prevent France's total humiliation. Only after
the Cent Jours was he assigned to the post of envoyé plénipotentiaire auprès du
roi des Pays Bas.

¹¹ The princesse d'Hénin was the aunt of M. de la Tour du Pin-Gouvernet
(vi, L. 575 n. 2).

¹² For Harriet Chastel de Boinville *née* Collins (*c.* 1773–1847), see L. 752,
and v, L. 425 n. 8. Widowed since 1813, she was a 'radical' both in Pimlico lodgings and later in her salon at Bracknell.

¹³ EBB and CRB took rooms, as they had previously, in Turnham Green, where
they remained except for occasional visits until 1817.

¹⁴ For CBFB's address, see L. 805 n. 8; for her reasons, see L. 735 n. 11.

necessarily hang wholly upon his uncle James,[15] for His Grand-father & Chelsea are now no more — —
I need not enlarge upon this subject.⌐

He cannot be left, mon ami, by us *both*: it would be *criminal*, to leave him, his singular character, precarious health, danger-ous propensities, & peculiar situation considered, it would be *criminal* for ME to leave him! Oh then weigh well *how* BEST we may be all re-united, & *when*, & *where*!

His love of Cambridge flows from seeing that life open to all sort of scientific honour, & that such honour is here the road to very high consideration in the best & highest classes of society: but he believes there is no spur to existence for an ambitious character in France out of the military line.

And in that line, the *exigeances* of *etiquette*, PUNCTUALITY, & *complaisance*, would, I am sure make life burthensome to him. |

⌐Always direct to Sloane Street, 63. Pray date yʳ Letters! till I give a new direction My letters will get to me safely.⌐

808   Senlis and Paris,
                                            23–29 July 1814
M. d'Arblay
To Madame d'Arblay

A.L. (Berg), 23 July 1814
Originally a double sheet folio, of which the cover was later discarded
2 pp.
Edited by FBA, p. 1, *annotated*:   +   20

Senlis ce 23 Juillet 1814

une calamité! oh ma Fanny quelle terrible decouverte — et quel *draw back* à tout ce que ma position pouvait m'offrir d'agreable! quel changement — et combien dejà je l'éprouve. Hier encore j'etais presqu'ivre de bonheur, en *songeant* que le plan que j'avais formé n'avait rien de romanesque; et qu'il devait te convenir, comme à moi. Deux mois disais-je à ma

---

[15] FBA had reservations about her brother's political sympathies. Moreover, she feared the possibly adverse effects on AA of JB's passionate fondness for whist and chess.

garnison, ou 4 au plus; 2 à paris pour mon service; et le reste (lorsque tout sera tranquile) par tout où nous voudrons. De cette maniere tu avais à ta disposition 6 mois entiers et peut-être 8. avec la liberté de les passer en Provence en Italie en Angleterre à ton choix. Jusqu'à l'entier retablissement de ta santé, Alex pour t'eviter le passage de la mer, serait venu passer ses congés avec nous; avec nous qui nous serions arrangés en consequence Helas! Tout cela paroissait si facile, si raisonnable! car enfin nous ne pouvions pas même trouver d'obstacle du côte de l'argent necessaire pour tout cela. En effet il est de toute impossibilité que je n'aye point, et cela avant peu, 10,000 f au lieu de 6,000 c'est à dire le double de ce que j'ai actuellement. *Une calamité!* Quel cruel mot! et pourtant je ne puis que te remercier de l'avoir prononcé, malgré l'irreparable mal qu'il a produit, et malgré que ce mal me paroisse absolument sans remede. En effet comment mettre fin à *cette calamité* dont tu te plains, et dont moi même je dois à present me plaindre: car tu ne peux l'ignorer, mon adorable amie, il ne peut plus y avoir, je ne dirai pas de bonheur, mais de paix, de tranquillité, pour moi, dans une situation qui te rend malheureuse; et mon voeu doit être et est effectivement d'en sortir aussitôt que je pourrai le faire sans manquer à tout ce qu'il y a de plus sacré. Daigne donc mon adorable amie, prendre patience; et reçois ici le serment que je te fais de *tout quitter des que tu le voudras,* pour te suivre où tu jugeras à propos de te fixer. Je dis *quand tu le voudras,* parceque je sais que ma Fanny ne voudra jamais que ce qui pourra s'accorder avec l'honneur et le devoir. L'un et l'autre, en ce moment, exigent que je reste jusqu'à ce que l'infortuné monarque au quel je suis attaché, soit parfaitement à l'abri des craintes que ne peuvent manquer de lui donner, comme à tous les Français vraiment dignes de ce nom, les projets audacieusement et presque hautement et publiquement avoués par ses nombreux ennemis.[1] Au surplus je ne doute nullement que malgré leur nombre, très considerable en ce moment, ils ne reussiront point à contrebalancer et à vaincre les efforts que doivent faire et que font effectivement les partisans encore plus nombreux

808. [1] See L. 799 n. 3, and the following by Lefebvre (p. 573): 'On ne tarda pas à conspirer. Fouché, convaincu que l'Europe ne tolérerait pas le retour de Napoléon, opinait pour le duc d'Orléans ou pour la régence de Marie-Louise à laquelle on gagnerait l'Autriche. Maret, au contraire, travaillait pour l'empereur. . . . Des généraux préparaient une sédition militaire.'

d'un ordre de chose, que tant d'interêts tendent à consolider. Amen! Amen![2]

(Paris ce 25) Tu es etonnée et peinée de ce que je ne te parle point des Beauveau. Ils sont toujours pour moi tout ce qu'il y a de plus aimable. Mais je ne puis te cacher que le chef de cette famille est bien mecontent de ce qu'il n'a pas été du nombre des pairs, quand il en peut citer plusieurs a qui ce titre a été accordé malgré leur opinion bien prononcée en faveur du Tyran detrôné,[3] quand tout le monde devrait savoir qu'il n'a jamais pour ce qui le regarde brigué la place qu'il avait près de ce Tyran, dont il s'est au contraire tenu eloigné autant qu'il l'a pu.[4] C'est en effet, ce que toi et moi nous pouvons attester. Au surplus ma bonne amie, tu sauras que toute cette interessante famille est actuellement aux eaux à l'exception d'Edmond[5] et de son frere[6] qui sont restés ici. Le premier est ainsi que Maxime[7] Lieutenant en premier dans le regiment du Roi Hussars. Quant à Charle;[8] il

[2] M. d'A's optimism was groundless, for by the end of July there was open military unrest. According to *The Times* (13 Aug. 1814): 'the guards at the barriers of Paris were suddenly doubled, and some symptoms of alarm were manifested. The occasion was understood to be, that the Duke D'Angouleme [late in July] . . . had met with a most ungracious reception from a regiment in garrison at Brest, which declared that it would march to Paris, to endeavour to restore the deposed government. The officers were said to be the ringleaders of this mutiny.'
[3] Several, who had held distinguished posts in Napoleon's government, received peerages or other marks of distinction shortly after the Restoration: e.g. Choiseul-Praslin, Gontaut-Biron, Talleyrand, Destutt de Tracy, Laurent Gouvion-Saint-Cyr, Jaucourt, Victor Latour-Maubourg, Bourdois de la Motte, Andréossi, La Tour du Pin-Gouvernet.
[4] The gossip about Marc-Étienne-*Gabriel* de Beauvau (1773–1849), prince de Beauvau-Craon, appears in a letter (Osborn) written on 20 June 1814 by Mary Harcourt to FBA. 'I wish I could give you any comfort about our poor friends in France, but the truth is that whether right or wrong, he [Gabriel] is supposed to have taken a part against the good cause & I fear did not in the beginning express his wishes as strong as he might have done—the rest of the family were so very violent that possibly they appeared cold & because they were losers by the Change it was natural to suspect them of being cold whether they were so or not—he is not popular but it is hard his Angel Wife should suffer—' For the relation between the Harcourts and the Beauvau family, see v, L. 513 n. 1.
[5] Edmond de Beauvau (L. 727 n. 4). In June 1814 he was made a lieutenant and the following month transferred to his old unit, the 1st régiment des Hussards.
[6] Charles-Just-François-Victurnien de Beauvau (1793–1864), officier de carabiniers.
[7] 'Maxime' de Maisonneuve. See L. 736 n. 2. In June 1814 he was transferred from the 19th régiment de Chasseurs à cheval to the 1st régiment des Hussards.
[8] Charles de Beauvau, wounded during the Russian campaign and permanently lamed, became aide-de-camp to the duc de Feltre in 1813. Although made prince de Craon in 1814, Charles de Beauvau hastened to join Napoleon during the Cent Jours. In 1815 he retired from the military, never having served during the Restoration as 'aide de camp d'un très grand personnage'.

espere être aide de camp d'un très grand personnage;[9] et ce qui vaut beaucoup mieux encore, il va jouir avant peu d'une fortune très considerable et tout à fait independante en epousant la soeur[10] du duc de Praslin,[11] avec qui j'ai formé, depuis ton depart, une liaison assez intime. Sa femme[12] m'a demandé aujourdhui, chez M^de de Tracy, de tes nouvelles, avec beaucoup d'interest. Si je voulais au reste te nommer tous ceux qui me font pareille question la liste que j'en ferais, ne me laisserait aucune place, pour tout ce que nous avons à nous dire. Je dois ajouter encore que quoique Charle soit extremement à la mode, par la justice qu'on rend à son excellent esprit et à sa conduite parfaite il n'evite aucune occasion de me prouver une amitié qui lui fait preferer ma societé à tous les jeunes gens de son age les plus elegans et les plus recherchés. Aujourdhui encore nous avons fait ensemble et tête à tête une ¦ promenade à cheval de plus de deux heures, et nous avons terminé notre soirée par une visite à Mad^e de ⟨Tracy⟩ qui est toujours ce que tu l'as connue. Il est vrai que moi même je suis un peu à la mode; et par exemple tu ⟨apprendras⟩ avec plaisir qu'après avoir eprouvé quelque difficulté et même un peu souffert du cheval, à peine y avais-je monté au 1º fois que j'ai reçu sur la maniere dont j'y etais placé des complimens très flatteurs puisqu'ils m'ont été donnés par le meilleur ecuyer des gardes du Corps le Comte de Chaumontal.[13]

Ce 27. Voici ma bonne amie une lettre de mon ami Entwistle que je te fais passer. Tu y verras que son opinion est qu'avant de

[9] M. d'A confused the two brothers. Edmond de Beauvau, like Charles, rallied to the Napoleonic cause during the Cent Jours. But Edmond was made aide-de-camp to général Joseph Gérard (1772–1832), one of the heroes of the Battle of Leipzig.

[10] Charles de Beauvau was to marry in 1815 Lucie-Virginie de Choiseul-Praslin (1795–1834).

[11] Claude-Raynald-Laure-Félix de Choiseul-Praslin (1778–1841), duc de Praslin. He attached himself to Napoleon, who made him chambellan (1805), comte de l'Empire (1810), and président du collège électoral de Seine-et-Marne (1811). Shifting his loyalty to the Bourbons in 1814, he was admitted to the Chambre des Pairs in June of that year. During the Cent Jours he joined Napoleon. For four years thereafter he was in disgrace but in 1819 returned to the Chambre des Pairs.

[12] Charlotte-Laure-Olympe le Tonnelier de Breteuil (d. 1861) had married the duc de Praslin in 1803.

[13] Victor-André-Thomas-Jean de Chaumontel (1752–1814), comte de Chaumontel, had in September 1780 entered the gardes du Corps du roi in the compagnie de Luxembourg. By 1792 he was fighting in the armée des Princes and from 1793 to 1800 in the armée de Condé. On rejoining the gardes du Corps, again in the compagnie de Luxembourg, he—like other *émigrés*—held a lower rank than his years of service would have warranted. But on his death certificate his rank was that of a colonel and his widow received a suitable pension.

nous decider, nous devrions avoir a fair evaluation of Camilla cottage; & he has written in consequence to one of his friends qu'il dit être trés versé dans cette matiere. Il ajoute que nous avons tout le tems d'attendre le resultat de cette estimation contradictoire, puisque Mr Hudson garde Camilla Cottage jusqu'au premier Novembre. En même tems, ma chere Fanny, il dit: que si par un malheur inoui William venait, ou à changer d'avis ou à mourir, nous n'aurions pas un sol à pretendre, et qu'enfin nous perdrions tout, aucun trustee en ce cas, ne pouvant nous faire avoir alors les 640 livres sterling qui nous sont offerts.

Tout cela bien pesé, je t'engage, mon amie, à terminer, après toutefois avoir fait une derniere tentative auprès de Mr Hudson qui m'avait fait entendre qu'il trouvait juste de me donner les *1000^f* que je demandais, mais ne m'a jamais fait la reponse qu'il m'avait annoncée. Bref je te donne carte blanche, et te prie d'user dans toute sa latitude de la procuration tout à fait illimitée que je t'ai remise à ton depart d'ici. Je n'ai pas besoin, je crois, de te dire que cette affaire et celle des livres reduits de plus de 20,000 volumes à moins de 5,000 m'a prodigieusement refroidi sur la passion que je ressentais pour le pays que tu habites.[14] Il est certain qu'en general de pareils traits ne sont pas communs en France, tandis qu'en Angleterre il parait que les plus honnetes gens trouvent ces choses là tout à fait simples; et pourvu qu'on agisse *legally* en mettant à part et conscience et delicatesse, on reste un trés honnorable et honnore gentleman!!! Quelle terrible epigramme que cet avis de Mr Haguette, et combien je serais honteux et desolé d'avoir fourni la matiere d'une pareille diatribe.[15] Grace au ciel je n'ai rien à craindre de ce coté; et certe l'affaire du Loan[16] est un peu differente de celle de Camilla Cottage.

(Ce 29) Je reçois à l'instant un billet de Madame de Cadignan qui m'engage à aller passer la soirée avec elle chez Mad^e

---

[14] See Ll. 790, 793. In the *Sale Catalogue* of CB's miscellaneous library 2,092 titles were listed, many of them multi-volumed.

[15] See L. 803.

[16] The loan had to do with the investment of M. d'A (along with William Locke and John Angerstein) in the omnium, of which there were two. On 20 June 1803 William Locke wrote (Archives Nationales) to M. d'A: 'Pray do not return upon the £1500 Omnium, which I before told you had been settled by an agreement between M^r A & me without any loss to you or myself. . . . —When I can get from him the Acc^t of the £2000 you shall have it.' Apparently M. d'A was indebted to the elder Locke for his investment in the £2,000 omnium. See L. 761 n. 7 and Appendix II.

Hottinger[17] qui lui a ecrit pour l'engager à me le proposer. En relisant ta lettre, je vois que tu me reproches de n'avoir pas parlé des Tra[cy]— en te parlant des Bea[uvaus]— je t'ai dejà fait connoitre les raisons de mon silence. Du reste les uns et les autres sont pour nous toujours de même, all kindness. M^r de Tr— est conserve *pair* — M^r de Be—aurait du l'être. Je t'ai mandé que les deux gendres de Mr de la Fay[18]— sont off^{ers} des gardes du Corps et consequement majors de cavalerie, tandis que le brave son trés distingue fils[19] n'est que capitaine dans un reg^t de ligne. I grieve that very much. Neanmoins je jouis beaucoup de l'avancement de Mr de Lasteyrie, mon camarade grenadier. C'est aussi un sujet très rare et un fort beau caractère; Mad^e de Cadignan tres sensible à ton souvenir est mieux. Le lait d'anesse a fait merveille; neanmoins je ne la trouve pas encore très bien, et la crois attaquée du foie. Son fils n'est pas encore placé, et cela la tourmente.[20] Si elle a paru un peu legère, elle est je t'assure bien changée, et n'existe absolument que pour son fils, qui heureusement promet d'être un excellent sujet; autrement il la tuerait — Je ne t'envoye pas une nouvelle procuration parce que je n'entens pas bien ce que tu me demandes, et ne puis concevoir que celle que tu as eue en partant ne soit pas suffisante.[21] Mr Entwistle que j'ai consulté m'a dit qu'il fallait que tu prisses la peine d'aller à la Banque,

[17] Martha Eliza Hottinguer *née* Redwood (1773–1830) was born in Newport, Rhode Island, the daughter of Abraham Redwood (1728–98), and she died in Paris. Her husband was Jean-Conrad Hottinguer (1764–1841), baron de l'Empire (1810), régent de la Banque de France, member of the legislature (1815).

[18] Married in 1798 to Anastasie de Lafayette (1777–1862), Jules-*Charles*-César de Fay de Latour-Maubourg was in July 1814 made a sous-lieutenant in the gardes du Corps in the compagnie de Luxembourg.

In 1803 Virginie de Lafayette (1782–1849) wed Louis de Lasteyrie du Saillant (1781–1826), whose army career was indecisive. Entering military service in 1792, he became within two years a sous-lieutenant in the régiment de Vaisseaux à Malte. Returning to France in 1802, he joined the 3rd régiment de Dragons, became a sous-lieutenant (1805) and a lieutenant (1807) in the same unit. In 1808 he left the service, aware that Napoleon's distrust of his father-in-law would prevent further military promotion. In 1814 he was made a capitaine in the Garde Nationale and with the Restoration he was a lieutenant-colonel in the gardes du Corps in the compagnie de Noailles.

For the marriage of Anastasie, see v. L. 485 n. 7.

[19] George Washington du Motier de Lafayette (1779–1849) had by 1806 become a capitaine in the 7th régiment de Chasseurs à cheval and in the same year served with général Grouchy in the 2nd division, 2nd corps of the Grande Armée. In 1807 he was placed 'en non-activité'. In April 1814 he was named capitaine aide-de-camp de ministre de la Guerre but failed to receive the post. In July of the same year he became capitaine in the 3rd régiment des Hussards.

[20] See L. 747 n. 4.

[21] The necessity for a procuration is explained in L. 805 n. 1.

ou l'on te donnera, quand tu auras bien fait connoitre ce que tu desires faire, le modele imprimé de ce que je signerai quand tu me l'auras envoyé. Je ne puis ma bonne amie, me consoler de l'idée de ne pas vous serrer dans mes bras Alex et toi. Si la chose est possible encore, comme je l'espere, venez tous deux, oui tous deux, dès que vous le pourrez, et il me semble que vous le pourrez aussitôt que l'affaire de Camilla Cottage sera terminée. Je sens que notre reunion me dédomagerait de l'enorme perte que nous eprouverons par cette *Sad business.* Oui ma bonne amie, Alex ne vint il ici que les quinze derniers jours de ses vacances, j'en serais ravi. D'ailleurs il protegerait ton retour, et je te promets ainsi qu'à lui de ne pas le retenir un moment au delà du tems dont il peut disposer. Le portrait que tu me fais de lui est tracé de main de maitre, et je me rens à tes excellentes raisons. |

809   63 Lower Sloane Street,
                                       5 August 1814
To Charles Chamier Raper

A.L.S. (Public Record Office, WO. 43/61), 5 Aug. [18]14
Double sheet 4to   1 p.
Addressed: Charles Raper, Esqr, / Cook's Grounds, / King's Road.
Annotated in pencil: Ls *from Mdme d'Arblay*
with an enclosure, an A.L.S. from Henriette-Marguerite (Guinot de Soulignac) Bidé, comtesse de Maurville, to FBA, 6 May [1814] ds.   4to
2 pp.   *Addressed*: A Madame / Madame d'arblay
Annotated by FBA, p. 4: The want of a right direction retarded my receipt of this Letter till within a short time.—

Lower Sloane Street,
August 5th
Dear Sir,
I enclose you the Letter of Mad^e la Comtesse de Maurville,[1]

809. [1] Henriette-Marguerite Guignot de Soulignac (*c.* 1761–*post* 1825), the widow of Jean-Louis-Bernard Bidé de Maurville (d. 1796). See iii, L. 237 n. 9. The enclosed letter is as follows:

a Bruxelle Ce 6 Mai
rue de la montagne 320
L'aimable acceuil, et Votre tendre interet, pour moi dans le sejour que j'ai fait a paris, Madame, m'enhardie aujourd'huit, a réclamer Vos bontés. Vous avez

for whose distress & petition I have solicited your assistance. You cannot give it for a more estimable person, either in principle or conduct. She sustained herself here by giving instructions, in French, &c, to several young persons, assembled for that purpose, under her roof, till the Truce of Amiens inspired her with better, but false hopes, of ameliorating her condition abroad. Once there, however disappointed, she found no means to return; & her present claims upon the generosity of This government, were precisely such as to annul all appeal upon that under which she lingered. She subsisted, therefore, almost wholly upon the hospitality of a Relation, M. de La Tour du Pin, of late Prefect at Brussels:[2] a place he never accepted till threatened with an Execution in his mouldering Chateau, near Bordeaux, from penury & revolutionary ruin. Louis 18 has lately, I am told, made him Ambassadour to Holland: but he has only his appointment; & his good Cousin, Mad^e de Mau[rville] anxiously desires to hang no longer wholly on his benevolen[ce.][3]

I beg my kindest love to my dear Fanny, & many *embrassa[des]* to my little Favourite,[4]—the Favourite of my dearest Father!— & pray ⟨believe⟩ me, Dear Sir, your affect^e Fr^d & Servt

F. B. d'[Arblay]

quelque fois Ecouter les details qui me consernoient avec Cette douceur et ce Coeur que j'ai si souvent rencontrée dans une amie qui Vous tenoit de près; eh bien, Madame je prend donc la Confiance de Vous ⟨entretenir⟩ de ce qui me regarde; j'avais comme j'ai eu le plaisir de Vous le dire, obtenue une pension de sa Majeste le Roi d'angleterre. apres avoir perdue mon mari a son Service, et deux beaufreres a quiberon, elle etoit de 30 £ Sterlings par an. en 1801 que je revins en france, il eut été aussi imprudent, que dangereux, de se charger de deux papiers, l'un Brevet de Capitaine au Regt de Mortemard, et l'autre de titre ou brevet de ma pension envoyer par Mr. Windam et signé Woofort. Les deux objets furent laisses a Mr. havilland Le Mesurier, a Londres, pere d'un ancien Lord-maire. à l'entré des allies en Belgique j'ai ecrit de suite, afin de réclamer des papiers, on m'a répondue que non seulement Mr Le Mesurier etoit mort, mais sa femme, et son fils, que j'ai eu chez moi pendant un an. Vous voyez Madame qu'elle suite de malheur, car j'en éprouve bien d'autres, oserai-je vous prier de me rendre le service de faire prendre des informations au Bureau de la guerre, si les Copies du brevet de pension y a été conservé. . . .'

[2] M. de la Tour du Pin-Gouvernet was 'préfet de la Dyle' from 1808 to 1813. 'Ce nouveau département fut crée, le 9 vendémiaire an IV, par la Convention. Bruxelles fut choisi comme chef-lieu' (Robinet).

[3] Because her pension was restored, Mme de Maurville was able to maintain her own house in Brussels. FBA's concern did not go unpaid. After her flight from Paris in March 1815, she spent several days in Mme de Maurville's house recovering from exhaustion. Moreover, the latter found another residence nearby in which not only FBA but also Mme d'Hénin and M. de Lally could live while refugees during the Cent Jours (viii *passim*).

[4] Catherine Minette Raper (i, p. lxxi), now 6.

810   63 Lower Sloane Street,
                               9 August 1814
To Mrs. Locke

L. excerpt in the hand of CFBt (Diary MSS. viii. 6018–[19], Berg),
9 Aug. 1814
    Double sheet 4to 2 pp. p. 1 foliated 59 Page 3 bears an excerpt
from FBA's letter of 24 Aug. 1814 to Mrs. Locke. See L. 814
    Edited at the Press. *See* Textual Notes.

To Mrs *Locke*

The Friends of M: d'A; in Paris are now preparing to claim
for him his rank in the Army as he held it under Louis XVI. of
Marechal de Camp: & as the Duc de Luxembourg will present,
in person, the demand *au Roi*, there is much reason to expect it
will be granted.[1]
    M: de Thuisy, who brought your Letter from Adrienne[2] has
given a flourishing account of M: d'A: in his new Uniform,[3]
though the Uniform itself, he says is very ugly: But so sought is
the Company of the *Corps de Gardes des Roi* that the very Privates,
M: de T[huisy] says are Gentlemen. M: d'A. himself has only
the place of *sous-lieutenant*—! but it is of consequence sufficient,
in *that* Company, to be signed by the King, who had rejected
two officers that had been named to him just before he gave his
signature for M. d'A.—

810. [1] See L. 806.
    [2] Adrienne-Adélaïde-Anne de Chavagnac (1795–1868). See v, L. 437 n. 3
for her relationship with the Lockes from 1795 to 1802.
    [3] The information that was communicated to FBA was also stated by CFBt in a
letter (Berg), dated 27 July 1814, to her aunt: '. . . [chevalier de Thuisy] told me
that he saw [M. d'A] in his uniform just before he (M. de Thuisy) left France.
"que cela lui alloit à merveille; but that the uniform is by no means so magnificent
or costly, as it was expected to be. he says that M: d'Arblays corps or regiment is
the best of all, the most sought after, & the one in which even the rank of a private
is most difficult to obtain. it seems that the very privates in this distinguished
corps are all *gentils hommes*. he says that there used to be only four regiments
of french guards, but now the king has made six. two new ones of which the command is given, par politique, to two of Bonaparte's former marshalls. & these two
are not filled up, and persons can hardly be obtained to take even the subordinate
commands in them; while volunteers are crowding to petition for admission as
mere privates in the corps which is commanded by the Prince de Luxembourg
& M. d'Arblay.—'

425

I need not say what spirits & what pleasure this has occasioned to him. I have heard much of him—all of cheerful import—lately through Miss. Planta,[4] whose sister has just accompanied Lady Rolle to Paris.[5]—that favoured Capital seems to be half peopled by English. The rage for Parisian ꞁ excursions is almost incredible[6]

811   [63 Lower Sloane Street,
                                    10 August 1814]
To M. d'Arblay

A.L. (rejected Diary MSS. 6022–[23], Berg), *n.d.*
Originally a double sheet 4to, of which the second leaf was later discarded   2 pp.
Edited by FBA, p. 1 (6022), *annotated and dated*: (23) August 10th 1814. 63. Lower Sloane St. Chelsea
Edited also by CFBt, *but rejected at the* Press. *See* Textual Notes.

Ah, Mon ami! with what mixt sensations do I now read those Letters which erst gave me such pure delight!—Your new honours & the restoration of your old ones, fill me with joy & exultation: I feel in its fullest force your just satisfaction, your deserved prosperity: I can neither blame nor wonder at the step you have taken —— but neither ought YOU at the deep distress which it occasions ME. Do I not see that either my own personal happiness, or the welfare, perhaps the existence, of Alexander must be sacrificed? I will not fatigue you with re-reading, or myself with re-writing, the painful & long details I have sent you so often upon this subject: but every hope I have for the future with regard to our dear Boy hangs upon his having a *watchful monitor*, & *confidential* Friend, within his reach, for the present.

[4] Margaret Planta.   [5] See L. 798 and nn. 12, 13.
[6] 'A peine les fêtes et les réjouissances, destinées à célébrer la victoire de l'Angleterre et de ses alliés, se terminèrent-elles que commença vers nos ports de la Manche l'afflux des visiteurs anglais. . . . Ces voyageurs de 1814 appartiennent non pas à une élite, mais à toutes les classes de la société et à toutes les conditions. . . . Les uns s'avancent en terre promise avec un bel enthousiasme, qui ne survivra pas toujours au contact des réalités. Les autres arrivent tout remplis d'une sainte indignation contre la nation vaincue et déchue, qui a donné au monde tant d'exemples fâcheux d'impiété et d'instabilité.' See Marcel Moraud, *La France de la restauration d'après les visiteurs anglais* (1933), pp. 15–17.

His character is still—though fair in promise—as unformed, as his Constitution, though visibly improving, is unsettled.

Left to himself, he is utterly careless of BOTH!

Can I then, hesitate?—would happiness, even with YOU, be mine in deserting such a charge?—

Oh who should have told me THE PEACE—the blessed PEACE should have brought to me so cruel an alternative!—

The anguish I have suffered during my struggles, my un-certainty, you would be sorry indeed to know: but, since your last Letter, without date, yet certainly last written, my mind is calmer.[1] I see my way with decision. My poor fluctuating Alex, little as he knows it, or is conscious of his various dangers, requires me for his health—his principles—his happiness *à venir*, & his reputation:—YOU, on the contrary, however kindly you may wish for me, could never so facilely spare me. A new world is opened to you; honours, well merited, pour upon you; you have all the security of constantly sustained, or honourably renewed connexions; Generously you may wish me at your side to share your prosperity, but 'tis to Alex alone I am essential; 'tis Alex alone I can serve.

Separated, therefore, we must remain—alas—Alas!—till the fate of Alex is fixed, or till you can procure a congée.—

In about 2 years & a half, if he takes a good degree, he will be at liberty to follow any course he pleases—all roads to honour, profit, & talents will be open to him; & he may travel whithersoever he will, yet return to the same advantages. But to miss *ONE TERM* in the interval, would destroy *all* his prospects, & throw away all his exertions & attainments.

Such are the University Laws.

I must yield with the best courage in my power, & since I have taken my decision,—since I have clearly seen my positive call, I am reviving, & constantly trying to chear myself with the thought of your happiness & occupations, opposed to poor Alex's inexperience & cruel insufficiency to himself. *Soignez* there-fore your health, as I will mine—. That yet we may meet, even here!—Oh *Soignez* it!—my heart is still too full, serene as I am comparatively with what I have been, to suffer me to give vent to its feelings & disappointment without paining you—

Therefore to business.

811. [1] The letter is missing.

427

I have given up the journey to Wales, which I found, upon examination, better relinquished than pursued.[2]

I have gotten Alex a private Tutor, whom he meets 3 times a week in town.[3]

Quant à *Mme la Baronne.* Dieu m'en garde![4] it would forfeit my fame! I could never pass, living as I live, so parsimoniously & obscurely, for your Wife!—⌐I have no doubt but it might ⟨gain⟩ upon Alex—but I think his vain-glory already his defect, & I would not give him any such reason.¬ In England, also, a Baron, who is newly made, & not a peer of parliament, is reckoned a Dentist, or a surgeon, &c & by no means as much respected for that title, as a powerful Esquire. A Title, unless of ancient or hereditary descent, is always *genant,* or *ludicrous,* unaccompanied by state or fortune. I earnestly hope that was an idea *passagere.*

Alex thinks—& *I* think, there is no credit or prosperity in France, for a young man, out of the military line. And *in* it, the sufferings of forming him would make his life a burthen to himself. I am sure of it. |

⌐Pray do not touch the Letter of Attorney till you have read 2¬[5]

⌐We have an annuity to pay to Letty Brookes of £13.3 on 1st of Jan^{ry} you remember.¬[6]

⌐I have still no intelligence whatever from Mess'rs ⟨Longman⟩ & Co!!¬[7]

---

[2] In L. 805 FBA first spoke of escaping from the 'melancholy' environment of Lower Sloane Street. In L. 807 she projected a visit to the Waddingtons at Llanover. Within nineteen days she realized her plans were ill-advised (L. 820).

[3] See L. 804 n. 6.

[4] M. d'A had a choice: 'le titre de Baron ou de Comte, car je serais maitre d'obtenir l'un ou l'autre.' See L. 817. M. d'A accepted no title at this time but in 1815 that of comte was bestowed upon him by Louis at Ghent. FBA was reluctant to use the title comtesse except when she signed French documents. Although it allowed the Princesses to invite her openly to the various royal houses, FBA dropped the title when, after the death of M. d'A, she considered it detrimental to AA's career as an English clergyman (*HFB*, p. 420).

[5] See the conclusion of L. 812.

[6] CB bequeathed 'the rent of [his] house in York Street, Covent Garden' to his niece Letitia Brooke. In 1807 the annual rent was £27. His will stipulated further that 'the said Rent may be continued to her during her life till the lease is expired, and afterwards the same annuity to be paid to her by my daughters, Esther, Frances, Sarah, and Grand daughter Fanny Phillips'.

[7] See Ll. 761 n. 5, 773 n. 19. The 'intelligence' she required was a cheque for £500, the second instalment of the initial £1,500 to be paid by Longman *et al.*

63 Lower Sloane Street,
15–[22] August 1814[1]

To M. d'Arblay

A.L. (rejected Diary MSS. 6024–[25], Berg), 15 Aug. 1814
Originally a double sheet 4to, the second leaf of which was cut into 3
segments (as described in the Textual Notes). The top segment is missing.
4 pp.
Edited by FBA, p. 1 (6024), *numbering retraced*: 24
Edited also by CFBt *and the* Press. *See* Textual Notes.

63. Lower Sloane St. Chelsea—
August 15. 1814.

⌐*Read This first.* The enclosed is older, & upon business—⌐

Enfin je respire, mon bien bon ami! Je viens de reçevoir une
Lettre qui me ranime à l'Esperance! helas! helas — que n'ai-je
pas souffert dernirement de ne voir point de lumierè pour notre
re-union! Votre Lettre du 6:[2] me donne la vie. ah mon ami,
calamité n'etoit nullement un terme trop fort pour ce que j'ai
éprouvé à la vue de ma position! Je ne veus plus en parler.
⌐Il faut que je vous envoie ce que j'ai écrit déjà! parce que je
n'aurai pas le temps de recommencer. Il faut bien que ca parte
tout de suite, ce que je prie à M. le d^c de la Châtre. Il devrait
passer en France au plus vîte puisque je le reçois au départ —
Je parle de la Lettre d'Alex & age.⌐

Is there, then, a hope you can come to us in October! how
has my heart lightened, how have my spirits risen, since I read
those words, in my dear thrice dear Yesterday's Letter! All that
may follow, we may then settle together. You will see & fully
comprehend all I have urged, painfully but essentially, about
our situation; mine & Alex's; & the positive necessity of duty &
affection & propriety that demands MY stay, or *his* departure.

⌐But to the Minors, I mean the young Indians. Certainly
we must take legal advice about them, as their legacies must
not be paid till they are of age, & as they have a right to *interest*
the whole of their minority.[3]

812. [1] Written piecemeal, the letter was completed 22 August (the Monday after
the end of the musical sale).
[2] M. d'A's letter, dated 6 Aug. 1814 and received in Chelsea on 14 August, is
missing; but as in L. 808, it probably questioned FBA's use of 'calamité' to define
her position.
[3] Eight children of Richard Burney (d. 1808) received £100 each.

The letter of Attorney I send is precisely such a one as Mr. Entwistle advises.[4] His advice I should think excellent but for the fear of any sudden event, & but that the | Cottage will not be estimated at 500 if not repaired this autumn—& Mr. Hudson cannot send an answer, for he *cannot*, it seems, buy, at any price what we have no legal power to sell! ! !

I am most glad indeed of your permission to finish the affair. Martin promises to obtain better terms — — than the 640 *if possible*. But—another year being now passed over without repairs, I gravely fear, we shall not augment the price.[5]

The Musical sale finished yesterday:[6] but no account has reached either me or Esther. Mr. White has had directions, I conclude, to send it to the Isle of Wight.[7]

I hope to clear the poor College Apartments next week, & to be off for Richmond with Alex. Wales I have explained is out of the question at present. Mr. Bellamy, the private Tutor, is also gone into the Country, but I mean & hope to have another Month of his assistance previously to Alex's return to Cambridge, which must take place about the middle of October.

I will strictly follow your directions in leaving the 5 G[s] to be settled from the next Tancred.[8]

Sunday Evening.

The Letter by Mrs. Hottinger[9] & the parcel arrives this moment. For the Letter, 10,000 thanks. The Brochure is admirable![10] I have sent it to Sarah by Alexander. But I cannot, mon ami, make her so much as *Write by Trade* as to *share the profits*—that is never professed[11] |

---

[4] See L. 808.

[5] For the probable sale price of Camilla Cottage, see L. 803 n. 11.

[6] The sale began on 8 August and lasted for nine days, i.e. until 17 August. But see L. 782 n. 12.

[7] The money gained from the sale was to be sent to CB Jr. at Ryde.

[8] AA had an unspecified college debt of five guineas that was to be absorbed by the next Tancred draft of £52. 14*s*. due on 11 Nov. 1814 (see 'Tutor's Account Book').

[9] See L. 808 n. 17.

[10] A brochure probably advertising SHB's *Traits of Nature* (1812). Popular in France, several of her works were subsequently translated: *Clarentine* (4 vols., 1819), *Le Jeune Cleveland, ou traits de nature* (4 vols., 1819), *Miss Fauconberg* (3 vols., 1825), *Le Naufrage* (2 vols., 1816), *Les Voisins de campagne, ou le secret de Miss Burney* (4 vols., 1820).

[*The top of the second leaf is missing*]

What is become of M. de Lally?[11] I languish to see him come forth from his noble obscurity to shine as he ought to do.

I am grieved about the de Beau[vau]s. L^y Harcourt had already given me their history. I am always eagerly occupied in clearing up all doubts of their real internal fidelity, & forced acquiescence.[12]

Désapprouver, mon excellent ami! jamais, jamais!—but what a misery for me to be forced to such a separation! I will think of it no more—your project for October is new life to me.

⸻

⸢What frightful & large expense is that of your present dress & equipage! I rejoice, indeed, you will *forbear applying* to our store for it. If you could not make your income do even for yourself there, & being alone, how shall we do all together? for you will never suffer me to contrive in œconomies so parsimonious as I now observe, when we are under one roof, & now, I must do it only till my income is increased, or again sell out, which will prevent our ever having any benefit from my melancholy legacy, save that of replacing, not augmenting our revenues. Alex, you know, resides but 10 months at Cambridge. We have now been saving for our Month or 6 weeks at Richmond,[13] for I cannot there, or any where, live as penuriously as here. Thus my whole heart & faculties are put upon avoiding to sell out any MORE. But how accomplish the journies you talk of so gaily?[14] What I *may* have when all is arranged, I yet know not, but I have now merely 80 in the 3^pr c^ts & 90 from Mr. Mathias. The Cottage ought to be 47, but has this ½ year, as you may remember, by Mrs. Lock's last account only been paid up by her to 7⟨bre⟩ and[15] —

[11] See L. 769 n. 14.

[12] For Lady Harcourt's version of the Beauvau scandal and the explanation of M. d'A, see L. 808 and n. 4. By 1817 FBA convinced Lady Harcourt of the royalist loyalty of the Beauvau family and urged her, when in Paris, to visit them. Lady Harcourt did so, and FBA wrote (Barrett, Eg. 3699, f. 43b), rejoicing that they 'had the infinite solace of your ladyship's protective Society at Paris'.

[13] FBA arrived in Richmond by 28 August (Diary Entry, p. 518) and did not leave until her return to France in November.

[14] See L. 808.

[15] See L. 807 n. 2.

[*The top of the leaf is missing*]

will do that. I have strongly had him recommended to M. & Mrs. M. Montagu,[16] who are just gone to Paris & are people of very large fortune & great vogue & fashion in town. I have hopes they will record my wishes powerfully & *comme il* est penetrat. I find the sweet wine, Mountain, which I have tried once is reviving immediately & immediately was relinquished. I shall recruit & restore needed warmth as fast as possible.

Alex is well—he is gone with Sarah to James Street. He was much pleased that your late M. J.[17] orders dancing. S. is highly cultivated & distinguished. She dances remarkably well & has read everything. Miss B. Planta has written warmly of your civilities.[18] Lady Keith, just returned from Bordeaux, is all courteous kindness. But every body, now has left London. Make yourself easy & happy mon bien cher ami, for your last Letter of Août 6 has quite restored me. How will I love October! Mais qu'avez vous ésperé? dites moi je vous en prie.

Parlez moi de Me de Maisonneuve. Dites à ma chere princesse[19] que j'ai much hope for Me de Maurville. J'ai visité upon her affair yesterday with Mr. Raper who will deliver my letter upon it to Lord Palmerston.⁊[20] Be well, & enjoy your honours, my most beloved! We will discuss nothing when you come but how we may All live together. *Here* or *There*. asundered no more!—I am yours, mon ami! yours wholly, solely, entirely!—for your son is still *you*—& you have no other rival. Duty, too, alone puts even Him on the same line. Be gay—be happy—enjoy yourself—I am all hope again! I am charmed you have recovered your Horsemanship. Yet I always dread too great *audace* after a remission of riding for 22 years. I always feel that that was the destruction of the for-ever lamented M. de Nar-

[16] In 1783 FB had met Matthew, 'Mrs. Montagu's nephew and heir, a very elegant man,—who *condescended* to talk a great deal to me' (*ED* ii. 307–8). For a biographical account of Matthew Montagu (1762–1831) and his wife Eliza *née* Charlton (*c.* 1765–1817), see i, L. 5 n. 14.

[17] Probably Gabriel Jouard (d. 1832). See vi, L. 595 n. 5.

[18] See L. 803 n. 3.

[19] Princesse d'Hénin (Ll. 807 n. 11, 809 n. 3).

[20] Henry John Temple (1784–1865), Viscount Palmerston (1802) and Baron Temple of Mount Temple (Irish, 1723). A Cambridge M.A. (1806) and M.P. (1807–65), he was a Lord of the Admiralty (1807–9), Secretary of War (1809–28), Secretary for Foreign Affairs (1830–4, 1835–41, 1846–51), Home Secretary (1852–5), Prime Minister (1855–8, 1859–65). As Secretary of War, Palmerston restored a widow's pension to Mme de Maurville, her husband having died during military service for England.

bonne. Disdain not caution mon très—très cher ami!—⌐Oh how I hope a little time will teach a juster appreciation of the ci-devant aide de camp de M. de Grouchy!²¹

Monday noon—I have just had very kind words from Mrs. Locke²²—notwithstanding my appeal against *Generosity*. But then she only answer'd to press my hastening that business for the too solid reasons I have argued, ie. that to me any adjustment is *SURTOUT* [res]tricting & our liberty must always be sure—

Nº 11
To be read Last⌐²³

813   Paris, 19 August 1814

M. d'Arblay
To Madame d'Arblay

A.L. (Berg), 19 Aout 1814
Double sheet 4to   4 pp.   The cover is missing.
Edited by FBA, p. 1, *annotated*: ⁂ ⌐(10)⌐ 25 *See further*, Textual Notes.

Paris ce 19 Aout 1814

Depuis deux jours, ma chere amie, j'ai commencé mon service au palais des Tuilleries. Assurement rien de moins fatiguant, et pourtant rien de plus assujetissant et de moins commode. Madame la Duchesse d'Angoulême est de retour bien mieux portante; et le Vᵗᵉ d'Agoult revenu avec elle est de plus en plus amical. En même tems il devient d'une paresse qui ne laisse pas que de me fatiguer un peu trop, et me contrarie singulierement aujourdhui. Imagine-toi je te prie que j'ai lu 22 lettres auxquelles il s'attend que je vais faire reponse tout

²¹ Emmanuel de Grouchy (1766–1847). Entering the army in 1781, he became général de brigade (1793) and général de division (1794), comte de l'Empire (1809), maréchal de France (1815, 1831), pair de France (1815, 1832).
²² This recent letter of Mrs. Locke is missing, but it perhaps recapitulated the theme and spirit of her letter, dated 19 June 1814 (L. 805 n. 7).
²³ The enclosed letter, 'upon business', is missing, but it was written *pre* 10 August. See L. 811.

de suite; et cela parceque, avant hier, le trouvant dans l'embarras et prêt à jetter toute sa correspondance au feu, j'ai eu la bonne homie de repondre pour lui à 3 ou 4 des lettres dont on l'accable. Il n'est heureusement que 5ʰ du matin, et comme je veux profiter de l'occasion de Lady Rolle[1] qui part demain de tres bonne heure je te dirai que trés heureusement je trouve que l'esprit public devient de jour en jour meilleur; et qu'ainsi, j'ai l'esperance d'aller te trouver dans les premiers jours de Novembre. Plutôt serait absolument impossible. Si tout est tranquille, nous pourrons passer ensemble cinq mois et demi c'est à dire jusqu'au premier d'avril. d'oú il suit que tu aurais mal fait d'avoir vendu nos meubles; car un logement garni nous ruinera. Il me semble, ma chere amie, puisque tu ne veus pas absolument venir me retrouver, que ce que nous pouvons faire de mieux, c'est de louer à Richemond ou près de Richemond une cottage ǀ ou il y aurait une ecurie pour deux chevaux et assez de logement pour nous deux un domestique et une femme de chambre sachant faire un peu de cuisine. Quant à Alex, le tems que je puis rester près de toi est precisement celui où il sera forcé d'être à Cambridge où nous irions passer une quinzaine de jours. J'ignore ce qu'il m'en coutera pour le passage de mes deux cheveaux et de mon cabriolet; mais ⌜cela ne peut être bien considerable, et⌝ il me semble qu'il vaut mieux faire ce sacrifice, que de laisser ici mon domestique avec mes cheveaux, qui seraient perdus. ⌜Il y aurait sans doute la ressource de les vendre; mais ce serait certainement avec une perte considerable du montant mais l'on saurait la necessité où je serais de le faire. En outre, il me serait impossible de les remplacer — jamais pour le double du prix qu'ils m'ont couté.⌝ N'est-ce rien d'ailleurs que d'être, à mon âge, parfaitement monté, et d'avoir deux chevaux qui ont fait la guerre, et me font honneur de toute maniere? J'avoue qu'il m'en couterait beaucoup de renoncer à l'avantage très grand que j'y trouve. ⌜Neanmoins, ma seule amie, je le ferai si cela te parait convenable, mais avant de te decider reflechis y bien.⌝

(à Sept hˢ du Soir),

Conçois un peu, ma bonne amie, l'espece d'activité passive à la quelle je suis quelquefois condamné. J'avais defendu ma

813. [1] See Ll. 798 n. 13, 803 n. 3, 810 and n. 5. Lady Rolle was in Paris from 15 July until 20 August.

porte pour t'ecrire et expedier les lettres du chateau. arrive un ancien aide de camp de M^r de La F[2] — nommé Geoffroi,[3] qui me fait dire qu'il n'a qu'un mot à me dire, qu'il n'est que pour un instant à Paris et qu'il ne me demande que deux minutes. Je le fais entrer, et ne puis me dispenser de lui offrir une tasse de caffé, qui lui donne le tems de commencer son histoire depuis notre separation. Rien n'a pu | l'interrompre, et quoique j'aye pu faire, quoique j'aye pu dire, malgré même tous mes baillemens, que j'ai fini par ne plus lui cacher, il en a eu pour plus de deux heures. Le pis est que j'en ai eu mal à la tête et une migraine qui m'a fait prendre le parti d'essayer de dormir un peu pour la faire passer. J'avais dit à Mad^e Desprez[4] de m'eveiller au bout de deux heures. J'en ai passé une entière avant de fermer l'oeil: mais lorsque je l'ai ouvert, j'avais au plus le tems de m'habiller bien vite pour arriver à mon service; après le quel j'ai passé deux grandes heures et demie à repondre à quelques lettres pressées. Tout cela n'a guere diminué mon mal de tête! de sorte que je n'ai de bon en ce moment que mon coeur toujours le même, c. à. d. bien tendrement devoué à ma chere Fanny. et notre cher & every day plus cher Alex. J'espere qu'il sera content de son livre, dont Lady Rolle veut bien se charger.[5]

Ma pauvre Fanny, es tu bien persuadée que la carriere qu'il y veut absolument suivre, soit bien celle qui le conduira le plus surement à jouir de la somme de bonheur à la quelle il peut pretendre; et surtout, peus tu croire reellement que *lui*, car je ne parle pas même de *moi*, sera suffisament payé des sacrifices enormes que nous coutera ce parti, une fois que nous l'aurons pris irrevocablement? Je ne puis que te repeter ce que je te disais ce matin. *Reflechis y bien*; mon adorable Fanny!

[2] Marie-Joseph-Paul-Yves-Roch-Gilbert du Motier de Lafayette (1757–1834). See vols. i and ii *passim*.
[3] Joseph-Louis de Geoffroy (1746–1835), chevalier, seigneur du Rouret, capitaine, then major des Vaisseaux du roi, and retired as contre-amiral honoraire, chevalier de Saint-Louis. He married Marie-Catherine Gallemard (d. 1850), who bore him one child, Adolphe (1790–1877), baron de Geoffroy du Rouret (1823), *dit* marquis du Rouret.   [4] M. d'A's *domestique* (see viii *passim*).
[5] In a letter (Berg), dated 7 July 1814, AA asked M. d'A for two books: *Histoire d'Hérodote*, traduite du Grec, avec des remarques . . . par M. Larcher (1786); Silvestre-François Lacroix, *Traité élémentaire de calcul différentiel et de calcul intégral* (1st ed., 1802; 2nd, 1806). AA was particularly interested in the Lacroix, reminding M. d'A on 13 July (Berg): 'Vous avez, je crois, la 2^{ieme} Edition, ou 1ere, en 2 petits octavos; l'Ouvrage est lû et relu pour l'Université.' It was the Lacroix that Lady Rolle was bringing to AA.

Quant à moi, je ne puis plus y penser longtems de suite, parceque ce sujet est pour moi trop melancholique. Tu me dis qu'Alex, s'il acheve son tems à Cambridge, verra ouverte devant lui une carriere très brillante. | Je te repons que celle dans la quelle il n'aurait ici qu'à se laisser aller, est infiniment plus sure et plus brillante, puisqu'il se trouverait tout naturellement placé de maniere à pouvoir pretendre à tout, tandis qu'en Angleterre il sera longtems confiné dans une cure ou un prieuré d'où il ne pourra jamais sortir qu'en faisant des efforts dont son caractere le rend et le rendra probablement toujours incapable.[6] Et cependant quel sera pour nous le resultat de ce parti, d'en être separé, et de vivre peniblement sur un revenu mediocre, qui ne nous mettra pas à même de mettre de coté l'argent necessaire pour aller le rejoindre de tems en tems. En restant ici, au contraire, je vois que nous pourrions, dans très peu de tems y vivre dans la plus grande aisance, en egard à la simplicité de nos gouts, et à notre peu d'ambition. mais surtout à l'eloignement que nous avons tous deux pour tout ce qui est representation c. à. d. sacrifice du bonheur à la vanité de rassembler quelques personnes qui le plus souvent vient de l'ennui qu'ils vous causent quand ils ne vont pas jusqu'à se plaindre d'en avoir eu leur bonne part.

Il est plus que probable, par exemple, qu'avant deux ans et peut être avant une, ma place sera doublée. à peu près dans le même tems, je serai Lieutenant general, et ensuite cordon rouge, pour peu que je vive.[7] En ce cas, je suis sur de pouvoir te donner une voiture qui te mettra pour jamais à l'abri des ravages que l'humidité te fait eprouver, et des craintes plus grandes encore qu'elle ne cesse de me donner. Dès lors aussi plus de calculs economiques en opposition avec ce qu'exige le premier de nos besoins, celui de ta santé. Permets, *my dearest Soul*! que je te prie — que je *t'ordonne* s'il le faut, de la soigner comme notre bonheur.

6 This statement suggests the struggle between M. d'A and his wife over AA's future: the desire of M. d'A that his son become an officer in the duc de Luxembourg's company and FBA's intention that the boy should become—as he seemingly agreed—'un bon clergyman' (L. 771). See L. 825, wherein FBA almost capitulated to the aim of M. d'A, and L. 827 n. 3, wherein she managed to keep AA at Cambridge.

7 See L. 806 n. 3. There is no evidence that M. d'A ever received the cordon rouge.

814   63 Lower Sloane Street,
                              24 August 1814
To Mrs. Locke

L. excerpt in the hand of CFBt (Diary MSS. viii. 6020, Berg), 24 Aug.
1814
Double sheet 4to 1 p. p. 3 foliated 60 Pages 1–2 bear an excerpt
from FBA's letter of 9 Aug. 1814 to Mrs. Locke. See L. 810
Edited at the Press. *See* Textual Notes *for* L. 810.

Augt 24. 1814
M: d'Arblay has obtained his rank, and the kind King has
dated it from the æra when the original Brevet was signed by
poor Louis XVI in 1792.[1]

815   [Chelsea, 24 August 1814][1]

To Charles Parr Burney

A.L. (Berg), *n.d.*
Double sheet 8vo 4 pp. *pmks* T.P.P.U. / Chel[sea] EO 27 AU
1814 27 ⟨AU⟩ 1814
Addressed: Revd Charles Parr Burney, / Greenwich.

The direction of M. d'Arblay for a visit, my dear Charles, is

          N° 8, Rue de Miromenil,
          fauxbourg St Honoré à Paris.
          For a Letter—
          A Monsieur, Monsieur
             Le Chevalier d'Arblay,
          Officier des Gardes du Corps,
          Rue— &c

814. [1] See the official letter of the duc de Luxembourg to M. d'A in L. 806 .

815. [1] The dating of this letter depends on its reference to the impending visit
of Mrs. Locke and Amelia Angerstein. According to Diary Entry, p. 518, this
visit took place on 25 August.

But for Heaven's sake send him no more sight-seekers,[2] who expect 'The Hero' to give dinners, & shew Lyons!—'The Hero' is equally without Fortune or Leisure for doing the honours of Paris.

I have never had an opportunity to thank you for the sight of that famous epistle,[3] which, at the time, ¹ was so valuable to me, that I shall always have a *sneaking kindness* for the way-ward Writer, in defiance of his flippancy, & even of his self-conceit. Besides, if he sports so facetiously with 'The Great Men' and to *You*—how could I expect *plus d'égard* for 'The Hero'?—

I found a Letter at my return to Chelsea from the same 'Great Man,' smoothing my retreat hence, by orders issued to Mr. White relative to the forlorn apartments, which I am always saddened in entering, & pained in quitting. Friday[4] I hope to bid them a last Adieu—& to set off for — — —

PARIS, you conclude? for who goes not to Paris?—

But no; 'tis for rather a shorter stage. Richmond, an please you.

By the way, *The Hero's* way of life ¹ is so little understood by the travelling English, that, the other day, a lady & gentleman,[5] by whom I had sent a Letter, wrote a billet to ask him What *were the Days* & hours they might have the pleasure of being sure to find him at home, to pass *la soirée* with him!

What answer he has made to *them*, I have not heard; but the answer he wrote to *me* was somewhat brief, though not the less expressive, namely—'! ! !'

My Brother tells me his return is still unfixed—He seems much better & perfectly happy in his domestic circle. This must compensate the great inconvenience, to us, (Mrs. B. & myself) of his long absence at this period:—though all goes as ill as if some foul fiend marred my dear Father's kind designs for us. No one could know his collection & credit its product. ¹

My kind Love to All *des nôtres* at Ryde if you write before I do: & pray add that I was much pleased with the Letter to

---

² Robert Finch, who by virtue of CPB's letter of 4 June 1814 (Bodleian), was 'placed . . . at once upon the footing of old acquaintance' with M. d'A.

³ Unidentified.

⁴ FBA probably spent another day (i.e. until Saturday 27 Aug.) to ensure that all valuables were removed from CB's apartment for sale by John White, or, if not sold, for storage at his warehouse. It was not until Sunday tha. she and AA left for Richmond.

⁵ Mr. and Mrs. Matthew Montagu. See L. 812 n. 16.

Mr. Dyer.[6] I have ample business, now, with my cargoes of mss. Letters, &c, for a week to come:[7] & to-morrow morning I devote to Mrs. Lock & Mrs. Angerstein, who come to me from Woodlands.[8] Alex sends his best Love. He works arduously at Algebra, but [I] fear never will fag at classics!—

Adieu, my dear Charles

ever truly yours FB d'A. |

816   Paris, 26 August 1814

M. d'Arblay
To Madame d'Arblay

A.L. (Berg), 26 aout 1814
Originally a double sheet 4to, of which FBA later discarded the second leaf 2 pp.
Edited by FBA, p. 1, *annotated*:   (26)   *See further*, Textual Notes.

Ce 26 aout 1814

Depuis quelques jours, ma chere Fanny, je suis à combattre contre un accès de melancolie insoutenable, que ta lettre datée *10*,[1] n'eut fait qu'augmenter: mais heureusement celle N^o *11*,[2] que mon bon ange y a jointe, me rend le courage et me donne l'espoir que tout ce qui nous concerne aura une bonne fin. Amen Amen!

┌Je ne reçois qu'à l'instant même ces deux lettres ⟨avec celles du Ministre⟩ que je me hâterai de te renvoyer aussitôt qu'elles auront été revetues de toutes les formalités requises. Malheureusement cela exigera quelques jours. M^r ⟨Gillet⟩[3] n'est

[6] George Dyer (1755–1841), writer, classicist, and bibliophile, lived at Clifford's Inn, London.

[7] At this time FBA began to sort out the vast collection of Burney papers for the three-volume *Memoirs of Doctor Burney* (1832), and, as she confessed to EBB in a letter (Barrett, Eg. 3690, ff. 129a–130b) on 28 Nov. 1820, an additional three volumes of CB's selected correspondence from and to various members of the Johnson circle and other celebrities. The three volumes of correspondence that she hoped 'the Press would cover . . . with gold' never appeared.

[8] See L. 724 and nn. 12, 14.

816. [1] L. 811.   [2] The missing portion of L. 812.

[3] Antoine-Louis Gillet (*fl.* 1801–51), a friend of the late Antoine Bourdois, and a notary (v, L. 450 n. 7). Maria Bourdois referred to him as 'the *honorable* notary' (Barrett, Eg. 3697, f. 18b).

pas ici. Il a accompagnè sa femme en voyage mais M͏ʳ De la Mare[4] est allé passer quelque tems ⟨mardy soir⟩ dernier pour savoir s'il est de retour. Je ne puis aller moi même ꜚ parcequ'il m'est arrivé ce matin un petit accident, qui ne doit pas plus t'allarmer que moi qui compte qu'il ne m'empêchera pas de monter demain ma premiere garde au chateau — Tu sauras que rien n'est plus regulierement etabli que le service qui s'y fait. Ce matin une maudite visite que je n'ai pu refuser m'a mis un peu en retard pour l'heure de la messe. Midy sonnaient quand je suis entré aux Tuilleries. J'ai eu beau monter les escaliers quatre à quatre je me suis trouvé face à face du Roi que j'aurais du preceder dans la chapelle. Je n'avais consequement d'autre ressource que de redescendre et monter les escaliers pour y arriver avant lui par une autre route. C'est ce que j'ai reussi à faire; mais dans ce trajet, fait à la hâte, je me suis embarassé dans mes longs eperons, et suis tombé ꜚnon pas en lesant la tête, mais ꜚ le genou sur le tranchant d'une marche, qui m'a fait eprouver une douleur trés vive à *la rotule*. Très heureusement Le Roi ne sort pas aujourdhui. J'etais commandé pour l'accompagner à cheval, et malgré une douleur, assez vive, j'etais resolu de ne pas m'en plaindre et de le suivre.[5] M'en voilà quitte, il ne sortira pas, et je suis accouru dans mon logement, où j'ai recours au *tout puissant* Opodelloc, qui dejà a fait des merveilles, puis qu'il m'est possible de m'entretenir avec mon adorable amie.

(à 6ʰ du soir) Une partie de ce que tu viens de lire a été ecrit auprès d'Edmund[6] toujours le plus aimable et le plus partial de mes amis ou plutôt de nos amis. il ne cesse de me parler d'Alex — aussi l'aime-je bien tendrement. Cette amitié au surplus est en ce moment un peu ruineuse: mais comment aurois-je pu eviter une depense que je regrette en songeant aux sacrifices que fait perpetuellement ǀ ma chere Fanny. Puisses tu O mon ange! en être autrement recompensée que par les benedictions que te donne en ce moment le plus tendre et le plus vrai ꜚdes amis,ꜚ le plus reconnoissant des epoux. Imagine

---

[4] Denys Huard de la Mare (*c.* 1783–*post* 1841), a notary, whose office was at 1, rue Ste. Croix d'Antin. A relative by marriage of M. d'A, he was the husband of Adélaïde-Louise-Thérèse *née* Gillet de la Jacqueminière.

[5] As a sous-lieutenant in the duc de Luxembourg's company, M. d'A was commander of the royal artillery guard assigned to the defence of the royal household and the King's person.

[6] Edmond de Beauvau (L. 808 n. 5).

toi qu'Edmund, en rougissant, m'a demandé s'il ne serait pas trop indiscret de me demander de partager mon diner, pour avoir le plaisir d'être plus longtems avec moi. Ma reponse a été ⌐que mon diner n'etait qu'une pauvre petite soupe aux herbes et un peu de pâté de jambon; et que n'ayant qu'une femme qui nuisance en ce moment, servait en même tems la princesse dont la cuisiniere etait absente et la femme de chambre malade, je n'avais de ressource que⌐ d'envoyer chercher un ⌐mauvais⌐ petit poulet et un plat de legumes et du poisson ⌐si cela pouvait lui convenir et à la fois s'il n'avait pas d'autre engagement. Sur cela, il est parti en disant qu'il allait le chercher et le ferait aussi accompagner d'un excellent melon qu'ils avaient à la maison. Bientôt il est revenu sans son frere[7] qui avait du partir pour la campagne et sans le melon qui avait été mangé et que j'ai remplacé par⌐ une omelette, qui a disparu comme tout le reste; malgré la honte que je me suis sentie en pensant que ma bonne et incomparable amie s'impose tant de privations. O ma Fanny, quel ange n'est tu pas! ⌐Tu ne me dis point quelle est la raison qui t'a fait commencer un voyage dans le Pays de Galles.[8] Tout ce que tu me dis à ce sujet est tellement vague qu'il m'est reellement impossible d'y rien comprendre. J'ai serieusement de la peine à me rendre raison de ce qui peut t'avoir decidée, surtout quand je lis dans ta lettre que *the private Tutor* est en ce moment parti lui même pour la campagne. *'Hope', do* you say *'to complete the journey you talk of so gaily?* J'imagine que cela n'a aucun rapport à ta visite chez M[de] Waddington dont j'aime tous les jours davantage la charmante fille mais bien aux voyages que Mr Larrey veut que tu fasses en Italie, ou au moins sur la frontiere de ce pays, à Nice par exemple. Eh bien, Madame, si vous êtes sage et moi aussi, c'est à dire si vous et moi Ma chere athanase nous sommes assez heureux et assez raisonnable pour ne pas separer du malheur trop reel de notre separation momentanée et qui j'espere ne sera jamais bien longue quoique jamais assez courte, la certitude d'une reunion confortable je dis que ces voyages d'Italie nous serons trés faciles. Et voici comment. Ecoute bien ceci. Je n'ai que 6000 en ce moment; la ration de deux chevaux et une indemnité de logement qui allait devoir n'être que de 6000[f]. Tout cela assurement n'est pas merveilleux. Chacun même est

[7] Charles de Beauvau (L. 808 n. 6).   [8] See L. 820 and n. 10.

sur cela d'accord et l'on pense assez generalement qu'aussitôt la liste civile etablie il doit y avoir une augmentation, en egard à la charité actuelle ⟨des vieus⟩ et generalement de tout *hors la paix*. Où donc⸬ |

[*The second leaf is missing*]

⸬Oui, oui mes bons, mes chers amis je serai prés de vous le plutôt possible non pas peut être en octobre, mais trés certainement en novembre.

Ne sois pas inquiete de tes lettres que j'ai toutes reçues. Adieu bonne bonne amie. Adieu cher cher Alex! J'espere que ce cher ami a reçu les livres de ⟨Calcul⟩[9] que je lui ai envoyés par Lady ⟨Rolle⟩ qui est charmante.

J'espere que la procuration que je t'envoye est telle que tu la desires. Je te prie d'en faire l'usage que tu trouveras convenable, ce que je t'ai ecrit à ce sujet dans cette lettre n'etant qu'une simple ⟨germination⟩ qui ne doit être d'autre part que celui d'un simple conseil d'un ⟨tenté⟩.

Eh mon dieu j'allais oublier de te prier de terminer au plus vîte l'affaire de *Camilla Cottage* sans même ecrire grand chose ⟨sur ce⟩ dont je rapelle ⟨tres bien⟩ d'avoir fait mention. En verité j'en ai honte d'après ce que ⟨tu rapelles depuis⟩.⸬

817   Paris, 27 August [1814]

M. d'Arblay
To Madame d'Arblay

A.L. (Berg), 27 Août
Double sheet 4to   4 pp.
Edited by FBA, p. 1, *annotated*:   22   27
Pinned to p. 2 was a cutting ($1·1 \times 0·9 \times 8·6''$), the *recto* and *verso* of which are printed at the end of the letter. For extensive obliterations *see* Textual Notes.

(27 Aout à $9^h \frac{1}{2}$)

En arrivant en voiture à 8^h à l'hotel des Gardes, je n'ai point

[9] See L. 813 n. 5.

trouvé de Marechal de Logis¹ puisque tout le monde etait à la manoeuvre à cheval pour se preparer, ou pour mieux dire pour faire une sorte de repetition de ce qui doit avoir lieu après demain 29 jour où le Roi dine à l'hotel de ville. Je suis en consequence monté chez un off^r de mes amis dont j'ai fait ouvrir la chambre, afin de pouvoir y attendre que la garde fut rassemblée. Quand elle l'a été je suis descendu, et j'allais la conduire clopin clopant au chateau lorsqu'un de mes camarades est arrivé pour me remplacer. Comme j'etais dans le fait assez souffrant et mal à mon aise, j'ai profité de son offre obligeante, et suis revenu sur mon lit, dans l'esperance que 24 heures de plus employées à me soigner et me bien frotter me permettront d'assister plus utilement à la fête projetée,² et dont pour rien au monde je ne voudrais être eloigné. Je serais très malade que j'irais; à plus forte raison quand je n'ai qu'un petit bobo qui ne peut avoir aucune suite fâcheuse et peut tout au plus m'arracher quelques grimaces. ⌐Ce soir entre 7 et 8^h j'irai donner et faire signer la procuration que tu m'as envoyée.³ Ce sera chez M^r De la Mare parce que Gillet est absent,⁴ et j'aurai pour temoin le ⟨Senechal prin.⟩ de France, La Tour Maubourg Senior⁵ et le Cte de ⟨Beaune,⁶ Qui,⟩ j'espere pourra la remettre demain dans les bureaux de Monsieur de ⟨Blacas⟩⁷ —J'ai été interrompu par

817. ¹ Guillaume-Jean-Baptiste de la Frangne (1776–1831), baron de Beaune (1827), maréchal des logis des gardes du Corps, écuyer de la duchesse d'Angoulême, chevalier de Saint-Louis.
² 'A magnificent fête was given to the King on the 29th ult. by the City of Paris, at the Hotel de Ville, which was continued . . . till the next morning.' Present at the Fête were the entire Royal Family, the ministers of State, and the important officers of the Royal household. 'Almost all the English of distinction in Paris were at this Fête [including Wellington]. In the evening the city was illuminated.' See *GM* lxxxiv² (1814), 277.
³ See L. 805 n. 1.
⁴ See L. 816 nn. 3, 4.
⁵ Marie-Charles-*César*-Florimond de Fay, comte de Latour-Maubourg, had been raised on 19 Aug. 1814 to the rank of lieutenant-général and two months earlier had been created a pair de France.
⁶ Possibly Joachim de Montagu-Beaune (1764–1834), marquis de Pouzols, vicomte de Beaune (v, L. 515 n. 13). In 1814 he served as capitaine in the régiment d'Artois, Dragons.
⁷ Pierre-Louis-Jean-Casimir Blacas d'Aulps (1771–1839), duc and pair de France (1824). Always devoted to the Bourbons, he lived from 1804 to 1808 largely in St. Petersburg as représentant officieux of Louis XVIII. He joined the King at Hartwell in 1808 and in 1810 Louis commissioned him chef de régler sa maison. Blacas corresponded with Talleyrand in 1813 to secure the return of the Bourbons. With the Restoration he became ministre de la maison du roi (2 June), maréchal de camp (8 Aug.), chevalier du St. Esprit, grand maître de la garde robe. With Talleyrand's departure to Vienna, he was made chef occulte du ministère.

l'arrivée de tous les d'Albizzi[8] et ⟨Monsieur d'antigny senior⟩[9] qui sortent de l'audience de Mad[e] la duchesse d'Angoulême qui est montée à cheval et ne pourra les recevoir que demain. Je reviens à la procuration que tu m'as adressée. Si j'avais de l'argent à te faire passer, je t'assure que je le garderais et remettrais à arranger cette affaire dans le tems que je compte être avec toi, soit à Londre, soit dans le voisinage. Il me semble bien etrange que Charle ait *omis* tant de choses dans une piece aussi importante que celle constatant la remise d'une somme de mille | livres stirling provenant d'un legs.[10] Ces omissions si singulières, sont elles involontaires? Ce que nous avons eprouvé jusqu'à présent non seulement me *permet* mais encore me fait en quelque sorte une loi d'en douter si c'est ce que c'est. Encore que la manière dont je suis designé en tête de cette procuration donnée par moi:[11] *To Alexander d'Ay* of Sloane Street *Chelsea Esquire now at Paris* &c—Je n'y conçois rien et te prie instamment avant de faire usage de cette piece contre la quelle je proteste. Si comme je le crains elle peut me compromettre je te prie, dis-je, de bien t'assurer qu'elle doit être ainsi conçue, loyalement et legalement. J'ai beau me dire que surement tu n'as pas l'intention de me faire signer une farce, il n'en est pas moins certain 1° que mon nom n'est pas *Alexander*, 2° que je ne suis point de *Sloane Street Chelsea*. Qu'est ce que tout cela veut dire?[12] et ce titre de *Esquire* que j'ai pu prendre quand j'habitais réellement l'Angleterre mais qui ne peut me convenir actuellement que je suis rentré en activité de Service en France ma Patrie, et qu'on m'y connaît comme off[r] des Gardes de Corps. Je le repete, ma chère amie. Ne fais aucune usage de cette procuration que tu ne te sois auparavant bien assurée que cela ne peut être autrement et qu'il n'y aucun risque à la laisser tel que cela est. L'epreuve que j'ai faite près de Mickleham nuit un peu comme tu sais à l'entiere confiance que j'ai eu jusqu'à present dans tous ceux qui habitent le Pays qui t'a vu naître!

[8] Pierre-Joseph Albizzy (1745–1826) was a cousin of M. d'A and adjutant to the Mayor of Joigny. He was accompanied by his wife Marie-Rose (d. 1818) and their five children.

[9] Charles de Damas d'Antigny, now 56 (L. 798 n. 9).

[10] M. d'A refers to FBA's inheritance of 'one thousand Pounds, five per cent Navy'.

[11] M. d'A distrusted most Englishmen in 1814 because of the forced sale of Camilla Cottage, the dwindled size of CB's miscellaneous library, and the relatively small sum of money received by FBA from its sale.

[12] For FBA's reassurance about these details, see the beginning of L. 820.

ah qu'il me coute de renoncer à cette tant douce mais trompeuse confiance. Je peus penser tout haut devant toi mon adorable et incomparable amie. Malgré tout ce que nous fait souffrir en ce moment le poste que j'occupe prés de mon Souverain, malgré le mal qu'en a eprouvé celle pour qui je suis et serai toujours prêt à donner ma vie, persuadé comme je le suis et le serai toujours que rien de ce que je puisse faire pour lui prouver la sincerité de l'hommage que je lui ai si justement fait de toute une existence qu'elle a daigné embellir, ne peut approcher de ce que je lui dois de reconnaissance et d'amour.[11] |

[xxxxx 3 *lines*] si malgré mon veu de ne pas survivre à tout ce qui m'attache à la vie, j'etais condamné à rester quelque tems avant de rejoindre ma chere Fanny si dieu m'en separait — ô ma tendre amie, quelle destinée est la notre, et combien la mienne en particulier a été etrange. Combien surtout ce que j'eprouve en ce moment est hors des limites d'une vie ordinaire, d'une destinée commune. Quel nuage affreux W^m L[ocke] a repandu sur toutes mes jouissances![13] Comme il a empoisonné ce qui aux yeux du monde peut me presenter sous un jour trompeur, comme il a détruit à jamais cette confiance sur la quelle reposait principalement mon bonheur en ce monde. ô ma pauvre amie, quel vilain monde que celui où nous vivons, quand d'aussi douloureuses epreuves vous tiennent sans cesse dans la crainte de ne pas faire un pas sans en rencontrer de semblables. Cette pretendue *generosité* de quelqu'un que ma conscience m'assure n'être pas même *juste,* me suffoque. Elle me rend peut être injuste envers d'autres; et je suis tourmenté à la fois et de la crainte d'être dupé de nouveau, et de celle de calomnier les intentions de ceux de qui j'attens un traitement que j'ai si peu merité. à cela se joint l'espece de honte de me montrer en opposition avec le caractere desinteressé que j'ai toujours eu, et qu'il me semble que je ne devrais pas avoir perdu: car j'ai beau descendre dans mon coeur, j'y retrouve les mêmes mouvemens, la même horreur de tout ce qui n'est que calcul personnel, et la même promptitude à me défaire, sans le moindre interêst, et peut être un peu trop legèrement de ce qui m'est le plus utile et le plus agreable, quand cela me parait necessaire à quelqu'autre. Je crois en même tems être sur que

---

[13] See L. 820, in which FBA asks M. d'A to 'drive . . . this W[illia]m L[ocke]' from his mind.

c'est bien moins les pertes d'argent qu'on nous fait faire, qui m'ont affecté, et m'affectent encore, d'une maniere si douloureuse, qui me touchent le plus sensiblement. Je souffre bien davantage de la triste et cruelle lumiere que j'ai reçue, et dont l'eclat a detruit une illusion bien chere. Je ne doute pas non plus que lorsque toutes nos affaires seront definitivement reglées, j'aurai bien vîte oublié les pertes que nous aurions faites, pour ne m'occuper que de donner quelque consistance à ce qui nous restera. Il semblerait d'après cela que nous ne pourrions ⌐pas trop nous depêcher de terminer et pourtant je suis tourmenté de la crainte qu'au debut on ne te ⟨prive⟩ de connoissance des affaires et du desir que nous avons l'un et l'autre de nous debarasser de celles que nous avons en ce moment. Je te demande donc de grace de ne pas agir trop precipitament et de consulter quelqu'habile et honnête jurisconsulte avant d'aller comme tu le dis *accepter le legs* que nous devons à ton pere justement et sincerement regretté par moi comme par toi. Prends surtout toutes les precautions dont on peut t'aviser pour nous degager de toute responsabilité vis à vis des mineurs actuellement dans l'Inde.[14] Je n'entens rien, absolument rien à ce genre d'affaire mais il est tenable qu'il faudrait laisser à la banque ce qui leur revient pour que les interêts s'y accumulassent et qu'ainsi leur legs s'ameliore. Tu sais que je n'ai pas attendu le mauvais succès de la vente de la bibliotheque reduite de près de 20,000 volumes à moins le quart pour regretter de n'avoir pas été tout simplement à partager avec tes freres et soeurs. Je te jure que le pretendu avantage de quelques centaines de livres sterling ne m'a pas fait changer d'avis, et Pardonne le moi, il ne s'est nullement prouvé que cet avantage soit reel mais le fait est en definitif, jamais il ne pourra entrer en compensation pour ce qu'il nous aura couté!!! Quelle etrange manoeuvre que celle constament mise en usage contre nous. Quoi? ta soeur et toi vous êtes legataires et comme telles exposées à une responsabilité envers des mineurs eloignés de plusieurs centaines de lieues, separés ⟨aussi par⟩ des ⟨insolences⟩ c'est à dire que vous leur devrez compte d'une succession pour la gestion de la quelle leur testataire vous a simplement nommé deux Conseils qu'il n'a autorisé qu'à vous aider d'avis que l'un[15] d'eux a

---

[14] For FBA's discussion of the bequests left to the children of Richard Burney, see L. 812 and n. 3.   [15] JB.

refusé de vous donner tandis que l'autre[16] a agi en souverain maitre, non seulement sans vous consulter mais sans même vous faire part d'avance de ses demarches, toutes inacceptables toutes tenebreuses, car il faut trancher le mot. ET VOUS, vous, vous aurez à rendre compte de ce que vous ignorez, de ce que vous n'avez aucune ⟨manière de savoir⟩, de ce qu'on a ouvertement refusé de vous faire connoitre. Tout cela repugne aux ⟨raisons et attens⟩ des moindres convenances. Tout cela me semble nous exposer au risque certain d'être depouillé de tout ce que nous avons au monde pour indemniser ces gens, au ⟨cout⟩ du quel on pourrait nous dire: Que ne vous êtes vous mis en regle. Il s'agit encore dans l'affaire de veiller, non pas de loyauté, mais de ⟨honneteté et ce sera assez⟩ cesser ⟨du premier coup d'etre⟩ encore trop genereux!

Tous nos amis se portent bien. Je les vois bien peu. Je suis furieux du peu de succès de ton ouvrage contre le quel on a été prevenu par vos journaux.[17] Ceux qui l'ont lu ici en Anglais, ceux mêmes à qui je n'ai pu refuser de le prêter, se taisent ou se contentent de dire que c'est un ouvrage inferieur à ceux qui l'ont precedé mais dans le quel l'auteur a mis cependant beaucoup d'esprit—Pardon mon amie. Je ne doute point que la cause de cela soit tes heroines dont les vraies experiences ont indigné tout le monde. Pardon pardon. Tu sais mon ange quel a été ma façon de penser sur cette ingenieuse production. ⟨Neanmoins⟩ je regrette que maintenant que ⟨la vie de Londres cesse⟩ et le desir de ⟨flatter comme tu l'as fait⟩ ta part, et aussi, tu te sois laissée aller à citer quelques ⟨enoncés⟩ qui pretent des armes à la malignité et à la jalousie que tes succès et merites ont excitées.⌐

J'ai ri et je ris encore de ta sainte colere contre le titre de Baron ou de Comte, car je serais maitre d'obtenir l'un ou l'autre.[18] Je n'y ai jamais pensé serieusement: mais il etait possible que cela put te flatter, et si notre fortune etait realisée en France et que nous puissions placer en fond de terre ni l'un ni l'autre de ces titres ne seraient *ludicrous*

⌐Ce qu'il y a de très sur c'est que j'ai une telle crainte de contrarier outre mesure ceux qui se preparent pour [xxxxx *a few*

---

[16] This view of CB Jr. by M. d'A is based on FBA's L. 782.
[17] For the reviews of *The Wanderer* that M. d'A may have seen, see Appendix IV. See also L. 796 n. 6.
[18] See L. 811 and n. 4.

447

words] que je n'hesiterais pas à renoncer à tout le monde [xxxxx *a few words*] de s'offrir se distinguerait de ce que je n'aurais fait.

En consequence, mon amie, je te conjure dans ton nom et dans celui de ton fils de te menager la possibilité de deplacer à volonté tout ce qui n'est point [xxxxx *a few words*] qui nous a valu tant d'envie, qui encore [xxxxx *a few words*]

[xxxxx 1 *line*]

Adieu my dear Friend. Give my best compliments to Mʳ ⟨Hagget⟩[19] and also my best respects to Lady Harcourt,[20] Lady ⟨Rolle⟩[21] and to [xxxxx *a few words*]

Imagine toi qu'Alec est obligé de retourner à Cambridge le 5 d'octobre. Dis lui ⟨que je repousse mon⟩ arrivée ⟨encore pour⟩ passer quelques jours avec lui on ⟨repartira vite⟩ [xxxxx *a few words*]ⁿ

[*To this letter was pinned the fragment*:]

dans ce genre ce qu'on a perdu une fois, ne peut se recouvrer, O toi ma chere Fanny toi qui sais si bien reunir tout ce qui peut flatter une ame delicate pourquoi ne peus tu être toujours avec celui qui ne peut trouver de bonheur que près de toi? Certainement, je sacrifierai tout hors l'honneur à ce bien si cher: mais helas, le pourrai-je, cette année? Mʳ de Luxembourg est pour moi

[*Verso of fragment*:]

et qui convienne à Alex. Je ne pense pas à autre chose: mais jusqu'à present rien lui va absolument, et je pense qu'il faut dans tous les cas, qu'il finisse son tems de Cambridge, c'est à dire les deux ans qu'il a encore à y passer. Tu vois d'après cela que je me suis [*line cut*] la seule

[19] In effect, M. d'A is acknowledging the sound advice of the Revd. Mr. Haggitt on the disposition of Camilla Cottage.

[20] For Lady Harcourt, and especially her concern for the Beauvaus, see L. 812 n. 12.

[21] For the sense of indebtedness that M. d'A felt toward Lady Rolle, see L. 813 and n. 5.

M. d'Arblay
To Madame d'Arblay

A.L.S. (Diary MSS. vii. 6026-[31], Berg), 28, 30 Août—3, 7 Sep^t 1814
Originally two double sheets 4to, greenish, of which the second leaf of
the second sheet was discarded   6 pp.
Edited by FBA, p. 1 (6026), *annotated*: 27 The Duke of Wellington's
Reception as ambassadour to Louis 18.
    p. 5 (0630) *annotated and dated*: 27 continued   1814
Edited also by CFBt *and the* Press. *See* Textual Notes.

                                          Paris ce 30 Aout 1814

Il n'y a que deux jours, ma bonne Fanny, que j'ai passé plus
de 8 heures entieres à m'entretenir avec toi, sans même me
douter que la position dans la quelle j'arrivais me faisait beaucoup de mal. N'importe aujourd'hui je ne puis resister au
plaisir de venir te confier l'extrême satisfaction que me fait
éprouver la manière dont la fête donnée hier au Roi par la
Ville, s'est passée. Tout a été non seulement bien, mais à merveille; et cela est d'autant plus important, que je n'ai actuellement aucun doute que notre réunion au mois de Novembre ne
souffrira pas la moindre difficulté, puisque la seule chose qui
pourrait s'y opposer,[1] c'est à dire le moindre doute sur la
stabilité du gouvernement paternel qui nous a été rendu si
miraculeusement, n'est plus même admissible. Ce n'est pas
simplement avec plaisir, mais avec transport, avec la plus
expansive effusion de coeur, que le Roi, | Madame la Duchesse
d'angoulême et nos Princes ont été accueillis à l'hôtel de Ville.
Si l'enthousiasme du Peuple a été comprimé dans la route, c'a
été uniquement parcequ'en ne voyant que des voitures tout à
fait simples, personne n'a imaginé qu'elles renfermassent notre
Père, qu'on s'attendait à voir dans la voiture surmontée d'une
couronne. Il est presumable qu'on ne s'en est pas servi parce que
cette couronne est impériale et non Royale.

---

818. [1] M.d'A was to journey to England in October, but not to remain there.
On 11 Nov. 1814 (Diary Entry, p. 519) he and FBA were to sail from Dover to
Calais.

Louis XVIII n'a pas fait sur tout cela le moindre changement, et son Palais est encore tel qu'il était il y a six mois,
parsemé d'abeilles, de N, et d'aigles, qu'on aurait pu au moins,
ce me semble, faire disparaître du thrône sur le quel siegeait sa
majesté le jour où elle a reçu le Lord Wellington, d'une manière
si flatteuse pour ce Héros.[2] Après lui avoir témoigné combien
elle était satisfaite des sentimens qu'il venait de lui exprimer de
la part du Prince Régent, elle lui avait dit qu'elle désirait infini-
ment | de voir établié sur des bases solides la paix qui vient
d'être si chèrement conclue.[3] S. M[té] a ajouté 'j'aurai besoin
pour cela de la cooperation puissante de Son Altesse Royale.
Le Choix qu'elle a fait de vous, Monsieur, m'en donne l'espé-
rance. *Il m'honnore* — —Je suis fier, | de voir que | *le premier
Ambassadeur que m'envoye l'Angleterre soit le justement célèbre Lord — —
Duc de Wellington.*'[4] Ce qui est entre deux guillemets est mot à
mot.

Tout ce que je viens de souligner a été prononcé d'une voix
forte et tellement accentuée qu'elle portait à l'âme, et qu'elle a
touché même les Marechaux,[5] un peu honteux des succès

---

[2] The Duke of Wellington, now Ambassador Extraordinary from England to
France, had his first public audience with the French King on 24 Aug. 1814.
Louis's words of welcome followed a predetermined formula later voiced by the
comte d'Artois when he was visited by Wellington. 'The King and all the Royal
Family see, with the greatest pleasure, the choice which the Prince Regent has
made of a Hero so worthy to represent him. Our desire and our hope is to see a
durable peace established between two nations, more formed to esteem than to
combat each other' (*GM* lxxxiv[2], 277).

[3] Louis XVIII had in mind not only the casualties sustained by both the French
and Allied troops but also the tense political manœuvring that secured his restoration and the subsequent peace. During the last months of military struggle, succession was fought over bitterly. The return of the Bourbons—as Louis knew—
became a shaky compromise, one that might be further shaken during the Congress of Vienna to begin in a month's time. Finally, the peace was costly in territory. According to the conditions of the armistice signed in mid-April 1814, 'La
France était réduite à ses limites de 1792. . . . [et] perdait même les conquêtes
de la Révolution qui lui avaient été reconnues à Lunéville' (Orieux, p. 586).

[4] The choice of Wellington as ambassador to France indicated to Louis that
Castlereagh's support of the Bourbons had not abated. As early as January 1814
Castlereagh had argued in favour of a Bourbon restoration against Metternich's
and Alexander's alternate proposals. Yet since the Treaty of London (29 June
1814), Louis was uneasy about Castlereagh and how his interpretation of Pitt's
policies would affect France's future.

[5] With the Restoration the newly created 6,000 'soldats d'élite' were aged
émigrés or Ultras. At the same time many of Napoleon's proven officers were either
on half-pay or bypassed for promotions. The professional officers were angered by
the new army. 'Il faut lire dans le *Journal* du maréchal de Castellane la façon dont
il souligne certains passedroits. . . . On fait une promotion ridicule d'officiers
généraux, de gens auxquels on compte pour une activité le temps passé chez eux,
pour la raison qu'ils auraient pu servir si Louis XVIII avait régné' (Bertaut,
p. 188). See also L. 799 n. 3.

constans de leur maître à tous. Quant au discours du héros, dont j'étais près comme de ton lit à ta cheminée, je n'en ai pas entendu un mot; tant il parlait bas, et d'une voix presque tremblante. Déjà je crois t'avoir mandé que nous avons l'ordre du Roi de ne pas avoir égard à l'etiquette, dès qu'il s'agit des Anglois, qui sont admis de quelque manière et à quelqu'heure qu'ils se presentent: mais la manière dont il traite celui qui représente ici leur Nation ne peut se decrire. Dès que le Duc de Wellington paraît, on en est instruit par l'extrême satisfaction qu'on voit repandue sur tous les traits du visage déjà si bon du Roi. Je voudrais que tu ⅼ eusses été temoin, hier soir, de la phisionomie si expressive du Héros qui était sur la première marche de l'estrade d'un thrône dont il parait être le principal soutien. Il avait bien un peu la mine de se dire, *je n'ai pas peu contribué à son rétablissement*—mais cela d'un air si modeste, qu'à peine pouvait on saisir au passage, cette idée fugitive; tandis qu'on trouvait toujours bien prononcée la plus sincère et la plus vive satisfaction du succès qu'ont eu les efforts si constans et si genereux de la brave nation. Personne dans toute la salle, n'a pu mieux le voir ni l'examiner que moi, indigne qui occupais à droite du thrône à peu près la même place que celle qu'il remplissait si noblement à la droite. Je crois bien qu'il a du un peu m'envier les jolies voisines qui s'étaient fait jour jusqu'à moi, et qu'à la verité j'avais un peu aidées dans les soins qu'elles s'étaient donnés pour y parvenir. La plus près sur tout était bien digne d'être remarquée. Le Ministre de la Guerre[6] qui était à ma Gauche, et consequement un peu plus rapproché du Roi, m'ayant demandé son nom tout bas, en me disant que Mʳ le Duc de Berry[7] ne quittait pas les yeux de dessus elle, je la

[6] Pierre Dupont de L'Étang (1765–1840) began his army career as a sous-lieutenant in the legion of Maillebois (1715–91) serving in Holland. Very successful in Napoleon's army, he was named in 1807 grand-aigle de la Légion d'honneur, commandant supérieur de Berlin, and in 1808 comte de l'Empire. Also in 1808 he was defeated at Baylen in Spain, where 17,000 Frenchmen surrendered. He was accused of high treason before a military tribunal, judged guilty, stripped of his rank, and interned first in the fortress of Joux and then in the citadel of Doullens, where he stayed until the fall of Napoleon. The provisional government of 1814 named him commissaire au département de la Guerre, and Louis XVIII confirmed him in that post. After the provisional government was dissolved, he was named on 13 May 1814 ministre de la Guerre, a title held until 3 Dec. 1814. In his favour, according to Vitrolles, was 'la haine que le général Dupont devait nourrir contre Bonaparte lui fut comptée comme un mérite' (ii. 36).
[7] Charles-Ferdinand de Bourbon, duc de Berry (1778–1820). The second son of the comte d'Artois, he served from 1792 to 1797 under Condé, with whom he

priai de me mettre à même de repondre à cette question, ce qu'elle │ ⌐a fait en m'apprenant¬ qu'elle etoit la femme du receveur general du dep^t du Calvados et qu'elle s'appellait Emilie[8] —j'ai oublié le reste, mais je me rapelle parfaitement qu'elle est Lyonnaise, qu'elle est très jolie, fort spirituelle et tout à fait aimable. [xxxxx 1 *line*] Lorsque nous quittions la salle pour suivre le Roi, après la 3eme ou 4eme contredanse, S.A.R.[9] s'est approchée d'elle, et l'a priée pour demain à Bagatelle,[10] au retour de la Chasse, ou même pour la Chasse qui doit avoir lieu dans le bois de Boulogne. Cette dernière version est je crois la bonne: car elle est venue ensuite me consulter pour savoir si elle suivrait en caleche ou à cheval, ce que je n'ai pu lui dire. Il aurait fallu que je puisse moi même sur l'etiquette des informations impossibles en ce moment, surtout lorsque Madame de Choisi[11] eut pris mon bras pour descendre l'escalier, assez long, par le quel il nous fallait passer pour gagner les voitures de la Cour. Cette dame, et Madame de Damas,[12] etant les seules qui ayent accompagné Madame d'Angoulême, dont nous nous sommes entretenus pendant tout

went to Russia as commander of a Cavalry regiment. From 1801 to 1814 he lived in England, began a liaison with Emma (or Amy) Brown, and sired two daughters. According to Mme de Boigne (i. 154–6), he was guilty of poor judgement but 'the only prince of his family who was . . . capable of generosity'. In 1814 he returned to France and in 1816 married Caroline of the Two Sicilies (1798–1870). On 13 Feb. 1820, as he was leaving the Paris Opéra, he was attacked by an assassin and died the next day.

[8] Leu-*Henri*-Alain Pellapra (1772–*post* 1816), born in Lyon, married 26 Thermidor an 13, Françoise-Marie-*Émilie* Leroy (1784–*post* 1820), also of that city. Pellapra was named 'receveur general du dep^t du Calvados' in 1808 and held that post until 1816. His wife's beauty attracted many notables, among them Napoleon. Mme Pellapra's liaison with the Emperor allegedly produced in 1809 a child who was named Émilie Pellapra (d. 1871, as the princesse de Caraman-Chimay).

[9] Here FBA supplied the superscript ^x and the explanatory note: 'le duc de Berry'.

[10] Bagatelle, a small chateau built in 1779 by the comte d'Artois, on the border of the Bois de Boulogne, not far from the Seine.

[11] Anne-Charlotte-*Henriette* de Choisy (d. 1841) was connected with the exiled court of Louis XVIII. In 1799 at Mittau it was proposed that despite her youth she should marry Louis-Alexandre-Céleste d'Aumont (1736–1814), duc de Villequier (1759), duc d'Aumont. But the King, seeing 'l'inégalité et l'inopportunité de cette union', forbade the marriage (Forneron, iii. 129).

Mlle de Choisy accompanied Louis and his entourage when they moved to Hartwell and there became a close associate of the duchesse d'Angoulême and Mme de Damas-Crux (n. 12).

In 1815 Mlle de Choisy married the vicomte d'Agoult (L. 793 n. 8), whose first wife Marthe *née* de Galland had died in London in 1808.

[12] Anne-*Simone*-Félicité de Serent (1772–1848) married in 1799 Étienne-Charles de Damas-Crux (1754–1846), lieutenant-général (1814), pair de France (1815), duc-pair (1817).

le tems qu'elle m'a fait l'honneur de garder le bras qu'elle avait pris, ainsi, sans se douter du peu de secours dont j'aurais pu lui être si par malheur elle avait eu besoin d'aide. En effet j'avais le genou tellement enflé ᴦqu'à peine pouvais-je me tenir de bout. Ne va pas croire pour celà que ce bobo soit le moins du monde sérieux. Je suis au contraire gueri: mais j'avais voulu absolument monter mon garde au Chateau. j'y avais passé la nuit, et cela m'avait fort echauffé: Le cheval en outre, et surtout l'effort necessaire pour y monter, n'avaient pas peu contribué à me mettre un peu mal à l'aise. Toutᵑ ˥ cela, au reste, n'a pas été la faute de Monsieur le Duc de Luxembourg, dont je ne puis me refuser à te transcrire ici le billet arrivé la veille chez moi une demie heure après mon depart pour aller prendre le commandement de la garde montante.

Le duc de L. souhaite le bon jour à Mᴿ d'Ay, et lui fait demander de ses nouvelles en lui recommandant expressement de ne pas sortir que son genou ne soit gueri. Cette recommendation est l'ordre le plus positif, au nom de l'amitié et de l'interêst qu'il lui porte.

Le duc de L— prie Monsieur le Chevalier d'Arblay de recevoir ses tendres complimens.

Paris le 28 Août 1814.

Dis moi, ma chère Fanny, si tu peus jamais, rien imaginer de plus aimable, toi qui n'est pas tout à fait bête, et que j'ai la *kindness* de desirer avoir *at my side*, quand pareille chose m'est adressée; dis moi si dans la situation de nos affaires, et avec l'espérance bien fondé de passer ensemble paisiblement et honnorablement, les jours quelque fois nebuleux d'une viellesse qui entraîne avec soi le besoin d'une certaine aisance, ce ne serait pas le comble de l'extravagance de quitter ce qui peut et doit me l'assurer?

Embrasse pour moi Alex, puis embrassez moi tous deux comme je vous aime.

Le Chevᴿ d'Ay.

P.S. ᴦJe vais diner chez le Ministre de la Guerre. Si j'y apprens quelque chose, je t'en ferai part. adieu ma chere amie! (De retour) Rien de nouveau. On dit, on assure que Du Pont a de l'esprit. Je le crois, mais il ne sait pas faire le ⟨Rousseau⟩[13] de chez lui. Il m'a pourtant bien traité

(le 3 Septembre) Tout à l'heure en passant près du Palais Royal, j'ai vu, tres distinctement vu John Angerstein entrant aux Français ou l'⟨   ⟩ Merope de Voltaire.[14] Quoi! lui aussi serait arrivé sans m'apporter de tes nouvelles! et sans venir m'en donner? Oh les anglais, les anglais sont bien etranges, et malgré toutes leurs qualités, malgré tous nos defauts, Je ne puis m'empêcher de penser qu'à tout prendre nous valons mieux qu'eux. Qu'il est cruel de reflechir, et surtout de regretter! J'ai appris ce matin une nouvelle qui m'a fait bien du mal. Ce pauvre Boinville[15] que je m'attendais à revoir incessament parce que quelqu'un digne de foi avait ecrit qu'en decembre dernier⊓ |

[*The second leaf is missing*]

(Ce 7 Sep^t) Je te donne ma parole que je ne me rappelle point la main que j'ai baisée! Ce que je sais c'est que j'aime et aimerai toujours infiniment et par dessus tout cette ingrate Athanase — George Lock[16] et John Angerstein sont venus me voir et nous dinons aujourd'hui ensemble⊓

819   [63 Lower Sloane Street,
                                              pre 4 September 1814]
To Mrs. Waddington

A.N. (Berg), *n.d.*
Single sheet 4to   cut down to 4·6″   2 pp.

I was preparing to come to you my dearest Mary—with Alexander, who was to deposit me in his way to his private

---

[13] Nicolas-Auguste-Marie Rousseau (1770–1858), comte de Saint-Aignan. See v, L. 456 n. 11.
[14] Voltaire's *La Mérope*, a tragedy in five acts, was first performed in 1743.
[15] See L. 654 n.12.
[16] The quarrel of the d'Arblays with William Locke did not alter the feeling of M. d'A for his friends George Locke and John Angerstein. In fact, the two men avoided involvement in the contretemps. Amelia Angerstein on 4 May 1814 wrote FBA (Barrett, Eg. 3697, f. 72b): 'My husband having *never* had any communication with my Father on the subject, or with William since, & only knowing of the business the grief of heart I have experienced, feels desirous of declining entering into it, without he could hope any benefit could arise from his assistance or interference.' FBA, however, was not so forbearing as M. d'A. See L. 820.

Tutor—& I should have awaited his return for me—but I must yield to your fears—though I truly believe a conference & meeting such as ours—each on our guard—could only soothe, not agitate your too too tender feelings. I relinquish painfully the beautiful though inadequate portrait, & I embrace my sweet lovely Emily with fond affection—pray let me know when you are informed whether dear Fanny has seen M. d'A.[1] Let my bright Augusta ǀ continue the correspondence she has so wonderfully well begun, when the loved Mother, & elder[2] are indisposed—but fail not to let me hear as soon as is possible how you All arrive at Lanover which I really & most sincerely grieve to be unable to inhabit with you at this quiet & therefore favourite period—& Alex is quite melancholy at the impossibility & wants me to take a Cottage in your neighbourhood for the last month of his vacation—

Adieu adieu adieu—My letters will always be safe here—& hence follow me—

820   Hill Street, Richmond,
                                         4 September 1814
To M. d'Arblay

A.L. (Berg), 4 Sept. 1814
Originally a double sheet 4to of which FBA later discarded the second leaf   2 pp. *paged* 1   2
Edited by FBA, *who numbered the pages and annotated*, p. 1 : 28 N⟨°⟩ (29 lost)
See further, Textual Notes.

Richmond, Sep^{tr} 4th 1814

I will not lose a day ere I thank you for the kind expedition with which you have returned the Letter of Attorney, ⌐from which I mean to *save*, not *run* any risk, for I shall sell out *purposely* to *buy in* with the due attention to your name so carelessly neglected. I must enquire, however, what is right, for the only important omission, I believe, is your family name *Piochard*, as I do not think your French title or residence ought to be

819.   [1] Frances Waddington and her father went to France soon after 25 July (L. 807), returning to Wales in mid-September (L. 827).
   [2] Since Frances Waddington was now in Paris, FBA could justly allude to Emelia as the 'elder' of Mrs. Waddington's daughters (L. 636 n. 1).

mentioned.[1] Should Mr. Waddington be still at Paris—where he told me he must go in the first week in September—he can probably inform you upon this subject with perfect accuracy.⌐

And shall I be less *empressée* to thank you, also, for a Letter so full of communication, confidence, kindness & consolation? Oh how do I require—& how gratefully receive all the support you can bestow!—⌐I have never quite recovered, either in spirits, or looks, or feeling, from the dreadful *5th* week that was elapsing of total silence from your Letter from Calais from May 31st to uly 3d[2] I knew not whether you were alive — — Let me fly this recollection, still always baleful to me.—

Mais ce *clopin-clopant* m'alarme beaucoup pour la Fête du 29.[3] Je crains infiniment trop d'exertion. J'espère bien que c'est â notre cher M. Larrey que vous vous êtes confié pour qu'il vous soigne? Dites-moi cela, je vous en prie.

Mr. Locke at Paris![4] alas, I knew it last week, when I wrote your consent to the sale of the house, previously to the Letter that demanded the purchase of the Ground. Mrs. Locke then mentioned that he was gone—& that George, & John Angerstein were going, & desired to carry Letters for me. I had been too little satisfied with George, for neither calling upon or writing to you on your return, to chuse to give him an introduction. I declined even any Letter sending by John A. to avoid any sort of measure that might lead to an interview with William, while the Cottage business was not settled.[5] I acquainted them, therefore, I had just written by M. de La Châtre.⌐

How do I wish ⌐this⌐ affair finished! Murray is provokingly out of town: or I should instantly catch at your spirited & noble determination to owe nothing to a computation so narrow as that of not taking yet greater advantage of our credulity. The Law is all against us! There is only one voice to confirm that: I have sent, therefore, proudly, your acceptance of the terms of their own surveyor, Burton, *620*!!![6] ⌐to Martin, who will decline

820. [1] FBA's soothing response to M. d'A over the form of his name and address on the procuration he signed. See L. 817.

[2] See especially Ll. 788, 790, 792, 794, 795, in which FBA expressed concern over the silence of M. d'A. L. 796 was her first communication from M. d'A since his note from Calais (L. 780).

[3] See L. 817.   [4] William Locke.

[5] For the cordial relationship of M. d'A with George Locke and John Angerstein, see L. 818 and n. 16.

[6] William Burton (1774–1825), bookseller and auctioneer, at 62 Cornhill.

it as soon as Murray returns from the country.⁷⁷ I feel with you
entirely, that the word *generosity*⁷ is a *suffocation* to Justice,
honour, & friendship, that would make any benefit a degrada-
tion. I am proud, I repeat, to be the medium of such a decision.

Mais Vous—Vous, aussi, vous parlez des *empoissonmens de
la vie — de vos jouissances*, that seemed so excelling? alas, what,
indeed, as you painfully cry, is this World!—Your *bonheur*,
so merited, & so enjoyed, is all that has made *me* patiently bear
our separation, & the contrast of the harrassing fatigue of my
own Position. | O drive, as fast as you can, this W[illia]m
L[ocke] who has broken so ungenially upon your happiness,
from your mind, & give me again the comfort to hear of your
complete prosperity. Avoid him, if it be possible—if not, be
distantly polite. To be otherwise, after your Letter, may seem
inconsistent.⁸ But oh never—never suffer yourself to forget our
exquisite attachment to his Father, who gave us to each other!—⁹

For ME—my only source of Felicity in your absence is a
source, also, of such deep apprehension & solicitude, that every
gleam of hope is followed by some cloud of despair! yet he
improves, in *every* thing, evidently, though uncertainly, & with
relapses that are nearly distracting: nevertheless, the tender love
I bear him makes the smallest amends pay me for whole worlds
of suffering—& how I shall support the wearying harrass of
mere & lonely melancholy business, & studious privations,
when he leaves me for Cambridge, I know not. For all my
BUSINESS is the revisal of my dearest Father's papers, Mss.
Letters—an endless employment! all my privations have been
to *spare nothing* for Alex, whose demands, between Books &
Tutors, are incredible.

If what I have *said* relative to *Le pays de Galles* is *vague*, so is
what I have experienced. A *manque de bonne foi* is clear—in an
invitation I had believed of the most ardent vehemence of
sincerity—till I was accepting it!!!¹⁰—I had received a Letter of

⁷ See the concluding paragraph of L. 812.   ⁸ See L. 776 nn. 3, 4.
⁹ In January 1793, FB visited Norbury Park when it was presided over by
the elder William Locke. It was then that she met M. d'A, who had recently
become a resident of Juniper Hall.
¹⁰ Mrs. Waddington was probably annoyed with FBA, who had refused to see
James Greene (Ll. 684, 691), to write frequently (L. 695), to chaperone Frances
Waddington during a London season (L. 718) and later during a Paris début
(L. 791). FBA had also refused to help a friend of the Waddingtons secure a
legation post in Paris (L. 802) and failed to send Mrs. Waddington a presentation
copy of *The Wanderer* (L. 753 n. 9).

such soft, supplicating, almost dying entreaty, that, finding the idea extremely pleasing to Alex, & being without any establishment to leave, & petitioned *à genoux* to take a vacant place in their carriage, I listened, for the first time, to pleas I had heard at least 50 with a deaf Ear. I then began to deliberate how to change the lessons of the private Tutor to our return: BUT— — when we went, with this plan, to a tea party with the family, the fair Inviter no sooner found my refusals relaxing, than her ardour relaxed also! The subject was dropt!—an appointment she had made to come to me, & talk it over, was broken! a Letter came, instead, without one word upon the subject! but the day before she went to Deal, she settled to call, & to renew her *earnest request*: She came not, however; her Daughter brought her apology of Headache—and never named the matter!!! Take no notice, *I ENTREAT,* of this detail.

⌐Let me not, however, use more paper ere I write what was my chief business to expound to you, i.e., my position with regard to money, which many things make essential you should know with detail, for surely, surely, you forget, or mistake it! 1.ʳᵉ I have yet received nothing but 100. pᵈ *à compte* from Charles,[11] for a necessary purpose I shall presently explain. The Cottage man's rent had been advanced, you may remember, in so much that 5 pᵈ only is due from the last Novʳ payment, & the 23.10 due last May, Mrs. Locke has never offered me, whether because it is expended in any repairs or kept for ⟨whole⟩ interests, I know not. This year, therefore, instead of the richest, is the poorest of any, nothing coming to me but 80. from the 3 pʳ cᵗˢ & 90 from Mr. Mathias: for 47, hitherto received for the Cottage has failed & will soon be reduced to nearly $\frac{1}{2}$!—⌐

⌐I often hear of you now; all the English enquire about you.⌐

[*The second leaf is missing*]

11 See L. 797 and n. 1.

M. d'Arblay
To Madame d'Arblay

A.L. (Berg), ⌈Samedy⌉ Dimanche 5 Sept.
Originally a double sheet 4to, of which FBA later discarded the second
leaf 2 pp.
Edited by FBA, p. 1, *annotated and date retraced*: 29   *See further*, Textual
Notes.

(*Dimanche* 5. Sept^{bre})

Je viens de passer près de 3 heures la tête dans mes deux
mains ou les coudes sur ma table, assailli par les idées les plus
contraires. Je n'en suis pas pour cela plus en etat de repondre, ma
chere chere amie, à ta lettre du 24 aout, dans la quelle Alex s'est
enfin expliqué d'une maniere selon lui et selon toi tout à fait
claire[1] — Quelle vie que la mienne! et quelle etrange position
que celle où je me trouve! à demain, la nuit peut être me sug-
gerera quelque moyen de voir un peu mieux et plus distincte-
ment ce à quoi je dois m'arrêter au milieu de l'espece de cahos
dont je suis environné. Je vais m'habiller pour me rendre au
Chateau. j'ai promis à M^{de} la C^{esse} de Vezé,[2] fille de Mme de
Germigney,[3] de m'y trouver un peu avant la messe du Roi, afin
d'y faire entrer sa societé.

(Dimanche soir) Helas, ma bonne amie nous n'aurons rien
à nous reprocher et mon tour est venu! Quel terrible désapointe-
ment! et combien je suis faché d'avoir été la cause bien inno-
cente du chagrin que tu as eprouvé, s'il approchait de celui que

821. [1] FBA's letter is missing, but in it she again rejected a military career for
AA. See Ll. 807 and especially 811, for AA's similar attitude.
  [2] Françoise-Émilie de Germigney (*fl.* 1772–*post* 1814) had married in 1789
Joseph-Luc-Jean-Baptiste de Mareschal-Vezet (1743–1816), comte de Vezet.
An adviser to Louis XVI and then to Louis XVIII, the comte de Vezet, once
président au parlement de Besançon, followed his King to Germany. Even while
Louis was at Mittau, Vezet returned to France often, assumed aliases, and became
part of a small subversive group called the agence de Souabe. Disapproving the
King's move to England, Vezet instead took up Swiss residence with his family.
He returned to France openly only with the Restoration. See Forneron, ii. 69,
77, 269; L. Pingaud, 'Le président de Vezet', *Revue historique* (Nov. 1882), pp.
317–18.
  [3] The mother of the comtesse de Vezet was Denise-Victoire *née* de Chastelier
du Mesnil (*fl.* 1750–1814), the wife of Jacques-François de Germigney (d. 1790),
2nd marquis de Germigney (iii, L. 145 n. 4).

m'a fait et me fait encore ta derniere lettre! *Is there then,* dis tu, *nothing else in France? absolutely nothing.* Helas non, non: il n'y a rien pour quelqu'un que le moindre petit assujetissement ou d'etiquete, ou de devoir, ou d'usage, effraye au point de se persuader que cette contrainte considerée par lui comme un esclavage insuportable, ne manqueroit pas de rendre sa vie un veritable fardeau. ⌐Ce qui m'etonne, et ce que je ne pourrai jamais concevoir c'est que ce soit aussi ⟨là⟩ ton opinion, et que tu puisses reellement pens[er] egalement que ton fils deviendrait bigot et resterait aussi, *à notre eternelle honte, si faible* de son ⟨corps⟩. Permets moi, ma chere Fanny, de te dire qu'en cela ta sagacité ordinaire est tout à fait en défaut. Bien loin qu'une originalité qui a sa source dans l'amour excessif des sciences abstraites rendisse notre fils ridicule, je te repons qu'elle le presenterait à ses camarades comme singulier mais tres respectable et que même ses irregularités seraient facilement excusées. Ces irregularités en surplus ne seraient point *invincibles.* J'en ai une assez forte garantie dans l'amour propre même qui se les exagere. Mais supposons qu'en effet elles fussent telles qu'elles résistassent à tout. Des lors, et par cela même celui qui en serait atteint ne pourrait devenir propre à rien. assurément les devoirs d'un ⟨clergyman⟩ par exemple sont d'une bien autre importance que ceux des gardes de Corps. La négligence à ses emplois et la moindre inexactitude auraient necessairement des suites bien plus facheuses et consequement bien plus redoutables. Mais c'est [xxxxx 4–5 *words*]⌐ | il avait oui dire qu'il etait bien portant, eh bien, nous l'avons perdu peu de jours apres son arrivée à Wilna! Le jeune Croismaire[4] ecrit que cet infortuné avait les pieds et les mains gelés, de maniere à ce qu'il etait impossible qu'il conservât ni les uns ni les autres! En ce cas son existence eut été si affreuse, qu'on ne peut le plaindre d'en avoir trouvé le terme. mais je n'en regrette pas moins cet ami veritable, dont de legers defauts ne peuvent à mes yeux qu'obscurcir et non detruire les excellentes qualités. ah! M. Angerstein! combien votre vue a renouvellé ce que m'a fait eprouver votre beau frere! et combien tous deux vous me rendez plus chere ma patrie en diminuant l'enthousiasme que j'eprouvais pour la vôtre plus admirable qu'aimable. Heureusement j'ai

[4] Charles-Louis de Croismaire (1792–1879), capitaine in the Chasseurs à cheval de la garde royale (retired in 1830).

eu aujourdhui quelques compensations. D'abord j'ai retrouvé de nouveaux amis, aussi devoués, aussi aimans qu'il y a vingt cinq ans; et ce qui me flatte le plus, c'est qu'ils ignoraient ma situation actuelle. L'un d'eux est le Marquis de la Baume,[5] neveu du Lieut^ant Gen^al Narbonne Frizlar,[6] grandpere de Mad^e la Duchesse de Chevreuse.[7] Il est là avec des parens fort riches, et dont il s'est separé, parce qu'ils font chez les restaurateurs une depense folle. Nous sommes convenus que nous irions ensemble faire quelques diners où nous ne depasserons pas 4 francs, ou 5 par extraordinaire. Je parie que ce prix là l'etonna; mais, ma chere amie, le passage des alliés, et l'arrivée des Anglais, a bien changé Paris, qui est à present fort cher. Il m'est d'ailleurs impossible actuellement d'aller comme je le fesais dans la premiere gargotte où j'etais et pouvais rester inconnu. À propos de diner, je dine demain chez le Vte de Narbonne, qui a epousé la princesse de Beaufremont Listenoy[8] que tu n'as surement pas oublié. Elle m'a beaucoup demandé de tes nouvelles. |

[xxxxx 3½ *lines of marginal writing*]

822
To Charles Burney

Hill Street, Richmond,
6 September 1814

A.L. (Berg), 6 September 1814
Double sheet 4to   4 pp.   *pmks* RICHMOND / 6 SP 1814   6 SP 1814   black seal
Addressed: Rev^d Dr. Charles Burney, / Rectory House, / Deptford
Docketed in pencil, p. 4: Maggs   2.20.   56

5 Possibly Pierre de la Baume (*fl.* 1789–1814). His mother was Marie-Françoise-Agnès de Narbonne-Pelet, who married a seigneur du Prat de la Baume.
6 Jean-François Pelet (1725–1804), *dit* comte de Narbonne-Pelet-Fritzlar, lieutenant-général (1784). He added the name Fritzlar to his own when in 1762 he distinguished himself in the battle of Fritzlar.
7 Françoise-Marie-Félicité-Hermessinde de Narbonne-Pelet (1785–1813) had wed in 1802 Charles-Marie-Paul-André d'Albert (1783–1839), duc de Luynes et de Chevreuse. She was 'young, pretty, and extravagant. . . . [holding] a special position in what was then known as the society of the *ancien régime*'. When compelled to accept appointment as dame d'honneur to the Empress, she performed her duties reluctantly. In time she outraged Napoleon, was exiled, and lived successively in Luynes, Lyons, and Grenoble. '[S]he eventually died of vexation in the third year of her exile' (Boigne, i. 235–7).
8 See L. 736 n. 20.

461

Hill Street, Richmond,
Septr 6th 1814.

I gladly followed your Counsel, my dear Carlos, almost the moment I received it, of delivering the keys to Mr. Yates,[1] *en attendant* that Mr. White completes the removal of the remnant articles.

But what is become of you? are you utterly amphibious? one foot at sea, one foot on shore?—or are you at length rectifying the World in your Rectory? I shall take my chance of directing thither.

What, also, is become of Messrs Leigh & Sotheby?[2] We were promised to receive our dues from them in a month: how many weeks do they count for the 12th part of a year?

I have just got my Letter of attorney returned from Paris, & I am going to put my 1000 stock from the 5 ^{pr} C^{ts} to the 4, in order to have a quarterly payment:[3] I should be very glad, indeed, to have at the same time all you can collect for me, from *Leigh's*, *White's*, & the *residuary*,[4] to Buy in immediately, i.e. during *September*, to make me a little current sum for *October*, that would enable me to wait till *January* for my other old dividend.[5] Otherwise, by again selling out, as I did in the spring, I am only *replacing*, instead of *augmenting* my income, when I buy in.

If M. d'A. can obtain a congée, with full honour, he will come over in October, here to winter: if not, I am to join him in Paris, when I have deposited my other Alex at Cambridge. I am very earnest, therefore, to hasten what is possible of my accounts & Receipts

Pray do the *best* & *quickest* you can for me. I shall not go to town to transfer my 1000 till I can do all the other business you can be so good as to forward for me at the same time.

M. d'Arblay has been obliged to relinquish his post at the Minister of the *interieure*, as derogatory to his military rank,

822. [1] See L. 794 n. 3.
[2] See Ll. 773 n. 10, 787 n. 12. FBA received £551 in cash from the sale (see L. 825).
[3] See L. 823 n. 4 for FBA's failure to negotiate the transfer of what CB's will designated as her 'sum of one thousand Pounds, five per cent Navy'.
[4] FBA wanted CB Jr., as executor of CB's will, to surrender her share of the funds from several sources: the sale of the miscellaneous books by Leigh and Sotheby, the sale of the music manuscripts and books by John White, the 'petty sale' of odds and ends also by White, 'the Sum in Funds' left with CB's banker.
[5] See L. 807 n. 4.

which is now restored, by an ordinance of the King, graciously dating his brevet from 1792, when he was made Marechal de Camp by Louis 16.—

This Honour, however, is HONOUR only! no pay is annexed. The Government is so poor, it pays only those in actual service: & he is in actual service only as an officer of the Corps des Gardes:⁶ as that, he is but sous-Lieutenant, which ranks, nevertheless, as a Colonel, though its pay scarcely buys its expensive embroidered uniform, & the 2 Horses necessarily required. The *fourage* of the Horses, and, I believe, the stabling, is allowed by the Government: but the buying them, & all accidents that may happen to them, fall upon the officers.

M. d'A. however, is truly happy, in a personal mark of the King's conviction of his fidelity & loyalty, ˡthe most honourable & flattering!

I wrote *my* thanks to Mr. Yates, when I sent the keys, upon quitting Chelsea, by Alexander: for Sarah was here: but I said *YOU* would wait upon him with *Yours*. But why Mr. White never came to his appointment, to take away the rest of the Chinese Instruments, & a screen & a sort of Desk, or Drawers, for our own *petty* sale, I knew not.⁷ He has fought shy of me, of late, though, before the sale, he had promised to report progress. I have no intelligence how the sale went off.⁸ Edward, I am told,

⁶ See Ll. 793, 806 n. 2.

⁷ The furniture, musical instruments, books, and prints left to his two eldest daughters, as well as other items not specifically distributed by the will, were to be sold at auction by Mr. White. The profits from the sale of these items were to become part of the inheritance of EBB and FBA. The 'Chinese Instruments, & a screen & a sort of Desk, or Drawers' are described in CB's will as 'two Gongs and oriental instruments in Chests sent from Canton by Mr. Matthew Raper and two of inferior quality brought by Lord Macartney when he returned from his Chinese embassy. [Also] A very curious and delicately painted procession of the Great Mogul through a triumphal Arch, on an Elephant, with his Wives, Concubines, and great Officers of State.' Undoubtedly a part of this sale was 'A curious Merlin Table, which may be formed into desks for 8 performers, with brass furniture for Candle light. By a winch it can be elevated to any height, for writing or playing standing, with drawers and various contrivances for secret deposits. . . . This to be sold for the profit of my three daughters, ESTHER, FRANCES, and SARAH.' See L. 825 and n. 8 for EBB's special contributions to this sale.

⁸ The 'petty sale' included items left not merely to the two residuary legatees, but to other members of CB's family. It became a continuation of Mr. White's sale of CB's 'MUSICAL LIBRARY' and was first advertised on 15 August in the *Morning Chronicle*. See L. 782 n. 12. Apparently the sale was suspended on 17 August but on the 24th the *London Gazetteer* advertised a sale 'this day' that concentrated on remnants from the musical sale as well as on pieces of furniture and *objets d'art* left from the 'petty sale'. Among the last to be sold were the Indian pictures from the collection of Governor Holwell and the portrait of Handel. Some of FBA's 'chattels' were not sold but stored at Mr. White's warehouse (L. 825).

attended:[9] but I have neither seen nor heard of him. Nor have I any news from Esther—I trust in ignorance!

Your Letter about my truly perplexing youth has so affrighted me, that besides a private Tutor at Cambridge, Mr. Gwatkin,[10]—(to whom I now owe 15^{pd}—; & Mr. Bellamy,[11] the Mathematical Tutor recommended by Mr. Haggitt, not yet paid, neither, & I know not his terms:) I have applied for one while we are here, of high eminence, Mr. Patterson[12]—who will give him daily Lessons for a Month—& is to have £20.! But I will gaily live in a Cell, rather than splendidly in a Palace, to save him from another *disgrazia*.— |

Mrs. James Burney met, to-day, with a young Cantab. who quite mournfully lamented his excentricities, saying that, but for those, he had the Character of bearing the highest expectations of any undergraduate through-out the university!— should he now again fail, I must run away with him to France! For Mr Chapman has sent word by Clement that he will certainly be *rusticated* if he does not entirely reform!![13]

He *now* works in a manner the most exemplary, quite as much as his health & strength will bear: but he has neither to attend the cold Chapel at 7. in a winter's morning; nor the dull lectures at any other hour!—How to secure him a little common sense, which he utterly wants, as well as judgment & foresight, I know not—but he *will* do well, *if he lives*, I feel sure, when

[9] Edward Francesco Burney was at the sale to watch the disposition of CB's bequests to him: the '42 prints, framed and glazed, most of them presents from . . . Sir Robert Strange'; the 'Piranesi views of Rome and the ffol° edit. of Leonardo da Vinci's Art of Painting'; 'Arnold's edition of Handel's works on large Paper' (the profits from this last item to be shared with his brother Charles Rousseau Burney).

[10] Richard Gwatkin (1791–*post* 1870) was a Senior Wrangler and winner of Smith's prize. He took his B.A. in 1814 and in the same year became a Fellow of St. John's, keeping that post until 1833. He took his M.A. in 1817, his B.D. in 1824; he was ordained deacon in 1820 and priest in 1821. According to the 'Tutor's Account Book', AA was tutored by Gwatkin during the Midsummer term of 1814 and the payment due was £14. Apparently, however, AA did not attend all the sessions scheduled by Gwatkin, who in November 1814 cancelled £7 of the £14.

[11] See L. 804 n. 6.

[12] James Paterson (1787–*post* 1820), of Greenwich, Kent, matriculated at Christ Church in 1804 and received his B.A. in 1809.

[13] Chapman's distrust of AA's working habits and character did not change even when the latter had migrated to Christ's. On 7 Mar. 1817 AA wrote (Berg) to FBA assuring her that he would be a Wrangler.

'*I am to make my Second and last appearance in the Schools before October on Monday— as Second opponent.—*

'When I called upon M. Chapman, he said: Well, when do you take your degree? —Next Xmas, Sir—Why not next term?—Because of an honor, Sir—I am afraid you will be too lazy for that.'

relieved from the shackles he has so little fortitude for enduring. Mr. Chapman, unfortunately, is the severest & most rigid of all the Tutors. At Clare & Trinity they would have winked at particularities, in seeing talent always working, though irregularly directed. This Cantab. Mr. Butler,[14] said he was both liked & admired & pitied & blamed by all the university; & that he excited a general interest. O my dear Charles! that these fearful 2 years were—*for him*— —over—happily![15]

adieu—adieu. Love to Rosette & *all* the Fannys & the *unique* (but one) Parr. |

I always reserve your oration for Cambridge—when— perhaps!—his watchful Flapper may be far away![16] |

I am not hurrying you for money to spend *out & out*; my hundred would still suffice for that; no, 'tis to *prevent* selling *out & out*, by deposing more *principle* & thereby existing on the *interest*. Otherwise—how am I to do every other year?[17] |

Alex wants the *Jesuit's Newton's* principia;[18] none other will suffice for his studies: now had I not better beg Mr. Payne to

[14] Either Brook Watson Butler (1795–1838) or John Olden Butler (*c.* 1794– *post* 1815). Since the former was a student at Trinity and the latter at Clare, one or the other could have supplied FBA with her conclusions about both colleges.

[15] FBA assumed that AA would receive his degree in 1816, three years after matriculation at Caius in the Michaelmas term of 1813.

[16] FBA was AA's 'flapper', referring to herself as such as late as 1 Apr. 1836. She used the Swiftian term as did Lord Chesterfield in writing to *his* son (Letter xcix, 1774). For CB Jr's 'oration', written to AA, see L. 804.

[17] FBA's desire to live on the interest from her investments explains some of the elaborate bookkeeping entries in the d'Arblay account at Hoare's opened on 20 Oct. 1814. They owned and deposited with the bank in October 1814, prior to departure for France, £1,350 in cash, and 3 per cent consols whose face value was £3,000 and whose semi-annual dividend amounted to £40.10. Also initially deposited at Hoare's was FBA's inheritance of 5 per cent Navy whose face value was £1,000 and whose semi-annual dividend was £22.10. On 7 Jan. 1815 the d'Arblays purchased 5 per cent Navy bonds whose face value was £1,800 (£1,705. 12s. 6d. in actual cost) and on 28 April more of the same bonds at a face value of £724. 3s. 2d. (actual purchase price £624. 11s. 9d.). On 23 and 27 Oct. 1815 (upon their return to England), they again purchased shares of 5 per cent Navy: £551. 14s. 6d. (a purchase price of £500); £424. 2s. 4d. (purchase price of £382. 15s. 4d.); £500 (purchase price of £451. 5s.). Thus by October 1815 the d'Arblays had a portfolio whose face value approximated £8,000 and whose investment income for that year amounted to £182. 15s. 10d. For further additions to this account, see vol. ix.

[18] FBA refers to Andrew Motte's translation of Newton's *Mathematical Principles of Natural Philosophy . . . To which are added The Laws of the Moon's Motion, according to Gravity. By John Machin . . .* (2 vols., 1729). In 1803 an expanded edition in three volumes appeared. In describing Andrew Motte's translation as the '*Jesuit's Newton's principia*', FBA probably confused the English translator with the French writer and critic Antoine de La Motte (1672–1731), who was Jesuit-trained.

take & *change* our superb Newton, for the Jesuit's, & for Euler,[19] &c, &c, &c i.e. such mathematical Books as he cannot do with-out? It is ill answering my dearest Father's meaning to keep a Book for *Alex*, at this expensive moment of his education, that is merely a *Picture*; for if he consults it only half an hour, it will be no better than a Book on a ¦ stall! Give me your notion. He has just made me send for *Playfair's* Euclid.[20] His demands are endless, yet necessary. Newton's *Principia*, (the *Jesuit's*,) is indispensable.

823

Hill Street, Richmond,
19 September 1814

To Charles Burney

A.L. (Berg and Osborn), 19 Sept. 1814
Double sheet large 8vo (Berg) and a single sheet 4to (Osborn) with a binding strip along right margin p. 2 in all 6 pp. (4 pp. 8vo and 2 pp. 4to) *pmks* RICHMOND / 19 SP 1814   19 SP 1814   seal
Addressed: Rev^d Dr. Burney, / Rectory House, / Deptford,

Hill Street, Richmond,
Sep^t 19. 1814.

My dear Carlos,
    I write now, a formal address to my Acting Executer & kind Brother, to tell him, in due form & order

That

    I absolutely decline being Administratrix, Trustee, or &c &c for the Minors:[1] — — for
Being myself rather a Major, I doubt whether the Infants of 5 or 6 years of age may be much the better for my acceptance of the management of their legacies

[19] FBA refers to the Swiss mathematician Leonhard Euler (1707–83). Of Euler's many works, AA probably wanted either *Institutionum Calculi Integralis* (3 vols., 1768–70); or *Elements of Algebra . . . translated from the French . . . with the . . . notes of Bernoulli . . . the additions of M. de La Grange, some original notes by the translator, memoirs of the life of Euler . . . and a praxis to the whole work* (2 vols., 1797).
[20] John Playfair (1748–1819) edited *Elements of Geometry; containing the first six Books of Euclid, with two books on the Geometry of Solids. To which are added, Elements of Plain and Spherical Geometry* (Edinburgh, 1795).

823. [1] FBA had in mind about five of Richard Burney's children who were still under age in 1814 and who had received bequests in CB's will.

And

Nothing is less certain than where I may fix my standard. M. d'Arblay will come over as early as he can next month, then to decide, as far as in him lies, our destiny—

But

once engaged in active service for | & by his King, he may not be his own Master for some years—
& *some years* at our Major time of life — — — I say no more. We ought, certainly, to form no tie that we may so ill be able to fulfil.

Sarah, *I think*, purposed being one of the Trustees for these poor Children—& to require Mr. S[tephen] Allen,[2] or Martin, to be the other.

This must be enquired into.

BUT

at all events,

previously to your resignation,[3] Let me know if there be any legal measure that should be taken to ASCERTAIN that no future demand, in any mode whatsoever, may be made upon me.

It is not that I doubt Alexander's | making an admirable steward & Guardian—attentive, adroit, skilful, & sharp-sighted to their interest — — — But still, I would rather let him *begin* with his own sons & Daughters!—

M. d'Arblay, a foreigner—

His Wife, his Rib—

May both be better re-placed by fixed *Inhabitants*, as well as *Natives*.

But my chief point is

That my declining this charge should be so legalised as to obviate any possible future application, or doubt, or dispute.

Our Sister Esther declines also, for *half* these reasons. But she will write herself. We talked the matter over to-day in

---

[2] The Revd. Stephen Allen (i, p. lxxiv) and Richard Burney had the same mother (Elizabeth *née* Allen, CB's second wife). Richard and SHB were brother and sister, the two children of Elizabeth and CB. In FBA's judgement, SHB and Stephen Allen had a closer familial relationship to 'the Minors' than had she and the other children of CB and Esther *née* Sleepe. But see L. 825 and n. 9.

[3] As executor of CB's will. In fact, CB Jr. continued as executor until the 'Irish mortgage' was legally foreclosed in March 1815 and the money received.

my new apartment, being the old one of our Sister Broome— ¦ where I shall be charmed to receive you for our grand conference, if you can spare a day amongst us—i.e. the Broome's, Barrett's, & *your humble.*

But pray be prepared upon this subject, as I must not even for a quarter of a moment take your discharge into *my* hands. If any expence be necessary for proper & positive & legal advice, I will chearfully pay it at once.

I have lost the 4 ᵖʳ Cᵗˢ—! — I knew not they were so soon to be shut,⁴ as I never see a news paper but by accident—or I should have begged to draw upon yʳ Banker for the 551.⁵— when I went, with Martin & Edward, last week, for my dividend in the 5 ᵖʳ ct.— ¦

My poor Alex frightens me to death! after working with an application the most energetic all this time, he now suddenly falls off, & has, evidently, something *morbid* in his constitution that *paralyzes his character*: for though he listens to my remonstrances, promises to heed them—& struggles so to do—all constancy in his principal pursuits is for the [mome]nt at an end, & he has a langu[or] in his frame, that leads to a species of apathy that resists all representations of consequences; to which, except for what regards ANALYTICAL Mathematics, he grows utterly insensible!! no reasoning conquers him, for he feels & agrees to all that can be urged; but he has a listlessness, in those moments, that seems to make him *INCAPABLE* when left alone—& *DESPERATE* when reproached or menaced!—

Yet—in another day or two, he will again be all vigour & spirit!—

Poor—poor singular Alex!—he has just owned to me he feels, at times, so ¦ [u]tterly without energy, that a total indifference comes over him for his lot in life!—which he only rouses from by his sole positive joy & propensity, Algebra!— He has not, nevertheless, fear of his own ultimate success—oh could I share his confidence!

Adio, my dear Carlucci—I hope you do not forget Mr. Yates

⁴ The 4 per cent consols were last sold on 6 Sept. 1814. It was not until 5 Mar. 1816 that the d'Arblays sold all their shares of the 3 per cent consols and those of the 5 per cent Navy held at Hoare's to buy 4 per cent consols with a face value of £4,136. 10s. See also L. 749 n. 16.
⁵ The extra money needed to transfer FBA's capital from 5 per cent Navy to 4 per cent consols. For the origin of £551, see L. 825.

& Mr. Long?[6] *The handsome thing*, WHEN YOU THINK OF IT, nobody can do in a more *handsome manner*.[7] M. d'A. has only had 3 falls from his Horse!—Imagine if I wish his waiting over! —

I am truly glad your sea & Ryde excursion did you service. I think it very long not to see you—though to press that now seems a matter of *business*; therefore I wait quietly. I am very well lodged, comfortably & healthily, & pretty near Broomes & Barretts, whom I [hav]e the consolation to embrace daily. How does Rosette? my kind Love & pray—if I may make so free—Do you ever hear anything of your shabby friend, Dr. Retardy—id est—our Archy?[8]—I think I have known people, in my life, almost as ⟨alert⟩ as his Grace!—you'll excuse my [being] jocular!—

824

M. d'Arblay
To Madame d'Arblay

Hôtel de la Marine, Paris, 19 [September 1814]

A.L. (Berg), Lundy 19
Double sheet 4to   4 pp.   *pmks* T.P.P.U. / LOMBARD ST   To be Delivered / by 10, o'Clock / on Sund Morn   SE 24 1814   wafer
Addressed: Angleterre / À Madame / Madame d'Arblay née / Miss Burney. at Mˢ Broome's / *Richmond* near London
Edited by FBA, p. 1, *annotated and dated*: ⫶ 30 (29 lost) 1814 (19 Septʳ). *See further*, Textual Notes.

Lundy 19 à 10ʰ du soir chez le portier de l'hotel de la Marine où sont logés MM. Angerstein et Lock (Georges) qui devaient partir aujourdhui, et sont restés pour voir la ceremonie de la

---

[6] Dudley Long North (1748–1829). On the death in 1789 of his widowed aunt Anne Herbert *née* North, Dudley Long, complying with the terms of her will, took on the name and arms of North (dropping his own surname Long) and acquired the family estate of Little Glemham, Suffolk. In 1812, upon the death of his elder brother Charles Long of Hurts Hall, Saxmundham, he resumed the name and arms of Long while retaining those of North. At the time of FBA's letter, he was M.P. for Richmond in Yorkshire (1812–18) and a distinguished Whig.

[7] Long-standing friends of CB, they were to have a token of remembrance, which CB Jr., as executor, could choose from the non-allotted remnants in the College apartment.

[8] See L. 804 n. 11.

benediction des drapeaux et etendards de la troupe de Ligne.[1]
Comme ces MM partent demain de grand matin, Je suis venu
causer ici un instant avec toi, ma chere amie, pour te dire que
cette ceremonie s'est si bien passée, que j'ai eu le courage
d'exposer de nouveau ma situation à M^r le Duc de Luxembourg
qui toujours inepuisable en obligeance, m'a deviné, et m'a dit
qu'il fallait que je partisse aussitôt après avoir achevé mon
service, malgré que je n'en aye fait aucun à la Garnison, où je
n'ai fait que paroitre deux ou trois jours à sa suite. Sur
l'observation que j'en ai faite, il m'a dit : je me charge d'arranger
tout cela. D'ailleurs, a t'il ajouté, vous irez à votre retour,
combien comptez vous rester en Angleterre? — au moins quatre
| mois, Monsr le Duc. l'*au moins* l'a un peu etonné. Je ne puis y
rester moins que cela, ai-je repris, en m'en appercevant. à la
bonne heure, s'est il ecrié;[2] commencez toujours par y aller. Tu
vois d'après cela, ma chere amie, qu'à moins de contrarietes que
je ne puis prevoir, car je ne doute pas que Mr de L., qui est en
faveur, n'obtienne mon congé, il est probable que j'arriverai
près de toi avant qu'Alex ne soit parti p^r Cambridge. C'est là
ma seule reponse à *l'injustice*, pardon!—à *l'injustice* de celle qui
a osé penser, et m'ecrire, que je ne desirais aller la rejoindre que
pour acquiter une dette! bien veritablement contractée, mais
absolument impossible à payer.[3] Ô mon amie! que t'est il donc
passé depuis quelque tems par la tête? Helas j'ai été bien
malheureux, mais en verité je n'ai jamais eu vis-à-vis de toi
qu'un tort apparent, mème quand j'ai été si longtems sans
t'ecrire; car jamais je n'ai passé un seul jour sans regretter de
toute mon ame de ne l'avoir pas passé avec toi. Tu le sais mon
amie, si cela | n'etait pas l'exacte verité, je ne le dirais point.[4]

824. [1] On 24 Sept. 1814 *The Times* transcribed the report in *Le Moniteur* 'of the
consecration of the colours of the different regiments of the line of the 1st military
division, which took place [19 Sept.] in the Champs de Mars. . . . Every regiment,
from respect to the wishes of these Princes [Angoulême and Berry], made it a duty
to receive [Louis and the duchesse d'Angoulême] in an attitude of immobility
and silence, the first characteristic of military discipline. . . . After the consecration,
all the regiments were drawn up in close column around the altar; and the colours
and standards having been brought by the Colonels to the front of each regiment,
Lieutenant-General Count Maison pronounced the oath with a loud voice, which
was spontaneously repeated by all the troops. . . . Acclamations of *Vive le Roi,
Vivent les Bourbons*, were incessant till the King left the field to return to the
Thuilleries.'
    [2] See L. 826 for the terms of M. d'A's furlough.
    [3] See L. 808 n. 16.
    [4] See also L. 826, wherein M. d'A denies as groundless the rumours heard by
FBA that his life in France was self-indulgent, even dissipated.

Quant à ce que tu m'écris d'Alex; ⌐j'avoue que les expressions me manquent pour rendre ici tout ce que m'a fait penser cette lecture. Jamais je te le jure, desappointement n'a été plus complete, et je suis en honneur ⟨horrified⟩.¬ Je ne sais en verité que faire, et pourtant j'ai bien reflechi sur ce sujet: mais sans en être plus avancé. Helas il n'est que trop certain qu'aucune carriere que celle militaire ne peut valoir ici pour lui la peine de s'en occuper. ⌐Comment doit ⟨alors⟩ songer à rester dans la ⟨même⟩ place quelconque quelqu'un de ce caractere, quelqu'un qui même pour ce qu'il desire le [plus n'a pas la] force de suivre une resolution raisonnable et [qui se laisse dep]artir de la raison et faute de savoir mettre d'accord ses ⟨accidents⟩ et son gout ou plutot sa passion dominante, s'expose au risque plus que certain de compromettre sa tranquillité et ruiner sa reputation.¬ Où trouver une place quelconque dans la quelle on ne soit pas assujeti à des heures reglées, à un travail obligé? Je n'en connois point, et je dirai plus: | je maintiens, qu'il n'y a aucun etat où l'on ne soit plus dependant que dans celui de garde du Corps. Ah — combien ta lettre, si tendre, si bonne, et pourtant si cruelle, m'a fait de mal! Comme les privations dont tu me parles me dechirent le coeur.⁵ O mon amie crois en le cri de ce coeur tout à toi!—Jamais je n'en éprouverai aucune auprès de ma Fanny, et du pain bis et un verre d'eau avec elle vaudront toujours mieux pour moi que tout ce que tu pourrais imaginer de plus tentant. Neanmoins, je t'avoue, mon coeur saigne de partir cette fois sans voir mon pauvre oncle, à son âge, et après l'avoir flatté que j'irais passer 8 jours avec lui. Tous les 4 jours il m'ecrit qu'il m'attend avec impatience. Je ne serais pas digne de toi, si je lui etais moins attaché, il t'aime tant

adieu, ma bonne amie, attens toi à me voir bientôt. Très certainement j'arriverai assez à tems pʳ passer quelques jours avec Alex! que je reconduirai à son College, si absolument ⟨il tient ⟩ y retourner; quant à toi, je ne pers pas l'esp[oir de te retr]ouver. Amen! Amen!

⁵ The response of M. d'A to FBA's financial anxiety and economies. See especially Ll. 812, 820.

825   Hill Street, Richmond,
                                           4 October 1814
To Charles Burney

A.L. (Osborn), 4 Oct. 1814
Double sheet small 4to   4 pp.   with mounting tape along right margin,
p. 4
Addressed: Rev^d Dr. Burney, / Rectory House, / Deptford.

                                      Richmond, Octr 4. 1814.
     O Charles—you have written me a dagger![1]—

     I have been too much overset by it either to answer by it
either to answer you, or to come to any resolution how to act
till within a few hours.—

     It is plain to me you have no hope!—for what will *my*
remaining 50 miles from the scene of action do more than
remaining 250?—& at C[ambridge]—*he* cannot bear to have me
stationed, & has made me, & even his Father, think such a
measure would expose him to ridicule, & *uselessly*; for I could not
be at his side before 7.—nor at the *preparatory* moments of other
attendance. And his PROMISES, like my injunctions, are all
rendered void by a miserable, pernicious absence of mind, that
makes both the one & the other escape his memory. Upon the
whole, there can be no doubt it would certainly be better for him,
& ultimately more profitable, to be left fallow for a year or two,
from any forced pursuits, & to work at strengthening & fixing
his constitution, as well as curbing his excentricities.—I have
thought, & wished this long—but the Tancred has withheld
me! an advantage so great, obtained with so much difficulty yet
Honour—to relinquish it!—how cruelly mortifying! how nearly
ruinous to all my best projects—& how | wounding to my
feelings![2]—nevertheless, to *risk* his being Rusticated were worse
than to *incur* any other & less evil.—

     I have written, therefore, the whole to M. d'A. who already is
sighing to have him by his side.[3]

     I have no doubt of the result — —

825 [1] Now missing, CB Jr.'s probable expression of reluctance to assume guardianship of AA, whose collegiate behaviour could only end in rustication.
     [2] See L. 673.   [3] See Ll. 796, 798 and n. 2.

I dare not enlarge—nor enter upon what it costs me. — —[4]
But give me some hints how the withdrawing should be done
—so as most gratefully to mark OUR sense of Dr. Davy's
goodness in particular, & of the kindness we owe to all the
other Trustees.[5]—

Alas!![6]— — —

For myself, my every winter here has been such a scene of
captivity, that M. d'A. & my sage Dr. Larrey have long pressed
me to pass the present in the South of France—Alex alone has
withheld me; for I believe it would fortify the rest of my life.
If, therefore, it be not too late, when my affairs are settled, for
so long a journey, I shall now oppose it no longer. *au contraire.*

But what is become of Mr. White? *Sept 18th* you wrote me
word you were to have his answer *to-morrow*?[7] Is the gentleman
gone to repose with the Sleeping Beauty in the wood for a few
40 years, or so? ┃ He took the whole of the Book cases & shelves,
for the difficulty where to deposit them, in my so uncertain
residence, & the desire, mutual, of my sister & myself to terminate our joint affairs, fixed us both, ultimately, upon holding
back NOTHING from a mutual sale. What was her's *separately*,
Mr. White has arranged with her *at ONCE.*—Why so tardy for
us unitedly? Her piano Forte, Purcel, Handel, &c are all, I
believe, paid.[8]

M. d'A. I trust & hope, will be here soon—his waiting, for
this season, was to finish last Saturday, & he has already the
promise of his Chief, M. le Duc de Luxembourg, to ask his
congée of the King.

I leave the 551 you have been so kind as to announce from
Sotheby at yr Banker's, till I hear from Paris upon that subject.

Have you got any information about the minors? Sarah
Declines, & assures me she *cannot*, in Law, take the responsibility,

[4] FBA refers to her struggle with M. d'A over AA's career and her refusal
to entertain the possibility of a military life for their son. See especially Ll. 793,
798, 803, 807, 811.
[5] For the Tancred trustees, see L. 670.
[6] 'Alas': FBA's dwindling hopes for AA's university career.
[7] See L. 822 nn. 7, 8.
[8] For the edition of Handel left to Charles Rousseau Burney, see L. 822 n. 9.
To EBB was left CB's 'large Piano Forte with additional keys at the top and
bottom, originally made by Merlin, with a Compass of six Octaves, the first that
was ever constructed . . . for duets à Quatre Mains in 1773'. There is no record
in CB's will of a Purcell memento left to EBB or her husband, although in White's
advertisement in the *Morning Chronicle* there is reference to a portrait of 'H. Purcell,
by Closterman'.

which must fall upon Charles Parr[9] & *little Blossom!*—i.e. *Your* Heirs.—So little Blossom becomes a personage pretty early. I don't know what all this means.

I am charmed with the word *delightfully well* for my dear Rosette. My kindest Love to her. But I am ⌐ truly concerned at your comfortless account of my amiable Name-sake—may she amend![10]

The Newton sent by M[r] Payne we have been forced to return, for it was not the *Jesuit's Ed*: nor the *Principia*[11] It was therefore, for Alex's present studies, wholly useless.

Poor simple youth! his whole inclinations—taste—choice are at Cam!—*certainly*, if my income will suffice, he shall *return*! It would break his heart not to open to his prospects that hope— but it hangs upon such promotion for his Father, as to suffice for both *Parents* to *live* upon, meantime, though not to *bequeath*: for, without the Tancred, Cam. itself, *sans* the vacations, is upwards of 200! p[r] ann. I shall drop no hint of the idea of *withdrawing*, till I hear from Paris, & from YOU—that it may, at least, be done respectfully & properly—& with no reference to our fears for my poor Alex, who must simply be called by his Father to France—which many expect—

I never know the Direction of Richard's widow.[12] As soon as you can possibly give me intelligence what to expect, and what *NOT* to expect, you will much help me in the embarrassment of my arrangements, therefore pray do not wait our final *MEETING* to put me out of mental suspense.—

Adieu, dearest Charles—Let me know how y[r] *feet* harden—& be sure keep your *Heart* from getting the same trick! Tell me, too, something of your *head*. I seem demanding an anatomical survey.[13] I am truly melancholy at this measure while I hold it right.

adieu—adieu—pray write to me—

[9] FBA's playful shifting of responsibility to CPB, now the executor for the bequests made by CB to certain of the children of Richard Burney. See L. 823 n. 1.

[10] CPB's elder daughter, who was now ailing.

[11] See L. 822 n. 18.

[12] The former Jane Ross (1772–1842), who had married Richard Burney in 1787, still lived in India. See i, p. lxxiii.

[13] FBA's 'anatomical survey' implies that CB Jr. suffered the ordeal of bloodletting or scarification of the feet and of blistering the scalp, a desperate remedy used when the gout induced in the head 'pain, vertigo, or palsy' (*Enc. Brit.*, 3rd ed., xi. 185, 186).

I hope my dear Parr has no serious *alarm* for his Fanny? How is *my* Bantling?[14]—— |

I have not even heard from M[r] White whether our poor chattels[15] have been yet sold—& Prints. — —

826   London, 7 [October 1814]

M. d'Arblay
To Madame d'Arblay

A.L. (Berg), Vendredy 7
Double sheet 4to, of which FBA later discarded the second leaf   2 pp.
Edited by FBA, p. 1, annotated, and dated from pmk: ∺   31   9 Oct[re] 1814.
See further, Textual Notes.

Ce Vendredy 7 chez le Vte d'Agoult en
attendant un rendez vous que m'a donne
le Ministre

Quoi bien reellement, ma chere amie tu as été inquiete et tu avais besoin d'être rassurée sur mes sentimens pour toi. ô mon amie à quel tourment effroyable tu as été en proie; et moi, j'en suis tourmenté comme si j'etais coupable de t'avoir fait eprouver un supplice au quel rien ne peut etre comparé. Je n'ai qu'un mot à dire ma chere Fanny; et le Ciel qui lit au fond des coeurs sait combien le mien est sincere quand je te dis, que jamais un seul instant je n'ai été tenté d'hesiter entre tout ce que tu trouves d'enivrant dans ma situation actuelle, et ce qui existe bien reellement dans le bonheur d'une union sans exemple! J'ai toujours esperé ce qui enfin est arrivé; et le parti que tu as pris est precisement ce que je voulais te proposer. Je suis tout à fait de l'avis d'Alex, et cette opinion est aussi celle de Mad[e] de Lav[al] et de tes autres amis qui tous pensent que tu dois revenir. Je me suis neanmoins arrangé pour rester près de toi jusqu'au printems,[1] dans le cas où tu aurais persister à

[14] Rosetta d'Arblay Burney (Ll. 761 n. 2, 829 n. 1).
[15] See L. 822 n. 8.
826. [1] See L. 818 n. 1.

resider où tu es. A la verité mon congé n'est que jusqu'au mois de Janvier, mais M^r le Duc de Luxembourg m'a fait entendre qu'à moins d'evenemens peu probables, il se fesait fort de me faire avoir une prolongation. En verité | ⌐ma chere Fanny, c'est une chose bien etrange que la conduite de William vis-à-vis de nous. Qu'entend il donc faire? Veut il à présent nous disputer même les 640£ offerts?!! Qui jamais l'aurait vu?! Ah mon cher ⟨Monsr⟩ Lock.⌐ Je ne veux m'appesantir sur rien de pénible et tu vois que j'ai dejà passé très legerement sur ce que tu me dis au commencement de ta lettre concernant l'extrême dissipation dans la quelle on t'a dit que je vivais, et sur les consequences qu'on paraissait en vouloir tirer. Ma chere Fanny, je te le repete, Nul être au monde ne peut se vanter d'avoir un moment balancé ni dans mon *coeur*, ni dans mon *esprit*, ni dans ma *pensée*, l'être ⌐*adorable*⌐ au quel j'ai le bonheur de voir mon sort lié. ⌐Pardonne moi cette expression adorable, qui t'a deplu n a guère. Elle est sortie de ma plume tout naturellement, et il me semble qu'autrefois elle ne te deplaisait point.⌐ oh! que nous avons besoin de nous revoir —— je ne m'en doutais pas je l'avoue, je ne soupçonnais guère que mon amie pût être malheureuse par son coeur, qui aurait du me rendre plus de justice. ⌐Que ceux sur les quels j'avais le plus compté après toi, me la refusent, et qu'ils soient bassement ⟨ser⟩ieux, quand ils devraient ce me semble être fiers de celle qu'on m'a faite, je ne dirai point que cela m'est égal, mais j'affirmerai avec vaillance que je ne suis pas⌐ |

[*The second leaf is missing*]

⌐Je m'aventure certainement à Londre ⟨un jour⟩, mais d'etre obligé de revenir quelque tems à Londre p^r rachetter les duperies de Grandmaison ⟨à notre⟩ ambassadeur.[2] Ce qu'il y a de sur, c'est que je suivrai de près cette lettre.

[xxxxx ½ line]: mais j'ai tort puisque cela ne sera pas long! [xxxxx ½ line]⌐

---

[2] Aubin-Louis, *dit* M. de Grandmaison, half-brother to Alexandre-Paul Millin de Grandmaison (1739–1811), whose widow continued to be a friend of the d'Arblays. Aubin-Louis de Grandmaison (1759–1818) was chef de division au comité de l'instruction publique, conservateur des médailles à la Bibliothèque nationale, botaniste. Made a member of the Institut in 1804, he became a chevalier de l'Empire in 1808.

827

To Mrs. Waddington

Richmond,
13–18 October 1814

A.L.S. (Berg), 13–18 Oct. 1814
Double sheet 4to   4 pp.   *pmks*   RICHMOND 25 OC 1814   25 OC
1814   25 OC .814   black seal
Addressed: Mrs. Waddington / Lanover / Abergavenny / Monmouthshire
Also L., incomplete copy in the hand of CFBt (Diary MSS. viii, not
numbered but after 5923, Berg), 13 Oct. 1814   Single sheet 4to   2 pp.

Richmond, Octr 13. 1814.

Eh bien, mes chères amies? are you becoming a little English-
ised? or are you still tout à fait Parisiennes?[1] In either case,
donnez moi, je vous en prie, de vos Nouvelles.—Did not my
fair name sake give me to understand that she had a *hundred
little details* to communicate that she knew would be interesting?
—I have let a month pass away without any demand, sure that
the fondest of mothers could not require less for her own private,
though never selfish information: but now, I may venture, I
hope, to put in my claim for some intelligence, both *general* &
particular, of this delightful excursion.

I wish, too, passionately, my dearest Mary, for a full &
faithful development of the points at which you hint in the
folding of your Letter—namely, Cambridge & Alexander. He
never, you say, can succeed at Cambridge — — unriddle to me,
I beg, what that never means? and tell me honestly what the
C. Men you have seen,[2] those expected after your Letter, as well
as those who had preceded it, have related or imagined upon
this too interesting subject. It is NOW that to know the *whole
truth* may be useful; for now, just NOW the conflict is at the
height which must subside by our fixing to which of his two
native Countries—that of his Birth or that of his Ancestors—he
will finally belong. Had I fears he would *never* succeed, all my
influence would take a new turn—M. d'A.'s *own* affairs, indeed,
must ultimately biass us both, as from our Alexander neither of

---

827.   [1] See L. 819 n. 1.
   [2] Professor Monk (L. 709 n. 15) was Benjamin Waddington's nephew. Accompanied and followed later by several colleagues, he visited the Waddingtons at
Llanover and reported on AA's activities at Caius.

us will be parted; but | even for the instant such a belief as your's would make me struggle hard against his return — —

Monday—October. 18th 1814

I have lost my post, & eternal avocation has kept my Letter back to this moment—but though I have a million of things to tell you, as well as to do, the pressure of my desire to have an answer to what I have already written forces me to remit all till I write again—& to beg you most earnestly to let me have as quick an answer as possible—for THIS WEEK decides Alex's return or not to Cambridge[3]—& I will hear & weigh & discuss ALL at once—& then—here after—on this theme— forever hold my tongue! various interruptions have brought me to the last moment of the post ere I have a minute to fill my paper—My so amiable name sake will write of France—& even of my poor Alex, if her dearest Mother is unhappily indisposed—

My next Letter shall try to make amends for this merely selfish scrawl—which I am sure you will forgive when you know the conflict of pros & Cons that now harrass

yr most affecte

F B d'A. |

I beseech you not to let your too ardent friendship disturb you about the Reviews & critics: & I quite supplicate you to leave their authors to their own severities or indulgence. I have ever steadily refused all interference with public opinion, or private criticism. I am told I have been very harshly mangled[4] —but I attribute it not to what alone would affect me, but which I trust I have not excited, personal enmity; I attribute it to the false expectation universally spread that the Book would be a picture of France[5]—as well as to the astonishing *éclat* of [a]

---

[3] The decision was made during the week of 18 October, for by the 25th of that month AA, accompanied by M. d'A, was *en route* to Cambridge with a stop-over at West Humble (L. 829). But see L. 828 n. 1 for evidence of FBA's indecisiveness.

[4] *The Wanderer* was not well treated by the reviewers. See Appendix IV.

[5] See *The British Critic*: 'Her long residence in a foreign country, it was conjectured, would have opened sources of information, of which her inventive powers were so well enabled to take a due advantage both in portraiture of character and the description of events. . . .

'To those who might have supposed that Mme. D'Arblay would have entered into long discussions on the events of the day, or unfolded the political intrigues of the neighbouring country, a few very sensible and feeling observations in the work of 5 Volumes being *all* bespoken before it was published.[6] The Booksellers, erroneously & injudiciously concluding the sale would so go on, fixed the rapacious price of 2 G[s7]—which again damped the sale—but why say *damped*, when it is only *their* unreasonable expectations that are disappointed? for they acknowledge that 3600 Copies are positively sold & paid before in the first half year? What must *I* be, if not far more than contented? I have not read, or heard, one of the Criticisms: my mind has been wholly occupied by grief for the loss of my dearest Father, or the inspection of his MSS. & my harrassing situation relative to my own proceedings. Why, then, make myself *black bile* to disturb me further? *No*; I will not look at a word—till my spirits & time are calmed & quiet ⎮ & I can set about preparing a corrected Edition.[8] I will then carefully read ALL; & then— the blow to immediate feelings being over, I can examine as well as read, impartially, & with profit, both to my future surveyors & myself.

Mille tendresses à ma chère Invalide[9]—aussi bien qu'a my namesake, & Augusta.—

828   Richmond, 14 October 1814

To Charles Burney

A.L. (Berg), 14 Oct. 1814
Double sheet 4to 4 pp. *pmks* RICHMOND / 15 OC 18⟨ ⟩
15 OC 1814   black seal
Addressed: Rev[d] Dr. Burney, / Rectory House, / Deptford,
Docketed in pencil, p. 1: From / Fanny / B.

preface are addressed, which clearly prove the impropriety of such allusions, and the ingratitude of such an exposure.'
But *GM* lxxxiv[1] (1814), 579–81, tended to view the novel as a political document *manqué*.

[6] The first edition of *The Wanderer*, consisting of 3,000 copies, was sold out two or three days before publication (Ll. 759, 760).

[7] FBA's statement about the price of the novel is just. Even the longer *Camilla*, printed by subscription, sold for one guinea in 1796. At that time FBA thought the price as high as might be *reasonably* expected for a novel.

[8] Such a plan was consistent with FBA's procedure. As late as 30 Aug. 1817, FBA, writing (Barrett, Eg. 3695, f. 97) to Longman & Co., intended 'to prepare a corrected & revised Copy for some future—though perhaps posthumous Impression'.

[9] Emelia Waddington.

Richmond, Octr 14. 1814

The RESULT I expected, my dear Charles, is just arrived: M. d A. could not support a *risk* that to *you* seems so strong as to make you withdraw your Guardianship, & therefore,—especially as we can neither of us consent to live a Divorced life any longer, and so *uselessly*,—he has demanded a *congée* for coming over to fetch me to a warmer climate for this Winter, and to try what a similar change of air will do for fortifying & strengthening & fixing the constitution of our too—too singular as well as single offspring.[1] We shall all 3, I trust, return hither in May.—

Do let me know then, I beg, what should be done relative to the Tancred? Certainly Dr Davy must be the FIRST informed —should it be by You or by me? or by both? As he may have some one he may wish to serve, he ought to have a few days acquaintance with the vacancy previous to its being known through Letters of thanks & regret to the Trustees at large.

I have said this before, but you have not answered it. Yet I cannot bear to act but through & with you, my dearest Carlucci, to whose affectionate exertions I owe — — — my present grief upon this subject!—that is not just the term, perhaps, that you expected; but in that grief there is as much of gratitude as of | disappointment. You will easily conceive where duty, Respect, & propriety call for my *next* formal avowal, relative to Alex, & my FIRST relative to myself. But this must not take place till after the arrival of my Chevalier; & as that depends upon circumstances which neither of us can command, I would not have the business transpire beyond Dr. Davy, till you hear from me again.

15 p^d was due to the Bills, over the Tancred & the Greek scholarship, sent by Mr. Chapman.[2] We must enquire whether

828. [1] Between 19 September (L. 823) and 25 October (L. 829), FBA's plans for AA were uncertain. From 4 to 14 October, she was prepared to withdraw him from Cambridge. On 18 October, she allowed herself a week to decide whether he should continue or terminate his studies. On 25 October, AA was on his way to Cambridge.

[2] The 'Tutor's Account Book' kept by Mr. Chapman lists the following fees accrued by AA from March 1813 to the beginning of the Michaelmas term in 1814: 'Admission fees [1813]—3.18.8; Mids.—3.11.4; Mich.—3.17.4; Xtmas—74.8.6; Lady [1814]—27.15.2; Mids.—28.19.9; Private Tutor—Mids.—14.' The following funds were deposited to cover his expenses: 'Ap. 13 [1813]: Excess of Caution . . .—1; Nov. 11: Tancred Draft—53.14; Feb. 17 [1814]: By Cash—31.1.10; May 6: Tancred Draft—55.14.' AA's deficit was approximately £15.

the opening of the *present* half year may be allowed to pay that sum.

There must, also, be some trifles due, I suppose, elsewhere. But the Furniture will be sold for *us*. How? & by whom? I know not, in the least, where or how to apply for all this.

Alex's Books, of course, & what he has left of Cloathes, & *oddments*, in poor Kitty Cooke's phrase,[3] we must get his *Gip*, Mrs. Parker,[4] to pack up & send us. |

I have been quite FLABERGASTED with surprise & something worse at this Bill for John's school of £40. I had wholly mistaken that business, believing the money for which I had applied to you for his MESS to India, to be to *save* the £40.— I knew not the 40. was *already* incurred, & unpaid.[5] I had misapprehended Sarah, & must now pay for my want of acuteness.—As I consider This a Bill which our dear Father meant to discharge, there can be no hesitation. But a demand was made on Sarah, by a *Tayler*, for £15—incurred by the *Captain's* (John's) order, before John had been received by his family: & to *that* I have positively objected payment. The Tayler should have made his claim while my dear Father *lived*—for it is now above a year—& a half since the Cloathes he speaks of must have been made: & the *Captain,* says the Tayler, desired the Bill might be *referred* to Miss Burney![6] I think this an *imposition*: but if *not*, Hetty & I can only be amenable, even by our own scruples, to accounts we *know* to have been considered as Debts of our dear Father. John *worked* his passage to England, & the *Captain* brought him by desire of his *Mother*, not of my Father. Ergo, it seems to me we have no more responsibility for John, in this, than for James, & the rest of the Ten.[7] Nor

[3] The term 'oddments' was a favourite of Papilian Catherine 'Kitty' Cook (*c.* 1731–97), whose use of dialect and idiom often mangled the language and delighted the Burneys when they visited Chessington Hall. As late as the summer of 1813, CB—now morbidly depressed—remembered her various expressions and almost jocularly referred to his toothache: 'Ah teeth, teeth, *thou art proosh^g things,* according to poor Kitty Cook' (Osborn).

[4] The bursary records of Gonville and Caius that might identify Mrs. Parker, AA's gyp, are not extant.

[5] On 26 Jan. 1814, SHB wrote to CB Jr. on behalf of her nephew John Burney (1799–1837), the thirteenth child of the late Richard Burney. In her letter (Osborn) she recommended her 'new protege' as a 'very worthy, active, considerate lad' for whom she wished CB Jr. to secure a cadetship aboard an East Indiaman. Unable to have the boy accepted as a cadet, CB Jr. agreed to pay his mess while John Burney served as a midshipman *en route* to India.   [6] SHB.

[7] In Richard Thomas's large family tree (Comyn) was a son referred to as Captain James (i, pp. lxxiii–iv). But see L. 669 n. 6 for James's rank.

can I believe a *Tradesman* would so long have neglected to claim a lawful debt. If you know otherwise, set me right. |

Nor do I think Mr. Sympson[8] very correct: to send an acc^t 5 months after his pupil has quitted him, & England. What has been his reason for not sending sooner, if he had a right to send at all? If any further demands come, now, I shall protest against them: for there can be no more reason Esther & I should be responsible for the Debts of John, *save what were meant to be paid by his Grandfather*, than for any other of the 10 Brethren. I hope when you write to Mrs. Burney of India, you will give her a *littel hint* that the Chief of the Family being now, alas, no more, the Uncles & Aunts are all fully supplied with Races of their own; & that, therefore, the rest of the Richardonian tribe must be contented to be educated where they were born, unless some circumstances peculiar to themselves, & independent of fallacious expectations from their Relations, induces them to travel.

Certainly, nevertheless, I do not mean to dispute paying *Mr. Sympson*, though he may wait till more cash is forth coming, as I cannot refund, though I must needs diminish. He cannot expect money never claimed to have been kept lying upon a shelf for him.

Adieu, dearest Charles, my kind Love to Rosette—to Parr—his Fannys—& Rosettina.

Mr. Payne has sent an excellent Newton[9]—& Lemprière[10]—alas alas!—all all in vain!—

Again I repeat my cordial thanks, my dear Brother—for your Brotherly care of us—!!!— |

Sweet Charlotte Barrett brought forth another Cupid 2 days ago: & mamma & Cherub both are in a fair way.[11]

[8] The school headed by Daniel Simpson (*c.* 1750–*post* 1814) in Mendlesham, Suffolk.

[9] See L. 822 n. 18.

[10] John Lemprière's *Bibliotheca Classica; or, a Classical Dictionary, containing a full Account of all the Proper Names mentioned in Antient Authors* (Reading, 1788). A popular reference work, it went through eight editions by 1814.

[11] CFBt's fourth child, Henry John Richard (1814–29).

To Charles Burney

A.L. (Osborn), *n.d.*
Double sheet 8vo   4 pp.   with mounting tape along right margin p. 4
pmks   RICHMOND / 25 OC 1814   25 OC 1814   black seal
Addressed: Rev^d Dr. Burney, / Rectory House, / Deptford.

Certainly, my dear Carlos, we will have written documents
for my poor—but dauntless Alexander—He has just left me!—
& for the first time!—& for 6 MONTHS CERTAIN!—should I not
rather precede that word by another syllable!—

pray beg my dear Parr to fix upon my representative, that I
may make over my directions in due form for my new little
bantling.[1]

Ah, poor Rosette!—

M. d'Arblay is gone to town with his darling son—& he will
go to-morrow to West hamble[2]—& I am not sure when he will
return—nor when, we make our final route—*final* for this year!—

When the Museum—Mr. White—&c—enable you to settle
with Esther I entreat my moiety may be paid to Mr. Merrik
Hoare, Fleet ⏐ Street, with whom we shall leave a Letter of
attorney for forwarding to *us*, or Alex, or the stocks, all that
of monies may be in question during our absence.[3]

I entreat you to rummage the Bureau & Closet, & to have the
goodness to send all of any sort of trash you can find, papers or
goods, to the care •of *Mr. White*, Auctioneer, Storey Gate, /
Great George Street / Westminster. / *for M. d'Arblay*— / *From
the Rev^d* / *Dr. Burney.*

829. [1] See L. 825 n. 14.
 [2] M. d'A went to Camilla Cottage to see which of his and FBA's possessions
could be stored for them by Miss Baker (viii, L. 843 n. 6) or sent to John White,
the auctioneer, either for crating to France or for sale. Having looked over
their property, M. d'A returned to Richmond by the first week in November.
There he consulted with FBA about the distribution of their goods. Obviously,
there was little in the cottage worth saving. In a letter (National Portrait Gallery),
postmarked 7 Nov. 1814, M. d'A asked his tenant, Bolton Hudson, 'qu'on envoye
le plutôt possible à *Monsieur White* . . . les deux boites dites *Caisonnes*'. He also asked
Hudson to send 'à la même adresse les coussins qui sont dans le Cabinet, notre
intention etant de les faire vendre pour eviter l'embarras de les emporter'.
 [3] See L. 721 n. 4.

And also my *select Theatre*!⁴—don't forget—I shall amuse myself *therewith* in Montpelier or Tours—or Nice

How sorry I am for Dr. Davy!—

But oh *how* sorry for Rosette & yourself!—

I certainly cannot go to Deptford—you knew my promise! M. d'A. will *if possible*. But *you* must come to *me*, if poz. make any stay in town, & Paris too. |

I do not fret myself, I thank Heaven, about the Reviews. I shall not read any of them, to keep myself from useless vexation —till my spirits & my time are in harmony for preparing a corrected Edition.⁵ I shall then read all—&, I expect, coolly & impartially. I think the public has its full right to criticise —& never have had the folly & vanity to set my heart upon escaping its late severity, while reminiscence keeps alive its early indulgence. But if, when all the effect of false expectation is over, in about 5 years, the work has ONLY criticism,—then, indeed, I shall be lessened in my own fallen fallen fallen hopes— fed, now, not by any general conceit, but an opinion That—if the others were worthy of good opinion, THIS, when read fresh, & free from local circumstances of a mischievous tendency, will by no means be found lowest in the scale.⁶ |

I beseech the packet may come immediately, as M. d'A. will pack all before I leave Richmond, & join what is to *go*, or *remain* at Mr. White's

---

⁴ Either *The Theatre: or, Select Works of the British Dramatic Poets* (12 vols., Edinburgh, 1768); or *The British Theatre; or, A Collection of Plays, which are acted at the Theatres Royal, Drury Lane, Covent Garden, and Haymarket . . . With Biographical and Critical Remarks, by Mrs. Inchbald* (25 vols., 1806–9, 1814). FBA probably had the first of these two multi-volumed works in mind.

⁵ See Appendix IV. CB Jr., like Mrs. Waddington, must have seen the attack on *The Wanderer* in *The Quarterly Review* (Apr. 1814) and the qualified praise of the novel in *The British Critic* (Apr. 1814).

⁶ See *The Quarterly Review* (Appendix IV), which attacked FBA as a supporter of Napoleonic tyranny.

To James Burney

A.L.S. (The Hyde Collection), *n.d.*
Two single sheets 4to   3 pp.   *pmks*   RICHMOND / 28 OC / 1814
28 OC 181⟨   ⟩   wafer
Addressed: Captain Burney, / James Street, / 26 / Westminster.

I thank you cordially for your hospitable invitation, my dear James, but I know nothing at this moment of what will be my movements, or powers;[1] I have received the most gracious commands (under the name of desire) to wait upon Her Majesty & the Princesses at Windsor before my departure, unless M.d'A's *furlough* will make it indiscreet.—I know not how even to ask him the question, as I am uncertain whether he is in town, at La Sablonierè,[2] or at West Humble. Should you see, or know of him, pray tell him of this matter: which may change his own plans. I am unwilling to answer till he knows of the invite, unless it become an absolute summons, which MUST be obeyed immediately.

our good Charlotte sends her love—her sweet Daughter is *tolerably* well only.[3]—Charles is going to Tunbridge to Lady Crewe.[4]

I expect very essential benefit from | a southern climate this winter. It will make me quit the relaxation of my fire side daily; which is necessary for restoring my strength & very shaken

---

830.   [1] The departure schedule arranged by M. d'A was not observed. In a letter (Berg) to FBA, AA commented on 1 Nov. 1814: 'I suppose you have quitted *Richmond* by this time—indeed you *must* . . . Papa had ordered a bed for you at le *Sablonniere* hotel for *Friday* last' [28 Oct.]. In fact, FBA and M. d'A did not leave Richmond until 10 November, their delay caused first by a royal invitation to FBA and then by her severe cold.

[2] La Sablonière Hotel, which absorbed what was once William Hogarth's house into its larger structure, was located on the east side of Leicester Square. M. d'A—like many *émigrés*—became acquainted with the hotel shortly after his arrival in England in 1792.

[3] CFBt recovered slowly after the birth of her fourth child on 12 October.

[4] According to *The Tunbridge Wells Guide* (1797), the watering place 'has . . . become the general rendez-vous of gaiety and politeness during the summer' (p. 115). In *Camilla* (1796), FBA acknowledges this fact, pointing out that the *ton* spends 'all the autumn at Bath'. In the two decades since this statement, the fashion did not alter. Lady Crewe in October missed the modish company that visited Tunbridge in the summer. CB Jr. often visited the spa in the autumn. See L. 728 n. 1.

nerves. I am glad you are, at least, not SURE my Alex is
not MORE FAT!—My kind Love to dear Mrs. B[urney] & to
Martin & Sally—your affe^cte sister

FB d'Arblay

I leave Alex for the First time in his [lif]e —— I have felt
myself not YET the stronger for [the] separation —— ¹

This is not to be looked at—

831   'Camilla Cottage',
                                       28 October 1814
M. d'Arblay
To Madame d'Arblay

A. L. (Berg), 28 Oct.
Double sheet 4to   4 pp.   *pmks*   EPSOM   29 OC 1814   29 OC 1814
wafer
Addressed: A Madame / Madame d'Arblay née Miss / Burney at M^rs
Broome's / Hill Street / Richmond / *Surry*
Edited by FBA, p. 1, *annotated, and dated from pmk*: 32   1814   Octr 29.
Written on a Last Visit to our dear—matchless Camilla Cottage—when we
were forced to relinquish it after the loss of our adored Mr. Lock.
See further, Textual Notes.

Poor Camilla's Lodge
28. 8bre 1814

O ma pauvre amie que je suis faché de n'être pas près de toi.
What a melancholy business I am employed in! Je t'assure que
de ma vie je n'ai autant souffert. à tout moment j'ai les larmes
aux yeux, et d'honneur je ne sais ce que je fais: mais je sais bien
ce que je pense, et j'espère que tu l'as dejà deviné. Je me dis
que jamais aucun être sensible n'a été plus veritablement
heureux que je ne l'ai été dans cette aimable cottage — aussi je
le regrette au delà de tout ce que l'on peut dire — ô mon amie
combien nous avons été dupes, et combien nous le sommes
encore! On t'a dit que notre maison avait beaucoup perdu. Eh
bien, je l'ai bien examinée sous tous les rapports. Je te jure que
rien n'est plus faux. ⌐Chaque ancien cabinet que j'ouvre
(toujours avec la même clef) me démontre ce qui autrement
m'aurait paru impossible. Je suis d'avis de the greatest sound-

ness in all what has been done in the whole of the building. *Quelques unes* des choses renfermées dans chaque nouveau cabinet, exhibit the marks of decay, mais on ne peut l'attribuer qu'aux premiers materiaux qui entrent dans leur composition, et le bois de ces cabinets est en general perfectly sound:⸜ J'en conclus que nous sommes maltraités à un ˡ point reellement inconcevable. Tache de me lire car je ne puis ecrire mieux. Je te griffonne ceci à 7 heures du soir à la suite d'un diner pris à la hâte et plutot que celui d'hier, car il etait 8ʰ quand je me mis à table en revenant de Norbury. J'y suis allé encore aujourdhui pour n'y plus retourner, et le congé que j'ai pris l'argent à la main et les larmes aux yeux ne me sortira de longtems de la memoire!!! ⸜J'ai ouvert ⟨les 2 derniers⟩ cabinets dans la chambre à la suite du drawing room et deux dans la chambre où nous couchions. Tout était dans le meilleur etat, tout soit dit le plus grand nombre des choses. Celles dans les quelles le bois entrait comme partie constituante ont seules souffert. Mais je te jure que les shelves les serrures et les portes sont *quite sound*. jamais je n'ai rien vu. de pourri sur une seule planche ⟨bien⟩ *travaillée*; et⸜ je te proteste que la maison est aussi bonne que si elle avait été bâtie il y a six mois — Quant aux reparations dont on nous a tant parlé!!!!!ˡ je t'avais dit qu'elles ne devaient pas couter 20 guinées et je te dis actuellement et avec connaissance de cause qu'elles n'en couteraient *pas deux*!!! Oh! comme ˡ nous sommes trompés!!! ⸜⟨Causons-en⟩ alors ensemble et si le pain et la viande n'etaient pas ⟨ici⟩ si chers, je te demanderais la permission de renier notre parole et d'acheter nous même le terrain au prix de Mʳ Bolton.² Nous en aurions le droit ⟨presqu'en 20⟩ jours encore de tems et qu'on nous fait attendre! Mais la viande coute ⟨60⟩ sols et le pain environ ⟨10s⟩!⸜ Oh! que je quitte ceci avec peine! j'y ai été si heureux! je comptais si bien y mourir! Je meurs de chagrin, et j'aurais bien besoin de quitter bien vite ceci. ⸜⟨Où mettrais⟩ je tout ce que j'ai bien de chagrin ⟨à laisser?⟩ j'ai de quoi remplir une maison entiere; et pourtant il y a des choses que je ne peus retrouver. Je ne sais ce qu'elles sont devenues. Ton edition de Pope par exemple en 8v[o ou] en 4°. Je ne l'ai vue nulle part. J'ai pourtant retiré tout

---

831. ¹ This is the belated reaction to FBA's complaint (Ll. 741, 798) that unless repairs were made, Camilla Cottage would depreciate further in value.
² See L. 803.

ce qui était à Norbury Park. Je n'ai vu non plus en aucun endroit *aucun* des dessins de William. Il est probable qu'ils sont avec notre *devant de cheminée*!!! Depuis ⟨10⟩ heures je travaille comme un forcé et je ne sais encore quand j'aurai fini. | Cela peut être ⟨bizarre⟩ mais tu seras bien plus surprise quand tu sais que le fils de Mr ⟨Hudson⟩³ a travaillé autant que moi, et que son Pere et lui sont venus ici *exprès*. Malgré leur obligeance et la gratitude qu'elle me fait eprouver, je n'ai pu m'empecher de leur reprocher la diminution ⟨des⟩ 200£. Ils m'ont dit comme je m'en doutais bien qu'ils avient voulu offrir une somme ronde de 600£ et non pas ⟨deux⟩ &c &c et ils ont ajouté que nous etions maltraités (ill used) parceque l'on a porté for the *ground* what was fairly due to us for the house & improvement of that ground. They say that if the house had been valued 800£ they should not have objected to it. Demain j'irai en ville par le stage de 3h ½ mais je ne [pour]rai probablement etre avec toi que Dimanche!!! What drawbacks!⁻ Mr Cambridge ne nous a pas dit qu'il etait venu visiter notre Cottage. Il devrait bien nous abriter ce que nous ne [pouvons] emporter

Amen

832 [Richmond, 28 October 1814]

To Charles Burney

A.L.S. (Osborn), *n.d.*
Single sheet 4to 2 pp. *pmks* RICHMOND ⟨ ⟩ OC 1814 28 [18]⟨1⟩4 black seal
Addressed: Revd Dr. Burney, / Rectory House, / Deptford

You meanest of Rectors!
If you write to me again upon a scrap that can hardly arrive —I shall answer upon a bit of Tea paper.
I shall begin preparing a collection of morsels, for that purpose, upon my next parcel from the Grocer's.

³ Thomas Hudson (*fl.* 1814–37). From the *Charity Commissioners Report* (1837), pp. 444, 446: 'Mr. Thomas Hudson, who, in the year 1820, had been appointed receiver and accountant on the death of his father, had been in the habit of appropriating to his own use large sums of money received on account of rent.' During the fifteen years that he served as an officer of Bridewell and Bethlem Hospitals, Thomas Hudson embezzled £10,066. 6s. 9d. After discovery of his theft, he disappeared on the Continent.

Send me at least, & immediately my *own mss.* which I beg
you to indorse with

> To be opened by / me / Mᵉ d'A.
> *Madame* d'Arblay—
> Nᴏᴛ Mʳ—

for I shall reserve them for our Evenings when better matter
fails.

I send another Kᴇʏ—& Hope[1]
But a lock may be picked without Hᴀᴍᴍᴇʀs, or ᴀɴʏ noise You
are a miserable House breaker—not to know that I'll never
employ you— |

N.B. I have laid a wager with myself that your next letter
will be on a full new bright gilt sheet!!! to reprimand my
reprimand.—

Send me back all my Keys if not the right [ones] —. — if
they belong not to your Lockes—Ten to one but I may miss
them from some other!— —

West Hamble M.d'A. visits at this moment as I believe—
Lady Crewe sent me no answer about her Letters—if I receive
them, I will seal them carefully up in the ⟨tin⟩ Trunk that will
hold all others, till my return, of my dearest Father.[2]

But present her my very best of ʙᴇsᴛs as you think she will
ʙᴇsᴛ like. I have written twice myself my thanks, &c which I
suppose has annoyed her abhorrence of ᴄᴇʀᴇᴍᴏɴʏ—but I
meant mere simple & true acknowledgement of a sample of her
constant kindness

Hᴏᴡᴇᴠᴇʀ I always ʙᴇᴡᴀʀᴇ of the 3ᵈ Time—& so shall now
make you my proxy

How truly am I grieved for poor dear Rosette! I have just
received gracious commands to wait upon Her Majesty before
my departure at Windsor on her return from Brighton.[3]—It will
be an impossible gratification Though a hurry past expression,
as I cannot sleep there even one night—

832. [1] CB Jr. inherited certain books kept 'in the glazed book-case standing in
[CB's] parlour' and CPB the 'models and coins contained in the drawers of the
said Case' as well as the case itself. CB Jr., in requesting a 'key', may have had this
'Case' in mind but more likely he meant a 'key' to the locked closet or bureau set
aside in his house for FBA's personal papers.

[2] FBA presumably requested the return of CB's letters to Lady Crewe. Of these
68 are extant. No evidence suggests the request was granted.

[3] The Queen and Princesses left for Brighton on Monday, 24 October, and
returned to Windsor on Saturday, 29 October.

833   Richmond, 8 November 1814

To Mrs. Broome

A.L.S. (Berg), 8 Nov. 1814
Double sheet 8vo greenish   1 p.
Addressed: Mrs. Broome,

Accept, my dearest Charlotte, & use—from your honoured remembrance of its first owner, & your tender love of its second, with pleasure this writing Box—which I shall trebly delight to present you, if you will make it the kind vehicle of those marks of partial affection which I shall charge it to invite you to send forth to

your forever faithful &
truly affect^{te} FB. d'Arblay,

Richmond, Novr 8th 1814

834   [Richmond, 8 November 1814][1]

To Charles Burney

A. L. S. (Osborn), *n.d.*
Double sheet large 8vo   2 pp.   RICHMOND / 9 No   9 NO 1814
wafer
Addressed: Rev^d Dr. Burney, / Rectory House, / 26 Deptford

Tuesday—

A furious Cold had decided M. d'Arblay not to let me execute any commission, or pay any visit, that will make me sleep from home:—even to Windsor, though graciously invited for 2 Days, I went but for 2 Hours[2]—

Yet we cannot bear to go without a sight & shake hands of all our Tribe—as far as attainable—Let me hope that you,

---

834. [1] Although postmarked 9 November, a Wednesday, the letter was written the day before.

[2] Since the Queen and the Princesses returned to Windsor only after five o'clock on 29 October, FBA probably visited them during the first week in November.

dear Carlos, so foremost in my desire, may be of the number
—We shall set off hence at 9 on Thursday Morn—stop at
Turnham Green—Chelsea College!—& Cook's Grounds—&
James Street and *Deptford Rectory* & Greenwich Institute[3]—but
we can merely receive your benediction

Give it *cordially*, dearest Charles, to your old best friend—&
— —

ever & ever truly affectionate love
F B d'Arblay

Tuesday—Richmond
We are to sleep at Canterbury[4]

If you wish for Mr. Malone's Book, of which Mr. Boswell[5]
stopt the sale,[6] pray tell Esther I have consented, if *she* does,
to present it you. If you don't care for it, say so, as then — — —
I hope you saw the Dainty[7]—

I thought you would have given me some answer from Lady
Crewe[8] — —

[3] FBA's parting visits to her family: to EBB at Turnham Green; to SHB (in a
new apartment) at Chelsea College; to Fanny Raper in Chelsea (L. 801 n. 1);
to JB at 26 James Street, Westminster; to CB Jr. and the ailing Rosette in Deptford (for FBA's change of plan, see L. 829); to CPB at the Greenwich School.

[4] FBA and M. d'A spent the first night of their 56-mile journey to Canterbury
at Sydenham.

[5] James Boswell, the younger (1778–1822), barrister and second surviving son
of Johnson's biographer. When still young, he became an intimate of his father's
friend Edmond Malone (1741–1812), the scholar whose first edition of Shakespeare's works appeared in ten volumes in 1790. Malone turned over many of his
manuscripts, notes, and books to the younger Boswell so that the latter could
complete a projected new edition of Shakespeare. 'Boswell's Malone', known as
the 'third variorum' edition of Shakespeare, appeared in 21 volumes in 1821.

[6] According to the *Sale Catalogue* of Dr. Burney's miscellaneous library (1814),
there were two items by Malone: No. 1041. *Malone's Inquiry into the Authenticity of
Certain Papers and* [Legal] *Instruments . . . attributed to Shakespeare* (1796); No. 1042.
Malone's *Account of the Incidents from which the Title and Part of the Story of Shakespeare's
Tempest were derived and its true Date Ascertained* (1808 [–9]). It was the second
(accompanied by a letter from Malone to Dr. Burney) that FBA wished to give to
CB Jr. This small work, privately printed in January 1808, traces the origin of *The
Tempest's* plot to the account of the discovery of the Bermudas issued in 1610 by
Sylvestre Jourdain (d. 1650). On the fly-leaf of Malone's pamphlet, after the presentation inscription, was written: 'Not published;—eighty copies only having been
printed. It is requested that this pamphlet may not be inadvertently put into the
hands of any person who may be likely to publish any part of it.' On the fifth day
of the sale of CB's library, the pamphlet was sold. But Boswell managed to cancel
the sale and persuade FBA and EBB that it would be better to retain the work
within the Burney family.

[7] Rosetta d'Arblay Burney was called 'the Dainty'.

[8] See L. 832 n. 2.

ADDITIONAL LETTERS*

633A   [Deal], 15 August 1812

To Charles Burney

A.L. (Burney-Cumming), 15 Aug. 1812
Double sheet 8vo   2 pp.   *pmks*   17 AU 1812   17 AU 1812   wafer
Addressed: The Reverend Doctor / Charles Burney / Greenwich.

Aug 15⟨th⟩ 1812

Alex from the ship announced last night my happy—happy
approaching arrival to my dearest Charles—I now announce
myself—that after difficulties *all but* insurmountable I am writing to him from Deal—where a Mr. Stone has already found
me out, & would have ensured my landing,[1] had not a sea
officer brought me from the ship *in triumph* in his own boat.[2]—
Oh my whole soul is full—full of joy!—I shall stay all to-
morrow to rest a little, for I feel as if I should be subdued by
such meetings as I am flying to if I did not recruit first, after
passing 3 nights without undressing. I have written to our
beloved Father[3]—but only my *intention* to-morrow I shall
acquaint him I am at Deal—if the post goes out—& the ˡ day
after I shall try to arrive at night at Chelsea[4]—but it is possible
the conveyances may be taken — — my charles—my dearest
Charles—a short adieu!—pity my excellent life's partner, who
could not obtain a passport—If he had — — for *life*, not for a
few months—would I re-join all my dear, dear native Friends—
Loves—Loves—Loves—around—

* As noted in the Acknowledgements, these are the ten Additional Letters for
which we are indebted to Mr. Burney-Cumming and the Kestner-Museum.
633A. [1] In all likelihood Charles Stone (*fl.* 1791–1812), a clerk in the Custom House
at Dover.
   [2] See L. 637 and n. 15.
   [3] See L. 632.
   [4] FBA's arrival 'at Chelsea' is described in L. 637 and nn. 26, 27, 28.

639A   [23 Chenies Street],
                              1 September 1812
To Madame Beckedorff

A.L.S. (Kestner-Museum), 1 Sept. 1812
Double sheet 4to 1 p. *pmk* 1 SEP 1812   wafer
Addressed: Mrs. Beckedorff / Windsor Castle / Windsor.

                              Ce 1st Septr 1812—
Madam,
    A Letter which I have just received from Miss Planta en-
courages me to hope for your kind offices in accelerating for me
the high & inestimable Honour of admission to Her Majesty.
    My Brother the Chaplain will convey me to Windsor to-
morrow Morning, & I now take the liberty to entreat that you
will have the goodness to give orders that I may be allowed,
upon my arrival, to wait in your Apartments for Her Majesty's
gracious commands.[1]
    I am, Madam, with great consideration,
                         Your Most humble Servant
                              F Burney d'Arblay.

640A   [23 Chenies Street,
                              9 September 1812]
To Charles Burney

A.L. (Burney-Cumming), *n.d.*
Double sheet 8vo 2 pp. *pmks* 10 SP 1812   10 SE 1812   red seal
(wafer)
Addressed: Rev^d Dr. Burney, / Rectory, / Deptford.

    How we missed you, Dearest Charles,—or rather how we
desired you, & dear Rosette, in James' Street[1] Yesterday!—
    If we must make the R[oyal] visit, I particularly wish it

639A. [1] FBA's visit to Windsor was postponed by one day. See L. 639 n. 2.
640A. [1] JB's house.

493

deferred as long as may be done without impropriety.[2] I will detail my reasons when we meet. And to this end, that no offence may be taken, I shall postpone Norbury till it is over. While I am merely with my own family, it is not possible any one can be rationally affronted: but I conceive that I must avoid being always *a gadding aside*.

What prodigious News![3] I am longing to greet my dear Father. Edward[4] comes to Dinner or I should not resist setting forth for Chelsea. But to-morrow I must give him 3 Cheers.

A Million of thanks for my Alex—& give half of them to dear Charles the second.[5] I never thought to like Charles the second so well! How we are turned topsy turvy in this World! I never thought or wrote of him before but with distaste, if not disgust.

I believe you know I have a desire to converse with the Duchess of Buccleugh[6]—Charlotte Barret, with great delicacy & propriety, has negociated, through a third person, for a meeting, which is to take place when Her Grace comes to town, at Montagu house,[7] though, with extreme & condescending politeness, she has offered to come to *me*. 'Tis upon an affair very important, though not personal, & I must not miss her. She goes in a fortnight to Scotland.

Alex is gone to see Westminster Abbey with James—I believe, but certainly with Mrs. J: B. & merry little fatty.

Every body joins in Love, to you & to dear Rosette—

God bless—

[2] FBA refers to a royal invitation to pay an extended visit to Windsor. For the date of that visit, see L. 657.

[3] See L. 641 and nn. 1, 6.

[4] FBA's cousin, Edward Francesco Burney.

[5] CPB.

[6] See Ll. 641 and n. 3, 642 n. 6.

[7] In Bloomsbury.

685A   Norbury Park,
                                        27 March 1813
To Madame Beckedorff

A.L.S. (Kestner-Museum), 27 March 1813
Double sheet 4to 3 pp. *pmk* EPSOM 27 MR 1813 wafer
Addressed: Madame Beckedorff, / Windsor Castle.

                                        27ᵗʰ March, 1813.
                                        Norbury Park,
                                        near Dorking,
                                        Surry
Dear Madam,
    Not till Yesterday did the melancholy tidings reach me of the
new affliction which has befallen the Royal Family.[1] I am so
deeply, & with my whole heart interested in whatever can
affect Her Majesty, that I cannot resist entreating you, Madam,
when you can steal a moment of leisure, to have the great
Kindness to afford me a few lines, with the real state of the
Queen's health. God grant this new event may not again
give a shake to what is so exquisitely precious! Oh may Her
Majesty preserve Herself in thinking of the immense value of
Her sacred life to all the loved & lovely Princesses in particular—
as well as to All the Princes—the Regent surtout—!—& the
Nation, in general! The highest of All claims to Her Majesty's
personal care & fortitude I dare not name—but That, I am
sure, is ever uppermost in her virtuous & reflecting Mind.
    I am the more concerned for this misfortune, though I had
never the honour even to see her late R: H. the Duchess,
because I have frequently observed that it has seemed a
pleasure to Her Majesty to visit Her R. H. & that Her Majesty
loved to speak of Her, & always named Her with distinction and
affection.—And when I think how few are the pleasures—how
rare is all relaxation of which Her Majesty can participate,
I feel every new deprivation as an afflicting calamity. God
spare Her Majesty—He who alone can bring them round—to
happier days!—We see not, it is true, the road by which they

685A. [1] For the death of the Duchess of Brunswick and FBA's preparations for
formal mourning, see Ll. 686 n. 2, 687 n. 5.

                                                            495

can now come—but neither did we *fore*-see the bitter evils by which—should they be granted—they have so mournfully been preceded.

All the sweet Princesses, too, appeared to me much attached to Their Royal Aunt, & to take delight in shewing Her R. H. their tender respect. How grieved I am that yet another source is cut off for the exercise of Their sweetness, & for according them some happiness! May I hope, Madam, you will also give me some news of Their Royal Highnesses? And particularly whether H. R. H. the Princess Sophia gains a little strength?

Your Kind wishes for me, Madam, here with my beloved Friend, Mrs. Lock, have a great chance to be realized, when once a little soft weather will suffer me to take the air upon this salubrious spot. But at present, though my fever is quite con-quered, my Cough retains all its obstinacy and irritation.[2] I have left my dear F [*tear*] remarkably well. My son is gone to some preparatory studies, previous to entering the university, at Greenwich.

My best Comp^ts always attend Miss Beckedorff and I beg you to believe me, Dear Madam,

> Your obliged
> humble Servant
> F. B. d'Arblay.

689A

To Charles Burney

[23 Chenies Street,
20 April 1813]

A.L. (Burney-Cumming), *n.d.*
Double sheet 8vo   1 p.   *pmks*   20 AP 1813   20 AP 1813   P.P.U. wafer
Addressed: Rev^d Dr. Burney, / Rectory House, / Deptford.

My dearest Charles,

I will do the most illiberally that I can exactly what I wish no one else to do, cut & slash unmercifully.[1]

---

[2] L. 684 n. 2.

689A. [1] Ever since her radical pruning of *Camilla* for the 1802 edition, FBA recognized verbosity and repetition as two of her literary faults. What held true for *Camilla* was also valid for her current work, *The Wanderer*.

I beseech you not to fail bringing on Wednesday a Coat, black or brown & a pair of shoes for Alex.[2]

AND

His part of Percy,[3]
Left in one of his pockets.
All the Girls are quite affronted at his leaving it.[4]

I have just this moment received a Letter from Mr. Colburn — — A *very handsome Letter*, well worth attention.[5]
& I have written an answer — —
a very civil answer—saying little, but leaving openings.

I am too busy to copy, so reserve the two Epistles for Wednesday.
Pray don't forget *COAT—SHOES & HALL*.[6]
Beg dear Rosette to take that Commission, with my Love.

695A   [23 Chenies Street,
                            c. 19] May—1813

To Madame Beckedorff

A.L.S. (Kestner-Museum), *n.d.*
Double sheet 4to   2 pp.   *pmk*   wafer
Addressed: Madame Beckedorff, / Windsor Castle, / Berks.

Dear Madam,
     How grateful are my feelings to Providence that once more— after a chasm of 11 Years, it is allowed me to join my small,

---

    [2] FBA insisted on AA wearing mourning for the death of the Duchess of Brunswick (L. 687 and n. 5).
    [3] This suggests preparation for home dramatics. AA was perhaps to play the leading part in Hannah More's tragedy *Percy*, the hero of which was the Earl of Northumberland. First performed at the Theatre-Royal, Covent Garden, on 10 Dec. 1777, *Percy* was popular for the remainder of the century.
    [4] Possibly the Waddington girls who were to arrive in London in June.
    [5] Mr. Colburn's letter had to do with his desire to purchase *The Wanderer* (L. 711 and n. 2).
    [6] A familiar allusion to *Percy*. The setting for three of its five acts was either 'A Gothic Hall' or, simply, 'The Hall'.

but true voice, in my dear native land, to the general Chorus of prayers, of benedictions, & of warm wishes, upon the return of Her Majesty's Natal Day![1] To word as I feel them I should try in vain: but there is no occasion; Her Majesty's judgement is generous as well as penetrating. I have nothing, therefore, to fear, for I cannot, I trust! pass for a Monster—& what less must I be if my attachment to Her Majesty were not a part of my existence?

I hope you are now, Dear Madam, recovered from your late disturbance? Your courageous efforts to save our Royal Mistress from alarm have done you credit through-out the Nation. It was not for that you so exerted yourself, I well know; &, indeed, had such been the *motive, such* would *not* have been the result. Let success then, joined to general approbation, act like two physicians, to fortify you after this shake, & complete your cure.[2]

I passed an hour or two very pleasantly yesterday Morning at Harcourt House, where even the subject upon which we met professedly to discourse, Madame de Beauvau, scarcely kept us ten minutes from pursuing the currency of our thoughts, in talking of the much loved Royal Family.[3]

I beg Miss Beckedorff to accept my best Compliments, & remain, Dear Madam,

> Your obliged
> humble Servt
> F B. d'Arblay.

May—1813

695A. [1] Queen Charlotte's birthday was 19 May. It had been officially celebrated in 1813 by the Queen who on 4 Feb. held a drawing-room and by the Prince Regent who on the next day gave a ball and supper in his mother's honour.
[2] L. 692 n. 6.
[3] Ll. 696, 808 n. 4.

23 Chenies Street,
14 September 1813

To Charles Burney

A.L.S. (Burney-Cumming), 14 Sept. 1813
Double sheet 4to   4 pp.   *pmk*   14 SE .813   wafer
Addressed: Rev^d Dr. Burney, / Sand Gate / Sussex or Kent
Docketed: M^r B—

Tuesday 14 Sept. 1813
23 Chenies Street,
Alfred Place—

My dearest Carlucci,

Whoso could read your cordial urgency, & resist it must be made of other paste than

Yours ever
F B d'A.

⌒

There is my answer, Dearest Carlucci.

For the rest, I received your Letter too late last night to write. I was out all the Morning

But this morning, all is arranged—& I have taken my place, & my measures, for setting off in the Canterbury Machine

on Friday morning, the 17^{th1}

I shall arrive at the Shrine of St. Thomas a Becket at 4 o'clock in the afternoon.

I am quite sorry I shall have so short a peep of dear Sarah & dear Charlotte & all the Barrets:[2] yet the departure from you of Sarah is what gives *universal approbation* to my joining You.

Those Guns you mention gave me the heart-ache — —[3]

I have heard nothing upon the subject here.

Alex *has* received a summons from Cambridge—Clement brought it from Mr. Chapman.

722A. [1] See L. 724 n. 2.

[2] The departure of the Barretts and SHB is described in a letter of CB Jr. to CPB (L. 724 n. 2).

[3] There was no major military action at this time, just minor skirmishes between the allies and the French following the battle of Dresden (L. 724 n. 18). Still the guns may have sounded the allied victory at Dennewitz on 6 September, a victory which endangered French forces along the lower Elbe.

Every body also, even of the highest class, expect him to be entered in October—& a recommendation has been given, for that period, to Mr. Herschal.[4]

I have had—I thank God! at last, a comfortable Letter from my best of all the best Friends I own & enjoy & love.— he has received himself one, at length, also, of mine, that brings us to an understanding, &, I stay, avowedly till spring.

May I, by that time, at least see my Boy settled in his new career, & be able to carry over to his fond father some account how he acquits himself, how he goes on, how he likes it, & what are his prospects & plans, &c—

For, if ignorant of all that, even from the beginning, the cruel slackness & uncertainty of Letters would drive us both non compos!—

Adieu, my dearest Charles! I am charmed, now once 'tis decided, to spend with you this truly social time, for, if you are but convalescent, truly, I trust, & mutually we shall enjoy it.

I take it for granted you can get Books—so I shall bring none.
Adieu till Friday, Caro il mio Frate.

travel that way at this time.
    Mrs. Darnley
      will enquire for the
      Reverend Doctor's Chaise & Man.
    Remember well!
    The lady whom your Groom, or postilion—
                  (pray don't send *TWO* — —).
will find at The Fountain Inn Canterbury[5]
is Mrs. Darnley. — —   No Outlandish Madames

---

[4] John Frederick William Herschel (1792–1871), B.A. (Senior Wrangler and 1st Smith's Prize) 1813, M.A. 1816, Fellow of St. John's, Cambridge (1813–29). In 1813 he was already a F.R.S. and co-founder of The Analytical Society at Cambridge. For his contributions to the study of mathematics, see *DNB* and Venn.

[5] The Fountain Inn, owned by Samuel Wright (*fl.* 1812–27), was a posting house in St. Margaret Street, Canterbury.

[63 Lower Sloane Street],
30 December 1813

To Charles Burney

A.L. (Burney-Cumming), 30 Decʳ 1813
Double sheet 8vo   4 pp.   *pmk*   31 DE 1813   black seal
Addressed: Revᵈ Dr. Burney, / Rectory House, / Deptford.

Decʳ 30ᵗʰ 1813
'Is This *THE FROLIC*?'

Is This the way, my poor dear Carlos, that my consent to our excursion was to CURE you![1] — — alas, how sorry I am for you! — — I can well conceive, indeed, what you must have suffered in disappointing your warm & cordial expectant, & I feel for you with all my heart.[2]

But with respect to myself, the procrastination is a real relief, in a thousand ways, though the circumstances that occasion it keep of its being an enjoyment. Indeed, besides my hurries, & worries, I think it would have been highly dangerous for me to make a two days journey through such a foggy atmosphere. I have been apprehensive I should have finished it on a sick bed at Althorp.!—& only your so warm desire, & my ⌐ own not to check, or chill, your cordial & so dear kindness, has kept me, these last 3 days, from writing you an excuse.

My writing to Lady Spencer is out of all question—thank Heaven! for I am already so overloaded with epistolary duties —& epistolary—Alas! neglects, that the last of the honours I enjoy at this period is the sight of a New Hand in an address to myself.

My dear Father continues well,—George tells me: but the fogs, & a threat of cold, impede my visits to the College.

Our poor James is by no means recovered, I hear, with extreme concern.[3] I long to get to him; but am an absolute prisoner in weather such as this.

Alexander is not yet arrived! — — nor have I any fresh news of him. Clement writes me word he is of opinion his Cousin

---

735A. [1] The invitation to Althorp came from Lady Spencer (L. 731 n. 1).
[2] For the lengthy attack of gout that CB Jr. suffered, see L. 737 n. 2.
[3] JB suffered from a 'slow fever' (Ll. 731, 737 and n. 1).

had business that would yet ⎸ detain him at Cambridge for a fortnight. I wrote for intelligence yesterday: & am not very tranquil, you will believe!⁴

I will keep this, to see what to night will produce, or to-morrow's post.

If Lady Spencer should not come to town before you are able to go to Althorp, pray make no new arrangement for *me* without giving me notice, lest it should interfere with one I have in view of my own.

I shall now, at least, pass my ever sad, ever sacred, yet ever dear 6ᵗʰ Janʸ as for 13 years I have done, in cherishing recollections: That day which Gave—& which took away my heart's darling Susan!—

Do you know the Primate of Ireland? the excellent Susan Adams lives with his lady, Mrs. Stuart, who has written me a long, & very kind Letter, with an account which much concerns me of the ill health of that faithful creature.⁵ I *ought* to call upon Mrs. Stuart—but—but—but!—

My kind Love to dear Rosette—& adieu dear Carlucci—

may yet we ⟨journey⟩

Thursday—No Alexander!—& no Letter!⁶

775A

To Charles Burney

[63 Lower Sloane Street],
12 May [1814]

A.L. (Burney-Cumming), 12 May
Double sheet 8vo   4 pp.   [*cover missing*]

Thursday May 12.

My dearest Carlos,

As I can no where find my asses skin memorandum Book, I conclude it to have gone, in some general mass of loose matters, to THE SALE¹ — —

---

⁴ See L. 738 and nn. 2, 3, 5.   ⁵ Ll. 666 and n. 1, 756 and nn. 5, 6, 7.
⁶ AA arrived at Lower Sloane Street on 1 January (L. 738 n. 3).

775A. ¹ The sale of CB's miscellaneous library was to begin on 9 June in the auction rooms of Leigh and Sotheby.

And as NO PRICE could pay me for the personal business contained in it, I must beg you to send a desire it may be set aside instantly when found; I shall write its description on the other side, to save your time for what seems, but by no means IS a trifle.

Alex, too, writes me word he has left at the College a Book of Nicholson's, the Librarian at Cambridge.[2] This I have sought in vain, for all the Books are gone. I will also write its description. He is in *l'agonies* for it, as the Bookseller sends for it daily. I If the cataloguers make any difficulty of hunting for these articles, I will solicit M. d'Arblay on one side—

& the Rev[d] Richard Burney on the other,

in all due form & order

to authorize themselves with a commission in your name to help making the search.

Professor Monk, also, claims your remembrance of a promise of some notes that Alex only marks by the name of *Alcestes*.[3]

The poor youth is *non-compos* with impatience to see his Father[4]—who has been stopt from the journey by the affair of the Cottage Camilla—which now, I trust, from his firm appeal, & superiour knowledge of business in general, (after 10 year's practice of business in particular) will be amicably as well as justly arranged. I It begins to wear quite a new face.[5] M.d'A. is at this moment gone to confer upon *legalities* with Martin. He will tell Martin, also, to dress up the Letter for M. de Coucy,[6] *according to Law*, which he will send for your approbation & signature, with all speed; the whole business being now necessarily at a stand.

We dined yesterday at Lady Crewe's Cottage.

M.d'A. left me with intention, if he had finished essential affairs in time, to go to Greenwich, to see dear Charles Parr, & my name's sakes.

---

[2] The Cambridge bookshop was opened by John Nicholson (1730–96). His shop was patronized by University students and those who could not afford his moderate charges were allowed free access to the books. After his death the business was continued by his son John (d. 1825), who in 1807 moved the shop from its original site in front of King's College to the corner of Trinity and St. Mary's Streets.

[3] See L. 709 n. 15.

[4] M. d'A arrived in England on either 28 or 29 April.

[5] For M. d'A's visit to Cambridge, see Ll. 776, 803 n. 6; for the difficulties over the sale of Camilla Cottage, see especially Ll. 776, 778, 781, 820.

[6] See L. 777 and n. 5.

Alex writes me word that Dr. Marsh,[7] 'my ┃ *uncle's friend*' has had an assembly, at which he invited all the *Fair Sex* of Cambridge, & to which He, Alex, was also a Guest. What a happy opportunity to display his gallantry! Mr. Chapman tells him he is to make the next Latin Speech, october 28.[8] upon the progress of medicine! Shall we ever be sick again? — —

Adieu, dearest Charles—I am sad—sad that my better half must soon again depart! I dread his being fastened upon!—

I will not grieve you by enquiries.!—for poor dear Rosette.— but it is not—& never can be forgetfulness!—

Friday Morn — —

Last night George came to me with the keys of the house— which he Beckey & Maria have finally quitted. But he puts in a claim, in the right, he says, of Beckey, to the gold Buttons in my dearest Father's shirt, worn at his last moments. I believe it is quite usual. She gave them, she says, to you.

The Family Seal Hetty & I have deemed right to offer to James—who has not *refused*—nor accepted—as yet. which delay I look upon as secret acceptance.

Pray tell Charles that M. d'A. has been warmly singing to me the praise of my name sake[9] — — and I hope You will allow *ME* to think M.d'A. is a judge of taste!— ┃

Many Thanks to C.P.B. for his warm-hearted Letter. Have you told him his minerals are from the Isle of Elba?

Lost, or Mislaid
In the Chelsea Library.

An asses' skin Memorandum Book, red morocco, with a gold border; & 4 leaves, long, narrow, old & shabby: but full of writing.

And

The *1ˢᵗ vol.* of *Tacitus Gronovie*—an Elzevirian type.[10]

---

[7] Herbert Marsh (1757–1839), B.A. (2nd Wrangler and Smith's Prize) 1779, M.A. 1782, B.D. 1792, D.D. 1808. At this time he was Lady Margaret Professor of Divinity (1807–39) and a F.R.S. (1807). He became Bishop of Llandaff (1816–19) and of Peterborough (1819–39). For his innovative contributions to the study of theology, see Venn.

[8] In fact, he was told in February.   [9] Rosetta d'Arblay (L. 757 n. 1).

[10] FBA refers to the first volume of *C. Cornelii Taciti Opera quae extant, J. Lipsii, . . . et selectis aliorum commentoriis illustrata. J. F. Gronovius recensuit, etc. 2 tom.* Apud

789A   [63 Lower Sloane Street,
                                              7 June 1814]
To Charles Burney

A.L. (Burney-Cumming), *n.d.*
Double sheet 8vo   3 pp.   *pmks*   7 JU 1814   T.P.P.U.   wafer
Addressed: Rev^d Dr. Burney, / Rectory House, / Deptford.

My dearest Carlos,
    The *Hist^y of France* is in the Catalogue, I now find; but not
under the Name of *Velly*, which belongs to it, but of so minor
an editor that I had never marked his Name, *Laureau.*[1]
    How unfortunate that the sale begins of so great a Drawing-
room day as next Thursday! when *all London* will be engaged,
either at the Palace, or in looking on![2] Is it impossible to let it
begin on *Friday*?
    What can have become of my dear Father's *20.000* volumes?
which, & UPWARDS, I find recorded repeatedly in various
Letters, & which appeared in the Catalogue?[3] *We* have not
5000 in All, counting every possible Volume, which I have done:
There are but *4601.* |
    In *partial* gifts, it is impossible to count more than a thousand,
including Your's, Sarah's, Fanny Raper's, Richard's, & M.d'A.'s
12 volumes, alex's 15. my 1.[4]
    In the Music Tracts there are perhaps, & probably, above
1000[5]—But all that will amount only to 7000. — — Where

Elzevirium: Amsterdam. First published in 1673, the work was reprinted many
times. CB's set was printed in Glasgow in 1743. It was sold (the first volume having
been found) on the eighth day of the sale for 8*s*.

789A. [1] See L. 787 n. 7.
    [2] On 8 and 9 June the Royal Family entertained the Russian Emperor, the
Prussian King, their parties, and the various foreign dignitaries that helped to
defeat Napoleon.   [3] See L. 808 n. 14.
    [4] For books bequeathed: CB Jr., L. 773 n. 6; Fanny Raper and SHB, L. 773
n. 11; M. d'A, L. 797 n. 7. The will also specified the books FBA and AA inherited. 'But such books in the [glazed book-case standing in the parlour of my
Apartments] as my Son Charles . . . may already possess I bequeath to my daughter
FRANCES D'ARBLAY, and my Grandson, ALEXANDER D'ARBLAY.' Richard Allen
Burney's bequest was peculiar, if a bequest at all. CB in his will intimated that he
had intended to leave his grandson his 'large Fol° MS. book of Voluntaries. . . .
But this Grandson has long out-grown such old-fashioned Studies and can play
extempore and compose for himself and others more modern and better music.
My Nephew, his father [CRB], may therefore do with the book what he pleases.'
    [5] The *Sale Catalogue* of 'The late Dr. Burney's Musical Library' numbered 822
items, many of them multi-volumed.

can be the rest? We must always lament that you did not let the *Catalogue* regulate the taking Away, & making the new one.

What answer has Mr. Leigh sent about the Prints?

I *earnestly* desire they may be sent to *me*, to make, as I proposed from the beginning a List before any Sale.

For the WORLD don't let them be sold ˡ in this miserable way, uncoun[ted] & unannounced. And, as they are not in the Catalogue, you may easily order them away, & let them be for Mr. White's sale, as there is time for mentioning them there.[6]

I thank you heartily for the money account, though I wish it more intelligible, I mean minute: & in particularly I do not understand why you class amongst Legacies *to be paid* the £1000 of Fanny Phillips, which, in the *Will*, is expressly called her *portion*.[7]

I conclude the Irish business to be now settled for proceeding, by your granting the £50, & the probate which Martin demanded; but I have not seen or heard from him.[8]

God bless you, my dear Carlucci. I hope to heaven you have had no new alarms, & that poor Rosette is amending.

Charlotte, who is with me, sends her love.

[6] L. 782 n. 13. [7] Fanny Raper was left £1,100 (L. 769 n. 2).
[8] L. 781.

DIARY ENTRIES (BERG)

Written on leaves torn from a Memorandum Book originally for 1811, redated by FBA: 1812

jeudi 20 Aout

                          Chelsea—

⌐visit Cathedral at Canterbury—
only one Traveller
Dine at Chatam   pass Gravesend—⌐ stop on some Common
clergyman—⟨stalls⟩—&c
Dr. Charles — — Has spent 3 y^{rs} in Parish
surprise—Joy—&c Lett^{rs} failing. &c
To Chelsea—George comes down—Beckey on stairs—
⌐In to Padre—on Sofa⌐—Chairs & Tables removed—
changed—weak—self-deserted for all effort yet re-animating by
starts in discourse—

vendredi 21 Aout

  ⌐James & *Sally*
Charles—
Fanny Raper—
Charlotte & *Clement*
write to Miss Planta⌐

samedi 22 Aout

⌐Letter Mrs. Lock—& Amine
Esther dear
Mrs. James & Sally⌐

dimanche 23 Aout

  ⌐3 James's & Sally⌐

lundi 24 Aout

                       ⌐Chelsea.

Charles & Rosette—well—& cordial
Caillebot—⟨De Bue⟩

507

consult Charles—
Alien office—
return—Mrs. Lock—Amine/Augusta /
written ⌐sent⌐ N° 3 to this Morning
Charlotte & Charlotta—& Clement⌐

mardi 25 Aout
⌐My Fredy—Amine & Augusta come again for all the Morning⌐

mercredi 26 Aout
Charles announces invitation to Pˢ of W.
⟨   ⟩ to Windsor
⌐Martin Clement Fanny Amelia Sally⌐

jeudi 27 Aout
⌐First Letter from Miss Planta
Charles comes with Rosette—Mʳˢ yᵍ Charles & Child—⌐

mardi 1 Septembre
⌐write to Mᵉ Beckerdorf
Esther dines with us at Charlottes
Archdeacon Mrs. George & Miss Baker come to me at Charlotte's Brings his Book
Edward comes to Tea⌐

mercredi 2 Septembre
⌐Go to Deptford with Alex
Fetched by Chaˢ's carriage charming Rectory Rosette well—⌐

jeudi 3 Septembre
⌐To Richmond with Charles—sweet Charlotte & her lovely dears—⌐
To Windsor Dine Mᵉ Beckerdorf—
Reception by Her Majesty—with Pˢ Sophia—deeply affected —reviving—delicacy goodness graciousness—
⌐sleep at sweet Charlotte Juniors—⌐

vendredi 4 Septembre
⌐Return to Rectory Day with Charles & wife & child
Archdeacon & Mrs. Geo. & Miss Baker pay us a long visit at
Charlottinas.⌐

jeudi 17 Septembre
⌐Return with Alex to d[ea]r Charlotte's⌐

vendredi 18 Septembre
⌐All to Esthers at Turnham Green—Edward accompanies—
& Charlotte—Clement & Alex & I all walk to Kensington—
meet there Charles & Rosette pleasant day, & walking &
chattery with dearest Etty—⌐

samedi 19 Septembre
⌐James—wife & Sally all come to dear Charlotte's.⌐

dimanche 20 Septembre
Go to Chapel Royal to hear Chaˢ preach excessively affected
by *that* place—& his being preacher
See dear James & family

Diary Entries (Berg)

Written on leaves torn from a Memorandum Book for the year 1814

Memorandums & Resolutions
At the Beginning of the Year 1814.

G⟨reat⟩ B⟨ookham⟩ Cobham, Surry.
Mrs. ⟨   ⟩. Frodsham, Ro⟨   ⟩s's Gardens ⟨   ⟩ Sᵗ
King's Road, Chelsea

⟨18⟩14

Saturday 1 January
1814.

This Month—of ever mournful recollection! was consigned
to correcting the press of The Wanderer, & ⟨numerous⟩ visits
to my dear Father with heart-harrowing disturbance from
the situation of Paris & my Heart's best treasure.

1) yet hesitate? ⟨   ⟩ I ordered a proper dress—& my sweet Mrs. Angerstein—to whom I sent Alex, undertook to help directing my apparel. She sent also to enquire of M. de la Châtre whether I might appear in deep Mourning—He answered to Mrs. Angerstein. (2) out that I had written ag^st the *Emigrés*! L^y C. indignantly mentioned my little essay for the Fr. Clergy—O, then, she cried, it was somebody else! But I'm glad I spoke out! A'nt *You*? because of this *eclaircissm^t* & jumped about the room crazily for 1/4 of an Hour.

L^y Crew. & D. Castries & Me de Gouvello. &c & D. Duras. & descent. crowd. vain waiting D^s Angouleme. Pr. Condé. Then The King. Desire to see him. position behind Chair: Gouvello—L^y Crewe. D. Duras. Presentations. alarm. D. Duras orders cards of name; & that all come behind the chair, & then walk off. Gives Eng. Ladies precedence sur tous les rapports—Buckingham's. Address. Affecting & charming reply in English. D. Duras recognized me in the interval—& sd. Mad^e d'Arblay ⟨   ⟩ je suis bien aise de vous voir ici! comment ça v-t-il? Comment vous trouvez vous?—&c I came forward quite chearful & relieved wh^n the K. had spoken so beautifully of England—& involuntarily began Les Anglois—mean^g to speak of their reconnoissance—but being named, the K. turned to me with such a sweet expression of pleasure & partial disposition to kindness.

Monday 25 April

My dear Boy left me, at 7 in the Morn—to return to Cambridge.

Thursday 28 April

This Day arrived from Paris the Friend & dearest Delight of my Existence.—well, though harrassed, gay, though worn with fatigue, and kind—oh kinder than Man ever was before him!—

Friday 29 April

Mon ami ⌈Breakfasted at Lady Harcourt's⌉ called on Amelia—James—Esther—Carbonneau

Sunday 1 May

Mon ami dined at Mr. Angersteins—& spent the Evening at Williams—

Tuesday 3 May

Mon ami Breakfasted at Lady Harcourts—whence I had a most kind Letter—

Tuesday 10 May

L'amico carissimo dined at Ld Harcourt's

Wednesday 11 May

Early dinner at Brumpton with Lady Crewe Mad^e de Gouvello, Miss Lloydd, Fanny Raper & Sarah—& my beloved.

Saturday 14 May

My amico went to our Alex, at Cambridge.   a terrible Letter through M. Murray preceded his journey.

Monday 16 May

Rec^d Sarah & Fanny Raper—

Tuesday 17 May

Wrote to Fredy & Amine.
My amico returned from Cambridge—enchanted with his visit & his Alexander.

Wednesday 18 May

Early dinner with Lady Crewe, at Brumpton, & Lady Douglas, Ly. Lambert, & L^y Dunnegal—&c

Thursday 19 May

Mon ami wrote an answer to Murrays Letter—severely dreadful—
We went together to sweet amelia—sad & overset—

Friday 20 May

Mon Ami went to Norbury Park & poor lost west Hamble—

Saturday 21 May

He returned—terrible conflicts about our cottage—

Sunday 22 May

He saw dear Amelia upon the subject—ah—

Monday 23 May

I received—alas! a Letter I deplore about our Cottage—&
my Life's First blessing received a summons from the Duc de
Luxembourg to be placed in the Corps du Garde—& He left
me to seek a Passport—

Tuesday 24 May

Nearly at Midnight my Heart's Partner left me again!—
Stranger to all happiness will be that Heart till he returns!—
I wrote, by his dear conveyance—to M. de La
3 weeks & 4 Days alone he stayed with me—

Wednesday 25 May

⟨ ⟩ I spent the melancholy day in business at the sad College, & in writing to my sweet Amelia—
Sarah & Fanny Raper both came with consoling kindness to
visit me in my sadness

Thursday 26 May

Again at the Mournful College!—& answering a Letter
more softening about our erst so dear Cottage—which we are
now threatened to lose, with nearly all the loved associations
that rendered it precious,

Friday 27 May

yet again at the College, & my papers—& a little chearing
myself with Sarah & Fanny in Sarah's apartments—

Saturday 28 May

A dreadful cold unjust & unkind Letter from one erst the
reverse of all that but thus changed from jealous envy of my
dear Father's favour!—ah, but what a Solace after wards, in a
Letter all reviving from Dover!

Sunday 29 May

rec^d his rough refusal of last offer of Irish 3^d fr^m James.
I answered—for ⟨1⟩
⟨I⟩ Re^d a few dear lines written at the Inn before departing
Lady Crew called

[*An entry on the right-hand Accounts page relating to Week 22, i.e. May 30–June 5*]

Wrote to Mon Ami—M. de La Châtre, Amine. Charles.
James Lady Harcourt. Esther. Mrs. Rishton. Mrs. Wadding-
ton. Alexander, Fredy. Me de Braamcamp. Charlotte. M^e
Beckerdorf.
Letters *from* Mon Ami from Calais—

[Monday] 30 [May]

⌐Wrote to Charles—& Amelia.
Rec^d—at length, a kind answer, of acceptance, from James.

[Tuesday 31 May]

Wrote to Lady Harcourt—M. de La Chatre—James—
W[*rote*]. to Mon Ami by M. de La Chatre—gave hist. ⟨   ⟩
for the sale argent: of alex's silence upon Exam. of new proposal
from Mr. W. L. not yet received.
Wrote to M. de La Châtre, enclosing No. 1. to Mon ami—

[Wednesday] 1 June

Wrote to Alexander—Fredy—Me de Braamcamp—Charlotte—and Madame Beckerdorf—

[Thursday 2 June]

Rec^d a sweet Letter from my Amine.

[Friday 3 June]

Wrote to Amine—Esther—

[Saturday 4 June]

Wrote to Mrs. Rishton—-& to Charles—

[Sunday 5 June]

Wrote to Mrs. Waddington—

Monday 6 June
⌐Received Esther—& Charlotte

Tuesday 7 June
My dear Charlotte spent the night, & this day with me—
Betty Blue & Amelia made a short visit.⌐

Wednesday 8 June

I went, by my gracious Queen's permission, to her palace,
to see the Emperor of Russia & the King of Prussia. I was first
honoured with a short audience of infinite sweetness by Her
Majesty, who, seeing me affected gave me Her hand—which I
kissed upon a bent knee. I was placed by Mᵉ Beckerdorf in the
Great Hall of entrance, which was filled with persons belonging
to the Household—amongst them I was recognized by my old
friend Genˡ Manners; & by Mrs. Ariana Egerton—& the Misses
Planta.—The Emperor of Russia has an air of the most perfectly native & unconscious goodness, unassuming, unpretending: his figure is tall, well made, & elegant; his face is modest,
intelligent, but rather russ, from the shortness of his nose, &
width of his mouth—nevertheless it is pleasing. But he looked,
I thought, embarrassed. The terrible Rˡ domestic difficulties
probably perplex if not alarm him in his conduct. His sister of
oldenbourg seems sensible, lively, intelligent, & seeking information with a zeal & sagacity that prove solid intentions of
turning it to profit. The King of Prussia engaged universal
approbation & sympathy by an air that spoke him still mourning his lost & loved & charming Wife, whose Aunt, our Queen,
he was visiting. And he interested all the more, by forming
around him, in this distant Country, a family group, of sons,
Brothers, Sister, Nephews & Cousins. All seeming to cling to
him with fond regard. The Emperor, in like manner, talked
with the most open pleasure with his Sister, who ran on in Russ
to him with unreserved freedom & vivacity. The Dˢˢ of York
appeared in the highest spirits & delight from the arrival of her
Brother, the K. of Prussia. Our Princess Charlotte was brilliant
yet more with youth & juvenile charms than with Diamonds,
though they were sparkling around her. The Dˢ of oldenbourg
was lavishly ornamented with them: I did not see Blucher nor

Platoff, to my great regret, but this was a Court only for Sovereigns & Princes & Princesses. The prince Regent alone was
away! all the Royal Dukes were there. The Queen I had the
high honour to see for a few minutes previously. Her Majesty
said 'What cold weather! I believe it is to compliment the
Russians!—' meaning That they may think our climate no
better than their own. I told her that to see Europe's Pacificator
had drawn me from my solitude. She answered that all applause
was certainly due to Alexander—for his forbearance & conduct:
but that we must not take the origin of the grand success from
its right owner Wellington. I loved her patriotism, which
warmed my heart: & most cordially joined in her opinion.

Thursday 9 June

⌜To Day the Sale opened of my dear & honoured Father's
miscellaneous Library! alas, what a dispersion of All that so
lately made his joy & pride!⌝

Friday 10 June

Drank Tea with my Brother James—& went with him to
view some of the Illuminations for Peace & the visit of The
Emperor & the K. of Prussia.

Sunday 12 June

⌜Wrote Mon Ami, enclosed to M. de La Châtre⌝
(2)

[Summary of visits, 6–12 June, at top of left-hand page]

Visits—to James. Queen's House to see The Emperor. Sarah.
—FROM Esther. Charlotte. Fanny Raper—Charles—

[Summary of letters, 6–12 June, at top of right-hand Accounts page]

Wrote letters to Lady Crew, James. Alexander. Amine—
Charles—Mon Ami. M. de La Chatre. Mrs. Waddington.
Fredy—
From—Charles—Lady Keith Mᵉ de Braamcamp:

Monday 13 June

⌜My dearest Alexander arrived from Cambridge⌝

Friday 17 June

⌐Alex. took my 3ᵈ Letter—sans reponse!—to M. de La Chatre—! —⌐

(3)

Saturday 18 June

⌐To day Finished the Sale of my beloved Father's miscellaneous Books—kind—dear—lamented Father!—⌐

[Summary of letters, 13–19 June, at top of right-hand Accounts page]

Wrote to Charles. Esther. Lady Harcourt. Amine. Lady Keith—Mon Amico. Mᵉ de Braamcamp:

From Mrs. Rishton—Esther: Mrs. Waddington:

Thursday 23 June

⌐Alex carried a 4. Letter to Day to M. de La Chatre—& heard that He only knew that M.d'A. had certainly arrived in Paris! but not by any Letter! He has promised to write to a common Friend for news Alas! how await it!—I am scarcely alive with heaviness or dread—though supported still by ultimate hope, nay *belief*, that mistake alone causes this⌐

(4) (1)

Friday 24 June

⌐Charles brought me the reviving tidings that his Son too, had a Letter from Mr. Finch, who has seen my heart's best Frᵈ in Paris! seen him in his own apartment—& walked with him to Le Palais du Corps Legislative.

Sunday 26 June

A 5ᵗʰ Letter went to my beloved This day, by a French officer, through Sarah—

(5)

[Summary of visits, 20–6 June, at top of left-hand page]

Visit Sarah—James—Blucher at covent G[arden] Theatre—

Visits from Esther. Charles. Mrs. Hoare. Miss Thrale—Fanny Raper

[*Summary of letters of week 27, i.e. 4–10 July, on right-hand Accounts page*]
Letters To Mon Ami, by M. Entwisle (7) Amine—Charles.
To—Lady Crewe Lady Liverpool—
From—Miss B. Planta—Amine—Charles—& from Mon
Amico Carissimo by the post. (5)

n ay 11 July
(8th) [letter sent]

Tuesday 12 July
Met Lady Rolle at The Miss Planta's; a sensible, polite &
very obliging woman. Received by the Duchess of Leeds most
affectionately—& presented to her delicately pretty Daughter—
Called on Me. de Braamcamp much melancholy talk upon poor
regretted M. de Narbonne!—Received by sweet Princess Eliza
most cordially—saw there sweet, also, Ps Augusta—Invited by
her most graciously to see the Fête from her R.H.s room—Ps
Sophia of Gloucester came in—Talked condescendingly to me,
& said Cecilia was her favourite Book in the whole World.

Thursday 14 July
Through M. de Thuisy
VII

[*Summary of visits, 11–17 July, at top of left-hand page*]
Visits To Mrs. Waddington—Miss B. Planta—Duchess of
Leeds—James—
To—The Queen's House—Made de Braamcamp—Lady
Crewe—M. de La Châtre—
From Miss F. Waddington. Fanny Raper—Sarah—Esther—

Tuesday 23 August
⌐2 sent by M. de La Châtre avec the power of Attorney to
mon ami.
10 11⌐

Wednesday 24 August
⌐Received a long Letter from Mon Ami through Miss B.
Planta⌐
I

Thursday 25 August

⌐Received a long Letter from Mon Ami through Miss B. Planta & L^y Rolle—

Heard my Letter through M. de La Chatre was just gone

My ever dear Mrs. Lock—& ever sweet Amelia came & spent the Morning with me in affectionate converse—all 3 avoiding the poor Cottage subject! I heard that William is gone to Paris!—whither George, & J Angerst[ein] are going!—⌐

Sunday 28 August

Arrived at Richmond, with my Alex—

Diary Entries (Berg)

Written on return to France, 1814, on a scrap of paper (5·7 × 3·2 to 3·4″)

(1)

Return to France 1814

Last Day at Richm^d

Fm. Charlottes—Ellerker—Baker
r^ms Furniture &c sweet Charlotte
In a Chaise from Mr. Herst—
1st to Turnham Green
   Hetty—Mr. B.

To Fanny Raper
   cadeaux—
      & leg[acy] remitted—
      My part

To James St!—
Found only Mrs. B—
Pay Wanderer & Camilla Bill
& Longman for Bind^gs
   & Mme—de Staël

Diary Entries (Berg)

Written on return to France, 1814, on a leaf of a Pocket Notebook of CB's for the year 1768

(2)

Return to France in 1814

Monday [7 November]
   visit Charles & Rosette
   print Porson

Tuesday [8 November]
   Call ⌐J[ames] Street⌐—at Greenwich
   Chaˢ Parr & Bicknell—
   Sleep Sydenham

Thursday [10 November]
   To Dover

Friday [11 November]
   Wrights—&c
   Cliff

Diary Entries

Written on leaves from a Notebook, 1814

Mᵐᵉ d'Henin

Mᵐᵉ de Maisonneuve

Mᵐᵉ de Maubourg

Mᵐᵉ Victor de Maubourg

Mᵐᵉ de Beauvau

Mᵐᵉ de Br

Mᵐᵉ de Segur

Mᵐᵉ de souza

Mᵐᵉ de Tessé

Mᵐᵉ de Germanie

Mᵐᵉ de Laval

Mᵐᵉ de Craon

Mᵐᵉ de Bourzac

Mᵐᵉ Meulan

Mᵐᵉ Guizot

Mᵐᵉ de Poix

Mᵐᵉ de Simiane

Mᵐᵉ de Tracy

Mᵐᵉ de La Fayette

Mᵐᵉ George de La Fayette

Mᵐᵉ de L'aube pîn

Mᵐᵉ Chastel

Mᵐᵉ Hix

Mᵐᵉ de Grandmaison

Mme Dupont de Nemours

Mme Rigaud

Mme de Scitivaux

Mme de Grivel

Mme Greffulh

Mme Meignen

Mme Bazille

Mme de Gassendi

Mme de Jarjaille

Mme Allart

Mme Bourdois

Mme Charle de Maubourg

Mme Bazille—la jeune

Mme Ragon

Mlle de La Jaqueminière

Mme Charier

Mme Mersenne

Mlle de Lally

Mlle de Beauvau

Mlle Gabrielle de Beauvau

Mlle D'Alpy

Mlle de Chavagnac

M. de la Bretonn⟨ière⟩

Mad^e de Chavagnac

Mrs. & Miss Potts

Mme de Boinville

Mrs. Turner, Cor⟨nelia⟩

Mme Pougens

Mme Hubert

Mrs. Gaudy

Mme de Montagu

Mme de Duras

Mme La Tour Du Pin

Mme Cherton

Mrs. Boyd

Mad^e Andreosi

Mad^e Malhouet

Mad^e de Gerando

Mad^e de Maurville

Mlle de Mortemart

Mme d'Yenville

Mme Heurre

Mme Larrey

Mlle Larrey

Preface to Appendix I

ON 25 July 1784 the newly married Mrs. Piozzi wrote to FB: 'Wish me Joy my dearest Miss Burney. . . . Wish me Joy then generously and like a Friend. . . . And be not sorry to see your Letter signed by the beloved and long desired name of your affectionate H: L: Piozzi' (*HFB*, p. 181). The next day, from Norbury Park, FB and SBP sent a letter (Barrett, Eg. 3690, f. 19) to their father: 'As to poor Mrs. Thrale—she only keeps retired till she finds who will seek her; she has no intention at all of *concealment*, but merely of present *obscurity*. . . . poor unhappy Mrs. Thrale! What a delusion she has to awake from! —alas!—'

Despite her misgivings, FB soon replied to Mrs. Piozzi's exuberant note, wishing her well but omitting all felicitations for her husband. In her turn Mrs. Piozzi reproached FB for this omission and told her 'to have done with all friendship, in which [Mr. Piozzi] has not his share!' On 10 Aug. 1784 FB wrote 'in a letter of ice' her protest against Mrs. Piozzi's reproaches. Three days later (13 Aug.) Mrs. Piozzi answered: 'Give yourself no serious concern, sweetest Burney. All is well, and I am too happy myself to make a friend otherwise; quiet your kind heart immediately, and love my husband if you love his and your H. L. Piozzi' (*Thraliana*, ii. 612–13 n.). Rejecting FB's further gestures of friendship, Mrs. Piozzi admitted to herself on 3 Sept. 1784: 'It hurts me to leave London without seeing Miss Burney tho' She has played a false & cruel part towards me I find— stimulating my Daughters to resist their natural Tenderness, & continue the steady refusal of a Consent wch alone c^d have saved my Life:—Very severe in Miss Burney, & very unprovok'd—I w^d not have serv'd *her so*' (*ibid.*, ii. 612). See also *HFB*, pp. 171– 82; Clifford, pp. 213–14, 216–17, 222–5; *Queeney Letters*, pp. 66–117.

APPENDIX I

FRENCH EXERCISE BOOK III
IN RETROSPECT: FBA ON MRS. THRALE

[*post* 13 mai 1804]

Je suis tellement en arriere pour mes thèmes que pour parvenir à l'instant actuel il faut que j'essaye d'ècrire quelques petites histoires: & je commencerai par vous dire, tant bien que mal, l'origine de ma liaison avec Me Thrale, et puis de[1] progrès de notre amitié, de ses suites, et, malheureusement, de sa fin! du moins quant à toute liaison, car mes souvenirs me feront toujours rester pour elle amie fidelle pour la servir, et pour la[2] vouloir du bien.

La premiere fois que je l'ai vue[3] c'étoit chez Mon cher Pere, dans la rue St. Martin. Enchantée avec mon Pere, qu'elle avoit connue dèjà[4] quelque tems, elle a voulu[5] voir toute sa famille, et surtout sa bibliotheque. Elle est venue,[6] donc, et l'Auteur le plus cèlèbre de nos jours et de notre pays a bien voulu[7] être de | la partie; mais je ne veux pas parler de lui comme auxiliare; je vous raconterai les honneurs[8] qu'il m'a fait separement. Elle étoit accompagnée par sa fille, Mlle Thrale, & par Mlle· Owen, une dame de la principalité[9] de Galles, ancienne amie de famille de Me· Thrale avant son marriage. Notre famille étoit re-unie pour les reçevoir, et nous avions aussi du monde.

J'avois dèjà beaucoup, mais beaucoup entendu parler de Me· Thrale, et je fus[10] assez curieuse de la voir. Elle m'a infiniment surprise; c'étoit de son erudition, de ses connoissances, de son instruction et de son esprit que j'avois entendu parler; mais à la voir on auroit cru que rien de tout cela ne l'avoit occupé: | elle fus[11] si

FBA designated her errors in the text by numbers, underscoring, and other symbols. At the bottom of each page in the Exercise Book, using the appropriate sign, she wrote out her emendations. For consistency we have underlined and numbered her intended changes.

[1] de *to* je parlerai du   [2] la *to* lui   [3] l'ai vue *to* l'a vis   [4] avec . . . connue dèjà *to* de . . . connu depuis   [5] a voulu *to* voulut   [6] est venue *to* vint   [7] a . . . voulu *to* voulut   [8] les honneurs *to* l'honneur   [9] la principalité *to* la principauté   [10] fus *to* étois   [11] occupé . . . fus *to* occupée . . . étoit

superbement mise, et parue[12] avec tant de soin, qu'on auroit imaginé
qu'elle n'eût guere penser[13] qu'à sa toilette, sur tout comme non
obstant tout ce qu'elle a[14] fait pour se decorer avec magnificence, il
n'y avoit nul[15] apparence du[16] goût, ni d'elegance naturel;[17] l'art
paru[18] partout, l'art, du travail, et surtout de la dèpense, de manière
que c'ètoit[19] evident que tout étoit l'effet d'une étude laborieuse; et
qui, par consequence, avoit demandée[20] beaucoup de tems et de
reflexion; car, dans ce genre, tout est travail, où la Nature ne donne
pas le secours du bon goût. Aussi ai-je trouvé, après, que tout-ce
qu'elle a le plus ambitioné[21] c'étoit de passer tout le monde de
surprise et d'admiration comme la dame la mieux parée de la
société. |

Ce n'est pas que cela sait ce qui lui a paru le plus admirable; au
contraire, elle avoit un haut mèpris pour ceux qui ne se donna[22] qu'à
la parure; mais comme pour l'esprit elle n'avoit point à ètudier, et
pour la celebritè rien à desirer, elle souhaité[23] a joindre au don de
la nature et à l'éclat de la reputation, l'apparence d'être mieux prise,
comme par chance, que ne fûrent toutes[24] les jolies petites maitresses
qui n'avoient à se vanter que de cela. Mais ici elle n'a jamais gagnée[25]
son but; on n'a rien vu qu'une vanité deplacée, et un dèpense
inutile. Elle avoit tant d'attraits, tant de titres à l'admiration, que
c'étoit bien, bien dommage qu'elle ne pouvoit[26] pas | enseigner à ses
desirs d'être borner[27] pas ses talens. Au reste, nous l'avons trouvé[28]
gaie, agréable, et spirituelle, quoique parlant un peu trop, et permet-
tant trop à ses yeux de chercher si elle étoit écoutée, et si de l'être
n'étoit pas bien assez pour être admirée. Moi, j'étois toujours,
comme à l'ordinaire, dans un coin n'osant jamais parler, n'y pensant
même pas, et jamais marqué d'etre[29] de la société, que quand[30] il
étoit question d'offrir quelque petite[31] service qui pourroit être fait[32]
en silence. M^e· Thrale, non obstant, m'auroit bien reconnu,[33] car
elle nous a tous bien remarquée, et ses yeux étoient toujours à
parcourir la salle, à tout regarder, et à tout examiner. |

---

[12] parue *to* parée   [13] n'eût guere penser *to* n'avoit guere pensé   [14] a
to avoit   [15] nul *to* nulle   [16] du *to* de   [17] naturel *to* naturelle
[18] paru *to* paroissoit   [19] que c'ètoit *to* qu'il étoit   [20] par consequence
. . . demandée *to* consequent . . . demandé   [21] ambitioné *to* ambitionée
[22] donna *to* donnent   [23] souhaité a *to* souhaitoit   [24] ne fûrent toutes *to*
toutes   [25] gagnée *to* atteint   [26] pouvoit *to* pût   [27] borner *to* bornés
[28] trouvé *to* trouvée   [29] marqué d'etre *to* remarquée faisant partie
[30] quand *to* comme   [31] petite *to* petit   [32] fait *to* rendu   [33] reconnu
to reconnue

Appendix I

Ce 27 mai [1804]

Elle avoit très peu, ou plûtot point de retenu[34] dans ses examins,[35] qu'elle a fait[36] pour le plaisir de s'amuser en cherchant quelques nouvelles idées, qu'elle croyoit pouvoir trouver sur chaque individu, en développant par leur traits ou leur phisionomies ce qui pouroit passer dans leur esprit. Quelque fois elle a divené[37] à merveille les caractères, les pensées, les projets de tout-ce qu'il l'environnoit; et ses heureuse instances l'a bien dedommager[38] de mille et mille meprises fait en autres[39] circonstances: car toujours elle se ressouviné[40] de ces succès, et toujours elle a oublie ceux qui ont manqué. Ce qu'elle a pensé de moi, je ne l'ai jamais sû; ainsi j'imàgine c'étoit[41] peu de chose. |

Cette visite ma mere a retourné[42] sans prendre personne de la famille avec elle si ce n'est pas[43] mon plus jeune frere, son propre Enfant, Richard, alors très jeune, gai, spirituelle, comique, et beau comme un Ange. Moi je ne l'ai revue aucun part dèpuis, pour bien[44] long tems, et je n'avois pas la moindre idée de jamais former avec elle aucune liaison particuliere. Combien peu ai-je prevu une amitié de sa part la plus confiante, de la mienne la plus fidelle qu'à[45] jamais été excitée ou eprouvée de part et d'autre! —

Ce fut bien, je crois, une année après ceci avant que je l'ai[46] revue. Quel jour memorable pour moi que celui-là[47] de notre seconde entrevue! c'étoit à Stretham, à la terre et à la villa de son epouse. |

Dèja Me Thrale étoit dans le secret du petit livre Evelina, qui avoit été imprimé plusiers[48] mois, & qu'une Dame avoit recommandé à[49] Dr Johnson lui meme, qui lui-meme l'avoit nommé à Me Thrale, et Me Thrale, par un hazard le plus singulier dans le[50] monde, avoit prié mon Pere de le lui acheter, et de le lui apporté[51] à Stretham: Il l'a fait,[52] avec une joie inexprimable, quoique melé avec la[53] crainte. Il n'avoit su lui meme que depuis peu que sa fille étoit[54] l'auteur; imaginez donc, car je ne puis pas essayer de vous le decrire, | ce qu'il doit avoir eprouvér[55] d'emotion quand un pareil[56]

---

[34] retenu *to* retinue   [35] examins *to* examens   [36] a fait *to* faisoit
[37] divené *to* deviné   [38] instances l'a . . . dedommager *to* examples l'avoient
. . . dedommagée   [39] fait en autres *to* faites d'autres   [40] ressouviné *to* ressouvenoit   [41] c'étoit *to* que c'étoit   [42] Cette visite ma mere a retourné *to* Ma mere rendit cette visite   [43] si ce n'est pas *to* excepté   [44] aucun . . . pour bien *to* aucune . . . pendant   [45] qu'a *to* qui ait   [46] l'ai *to* l'aye
[47] celui-là *to* celui   [48] plusiers *to* depuis   [49] à *to* au   [50] dans le *to* du
[51] apporté *to* apporter   [52] l'a fait *to* le fit   [53] melé avec *to* melée de
[54] étoit *to* en étoit   [55] eprouvér *to* eprouvé   [56] un pareil *to* une pareille

commission lui avoit été donné![57] quand il a trouvé que la celebre
M[e.] Thrale desiroit de le lire, & que c'étoit Dr. Johnson lui meme
qui lui avoit[58] chargé de le chercher! Je suis etonné[59] qu'il a[60] pu se
taire un instant quant à[61] l'heureuse auteur — mais il voulut
premierement savoir l'opinion que M[e.] Thrale pourroit former du
livre. . . . Eh bien, tout etant favorable, et tout etant decouverte[62]
par mon Pere enchanté, Me Thrale prioit mon Pere, qui la quitta
pour aller me trouver à Chesington, ou j'étois avec mon meilleur
ami, M. Crisp, de revenir, chemin fassant,[63] | et de lui amener sa
fille, pour diner, et pour rester la nuit. Quel jour que ce jour là pour
moi! C'étoit comme le commencement d'une nouvelle existence.
Jamais avant ce jour m'étoit il-passé par la tête que j'étois regardée
par qui que ce soit, jamais n'ai-je eu le[64] moindre inquiétude sur ce
qu'on pourroit penser de moi, car jamais n'ai-je imaginer qu'aucun
observation ne fût[65] dirigé contre moi. Ce jour ci j'étois bien sure du
contraire; mon secret étoit connu de Me Thrale, . . . peutêtre par[66]
toute la maison, — j'esperoit[67] bien que non, mais je ne pouvois être
sans des doutes et solicitudes: — — quoique tout occupé par[68] la
certitude que M[e.] Thrale étoit de la[69] comité secret, que j'avois à
peine tems de penser à aucun autre.[70] |

Eh bien, me voilà arrivé.[71] La villa de M. Thrale étoit assez jolie,
mais ni large[72] ni belle ni magnifique. Elle doit l'avoir[73] appartenu
avant qu'il jouissoit[74] d'une si grande fortune: ou, plutot, je crois
qu'elle ètoit à son pere, qui fût le veritable brassier,[75] M. Thrale son
fils ayant été toujours élévé comme un homme du premier rang,
finissant son education à l'université, & apres faissant le tour de
l'Europe avec un precepteur. Aussi, je me rappelle à present qu'il
avoit effectivement beaucoup ajouté à la maison, qui, d'origine,
n'avoit que de très petites chambres: il bâtit une apartement pour
salle à manger,[76] qu'il avoit decorè[77] avec tous les ouvrages de
Hogarth; un salle de compaignie, qui étoit ornée avec | les meilleures
gravures de Strange, et quelque autres digne de leur faire des

---

[57] donné *to* donnée   [58] lui avoit *to* l'avoit   [59] etonné *to* etonnée
[60] a *to* ait   [61] quant à *to* sur   [62] decouverte *to* decouvert   [63] fassant
to faisant   [64] le *to* la   [65] imaginer qu'aucun . . . ne fût *to* imaginé
qu'aucune . . . fût   [66] par *to* de   [67] esperoit *to* esperois   [68] occupé
par *to* occupée de   [69] de la *to* du   [70] tems . . . aucun autre *to* la tems . . .
personne autre   [71] arrivé *to* arrivée   [72] large *to* grande   [73] l'avoir
to lui avoir   [74] jouissoit *to* jouêt   [75] fût . . . brassier *to* étoit . . .
Brasseur   [76] apartement pour salle à manger *to* salle à manger   [77] decorè
to decorée

compagnons;[78] et une bibliotheque charmante, large, simple, commode, et fourni[79] de ses trèsors de literature à la[80] choix du D[r.] Johnson, que M. Thrale avoit eu le bon sens, la modestie, et le bon goût de prier de lui choisir et acheter des livres à son grè: commission delicieuse pour cet admirable homme, pour qui C'étoit un vrai[81] fête. . . . Des offices, aussi, innombrables avoient été ajouté[82] à la maison, surtout un Dairy de marbre entiere,[83] pour les vaisseaux, pour le plafond, pour les murs, et pour le parquet,[84] . . . c'etoit un endroit à montrer à tout le monde, extremment agrèablé et frais. |

Ce 3. Juin, 14. prairial

Me voilà, donc, arrivée, et quelle fût ma reception! avec quelle bonté j'étois accuelli![85] Me Thrale s'avança à[86] me prendre la main avec un air qui a bien demontré que son parti fût[87] pris de faire la conquête de mon coeur, et Dr. Johnson avec des manieres qui m'ont assurées[88] que déjà il étoit resolu de m'abandoner, de sa façon, le sien. M[lle.] Thrale s'étoit recueilli,[89] pour tout observé[90] en silence, mais sans jamais sortant[91] de la chambre, et sans me perdre jamais de vu.[92] M. Thrale étoit poli, attentif, aimable; et il n'y avoit pas même un domestique qui n'a pas[93] marqué, par des attentions d'un respect peu commun, combien tout le monde étoit preparé avant mon arrivé, de[94] me faire honneur, et de me[95] fêter. |

Je passe par les détails de ce[96] journée pour continuer mon histoire avec Me Thrale. M'ayant comblé de toute espece de bonté et d'obligience jusqu'au dejeuné[97] le lendemain, alors, dès qu'il étoit question de notre depart, elle a prié[98] mon Pere de me laisser jusqu'à son retour à la fin de la semaine; priere secondé[99] par M. Thrale, à moitié prononcé[1] par M[lle.] sa fille, et tout à fait enforcé,[2] avec une energie invincible, par le Docteur Johnson. Mon cher pere, qui ne souhaitoit rien au monde tant que de me voir accuelli[3] par des Gens

[78] digne . . . faire des compagnons; et *to* dignes . . . tenir; et compagnie   [79] large . . . fourni *to* grande . . . fournie   [80] à la *to* au   [81] un vrai *to* une vraie   [82] ajouté *to* ajouter   [83] un Dairy de marbre entiere *to* une laiterie toute en marbre   [84] pour les vaisseaux, pour le plafond, pour les murs, et pour le parquet *to* les vaisseaux, le plafond, les murs, et le parquet   [85] étois accuelli *to* fus accuellie   [86] à *to* pour   [87] fût *to* étoit   [88] assurées *to* assuré   [89] recueilli *to* recuellie   [90] observé *to* observer   [91] mais . . . sortant *to* sortir   [92] vu *to* vue   [93] n'a pas *to* n'ait   [94] arrivé, de *to* arrivée, à   [95] de me *to* me   [96] ce *to* cette   [97] dejeuné *to* dejeuner   [98] étoit . . . a prié *to* fût . . . priâ   [99] secondé *to* secondée   [1] prononcé *to* prononcée   [2] enforcé *to* appuyée   [3] accuelli *to* accuellie

de Lettres, étoit d'un enchantement qui n'a pas de nom, et moi . . . etonnée, embarrassée, flattée, effrayée, et charmée . . . que d'emotion, que de plaisir, et surtout que de surprise n'ai-je pas eprouvé.[4] |

Dans les trois jours que je passai ici[5] dans ce tems, je jouai d'un bonheur complette;[6] M⁻ᵉ Thrale me traita avec les egards flatteusses qui annonça[7] un veritable desir de me plaire, et de gagner[8] mon amitié en me montrant une confiance et une partialité qui ne pouvoient naiquit[9] que d'un estime[10] marqué dont elle étoit decidée, dès notre premier entrevue, chez elle de moi[11] croire digne — Jugez, mon ami, si elle ne m'a pas trouvé[12] reconnoissante! Hors de ma famille, et d'un très petit, très etroite[13] circle d'amis, à peine étoit[14] connue, à peine avois-je jamais parler[15] à qui que ce soit du moins excepté quand le[16] chance m'avoit fait voir quelqu'un — tête à tête, — chose extremmement rare . . . |

Mais à present, quel[17] difference! on m'addressoit[18] à chaque minute, rien n'étoit discuté sans demander mon avis, rien n'étoit decider,[19] sans que j'eusse prononcé mes opinion. J'étois forcée de parler, et tout ce que j'ai dit étoit non seulement ecouté, mais respecté. Il n'y a pas de phrase pour décrire le millieme parti[20] des distinctions, des egards, des flatteries dont j'étois l'objet. C'étois[21] vraiment pour moi une existence nouvelle — et le premier à diriger tous ces honneurs ce fut le Docteur Johnson. Déjà il avoit beaucoup aimer[22] mon pere — avec quel plaisir a-t-il saisi cette occasion de lui montrer son amitié! |

Mais comment est-ce que je ne puis pas m'abstinir de parler tant de Dʳ· Johnson quand c'est de M⁻ᵉ Thrale que je voudrois parlé?[23] . . . Quand mon pere vint me chercher, des solicitations generales-lui furent faits pour que je serois permis[24] de retourner bien tot passer une semaine à Streatham. Cela fut bientôt accordé, et c'etoit[25] arrangé qu'il m'y rammena[26] à sa premiere visite. Neanmoins, M⁻ᵉ Thrale m'avoit tant[27] prise en gré, qu'elle ne pouvoit pas attendre

[4] eprouvé *to* eprouvés   [5] ici *to* là   [6] complette *to* complet   [7] annonça *to* annonçoient   [8] et de gagner *to* et non de m'examiner, mais de gagner   [9] naiquit *to* naître   [10] un *to* une   [11] premier . . . de moi *to* premiere de me   [12] trouvé *to* trouvée   [13] etroite *to* etroit   [14] étoit *to* étois-je   [15] parler *to* parlé   [16] le *to* la   [17] quel *to* quelle   [18] m'addressoit *to* s'addressoit à moi   [19] decider *to* decidé   [20] le millieme parti *to* la millieme partie   [21] C'étois *to* C'étoit   [22] avoit beaucoup aimer *to* aimoit beaucoup   [23] parlé *to* parler   [24] faits pour que je serois permis *to* faites pour qu'il me permêt   [25] c'etoit *to* il fut   [26] rammena *to* rameneroit   [27] tant *to* tellement

ce periode,[28] et j'eus d'elle une lettre charmante pour me demander de me tenir prête pour retourner deux jours après que je l'avois quitté.[29] Alors elle vint elle-meme de Streatham me chercher. Et, alors, elle me montra encore plus de partialité que jamais; elle me combla de toute sorte[30] de bonté. |

A cette seconde visite une liaison étoit formée qui dura bien bien d'années,[31] et qui devroit durer encore. M^e· Th. n'attendoit[32] pas à me connoître davantage pour se lier avec moi d'une amitié complette: c'étoit une obligeance, un desir, ou plutôt un besoin de me plaire, qui bientôt devenoit[33] une espece de besoin de me voir toujours auprès[34] d'elle: et c'étoit une estime si decidée, qu'elle prenoit en moi une confiance sans limites, sans bornes quelconque,[35] tout m'étoit dit, et non seulement avec une franchise sans reserve, mais avec insistence de savoir mes idées, mes opinions, egalement sur les evenemens dejà passées,[36] et sur les plans, les projets pour l'avenir. |

Dès ce temps, elle insista que je comptasse Streatham comme un autre chez moi, et, en effet c'étoit bientôt le seul où elle pouvoit endurer de me voir établi.[37] Elle étoit presque offenser,[38] et tout à fait chagrin[39] au moindre mot de la quitter, et à peine pouvois-je, sans la rendre malheureuse, echapper pour passer même une semaine de suite à la maison paternelle. Tant d'agrèmens s'unit à[40] me rendre Streatham agrèable, que cette extreme partialité n'auroit été qu'un source de bonheur, si elle ne m'avoit pas separé de la premiere amie de mon ame — la soeur de toute ma tendresse, de mon coeur entier! — car quant à mon cher pere, j'étois toujours sure de la voir une fois par semaine, et cela de la maniere la plus gaie et la plus agrèable |

Ce 10 Juin.

et[41] mes autres freres et soeurs & ma famille et mes amis, je les voyois de temps en temps aussi: mais jamais je n'ai pu me passer d'elle — jamais ai-je[42] trouvé ce que c'étoit[43] de me contenter de ne pas la voir! ... Hélas — Hélas! ... à cela près, Streatham étoit pour moi un paradis terrestre. M^e· Th. étoit d'un caractère rare, et difficile à connoître, mais d'une humeur si gaie, des[44] manières si carressantes,

---

[28] ce period *to* cette epocque   [29] quitté *to* quittée   [30] toute sorte *to* toutes sortes   [31] d'années *to* des années   [32] n'attendoit *to* n'attendit   [33] devenoit *to* devint   [34] auprès *to* près   [35] quelconque *to* quelconques   [36] passées *to* passés   [37] établi *to* établie   [38] offenser *to* offensée   [39] chagrin *to* chagrine   [40] s'unit à *to* se reunissoient pour   [41] et *to* quant à   [42] ai-je *to* je n'ai   [43] c'étoit *to* c'étoit que   [44] gaie, des *to* gaie, avec

d'un[45] discours si franc, qu'on imaginoit dévellopper tout ce qu'elle étoit dans un quart d'heure. Elle aimoit infiniment la plaisanterie, et elle étoit plein[46] d'esprit, et remplie de connoissances. Elle savoit le latin comme un vrai savant et l'Italiene et l'espagnol et le françois parfaitment, pour les lire ou écrire, quoique pas[47] bien pour les parler, quant à la prononciation. |

Elle m'arranga[48] une chambre à coté de sa Dressing room[49] pour que nous puissions[50] toujours être près l'une de l'autre; cette chambre me fût appropriée, même dans mon absence, et elle me donna les clefs des armoirs,[51] &c, qu'elle ne voulût jamais me permettre de lui laisser quand je m'en allais. C'étoit une chambre des plus large et commode[52] de la maison, mais jamais elle ne m'a permis de l'offre[53] à qui que ce fût, même quand la maison fût[54] remplie de monde. M. Thrale me presenta d'une[55] pulpitre, qu'il causa de m'avoir faite, à[56] des ordres particuliers, & qui m'étoit assigné pour ecrire à Streatham, car il avoit un grand desir que j'ecrivisse à Streatham ... chose, neanmoins, de toute impossibilité, si peu j'avis du[57] temps à moi meme. J'en ai trouvé, cependant, pour | écrire à mon ange! — à Elle toujours j'ai consacré tout-ce que j'avois de temps pour moi même. Mais la toilette fut,[58] alors, une chose très serieuse: comme M^e· Th. aimoit beaucoup la parure, tout le monde chez elle se paré[59] beaucoup: et cela demanda[60] pas mal de temps. Surtout pour moi, qui avoit toujours bien de[61] choses à arranger, à faire, à changer tous les jours, outre le temps de m'abbiller. Mais ce n'étoit pas du temps perdu; car alors elle s'est montée dans sa Dressing room, pour[62] causer au travers les[63] portes, si nous etions à faire nos toilettes, où de chambre, en chambre[64] les portes ouvertes, si je fus[65] à travailler. Si par hazard elle fût[66] forcée d'aller en ville sur[67] des affaires, je n'étois pas plus à moi pour cela; | Mais ce sera un autre histoire que ma maniere d'être avec la Dr Johnson. &c.

Ce n'étoit pas seulement chez elle que M^e Th. voulu que nous

---

[45] d'un *to* un   [46] plein *to* pleine   [47] pas *to* moins   [48] m'arranga *to* m'arrangea   [49] sa Dressing room *to* son Cabinet de toilette   [50] puissions *to* pussions   [51] armoirs *to* armoires   [52] large et commode *to* larges et des commodes   [53] l'offre *to* l'offrir   [54] fût *to* étoit   [55] presenta d'une *to* fit présent d'un   [56] qu'il causa de m'avoir faite, à *to* pour lequel il avoit donné   [57] avis du *to* avois de   [58] fut *to* étoit   [59] paré *to* paroit   [60] demanda *to* ne demandoit   [61] de *to* des   [62] s'est montée dans sa Dressing room, pour *to* montoit dans son Cabinet pour de toilette   [63] les *to* des   [64] de chambre en chambre *to* d'une chambre à l'autre   [65] fus *to* étois   [66] fût *to* étoit   [67] sur *to* pour

fumes[68] ensembles; elle ne faisoit nul parti, elle n'iroit nul[69] part, sans le plus vif desir de me faire l'accompagner. Et toujours elle eut[70] soin de me faire reçu[71] avec et de même que Mlle Th. qui, loin d'être jalouse, faisoit toujours de son coté tout-ce qu'elle a pu[72] pour m'engager de même. Elle étoit froide de nature, peu demonstrative, ou plutôt glaciale; mais elle conçevoit[73] pour moi une haute estime, qu'elle a fidellement conservée jusqu'à cette heure: et avec cela, quand j'étois gaie, elle m'aimoit à la folie. O comme elle étoit toujours dans l'enchantement quand on l'a[74] faisoit rire! |

Et cela m'a[75] arrivé à plaisir, car je n'avois que[76] bavarder en disant tout ce que me passa[77] par la tête pour l'amuser; tout ce qui étoit bizarre lui plaissoit hors de tout[78] expression; et moi, dans ce temps, j'avois souverainement le don de la bizarrerie, de la gaiété grostesque, burlesque, et ridicule. Et comme par caractere elle étoit serieuse, elle trouva[79] rarement de quoi s'amuser elle même, quoique toujours de quoi s'occuper, et de quoi faire des progrès en toutes sortes d'etudes; ainsi, elle avoit une espece de besoin d'être secouer[80] par les plaisanteries d'autrui: et quand cela lui arrivera[81] pour moi, du moins, elle étoit comme folle de plaisir, et me devenoit devoué[82] comme si elle me devoit le plus singulier d'obligation.[83]

Egalement bon pour moi étoit aussi[84] M. Th. qui se mettoit toujours en avant pour decider mon pere de[85] me laisser aller avec eux partout. À Brighthelmstone, j'étois[86] de la partie, deux ou trois fois; à Bath de même; de même à Tunbridge. Et à Londres, ils ne faissoient aucune[87] engagement, presque, dans laquelle[88] je n'étois pas inclue. Toutes[89] leurs connoissances devinoient les miennes; toutes leurs amis me montroient de confiance et d'estime;[90] toutes les lettres que M[e] Th. recevoient me nomma,[91] et avec cette espece d'interêt qui marquoit la certitude que de me montrer des egards

---

[68] voulu que nous fumes *to* vouloit que nous fussions   [69] nul parti, elle n'iroit nul *to* aucune partie, elle n'alloit nulle   [70] eut *to* avoit   [71] reçu *to* recevoir   [72] a pu *to* pouvoit   [73] conçevoit *to* avoit conçu   [74] l'a *to* la   [75] m'a *to* m'est   [76] que *to* qu'a   [77] que me passa *to* qui me passoit   [78] tout *to* toute   [79] trouva *to* trouvoit   [80] secouer *to* secouée   [81] arrivera *to* arrivoit   [82] devoué *to* devouée   [83] me devoit le plus singulier d'obligation *to* m'avoit eu la plus grande obligation   [84] Egalement bon pour moi étoit aussi *to* J'ai trouvé egalement bon pour moi aussi   [85] de *to* à   [86] étois *to* ai été   [87] faissoient aucune *to* faisoient presque aucun   [88] presque, dans laquelle *to* dans lequel   [89] Toutes *to* tous   [90] de confiance et d'estime *to* de la confiance et de l'estime   [91] nomma *to* nommoient

étoit cru être le[92] moyen de lui plaire. Enfin, en tout, c'est[93] bien impossible d'imaginer plus des attentions, des obligeances,[94] de respecte, d'amitié, et d'agrémens que je n'ai[95] regulierement | trouvé dans ce sejour, et par tout ailleurs où j'ai accompagné M^e· Th.

La gaiété de cette liaison étoit[96] bientot interrompue, quoique sa tendresse n'étoit[97] que reservée par le malheur qui l'attaqua. M. Th. étoit[98] saisi d'une apoplexie, qui menaça premierement ses Jours, et après sa raison. Une partie étoit[99] formée pour Streatham, où étoient priés les demoiselles Streatfield & Brown, les deux favourites de la maison, le jeune et gai capitaine Fuller, Mr. Seward, et je crois quelques autres. M^e Th. m'ecrivît le terrible countretemps qui arrivît,[1] mais me chargea de ne rien dire, & de n'avoir pas l'air de rien savoir. M. Th. avoit vu ses medicins, qui avoient prononcés que l'attaque étoit très peu alarmante, et pouvoit bien tot passer, s'il suivoit leurs ordonnances. |

Ce 17 Juin

Mais helas il n'a jamais voulu les suivre; et cette attaque, que les saignées et les medicines auroient bientot fait passé,[2] n'étoit que le precurseur d'une autre, par son mepris total de regime, regime, qui seul pouvoit[3] l'avoir retabli; de sorte qu'attaque suivit attaque, et sa santé, ses jouissances, son bonheur, et finalement sa vie furent les sacrifices d'un entetement de ce faux mepris du danger. Dès ce temps, beaucoup d'anxieté se mela dans tout-ce que nous fessons,[4] et dans tout-ce que nous avions le projet de faire; mais ce ne fut que meler, puisque nous ignorimes le vrai[5] etat des choses, et moi je ne doutois pas pour long tems[6] que chaque attaque n'étoit pas[7] la derniere, et que chaque convalescence n'étoit pas[7] une guerisonne[8] complette. |

Dans[9] tout ce temps, M^e· Th. avoit l'air de m'aimer tous les jours davantage; ou plutôt toutes les heures, car c'étoit une espece de passion, puisque elle ne savoit pas ce que c'étoit que la tranquilité si je ne fus pas à son côté. Elle me confit toutes ses soucies,[10] toutes

---

[92] étoit cru être le *to* été reconnu comme un   [93] c'est *to* il est   [94] plus des attentions, des obligeances *to* plus attentions, obligeances   [95] n'ai *to* n'en ai   [96] étoit *to* fut   [97] n'étoit *to* ne fut   [98] étoit *to* fut   [99] étoit *to* fut   [1] arrivît *to* étoit arrivé   [2] passé *to* passer   [3] pouvoit *to* eut pu   [4] fessons *to* fessions   [5] ignorimes le vrai *to* ignorions le veritable   [6] et moi je ne doutois pas pour long tems *to* et pendant long tems moi je ne doutois pas   [7] n'étoit pas *to* ne fut   [8] guerisonne *to* guerison   [9] Dans *to* Pendant   [10] ne fus . . . confit toutes ses soucies *to* n'étois . . . confioit tous ses soucis

ses craintes, toutes ses chagrin.[11] Elle ne sembla reçevoir de la consolation qu'avec[12] moi. Toujours gaie dans la société, elle devint[13] presque toujours la proie d'inquiétudes[14] et des alarmes en s'eloign-ante[15] du monde: et ce fût alors que j'ai aprise par mon[16] propre experience combien peut[17] etre separé l'un de l'autre le bonheur et la gaiété. La maladie de son mari n'étoit pas, à beaucoup près, tout ce qui l'acabla; elle aimoit,[18] ou plutot, elle l'estimoit en[19] bien bon ami, bien bon maître de sa maison, de ses Enfans, de ses domes-tiques, et d'elle même: Mais elle n'avoit point pour lui ou tendresse ou gout.[20] Je ne soupçonrai pas Cela, neanmoins, à l'epoch ou[21] je parle; je ne l'imaginai même pas: quoique j'ay bien pris garde que la moitié de ses chagrins roulerent[22] sur ses craintes que son mari fesoit quelque erreur dans ses affaires, qu'il ne pourroit plus les regler, et qu'il pourroit bien deviner le dupe de quelque friponnerie d'autrui, ou de quelque manque de jugement de lui-meme. Mais cela, je l'ai tout vu comme appartenant à son[23] consideration person-nelle, qui ne pourroit pas[24] supporter l'idée de voir ce change[25] dans un homme jusqu'à là[26] renommé pour son jugement et sain[27] con-duite. Et quand je l'ai vue inquiete sur la fortune, j'ai pensé de[28] ses Enfans, et tout m'a paru aussi respectable que naturel. Ce fut bien long temps après que j'ai su[29] la verité de ses sentimens à cet egard. O comme je m'interressoit[30] vivement de tout-ce qu'elle me disoit de ses souffrances, et de tout-ce que j'en ajouté[31] par mes propres idées de ce qu'ils doivent[32] être! Je l'aimoit[33] avec la plus vive et la plus sincere amitiès, et je m'abandonnée[34] à elle pour soulager ses peines en particuliere,[35] et pour partager ses jouissances en general et en public. Souvent m'a-t-elle[36] rendu souverainement triste, quand je l'ai vu[37] elle meme, tout de suite après la conference

[11] toutes ses chagrin *to* tous ses chagrins qu'avec *to* sembloit . . . consolation que de *to* des [15] s'eloignante *to* s'eloignant ma [17] peut *to* peuvent l'aimoit [19] en *to* comme un pour lui ni tendresse ni gout roulerent *to* j'aye . . . rouloient pouvoit [25] change *to* changement *to* sa [28] de *to* à [31] de . . . j'en ajouté *to* à . . . j'y ajoutais [33] l'aimoit *to* l'aimois liere *to* particulier [36] m'a-t-elle *to* elle m'a

[12] sembla . . . la consolation [13] devint *to* devinoit [14] d' [16] j'ai aprise par mon *to* j'apris par [18] l'acabla; elle aimoit *to* l'acabloit; elle [20] point pour lui ou tendresse ou gout *to* [21] l'epoch ou *to* l'epoque dont [22] j'ay . . . [23] son *to* sa [24] ne pourroit pas *to* ne [26] jusqu'à là *to* jusque-là [27] sain [29] ai su *to* sus [30] m'interressoit *to* m'interressois [32] ils doivent *to* elles devoient [34] m'abandonnée *to* m'abandonnois [35] particu-[37] vu *to* vue

qui m'avoit attristé, gaie et enjouée elle-meme comme s'il n'y étoit de rien.[38]

De cette maniere, au milieu de toutes ces inquietudes, et des scenes les plus effrayantes du danger,[39] nous allâmes aux bals, aux spectacles, aux assemblées, comme si tout étoit à merveille; car les attaques de M. Th. furent ordinairement très courtes, et il fût le premier de[40] nous indiquer les amusemens que nous devions prendre, et qu'il voudroit[41] bien partager. Il n'avoit qu'une longue maladie tout le tems; et[42] cela fut à Southwark à sa propre maison, où est le[43] braisserie; et l'attaque qui l'a précédé, ou amené[44] lui arriva le soir meme ou plus de cinquants personnes furent invités[45] à souper. Cette attaque fut des plus terrible imaginable;[46] il sembla mort long tems — mais le fameux Dr. Jebbe le re-sussita, et l'auroit surement rétabli, si'il auroit[47] voulu se soumettre à ses ordonnances. Je me rappelle qu'alors les domestiques fûrent frappés de ce que je ne voyois pas, l'indifference de M^e Th. pour son mari; et l'un d'eux, le Butler m'a dit d'un air indigné, à mon eternel[48] surprise, "Mad^e, quand M. Th. fut d'avoir[49] une autre attaque, M^e· a souris! —[50] j'étois très indignée moi-même de[51] cette assertion, et comme cet[52] domestique compta bientot de[53] se retirer de la maison, je l'ai cru une calomnie de[54] dèpit, et je l'ai meprisé[55] tout à fait. Mes propres sentimens m'ont peint les siennes,[56] et je n'ai jamais ajouté foi à rien qui n'étoit pas à son honneur.

Enfin, le voilà venu passer[57] le printems en Grosvenor Square, où il avoit pris une belle maison. Tout fut arrangé pour une fête chez lui, où devroient être des ambassadeurs nouvellement arrivés d'Afrique, &c. Moi, le jour avant, j'étois très occupée à des preparatifs pour mettre une robe neuve, qui n'etois pas encore finie, quant à la garniture,[58] quand M. Th. venoit[59] me chercher pour me

---

[38] attristé . . . n'y étoit de rien *to* attristée . . . n'eût été question de rien [39] des scenes les plus effrayantes du danger *to* de scenes d'un danger le plus effrayant [40] de *to* à [41] voudroit *to* vouloit [42] n'avoit . . . tout le tems; et *to* n'eût . . . durant tout-ce tems [43] le *to* la [44] précédé, ou amené *to* précédée, ou amenée [45] furent invités *to* étoient invitées [46] terrible imaginable *to* terribles [47] auroit *to* avoit [48] le Butler m'a dit . . . eternel *to* le maître d'Hotel me dit . . . eternelle [49] M. Th. fut d'avoir *to* on a annoncé que M. Th. avoit [50] souris *to* souri [51] moi-même de *to* de [52] cet *to* ce [53] compta bientot *to* devoit bientot [54] de *to* dictée par le [55] meprisé *to* meprisée [56] les siennes *to* ceux de M^e· Th. [57] le voila venu *to* violà M. Th. venu pour [58] qui n'etois pas encore finie, quant à la garniture *to* dont la garniture n'étoit encore finie [59] venoit *to* vint

promener en sa voiture.[60] Combien n'ai-je pas toujours regretté que j'ai [61] refusé d'y aller, & que j'avois donné des ordres pour dire que je n'étois pas visible! comme cela, j'ai perdu la derniere vue que j'aurois eu[62] de ce respectable et respecté ami: car le jour apres, de bien bon matin, avant que je fus[63] levée, on m'a porté[64] un billet de Me Th. pour me dire Qu'elle partiroit[65] sur le champ pour Brighthelmstone, & pour me prier de la plaindre, et de l'aimer toujours. |

Ce 24 Juin

J'étois choquée, on ne peut pas davantage, et ne pouvois rien comprendre: Je me levai vîte, pour repondre, et demander ce qu'elle fera[66] quant à l'assemblée; mais quand j'ai voulu[67] remettre ma reponse au domestique, on m'a[68] dit qu'il étoit parti, et qu'il avoit annoncé en bas que M. Th. n'étoit plus! qu'il avoit morru[69] à minuit! . . . Effrayée, affligée, Je me hatai d'aller à Grosvenor Square, pour m'informer davantage. Là J'ai appris[70] que ce n'étoit qu'à Stretham que Me· Th. étoit & sa fille étoit[71] allées, & que de là elles iroient à Brighton. Sur cela, Je me décida tout de suite de leur[72] suivre, pour tâcher de leur[73] consoler. Je retournai à St. Martin's St. pour demander | permission pour cette absence de mon Pere, ce qui me fut tout de suite accordé. Une voiture de Me· Th. étoit sur le point de partir pour Streatham; Je l'engagea[74] de venir me prendre; & J'arriva, bien peu attendu,[75] à Streatham cette nuit. J'ai trouvé[76] Me & Mlle Th. et M. Seward, qui m'avoit davancer[77] dans le même dessein que le mien. Là j'ai resté[78] quelques jours, toujours occupée à leur[79] soigner, mais trouvant[80] ni l'une ni l'autre inconsolable. La peur que ce pauvre M. Th. auroit pu devenir imbecile, par une plus longue vie, puisque il ne pourroit[81] jamais gagner sur lui de suivre le regime, severe, et la diete prescrit[82] par Dr. Jebb, sembloit de leur[83] rendre sa perte un malheur moindre à craindre que sa conservation. Je n'ai jamais pu raisonner comme

---

[60] en sa voiture *to* en voiture   [61] ai *to* aye   [62] eu *to* eue   [63] fus *to* fusse   [64] m'a porté *to* m'apporta   [65] partiroit *to* partoit   [66] fera *to* feroit   [67] ai voulu *to* voulus   [68] m'a *to* me   [69] avoit morru *to* étoit mort   [70] ai appris *to* appris   [71] Me· Th. étoit & sa fille étoit *to* Me· Th. & sa fille étoient   [72] décida . . . de leur *to* décidai . . . à les   [73] leur *to* les   [74] l'engagea *to* l'engageai   [75] arriva . . . attendu *to* arrivai . . . attendue   [76] ai trouvé *to* trouvai   [77] davancer *to* davancée   [78] ai resté *to* restai   [79] leur *to* les   [80] mais trouvant *to* mais ne trouvant   [81] pourroit *to* pouvoit   [82] prescrit *to* prescrite   [83] de leur *to* leur

cela moi meme, mais | je conçus la possibilité que d'autres pouvoient
raisonner comme cela,[84] quoique aimant bien l'objet devoué à la
mort. Neanmoins, je ne tardai pas à appercevoir que la douleur ne
fut[85] pas accablante (que cet evenement avoit occasionné.)[86] J'aurois
bien voulu voir davantage; mais j'ai toujours trouvé des moyens de
m'offrir[87] à moi meme et à mon coeur des excuses pour tout-ce que
faissoit ma chere et aimé[88] amie, M^e· Th. Je la suivai bientot à
Brighton; je la joinis encore à Streatham; je me donna à elle pour
tout le tems que j'avois à ma disposition et cela autant par recon-
naissance que par affection, puisque j'avois partagé ses jouis de fête,
j'etois bien disposée de partager ceux de douleur, du moins du
chagrin et de solitude. Mais ceci n'étoit pas bien long tems dans mon
pouvoir: J'étois engagée à écrire Cecilia, & mon pere | avoit une
impatience de me faire écrire qui n'avoit point de bornes. It étoit
miserable de me voir la negliger; et, quelque tems aprés, il me
chargea de me mettre tout à l'ouvrage, & de refuser toute invitation
quelque conque,[89] même de M^e· Th. — comme cela, je la voyois très
peu; quoique dans ce tems, quand j'avois une petite maladie à
Chesington, elle avoit la bonté et l'amitié et l'energie de venir me
voir, un milieu d'hyver,[90] & quand elle étoit accablée d'affaires.
Combien cela m'a tendrement attachée! et mon inestimable M. Crisp
pour moi! — Enfin, Cecilia fini, je me retournerai[91] encore à Streatham comme auparavant. — Mais je ne trouvai plus la[92] meme
Streatham! . . . Le maître n'étoit plus, et la maîtresse n'étoit plus
connoissable. Ce n'est pas qu'elle fut changée pour moi; non, elle
étoit aussi intimante, aussi empressée à me plaire qu'auparavant,
mais elle étoit changée en elle meme, — changée d'une | maniere et
à vu[93] point inconçevable. Elle étoit reveuse, distraite, occupée;
toujours ou écrivant pour la poste, ou attendant son arrivée, sans
s'expliquer,[94] comme autre fois, de qui venoit[95] ses Lettres, ni à qui
elle destinoit les siennes. Elle soupiroit souvent du fond du coeur, . . .
quoique il étoit[96] tous les jours plus clairs que-ce n'étoit pas son mari
qu'elle étoit à regrettée.[97] J'étois troublée et tourmentee de la voir
comme cela, mais bien loin[98] de deviner ce qui se passé[99] dans son esprit.

---

[84] pouvoient raisonner comme cela *to* le pussent   [85] ne fut *to* n'étoit
[86] occasionné *to* occasionnée   [87] de m'offrir *to* d'offrir   [88] faissoit . . .
aimé *to* faisoit . . . aimée   [89] quelque conque *to* quelleconque   [90] d'hyver
to de l'hyver   [91] fini . . . retournerai *to* finie . . . retournais   [92] la *to* le
[93] changée d'une maniere et à vu *to* changée a vu   [94] s'expliquer *to* expliquer
[95] venoit *to* venoient   [96] quoique il étoit *to* quoiqu'il fut   [97] regrettée *to*
regretter   [98] loin *to* eloignée   [99] passé *to* passoit

Appendix I

Un Soir, nous étions à lire Penser. Rever. Songer, dans les Synonimes de l'abbé Gerard: qui dit, à peu pres, "on pense de ses amis, on songe de ses affaires, on rève de[1] ses amours: Elle étoit[2] bien bien serieuse après cette lecture, et n'a rien dit. Nous avons causés,[3] Dr. Johnson, ǀ Mlle Th. & moi long tems, sans qu'elle ouvrit la bouche; Je l'ai approché, doucement, et lui dit,[4] à l'oreille, "Mais qu'est que c'est que ce silence, ma chere Madame? Est-ce penser, songer, ou rever?" . . . Dieu! comme elle avoit[5] l'air de se reveiller en sursaut!— Elle me regarda avec un air d'effroi, sembla desirer lire d'un coup d'oeil au fond de mon penser,[6] et presque au même instant crainagant[7] de le savoir, elle cacha[8] les yeux et le visage avec ses[9] deux mains; et avec une precipitation qui n'a point de nom, elle vola hors de la chambre. Toute etonnée, Je la suivi.[10] C'étoit en vain; elle gagna sa chambre dans[11] un trait, et s'enferma dedans.[12] Je la pria[13] de me laisser entrer. Point de reponse. Je reiterera[14] mes instances. Pas un seul mot. Toute consterné[15] à mon tour, je fut forcée de ǀ me retirer, par[16] l'approche de quelques domestiques. C'étoit pour annonçer le souper. Je descendis avec inquiétude, presque avec terreur. Point de M[e.] Th. Elle avoit envoyé dire à sa fille qu'elle avoit mal de Tête, & qu'elle se coucheroit. Alors, j'étois presque hors de moi-même de surprise, de suspense, de mille emotions alarmantes. J'avois[17] bientôt fini, et dès que je pouvois[18] me debarrasser du D[r.] J. et M[lle.] Th. Je volai à la chambre de M[e.] Th. La Porte étoit toujours fermée; je l'a[19] priai avec les plus vives instances me recevoir; elle ouvrit la Porte enfin; mais m'empecha d'entrer; je voyois qu'elle étoit tout en larmes; je voudrois[20] l'embrasser, — elle me donna avec precipitation un billet, prononça en sanglottant un Farewell! & ferma la porte avec une main resolue, quoique tremblante. — ǀ

. . . . .

Je vais resumer mon histoire avec M[e.] Thrale. Vous conçevez avec quel empressement mais quel[21] emotion, et quelle terreur je corru dans ma chambre pour lire ce billet: ah, tout étoit loin de ce que

---

[1] pense de . . . songe de . . . rève de *to* pense à . . . songe à . . . rève à   [2] étoit *to* fut   [3] avons causés *to* causames   [4] l'ai approché . . . dit *to* l'approchai . . . dis   [5] avoit *to* eût   [6] mon penser *to* ma pensée   [7] crainagant *to* craindre   [8] cacha *to* se cacha   [9] ses *to* les   [10] suivi *to* suivis   [11] dans *to* comme   [12] s'enferma dedans *to* s'enferma   [13] pria *to* priai   [14] reiterera *to* reiterai   [15] consterné *to* consternée   [16] par *to* à   [17] avois *to* eûs   [18] pouvois *to* pus   [19] l'a *to* la   [20] voudrois *to* voulois   [21] quel *to* quelle

536

j'eprouvois en le lisant. C'étoit un aveu que j'avois deviné ce que c'etoit que ses reveries, quoique Dieu sait je n'avois rien deviner[22] du tout! ce que j'ai[23] dit étoit un pur hazard, un simple Badinage. Mais elle me l'avouoit, & d'une manière qui m'a bien montré que c'étoit une malheureuse passion, et une qu'elle avoit bien voulu dompter, mais qui l'avoit dompté elle-même. J'étois on ne put pas plus affligée, consternée et embarrassée. Je l'écrivis d'un[24] ton le plus tendre, mais je n'ai rien osé[25] demander. . . . Je l'ai seulement protesté[26] que je lui étoit[27] devouer pour la vie — ce qui auroit été bien vrai si elle l'avoit voulu — Alors elle m'a encore ecrit, et avec une emotion presque folle — elle me disoit qu'elle ni pouvoit plus garder un secret — que je lui avoit[28] arraché le seul | qu'elle avoit jamais essayé de garder avec moi — et que, puisque je savois maintenant la position de son coeur, il falloit tout savoir — et elle me pria de deviner moi-même la personne qui l'avoit mis dans cet etat — mais pour l'amour du dieu de ne pas me tromper; que d'hesiter, ou de nommer un autre que le vrai, seroit la tuer! — Ce que j'ai souffert moi-même alors est inexprimable. Evidement cette person qui l'avoit[29] tant eprise étoit quelqu'un qu'elle avoit honte de nommer: J'ai pensé[30] à tout-ceux[31] qui l'environnoient ordinaire-ment, et à tout-ceux avec qui elle avoit quelque correspondence;[32] il n'y[33] avoit pas un qui devoit[34] la faire rougir. . . . Mais c'étoit clair qu'elle rougissoit. . . . Que penser? — Dans le monde on avoit parlé de Piozzi, — Mlle. Palmer, surtout, m'a[35] demandé s'il n'étoit pas singulierement favorisé? — Cela m'avoit offensé, revolté, — et voilà tout; je n'avois[36] plus pensé. |

Mais tout cela me revennoit à cette heure dans l'esprit, — et tout d'un coup mille choses et mille que je n'avois pas pesé dans le tems se presentoient a mes souvenirs. Ce seroit sans fin de vous les reciter, mais l'un venoit si vîte à l'aide de l'autre, que la verité sembloit me percer les yeux comme si c'étoit par un eclaire.[37] C'est donc comme cela! m'en ai-je? C'est . . . . . Piozzi!!! — ! — Je vous fais grace de mes commentaires, de mes chagrins, je puis dire de ma honte — car Je l'avois aimée et honorée à un point d'avoir cru impossible une

---

[22] deviner *to* deviné   [23] ai *to* avois   [24] l'écrivis d'un *to* lui écrivis du [25] n'ai rien osé *to* n'osai rien   [26] l'ai seulement protesté *to* lui protestai seule-ment   [27] étoit *to* étois   [28] avoit *to* avois   [29] qui l'avoit *to* dont elle étoit   [30] ai pensé *to* pensai   [31] tout-ceux *to* tous-ceux   [32] correspon-dence *to* correspondance   [33] n'y *to* n'y en   [34] devoit *to* dût   [35] m'a *to* m'avoit   [36] offensé, revolté . . . n'avois *to* offensée, revoltée . . . je n'y avois [37] pesé . . . mes souvenirs . . . eclaire *to* pesées . . . ma memoire . . . éclair

pareille oublie, une pareille sacrifice fait à toutes ses devoirs pour[38] l'indulgence d'une passion si peu respectable, si étrange, si extraordinaire! Elle étoit instruite au delà de presque toute personne de son séxe, et lui, il l'avoit[39] l'air de n'avoir rien appris que la musique; elle avoit d'esprit[40] | comme un ange; et lui, il ne parla[41] presque jamais que de la musique, de ses écoliers, de l'argent qu'il compté gagné,[42] ou de l'argent qu'il craignoit avoir perdu: elle étoit d'une haute origine, dont elle avoit, jusqu'alors, étoit fiere au dela de[43] raison — mais je ne veux plus parler d'une contraste si étonnante, lequelle,[44] dans le tems, m'a causé tant de peine — ce que j'ai senti le plus, c'étoit le tort qu'une pareille[45] attachement feroit à ses filles; et la honte qu'elle causera dans le monde; et la rage du Docteur Johnson, etc. . . . enfin, tout étoit terrible — Je ne savois où me tourner la tête, ni comment avaler[46] mon chagrin, mon affliction. Je passois la nuit en versant des larmes, quoique je me ferçois[47] de voler chez elle, cachant, | en l'embrassant, ma honte pour la sienne dans ses bras — Elle étoit toute rouge et confuse, mais elle ne trouva rien de si[48] pressé que de me faire savoir son dessein inalterable de l'epouser. Elle mettoit apart[49] toute delicatesse pour la declarer; poussé[50] apparement, par la crainte de mes remonstrances, qu'elle cherchoit a rendre plûtot nulle que vaine.[51] Ah, comme j'étois malheureuse pour elle à cet epoch![52] n'osant rien dire à personne, puisque j'avois en quelque sorte arracher d'elle[53] le secret, — pendant que tout le monde me questioné[54] sur l'étrange influence qu'avoit pris sur elle ce chanteur. — Enfin, c'étoit un tems bien triste pour moi, de toutes manières. . . . mais, bientot après, elle avouat[55] le tout à M[lle.] Thrale: qui egalement froide et haute de nature la reçu[56] avec une espèce de sangfroid etonnante.[57] |

.   .   .   .

[38] une pareille oublie, une pareille sacrifice fait à toutes . . . pour *to* un pareil oubli, un pareil sacrifice de tous ses . . . à   [39] l'avoit *to* avoit   [40] d'esprit *to* de l'esprit   [41] parla *to* parloit   [42] compté gagné *to* comptoit gagner   [43] au dela de *to* hors de   [44] d'une contraste si étonnante, lequelle *to* d'un contraste si etonnant, qui   [45] qu'une pareille *to* qu'un pareil   [46] me tourner . . . avaler *to* donner de . . . contenir   [47] en versant . . . ferçois *to* à repandre . . . forçasse   [48] trouva rien de si *to* eut rien de plus   [49] apart *to* à part   [50] poussé *to* poussée   [51] nulle que vaine *to* nulles que vaines   [52] epoch *to* epoque   [53] arracher d'elle *to* arraché de son   [54] questioné *to* questionoient   [55] avouat *to* avoua   [56] de nature la reçu *to* de son naturel la reçut   [57] etonnante *to* étonnant

Appendix I

[Après 19 Août]

Je recommence mon histoire avec Me Thrale. Ce sangfroid de Mlle. sa fille n'étoit, dans ce cas, qu'apparent; elle sentit un fort, quoique pas un vif dépit, et elle souffrit d'autant plus interierement qu'elle affectoit de calme en[58] dehors. Je ne savois[59] que trop tous ses sentimens, puisque sa mere, dans ses difficultés, M^e sa Mere l'a[60] dit, devant moi; Je vois, Je sais que vous sentez bien la necessité de la plus scrupuleuse discretion; et que vous garderez bien mon sécret; mais je ne puis exiger que tout cela restera[61] toujours enfermé dans votre sain. Ce sera à[62] vous faire crever. Dites, donc, tout-ce qui vous passe par l'esprit, et par[63] le coeur, à Mlle. Burney. Confiez à elle[64] toutes vos pensées. Je vous la donne, cette amie que j'aime et qui je cherisse la plus,[65] je vous la donne, et je ne demanderai jamais à elle[66] ce qui peut se passer entre vous. |

Cet arrangement me causa une melange la[67] plus compliqué de plaisir et de peine. J'étois enchantée de pouvoir agir ouvertement avec la personne auquelle[68] cette liaison seroit la plus nuisable,[69] et de la[70] faire voir que je n'étois pas aveuglée par l'amitié au point de trouver bien un tel projet, ni intimidié, ou par prudence, ou par timidité, ou par reconnoissance pour[71] ses bontés innombrables envers moi, à[72] lui déguiser mes sentimens, ou meme à menager les siennes[73] par la plus legere marque d'approbation. Bien, bien loin de cela, je lui ai toujours étois[74] sincere, toujours triste et franche sur la partie[75] qu'elle étoit resolu[76] de prendre — une partie[77] si contraire à ses devoirs essentiels de mere, | si opposé a son caractère[78] d'esprit, sa façon de penser jusqu'à cette heure, à sa celebrité, à sa famille, à sa naissance, et à sa manière d'être. Dont cela j'ai pris mille occasions de lui dire, quoique avec beaucoup plus de respect et de retenu que je n'avois jamais pratiqué[79] envers elle depuis ma premiere visite à Streatham, lorsque j'avois peur de tout le monde, et d'elle surtout. Mais il falloit bien montrer tous les menagemens possibles en disant de pareilles verités; vérités d'autant plus cruelles pour elle que tout

---

[58] de calme en *to* plus de calme au   [59] savois *to* connoissois   [60] l'a *to* lui a   [61] restera *to* reste   [62] sera à *to* seroit   [63] par *to* dans   [64] à elle *to* lui   [65] qui je cherisse la plus *to* cheris le plus   [66] demanderai jamais à elle *to* lui demanderai jamais   [67] la *to* le   [68] auquelle *to* à laquelle   [69] nuisable *to* nuisible   [70] la *to* lui   [71] par prudence, ou par timidité, ou par reconnoissance pour *to* par la prudence, ou par la timidité, ou par la reconnoissance de   [72] à *to* jusqu'à   [73] siennes *to* siens   [74] étois *to* été   [75] la partie *to* le parti   [76] resolu *to* resolue   [77] une partie *to* parti   [78] caractère *to* genre   [79] retenu . . . pratiqué *to* retenue . . . pratiquée

en ne pouvant pas les repousser, elle ne voudroit[80] jamais agir selon leur conviction. De sorte qu'elle menoit[81] pour long tems la vie la plus agité,[82] la plus insoutenable: jusqu'à ce frappé,[83] tout d'un coup, elle-meme de la vérité de sa position, | elle prit la resolution de ceder à mes instances, ou, plutôt, à ses propres convictions, et de renoncer à son projet et à[84] Sig.r Piozzi. Avec quelle tendresse n'ai-je[85] accueilli cette declaration! Je l'ai presque adorée, — mais, hèlas, quelle malheureuse periode que tout cela! — Elle eloigna Piozzi, dit fierement à sa fille, vous serez contente! votre orgueil ne sera pas blessé par le bonheur de votre mere! Et à moi; M.lle Burney, je sais que vous m'aimez, mais votre cruelle amitié me tue! Je vais mourir! — Et, effectivement, elle ne savoit plus ce qu'elle disoit ni qu'elle[86] fesoit, elle étoit comme quelqu'[87] une folle, parlant, tout haut à elle meme sur les escaliers, dans sa chambre, et même dans les rues; ne se souciant pas si | les domestiques, ou les passans, l'entendirent[88] ou non; dormant au milieu du Sallon tout droit,[89] & parlant tout le temps, haut, mais indistinctement. . . . Dieu! comme tout cela m'a attristée, m'a allarmée! une fiévre lente en fut la suite, & Sir Lucas Pepys fut appellé à son secours. Il trouvoit[90] bien vîte que la maladie venoit du coeur, et, à la vérité, — elle été[91] trop déséspérée pour chercher à cacher son etat veritable. Tout lui fut bientôt avoué: son étonnement étoit extreme: mais il garda le secret avec une prudence inebranlable. Cet etat penible, effrayable,[92] terrible ne dura pas long tems; elle ne pouvoit, ou ne vouloit pas essayer de faire plus sagement la conquête de ses sentimens, . . . moi, je ne pouvois pas la voyer[93] comme cela, et | presser plus fortement la perseverance. . . . M.lle Thrale, aussi, quoique pas adoucie, fut confondu[94] . . . et, enfin, nous étions tous dans un consternation à ne[95] pouvoir plus respirer, quand . . . tout d'un coup, je reçus une lettre de M.e Th. pour m'annoncer qu'elle ne pouvoit plus, qu'elle étoit à la mort, et que, pour lui sauver ce qu'il lui resta[96] de tête, . . . elle avoit expedié une expresse[97] pour demander le retour de Piozzi! . . . je ne vous parle pas de mon etat dans ce moment. J'étois plus que affligée, j'étois humiliée, mais J'ai pris courage de[98] faire un dernier essaye:[99] J'ai pris[1] la plume,

---

[80] voudroit *to* vouloit   [81] menoit *to* mena   [82] agité *to* agitée   [83] ce frappé *to* que frappée   [84] à *to* au   [85] n'ai-je *to* n'ai-je pas   [86] qu'elle *to* ce qu'elle   [87] quelqu' *to* comme   [88] entendirent *to* entendoient   [89] tout droit *to* toute droite   [90] trouvoit *to* trouva   [91] été *to* étoit   [92] effrayable *to* effroyable   [93] voyer *to* voir   [94] pas adoucie, fut confondu *to* non adoucie, fut confondue   [95] ne *to* n'en   [96] qu'il lui resta *to* qui lui restoit   [97] une expresse *to* un exprès   [98] ai pris courage de *to* pris courage pour   [99] essaye *to* essai   [1] ai pris *to* pris

et vîte, sans hesiter, je lui ai ecrit[2] la lettre la plus forte contre cette procedée,[3] mille fois plus forte qu'aucune que je n'avois[4] jusqu'ici hazardée. Je lui ai fait[5] toutes les representations possibles des maux et des torts et des chagrins qui pouvoient[6] suivre une pareille dèmarche — |

. . . . .

Bien, bien inquiete de savoir si cette lettre la facheroit par son extreme franchise, ou si elle la feroit encore une fois au moins hesiter avant de se décider, J'attendis la rèponse presque dans l'angoisse: — mais conçevez ma surprise, lorsque dans moins de deux heures ma lettre même m'a été rendue![7] J'étois stupifaite d'etonnement, du[8] chagrin, de dépit, — presque du desespoir d'être si mal compris,[9] ou si mal payée de ma sincerité, — lorsque j'appercevoit[10] quelques mots dans l'envellope. Je les ai lu[11] avec une crainte inexprimable— mais je les ai trouvé conçu dans sa manière ordinaire de tendresse[12] | et des egards,[13] quoique ils n'étoient écrit[14] que pour me dire quelle me renvoye ma lettre, peur d'être tentée de la montré[15] dans l'avenir à Piozzi! — !! — Hèlas, j'ai vu, alors, qu'il n'y avoit plus d'espoir. Et alors c'étoit[16] que j'étois d'un embarras personel extreme. J'avois toujours gardé le secret avec mon Pere et le d[r] Johnson; aussi je m'étois toujours flattée que c'étoit un secret qui cesseroit d'exister à tems pour n'être jamais su. À present, que je perdois cet espoir, j'étois presque au dèsespoir de ma propre position. Ma fidelité étoit engagée d'un coté, mon devoir, mon honneur, sembloient engagées à[17] l'autre! Que de combats interieurs n'eus-je pas dans le tems! La fidelité, neanmoins, avoit toujours le dessus, et pas un mot ne m'a jamais echappé . . . bien plus que cela, j'ai resisté à mille et mille interrogations de la part de tout le monde — excepté seulment[18] ces deux chers[19] & tres honorès[20] personnes. |

. . . . .

---

[2] ai ecrit *to* ecrivis   [3] procedée *to* conduite   [4] n'avois *to* avois   [5] ai fait *to* fis   [6] des maux et des torts et des chagrins qui pouvoient *to* sur les maux, les torts et les chagrins qui pourroient   [7] m'a été rendue *to* me fut rendu   [8] stupifaite . . . du *to* stupefaite . . . de   [9] du . . . compris *to* de . . . comprise   [10] appercevoit *to* apperçcus   [11] ai lu *to* lus   [12] ai trouvé conçu . . . ordinaire de tendresse *to* trouvai conçus . . . c. a. d. pleine de tendresse   [13] des egards *to* d'egards   [14] n'étoient écrit *to* ne fussent écrits   [15] renvoye . . . peur . . . montré *to* renvoyoit . . . de peur . . . montrer   [16] alors c'étoit *to* ce fut alors   [17] engagées à *to* engagés de   [18] seulment *to* seulement   [19] chers *to* cheres   [20] honorès *to* honorées

Et pour ces deux personnes, ou ils furent les derniers[21] à savoir quelque chose à ce sujet, ou ils m'ont crus engagé[22] à ne rien dire ou ils se sont imaginés[23] que je ne savois rien moi-même, & ils ne vouloient pas être les premiers[24] à me dire une si facheuse nouvelle. Dans fond les cas, ils ne m'ont pas parlés[25] la dessus que bien après[26] tout fut finalement arrangé. En attendant, voici Piozzi revenu, et reçu par Mᵉ· Thrale en amant accepté | en Mari decidé: . . . mais tout cela en cachette, comme bien vous pouvez imaginer. Mˡˡᵉ Th. l'a vu, moi, je l'ai su, . . . mais jamais je ne l'ai vu — invité,[27] comme à l'ordinaire, j'ai parlé franchement, j'ai dit que de recontre[28] Piozzi en particulier chez elle, sachant ce qu'il doit[29] devenir, pouvoit me causer des vraies difficultées et chagrines,[30] puisque cela pouvoit me donner l'air, même avec mon Pere, et Dr.[31] Johnson, d'avoir approuver, et même aider[32] à une liaison qu'ils ignoroient, et qu'elle ne pouvoit esperer qu'ils pouvoient approuver. Elle n'a pas bien gouter[33] tout cela, comme de raison; mais elle avoit tort de me m'etre[34] dans le cas de lui dire pareil[35] chose, ou courir pareil risque. Hèlas elle ne pensa[36] plus à moi, à ses Enfans, à ses amis, au monde entier! Elle n'étoit plus qu'à Piozzi! — Alors elle fixa[37] de retarder son mariage jusqu'à ce que Mˡˡᵉ· Th. étoit[38] en age, epoch[39] à laquelle elle declareroit son intention aux demoiselles Sus. et Sophie, en leur donnant le choix de vivre avec Elle et Piozzi, ou avec Mˡˡᵉ· Thrale, qui avoit | dessein à cet epoch de faire une établissement à elle.

Jan. 20 [1805]

Ceci arrangé, Elle devint plus contente, &, pour plaire à Mˡˡᵉ· Th. Elle avoit de tems en tems des assemblées: jamais, de lors,[40] je n'ai vu Piozzi que quand il y avoit beaucoup de monde rarement il est venu chez nous, quoique auparavant il s'y presenta[41] souvent; mais de me voir devenoit pour lui autant d'embarras[42] que de lui[43] voir

[21] ils . . . derniers *to* elles . . . dernières   [22] ils . . . crus engagé *to* elles . . . crues engagée   [23] ils . . . imaginés *to* elles . . . imaginées   [24] ils . . . premiers *to* elles . . . premières   [25] ils ne m'ont pas parlés *to* elles ne m'ont parlé   [26] après *to* après que   [27] invité *to* quoique invitée   [28] de recontre *to* que rencontrer   [29] doit *to* devoit   [30] des vraies difficultées et chagrines *to* de vrais difficultés et chagrins   [31] Dr. *to* le Dr.   [32] approuver . . . aider *to* approuvé . . . aidé   [33] gouter *to* gouté   [34] m'etre *to* me mettre   [35] pareil *to* pareille   [36] pensa *to* pensoit   [37] fixa *to* decida   [38] étoit *to* fut   [39] epoch *to* epoque   [40] de lors *to* dans ce tems   [41] presenta *to* presentût   [42] autant d' *to* un aussi grand   [43] lui *to* le

étoit pour moi une peine. Après ceci, M^e Th. alla à Bath, ou elle sembloit[44] se fixer, et ou elle restoit hors de[45] quelques visites à Londres, jusqu'au periode[46] critique. . . . Enfin, tout de suite après que Mlle· T. avoit atteinte[47] sa 22me· année, sa mere donna sa main à ce signore. Ce fut à Bath. Elle n'avoit personne avec elle de sa famille, de ses parens, ni de ses anciens amis. Elle avoit des nouvelles connoissances, fait[48] avec le signore, et des amis egalement à lui.[49]

Le Jour même de ce Marriage à jamais étonnant Elle m'ecrivit, pour me faire part de son bonheur, et pour me demander mes felicitations. Cela m' étoit[50] trop. Je n'ai vu ce[51] fin de tant de surpris, de chagrins, d'efforts inutiles, qu'avec la douleur la plus vive, et affecter[52] de la joie m'auroit été aussi impossible que de la[53] sentir. Je répondis tristement à sa demande, et quoique toujours avec affection et tendresse, car je l'aimai[54] de tout mon coeur, je n'avois pas la force, ou plutôt l'hipocrisie, de lui faire des felicitations quelconques. — Au reste, je l'ai fait aussi peu disagréable que je l'ai pu:[55] Mais certes c'étoit une lettre à marquer que rien ne m'avoit fait changer d'avis à son égard. Quelle étoit ma[56] réponse (— peut on imaginer une telle?[57] — c'étoit un court, sec réproche du froideur avec laquel[58] j'avois reçu l'avis de son bonheur! une lettre commençant Chere Mlle· Burney —: & finissant — votre tres obeissante servante — et ceci après des lettres, jusqu à la,[59] d'une telle chaleur de tendresse, que plutot elles avoient l'air d'être écrites avec passion qu'avec amitié! — ! Je fus cruellement choquée, blessée — comment a t-elle pu croire que de changer son caractère changeroit le mien? que de la voir oublier tous ses premiers sentimens aussi bien que de renoncer[60] à tous ses premiers devoirs, seroit pour moi un sujet de felicitation, et que j'aurois du ou pu avoir un air de satisfaction pour une conduite que j'avois[61] regulierement autant que j'ai pu opposé?[62] — et elle, qu'auroit elle du penser d'une pareil[63] et indigne inconsequence. |

---

[44] sembloit *to* sembla   [45] hors de *to* hors le tems   [46] jusqu'au periode *to* jusqu'a l'epoque   [47] avoit atteinte *to* eut atteint   [48] fait *to* faits   [49] à lui *to* les siens   [50] m'étoit *to* étoit   [51] ce *to* cette   [52] et affecter *to* affecter   [53] de la *to* d'en   [54] l'aimai *to* l'aimois   [55] l'ai fait . . . disagréable . . . l'ai pu *to* les fis . . . desagréables . . . pus   [56] étoit ma *to* fut sa   [57] on . . . telle *to* en . . . pareille   [58] du . . . laquel *to* de la . . . laquelle   [59] jusqu à la *to* jusque la   [60] que de renoncer *to* que renoncer   [61] que j'avois *to* contre laquelle je m'étois   [62] ai pu opposé *to* avois pu opposée   [63] pareil *to* pareille

Appendix I

Jan. 27 [1805]

C'est à Norbury que j'ai reçu cette cruelle Lettre qui m'a affligée au fond du coeur, — quoique j'étois[64] avec deux amies — ah Ciel! combien plus choses encore que celle qui[65] des ce tems j'ai perdue! — quelles anges consolatrices! . . . passe! passe! — ou mon histoire ne finera[66] jamais. J'étois long[67] avant que de répondre à cette Lettre — et ma reponse fut aussi soignée que melancholique! Je n'osais pas écrire tout de suite, et dans la chaleur de mon ame offensée, de peur que[68] de lui dire ce que sa lettre m'a peine[69] meriter pourroit la compromettre avec son mari, et puisqu'elle étoit enfin à lui, je ne voulois pas pour tout au monde avoir couru le moindre risque de l'embrouillir[70] avec lui pour qui elle avoit perdu ou renoncé tout autre. Je lui ai simplement ecrit[71] que je ne voudrois[72] pas lui parler de la douleur avec laquelle j'avois lu les premières lignes[73] tracées par sa main qui m'avoit fait de la peine;[74] mais | que je me recommenderois pour ma seule défense à sa memoire, et que jusqu'à ce qu'elle me rendroit[75] la justice que j'attendrois d'elle, je la prierois[76] de ne plus m'écrire. Je ne me rappelle pas si c'étoit tout de suite, ou quelque tems apres que j'eusse[77] sa réponse; mais c'étoit[78] écrite d'une tout autre manière, — c'étoit pour me faire part de son dessein de partir tout de suite pour l'Italie, de m'assurer[79] de son bonheur, en ajoutant: ainsi,[80] tranquilizer votre bon coeur, je vous en prie, ma très cher — . . . J'ai oublié de vous dire que j'avois dit en p. s. de ma lettre, que je desirois presenter mes complimens à M. Piozzi, contre qui[81] je n'avois jamais rien voulu[82] puisque je n'avois jamais rien vu à blâmer. . . . Après tout ceci je lui écrivis une lettre pleine de tendresse et contentement, avec les meilleurs souhaits pour | que sa felicité seroit[83] permanente, et l'assurant que je brulerois la seule de ses Lettres que je ne pourrois pas revoir avec plaisir, afin qu'il n'y auroit[84] aucun reste de rien qui pourroit[85] en aucun sorte nuire à l'amitié et à la reconnoissance je lui avois vouée.[86] Nous voici, donc, retabli[87] dans notre veille amitié, et nos premieres liaisons — n'est-ce

---

[64] étois *to* fusse   [65] qui *to* que   [66] finera *to* finira   [67] étois long *to* fus longtems   [68] de peur que *to* craignant   [69] m'a peine *to* me sembloit   [70] avoir couru . . . l'embrouillir *to* courir . . . la brouiller   [71] ai . . . ecrit *to* écrivis   [72] voudrois *to* voulois   [73] lignes *to* lignes qui   [74] qui m'avoit fait de la peine *to* me suffert   [75] rendroit *to* rendit   [76] prierois *to* priois   [77] que j'eusse *to* j'eus   [78] c'étoit *to* elle étoit   [79] de m'assurer *to* et pour m'assurer   [80] ajoutant: ainsi *to* ajoutant   [81] contre qui *to* auquel   [82] rien voulu *to* voulu de mal   [83] seroit *to* fut   [84] auroit *to* eut   [85] pourroit *to* put   [86] vouée *to* vouées   [87] retabli *to* retablies

544

pas? je l'ai vu comme cela bien sincerement — mais, la semaine passa sans réponse, — le mois . . . et, bref, jamais n'en ai-je reçu aucune! Jusqu'à cette heure, pas un mot d'elle ne m'est revenu! Le pourquoi m'est entierment inconnu: tout ce que j'ai toujours imaginé, c'est qu'elle avoit montré mes Lettres contre le marriage à Piozzi, en lui contant aussi tout ce que je lui ai toujours dit pour l'empêcher. Je ne pouvois pas attendre de lui la grandeur d'ame de pardonner à des torts contre son ambition, quoique j'aurois faits des torts[88] plus reëls contre ma verité | d'avoir agi[89] autrement. Neanmoins, c'est possible que sa silence a été[90] l'effet du pur hazard, ou meprise, de sa part, puisque la premiere nouvelle que j'ai entendu[91] d'elle après ma derniere Lettre, c'étoit[92] son départ pour l'Italie. C'est toujours possible que ma Lettre ne l'avois[93] jamais atteint. Pour m'assurer[94] la dessus, j'ai conté la[95] circonstance à toutes ses amis[96] que j'aye vu[97] dépuis: surtout à M. Seward: et tout au longue[98] à Mlle. Th. dans l'espoir de me raccommoder avec une amie jàdis si chere à mon coeur en trouvant qu'elle n'avoit pas le tort de m'avoir trahi de deux manières. Mais jamais je n'ai reçu aucun eclaircissement. Je l'ai vu[99] deux fois seulement dépuis son marriage. Le premier fois, c'étoit[1] chez M. Lock, Mad[e] Lock donna une Balle[2] à ses filles, ou toute les demoiselles de leurs connoissances[3] furent invitées.[4] Entre autres, Mlle. Cecilia Thrale. Je hesitai beaucoup si ou non je devrois[5] m'y trouver. J'avois un desire[6] profonde de revoir ma ancienne amie, et une | crainte presque aussi forte des suites. Enfin j'ai* parlé même à la reine. Elle me donna permission d'être de la partie. J'y fus. J'arrivai tard; M[e]. Lock m'a reçu* avec plus que sa tendresse ordinaire. M[e]. Piozzi étoit dans un chambre en dedans.* Je restai long tems dans la première* apartement, irresolu.* Ma bien aimée — O bien bien aimée, ma Susanne m'accompagnera,* enfin, dans l'autre. C'etoit là que fut* la danse. En tremblant j'entrerois.* Je m'arreterois* à chaque personne, par contenance, que je connusse.* Et la chambre en étoit pleine; — ma soeur Burney,

---

[88] faits des torts *to* fait une faute   [89] reëls . . . verité d'avoir agi *to* reëlle
. . . conscience si j'eusse fait   [90] c'est . . . sa . . . a été *to* il est . . . son . . .
ait été   [91] ai entendu *to* aye eue   [92] c'étoit *to* ce fut   [93] avois *to* ait
[94] m'assurer *to* m'en assurer   [95] la *to* cette   [96] amis *to* amies   [97] aye
vu *to* ai vus   [98] longue *to* long   [99] vu *to* vue   [1] Le premier fois,
c'étoit *to* La premiere fois, ce fut   [2] une Balle *to* un bal   [3] leurs connoissances *to* leur connoissance   [4] invitées *to* invitée   [5] Je hesitai . . .
ou non je devrois *to* J'hesitai beaucoup si je devois ou non   [6] desire *to* desir
* The asterisk indicates an error marked as such but left uncorrected and
frequently without underscoring.

Marianne, qui dansa* alors superierement pour une anglaise, Augusta, Amelie, les jeunesse, Fanny & Norbury alors tout deux tout à fait Enfans. . . . Me Piozzi étoit assise sur une banc, son mari à son coté. J'avançai toujours vers elle, esperant qu'elle se leverois pour me parler. Pas du tout. Enfin, j'apperçus Mlle. Cecilia. Je m'attacha* à elle. Je lui parlé* avec empressement et affection, long tems: et, enfin, je lui* prierit* de me conduire où étoit sa maman. Me voyant alors, | s'approcher, avec sa fille, elle disoit* tout haut, comme si elle m'appercevoit* pour la premiere fois. "Ah, c'est Mlle Burney!" Je l'approchois* alors plus vivement, elle se leva, et me fit une reverence profonde. Je ne sais comment je l'ai abordé,* je me trouvai mal, presque pret* d'evanouir, si fortes furent mes emotions à cet* rencontre. Da sa part, c'étoit un embarras extreme, melé d'une fierté qui disoit Voyons si elle me traite* comme autre fois! — Pour adoucir cette crainte, je l'addressois* avec toutes les marques possibles de la plus haute consideration. Appraisé* elle commença à causer, sur la danse, et les danseuses, surtout [1 *word* xxx] louanges de Marianne, qui, effectivement, étoit alors bien belle. Bientot, on m'a appelé* pour parler à quelqu'un — j'oublie qui, — mais c'étoit Me Lock | qui m'a fait* chercher, craignant que de rester plus long tems pourra* me rendre malade. Je me remettrois* dans l'autre chambre, après quoi, je me suis retournée.* C'étoit* alors que je l'ai un peu retrouvé.* Ne pouvant plus douter que c'étoit elle que je ⟨lui⟩ repasser, elle m'a d'avançai,* toute* souriant, & m'a pressé* de m'assoir à coté d'elle. Je le fis: et j'ai resté causant avec elle jusqu'à l'heure où j'étois forcée de me retirer. Nous n'avons rien dit au tems passé, rien prononcés que sur tout-ce qui étoit devant nos yeux. Elle a voulu me conduire chez moi; je n'ai* oser* accepter* cette offre. J'ai bien fait, car la reine me disoit* apres qu'elle sera* bien aise que je ne renouvellerois* pas plus intimmement cette veille liaison. Apres cela, la seconde et dernière fois que je la vis, ce fut en sortant de le* palais à Windsor pour aller à l'eglise.

APPENDIX II

M. D'ARBLAY'S STATEMENT RESPECTING HIS FINANCES

A. (Berg), n.d., being an account of the d'Arblays' financial affairs
from 1801 through 4 July 1813
Double sheet folio 4 pp.
Addressed: A Madame / Madame d'Arblay née Burney / chez le
Docteur Burney / à Chelsea / Londre —
Edited by FBA, p. 1, *annotated and dated*: ⁂ le 4 Juillet. 1813 ⌐
HISTORICAL ⌐
p. 4: ⁂ 4ᵗʰ July—1813. (37)
N.B. The early part of this memorial, rather than Letter, to be
preserved for our *Parens et amis*, by my dear Alex, as a model of
moderation, in its candid, impartial, & impressive statement of our
past, but astonishingly disappointed expectations relative to our own
Rights in our dear & own-built Cottage of West Hamble—constructed as an Inheritance for our son!—& by means wholly fur-
nished from a work—Camilla—of his mother, & of which the sole
Architect was his honored Father.

To the account of our beloved cottage is subjoined a compleat
statement of our money possessions & dealings with Messʳˢ Coutts—
& with our honoured Mr Locke, sent, himself—up to the year 1813.—
L'objet de cette lettre ecrite en *quintuplicate* au detriment de ma
Santé, puisque mes occupations, très multipliées à cause de l'arriere
resultant de ma longue maladie, m'obligent à prendre sur le tems de
mon repos celui de la faire, est d'eclairer nos amis et toi même sur le
veritable etat de nos affaires d'argent; et de detruire l'erreur reellement inconcevable qui leur fait croire qu'il ne nous revient rien,
absolument rien de tout l'argent que tu avais à la banque, lorsque
j'ai quittè l'Angleterre pour me rendre à St. Domingue en passant
par Paris pour y prendre mes derniers ordres et y recevoir mes
instructions. A cette epoque, ma chere Fanny, je te laissais dans une
jolie habitation champêtre batie avec une partie du produit de la
souscription de Camilla, sur un terrain que nous n'avons pas même
à bail ni à terme, mais sur la seule parole de Mʳ Lock à qui je payais

547

5£ du rente du terrain que je pouvais en prendre ainsi au moyen d'un bail amphitheotique d'autant plus long qu'il serait passé plus tard, ou payer un dernier 20. Tout cela quelque romanesque qu'il puisse paroitre, etait de même que ce qui va suivre suffisament justifié par le noble caractere non seulement de Mʳ Locke, mais de toute sa famille, objet de la juste admiration de tous ceux qui l'ont connue, et d'une sorte *d'enthousiasme* amical *bien naturel* de la part de ceux qui comme nous etaient admis dans leur intimité. Outre cette maison, tu avais à la Banque *dix sept cent cinquante livres sterling* (1750 £) à 5 p % et chez Mʳ Coutts cinquante et quelques livres sterling et la recette d'un quartier de ta pension de 100 £ fesant *en tout 75 £* outre le courrant pour ta pension. Sur cela j'emportais avec moi 1º une lettre de change de 100 £ sterling sur Mʳ Perregault qui me l'a payée, et en cas d'accident un credit de 500 £ sur la Jamaïque, credit que j'ai renvoyé depuis à Mʳ Coutts qui l'a reçu comme le prouve une de ses lettres, et son compte de Balance envoyé en 1803 comme tu le verras plus bas. Trompè dans mon esperance, et n'allant plus à St. Domingue, mais restant à Paris hotel de Marengo rue de Miromenil pour y solliciter une pension que j'ai obtenue [*blank*] ans après, je t'ecrivis que si ta santè te le permettait, car je t'avais laisseè assez mal portante, je te priais de venir me rejoindre, ce que tu fis aussitôt, m'apportant tout ce que nous avions en argent chez *Mʳ Coutts à qui tu laissas une procuration pour toucher ta pension durant ton absence.* Nos projets alors etaient de passer chaque année à peu pres autant de tems dans ton pays que dans le mien que *je ne revoyais que grace à ta generosité,* puisque j'avais pris lorsque tu voulus bien unir ton sort à celui d'un malheureux proscrit denué de tout, l'engagement formel de ne jamais t'obliger de renoncer à ta patrie, mais d'y vivre avec toi, eloigné du monde et dans un hermitage ou l'amitié la plus intime pouvait seule penetrer. Tu n'avais pu supporter le spectacle de l'insurmontable melancolie qui s'etait emparée de moi, aussitôt que j'avais entrevu la possibilité de revoir cette France qui m'a vu naitre et où tu as été depuis si bien accueillie par mes amis dont les moins anciens datent ⌜datent⌝ de pres de 30 ans. Notre unique ambition etait lorsque j'aurais obtenu ma pension de pouvoir suivre le plan de vie cité plus haut. Mais il fallait en attendant nous establir dans l'un et l'autre pays un petit revenu qui suffisant à nos gouts très moderés nous laissât dans l'independance. Pour cela tu consentis à me laisser tirer de la banque *750 £* que m'envoya Mʳ Coutts et que Mʳ Perregault m'a payés vers la fin de 1802. Une partie de cet argent nous fut malheureusement enlevée par MM Coulon chez qui je ne l'avais placée que parceque nous avions lu sur les murs de Paris une affiche imprimée dans la quelle on proposait comme les modeles les plus respectables ces fournisseurs dont la speculation tout à fait neuve a été de faire rehabiliter la memoire de leur Pere en faisant pour payer les dettes de sa banqueroute un sacrifice d'environ deux millions, au moyen des quels peu de mois après ils en ont emporté une vingtaine aux dupes de notre espece. 27 p % furent ensuite offerts et j'avais accepté, mais n'ai jamais rien touché; et Mr Locke ayant pris, pour un usage que je vais faire connoitre 700 £ sterling chez MM. Coutts tu consentis encore à ce que je retirasse le reste de chez ce banquier qui d'après sa *derniere lettre* de 22 Avril 1803 n'avait plus à nous que *38$^£$ 17^{sch} 8^d aux quels pour le nouveau compte qu'il doit nous rendre il faudra ajouter jusqu'à ce jour 28 juin ou plutôt jusqu'au 1er juillet 1813 dix années et demie de ta pension de 100$^£$ sauf la diminution qu'elle a subie à dater de l'epoque de l'impôt sur les pensions.* Ce qui doit suivre prouvera jusqu'à l'evidence, qu'une somme de 45,000 francs environ etait de trop peu d'importance pour qu'ils y fissent beaucoup d'attention, puisque dans le court espace de [*blank*] mois ils se sont trompés trois fois dans les comptes qu'ils en rendaient. La 1ere erreur *à notre desavantage* etait de 4800^f. La seconde de même etait de 2400^f et la troisieme moins bien prouvée et qui aurait été *à leur desavantage* etait de 600^f c.à.d. 25 livres Sterling evaluées chacune à 24^f. Ces messieurs doivent en consequence être peu surpris que je leur demande *un compte de balance* qui fesant suite à celui qu'ils m'ont adressé en 1803 et dont je joins ici copie, etablisse d'une maniere claire et precise l'emploi des sommes qu'ils ont recues en vertu de la procuration que tu leur as laissée p^r toucher ta pension, et des interêts que les sommes en provenant doivent nous avoir valu, si dans la procuration que tu as laissée on a pris à ce sujet les precautions convenables. Malheureusement, nos demanagemens et ta maladie m'ont fait perdre les notes d'après les quelles je pourrais dire positivement ce que nous avons reçu de cette pension chez Mr Perregault depuis que par le Conseil du grand juge j'ai consenti à la toucher jusqu'au moment où l'enorme perte qu'il fallait faire m'a decidé à cesser de profiter de cette ressource trop onereuse quand à 5 et 6 p^r % au plus je pouvais me procurer ici l'argent dont nous aurions eu besoin. heureusement la perte de ces notes qui peut être ne sont qu'egarées est peu importante: et que c'est à MM. Coutts à établir leur compte de balance d'après les reçus de nous à Mr Perregaux; qui je crois ne nous a payés que quatre années *au plus* de la pension. Une année a été touchée en notre nom par M^{de} de Boinville à ses risques et perils c.à.d. en supportant l'enorme perte du change. Mais la somme qu'elle a ainsi reçue a due être jointe depuis à celles *que nous avons* *chez Mr Martyn Banquier de Mr Locke* d'aprés le compte qui en sera fait plus bas. Il m'est consequement impossible de concevoir ce qui a pu te faire m'ecrire, dans trois lettres differentes *qu'excepté la maison; nous n'avons rien, absolument rien que cinq années de ta pension qui etaient chez MM. Coutts et qui suffiront à peine pour ton voyage.*

Preuves de ce qui vient d'etre exposé relativement à mon compte avec MM. Coutts extraites de lettres que j'ai reçues.

[*in the left margin*]

1ere lettre de MM. Coutts du *4 May 1802* cotée *A* et numerotée 2 parceque le N° 1 au brouillon de la lettre que je leur avais ecrite p^r reclamer contre une note qu'ils avaient remise à M^de D'Ay, et dans la quelle il etait dit que nous n'avions plus chez eux c.à.d. à la banque en leur nom, que 1450£ sur 1750 que je leur avais laissées, et qui ne pouvaient être diminués que de 100£ que m'avait payés Mr Perregaux.[1]

2eme lettre de MM. Coutts du *10 aout 1802* cotée *B.* et numerotée 3 les fonds vendus p^r se procurer les 750£ que j'avais demandés ne sont montés qu'à 745£ y compris 18 schellings pour le droit de courtage

3eme lettre de MM. Coutts du *25 Janvier 1803* cotée *C* et numerotée [*blank*]

[*each letter was copied by M. d'A in the original English, giving a French translation underneath*]

We have been favoured with your letter in duplicate of 23 April returning the letter of credit we gave you on Jamaica for £560 cancelled and a memorandum which we had given to Mad^me d'Arblay previous to her departure relative to your 5 p^r C^t 1797 wherein the sum of stock stated in that fund was £1450, but you have exclusive of this stock a further sum of 200 in the stock called Navy 5 p^r Cent making together £1650 five p^r C^ts.

We are sorry we did not state this in the memorandum given to Mad^e d'Arblay as it would have prevented you the trouble of writing for an explanation, &c. &c.

[1] See the tabular account, pp. 558–9.

Appendix II

Second extrait

We have been favoured with your letter of 12 Thermidor inclosing Made D'Ay's power of attorney to enable us to receive her pension of £ 100 annm

Agreably to your desire, we now transmit a letter of credit in your favour for 750^g on MM Perregault to provide for which we sold on the 7th inst^t the following stock belonging to you; Viz: &c. &c.

Troisieme extrait

We have been favoured with your letter of the 28th of december, and are very sorry that the mistake in the information given to Mr Locke regarding your 5 pr C^t 1797 in our name should have occasioned you the trouble of writing so long a letter. It arose from the person who wrote to Mr Locke not observing that the credit for £100 given to you on Mess^r Perregaux & Co. had been drawn for & charged to your account the 24th March last, consequently had no claim upon your property in the funds, &c.

[note in left margin] 3eme et derniere lettre de MM. Coutts du 22 avril, 1803 cotée D

We received the favour of your letter of the 24 March inclosing M^e D'Ay's certificate of life in consequence of which we received two quarters pension

due to her the 5 January	50 £
Deduct for entering the power of attorney	3 sh
Placed to the credit of your account	49 . 17

In our letter to you 25 January, it was mentioned, by mistake that 3 quarters were due the 5 of that month, but you would observe by the copy of your account then sent, that you had credit for the quarter to 5 July in August; consequently only two quarters were due in January——We expect to receive the quarter to 5 April in the course of a fortnight.

Agreable to your desire we have purchased for you as much 5 pr C^t 1797 as will make your capital three hundred pounds in the stock viz:

£43:15:10 five p^r C^t 1797 at 98 p^r C^t	£42.18.4
Brokerage	1.2
	42.19.6.

To be transfered for you into our name when the Bank books open & to be charged to your acc^t after which, there will remain a balance of cash in your favour of £38.17.8.

We have the honour to be &c —

Depuis cette lettre et la compte qui la procede, je proteste n'avoir rien reçu de MM. Coutts concernant nos affaires.

A. P. d'Arblay

Après avoir ainsi terminé ce qui concerne MM. Coutts & Co, je passe à notre compte avec Mr Locke; et je supplie nos chers amis de

Norbury park c.à.d. la digne epouse et les dignes enfans de cet ange de vouloir bien lire avec la plus grande attention ce qui va suivre.

Ils n'ont point sans doute oublié qu'à l'epoque où je reçus l'instruction de regarder comme non avenues mes lettres de service à St Domingue Mr Locke et son ami Mr Angerstein touchés de la triste situation où me mettait ce contr'ordre, nous donnerent sans même vous en prevenir un interest assez considerable dans l'emprunt du Gouvernement appellé *l'Omnium*. Ils voulaient et esperaient par là nous faire gagner quelques centaines de louis, et pour cela ils nous donnerent une portion de *2000* £ dans cet omnium qui ne fut en hausse que très peu de jours, et baissa ensuite très rapidement. Durant cette degringolade que je ne voyais pas prête à s'arreter, je ne cessais d'ecrire p^r supplier et même pour conjurer mon cher Mr Locke de vendre promptement; parceque, lui disais-je, je ne pouvais souffrir plus longtems qu'on me fît chaque mois l'avance d'un douzieme des *2000* £ qu'il fallait payer. Je ne pouvais m'expliquer plus clairement sans donner à entendre ce que je ne pouvais conscientieusement ecrire, que les affaires n'allaient pas aussi bien que le pensaient ceux qui mal informés, croyaient à un prompt arrangement definitif. Aussi, bien loin de vendre mon omnium à une tres faible perte, ce cher Mr Locke à l'epoque d'une hausse momentanée, acheta en mon nom 2000 livres sterling de plus dans ce maudit *Omnium*. De cette sorte, nous avons perdu 428£ 4^{shg} c'est à dire *10,267* francs cinq centimes. Sur 700 £ de l'argent que nous avions chez MM. Coutts il ne nous revenait que 271:15:3 que Mr Locke, à l'exception des 15^{sh} 3 a placés chez Mr Martyn son banquier. Depuis le mois de Juillet 1803 nous avons / donc / sous le nom de Mr Locke dans les 3 pour cent ce que cette somme de 271 livres sterling a pu acheter à cette epoque; et la somme ainsi placée doit s'etre accrue 1° des interets depuis ce tems, 2° des produits des loyers de notre maison 3° de l'annèe de ta pension avancée à Mad^e de Boinville qui a pris l'engagement de les remettre à William ou à toute autre personne de Norbury-park.

Preuves de ces faits

[*note in left margin, in M. d'A's hand*]

Lettre de Mr Locke du 10 Juillet 1803 cotée F. Ce que je copie est entierement de la main de Mr Locke et Madame Locke a ecrit à ma femme le reste.

At length, My dear friend, I have obtained the amount of your omnium which I inclose & to explain wich I must inform you that acting for you as I did for myself & on A's advice, I bought on the 10th April £2110

Mr D'Arblay account with Julius Angerstein

1803	To		1803	By	
April 16	To balance of cash payements on 2000 Omnium	£1300. —. —	April 16	By sale of 2110 Consols at 63 1/2 pr Ct to pay the Interest	£1339. 17. —
30	To interest on dito	40. 16. 5	May 20	By sale of 1300 £ consols at 59 5/8 per Cent	775. 2. 6
30	To £2110 Consols bought for the May account	1350. 8. —	30	By d^{to} of 1200 reduced at 58 5/8 pr Cent	713. 10. —
30	To Brokerage on £2110 at 1/8 pr Cent	2. 12. 9	30	By D^o of 139.5 defered at 47 p^r cent	65. 8. 11
May 20	To Brokerage on the sale of £2639. 5. Consols reduced & defer'd stocks	3. 6. —		By one year's dividend due £ 1300 Consols	39. —. —
		2697. 3. 2 X		By one D^d d^o 1200 reduced	36. —. —
	To Balance	271. 15. 3			
		£2968. 18. 5			2968. 18. 5

X les 271.15. 3 qui nous sont restés des 700
qu'a touchés Mr Locke ——

Je proteste que depuis l'arrivé de cet etat et de la lettre qui la transmettait et dont la copie le
⟨prouve⟩ ici j'n'ai rien reçu ni de Mr Locke ni de sa part.

A. P. d'Arblay

consols for the May account, in the hope that the pending negotiation might issue in a pacific arrangement, by which I flattered myself that you might recover your whole loss. The event was different from my expectations, & those of some of the best heads in the Country. That speculation has added to your loss, into the proportion of the difference between the price of stock on the day on which I made the bargain, & the day of settlement.

You will therefore recover upon the £700 which I received of Coutts, only £271:15:3 having lost on the loan £428:4:9.

Shall I remit you the remaining £271:15:3? or shall I invest it here? & in what manner? Until I hear your determination, it will remain in my hands, at the same interest which I make of my own money.

20th July Since the above, which I have delayed sending in the hope of a shorter & safer conveyance (a Russian Messenger) I have thought it best to invest £271, part of the above mentioned 271:15:3 in 3 pr Cent in my own name where it shall remain till you send me farther directions. I have received your letter of the 25th June; & another of the 29th rendering the inclosed orders of the 25th to Messrs Coutts or Messrs Donat useless. So much for business. Fredy will express better than I, what we have nearest our hearts, our regrets, our wishes, all that we have to lament in your absence, & all we look forwards in your return. Embrassés pour moi paternellement mais tendrement votre chere femme et mon petit ami. Remember us very kindly & with our best wishes to M et Mme Bourdois.

J'espere, ma chere amie, que si cette lettre te parvient comme j'ai lieu de le presumer, tu voudras bien m'en accuser reception par *duplicata.* car je t'avoue que j'ai le plus grand besoin d'être tranquillise sur son contenu. C'est bien assez, ce me semble, que d'avoir été completement ruiné, d'avoir ensuite perdu une partie de ce qui t'appartenait, et qu'il est plus que suffisant d'avoir / perdu plus de 10000f / par suite d'une speculation à la quelle nous n'avons eu dans le principe aucune part, sans perdre encore en ce moment une somme au moins aussi considerable, par un simple defaut de forme. Le fait est neanmoins que si nous n'avions pas affaire à des amis et aux plus honnêtes gens du monde, on pourrait d'autant mieux nous chicanner que la lettre de Mr Locke n'est point signée et que Mde Locke qui a ecrit sur cette même lettre n'a pas non plus mis de signature. Plein de confiance neanmoins dans le souvenir qu'a laissé le cher Mr Locke, et bien sur que ses heritiers reconnoitront son ecriture, et feront ce qu'il ferait lui même si nous avions eu le bonheur de le conserver, je n'ai d'inquietude que relativement à la difficulté de leur faire connoitre le veritable etat des choses. Ce qu'ils ne manqueront pas surement de faire sera de commencer par savoir quel etait le prix des 3 pour cent consolidés du 10 au 20 Juillet epoque à la quelle nos 271 livres sterling ont été placés. Le reste du compte ne sera pas difficile à etablir. Dans tous les cas je te supplie de *n'arrêter ce compte* qu'en y mentionnant comme on le fait toujours ici, que c'est *sauf erreur de calcul et omission*. De grace ma bonne Fanny n'oublie point de faire inserer l'equivalent de ces mots. Je te demande pardon de te tourmenter ainsi. Tu le sais je ne suis guere plus porté que toi à m'occuper des ces sortes d'affaires d'argent, et je ne fais volontiers et bien que les comptes des autres. Mais tu vois ce qui en resulte. Daigne donc condescendre à t'occuper serieusement de nos affaires, et termine mais dans le sens ce cette lettre. Le *sauf erreur de calcul et omission* doit être egalement placé dans l'arreté du compte de Mess. Coutts, si ce compte est tellement clair qu'il ne puisse laisser aucun doute. Ce dernier, je te le repete, est on ne peut pas plus facile à etablir.

Suivant le compte de balance qu'il m'a adressé et la lettre qu'il m'a ecrite le *22 avril 1803* il nous restrait redevable de 38$^£$: 17^{Sch}: 8^d au mois de janvier 1803.

Depuis le 1er janvier 1803 jusqu'au 1er Juillet 1813. il a du recevoir dix années et demie de ta pension.

Depuis cette epoque il nous a payé, comme il doit le prouver par les quittances ou de nous ou de ceux à qui il a payés pour nous, une somme de [*blank*]. Tels sont les elemens du nouveau compte de balance qu'il doit te remettre et que je prie Alex d'examiner. Je ne puis faire ce compte d'ici parceque j'ignore et nous n'avons jamais su à quelle epoque ta pension a été diminuée, et que je ne sais pas davantage quelle est cette diminution.

Quant à ton ouvrage qui j'espere est avancé, je t'avoue mon amie que je ne puis concevoir que tu n'ayes pas eu le tems de le finir, surtout quand je pense que tu es restée plus de cinq mois sans sortir plus de *deux fois*. Je ne veux pas m'appesantir sur cette idée, de peur de trouver, dans l'examen au quel je crains de me livrer, la confirmation de ce qu'il ne tiendrait qu'à moi de soupçonner d'apres plusieurs traits echappés à cette aimable M^{de} Solveyns, c.à.d de peur d'être forcé de reconnoitre que tu as été très serieusement malade et non pas simplement incommodèe. Je sais combien il repugne à ta delicatesse de faire par toi même un arrangement pour la proprieté de ce nouvel ouvrage, et d'ailleurs je suis bien sur que l'on ferait une dupe de toi. D'un autre côté, j'ai lieu de craindre depuis ce que m'a dit M^{de} Solveyns que tu n'ayes personne de bien empressé à faire pour cela les demarches necessaires. Cette ressource dans l'etat actuel de nos affaires viendrait cependant bien à propos. Neanmoins je dois t'avouer que pour rien au monde je ne pourrais supporter l'idée d'un arrangement qui ne serait point convenable, et que je desire et te demande instament la plus grande attention sur cet article. Dans le cas où les libraires de Londre voudraient abuser de ta position, et calculeraient sur ton prochain depart, et sur l'esperance de te voir condescendre à tout ce qu'ils voudraient. Voici ce que je te propose. Renonce pour le moment à faire imprimer en Angleterre, et rapporte ton manuscrit après l'avoir achevé et en avoir deposé dans une boëte copie chez une des tes nieces, de peur d'accident. Pour lors Lally, moi et quelques autres de tes amis nous en ferions ici la traduction qui très certainement nous rapporterait beaucoup. Très certainement aussi personne ne s'aviserait de traduire en anglais un ouvrage dont l'original ecrit par toi aurait été composé dans cette langue. Ainsi nous pourrions à la paix le faire imprimer à Londre après en avoir joui dejà en France. Reflechis à ce que je te propose, et peut être ne le trouveras tu pas deraisonnable. Mad^e Allard nous aiderait bien volontiers p^r la traduction à la quelle je ne pourrais donner que bien peu de tems. Quant à la copie qu'il faudrait que tu fisses faire j'imagine que tu pourrais y employer nos aimables nieces et Alex, en l'empêchant d'y trop [*page curled up*] de son amour-propre en s'asseyant sur les bancs d'une ecole avec des enfants de 10 à 13 ans: mais j'aimerais mieux que s'en tenant aux seules mathematiques il eut cherché à se dissiper et à acquerir un peu plus de connoissance du monde. Sa santé d'ailleurs m'inquiete beaucoup. Embrasse le tendrement pour moi et fais de ce que je te dis à ce sujet l'usage que tu trouveras le plus convenable.

Tous nos parens et amis me chargent de les rappeller à ton souvenir. M^{de} de Tessé dont la santé nous a donné quelques inquietudes est tout à fait retablie. M^{de} de Montagu vient de marier sa fille à un de nos anciens camarades Mr Legroing de Laromagère. Melle de Chavagnac est aussi mariée à quelqu'un que tu ne connais pas. Melle de Gre⟨feuil⟩ l'est à Mr de Castelane Col^{el} major du 1er Reg^t des Gardes d'honneur. — — Adieu ma bonne amie. je te souhaite une bonne santé et un prompt retour aussitôt que tu auras terminè tes affaires.

A. P. d'Arblay

[*marginal writing*]

⌐Mon cher docteur et son ami le Noir ont été bien sensibles à ce que tu m'as ecrit d'aimable sur leur compte. Tous deux m'ont expressement chargé de t'en remercier. Tout le monde de ta connoissance voudrait que je le nomasse mais je n'ai plus de papier — — Mad^e Victor de Maubourg toujours à la campagne y jouit d'une santé miraculeuse d'après l'etat où tu l'as laissée. Mad^e de Maisonneuve est toujours la même — c. à. d. l'amie la plus tendre de ma Fanny. Il y a à Chelsea une dame dont le nom est je crois Martyn qui doit partir dans deux mois pour venir ici. Ah si tu pouvais l'accompagner! Je ne puis me ressouvenir de son adresse que des dames anglaises qui demeurent près de l'habitation de Mad^e Victor ont donnée à M^de de Maisonneuve qui me l'a envoyée mais je l'ai [*breaks off, apparently for lack of space*] ⌐

⌐J'oubliais ma bonne amie une chose infiniment essentiele et que je t'ai dejà ecrite plusieurs fois. J'ai remarquè que tes lettres ecrites en français me sont parvenues presque tout de suite. Aye donc la bonté d'ecrire toujours ainsi. Je t'en conjure. Tu m'as mandé que tu ne croyais pas pouvoir venir avant le mois de septembre. Je le crois facilement puisque tu as été tant de tems sans pouvoir sortir plus de deux fois. Je te donne en consequence jusqu'à la fin d'octobre parce qu'alors en se couvrant bien il n'y a pas de risque: mais ce que je te prie d'eviter c'est de t'embarquer dans la quinzaine de l'équinoxe. Et ce que je te recommande par dessus tout c'est de profiter d'un ⟨parlementaire⟩ si l'occasion s'en presente. ⟨   ⟩ et amis. d'A⌐

⌐Mon oncle avec qui j'ai celebré [½ *line illegible*] de sa 82^ieme année n'a jamais été plus gai et plus aimable. Il me charge de te dire mille choses tendres, et de te temoigner l'impatience avec la quelle il attend ton retour. L'aîné de ses petits fils est je crois entré dans la garde d'honneur. Heureusement je connais son Colonel major et j'ai été lié jadis avec le Gen^al de division qui commande encore une garnison interessante.⌐

$£$ *s.* *d.*

Account with Mr. M. Coutts

Debit

1802			£ s. d.
Feb^y	16	To cash p^d Bearer	£24. 4. —
d^o	18	To D^o	36. 15. —
March	24	To Perregaux ⟨H^o⟩	100. —. —
April	9	To M^{rs} D'Arblay's bill	9. —. —
	13	To D^{to}	36. 16. 8
		To a power of Attorney for receiving M^{rs} D'Arblay's pension	.15. 3
	14	To Wm Lock's D^{ft}	350. —. —
	15	To M^{rs} D'Arblay's D^{ft}	19. 14. —
	21	To D^{to}	3. —. —
May	20	To Mr Martin dt on account of Wm Locke	350. —. —
Augst.	14	To Bearer	2. 10. —

Credit

1802				£ s. d.
Feb.	15	By balance of this date		£65 9. 8
	24	By cash rec^d for a quarter's pension to 5 January last		25. —. —
April	6	By £100 five pc^t from our name at 100. 1/2 p^r Ct	£100.10	
		Private transfer 2s.6p		
		Brokerage 2 .6 — 5.		100. 5. —
	9	By the Lady day Div^{de} on £1550 five pr C^t 1797		38. 15. —
May	4	By £332: 1: 8 five pr C^t 1797 at 105 3/4 pr cent	£351. 5. 6	
		Brokerage	8. 3	350. 15. 3

Date	To (Debit)	£ s. d.		Date	By (Credit)	£ s. d.
1803				21	By £337.15.2 D° D° a 103 3/4 pr Ct	
Jan 28	To Perregaux	750. —. —			Brokerage £350. 8. 6 / 8. 6	350. —. —
31	To Postage of letters to this day	12. —		July 10	By the Midsummer div^d on £200 Navy 5 pr C^ts	5. —. —
		1683. 6. 11		Aug 10	By £200 Navy 5 pr C^ts a 100 1/2 p^r C^t	201.
	To Balance carried to your credit in a new account	28. 6. 1			and £523.19. five p Ct 1797 à 104 p Ct	544. 18
		£1711. 13. —				745. 18
					Brokerage .18	745. —. —
				19	By our rect for 1/4 pension on 5 April last	25. —. —
				Oct. 14	By the Mich^as div^d on the £256.4.2 five p^r Ct 1797 in our name	6. 8. 1
						£1711. 13. 1

APPENDIX III

THE OCCUPATION OF JOIGNY

Notices historiques sur l'occupation de la ville de Joigny par les Cosaques le 30 janvier 1814 au soir, rédigées au nom du Conseil municipal et des Notables de la ville peu de jours après cette occupation et au milieu du mouvement des troupes alliées, pour répondre au reproche fait aux habitans de Joigny par ceux d'Auxerre et autres de s'être laissé envahir par 30 cavaliers.

Les originaux de ces notices sont à la Mairie de Joigny. . . . Manuscrit conservé à la Bibliothèque Municipale.

Le 22 janvier 1814, plusieurs personnes de Tonnère et notamment le Sous-Préfet arrivant en poste apprennent à Joigny que l'ennemi est à Laignes, à Ancy-le-Franc, distans de Joigny de 15 lieues environ et va arriver le lendemain. Le soir même, l'ordre du Général Commandant à Auxerre est donné au dépot du 24ᵉ chasseurs à cheval et à 1500 hommes du 153ᵉ régiment d'infanterie qu'étaient en garnison d'évacuer à l'instant sur Orléans. On fit partir jusqu'aux malades.

Ce départ précipité jette l'allarme parmi les habitans, ils se forment en garde urbaine; 300 habitans se répartissent 80 fusils de différents calibres, dont 15 seulement en état de servir et quelques fusils de chasse, mais point de munitions. Cette garde urbaine ne pouvait servir qu'à maintenir l'ordre de l'intérieur.

Le 25, deux envoyés de Joigny à Troyes en reviennent et rapportent qu'une colonne de Cosaques occupant Auxon, Villeneuve-aux-Chemins, Neuvy, à 8 lieues de la ville les avait arrêtés et chargés d'une lettre et de proclamations pour le Maire de Joigny; il les porte lui-même au Préfet, aux Généraux Moreau, Vaux et Bellaire. Le 27, deux pièces de canon son envoyées d'Auxerre à Joigny au Commandant de la place, mais sans aucune munition, déjà une compagnie de cannonniers s'était organisée pour les servir, elle devient inutile, le lendemain à 5 h. du matin, l'ordre arrive du général d'Auxerre de les faire partir pour Sens; le même jour le commandant de place nous quitte; les officiers, dragons, gendarmes, fantassins, tous armés arrivent d'Auxerre au milieu de la nuit. Ils emmènent avec eux des canons, des munitions. On aurait voulu garder une caisse de cartouches, ils s'y opposent; ils s'embarquent tous dans des bateaux avec précipitation; le général Vaux assure que l'ennemi est à leur poursuite, qu'il arrivera dans la journée; il s'irrite du moindre retard; tous filent sur Sens, et Joigny reste dans la consternation; il est le dernier poste ouvert à l'irruption de l'ennemi, il en voit plus aucun secours devant lui; toutes les forces qui se replient par derrière ne lui laissent que le désespoir de ne pouvoir se défendre.

D'un autre côté, on avait la certitude par les piétons, par les Maires de la forêt d'Othe qui borde la ville au Nord que 7 à 8000 ennemis avec de l'artillerie étaient à Arcis, à Dilo, à 4 lieues de Joigny; on en informait journellement le Préfet et le Ministre de la Police générale.

On ferme les portes de la ville sur la forêt, les autres portes sur la grande route, n'ayant pas de grilles fermantes restent ouvertes, et d'ailleurs la partie de la ville consacrée à l'exercice des troupes est ouverte. Un corps de garde néanmoins est établi de la caserne sur le quai où passe la route.

Des gardes forestiers et champêtres de l'arrondissement réunis au chef-lieu restent pendant deux jours pour faire quelques reconnaissances et se dispersent à la vue des troupes de ligne qui filent; la brigade de gendarmerie, l'unique force militaire qui restait disparaît aussi, et les habitans de Joigny, privés de tout secours et sans armes sont abandonnés à eux-mêmes dans l'impossibilité de rien entreprendre.

De toutes parts on apprend que 4000 hommes avaient traversé la forêt pendant la nuit à deux lieues de Joigny et s'étaient campés sous Villeneuve-sur-Yonne, qu'une autre colonne est dans les communes voisines, à une lieue. En effect, le 30 janvier une troupe de cosaques à cheval commandée par plusieurs officiers dont un major décoré et guidée par un habitant de la commune de Brion et descendue par le Chemin de la Guimbarde, côté de la Forêt, entre à la nuit par la porte de Saint-Florentin, la lance en avant, tombe sur la sentinelle qui avait en vain crié: "qui vive!", désarme le poste qui n'avait pas un coup à tirer, le disperse, fouille les casernes et monte à cheval à l'Hôtel de ville, en annonçant qu'elle n'est que l'avantgarde de 4000 hommes qui arrivent après elle. (On avait remarqué qu'un cosaque s'était détaché et était sorti de la ville, pour apparemment aller prévenir qu'il n'y avait aucune force militaire à Joigny.)

Le Commandant demande à l'adjoint (Mr d'Albizzi) (le Maire s'étant retiré) des vivres et des fourrages pour sa troupe, lui prescrit de préparer les rations pour les 4000 hommes qui le suivent et après avoir établi des postes à toutes les issues vient bivouaquer le long du quai, y passe la nuit et part le lendemain pour Villeneuvé. Le Sous-Préfet au moment de cette invasion traverse les postes ennemis pour se retirer dans la partie de l'arrondissement non occupée.

Après cette prise de possession par l'ennemi, la garde urbaine reprend encore son service, le 30 janvier pour le maintien de la tranquillité. Le Maire, de retour, donne l'ordre de n'arrêter aucun cosaque passant, mais le 1er février à midi, un officier, un de ceux qui commandaient l'envahissement de la surveille, et un cosaque dans une voiture de poste et prenant la route de Saint-Florentin son avertis par la sentinelle de s'arrêter; ils n'en pressent pas moins le postillon d'avancer; un militaire d'une commune voisine, (Colinet, de Senan) se jette à la voiture et à l'aide de quelques particuliers les force à en descendre; ils sont conduits par le garde et une foule de peuple à l'Hôtel de Ville devant le Maire, qui les fait retenir.

Oubliant sans doute l'ordre qu'il avait donné, il se proposait de les faire conduire à Auxerre; il finissait une lettre au Préfet pour le prévenir de cet événement, où allait l'envoyer, lorsqu'à l'instant même un envoyé de Joigny arrivant de Sens fait le rapport qu'il avait été arrêté la veille au soir par les Cosaques qui l'avaient conduit au camp Villeneuve-sur-Yonne où il avait passé la nuit; que ce camp pouvait être composé de 7 à 8000 hommes, était garni d'artillerie et commandé par le comte de Platov général russe, qui, le matin, avait fait relâcher notre envoyé avec un sauf-conduit.

Cette confirmation d'une force aussi considérable à 4 lieues de Joigny y jette la plus juste alarme; d'est de ce camp que sortent ceux que l'on vient d'arrêter; que faire contre les 8000 qui viendront redemander leurs hommes ⟨sans⟩ aucun moyen de résistance, la ville ouverte de toutes parts, nul espoir de secours prochain, aucune nouvelle des armées françaises; il fallait plutôt sauver la ville de l'incendie que de vouloir retenir les gens d'un ennemi qui ne manquerait pas le lendemain d'en tirer vengeance.

Dans cette crise, le Maire s'entoure du Conseil municipal, de tous les Notables et principaux propriétaires de la ville et d'anciens militaires au fait des lois de la guerre. Tous apportent un coeur français, mais aucun moyen de défense. On traite la question importante de savoir si la ville ayant été occupée par l'ennemi et n'ayant plus été reprise était devenue pays conquis. L'avis unanime est que la ville ayant été conquise est au pouvoir de l'ennemi et qu'elle n'a le droit de retenir aucun des siens sans s'exposer à une exécution militaire. En conséquence, les deux cosaques sont relâchés, ils repartent le soir pour Villeneuve d'où ils étaient venus. Le Maire quitte la ville dans la nuit et n'a pas encore reparu.

Le lendemain 2 février sur les 10 heures du matin, environ 7 à 8000 hommes de cavalerie russe avec 4 pièces de canon et 2 obusiers se présentent à l'entrée de la ville du côte de Paris, s'emparent en un instant de toutes les issues; 600 franchissent rapidement les hauteurs des vignes, s'établissent sur les montagnes qui nous dominent, y placent leur artillerie et y allument des feux. En un instant la ville est cernée de toutes parts.

Le Commandant à la Tête de son Etat-Major et d'une troupe en bataille sur la grande route et sur le quai somme l'Adjoint de lui livrer à l'instant le militaire et la sentinelle qui avaient arrêté ses envoyés. Il annonce les ordres du Général de les faire fusiller, et de réduire la ville en cendres pour réparation de l'insulte faite à ses envoyés.

Des explications ont lieu, des observations sont faites; le commandant s'apaise. Mais il ordonne que dans l'heure, sous peine d'exécution militaire, tous les habitans apportent les armes de toute espèce qu'ils peuvent avoir. Après la remise des armes, il fait assembler la garde, la passa en revue, la constitue prisonnière de guerre, mais de suite il fait proclamer qu'en considération de ce qu'il ne voit dans cette garde que des citadins pères de famille il leur rend la liberté et qu'il espère que son Prince le trouvera bon.

La remise des fusils de la garde urbaine et des fusils de chasse ainsi que du restant des munitions a assez justifié qu'il n'y avait pas lieu à la moindre résistance.

Depuis la ville est en proie aux passages journaliers et à toutes les réquisitions de l'ennemi.

Les habitans de Joigny réunis à l'Hôtel de Ville après la lecture du présent rapport en ont tous approuvé le contenu; ceux même qui n'ont pu se trouver à la journée de 1er février pour le renvoi des Cosaques reconnaissant que la mesure prise a été impérieusement recommandée par les circonstances et a sauvé la ville.

A Joigny, le 2 février 1814.

APPENDIX IV

EXCERPTS FROM REVIEWS OF
THE WANDERER

FROM the *Quarterly Review*, xi (Apr. 1814), 124:

If we had not been assured in the title-page that this work had been produced by the same pen as Cecilia, we should have pronounced Madame D'Arblay to be a feeble imitator of the style and manner of Miss Burney— we should have admitted the flat fidelity of her copy, but we should have lamented the total want of vigour, vivacity, and originality; and, conceding to the fair author . . . some discrimination of character, and some power of writing, we should have strenuously advised her to avoid, in future, the dull mediocrity of a copyist, and to try the flight of her own genius in some work, that should not recall to us in every page the mortifying recollection of excellence which, though she had the good sense to admire it, she never would have the power to rival.

The same journal (pp. 129–30) also attacked FBA as a supporter of Napoleonic tyranny.

We learn from the preface . . . that these volumes were written between the years 1802 and 1812, in Paris, where she enjoyed, as she informs us, under the mild and beneficent government of Napoleon the Great, 'ten unbroken years'—'neither startled by any species of investigation, nor distressed through any difficulties of conduct, by a precious fire-side, or in select society, a stranger to all personal disturbance.'
Now really we should have expected, if Madame D'Arblay were restrained by her feelings, whatever they might be, from expressing her detestation of the gigantic despotism, the ferocious cruelty, the restless and desolating tyranny of Buonaparte, that, at least, she should not have sought for opportunities of insinuating her gratitude for the blessings, the tender mercies which France enjoyed under the dominion of that tyger. . . .
This fault, however,—if the work should come to another edition— Madame D'Arblay will probably correct; because, since the publication of the last, Buonaparte has been overthrown and exiled; and we think we may assume . . . that Madame D'Arblay is not likely to continue to flatter, when her flattery can no longer conduce to her personal convenience.

Equally censorious was William Hazlitt's evaluation in the *Edinburgh Review*, xxiv. 320–38, which had been bruited long before its appearance in February 1815. It argued on p. 337 that '[t]here is little other power in Miss Burney's novels, than that of immediate observation: her characters, whether of refinement or vulgarity, are equally superficial and confined. . . . The difficulties in which she involves her heroines are indeed 'Female Difficulties;'—they are difficulties created out of nothing.

In the nearly sympathetic review found in *The British Critic* (Apr. 1814, p. 376), there is an attack on the language of *The Wanderer*. 'During her long residence in France, she appears to have forgotten the common elegancies of her native tongue; and, throughout her preface, to have indulged her impartiality between the rival nations, by adopting a phraseology which is neither French nor English, but uniting the bombast of the one with the awkwardness of the other.'

Probably the most favourable of all *The Wanderer* reviews was that which appeared in the *Gentlemen's Magazine* (lxxxiv[1]. 579–81) for June 1814:

Whatever proceeds from the pen of Madame D'Arblay has two most powerful advocates in the public breast—an universal respect attends her parental name; and each individual who has perused her almost matchless 'Cecilia' will feel convinced that every work of her production will come before them fraught with the strongest incitements to the practice of every degree of honour and virtue. 'The Wanderer' is an example of inflexible rectitude, suffering every privation that a fertile imagination could invent, and at length emerging from her miseries, with an unsullied reputation, a pure mind, and a reward such as poetical justice should ever bestow as a return for the exercise of the best qualities of our nature. The Wanderer is a young and beautiful female, driven alone from France during the reign of terror, who is compelled by her peculiar situation to parry every attempt to discover her name and family, either through the efforts of curiosity or malignity, or of the most unwearied and active benevolence. A person thus situated may be supposed to have fallen into a variety of 'difficulties,' and amongst a variety of characters, which characters and difficulties are delineated with various success. That of Albert Harleigh, the ultimate husband of the Incognita, is as amiable as the conceptions of the Writer are pure and instructive; but they all fade before the ardent, the independent assertor of the 'Rights of Women,' Miss Elinor Joddrel, a young lady who, sent to the South of France for the recovery of her health, returns (*driven thence by the terrors of the guillotine*) a genuine Republican and Free-thinker, completely released from all human prejudices, and willing to act in defiance of each friend and relative who wished to oppose her opinions. Elinor is decidedly the second person of the drama; and we find her exhibited in every light which is calculated to excite abhorrence for those doctrines that, the French themselves now blush to remember, once rendered their Nation infamous in the eyes of all dispassionate persons. The Reader will expect, in consequence of this information, much extravagance in the speeches and conduct of Miss Joddrel; nor will he be disappointed, or displeased to find the Authoress leaves room to suppose she returns to the good old maxims from which she had been perverted. Had this Novel appeared when the infatuation alluded to reigned in full force, it must have made a much stronger impression upon the public mind than it will at present; but as there are juvenile readers continually immerging into life, we trust 'The Wanderer' will have its use, and serve as an historical antidote to any lurking remnants of poisonous doctrines that still make their appearance at intervals, as our courts of justice too plainly testify.

Almost as laudatory was William Taylor's examination of the novel in the *Monthly Review* (lxxvi. 412–19) a year later in April 1815. Still there is a caveat on p. 419: 'When a new edition of this novel is undertaken, we should recommend something of abridgment, especially of the comic portions; and of those dialogues which continue indeed a consistent behaviour of the inferior characters, but which add no new traits to an individuality that is sufficiently peculiarized on their first introduction.'

APPENDIX V

A FIRM of booksellers, at the sign of the 'Ship and Black Swan, in Paternoster Row', was initiated by Thomas Longman (1699–1755). In 1754 his nephew Thomas II (1731–97) became a partner and from 1755 onward its director. In 1792 he began to withdraw from the firm's management in favour of his son Thomas Norton Longman (1771–1842). Owen Rees was admitted a member in 1794 when 'T. & T. Longman' became 'Longman & Co.' and *c.* 1800 'Longman & Rees'. By 1812 Cosmo Orme, Thomas Hurst, and Thomas Brown had joined 'Longman & Rees' so that the firm was now 'Longman, Hurst, Rees, Orme & Brown' of 39 Paternoster Row. Prior to his membership Thomas Hurst had his own bookshop at 32 Paternoster Row.

John Murray II (1778–1843), on the death of his father John MacMurray (1745–93), assumed control of a firm of booksellers and publishers at The Ship, 32 Fleet Street, opposite St. Dunstan's (1768–93). Under his own name and (briefly) that of Murray & [Samuel] Highley, he functioned at this address. (From 1805 to 1807 he had two other shops—326 Oxford Street and 13 Prince's Street, Soho, as well as at 32 Fleet Street.) Sometime between 1812 and 1815 his address is listed as Albemarle Street.

Henry Colburn (d. 1855) conducted a publishing business and lending library at 50 Conduit Street, New Bond Street (and *post* 1815 in New Burlington Street, for a short time in Windsor, and finally in Great Marlborough Street). Despite financial cunning, he was fair, even generous in his transactions.

'Honest Tom Payne' (1719–99), JB's father-in-law, began his long bookselling career as assistant to his elder brother Oliver at Round Court in the Strand. Through his marriage to Elizabeth Taylor (1745), he succeeded his brother-in-law, who had a bookshop in Castle Street next the Mewsgate, Charing Cross. When he retired in 1790, his son Thomas II (1752–1831) owned the firm and moved to larger quarters in 1806 at 88 Pall Mall. He continued at this address, taking his apprentice Henry Foss as a partner in 1813.

A firm of booksellers was begun in 1763–4 by George Robinson (1737–1801) and John Roberts (d. 1776). In 1784 Robinson (later known as 'the king of booksellers') made his brother John Robinson (1753–1813) and his own son George (d. 1811) his partners. After 1812 the firm's name was changed from 'George' to 'John Robinson', although its address remained 25 Paternoster Row.

Possibly in 1725 Benjamin White became a bookseller. After his death in 1794, the business was carried on at Horace's Head, 64 Fleet Street, by his sons Benjamin and John White (1794–9), and undergoing management changes (John Wright, 1800–2; G. Wright, 1805–10), it operated between 1812 and 1816 as Wright, Cochrane & Co.

The firm of booksellers and publishers founded in 1711 by Charles Rivington I (1688–1742) continued to prosper under the management of his fourth son John (1720–92) from 1740 to 1792. After the latter's death, the house of Rivington, located at 62 St. Paul's Churchyard (also at 59 Paternoster Row) was directed by his sons Francis (1745–1822) and Charles (1754–1831).

Edward Williams (d. 1838) owned a bookshop at 11 Strand that was founded in 1760 by his more celebrated father John, pilloried as a 'Wilkes & Liberty' man.

James Malcott Richardson was a bookseller and stockbroker at 23 Cornhill from 1810 to 1853.

Established by Thomas Hookham and maintained at various addresses (notably 100 New Bond Street, corner of Bruton Street), the firm in 1813 was operated by E. T. and Thomas Hookham Jr. at 15 Old Bond Street.

Samuel Leigh was a bookseller and publisher at 18 Strand until 1831. George Leigh (d. 1815) was a bookseller and auctioneer at 9 York Street, Covent Garden, and then at 145 Strand.

The bookselling business conducted by James Mathews (d. 1804 at 18 Strand was continued at that address by Mrs. Elizabeth Mathews, presumably his wife.

Joseph Booker (d. 1837) was a bookseller at 61 New Bond Street.

John Hatchard (1769–1849), who identified himself as 'Bookseller to her Majesty', had his bookshop at 190 Piccadilly. He began his career as an assistant to Thomas Payne the elder.

The booksellers listed above have been identified from the following sources: H. R. Plomer, G. H. Bushnell, E. R. McC. Dix, *A Dictionary of the Printers and Booksellers who were at Work in England, Scotland, and Ireland from 1726 to 1775* (1932); *Kent's Directory* for 1800; *Post Office Annual Directory* for 1812 ff.; *Holden's Triennial Directory* for 1805 ff.; *DNB*; P. A. H. Brown, *London Publishers and Printers: 1800–1870* (1961); John Nichols, *Literary Anecdotes of the Eighteenth Century* (9 vols., 1812–15). See also William B. Todd, *A Directory of Printers and Others in Allied Trades London and Vicinity 1800–1840* (1972).

INDEX

to Volume vii

Members of the British nobility are listed under family names with cross-references to titles.

Members of the French and European nobility are listed under the name and title by which they are best known, with cross-references to other names and titles.

Women are listed under their married names, with cross-references to maiden names and earlier married names.

In listing members of family groups, the alphabet is normally disregarded in order to clarify family relationships.

Short biographies or concentrations of biographical information are marked by numbers in bold face.

Index

Alexander I, H.I.M. (1777–1825), Tsar of Russia:
ally of England in 1812, 17 n.;
appearance, 514–15;
as Europe's 'Pacificator', 515;
as hero of France, 287;
his arrival in England, 366;
fêted by English Royal Family, 361 n., 514–15;
tours in London, Greenwich, and Chelsea, 406 n.;
mentioned, 100 n., 270 n., 284 n., 318, 332, 362 n., **366 n.**, 376, 397, 414 n., 450 n., 515.

Alien Act. *See* England.

Alien Office. *See* England.

Alison, the Revd. Archibald (1757–1839), prebendary of Sarum, 131 n.;
—— *Essays on the Nature and Principles of Taste* (1790), **173.**

Alison, Dorothea, *née* Gregory (*c.* 1755–1830), wife of the preceding, 131.

Alison, —— (d. 1812), daughter of the above, 173.

Allart, Marie-Françoise, *née* Gay (1765–1821), novelist, 229 n., 520, 556.

Allen, Elizabeth. *See* Burney, Elizabeth.

ALLEN, John Bartlett (1733–1803), of Cresselly, Pembrokeshire, **54 n.**

Allen, Lancelot Baugh (1774–1845), son of the preceding, master of Dulwich Academy, 237 n.

Allen, Catherine, sister of the preceding. *See* Mackintosh, Catherine.

Allen, Mary (d. *pre* 1812), sister of the preceding, 54 n.

Allen, Jessie, sister of the preceding. *See* Sismondi, Jessie.

Allen, Emma (1780–1866), sister of the preceding, 54 n., 184.

Allen, Frances (1782–1875), sister of the preceding, 54 n., 184.

Allen, Maria, sister of the following. *See* Rishton, Maria.

Allen, Martha. *See* Young, Martha.

Allen, the Revd. Stephen (1755–1847), FBA's stepbrother, 190 n., 467.

Alpy, Bonne-Jeanne d' (1777/8–1839), 520.

Alsace-Hénin-Liétard. *See* Hénin, princesse d'.

Alsace-Hénin-Liétard, Laure-Auguste

d', *née* de Fitz-James (1744–1814), princesse de Chimay, **20 n.**

Althorp, Northants, seat of the Spencers, 63 n., **70**, 75, 200, 201–2, 208, 218, 222, 223 n., 224, 232, 415, 501, 502.

Althorp, Viscount. *See* Spencer, George John, 2nd Earl Spencer.

Alty, John (1789–1815), of Jesus College, Cambridge, **246**, 249, 259.

Ambrugeac, Louis-Alexandre-Marie de Valon du Boucheron d' (1771–1844), comte d', **378.**

Amelia, H.R.H. Princess (1783–1810), 16 n., 106 n., 117 n., 118 n.

Analytical Society. *See* Cambridge University and Herschel, John Frederick William.

Andréossi [or Andréossy], Antoine-François d' (1761–1828), comte d', général, **419 n.**

Andréossi, Marie-*Stéphanie*-Florimonde d', *née* de Fay de Latour-Maubourg (1790–1868), wife of the preceding, 520.

Angerstein, John Julius I (1735–1823), 184, 185:
his residence: in London; at Woodlands, Blackheath, 185 n.;
M. d'A's financial account with, 421, 547–59, **553.**

Angerstein, Anna, *née* Muilman (Crokatt) (d. 1783), wife of the preceding, 185 n.

Angerstein, John (*c.* 1773–1858), M.P., son of John Julius (*supra*), 46, 82 n., 83, 93, 313, 324, 346, 454, 456, 460, 469–70,

Angerstein, Amelia, *née* Locke (1776–1848), wife of the preceding:
as Amelia Locke, 546;
corresponds with FBA *re* sale of Camilla Cottage, 338, 345;
fondness for AA, 415;
her residence at Great Cumberland Place, 313;
mentioned, 26, 49, 117, 141, 284, 285, 290, 293, 296, 314, 345, 368 n., 454 n., 507, 508, 510, 511, 512, 513, 515, 516, 517, 518.

Angerstein, Juliana, sister of John. *See* Sablonkoff, Juliana.

Anglo-Russian Peace Treaty. *See* Russia.

travels:

plans for holidays in Italy and southern France, 441, 480;

return to England in spring 1814, 6 n., 333, 335;

return to France, 341;

safe arrival in Paris, 341 n., 343 n.;

return to England, autumn 1814, departs for France with FBA, 442, 453, 467, 470, 473, 476, 512, 516;

death, 295 n., 329;

mentioned, 2, 5, 11, 18, 20, 24, 42 n., 44, 56, 92, 104, 106, 175, 189, 198, 235, 255 n., 261, 262, 264, 295, 312, 322, 343, 368 n., 401 n., 467, 473, 477, 480, 485, 492, 500, 503, 509, 513, 515, 516, 517.

Arblay, Frances d', *née* BURNEY (1752–1840) [FB/FBA]. The entries for Madame d'Arblay are classified under the following headings:

I. Chief events of her life (annual outlines).

II. Biographical data.

III. Travel and tours.

IV. Works read.

V. Works written or in progress; editorial work.

VI. Mentioned.

I. CHIEF EVENTS OF HER LIFE (ANNUAL OUTLINES)

1812: FBA arrives in England (1–12), where she has a reunion with her family (10–34). She moves about from residence to residence— Chelsea College, Deptford Rectory, Chenies Street (19–55). Her financial concerns involve the disposition of Camilla Cottage and the disentanglement of her pension from CB's account (34, 47, 49–50). She spends her mornings working on *The Wanderer*, which has already crossed the Channel twice (34, 51, 107). She refuses to return to France at her husband's summons because she feels too much is at stake in England (22–3, 24–7). AA is enrolled at Greenwich School where he prepares for eventual matriculation at Caius College, Cambridge

(44). The absence of M. d'A is a constant source of anguish for FBA (35 *passim*).

1813: She spares neither herself nor others to obtain a Tancred Scholarship for AA and she is successful in her efforts (71–8, 82–95, 97–100). *The Wanderer* nears completion and is negotiated for sale largely through the efforts of CB Jr. and later of Martin Burney (102–5). FBA suffers from influenza (caught from AA) and a lingering low-grade fever (101, 105). In a desire for renewed health and for the sake of friendship she visits Norbury Park in the spring (105–11). But in London her efforts to renew her friendship with Mrs. Piozzi (with MF as intermediary) come to nothing (118, 120–3). With the help of certain members of her family and Sharon Turner as consultant, she begins serious negotiations with the House of Longman for the sale of *The Wanderer* (138, 145–8, 152–3, 153–5, 165–6, 187 n.). Longman's offer is accepted against strong competition and the manuscript of *The Wanderer* is completed (156–7, 159, 166, 189, 190). AA is tutored at Greenwich School for matriculation at Caius (Michaelmas term, 1813) (161, 168, 180–1 n., 183 n., 189, 190).

1814: *The Wanderer* is published 28 Mar. 1814 (184, 200, 217, 222, 237–8, 256, 260–1). CB dies in his sleep 12 Apr. 1814 and is buried 20 Apr. (272, 280–1, 283–6, 290). Despite her mourning FBA is urged to attend the reception of Louis XVIII in London and to wait upon the duchesse d'Angoulême (289–317). As the Bourbons return to France and the Restoration begins, M. d'A loses his post as a civil servant (274). Wishing to become a French consul in England, he is forced to be a sous-lieutenant in the 'compagnie de Luxembourg des gardes

573

need to retrieve pension from
CB's account, 33–4, 47, 48 n.,
149, 548, 549;
need to sell and transfer stocks,
250, 407–8, 414 n., 455, 462;
need of procuration to handle
business affairs, 407, 408, 455,
462;
parsimony, 44, 133–4, 294,
326–9, 431, 465;
pension, 33–4, 47 n., 48 n., 50 n.,
133–4 n., 149, 328;
rejection of indebtedness, 161 n.,
222, 250, 264, 281, 333;
residuary legatee for CB's estate
and inheritance, 325, 355,
357–8, 390, 407–8, 414, 463 n.,
505–6;
sale of *The Wanderer* and gamble
upon editions, 48 n., 271;
statement of financial affairs
(1802–3, 1814), 326–9, 547–59;
stress upon financial stringency
for M. d'A, her refusal to
attend Louis's coronation,
332 n., 413–14, 431, 463;
struggle against need to think of
or handle money, 133–4, 153;
transfer of rents and other capital held by the Lockes, 48 n.,
149, 176;
trustees, 176.
3. *Family relations with:*
her father [CB]:
writes cheerful letters to. *See* CB,
Letters to.
as self-made man, 352;
first meeting with, 4 n., 10–11;
many visits to, 116, 195–6, 509;
his declining health, 10–11;
his depression and FBA's re-
medies, 11, 17–18, 46–7,
69–71, 74–5, 79–80;
seeks his help on behalf of the
Tancred for AA, 73–5, 76;
temporary therapeutic effect on,
11 n.;
presence at his death, 322–3;
mourns the death of, 283–4,
322, 324, 516;
his will justified by, 283, 291
passim, 325–6, 352, 438;
works on CB's papers, 457, 479;

her brother Charles [CB Jr.]:
awaits CB Jr. at Deal, 9–10;
accidental meeting upon a common, 10, 507;
encourages his desire for a
bishopric, 269;
pride in his religious reputation
and preaching at the Chapel
Royal (q.v.);
CB's will and CB Jr. as an
executor; her quarrels over
the will and peace-offerings,
346 *passim*, 462, 491;
visits at Deptford, 20, 44–5, 54
passim, 491, 508, 509;
worry about his health, 409, 438;
her brother James [JB]:
first meeting with, 12;
his concern for her health,
15–16;
fears ill effects of, on AA, 417;
makes peace with, over CB's
will, 349–50;
visits, 17, 268, 350, 361–2, 509,
515, 517, 518;
wishes JB or his family to share
in profits of 'Irish mortgage',
337, 342, 506;
her sister Esther [EBB]:
her courage, 25;
her animation, 25;
concerned that EBB receive
share of CB's estate, 348;
visits in John Street and at Turnham Green, 20, 70, 509;
finds EBB's husband good but
indecisive, 25, 31;
her sister Charlotte [CBFB]:
first meeting, 3 n., 12;
concern over her health, 41;
lives with her in Chenies Street,
'picnic' style, 21 n. *passim*;
moves to Richmond to be near
her, 430, 431 n.;
visits, 14, 20, 194 n., 351–2, 430,
438;
sends her a writing box as farewell gift, 490;
her sister Susanna [SBP]:
grieves for, 126, 248, 502, 509;
regards Molesworth Phillips as
responsible for SBP's death,
248;

Index

Index

Barrett, Henry (1756–1843), 31, 41, 51, 63, 166, 223, 250, 264, 282, 333, 353, 468, 499.

Barrett, Charlotte, *née* Francis (1786–1870), wife of the preceding, FBA's niece [CFBt]:
Letters to, Nos. 662, 714, 738, 749;
exchange of letters with MF, 31 n., 33 n., 34 n., 38 n.;
FBA receives letter from, 3 n.;
FBA invited to visit, 3 n.;
her third child born, 62;
her fourth child born, 482;
her visit to Sandgate, 156, 160, 183 n.;
receives a presentation copy of *The Wanderer*, 262 n.;
receives a set of Molière from CB's library, 351;
mentioned, 12, 17, 39, 41, 51, 88, 120 n., 124, 161, 166, 181, 196, 202 n., 250, 264, 282, 334, 354, 482, 485, 494, 499, 508, 509, 518.

Barrett, the Revd. Richard Arthur Francis (1812–81), son of the above, 39 n., 62, 70, 166, 223, 251, 333.

Barrett, Henry John Richard (1814–29), brother of the preceding, 482.

Barrett, Julia Charlotte, sister of the preceding. *See* Maitland, Julia Charlotte (Thomas).

Barrett, Henrietta Hester (1811–33), sister of the preceding, 52 n., 166, 223, 250, 333, 499.

Bassano, duc de. *See* Maret, Hugues-Bernard.

Bateman, Anna Maria, *née* Hedges (1727–1802), 165 n.

Bath, Somerset, 98 n., 123 n., 414, 530–1;
the Thrales visit, 530, 543;
Piozzi marriage at, 543.

Bath and Wells, Bishop of. *See* Eden, Robert John.

Bath Easton [Batheaston], Somerset, Maria Bourdois's residence there, 26 n.

Bathurst, Henry (1762–1841), Earl of, statesman, 129 n., 256 n.

Batty, Robert (1788–1848), Lieutenant-Colonel, writer, **77 n.**, 99 n.;
A Sketch of the Late Campaign in the Netherlands (1815), 77 n.

Bauffremont, Hélène, princesse de. *See* Choiseul-Gouffier, Hélène de.

Bauffremont, Hortense-Geneviève-Marie-Anne de. *See* Ferari de Romans, comtesse de.

Bayonne. *See* France.

Bazille, Jean-Baptiste-*Gabriel* (1731–1817), M. d'A's maternal uncle, 137, 284, 332, 382, 384 n., 392, 412, 471, 557.

Bazille, Marie-Euphémie-Claudine, daughter of the above. *See* Meignen, Marie-Euphémie-Claudine.

Bazille, Marie-Julie, *née* Ragon (1772–1840), daughter-in-law of Jean-Baptiste-*Gabriel*, 520.

Bazille de Précourt, Gabriel (1794–post 1813), eldest grandson of Jean-Baptiste-*Gabriel*, 557.

Bazille du Clos, Claudine, *née* Girardin (c. 1740–1827), sister-in-law of Jean-Baptiste-*Gabriel*, 520.

Beaufort, Dukes of. *See* Somerset, Henry Charles and Charles Noel.

Beaufort, Frances. *See* Edgeworth, Frances.

Beaumont, George Howland (1753–1827), **290 n.**

Beaunay, Louise-Étiennette de. *See* Beauvau, Louise-Étiennette de.

Beaune, vicomte de. *See* Montagu-Beaune, Joachim de.

Beaune, baron de. *See* La Frangne, Guillaume-Jean-Baptiste de.

Beaupré, comte de. *See* Choiseul-Gouffier, Marie-Gabriel-Auguste de.

Beauvau, Louise-Étiennette (de Beaunay) de, *née* Desmier d'Archiac de Saint-Simon (c. 1747–1831), sister-in-law of Charles-Just (1720–93), 2nd prince de Beauvau-Craon, 519.

BEAUVAU, Marc-Étienne-Gabriel de (1773–1849), 3rd prince de Beauvau-Craon, son of Louise-Étiennette, **419,** 422, 431 n.

Beauvau, Nathalie-Henriette-Victurnienne de, *née* de Rochechouart de Mortemart (1774–1854), princesse de Beauvau-Craon, wife of the preceding, **332,** 419, 498, 519.

Beauvau, Charles-Just-François-Victurnien de (1793–1864), officier de Carabiniers, aide-de-camp to the

Index

duc de Feltre, son of the above, **419 n.**, 420.

Beauvau, Lucie-Virginie de, *née* de Choiseul-Praslin (1795–1834), princesse de Beauvau-Craon, wife of the above, sister of the duc de Praslin, **420 n.**

Beauvau, Edmond-Étienne-Victurnien de (1795–1861), brother of Charles, **193 n.**, 420, 441.

Beauvau, Nathalie-Irène-Marie-Victurnienne, sister of the preceding. *See* Le Lièvre, Nathalie.

Beauvau, Henriette-Gabrielle-Apolline de, sister of the preceding. *See* Talon, vicomtesse de.

Beckedorff, Charlotte (*fl.* 1802–18), Keeper of the Robes to Queen Charlotte, 82 n.;
Letters to, Nos. 786, 639A, 685A, 695A;
FBA writes to, 15 n.;
FBA dines with, 15 n.;
protects Queen from mad woman, 117 n., 498;
writes to FBA about the royal interest in the Tancred, 90 n.;
mentioned, 35 n., 74 n., 83 n., 93 n., 109 n., 118, 148 n., 261 n., 295, 508, 513, 514.

Beckedorff, Sophia (*fl.* 1807–18), daughter of the preceding, 74 n., 81 n., 148 n., 496, 498.

Belcotton, County Louth, residence of Molesworth Phillips, 342 n.

Belfast, Marchioness of. *See* Donegall, Anna May.

Bellaire, Antoine-Alexandre-Julienne (1775–1838), baron de Bellaire, général, 560.

Bellamy, the Revd. James (1788–1874), Headmaster of Merchant Taylors' School, **407 n.**, 430, 454–5, 464.

Belloy, Henriette de. *See* Malouet, Henriette.

Bénévent, prince de. *See* Talleyrand-Périgord, Charles-Maurice de.

Bentinck, William (1709–62), 2nd Duke of Portland, **19 n.**

Bentinck, Margaret Cavendish, *née* Harley (1715–85), Duchess of Portland, wife of the preceding, **19 n.**

Bentinck, William Henry Cavendish, 3rd Duke of Portland, son of the above. *See* Cavendish-Bentinck, William Henry Cavendish.

Bentley, Richard (1708–82), son of the Revd. Richard Bentley (1662–1742), classical scholar, 35 n., 252 n.

Bernard, Jeanne-Françoise-Julie-Adélaïde. *See* Récamier, Jeanne-Françoise-Julie-Adélaïde.

Berry [Berri], Charles-Ferdinand, duc de. *See* Bourbon, Charles-Ferdinand de.

Berry, duchesse de, wife of the preceding. *See* Bourbon, Marie-*Caroline*-Ferdinande-Louise de.

Berry, Agnes (1764–1852), sister of the following, 46, 52, 130.

Berry, Mary (1763–1852), 46, 52, 54 n., 130, 207 n., 223 n., 287 n.;
The Berry Papers (1914), ed. Lewis Melville, 54 n.

Berthier, Louis-Alexandre (1753–1815), prince de Neuchâtel et de Wagram, maréchal de France, 359 n.

Berulle [Berule], Catherine-Philiberte-Françoise. *See* Thuisy, Catherine-Philiberte-Françoise de.

Bessborough, Countess of. *See* Ponsonby, Henrietta Frances.

Beurnonville, Pierre de Riel (1752–1821), marquise de, maréchal de France, 359 n., **376 n.**

Bexley, Baron. *See* Vansittart, Nicholas.

Bickerstaffe, Isaac (*c.* 1735–1812), dramatist, 46 n.;
Lionel and Clarissa (1776–7), 46 n.

Bicknell, Sabrina, *called* Sidney (*c.* 1757–1843), housekeeper for CB Jr., **65 n.**, 89, 114, 162, 191, 519.

Bicknell, John Laurens (*c.* 1786–1845), barrister-at-law, son of the preceding, 45.

Bicknell, Henry Edgeworth (1787–1879), brother of the preceding, 45.

Billy, Joachim-Nicolas (1748–1837), merchant, **294 n.**, 395.

Bingham, Charles (1735–99), 1st Earl of Lucan, **199 n.**

Bingham, Lavinia, daughter of the preceding. *See* Spencer, Lavinia, Countess Spencer.

Biren, Anne-Charlotte-Dorothée de, *née* de Medem (1761–1821), duchesse

Index

Biren (*cont.*):
de Courlande, 3rd wife of Pierre II (d. 1800), duc de Courlande et Sagan, 201 n.

Blacas d'Aulps, Pierre-Louis-Jean-Casimir (1771–1839), duc de, pair de France, **443**.

Blaenpant, Cardiganshire, estate of William Owen Brigstocke, 358–9 n.

Blaquiere, Anna Maria de. *See* Fitz-Maurice, Anna Maria.

Blaquiere, John de (1776–1844), 2nd Baron of Ardkill, brother of the preceding, 26 n., **173**.

Blücher, Gebhard Leberecht (1742–1819), prince von Wahlstadt, Commander-in-Chief of the Prussian army, 256 n., 257 n., **397 n.**, 514, 516.

Boinville. *See* Chastel de Boinville.

Bolingbroke, Viscount. *See* St. John, Henry.

Bonaparte, Napoléon. *See* Napoléon I.

Bonaparte, Caroline, grande-duchesse de Berg et de Clèves, Queen of Naples, sister of the preceding. *See* Murat, Caroline.

Bonaparte, Lucien (1775–1840), prince de Canino, brother of Napoléon I, 290 n.

Bontemps, Marie-Charlotte. *See* Jaucourt, Marie-Charlotte-Louise-Aglaé-Perrette de (La Châtre).

Booker, Joseph (d. 1837), bookseller, 103, 568.

Boscawen, Frances, *née* Glanville (1719–1805), 262 n.

Boswell, James (1740–95), barrister-at-law and biographer, 104 n.

Boswell, James (1778–1822), barrister-at-law and 2nd surviving son of the preceding, **491**.

Boswell's Malone (1821), 491. (*The Plays and Poems of William Shakespeare*, ed. James Boswell the younger.)

Boucherett, Ayscoghe (1755–1815), M.P., **185**.

Boucherett, Emilia, *née* Crokatt (*c.* 1761–1837), wife of the preceding, **185**.

Boughton, Elizabeth. *See* Upton, Elizabeth.

Bouillé du Chariol, Louis-Joseph-Amour de (1769–1850), *Souvenirs et*

fragments pour servir aux mémoires de ma vie et mon temps . . . 1769–1812 (1906–11), 282 n.

Bourbon, Charles-Ferdinand de (1778–1820), duc de Berry, 2nd son of the comte d'Artois, 359 n., **451–2 n.**, 470.

Bourbon, Marie-*Caroline*-Ferdinande-Louise de (1798–1870), daughter of Francis I of the Two Sicilies, duchesse de Berry, wife of the preceding, **451–2 n.**

Bourbon, Louis-Henri de (1692–1740), duc de, prince de Condé, **307 n.**

Bourbon, Caroline de (1714–41), de Hesse-Rheinfels-Rothenbourg, daughter of Landgrave Ernest and Éléonore de Loewenstein-Wertheim, wife of Louis-Henri, **307 n.**

Bourbon, Louis-Joseph de (1736–1818), 8th prince de Condé, son of Louis-Henri and Caroline (*supra*), 6 n., 296 n., **307 n.**, 319 n., 395 n., 510.

Bourbon, Louis-Henri-Joseph de (1756–1830), duc de, 9th prince de Condé, son of the preceding, 296 n., 319 n., **373 n.**

Bourbon, Louis-Antoine-Henri de (1772–1804), duc d'Enghien, son of the preceding, **373 n.**

Bourbon-Busset, Gasparde–Louise–Julie de. *See* Gouvello, Gasparde-Louise-Julie de.

Bourbon genealogy. *See* Vrignault, Henri.

Bourdois de Bréviande, Hannah Maria 'Marianne', *née* Burney (1772–1856), daughter of EBB and niece of FBA, **25–6 n.**, 29, 116, 414, 439 n., 546, 554.

Bourdois de Bréviande, Lambert-Antoine (*c.* 1761–1806), husband of the preceding, **26 n.**, 439 n., 554.

Bourdois de la Motte, Edmé-Joachim (1754–1837), physician, brother of the preceding, **377 n.**, 419 n.

Bourdois de la Motte, Marie-Geneviève, *née* d'Hermand de Cléry (*c.* 1757–1838), wife of the preceding, 520.

Bournon, Jacques-Louis (1751–1825), comte de, mineralogist and friend of M. d'A, **6 n.**

Bournon, Henriette-Marie-Anne-

Crewe, Sir David Dundas, Dr. Benjamin Moseley, Frederick North, J. P. Salomon, Samuel Rogers, the Thrales, John Townshend, Samuel Wesley (q.v.);

health: ailments and death, 11 n., 34, 58, 61, 177, 264, 268, 272, 280–1, 283–4, 292, 507;

funeral, 292;

will, 292, 324–7, 352, 438, 463 n., 512–13;

library:

its size diminished, 363, 382, 421, 505–6

monetary value, 326 n., 386;

sale of miscellaneous books, 326 n., 349 n., 356, 363, 388, 404 n., 504, 515, 516;

sale of musical library, 326 n., 347, 386, 430;

membership in Institut, 13, 124, 130;

relations with the Royal Family, 55;

Works:

'Astronomy, an Historical and Didactic Poem' (1796–99), 70 n.;

History of Music, 325 n.;

Memoirs, ed. FBA, 439 n.;

portrait of, frontispiece;

biographies of, by Scholes, and by Lonsdale;

mentioned, 3, 4 n., 14, 26 n., 31 n., 52, 104, 111, 113, 114, 116, 133–4 n., 144, 202, 215 n., 218, 224, 229, 237, 240 n., 246, 251, 265 n., 274, 295–6, 297–8, 335, 337 n., 356–7, 360, 368–9, 414, 481, 492, 494, 501, 522, 527, 534, 541, 542.

Burney, the Revd. Charles Jr. (1757–1817), D.D., FBA's brother [CB Jr.]:

Letters to, Nos. 632 (written by AA), 639, 644 (written with CBFB), 647, 648 (written with SHB), 652, 663, 668, 669, 674, 678, 680, 681, 685, 687, 688, 690, 698, 709, 711, 712, 713 (written with Martin Burney), 716, 722 (written with CFBt and SHB), 725, 726, 730, 731, 739, 740, 748, 750, 758, 760, 761, 787, 792, 797, 804, 822, 823, 825, 828, 829, 832, 834, 633A, 640A, 689A, 722A, 735A, 775A, 789A;

agent for FBA's 'works', 67 n., 113–14, 144–5, 145–6, 148 n., 153–5, 161, 262 n.; and FBA's pension, 133–4;

awaits FBA's arrival from France and their meeting, 1, 10;

career at college and theft of books, 58 n., 88 n.;

Chaplain to George III; his sermons at Chapel Royal, 27 n., 34, 49 n., 65, 138 n., 139 n., 509;

connections with Caius College, 58 n.;

Deptford Rectory and FBA's visits there, 14–15, 20, 23–4, 37–8, 39, 41;

desire for bishopric, 108 n., 110 n., 113–14 n., 139 n., 149, 252;

encourages FBA's visits with the Royal Family, 15 n., 54, 354, 493;

executor for CB's will and quarrel with FBA, 283 n., 284, 292, 325, 346–9;

friends: Lady Crewe, Martin Davy, Charles Manners-Sutton, the Spencers, John Young (q.v.);

AA's godfather and guardian, 23, 44, 176, 190, 195, 327, 472 n., 480;

illnesses, 51, 53, 63, 91–2, 138 n., 163, 164 n., 167–8, 218, 231–2, 252, 266, 371 n., 474, 501;

inheritance from CB, 291 n., 325 n., 505;

invites FBA to Sandgate and arranges for arrival, 183;

involvement with FBA's pension, 34;

library, its worth and ultimate sale, 34 n., 44 n.;

preferments, 27 n.;

receives presentation copy of *The Wanderer*, 262;

reputation as a Hellenist, 40;

scholarship, 34–5 n., 163;

schools: Chiswick, Hammersmith, and Greenwich, 45 n., 88 n.;

seeks Tancred scholarship for AA, 71;

underwrites education of several nephews, 45;

visits:

Althorp, 70. *See under* Althorp;

Ramsgate, 180 n., 181 n., 183, 194 n.;

Index

Burney, Sarah (*cont.*):
 mentioned, 64, 156, 166, 205, 245, 337, 464, 486, 494, 507, 509, 519.
Burney, Sarah 'Rosette', *née* Rose (1759–1821), wife of CB Jr.:
 as 'invalide', 52, 162 n., 178 n.;
 depressive retreats, 164;
 illnesses and recoveries, 64, 354, 390, 489, 504, 506;
 irresponsibility and instability, 52, 64;
 visit to Sandgate and flight, 153;
 parting visit of FBA, 491;
 mentioned, 15, 20, 24, 37, 43, 51, 73, 75, 77 n., 92, 109, 111, 114, 139, 141 n., 148, 153, 160, 191, 200, 218, 224, 246, 252, 270, 272, 284 n., 295 n., 371, 391, 407, 465, 469, 474, 482, 484, 493, 497, 502, 507, 508, 509, 519.
Burney, Sarah Harriet (1772–1844), novelist, FBA's half-sister:
 Letter by, conjointly with FBA to CB Jr., No. 648;
 Letters by, quoted or cited, 4 n., 11–12 n., 44, 74 n., 481 n.;
 Note to, No. 722;
 concern for children of Richard Thomas, 337, 467 n., 481;
 governess, 62 n.;
 inheritance from CB, 231 n., 291 n., 327, 347, 351, 363, 505;
 presentation copy of *The Wanderer*, 262;
 relationship with JB, 18 n.;
 rheumatism, 11–12 n., 21, 168;
 removal to smaller apartment after CB's death, 348;
 visits:
  Lymington, 11, 33, 168;
  Sandgate, 166, 168, 177;
 FBA's farewell visit to, 491;
 her fiction, 61–2 n., 119;
  Clarentine (1796), 61 n., 430 n.;
  Geraldine Fauconberg (1808), 61 n., 430 n.;
  Traits of Nature (1812), 61 n., 107 n., 119 n., 166, 430;
 mentioned, 18 n., 21, 38, 59, 61, 71, 80, 82, 100, 131–2 n., 136, 139, 151, 156 n., 177, 181, 196, 199, 202 n., 281, 296, 410, 499, 511, 512, 515, 516, 517.

Burney, Sophia Elizabeth (1777–1856), daughter of EBB and FBA's niece:
 lives with Hannah Bourdois, 25–6;
 mentioned, 30, 101, 206.
Burney, Susannah Elizabeth, FBA's sister. *See* Phillips, Susannah Elizabeth.
Burton, William (1774–1825), bookseller and auctioneer, **456 n.**
Burton's Court at Chelsea College, 11.
Bute, 4th Earl of. *See* Stuart, John.
Bute, 5th Earl of. *See* Crichton-Stuart, John.
Butler, Brook Watson (1795–1838), 465.
Butler, John Olden (*c.* 1794–*post* 1815), 465.
Butler, Samuel (1612–80), poet and essayist, his *Characters and Passages from Note-Books* (1759), 300 n.
Byron, George Gordon (1788–1824), 6th Baronet, poet, 145 n.;
 Byron's Letters and Journals, ed. Leslie A. Marchand, 145 n.

Cadell, Thomas I (1742–1802), bookseller, **154 n.**
Cadell, Thomas II (1773–1836), bookseller, son of the preceding:
 publishes *Camilla* (1796), 67 n.;
 publishes *Camilla*, 2nd ed. (1802), 192 n.;
 mentioned, 154 n., 238.
CADIGNAN, Anne-Charles-Guy-Gérard Dupleix (1767–1804), comte de, 276.
Cadignan, Catherine Dupleix, *née* Hunter (1773–1860), comtesse de, wife of the preceding, **216;**
 mourns the loss of her husband and second son, 276;
 borrows money from the d'Arblays, 242;
 mentioned, 229, 395, 421–2.
Cadignan, Charles-Frédéric-Louis Dupleix de (1797–*post* 1845), son of the above, 216 n., **242 n.,** 276, 422.
Cadignan, Samuel Dupleix de (d. 1805), brother of the preceding, 276.
Cadmus, an English brig, 320 n.
CAILLEBOT, Marie-Louis de (1764–1831), marquis de La Salle, **6 n.,** 36.

Index

Index

Choiseul-Praslin, Charlotte-Laure-Olympe le Tonnelier de, *née* de Breteuil (d. 1861), duchesse de Praslin, wife of the following, **420 n.**

Choiseul-Praslin, Claude-Raynald-Laure-Félix de (1778–1841), duc de Praslin, member of the Chambre des Pairs, 419 n., **420 n.**

Choiseul-Praslin, Lucie-Virginie de. *See* Beauvau, Lucie-Virginie de, sister of the duc de Praslin.

Choisy, Anne-Charlotte-*Henriette* de. *See* Agoult, Anne-Charlotte-Henriette d'.

Cholmondely, Mary 'Polly', *née* Woffington (*c.* 1729–1811), 151 n.

Christian, Jeanne. *See* Gregory, Jeanne.

Christ's College. *See* Cambridge University.

Clapham sect, 71 n.

Clare College. *See* Cambridge University.

Clarence, Duke of. *See* William IV.

Clarke, Henri-Jacques-Guillaume (1765–1818), comte d'Hunebourg, duc de Feltre, général, maréchal de France, **303 n.**, 341 n., 419 n.

Clarke, d'Hunebourg de Feltre, Henriette-Mathilde, daughter of the preceding. *See* Montesquiou, Henriette-Mathilde de.

Clifford, James, L., *Hester Lynch Piozzi (Mrs. Thrale)* (1941), 521.

Closterman [or Cloosterman, Clostermann, Klosterman], Johann Baptist (*c.* 1660–1713), painter; his portrait of Henry Purcell, 473 n.

Cochard, Pierre (*fl.* 1763–1814), painter, 414.

COCHEREL, Nicolas-Robert de (1741–1826), marquis de.

Cocherel, Françoise-Charlotte de, *née* Gallien de Préval (*fl.* 1755–1812), wife of the preceding, **6 n.**

Cocherel, Louise-Élisabeth-Marguerite de (*fl.* 1772–1814), daughter of the above. *See* Roncherolles, Louise de.

Cocherel, Philippine-Louise-Geneviève 'Virginie' de (*fl.* 1790–*post* 1812), sister of the preceding, **6 n.**

Coëtnempren de Kersaint, Claire-Louise-Rose-Bonne de. *See* Durfort de Duras, Claire.

Colburn, Henry (d. 1855), bookseller: Colburn's English and Foreign Public Library, 104, 267; desires to publish *The Wanderer*, 497; mentioned, 104 n., 148 n., 153, 112–13, 567.

Colchester, Baron. *See* Abbot, Charles.

Coleridge, Samuel Taylor (1772–1834), poet and literary critic: *The Lyrical Ballads*, published by Longman, 154 n.

Collet, Marie-Joséphine-Catherine. *See* Damas, Marie-Joséphine-Catherine de.

Collins, Harriet. *See* Chastel de Boinville, Harriet.

Comte, François-*Charles*-Louis (1782–1837), editor of *Censeur*, **396 n.**

Condé, 7th prince de. *See* Bourbon, Louis-Henri de.

Condé, 8th prince de. *See* Bourbon, Louis-Joseph de.

Condé, 9th prince de. *See* Bourbon, Louis-Henri-Joseph de.

Conegliano, duc de. *See* Moncey, Bon-Adrien-Jannot de.

Connaught, Earl of. *See* William Henry, H.R.H.

Constant de Rebecque, Benjamin (1767–1830), political writer, **396 n.**

Cooke [or Cook], Papilian Catherine 'Kitty' (*c.* 1731–97), **481 n.**

COOKE, the Revd. Samuel (1741–1820), M.A., **93 n.**, 166 n.

Cooke, Cassandra, *née* Leigh (1744–1826), wife of the preceding, 166 n.

Cooke, Mary (1781–*post* 1820), daughter of the above, **166 n.**

Cooper, Astley Paston (1768–1841), surgeon, **16.**

Cope, Arabella Diana. *See* Whitworth, Arabella Diana.

Copinger, W. A., *On the Authorship of the First Hundred numbers of 'The Edinburgh Review'* (1895), 207 n.

Coppin, Sarah. *See* Lambart, Sarah.

Coulon, Henri-François-Grégoire (*fl.* 1802–3). *See* Coulon et Cie.

Coulon, Marc-Antoine (*fl.* 1802–3). *See* Coulon et Cie.

Coulon et Cie., bankers, 548–9.

Courlande, duchesse de. *See* Biren, Anne-Charlotte-Dorothée.

Index

Dubster, a character in *Camilla*, 22.

Dubuc, Pierre-Louis (*fl.* 1780–1820), translator, **217 n.**

Dubue [or De Bue], St. Olimpe (*fl.* 1765–1814), **9 n.**, 507.

Dudley, Earl of. *See* Ward, John William.

Dumfries, Earl of. *See* Crichton-Stuart, John.

Dundas, Sir David (1735–1820), Governor of Chelsea Hospital, knighted (1803), **72 n.**, 77, 82 n., 83 n., 85 n., 87, 88 n., 90, 94, 99.

Dundas, Charlotte, *née* De Lancey (d. 1840), wife of the preceding, 77 n., 84, 85 n.

Dunkirk:
FBA's departure from, 1;
hospitality shown FBA there, 7;
mentioned, 165 n., 172.

Dupleix. *See* Cadignan.

Dupont de L'Étang, Pierre (1765–1840), ministre de la Guerre: his military career, **451.**

Du Pont de Nemours, Françoise (Poivre), *née* Robin (1748–*post* 1834), 520.

Duras. *See* Durfort de Duras.

Durfort, Étienne-Narcisse de (1753–1832), lieutenant-général, 395 n.

Durfort de Civrac, Émilie de. *See* Destutt de Tracy, Émilie.

Durfort de Duras, Amédée-Bretagne-Malo de (1771–1838), duc de Duras:
presents FBA to Louis XVIII, 304, 309, 310, 311–12, 330;
rumoured to be one of Napoleon's chamberlains, 330;
mentioned, 282 n., 288–9, 304 n., 344, 378, 399 n., 510.

Durfort de Duras, Claire-Louise-Rose-Bonne de, *née* de Coëtnempren de Kersaint (1778–1828), wife of the preceding, 282 n., 373, 377, 520.

Duval, Mme, a character in *Evelina*, 301.

Dyer, George (1755–1841), classicist and bibliophile, **439.**

Eagle Feast, FBA's attendance at, 35.

Eastburn, Kirk and Co., New York booksellers, 172 n.

École militaire de Saint-Cyr. *See under* Gouvion-Saint-Cyr.

École Polytechnique. *See* Paris.

Eden, George (1784–1849), 2nd Earl of Auckland, statesman and governor-general of India, **136 n.**

Eden, William (1744–1814), 1st Baron Auckland, statesman and diplomat, 136 n.;
The Journal and Correspondence (4 vols., 1861–2), ed. Robert J. Eden, 3rd Baron Auckland, 136 n.

EDGEWORTH, Richard Lovell (1744–1817), writer and educator, 138 n.

Edgeworth, Frances, *née* Beaufort (*fl.* 1798–1849), 4th wife of the preceding, 138 n.

Edgeworth, Maria (1767–1849), 2nd daughter of Richard and his first wife Anna Maria, *née* Elers (d. 1773), **138**;
Scènes de la vie du grand monde, a translation, 217 n.;
mentioned, 299 n.

Edinburgh, Bishop of. *See* Sandford, the Rt. Revd. Daniel.

Edinburgh Review:
The Wanderer reviewed by William Hazlitt, 564–5.

Edward Augustus, H.R.H. (1767–1820), Duke of Kent and Strathern, 366.

Egerton, the Hon. Ariana Margaret (*c.* 1752–1827), Woman of the Bedchamber, 514.

Elba, Kingdom of, 287 n., 320 n., 355 n., 504.

Elbe River. *See sub* Russia.

Elers, Anna Maria. *See* Edgeworth, Anna Maria, mother of Maria.

Elizabeth, H.R.H. Princess (1770–1840), Landgravine of Hesse-Homburg, 55, 61, 81 n., 124, 146 n., 146–7 n., 149 n., 172, 208, 268 n., 351 n., 517.

Ellerker. *See* Mainwaring Ellerker.

Elliston, Martha. *See* Martyn, Martha.

Elphinstone, George Keith (1746–1823), Viscount Keith, Admiral, **72 n.**, 78 n., 82 n., 83, 84, 90, 101 n., 360 n.

Elphinstone, Hester Maria 'Queeney', *née* Thrale (1764–1857), wife of the preceding:

597

Index

Fox, Henry Richard. *See* Vassall Fox, Henry Richard.

Fox-Strangways, Henry Thomas (1747–1802), *styled* Lord Stavordale, 2nd Earl of Ilchester, father of the following, **130 n.**

Fox-Strangways, Louisa Emma. *See* Petty-Fitzmaurice, Louisa Emma.

France:
diplomatic activities:
signs Peace Treaty 30 May 1814, 274, 281;
Constitutional Charter, 286 n., 294 n.;
territories diminished by armistice, 1814, 450 n.;
Treaty of London, 450 n.;
military activities:
rioting against French Troops in German states, 100 n.;
failed armistice, 4 June–10 Aug. 1813, 186 n.;
Dresden, Battle of (q.v.);
Leipzig, Battle of (q.v.);
army's retreat toward the Rhine, 186 n.;
losses in manpower, autumn 1813, 186 n., 204 n.;
open to invasion from south after defeat at Vitoria, 191 n.;
army's retreat to the Elbe, 191 n., 499 n.;
declaration of war by Bavaria against, 191 n.;
army's retreat west of the Rhine, 208 n.;
exhausted morale, 209 n.;
approaching defeat, 241, 252;
fall of Paris, 266;
fighting at Bayonne and Toulouse after defeat of Paris, 275 n., 282 n.;
soldiers as *fricoteurs*, 287;
places:
Aube, département of, Russians at Arcis-sur-Aube, Auxon [Auxonne], Troyes, 560;
Bayonne, 275 n.;
Bordeaux, 268 n.;
Calais, 7 n., 101 n., 165, 172;
Côte d'Or, département of, Russians at Laignes, 560;
Dunkirk (q.v.);

Joigny (q.v.);
Morlaix, 101, 172;
Orléans, 560;
Paris (q.v.);
Toulouse, 275, 282;
Yonne (q.v.);
Restoration:
Louis's *Address to the People of France*, 100 n.;
Bourbon Restoration and royalist organizations, 268 n.;
Les Bannières du Roi, 209 n.;
Les Chevaliers de la Foi, 209 n., 213 n.;
Gouvernement provisoire, 376;
déchéance of Napoléon, 294;
return of Bourbons and celebrations, 294 n., 355 n., 470 *passim*;
Louis XVIII's inauguration, 294;
undermines morale of professional soldiers, 287, 450 n.;
unrest after Bourbon return and conspiracies against, 396 n., 418–19 n., 424 n., 449 *passim*;
unrealistic prices, inflation (*see* A. Chabert);
La France de la restauration . . ., by Marcel Moraud, 54 n.

France, children of. *See* Louis XVI, Louis XVIII, Charles X.

Francis, Clement (d. 1792), 1st husband of CBFB, 326 n.

Francis, Charlotte Ann, *née* Burney, wife of the preceding. *See* Broome, Charlotte Anne (Francis).

Francis, the Revd. Clement Robert (1792–1829), son of the above:
writes to Mrs. Piozzi, 11 n., 88 n., 196 n.;
to FBA, 82 n.;
attitude toward CB Jr., 88 n.;
career at Caius, 195;
considers deferring a university career, 326 n.;
friendship with AA, 21 n.;
knowledge of geometry, 32;
matriculation at Caius (Nov. 1811), 326 n.;
studious habits, 394 n.;
mentioned, 14 n., 28, 45 n., 80, 219, 221 n., 225 n., 246, 249, 265, 322 n., 333, 354, 381, 464, 499, 501, 507, 508, 509.

600

Index

Harcourt, Élisabeth-Sophie d'. *See* Harcourt-Olonde, Élisabeth-Sophie d'.

Harcourt, Mary (Lockhart), *née* Danby (*c.* 1750–1833), wife of the following, 128, 129 n., 415, 419 n., 431, 448, 498, 511, 513.

Harcourt, William (1742/3–1830), 3rd Earl, General:
Deputy Ranger of Windsor Great Park, 128 n.;
his will, 129 n.;
mentioned, 511.

HARCOURT-OLONDE, Amédée-Louis-*Charles*-François (1771–1831), marquis d', Colonel in the British Army:
as courier between the d'Arblays, 27 n.;
as heir to Lord Harcourt's estate, **128**, 129 n.;
mentioned, 290.

Harcourt-Olonde, Élisabeth-*Sophie* d', *née* d'Harcourt, wife of the preceding, **128 n.**, 129.

Harcourt-Olonde, William-Bernard d' (d. 1846), son of the above, **128 n.**, 129 n.

Harcourt-Olonde, Georges-Douglas-Trévor-Bernard d' (1808–83), brother of the preceding, marquis, ambassadeur de France, **128 n.**, 129 n.

Harcourt-Olonde, Maria-Augusta d' (*c.* 1810–*post* 1833), sister of the preceding, **128 n.**, 129 n.

Harford, John S., *Recollections of William Wilberforce* (1864), 182 n.

Hargrave, Francis (*c.* 1741–1821), Treasurer of Lincoln's Inn, parliamentary lawyer, **77 n.**, 90, 97, 99 n.

Hargrave, Francis, Jr. (*fl.* 1786–1805), son of the preceding, 45 n.

Harley, Edward (1689–1741), 2nd Earl of Oxford, **19 n.**

Harley, Lady Margaret Cavendish. *See* Bentinck, Lady Margaret Cavendish.

Harness, the Revd. William (1790–1869), author, friend of Byron, 145 n.

Hart, Frances. *See* Milman, Frances.

Hart, William (1741–1804), father of Frances, 254 n.

Hartwell, Bucks., Louis XVIII's residence at, 294 n., 295 n., 316, 374.

Hatchard, John (1769–1849), bookseller, 103, 568.

Hawkins, Ann, *née* Burney (1749–1819), FBA's cousin, 30, 33, 43, 49, 52, 295 n.

Haydn, Franz Joseph (1732–1809), composer, 13 n.;
Notice . . . sur la vie . . ., by Joachim Le Breton, 13 n.

Hayman, Anne (1753–1847), Keeper of the Privy Purse to Princess Caroline, 297.

Hazlitt, William (1778–1830), critic and essayist:
reviews *The Wanderer* for the *Edinburgh Review*, 564–5.

Heber, the Rt. Revd. Reginald (1783–1826), Bishop of Calcutta, 207 n.

Hedges, Anna Maria. *See* Bateman, Anna Maria.

Heinrich, H.R.H. (1781–1846), Prince, brother of Friedrich Wilhelm III, 366.

Hénin, Adélaïde-Félicité-*Étiennette* d'Alsace-Hénin-Liétard, *née* Guinot [or Guignot] de Monconseil (1750–1824), princesse d', 228, 284, 295 n., 332, 349, 416 n., 432, 519.

Herbert, Anne, *née* North (d. 1789), 469 n.

Hermand de Cléry, Marie-Geneviève d'. *See* Bourdois de la Motte, Marie-Geneviève.

Herschel, John Frederick William (1792–1871), mathematician, F.R.S., **500.**

Herst, Mr. (*fl.* 1812–14), of Richmond, 518.

Hervey, Frederick Augustus (1730–1803), 4th Earl of Bristol, Bishop of Cloyne, of Derry.

Hervey, Frederick William (1769–1859), *styled* Lord Hervey, 5th Earl of Bristol, 1st Earl Jermyn of Horningsheath and of Bristol, **9 n.**

Hervey, Elizabeth Albana, *née* Upton (1775–1844), wife of the preceding, 9 n., 135 n.

Hervey, Theodosia Louisa, daughter of Frederick Augustus (*supra*). *See* Jenkinson, Theodosia Louisa, Countess of Liverpool.

Hesse-Rheinfels-Rothenbourg, Caroline of, daughter of Landgrave Ernest. *See* Bourbon, Caroline de.

Highley, Samuel (d. 1821), bookseller, 567.

Hill, Rowland (1772–1842), Baron, General, 369 n.

Hinner, Louise-Marguerite. *See* Jarjayes, Louise-Marguerite de.

Hirst, Hannah (d. 1845), FBA's landlady at Lower Sloane Street, 363, **364 n.**

Hix, Jacques-Antoine (*fl.* 1800–16), schoolmaster in Paris, 40 n.

Hix, Mme (*fl.* 1806–14), wife of the preceding, 519.

Hoare's Bank (1672–   ), 176 n., 464 n.

Hoare, Charles (1767–1851), 176.

Hoare, Henry Merrick [or Merrik] (1770–1856), 118 n., 176 n., 360, 483.

Hoare, Sophia, *née* Thrale (1771–1824), wife of the preceding, 118, 167, 187, 295 n., 360, 415, 516, 521.

Hoare, Peter Richard (1772–1849), brother of Henry Merrick (*supra*), 253 n.

Hoare, Arabella Penelope, *née* Greene (1782–1865), wife of the preceding, 253 n.

Hoare, George Matthew (1779–1852), of Morden, Surrey, **254 n.**

Hoare, Angelina Frances, *née* Greene (*c.* 1791–1846), wife of the preceding, **254.**

Hodgson, the Revd. Francis (1781–1852), provost of Eton, author, Byron's friend, 145 n.

Hogarth, William (1697–1764), painter and engraver, 485 n., 525.

Holden's Triennial Directory, 568.

Holland: La Tour du Pin-Gouvernet as ambassador to, 416.

Holland, Baron and Baroness. *See* Vassall Fox, Henry Richard and Elizabeth.

Holwell, John Zephaniah (1711–98), Governor of Bengal, 463 n.

Hood, Samuel (1724–1816), Admiral of the Red, 1st Viscount, 75 n., **77,** 78 n., 83, 84, 85 n., 90, 99.

Hookham, Thomas (*fl.* 1772–5), bookseller, 568.

Hookham, E. T., and Thomas Jr., (*fl.* 1813), booksellers at 15 Old Bond Street, 103, 568.

Horne, the Rt. Revd. George (1730–92), *A Father's Legacy . . . to which is added Mr. Tyrold's Advice . . . from . . . "Camilla" . . . Also, A Picture of the Female Character . . . by G. Horne* (1809), 131 n. *See* Gregory, John.

Hottinguer, Jean-Conrad (1764–1841), régent de la Banque de France, **422 n.**

Hottinguer, Martha Eliza, *née* Redwood (1773–1830), **422 n.,** 430.

Howard, Fulke *Greville* Upton (1773–1846), 82 n., 83, **84,** 85 n., 93, 135, 381.

Howard, Mary, *née* Howard (d. 1877), wife of the preceding, **135.**

Howard, Richard (d. 1818), father of the preceding, **135 n.**

Hoxton, an institution for the insane, 117.

Huard de la Marre, Adélaïde-Louise-Thérèse, *née* Gillet de la Jacqueminière (*c.* 1773–1842), wife of the following, **440 n.,** 520.

Huard de la Marre, Denys-Victor (*c.* 1783–*post* 1841), notary, **440,** 443.

Hubert, Philippine-Louise-Hortense, *née* Le Roy de Saint-Lau (1746–1813), *styled* marquise Des Essars, 520.

Hudson, Bolton (*c.* 1755–1820), official of Bridewell and Bethlehem Hospitals:
as tenant of Camilla Cottage, **33 n.,** 230 n., 343, 394–5, 403, 421, 430, 458, 483 n., 487, 488.

Hudson, Thomas (*fl.* 1814–37), son of the preceding, **488.**

Hugot, Pierre (*fl.* 1800–12), Hellenist, 40, 43, 199.

Hunebourg, comte d'. *See* Clarke, Henri-Jacques-Guillaume.

Hunter, Anne. *See* Palézieux-Falconnet, Anne de.

Hunter, Catherine, sister of the preceding. *See* Cadignan, comtesse de.

Hunter, Elizabeth [Eliza], (1762–1849), sister of the preceding, 276 n.

Hurst, Thomas (*fl.* 1790–*pre* 1827), bookseller, 103, 153 n., 155 n., 159 n., 187 n., 567.

Hutton, James (1715–95), bookseller, 171 n.

Hyde, Susannah. *See* Gardner, Susannah.

Index

Index

Index

Liddell, Anne. *See* Fitzpatrick, Anne (Fitzroy).

Lincoln, Bishop of. *See* Kaye, the Rt. Revd. John.

Lisbon, Portugal, earthquake, 219 n.

Listenois. *See* Bauffremont.

Literary Anecdotes of the Eighteenth Century (1812–15), by John Nichols, 568.

Little Glemham, Suffolk, 469 n.

Liverpool, Earl of. *See* Jenkinson, Robert Banks.

Llandygwydd, home of the Brigstockes. *See* Wales.

Llanover, home of the Waddingtons. *See* Wales.

Llanover, Lady. *See* Hall, Augusta.

Llansantfraed, home of James Greene. *See* Wales.

Lloyd, Miss, 511.

LOCKE, William (1732–1810), of Norbury Park:
and d'Arblays's financial affairs, 149 n., 547, 552–4;
character of, 547;
informs the d'Arblays of SBP's death, 56 n.;
provides the land for Camilla Cottage, 547;
mentioned, 9, 26 n., 60, 279, 421, 457, 476, 545, 547–72, App. II *passim*.

Locke, Frederica Augusta, *née* Schaub (1750–1832), wife of the preceding:
Letters to, Nos. 733, 754, 775, 776, 778, 799, 810, 814;
writes conjointly with FBA to M. d'A, No. 766;
writes to FBA in defence of William II, 338–9 n.;
as banker and house agent for the d'Arblays, 149 n., 176, 404, 431;
her involvement in the sale of Norbury Park, 345;
offended by M. d'A's letters to William II, 403;
prepared to confirm AA's English birth, 93;
receives presentation copy of *The Wanderer*, 262;
sends CB a gift, 108;
urges end to quarrel over Camilla Cottage, 368 n., 433;

mentioned, 26, 33 n., 38, 45, 48 n., 56 n., 63, 64, 82 n., 84, 93, 95, 98, 109–11, 117, 131, 139, 141, 185 n., 196, 198 n., 229 n., 240, 272, 279, 281, 328, 337, 456, 496, 511, 513, 515, 518, 544–6, 552, 554.

Locke, William II (1767–1847), son of the above:
exchange of letters with M. d'A about Camilla Cottage, 336;
and FBA's financial affairs after 1810, 149 n.;
decides to sell Norbury Park, **60 n.**, 230;
forces sale of Camilla Cottage, 60 n., 365, 421;
offends M. d'A by use of lawyer, 445;
sends proposals about the sale price of Camilla Cottage, 345 n., 368 n.;
visits Paris, 456, 518;
mentioned, 48 n., 176, 196, 279, 286, 343, 387–8, 395, 402, 454 n., 460, 476, 488, 511, 513, 552.

Locke, Elizabeth Catherine, *née* Jennings (c. 1781–1846), wife of the preceding, 64 n., 286.

Locke, Charles (1769–1804), 2nd son of William Locke I (*supra*), 9 n.

Locke, Cecilia Margaret, *née* Ogilvie (1775–1824), wife of the preceding, **135**, 142.

Locke, the Revd. George (1771–1864), 3rd son of William Locke I, 139, 198 n., 286, 329 n., 454, 456, 469, 518.

Locke, Harriet, *née* Thomson (c. 1783–1837), wife of the preceding, 139 n.

Locke, Frederick Augustus (1785–1805), youngest son of William Locke I, 9 n.

Locke, Amelia, sister of the preceding. *See* Angerstein, Amelia.

Locke, Mary Augusta, sister of the preceding. *See* Martin, Mary Augusta Lady.

Lockhart, Marianne Matilda. *See* Aufrère, Marianne Matilda.

Lockhart, Mary. *See* Harcourt, Mary, *née* Danby.

LONDON:
I. *General*: 36, 120;
fogs during last week of 1813, 218–19;

611

Index

Index

Maturin, Gabriel (1767–1840), 247 n.

Maturin, Henry (c. 1771–1842), brother of the preceding, tutor to Norbury Phillips, 247 n.

Maturin, Elizabeth, née Johnston (fl. 1802), wife of Henry, 263 n.

Maubourg. See Latour-Maubourg.

Maulnoir, Louis-Joseph (1755–post 1815), civil servant, **242 n.**

Maupertuis, Nicolas-Pierre Desvergers de Sannois, seigneur de (d. pre-1812), 35.

Maupertuis, Gertrude-Constance de, née Desvergers de Maupertuis (fl. 1812), wife and cousin of the preceding, mother of Mme de Caillebot, 35.

Maupertuis, Anne-Renée-Marguerite-Henriette Desvergers de Sannois de. daughter of the above. See Caillebot, Anne-Renée-Marguerite-Henriette de.

Maurville, Henriette-Marguerite Bidé de, née Guinot de Soulignac (c. 1761–post 1825):
petition for an English pension, **423–4**;
residence in Brussels, 424 n.;
mentioned, 432, 520.

Maurville, Jean-Louis-Bernard (d. 1796), husband of the preceding, 423 n.

May, Sir Edward. See sub Donegall, Anna May.

Mayence (Mainz), 211, 215 n.

Medem, Anne-Charlotte-Dorothée de. See Biren, Anne-Charlotte-Dorothée.

Megarry, R. E., and Wade, H. W. R., The Law of Real Property (3rd ed., 1966), 402 n.

Méhul, Étienne-Nicolas (1763–1817), musician, **140.**

Meignen, Gabriel-Antoine (1795–1830), grandson of Jean-Baptiste-Gabriel Bazille, son of the following, 557.

Meignen, Marie-Euphémie-Claudine, née Bazille (1772–1833), 520.

Mendlesham, Suffolk, site of Daniel Simpson's school, 482 n.

Merlin, Joseph (1735–1804), inventor, 364 n., 463.

Metastasio, Pietro Antonio Domenico Bonaventura [actually Trapassi] (1698–1782), 351.

Metternich-Winneburg, Klemens Wenzel Nepomuk Lothar (1773–1859), Prince von, Austrian statesman, 186 n., 450 n.

Meulan, Marie-Joseph-Théodore (1778–1832), comte de, **217 n.,** 275, 284.

Meulan, Alexandrine-Louise-Élisabeth-Lancelot de, née de Turpin-Crissé (d. 1846), wife of the preceding, 332, 519.

Meulan, Élisabeth-Charlotte-Pauline de, sister of Marie-Joseph-Théodore. See Guizot, Élisabeth-Charlotte-Pauline.

Mézeray. See Eudes de Mézeray, François.

Mickleham, Surrey:
as home of SBP, 26 n.;
Juniper Hall, 36 n., 206 n.;
Norbury Park (q.v.);
mentioned, 444.

Middlesex, Archdeacon of. See Cambridge, the Revd. George Owen.

Milman, Frances, née Hart (d. 1836), wife of the following, 254.

Milman, Sir Francis (1746–1821), M.D., **77 n.,** 85, 90, 99, 254 n.

Miremont, marquis de. See Simiane, Charles-François de.

Moncey, Bon-Adrien-Jannot de (1754–1842), duc de Conegliano, maréchal de France, 288 n.

Monk, James Henry (1784–1856), Regius Professor of Greek, Cambridge University, 82 n., **150 n.,** 477 n., 503.

Monmouth. See Wales.

Montagu, Lady Elizabeth. See Scott, Lady Elizabeth.

Montagu, Elizabeth, née Robinson (1720–1800), bluestocking, 131 n., 432 n.;
The Letters of . . . with some of the Letters of her Correspondents (4 vols., 1809–13), 209.

Montagu, Matthew, formerly Robinson (1762–1831), 4th Baron Rokeby of Armagh, adopted son of the preceding, 209 n., **432,** 438.

Montagu, Eliza [Elizabeth], née Charlton (c. 1765–1817), wife of the preceding, **432,** 438.

Montagu-Beaune, Joachim de (1764–1834), marquis de Pouzols, vicomte de Beaune, 443.

Montagu-Beaune, Anne-Paule-Dominique 'Pauline' de, *née* de Noailles (1766–1839), wife of the preceding, 379, 520, 556.

Montagu-Beaune, Pauline-Adrienne-Frédérique-Marie-*Stéphanie* de, daughter of the above. *See* Legroing de La Romagère, Pauline.

Montalivet, comte de. *See* Bachasson, Jean Pierre.

Montault [or Montaut], Augustin-François (d. 1790), comte de Montault-Navailles, 316 n.

Montault de Navailles, Marie-Louise-Joséphine de, daughter of the preceding. *See* Gontaut, Marie-Louise-Joséphine, duchesse de.

Montesquiou-Fézensac, François-Xavier-Marie-Antoine de (1756–1832), abbé de Beaulieu, 243 n., **374 n.**;
convictions on politics, 374 n.;
member of the gouvernement provisoire, 376;
ministre de l'Intérieur, 374;
mentioned, 243 n.

Montesquiou, Philippe-André-François de (1753–1833), *dit* comte de Fézensac, brother of the preceding, général, **236 n.**, 242 n., 374 n.

Montesquiou, Louise-Joséphine de, *née* de Lalive du Châtelet (d. 1832), comtesse de Fézensac, wife of the preceding and M. de Narbonne's cousin, 212 n., 235, **236 n.**, 279, 374.

Montesquiou, Raymond-*Aimery*-Philippe-Joseph de (1784–1867), baron de Montesquiou-Fézensac, son of the above, 279 n., **301**, 375.

Montesquiou, Henriette-Matilde, *née* Clarke d'Hunebourg de Feltre (1790–1831), baronne de Montesquiou-Fézensac, **301 n.**, 510.

Montmorency-Laval, Catherine-Jeanne de, *née* Tavernier de Boullongne (*c.* 1748–1838), vicomtesse de Laval:
friendship with M. d'A, 373–4, 377;
relations with Narbonne and grief at his death, 206–7 n., 213, 214–15;

salon, 204 n.;
mentioned, 59 n., 213, 387, 395, 475, 519.

Montmorency-Laval, Mathieu-Jean-Félicité de (1767–1826), vicomte de Laval, *later* duc de Laval, son of the preceding, 204 n., 213.

Montmorency-Laval, Guyonne-Élisabeth-Joséphine de, aunt of Mathieu (*supra*). *See* Luynes, Guyonne-Élisabeth-Joséphine, duchesse de.

Montmorency-Luxembourg, Charles-Emmanuel-Sigismond de (1774–1861), *dit* duc de Piney-Luxembourg et de Châtillon, **293 n.**;
friendship for M. d'A, 410, 453, 470;
carries letters, 27 n.;
invites M. d'A to join his 'compagnie de gardes du Corps', 344, 359, 380–1, 387, 396;
mentioned, 297, 318, 330, 343 n., 425, 448, 473, 476, 512.

Montmorency-Luxembourg d'Ollone, Bonne-Félicité-Marie. *See* Serent, Bonne-Félicité-Marie de.

Monthly Review:
William Taylor's review of *The Wanderer*, 566.

Moore, Anne Matilda, *née* Trefusis (1790–1876), wife of the following, **129 n.**

Moore, the Revd. Edward George (1798–1876), Canon of Windsor, **129 n.**

Moraud, Marcel, *La France de la restauration d'après les visiteurs anglais* (1933), 426 n.

More, Hannah (1745–1833), bluestocking, author of *Percy*, 497.

More, Mary or Maria. *See* Walker, Mary.

More, Rebecca (*fl.* 1794–1819), CB's servant, sister of the preceding, 10 n., 18, 21, 88, 131, 196, 281, 291, 504, 507.

Moreau, Jean-Claude (1755–1828), baron, général, 560.

Morgan, Sydney, *née* Owenson (*c.* 1783–1859), novelist, 217 n., 376 n.;
The Missionary (1811).

Morning Chronicle, 320, 463 n.

Index

Mornington, Earl of. *See* Wellesley-Pole, William.

Mortemart, Victurnien-Jean-Baptiste-Marie de Rochechouart (1752–1812), duc de.

Mortemart, Nathalie-Henriette-Victurnienne de Rochechouart de, daughter of the preceding. *See* Beauvau-Craon, princesse de.

Mortemart, Antonie-Louise-Victurnienne de Rochechouart de. *See* Forbin-Janson, Antonie de, comtesse de Janson.

Mortemart, Alice-Elfrède-Victurnienne de Rochechouart de. *See* Noailles, Alice-Elfrède-Victurnienne de, duchesse de.

Mortier, Adolphe-Édouard-Casimir-Joseph (1768–1835), duc de Trévise, maréchal de France, 288 n.

Moseley, Benjamin (1742–1819), M.D., 11–12 n., 280, 290 n.

Mostyn, Cecilia Margaretta, *née* Thrale (1777–1857), 119 n., 545.

Motte, Andrew (d. 1730), his translation of Newton's *Mathematical Principles of Natural Philosophy*, 465 n., 474.

Muilman, Anna. *See* Angerstein, Anna (Crokatt).

Mumby, Frank A., *Publishing and Bookselling* (1954), 104.

Mun, Jean-Antoine-Claude *Adrien* de (1773–1843), comte de, marquis de, 331.

Murat, Caroline, *née* Bonaparte (1782–1839), 241 n.

Murat, Joachim (1767–1815), husband of the preceding, maréchal de France, King of Naples (1808), 241 n.

Murray, Alexander (d. 1830), solicitor for William Locke II, 336, 339 n., 343 n., 345, 365, 368 n., 394, 457, 511.

Murray, John II (1778–1843), bookseller and publisher at The Ship, 32 Fleet Street, 103, 567.

Murray, Lindley (1745–1826), his *English Grammar* published by Longman, 154 n.

Musée National. *See* Paris.

Napier, Lady Sarah (Bunbury), *née* Lennox (d. 1826), 136 n.

NAPOLÉON I (1769–1821), Emperor of the French:
attempt on his life, 72 n.;
defeat at Moscow, and troop withdrawal, 60 n., 64 n., 72 n.;
defeat in Russia a presage of peace, 64 n., 70 n.;
defeat at Vitoria, 191 n.;
defeats in 1813, 208;
deserts troops at Wilna, 64 n.;
exile of Mme de Staël, 207 n.;
growing resistance to him in 1813, 100 n.;
military machine crumbling, 191;
recall of troops, 86–7 n.;
'return' to Paris, 86–7 n.;
south of France in revolt against him, 268 n.;
ultimate defeat, the *déchéance*, 284 n.;
withdraws to Elba, 355 n.;
Memoirs, ed. F. M. Kircheisen, tr. Frederick Collins, 376.
mentioned, 106 n., 206 n., 212 n., 215 n., 216 n., 236 n., 256 n., 274 n., 287 n., 303 n., 380 n., 418 n., 419 n., 451 n., 452 n., 461 n., 505 n.

Narbonne-Lara, Hortense-Geneviève-Marie-Anne de, *née* de Bauffremont, wife of Joseph-Augustin. *See* Ferrari de Romans, comtesse.

Narbonne-Lara, Joseph-Augustin de (1767–1825), vicomte de Saint-Giron, 215 n., 461.

Narbonne-Lara, Amable-Riom-*Louise*-Françoise de, daughter of the following. *See* Braancamp de Sobral, Amable-Riom-Louise-Françoise de.

Narbonne-Lara, Louis-Marie-Jacques-Almaric (1755–1813), comte de, général:
character, 236, 279;
aide-de-camp to Napoléon, 212;
ambassador at Vienna, 215;
relationship with Mme de Staël, 206–7 n.;
retreat from Russia, 212;
war experiences, letters about, 279 n.;
Torgau and death, 201, 212;
mentioned, 59 n., 171 n., 204, 206, 211 ff., 222, 241, 273–4, 432–3, 517.

Index

Playfair, John (1748–1819), mathematician and geologist, *Elements of Geometry containing the first six Books of Euclid* (1st ed., 1795), **466.**

Plumer, Marianne, *née* Turton (1775–1857), wife of the following, **29.**

Plumer, Sir Thomas (1753–1824), Attorney-General, Master of the Rolls, knighted (1807), **29.**

Plymouth. *See* England.

Poivre, Françoise. *See* Du Pont de Nemours, Françoise.

Poix, prince and princesse de. *See* Noailles, Philippe-Louis and Anne-Louise de.

Ponsonby, Henrietta Frances, *née* Spencer (1761–1821), Countess of Bessborough, 265 n.

Pope, Alexander (1688–1744), poet, 487.

Porson, Richard (1759–1808), Greek scholar, 35 n., 519.

Port, John (d. 1807) of Ilam (formerly Sparrow), 368 n.

Port, Mary, *née* d'Ewes [or Dewes] (1746–1814), wife of the preceding, 367–8;
intellectual superiority, 368 n.;
marriage, 368 n.;
mental disorder, 368 n.

Port, Georgiana Mary Ann, daughter of the above. *See* Waddington, Georgiana Mary Ann.

Porter, Jane (1776–1850), novelist, 217 n.

Portland, Dukes and Duchess of. *See* Bentinck and Cavendish-Bentinck.

Post Office Annual Directory (1812 ff.), 568.

Pott, Elizabeth. *See* Potts, Elizabeth.

Potts, Elizabeth, *née* Pott (*fl.* 1780–1814), wife of Samuel (*c.* 1735–1816), 520.

Potts, Anna (*c.* 1787–*post* 1814), daughter of the above, 7, 520.

Potts, Caroline (*c.* 1793–*post* 1814), sister of the preceding, 7, 520.

Pougens, Frances Julia de, *née* Sayer (1756–1850), 520.

Pouzols, marquis de. *See* Montagu-Beaune, Joachim de.

Powell, the Revd. William (1770–1838), of Abergavenny, 253.

Poyntz, Margaret Georgiana. *See* Spencer, Margaret Georgiana.

Poyntz, Stephen (1685–1750), diplomat, 265 n.

Priestley, the Revd. Joseph (1733–1804), scientist and theologian, 138 n.

Prosser, Edmund Bond (*c.* 1780–1855), surgeon in Monmouth, 253.

Provence, comte de. *See* Louis XVIII.

Provence, comtesse de. *See* Louise-Marie-Joséphine de Savoie, wife of the preceding,

Prussia:
Dresden, Battle of (q.v.);
Leipzig, Battle of (q.v.);
Treaty of Kalisch (q.v.);
Treaty of Tilsit, 366 n.;
See also King Friedrich Wilhelm III and the Royal Family.

Pully, Jeanne-Pauline-Louise Randon de. *See* Aubusson de la Feuillade, comtesse d'.

Purcell, Henry (*c.* 1658–95), composer, 347 n., 473 n.

Quarterly Review:
sees FBA as supporter of Napoleonic tyranny, 484 n.;
critique of *The Wanderer*, 207, 389 n.

Quelpée de la Borde, Louise-Marguerite. *See* Jarjayes, Louise-Marguerite de.

Quotidienne, La, royalist newspaper, 396 n.

Ragon, Marie-Julie. *See* Bazille, Marie-Julie.

Ragon, Rose, *née* Gillett (*fl.* 1806–14), 520.

Ragon des Essards, Louis-Hyppolyte (*fl.* 1783–1819), 243.

Raguse, duc de. *See* Marmont, Auguste-Frédéric-Louis Viesse de.

Rambuteau, Claude-Philibert-Barthelot (1781–1869), comte de, *Mémoires*, 213 n.

Ramsgate. *See* Kent.

Raper, Charles Chamier (*c.* 1777–1845), 31;
Letter to, No. 809.

Raper, Frances, *née* Phillips (1782–1860), wife of the preceding, FBA's niece, 12, 21, 26, 28, 64, 131, 231 n.,

623

Index

Raper, Frances (*cont.*):
247, 252, 258 n., 262 n., 291 n.,
327, 370, 398, 424, 491, 505, 507,
511, 512, 515, 516, 517, 546.

Raper, Catherine, 'Minette', daughter of the above. *See* Kingston, Catherine.

Raper, Matthew (*fl.* 1771), 463 n.

Rapin, René, called le père Rapin (1621–87), literary critic, 334 n.

Rathsamhausen, Marie-Anne. *See* Gérando, Marie-Anne de.

Récamier, Jacques (1751–1830), banker, 26 n., **132 n.**, 262.

Récamier, Jeanne-Françoise-Julie-Adélaïde 'Juliette', *née* Bernard (1777–1849), wife of the preceding, 132 n., 171 n.;
Memoirs and Correspondence . . . (1882), ed. Isaphene Luyster, 171 n.

Récamier, Marie, sister of Jacques. *See* David, Marie.

Redwood, Abraham (1728–98), 422 n.

Redwood, Martha Eliza, daughter of the preceding. *See* Hottinguer, Martha Eliza.

Rees, Owen (d. 1837), bookseller:
as negotiator for Longman's purchase of *The Wanderer*, 103, 147, 153 n., 154 n., 155 n., 157, 159, 161, 187 n., 567.

Reeves, John (*c.* 1752–1829), Superintendent of Aliens, King's printer, **36 n.,** 48 n., 87 n., 129, 257, 258, 340 n.;
History of the English Law . . . (5 vols., 1783–1829), 36 n.

Riccé, Gabriel-Marie de (1758–1832), comte de, *later* marquis de, général, 204 n., **214.**

Richardson, James Malcott (*fl.* 1810–53), bookseller at 23 Cornhill, 103, 568.

Richardson, Samuel (1689–1761), novelist, 240 n.

Richmond, Surrey:
residence of Sarah Baker and Charlotte Cambridge, 50 n. *passim*;
residence of the Barretts, 3 n., 20, 24 n., 27 n., 29 n., 37, 39, 508 *passim*;
residence of CBFB, 208 *passim*;
residence of FBA, 431 *passim*;

the d'Arblays' departure from, *en route* to France, 490–1.

Richmond, Yorkshire, 469 n.

Rigaud, André (1761–1811), général, **242–3 n.**

Rigaud, Marie-Anne, *née* Villeneuve (*fl.* 1780–1820), wife of the preceding, 242–3, 520.

Rijssel, Petronella-Jacoba van. *See* Latour-Maubourg, Petronella-Jacoba de Fay de,

Rimpton, Somerset, living of the Revd. Richard Allen Burney (q.v.), 29 n.

Risborough, John (*c.* 1781–1859), of Portsmouth, New Hampshire, sea captain, 8 n.

Rishton, Maria, *née* Allen (1751–1820), FBA's stepsister, 64 n., 74 n., 190 n., 292 n., 295 n., 513, 516.

Rivington, House of, 568.

Rivington, Charles I (1688–1742), bookseller, 568.

Rivington, John (1720–92), 4th son of the preceding, bookseller, 568.

Rivington, Francis (1745–1822), son of the preceding, bookseller, 103, 568.

Rivington, Charles (1754–1831), brother of the preceding, bookseller, 103, 568.

Roberts, John (d. 1776), bookseller, 567.

Robin, Françoise. *See* Du Pont de Nemours, Françoise.

Robinson, Elizabeth. *See* Montagu, Elizabeth.

Robinson, Matthew. *See* Montagu, Matthew, adopted son of the preceding.

Robinson, George (1737–1801), bookseller at 25 Paternoster Row, 567.

Robinson, George (d. 1811), son of the preceding, bookseller, 567.

Robinson, John (1753–1813), brother of George I, uncle of the preceding, 103, 567.

Rochdale, Lancs., 400 n.

Rochester, Bishop of. *See* King, Walker.

Rochford, 5th Earl of. *See* Zuylestein, William Henry Nassau de.

Rogers, Samuel (1763–1855), banker, poet, collector, traveller, 136, 148, 151, 290 n.;
The Pleasures of Memory (1792), 136 n.

Index

Index

Staël-Holstein, (*cont.*):
  her season in England (1813):
    guest at Mansion House, 320 n.;
    invited to the Prince Regent's ball,
      149 n.;
  liaison with Narbonne, **206 n.**;
  Paris, social and political life in:
    parties, 369;
    political dinners, 396 n.;
  residence in Clichy, 369, 396 n.
  publications:
    De L'Allemagne (1813), 171;
    *De l'influence des passions sur le
      bonheur des individus et des nations*
      (1796; reissue in English and
      French, 1813), 171;
    Réflexions sur le suicide (1813), 171;
  mentioned, 170–1, 182 n., 184,
    206–7, 209, 237, 240, 250, 257–8,
    305, 518.
Stafford, Baron. *See* Jerningham,
  George William.
Staffordshire:
  Elford (home of Richard Howard),
    135 n.;
  Ilam, home of John Port, 368 n.;
  Stafford (Richard Howard's pro-
    perties there), 135 n., 368 n.
Stanhope, Philip Dormer (1694–1773),
  4th Earl of Chesterfield, 465 n.
Stapleton, Gloucestershire, 254 n.
Starot de Saint-Germain, Marie-
  Louise-Françoise Adélaïde. *See*
  Bachasson de Montalivet, comtesse
  de.
Stephen, Sir James (1789–1859), *Essays
  in Ecclesiastical Biography* (1849), 182 n.
Stewart, Charles William (*later* Vane)
  (1778–1854), 3rd Marquess of Lon-
  donderry, half-brother to the follow-
  ing, 270 n.
Stewart, Robert (1769–1822), *styled*
  Viscount Castlereagh, 2nd Marquess
  of Londonderry, **233 n.,** 256 n.,
  278, 293, 399 n.
Stone, Charles (*fl.* 1791–1812), civil
  servant, **492.**
Stothard, Thomas (1755–1834), painter
  and book illustrator, **151 n.**
Strahan, Andrew (1749–1831), printer,
  197, 200, 201, 238, 327 n.
Strahan, William (1715–85), printer,
  father of the preceding, 197.

Strange, Sir Robert (1721–92), en-
  graver, knighted (1787), 464 n., 506.
Strange, Isabella, *née* Lumisden (1719–
  1806), wife of the preceding, **119 n.**
Strange, Isabella Katherina (*c.* 1759–
  1849), daughter of the above, **119.**
Streatfeild, Sophia (1754–1834), friend
  of the Thrales, 531.
Streatham Park, the Thrale house at,
  524, 534–9;
  described, **526–9.**
Stuart, John (1744–1814), 4th Earl of
  Bute, 77 n., **92.**
Stuart, Sophia Margaret, *née* Penn
  (1765–1847), 262, 502.
Stuart, the Rt. Revd. William (1755–
  1822), Primate of Ireland, husband
  of the preceding, 262 n., 266, 502.
Sunderland, Earl of. *See* Spencer,
  Charles.
Surrey:
  Chessington (q.v.);
  Cobham, 509;
  Dorking (q.v.);
  Mickleham (q.v.);
  Morden, 254 n.;
  Norbury Park (q.v.);
  Richmond (q.v.);
  West Humble (q.v.);
  Wimbledon, 265, 270;
  mentioned, 98, 135 n.
Sussex, Duke of. *See* Augustus Fred-
  erick, H.R.H.
Sussex:
  Brighton:
    FB accompanies the Thrales there,
      530;
    Mrs. Thrale and Queeney visit
      there, 535;
    mentioned, 156 n., 166, 172, 353,
      489.
Swansbourne, Bucks., 129 n.
Switzerland: Lausanne, an *émigré*
  colony, 206 n.
Sydenham, Lewisham Parish. *See under*
  London.
Sydenham, Thomas (1624–89), M.D.,
  138 n.

Tacitus, *Opera* (1743), 504–5.
Talleyrand-Périgord, Charles-Maurice
  de (1754–1838), prince de Bénévent:

628

629

Thrale, Cecilia Margaretta, sister of the preceding. *See* Mostyn, Cecilia.

Thucydides, AA's interest in, 26 n., 81 n.

THUISY, Jean-Baptiste-Charles de Goujon de (1751–1834), 4th marquis de, **282 n.**; family of, 87.

Thuisy, Catherine-Philiberte-Françoise de, *née* de Berulle [or Berule] (*c.* 1760–*post* 1824), wife of the preceding, 62 n., **282 n.**

Thuisy, Amable-Jean-Baptiste-Louis-Jérôme de Goujon de (1781–1829), comte de, son of the above, **282 n.**

Thuisy, Eugène-François-Sixte de (1782–1809), brother of the preceding, **282 n.**

Thuisy, Charles-François-Emmanuel-Louis (1784–1857), 5th marquis de, brother of the preceding, **282 n.**

Thuisy, Auguste-Charlemagne-Maccabée de (1788–1836), brother of the preceding, **282 n.**

Thuisy, Georges-Jean-Baptiste de (1795–*post* 1814), brother of the preceding, **282 n.**

Thuisy, Albertine-Louise-Mélanie de (1785–1847), sister of the preceding, **282 n.**

Thuisy, Amable-Jean-Baptiste-Louis-Jérôme de (1749–*post* 1815), commandeur-chevalier de Malte, brother of Jean (*supra*), **331 n.**, 402, 408–9, 425, 517.

Tilsit, Treaty of. *See* Prussia.

The Times, 354.

Titchfield, Marquess of. *See* Cavendish-Bentinck, 3rd Duke of Portland.

Todd, William B., *A Dictionary of Printers . . . 1800–1840* (1972), 567.

Tooke, the Revd. William (1744–1820), the elder, historian, editor, translator, 231 n.

Torgau, Austria, 201 n., 212.

Totnes, Devon., 253 n.

Toulouse. *See* France.

Townshend, George (1723/4–1807), 4th Viscount, 1st Marquess Townshend, 355 n.

Townshend, John (1757–1833), 2nd son of the preceding, 290 n., **355 n.**

Trapassi. *See* Metastasio.

Treatise on the extraordinary Virtues and Effects of Ass's Milk . . . (1753), 162.

Trefusis, Robert Cotton St. John (1787–1832), 18th Baron Clinton, Colonel, **128 n.**, 129.

Trefusis, Anne Matilda. *See* Moore, Anne Matilda.

Trefusis, Louisa Barbara. *See* Rolle, Louisa Barbara.

Trévise, duc de. *See* Mortier, Adolphe-Édouard-Casimir-Joseph.

Trinity College. *See* Cambridge University.

Trinity College, Dublin, 28 n., 247 n.

Tunbridge Wells. *See* Kent.

Tunbridge Wells Guide (1797), 485 n.

Turner, Charlotte. *See* Smith, Charlotte.

Turner, Cornelia, *née* Chastel de Boinville (*fl.* 1795–1814), 520.

Turner, Sharon (1768–1847), F.S.A., solicitor and writer, **47 n.**, 153, 154, 343 n.; *History of England* (3 vols., 1814–23).

Turnham Green, Middlesex. *See* EBB and London.

Turpin-Crissé, Alexandrine de. *See* Meulan, Alexandrine de.

Turton, Marianne. *See* Plumer, Marianne.

Twickenham Meadows. *See* Cambridge, the Revd. George Owen; *also* London.

United States, at war with England (1812–1814), 8, 22, 136 n.

Upper Ossory, Countess of. *See* Fitzpatrick, Anne (Fitzroy).

Upton, Elizabeth, *née* Boughton (1746–1823), Baroness Templetown, wife of Clotworthy (1721–85), 119, **135 n.**, 151, 315.

Upton, John Henry (1771–1846), 2nd Baron Templetown, 1st Viscount, son of the preceding, **135 n.**

Upton Fulke *Greville*, brother of the preceding. *See* Howard, Fulke *Greville* Upton.

Upton, Elizabeth Albana, eldest sister of the preceding. *See* Hervey, Elizabeth Albana.

Upton, Caroline, sister of the preceding. *See* Singleton, Caroline.

Upton, Sophia (1780–1853), sister of the preceding, 135 n., **315.**

Index